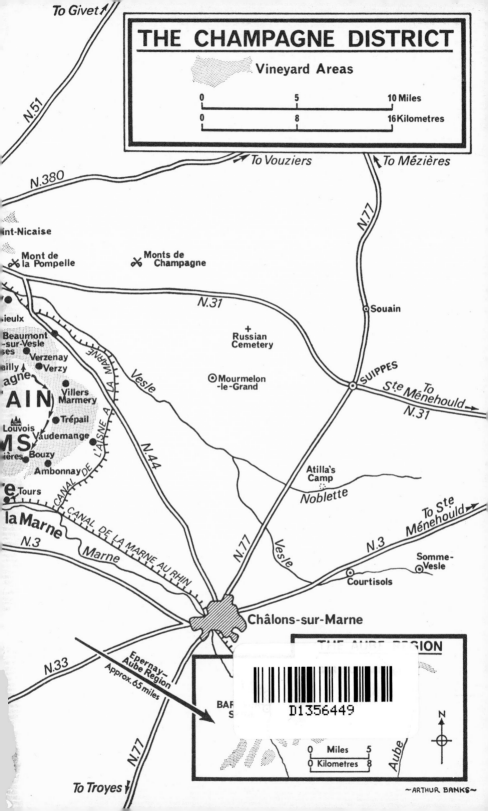

CHAMPAGNE

CHAMPAGNE

The Wine, The Land and The People

by

PATRICK FORBES

LONDON
VICTOR GOLLANCZ LTD
1982

First published September 1967
Second impression May 1972
Third impression January 1977
Fourth impression June 1979
Fifth impression July 1982

ISBN 0 575 00948 9

*Printed in Great Britain at
The Camelot Press Ltd, Southampton*

CONTENTS

LIST OF ILLUSTRATIONS

Photographic Credits

1 (René Jacques), 2 (Pietro Mele), 4 (Francis Goodman), 22 (Almasy), MOËT & CHANDON; 3, 5, 6, 7 (G. Lienhard), 8, 9, 10, 11, 12, 13, 15, 16, 17, 18, 23, COMITÉ INTERPROFESSIONEL DU VIN DE CHAMPAGNE; 14, POMMERY & GRENO; 19, BOLLINGER; 20, 21, 25, LANSON; 24, PIPER-HEIDSIECK.

MAPS

Line drawings by Graham Rust

ACKNOWLEDGEMENTS

A very large number of people who live and work in Champagne or are in some way connected with the wine and the winefield gave me unstinting help while I was writing this book. They were so numerous that a list of their names, though impressive, would be absurdly long. I ask them to accept this expression of my most sincere and lasting gratitude.

Of the many people who, although they have no direct connection with Champagne, also helped me in a variety of ways I should particularly like to thank: Mr. Hugh Murray Baillie, M. Emile Beauvais of the Laboratoire de Géologie de la Sorbonne, Major George Bolster, Mr. James Elton Brassert, Mrs. Winthrop Buckingham, the late Captain H. J. Buckmaster, Mr. G. H. Buller, Lady Diana Cooper, Mr. George Dennistoun-Webster, Mr. C. L. Drage, Herr Hasso von Etzdorf, Baronne Frachon, Frau Karin Gleisberg, Miss Anne-Marie Hartmere, the staff of the London Library, M. Edmond de Marcilly, Mr. Mark Morford, M. and Mme Bernard de Rham, Mrs. W. F. Stirling, Sir George Taylor, Dom Columba Thorne, O.S.B., the staff of the Treaty Department of the Foreign Office, M. Michel Triviaux, Mr. Peter Vaughan, Lord Vernon, Mr. David Wada, Lady Waterpark, Dr. Joan Wake and Mr. John Wedderburn-Maxwell.

I am greatly indebted to Miss Sheila Hodges for her editorial advice.

Finally, I should like to record my special gratitude to Mrs. Robert Sharwood for the unfailing assistance and encouragement which she gave me while I was engaged upon this book.

PART I

THE THREE CHAMPAGNES

CHAPTER I

THE PROVINCE

THERE ARE MANY Champagnes, as will soon become apparent, but there are three principal ones: the province (*la Champagne*), the wine-field within the province (*Champagne viticole*), and the wine itself (*le Champagne*).

My intention in these opening chapters is to explain certain basic facts about these three Champagnes, and to describe very briefly certain matters of which some knowledge is necessary at this stage, although they will be treated more fully later on.

Henceforth, to avoid confusion in genderless English, I shall refer whenever possible to the province as "Champagne", to the winefield as "the Champagne district" and to the wine as "champagne".

Strictly speaking, the geographical name "Champagne" belongs to that part of eastern France which in the Middle Ages formed the County of Champagne. Today this area almost exactly comprises the *départements* of Ardennes, Marne, Aube and Haute-Marne. For some considerable period in France's history Brie (famous for its cheese), which stretches westwards towards Paris between the Marne and the Seine, also came within the jurisdiction of Champagne; but over the years successive slices were taken into other administrative units, and nowadays it is a moot point whether the term "the province of Champagne" embraces any part of Brie, and if so how much. Even so, most of the inhabitants of Brie still call themselves Champenois. But, as Brie has little to do with this book, the references in my text to the province of Champagne mainly apply to the smaller territory, and it is shown thus on the accompanying map.

Champagne, without Brie, is still a huge province: the distance from north to south—from Givet, on the Belgian border, to the province's southern limits, which are virtually the approaches to Dijon—is close on 200 miles. Champagne, in fact, is very nearly the size of Belgium. Its inhabitants, however, number a mere 1,200,000, compared to Belgium's 9 million. Such a chronic dearth of population is a great handicap to the province's present and future development.

From the middle of the ninth century, when Charlemagne's great empire was divided into three kingdoms, Champagne's geographical

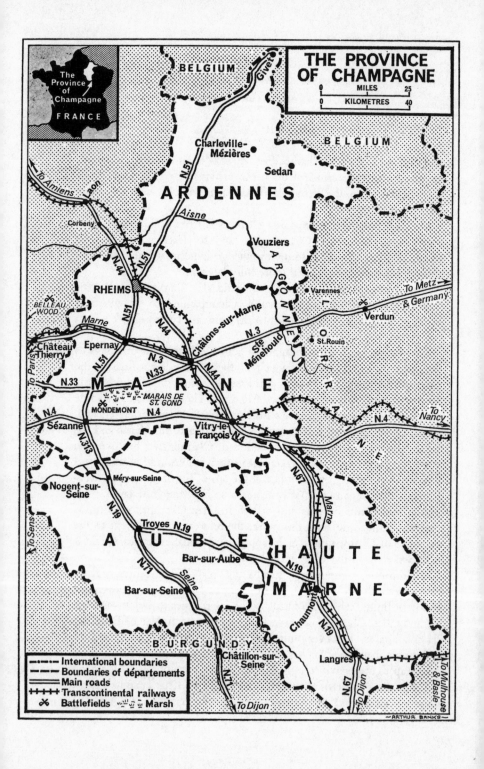

position brought her within the sphere of influence of France. While the Counts of Champagne reigned the province was more or less a satellite of that country. But in 1285 Jeanne, the heiress of Champagne and Navarre, married the heir to the French throne, Philip the Fair, and in the following year Champagne slipped effortlessly and permanently into the bosom of France. To have been spared the turmoil that its neighbour, the Middle Kingdom, had to live through to achieve its present form of an independent Belgium and Luxembourg, a German Saar, a French Alsace and Lorraine and an independent Switzerland was the luckiest thing that ever happened to Champagne: it was granted the leisure, as Michelet put it, "to cultivate the delicate flower of civilization".

Its geographical position has helped the province in another way. Champagne has always been a meeting point between north and south, and between the French and German worlds. In earliest times, by the rivers that traverse the province—the Aisne, the Marne, the Seine and the Aube—and, later, along the network of roads built by the Romans, there has come a never-ending stream of pilgrims, migratory people and merchants who have brought with them new ideas, new stimuli, and trade. Today Champagne is more of a crossroads than ever. Across the province hurtle three crack transcontinental expresses—Calais–Basle, Paris–Frankfurt–Berlin and Paris–Strasbourg–Vienna. At Châlons-sur-Marne the main road from the Channel ports to Switzerland meets the main road from Paris to Germany. And the Canal de la Marne au Rhin, which begins at Epernay, links Rouen with the Rhine.

In one respect, however, the province's geographical position has proved a bane. Lying spreadeagled across the direct route from Germany to Paris, Champagne has been invaded, fought over and ravaged with more monotonous persistence throughout its history than any other French province. It might, indeed, be called the battlefield of France.

Geologically, the province of Champagne is divided into five distinct areas, and the geological make-up of each one has largely determined its destiny.

The whole of Haute-Marne and the north-eastern part of Ardennes is Jurassic territory: hilly, thickly forested, with an extremely rigorous climate. The cultivation of potatoes, the extraction of minerals from the soil and trades connected with metals have brought some sustenance to the area, but not nearly enough, particularly to Haute-Marne, which

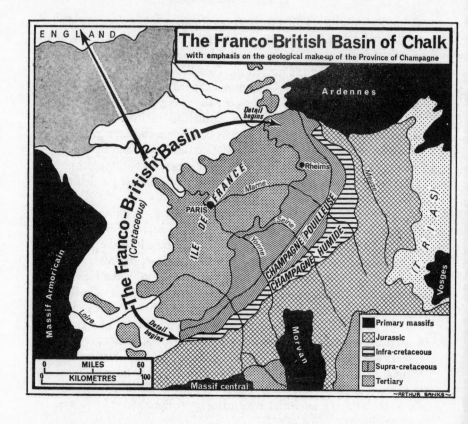

The Franco-British Basin of Chalk
with emphasis on the geological make-up of the Province of Champagne

ENGLAND

Ardennes

Detail
begins

The Franco-British Basin
(Cretaceous)

ILE DE FRANCE

Rheims

Marne

Seine

Yonne

PARIS

CHAMPAGNE POUILLEUSE

CHAMPAGNE HUMIDE

Meuse

(TRIAS)

Vosges

Massif Armoricain

Loire

Detail
begins

Morvan

MILES   60
0
KILOMETRES   100
0

Massif central

Primary massifs
Jurassic
Infra-cretaceous
Supra-cretaceous
Tertiary

~ARTHUR BANKS~

is one of the poorest and most under-populated *départements* in France.

West of the Jurassic territory, extending south in the shape of a crescent, lies an area commonly known as *Champagne humide*. This is infra-cretaceous territory, the eastern edge of the Paris Basin. Here, when the sea that filled the Paris Basin dried up, roughly 69 million years ago, it left behind not a sediment of chalk, as it did elsewhere, but rich clayey soil. Where the land is flat in *Champagne humide*, as it is in a region close to Vitry-le-François known as *le Perthois* and in another close to Charleville-Mézières known as *la Provence ardennaise*, the clayey soil is of remarkable fertility, a farmer's dream. But where the land is hilly, as it is in south-eastern Aube and in the Argonne region (150,000 men perished there in the First World War), the climate is as rigorous as in Haute-Marne, and the countryside is mostly covered in thick forests. In the Argonne forest there are on average 180 days of rain and 80 days of frost a year.*

Farther to the west still, extending down the centre of the province between the tips of the *Champagne humide* crescent, lies an area of flat chalky land known as *Champagne pouilleuse*. This is the most easterly section of the supra-cretaceous part of the Paris Basin. From here the seam of chalk, in places over a thousand feet deep, extends almost as far south as the *Massif central*, west to the *Massif amoricain* and north-west through Picardy and Artois to the English Channel, beyond which it appears again in the white cliffs of Dover and the South Downs (hence the term "the Franco-British Basin of Chalk" which geologists use to describe the whole area covered by the former sea). But what differentiates *Champagne pouilleuse* from the rest of the former sea-bed is that the chalk there is so fissured that rain-water tends to disappear through it like vegetable-water through a sieve.

For centuries *Champagne pouilleuse* was a joke—to everyone except the Champenois. "The land there's worth a farthing an acre—if there's a rabbit on it" was the type of remark a Frenchman from another province would make if he wished to enrage a Champenois. Kind souls have suggested that in fact the word *"pouilleuse"* has nothing to do with *"pouilleux"*, meaning "lousy", and that it derives from *poilot* or *pouillot*, which, in the local dialect, is the name given to the wild thyme that carpets the area in summer and exudes a sweet scent at night; La Fontaine often mentioned this charming flower and the enjoyment he derived from watching Jeannot Lapin romping about in it. But, whatever the origin of the word, there can be no doubt that *Champagne pouilleuse* used to be one of the bleakest spots in Europe: "an expanse of white chalk, dirty, poor . . . a sea of stubble stretched across an immense plain of plaster" was how Michelet described it. No crop would grow on it, owing to the exceptional dryness, and the only animal that could survive on it was the sheep. In consequence its unfortunate inhabitants, whose villages were perforce situated beside

* Knowing that he would find solitude and silence in such an inclement spot, St. Rouin, an Irish hermit, settled there in the seventh century. Near the site of his hermitage there is a clearing in the forest which forms an open-air cathedral; chunks of local stone, with the Stations of the Cross set in them in silver relief, have been embedded in the surrounding beeches and oaks. In 1953 a tiny chapel, designed by Father Rayssiguier, O. P., the architect of the Matisse chapel at Vence, was erected nearby. A concrete cube resting on concrete piles, it might be a block-house of the Maginot Line; concrete was chosen because it weathers better than stone—the former stone chapel collapsed in 1946.

rivers and streams, turned to spinning and weaving for their livelihoods. For this reason, Rheims and Sedan became centres of the cloth
trade and Troyes a centre of the hosiery and millinery trade—as it
still is.

In the middle of the eighteenth century, an enterprising Governor
of Champagne decided that an effort must be made to heal this festering
sore at the heart of the province. He imported Scots pines from the
Black Forest and planted them on the crests of the chalky ridges, where
nothing had ever grown before. They thrived, and at the beginning of
the nineteenth century the planting of trees began in earnest. It was
found that, in addition to the Scots pine, the black pine of Austria,
the Corsican pine, even laburnum and birch trees could survive on the
chalk. Humus, formed by dead needles and mosses beneath the trees,
slowly covered the chalk; in the spring anemones, orchids, eglantines
and broom burst into flower. By the second decade of the nineteenth
century the trees and the humus had rendered *Champagne pouilleuse*
fairly salubrious, and little by little the rearing of sheep gave way to
the raising of crops of rye.

However, the real transformation of *Champagne pouilleuse* did not
begin until 1947. In that year a small group of local farmers came to
the conclusion that if the pines were cut down and the most modern
fertilisers and farming equipment were used *Champagne pouilleuse*
could be turned into a vast wheatfield. Their experiments proved
sensational. Before long the activity in the area smacked of colonial
days: every available bulldozer in France was at work, people were
sleeping out under canvas, and rich families were buying up land for
younger sons. Today *Champagne pouilleuse* is the Kansas of France.
Each summer it is carpeted in gold, and giant barges leave Châlons-sur-
Marne daily, laden with wheat for Luxembourg and Switzerland.

But, although the face-lift has been a huge success, the past has left
scars on *Champagne pouilleuse*. The area is still thinly populated:
seventy-five inhabitants per square mile is the average density—less,
even, than in Haute-Marne (not that it matters now, so mechanized
is the farming). To English and Belgian tourists, accustomed to the
overcrowding of their homelands, this makes a drive across it a continual surprise and refreshment. For long stretches at a time no village,
man or beast is to be seen; the beautifully cultivated land appears to
be tilled by phantoms.

And there still exist small areas where the face-lift has not been
attempted. One of them is beside N. 77, between Châlons-sur-Marne
and Troyes. There the pines, planted in rectangular parcels, are stunted,

there are no crops, not even any sheep; the chalk remains virgin white, except in summer when the wild thyme shrouds it in mauve. But if you wish to avoid irritating the Champenois, you never mention what you have seen: old legends die hard, and they are still sensitive about *Champagne pouilleuse*. In fact, it is more tactful not to mention the word *pouilleuse* at all, and instead to talk of "the great agricultural plain of Champagne".

The supra-cretaceous plain extends west from *Champagne pouilleuse* to the Ile-de-France, forming the fourth of the geological divisions of Champagne. Here the chalk is not nearly so fissured as in *Champagne pouilleuse*, and crops have been grown on it since time immemorial. But there have never been many trees on this part of the plain, which probably explains how the province came to be called "Champagne". The Romans used the word *"campagna"* to describe tracts of open land. In France and in England, during the Middle Ages, a distortion of the word—"champaign"—had a similar meaning; Browning used it in *Two in the Campagna*; Christopher Columbus used the Spanish form of the word in a letter describing the wonders of Hispaniola. That is certainly how the Petite and Grande Champagne districts of the Cognac winefield obtained their names. But it has also been suggested that the name of the province may derive from two Celtic words, *"Kann Pann"*, meaning "white country", which is an equally apt description of the plain.

Now we come to the fifth of Champagne's geological divisions, the small part of the province which lies on the eastern edge of the Ile-de-France. It is a freak area, a fragment of the earth's surface as unique in its own way as the Kentucky Blue Grass Ribband or the hill-sides in Cuba where the tobacco for Havana cigars is grown. This is the mere dimple on the fair face of France that is the fount of all true champagne and is sometimes known as *Champagne viticole classique*. This is the Champagne district proper.

The dimple is really a pimple; this is what happened. Early in the Tertiary era, roughly 30 million years ago, the whole of the vast area in the centre of the Paris Basin that is now known as the Ile-de-France was shaken by earthquakes. These earthquakes raised the floor of the sea which had once covered the area between 100 and 300 feet, folded, twisted or broke the layers of chalk resting upon it, and covered the surface of the chalk with debris—debris composed partly of fragments of chalk and partly of rich mineral matters that had been vomited up from the bowels of the earth through the cracks in the chalk. Much later, in the final period of the Tertiary era, roughly 11 million years ago, an earthquake of considerably greater violence than the others struck the eastern edge of the Ile-de-France. The level of the former sea was raised a further 300 to 500 feet, and a chain of hills was formed upon whose steep sides the seams of chalk remained for a time exposed to the elements, but were later covered with a thin layer of topsoil composed of chalk fragments and Tertiary debris. The hills are known as les Falaises de Champagne. Their height, their steep sides and the topsoil on their sides have rendered possible the growing of the vines that produce the grapes for champagne; for without steep hill-sides the widespread cultivation of vines would be an unrewarding occupation in such a northern climate as the Champagne district, and without the topsoil it would be an impossibility.*

A glance at the accompanying physical map of northern France will show the singularity, as regards height, of the Falaises. From the English Channel to the foothills of the Jura, from Normandy's "little Switzerland" to the foothills of the Vosges, there is a blight of altitude, relieved alone (or almost alone) by the Falaises. This singularity is revealed more forcibly still to anyone driving from Châlons-sur-Marne along N. 3 towards Epernay. The road runs ramrod straight across the flat plain. As Epernay approaches, the two most important Falaises loom on the horizon: on the right (to the north-west), the one known as the Mountain of Rheims, which is shaped like an iron with its tapering front projecting into the plain; and on the left (to the south-west), the one called the Côte des Blancs, which rises along its full extent directly out of the plain.

The singularity of the Falaises, however, is not restricted to their height, their steep sides or the topsoil. What makes them precious beyond description, from a viticultural point of view, is the type of chalk that lies underneath the surface. The sediment left behind by the

---

* The healthiest, best matured grapes are generally found on vines situated between 450 and 550 feet above the plain or the bed of the valley. There are many reasons why this is so. Below 450 feet the danger from spring frosts is particularly great, and the soil tends to be too rich in humus. Above 550 feet the vine is exposed to sudden inrushes of cold air, caused by the intense transpiration of the trees on the summits. At the intervening altitude, however, the vines enjoy protection from wind, an optimum amount of sun and light, and excellent aeration. Also, soil conditions are particularly propitious: the chalk foundation is solid, the topsoil gravelly. The gravel not only enables the air to circulate freely through the soil, but also ensures that no more moisture is retained than is necessary to quench the vine's thirst. The vine-roots are thus kept warm, as dry soil holds the heat of the sun better than wet soil.

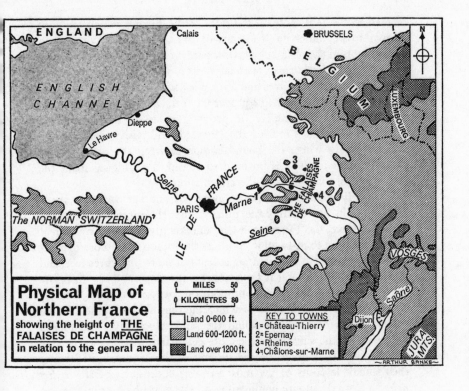

Physical Map of Northern France
showing the height of THE FALAISES DE CHAMPAGNE in relation to the general area

MILES 50
KILOMETRES 80

Land 0-600 ft.
Land 600-1200 ft.
Land over 1200 ft.

KEY TO TOWNS
1=Château-Thierry
2=Epernay
3=Rheims
4=Châlons-sur-Marne

~ARTHUR BANKS~

sea as it retreated from the Paris Basin is composed of marine organisms such as sponges, sea-urchins, sea-mosses, rhabolithes and coccolithes, and of minerals such as quartz, rutile, zircon and tourmalin; and the presence in the chalk, to a greater or a lesser degree, of these constituents determines its type. Now, it so happened that most of the top layer of chalk found on the Falaises is of a type known as *Belimnita quadrata*, which is markedly different from the micraster chalk found on the plain below. Had the top layer of chalk beneath the surface soil of the Falaises been mostly of the micraster type, it is extremely improbable that there would ever have been champagne. *For only where there are seams of* Belimnita quadrata *chalk, covered by a layer of Tertiary debris, will the vines produce radiant crops on the Falaises, and grapes that can be turned into a champagne which has champagne's unique, inimitable flavour.*

This most elemental fact was recognised by vineyard owners long before chairs of geology existed in the universities. Vines were never

planted in the few spots on the sides of the Falaises which are now
known to be underlaid by seams of micraster chalk; whereas on
certain spots in the plain below, which are now known to be underlaid
by seams of the *Belimnita quadrata* variety, they did plant vines, no
doubt having found by trial and error what science has taught vineyard
owners today: that the magic properties of the *Belimnita quadrata* chalk
outweigh the disadvantages of growing vines on flat ground. It
follows that if one is touring the vineyards and wishes, for interest's
sake, to know where the boundary line between the two types of
chalk is situated, there is no need to consult a geological map:. the
plantations of vines provide the information.

The early vine-growers were aware of another basic fact about
viticulture in the Champagne district: that the topsoil with which
nature covered the Falaises must be unceasingly renewed by man if
robust vines are to grow in it. In places the topsoil is no more than six
inches deep; seldom does it attain a depth of more than three feet; and
rain is for ever carrying it farther down the slopes.* They therefore
started scouring the neighbourhood for deposits of the Tertiary
debris and the other matters of which the topsoil is composed. In the
valley of the Marne they found the sand which gives the topsoil
lightness; on the summit of the Côte des Blancs they found the clay
which gives it cohesion; on the summit of the Mountain of Rheims
they found desposits of the most valuable constituent of all, *cendres
noires*, a form of impure lignite, so rich in its nourishing properties, on
account of the iron, sulphur and other oligo-elements which it contains, that it is sometimes referred to as the "black gold of Champagne".
Having found these deposits, they proceeded to quarry them, and then
to coat the topsoil with them every four years or so—a laborious and
costly operation, as many of the quarries and vineyards are not easy
of access. Each subsequent generation of vineyard workers has continued the job, so that through the centuries not only has the thickness
of the topsoil been maintained but its potential, as a source of great

---

* When one walks through a vineyard, with earth clinging to one's shoes, it
is difficult to grasp how thin the topsoil may be. Here and there, however, one
comes across a slope which has been cut away to make room for a road, and the
sides of the cutting provide a kind of elevation drawing of the soil and subsoil.
It is a revelation to see that generally there is only a foot or so of earth underneath
the grass; below that everything is solid chalk. For the agriculturalist, whose
plants are in the ground a year or less, such shallow soil would be a nightmare.
The vine, however, is in the ground for decades; it has a permanent root system
which explores a great area of soil and stores up important reserves of nourishment. Shallow soil, suitably constituted, suits the vine.

wine, has been enhanced. In effect, the topsoil of the vineyards is now an artificial creation, a creation, furthermore, of such complexity that it is never likely to be successfully reproduced or imitated elsewhere.

There is nothing particularly remarkable about the climate of the Falaises. Yet it has a considerable influence on the quality of champagne: it undoubtedly helps to give the wine its remarkable freshness and its cleanness on the palate. Growing grapes in such a northern climate, however, is a difficult and often a disheartening business. It is not the rigours of winter—the cold, the grey skies, the snowfalls in January—that are a problem: only if the temperature falls below − 15°C., which seldom happens more than once a decade, do the vines suffer (such extreme cold has much the same effect on their branches as it has on water-pipes: they burst, and have to be cut back). Nor are the winds much of a problem: the prevailing ones are from the west and south-west, and in the main they are warm and humid. Nor is lack of sunshine in summer the true cause of the trouble. The annual mean temperature of the Falaises is 10·5°C., which is a good half-degree above the minimum required for the successful cultivation of the vine; and in any case the total amount of warmth which the vines enjoy each year is considerably greater than the thermometer indicates, for the chalk fragments in the soil of the vineyards reflect the rays of the sun back into the foliage of the vine, giving it a second helping of sunshine, so to speak. (From an aesthetic point of view the phenomenon is astounding: it tones down colours, softens outlines, and gives the countryside a hazy, out-of-focus look, reminiscent of an Impressionist painting.)

What renders viticulture so difficult on the Falaises is (a) the frequency and the severity of the late spring frosts, and (b) the fact that, of the annual rainfall—160 rainy days a year on average, only twenty less than in the Argonne region—four-sevenths descends in summer and early autumn, July being the wettest month of all. For a late spring frost, if it is severe, and if it occurs when the vines are in flower, can prevent them from bearing any grapes at all that year. And rain, when the grapes are on the vines, can do almost as much damage. If it falls during or just after a warm spell, the resulting humidity will stir into action a whole range of pests and diseases, whose onslaught it may be beyond the power of the vineyard worker to control. And if it falls during a cold spell it may turn to hail. A vineyard that has been attacked by hail is as sorry a sight as an orange grove that has been visited by a plague of locusts: the vines look as if they have been spattered with machine-gun bullets, the leaves have holes the size of halfcrowns in them, and the bunches of grapes are bruised, battered, useless. On average, misfortunes such as these affect the quality or the quantity of grapes produced on the Falaises five or six times a decade, and not infrequently two or three years running.

CHAPTER 2

THE WINEFIELD

THE CÔTE DES BLANCS, as the name implies, is the domain of the vines that bear white grapes. A lozenge-shaped hill, approximately 600 feet high, it stretches south of the road between Epernay and Châlons-sur-Marne, at right-angles to the Marne and the Mountain of Rheims, for approximately thirteen miles. Throughout this distance the vines cling to its eastern slopes, which extend from the forests on the flat summit to the plain beneath in an unbroken belt varying in breadth from 400 yards to one-and-a-quarter miles. The contrast between the luxuriance of the vineyards and the immensity of the plain at their feet makes the Côte des Blancs one of the most spectacular vine-growing areas in the world. In summer, when the plain is covered as far as the eye can see with golden corn ablaze with poppies, corn-flowers and marguerites, the view from the higher vineyards is breath-taking.

Strung along the sides of the Côte lies a succession of vineyard villages. The most northerly of them is Chouilly, the most southerly Bergères-les-Vertus. These villages, as is the custom elsewhere in the winefield, give their names to the vineyards that surround them. Since 1911 each group of vineyards—each *cru* or growth—has been classified according to the quality of the grapes it produces. Altogether there are seven categories, headed by a *catégorie hors-classe* in which the ten plum growths of the winefield are grouped. These are the ratings of the Côte des Blancs growths:

Catégorie Hors-classe	*Première Catégorie*	*Deuxième Catégorie*
Avize	Le Mesnil-sur-Oger	Bergères-les-Vertus
Cramant	Oger	Chouilly
	Oiry	Vertus

The Mountain of Rheims is twelve miles long and approximately six miles broad; its highest point (near Verzy) lies 600 feet above the plain and 900 feet above sea-level. The plateau on top, across which runs the main Rheims-Epernay road, is covered by thick forests, 25,000 acres in extent, planted mainly with oaks, beeches, birches and many different sorts of pines. One of these forests—it is on the outskirts of Verzy—contains some of the most remarkable trees in the world: parasol beeches (*fagi sylvaticae*), known as *les Faux de Verzy*, "*faux*" being the plural of the old French word for beech, "*fay*". They were planted nearly 1,500 years ago by the monks of the Abbey of Saint-Basle, the ruins of whose chapel can be seen nearby. Few of them are more than ten feet high, but their hideously deformed, corkscrew branches stretch far out to form umbrellas so macabre that they would make a perfect setting for the witches' dance in *Macbeth*. The forests are broken now and then by the wood-cutters' villages, by deep ravines, meres, patches of heather and the quarries from which Tertiary debris for the vineyards is extracted. Wild boar haunt them, and are hunted in winter; in summer, Champenois and Parisian pot-holers descend deep shafts in the forests to explore underground streams that have no known source.

There are two distinct stretches of vineyard on the Mountain; both of them are mainly planted with vines that bear red grapes. The one which produces what are known as *vins de la montagne* extends almost continuously along the Mountain's northern slopes from Villers-Allerand to Mailly, along its north-eastern slopes from Verzenay to Villers-Marmery, and along its south-eastern slopes from Trépail to Tauxières, a total distance of approximately fifteen miles. On the western outskirts of Verzenay there stands a disused windmill, called the Moulin de Verzenay,* which is a vantage point without rival in the entire Champagne district. Nowhere else, not even on the Côte des Blancs, are vines to be seen in such stupendous array: you have the feeling you are on the bridge of a ship, ploughing through a billowing brilliant green sea. In the far distance to the left Rheims is just visible,

* The windmill, which is constructed entirely of wood, was put up in 1820 and was used to grind cereals. In 1901 the miller who owned it decided that it should cease working, as he did not wish its great wings to go on turning after his death. In 1904 his heirs, who had scrupulously respected his wishes, sold the windmill to the present-day champagne firm of Heidsieck & Co Monopole. The bill of sale, so the story goes, stipulated that the price should be one thousand gold francs for each child in the owner's family, an arrangement which resulted in Heidsieck Monopole having to pay ten thousand gold francs, as the owner's wife gave birth to her tenth child the day the bill was signed. Although its wings no longer turn, the windmill has never ceased to serve a useful purpose. During the First World War a concrete pill-box was built into its northern foundations, and many a distinguished visitor to the front line was taken there, handed a rifle and allowed to have a pot shot at the enemy, whose trenches throughout the greater part of the war were within firing distance. In 1944 it was used as an observation post by the American Army. Today Heidsieck Monopole use it, and the attractive little garden surrounding it, for receptions.

apparently pinned to the ground by a large gey cat, which in fact is its cathedral looming majestically above it. In the far distance to the right the valley of the Vesle is for ever broadening, until it finally merges into the grey flatness of *Champagne pouilleuse*.

These are the ratings of the *vins de la montagne* growths:

Catégorie Hors-classe	*Première Catégorie*	*Deuxième Catégorie*
Ambonnay	Tauxières	Chigny-les-Roses
Beaumont-sur-Vesle	Verzy	Ludes
Bouzy		Rilly-la-Montagne
Louvois		Trépail
Mailly		Vaudemanges
Sillery		Villers-Allerand
Verzenay		Villers-Marmery

The stretch of vineyard which produces what are called *vins de la rivière* extends for nine miles along the mountain's southern slopes from Tours-sur-Marne to Cumières. Virtually all these vineyards overlook the Marne. Sometimes they are referred to as forming part of the Grande Vallée de la Marne region, or the Grande Marne region, as the valley is nearly a mile wide at this point. These are the ratings of the *vins de la rivière* growths:

Catégorie Hors-classe	*Première Catégorie*	*Deuxième Catégorie*
Ay	Dizy	Avenay
	Mareuil-sur-Ay	Bisseuil
		Champillon
		Cumières
		Hautvillers
		Mutigny

In most of the *vins de la montagne* all the latent possibilities of the vines are found developed to their maximum extent. Most of them are wines that possess exceptional strength, marvellous freshness and a powerful bouquet.* A Champenois has written that you would not

---

* It is astounding that the wines should be so exceptional, because many of the growths that produce them face due north, and this, in theory, is the worst aspect of all for a vine in Champagne. The phenomenon is explained, some Champenois say, by the protection from winds which these vineyards are afforded by the Mountain of Rheims, and by the fact that the gradient of the slopes is not heavy: as long as the gradient is less than 1 in 20, they say, exposure to the north is not a drawback. But by far the most convincing explanation that I have come across

say of a wine of Verzy, for example, that it had an aftertaste of goose-berries, but that it had a real grapey taste. This highly developed vinosity of the *vins de la montagne* gives champagne its backbone. The *vins de la rivière* are also strong, fresh and possessed of a penetrating bouquet, but in them these qualities are slightly more refined, less overwhelming: one could say, for example, of a wine of Avenay that it had an aftertaste of strawberries, or of a Hautvillers wine that it had a nutty one. Thus, in a blend or *cuvée* ("*cuvée*" is the word the Champenois use for "a blend"), the *vins de la rivière* act as a perfect complement to the *vins de la montagne*, mollifying, so to speak, their obtrusiveness; and when the mollification is completed by the addition to the *cuvée* of a proportion of wine from the Côte des Blancs there results the harmony, the delicacy, the elegance that are the hallmarks of an out-standing champagne.

The Côte des Blancs and the two stretches of vineyard on the Mountain of Rheims are the prize vine-growing areas of the Falaises de Champagne, and every presentable champagne contains a percent-age of their produce. But even the most outstanding champagnes may contain the produce of vines grown in four less favoured areas of the Falaises: the valley of the Cubry, the valley where the village of Grauves lies, la Petite Montagne and the valley of the Marne. None of these less favoured areas has a *catégorie hors-classe* or a *première catégorie* growth. The valley of the Cubry runs north towards the Marne valley,

is in a book which is much less forbidding than its title: *A Treatise on the Origin, Nature and Varieties of Wine* by J. L. W. Thudichum and August Dupré, published in 1892. A local vine-grower told the authors that the secret of the quality of these north-facing vineyards lies in their special relation to *Champagne pouilleuse*. He maintained that the prevailing current of air over *Champagne pouilleuse*, which throughout the summer is a sun-trap, is in the direction of the northern slopes of the Mountain. As it passes over *Champagne pouilleuse* the air current abstracts heat from the soil there, and, on reaching the vines, not only adds to the direct effect of the sun on them but, in the evening and throughout the night, invests them with exceptional warmth. The fact remains, however, that grapes in these vineyards ripen on average eight days later than do those grown in vineyards facing south; evidently the accommodating air current does not entirely make up for the obliqueness and short duration of the sun's rays.

There are vineyards in the Champagne district facing every point of the compass, but the majority of the great growths face south, south-east or east. On the whole, south-east is considered to be the ideal aspect. Thus placed, the vine enjoys ample sunshine, heat and light; the one danger of a full southern aspect—roasting during heat waves—is avoided; and humidity, caused by dew or mist, is dispersed first thing in the morning by the sun rising in the east.

which it joins at Epernay; nowhere else on earth can there be so great a concentration of growths with such soothing names: Moussy, Pierry, Vinay, Saint-Martin-d'Ablois, Monthelon. Pierry is of the *deuxième catégorie*, and is remarkable because the flint in the soil gives the wine a flinty flavour ("*pierreux*", derived from the Latin "*petrosus*", means "flinty"). The valley of Grauves lies a mile or so east of the Cubry, at the back of the Côte des Blancs; it is very secluded and still wonderfully unspoilt. Two of its growths—Cuis and Grauves—are of the *deuxième catégorie*.

La Petite Montagne is situated a little to the north-west of the Mountain of Rheims, between the rivers Ardre and Vesle; its vineyards form a sort of appendage to those of the Mountain. They lie farther north than any others in the Champagne district. The growth of Ville-dommange is of the *deuxième catégorie*.

The valley of the Marne vineyards are a continuation—westwards, in the direction of Paris—of the vineyards that produce the *vins de la rivière*. From Cumières onwards they hug the slopes on both sides of the valley—but predominantly the slopes on the northern or right bank—for nearly forty-five miles, thinning out into little pockets the farther west they extend. Not one of them is in the three top *catégories*: in fact, the more westerly of them rank very low indeed as regards the quality of the wine they produce. Yet—great is the irony—it is they that give most casual visitors to the winefield their impression of what a Champagne vineyard looks like. This is because virtually all the top quality vineyards lie tucked away, well off the beaten track, on the road to nowhere, whereas the valley of the Marne is one of France's grand thoroughfares. Along it run both N. 3, the main road from Paris to Germany, and the railway line linking Paris with Strasbourg, Frankfurt, Berlin, Vienna and Istanbul.* And through it passes one of Europe's great inland waterways: from Charenton, where it flows into the Seine, the Marne is navigable as far as Epernay;† from Epernay

---

* Before the Second World War it was a common sight at Epernay to see Balkan noblemen, en route to Paris in the Orient Express, alighting to drink a glass of champagne at the Buffet de la Gare—thereafter they felt they really were in France.

† It can be imagined what an inestimable advantage the navigability of the Marne has been to the wines of the Champagne district: no other French wine-field has been blessed with such a quick and cheap means of conveying its produce direct to Parisian dining-tables. Today the navigability of the Marne is proving a boon to holiday-makers wishing to "get away from it all": the S.A.I.N.T. Line hires out superbly equipped yachts at Poincy (near Meaux) for one- or two-week cruises up the river to Epernay or Vitry-le-François and back.

the Canal de la Marne au Rhin cuts right across Champagne, Lorraine and Alsace to the Rhine at Strasbourg.

It is no disadvantage to the winefield's reputation that the vineyards which the average tourist sees are those of the Marne valley, because what they lack in quality they make up in beauty. There is an enchantment about everything appertaining to the Marne in this stretch of its waters, where it ranks as one of the great vineyard rivers of the world, that is more pronounced than in the rest of its 325-mile passage from Haute-Marne to the Seine. At Cumières the valley narrows and becomes much more enclosed (hence the viticultural nomenclature "Vallée de la Marne" or "Petite Marne" for this region, in contradistinction to "Grande Vallée de la Marne" or "Grande Marne" for the *vins de la rivière* region); and thus it continues, curving gracefully, the most classic and complete of valleys, as far as Dormans. Forests crown the slopes; sometimes the vines descend so close to the river that they are reflected in its green waters. (Of course the Marne is not always that colour; it is the most chameleon-like river I know. In winter it is often light brown, even, sometimes, a dull mouse-colour; during the rest of the year it is no surprise to find it a vivid blue or silvery grey; but in their happiest mood the waters of the Marne are a deep, shimmering emerald green.) The ubiquity of the vineyards and their orderliness—the latter fit to soften a sergeant-major's heart—confer an idyllic, almost Virgilian quality on the scene.

At Dormans the valley widens slightly; the curves of the river become longer, slower; on its banks, in summer, half-hidden by sun-dappled poplar brakes, are to be espied the orange tents and the caravans of the twentieth-century holiday maker. Vines disappear almost completely from the southern slopes of the valley now, and are replaced by orchards: in the eighteenth century Dormans was famous for its cherries, and some still find their way to English grocers. On the northern slopes the vineyards are starting to thin out, and to be separated by fields and woods; but vineyard villages still abound, some so close to the river's bank that many of the houses are reflected in the swift yet stately current, some so high up the side of the valley that only their red roofs and a Romanesque church tower are distinguishable from below. Dormans is on the boundary between the *départements* of Marne and Aisne, and these vineyards west of Dormans are often, for convenience, called "the Aisne vineyards". One stretch of the valley between Dormans and Château-Thierry is known as "*la Varoce*": it is an area where everyone knows perfectly well that the soil is not conducive to the growing of first-class grapes, yet the locals

The Abbey of Hautvillers—birthplace of champagne

The stupendous view from Hautvillers across the Marne Valley

will never admit it, and they go on tending their vines because their ancestors did and because they cannot bear to part with them.

Beyond Château-Thierry the little pockets of vineyard continue as far as the village of Nanteuil-sur-Marne, which lies just within the border of Seine-et-Marne. Nanteuil is the most westerly growth in the Champagne district, and the one situated nearest to Paris, which is only thirty-two miles away as the crow flies. For harmony, peace and luxuriant beauty, this stretch of the Marne valley compares with parts of the Dordogne, parts of the Wye, and the Tauber below Rothenburg. Forests of beech, oak and elm cover the crests; fruit trees and the little vineyards dot the slopes; rich corn flutters below; pleasant country houses peep out from behind poplar trees; and in the river are mirrored a succession of mellow villages and hamlets. Here Corot set up his easel; here La Fontaine wandered, composing his Fables.

The propriety of mentioning those vineyards of the Marne valley that lie in the *départements* of Aisne and Seine-et-Marne in the same context as the Falaises de Champagne is open to question, as the Falaises are definitely situated in the *département* of Marne. I feel justified in doing so because the belt of vineyard in the Marne valley is an almost continuous one, the subsoil throughout is *Belimnita quadrata* chalk, and the soil conditions prevailing are to some extent the result of the violent upheaval that gave birth to the Falaises. Besides, the variation in climatic conditions between the most easterly and the most westerly of the Marne valley vineyards is infinitesimal. There exists, however, yet another less favoured vine-growing area of *Champagne viticole*, and this cannot by the remotest stretch of the imagination be considered to have anything to do with the Falaises. It is known as the Aube region. The vineyards that comprise it cover the slopes of a mass of little hills and valleys situated in the extreme south-west corner of the *département* of Aube, in the vicinity of Bar-sur-Aube and Bar-sur-Seine, sixty miles from the southern tip of the Côtes des Blancs. The region forms part of *Champagne humide*, and thus the climate is harsher than on the Falaises; also, the soil conditions are in general quite different: the subsoil is mostly kimmeridge clay (as it is in the Chablis winefield, which lies close by), not *Belimnita quadrata* chalk.

In actual fact, the wine produced by the Aube vineyards—like that produced by numerous small pockets of vineyards which also lie completely cut off from the Falaises de Champagne—is not widely used to make champagne. Most of it is sold to makers of other wines, in France and abroad. Nevertheless, it has the right to enter *cuvées* of champagne.

At the time I write, there are about 44,478 acres of land in *Champagne viticole* planted with vines, a surface area roughly equal to that of Paris. This is just about a hundredth part of the total area of French soil planted with vines, about a third of the area covered by the Burgundian winefield and about a sixth of the area covered by the Bordeaux winefield. The distribution by regions is roughly as follows:

Côtes des Blancs	6,000 acres
Mountains of Rheims:	
vins de la Montagne area	8,000 acres
vins de la rivière area	4,000 acres
Valleys of the Cubry and of Grauves	3,000 acres
Petite Montagne	3,000 acres
Valley of the Marne	9,000 acres
Aube	4,000 acres
Isolated Pockets	5,000 acres

The distribution by *départments* is:

Marne	37,000 acres
Aube	5,000 acres
Aisne	2,000 acres
Haute-Marne	1 acre
Seine-et-Marne	38 acres

The quantity of wine produced by the vineyards each year varies enormously, depending on the weather conditions that have prevailed and on the incidence of disease. In 1893 wine was so plentiful and water so scarce that coachmen were seen washing down carriages with still Champagne wine. In this century the worst harvest so far has been the 1910 one, when only 14,182 hectolitres (312,004 gallons) were produced. Since the First World War the most plentiful harvest has been 1934 (767,570 hectolitres, 16,886,540 gallons); the least plentiful, apart from the Second World War period, has been 1927 (112,411 hectolitres, 2,473,042 gallons). During the decade 1957–1966 the average annual yield of the whole winefield was 564,833 hectolitres (approximately 12 million gallons), and the average annual yield of each acre worked out at about 350 gallons.

In 1908 the plantations in the winefield were valued for taxation purposes at £5,800,000; it is estimated, conservatively, that their value today is well over ten times that figure. Certain growths (planted) in Aube are not worth very much more than farmland, say £23 to £60 an acre; but in Marne a minor growth (planted) is worth between £900 and £1,500 an acre; and the growths in the *catégorie hors-classe* (which are practically never on the market) are worth (planted) between £3,000 and £6,000 an acre. The latter rate was paid by the purchaser of a portion of a planted *hors-classe* vineyard in 1963.

The champagne vines, like all the other great wine-producing vines of Europe, belong to the genus known as *Vitis vinifera*. It has been cultivated in Europe without interruption since the days of the Phoenicians. In 1844 no less than 2,000 distinct species of the genus that were being grown in French vineyards were displayed at the Luxembourg Gardens in Paris; the number today is about 100.

The law allows champagne to be made from the grapes of four of the species: the Pinot, the Chardonnay, the Arbanne and the Petit Meslier. However, less than 1 per cent of the winefield is planted with Arbanne and Petit Meslier vines. Champagne's life-blood is the juice of the Pinot and the Chardonnay.

The Pinot is an aristocrat. Like the Cabernet-Sauvignon and the Riesling, it makes wines which have that most elusive and attractive of all wine-virtues, which, for lack of a better word, is often called "breed". It is the vine that produces most of the great burgundies (the Burgundians call it the Noiren); and it may even be said to be the *éminence grise* of port, for the vines planted on the Douro originally came from Burgundy. Port, burgundy and champagne, each the issue of the noble Pinot, could thus be described as first cousins. The Pinot has been much transplanted to other parts of the world to give tone to otherwise undistinguished growths.

The name is believed to derive from the Latin word *pinus*: the vine's small grapes grow densely in the bunch, roughly in the shape of a pine-cone. There is a reference in *De Re Rustica* by Columella, published in the first century A.D., to a vine whose bunches of grapes grew in this fashion. No one knows when the Pinot was first introduced into the Champagne district and whether Champagne gave it to Burgundy or vice versa. The vine is mentioned in a fourteenth-century Champenois ballad, but the best evidence of its long connection with the district is to be found in the sculptures in the churches. The Champenois artists of the thirteenth, fourteenth and fifteenth centuries depicted a vine which looks exactly like the Pinot, although the periphery of the leaves is somewhat craggier. The explanation of this unevenness may well be that in those days the vines were not so well tended as they are today.

The Pinot is not an easy vine to grow. It is extremely fastidious as regards soil and climate, and demands careful valeting. It is also what is called a "shy bearer": several other wine-producing vines yield two-thirds more grape-juice. But the grower who accepts and panders to these characteristics is amply rewarded. The Pinot is full of vigour: it flowers early and its fruit matures early. The sugar content of its grapes is sometimes sufficiently high for a wine of 14 degrees alcohol to be produced. Its wine is delicate, possesses an incomparable bouquet, and, given time, can be depended upon to show the breed of its noble parentage.

The varieties of Pinot are very numerous: one vineyard owner in the Champagne district has no less than eighty-two. Many of the varieties have been produced by cross-breeding; others have resulted from the natural adaptation of the plant, during a period extending over several generations, to the chemical composition of a particular soil and to a particular microclimate.* Great experience is required to tell the different varieties apart: in order to do so, it is often necessary to know the shape and colour of the grape, the size of the pips, the shade the leaves turn in the autumn, as well, of course, as the taste of the juice.

The Pinot Noir, which dominates the Mountain of Rheims, and the Pinot Meunier, which is mainly grown in the valleys of the Cubry and of Grauves, on La Petite Montagne and along the Valley of the Marne, are the varieties most widely planted in Champagne.

The most striking characteristic of the Pinot Noir is that its grape-crop is small but of unbeatable quality. It thrives in calcareous soils and dislikes those that are argillaceous or humid. It is just about the most precocious of all the Pinots in its seasonal development, which makes it highly susceptible to spring frosts; in an average year its fruit matures well. The grapes are spherical and thin-skinned; when they

---

* Vineyards separated by a fold in the hills or a strip of forest can be exposed to astonishingly different climatic conditions in the course of a year: one may miss a hail-storm which sets the others back for weeks, or enjoy a shower of rain while the others remain parched. Climatically, the Champagne district is composed of a number of microclimates. In a region where an unblended wine is made, this might be a drawback; in one where wines of widely differing types are required to produce the final blend, it is an advantage.

mature they turn violet. They develop an abundance of waxy substance on their skins, and are therefore covered in thick bloom by the time they are picked.

The Pinot Meunier produces a wine that ages more rapidly and has a less fine bouquet than that produced by the Pinot Noir, but it is a useful vine in that it is exceptionally robust, buds late (a great advantage when spring frosts strike), and flourishes in soils that do not suit the Pinot Noir. It has been in the Champagne district since the sixteenth century. It was named the Meunier because the white down on its leaves—on its shoots, too, but there is more on the leaves—gives it the appearance of having been sprinkled with flour, a peculiarity which makes it easily identifiable. The bunches of grapes are egg-shaped and strikingly dense. The grapes are spherical and thin-skinned; they turn jet black just before reaching maturity.

The Chardonnay is sometimes erroneously called the Pinot Blanc Chardonnay or the Pinot Blanc de Cramant; in reality, it is not in any way related to the Pïnot family of vines. A Pinot vine that bears white grapes does in fact exist, and there are plantations of it in the Champagne district and in Burgundy, but it is in process of disappearing from both winefields. The Chardonnay produces some of the best white wines in the world. It is responsible for many famous white burgundies; it is the vine grown in Chablis. On the Côte des Blancs in Champagne it produces a wine remarkable for delicacy, richness of colour, freshness and bouquet.

The Chardonnay has been in the Champagne district for many centuries, but exactly how long no one is sure. Alleman, a learned monk of the ninth century, mentioned the *raisins brillants et dorés* of the area, which might be a reference to it. It is often stated that Thibault, Count of Champagne, brought it back from Cyprus during the Crusades. More probably it is of Burgundian origin, from the village of Chardonnay near Châlon-sur-Saône. The Chardonnay is a more prolific bearer than the Pinot Noir. It buds even earlier, and is therefore dreadfully susceptible to damage from spring frosts; on the other hand, its grapes mature more slowly; usually they are ready for picking a week later than those of the Pinot Noir. It thrives in marly and chalky soils. The clusters of grapes are much less compact than those of the Pinots. The individual grapes are round, more or less transparent and golden-green. Their skins are tender. They nearly always contain slightly less sugar than Pinot grapes.

Seventy-six per cent of the winefield is planted with vines that bear red grapes; the remaining 24 per cent is devoted to the white-graped

Chardonnay vine, which is mainly found on the Côte des Blancs. Between them, the soil and the subsoil tend to tie the hand of the vineyard owner: he may want to plant a Pinot Noir where at present a Pinot Meunier is growing, or to devote part of a Pinot Noir vineyard to the Chardonnay; long, long experience has taught him that such experiments are fraught with danger and seldom succeed.

CHAPTER 3

THE WINE

Up to the end of the seventeenth century, the wines made from the grapes that grew on the Falaises de Champagne were still ones; some were whitish in colour, but the majority were of a reddish hue. They were made, as burgundy and bordeaux and every other still wine are made today, according to the same basic principle used by the first man ever to make wine, who may have been a Chinese but was more probably a Sumerian: the grapes were pressed, the natural phenomenon of fermentation turned the grape-juice into wine, and the wine was then kept in a suitable vessel until it was ready to drink.

However, although the method of manufacture was the same as that used for all other wines, there was always, about the still wine produced on the Falaises, a peculiarity which, though not confined to them, was more noticeable than in other wines. In the spring, the wines began to fret. In some years the disturbance was strong enough for the wines to be described as being *"en furie"*; in others it was no greater than what modern Frenchmen associate with a *vin pétillant*; in others still it was so slight as to be invisible, merely enough to tickle the tongue—a degree of effervescence which today denotes a *vin perlé*. Nearly always the disturbance vanished as mysteriously and swiftly as it had appeared: *"Pasques passé,"* wrote a seventh-century vine grower, *"c'en fait."*

The first Champenois to grasp the significance of the phenomenon was a Benedictine monk called Dom Pérignon, who in about 1668 was appointed chief cellarer of a monastery on the Mountain of Rheims called Hautvillers. It occurred to him that it might be possible to develop the natural sparkle so that the wine became a fully sparkling one, what the French today call a *vin mousseux*. He embarked on experiments which lasted for nearly twenty years. Around 1690 he achieved his ambition—which many people will say was one of the most worth-while ambitions a man ever had—of manufacturing a bottle of truly sparkling champagne.

It is perfectly easy to understand the basic principle of the method which he used to develop the natural tendency of his wines to sparkle, once it is understood why grape-juice ferments. It does so because the yeasts which attach themselves to the grape-skins in the vineyards behave in the most extraordinary manner as soon as the skins are broken in the presses. Contact with the sugar which the juice contains sends the yeasts berserk. They attack the sugar and convert it into two things, alcohol and carbonic acid gas. If the vessel containing the grape-juice is an open one, the carbonic acid gas escapes into the atmosphere, but the alcohol remains and mixes with the grape-juice. The resulting mixture is wine.

Now, yeasts are sensitive creatures, and in very cold weather they wisely go to sleep. In a northern climate, such as that of the Falaises, where the grapes ripen and are pressed in the late autumn, their slumbers often create the following situation: the yeasts have not finished converting the sugar when the winter cold sends them to sleep, so that, although the conversion has proceeded far enough for the grape-juice to have become wine, that wine still contains sugar—and yeasts. In the spring, when warm weather returns, the yeasts wake up, realise that they still have a little sugar to play with, attack it, and convert it, as before, into alcohol and carbonic acid gas. The alcohol mixes with the wine, and the carbonic acid gas escapes into the spring air. As it rises to the surface the gas produces bubbles: it was these bubbles, this disturbance, that regularly each spring mystified and often alarmed people before Dom Pérignon's time.

In all probability Dom Pérignon had not the faintest idea what was the agent responsible for the fermentation of grape-juice, because it was not until the late nineteenth century that Pasteur unveiled the secret life of yeasts. But Dom Pérignon understood wine as well as any man in history, and he was determined to produce a wine that contained bubbles galore and could be enjoyed in a sparkling state at any time of the year, not just in the spring. His observations convinced him that he might succeed if he could find a substance which, without imparting a nasty taste, would hermetically seal a bottle filled with wine that had a natural tendency to sparkle. Strange as it may seem to us, this was a most difficult problem. At that time in France a bottle used as a container for wine was stopped with a piece of wood wrapped in hemp which had been dipped in olive oil: an entirely adequate contrivance for keeping dust away from a still wine, but quite hopeless as a hermetic seal. The story of how Dom Pérignon finally hit upon the ideal substance for his purpose is a strange one, and it will be a delight to relate it farther on. All I want to say here is that the substance was cork.

Once he had cork, the way ahead was clear. For in the spring, just before the wine showed signs of becoming disturbed, he could bottle it and for the first time hermetically seal the bottle with a cork. The disturbance would thus take place inside the bottle. When, weeks later, this disturbance, or the second fermentation of the wine as it is now called, was over, Dom Pérignon must have pulled the cork of one of his bottles in a state of considerable excitement. Would a true sparkle, a heavenly sparkle, an energetic sparkle that endured, emerge from the wine when it was poured? We know, of course, that it was bound to appear, because the cork had given the carbonic acid gas produced in the second fermentation no alternative but to suspend itself in the wine until such time as the cork was pulled, at which juncture out it would come, passing through the wine into the atmosphere, leaving in its wake a million bubbles.

The champagne which Dom Pérignon made was probably what the French today call a *crémant* wine, one possessed of more sparkle than a *pétillant* wine but not as much as a *mousseux* one. It cannot have been a fully sparkling wine because there could never have been a sufficient amount of unconverted sugar left in the wine at the time it was bottled for a fully sparkling wine to result from the second fermentation; nor would the bottles in those days have been able to withstand the pressure exerted on them by a fully sparkling wine. As the quality of champagne bottles improved, however, it gradually became the custom to add what is called a *dosage* of cane sugar to the wine at the time it was bottled, so that the quantity of carbonic acid gas produced by the yeasts increased. Today the pressure that is built up inside a bottle of champagne in the course of the second fermentation amounts to the astounding figure of ninety pounds per square inch. Buses run on tyres pumped up to that pressure.

This fact causes a problem in connection with the sediment which does not arise in the case of still wine. For one thing, the percentage of sediment and dead yeasts in a bottle of champagne will be considerably greater than in a bottle of still wine; secondly, filtering or decanting— the method used in the manufacture of still wine—is out of the question, for by the time either process was accomplished the pressure would have vanished into thin air and the champagne would be as flat as a pancake.

No one knows for certain how Dom Pérignon coped with this difficulty. However, as champagne became more widely known and people grew more fastidious in their tastes, the absolute necessity of selling it in a perfectly clean and limpid state inspired the Champenois to work out a system of getting rid of the sediment without losing more than a fraction of the pressure inside the bottle. The system, which is divided into two stages, known as *remuage* and *dégorgement*, is extremely ingenious. Watching it in operation is one of the things that draw hundreds of thousands of visitors each year to champagne cellars. It is described in detail in Chapter 28.

The process by which wine is put through a double fermentation— one in an open receptacle, the other in an hermetically sealed bottle— is known as the *méthode champenoise*. The law of France insists that champagne must be made according to this method. In other parts of the country wine-makers are at perfect liberty to make sparkling wine in whatever way they wish, but in no circumstances may they call it champagne; if, however, the sparkling wine was made by the *méthode champenoise*, that fact may be mentioned on the label. Since French law only applies within the boundaries of France, there is often nothing to prevent wine-makers in other countries from calling their sparkling wine "champagne". No one in his senses, however, would try to pretend that these so-called champagnes—or, for that matter, spark- ling wines made elsewhere in France—approach champagne in quality.

Many people who have been swigging champagne for a lifetime are unaware of the fact that the wine is made predominantly from the juice of red grapes. This apparent anomaly is rendered possible because the actual juice of the red grapes grown in the winefield, like the juice of most red grapes, is white, the pigmentation being in the skin. By pressing the red grapes in a special manner and removing the skins immediately after the pressing, juice which has hardly a trace of red in it is obtained. This juice imparts a "body", an importance, one might say, to champagne which the juice of white grapes alone can seldom give it. But if it were all "body", all importance, champagne would not be champagne. It is the addition of a judicious quantity— the ideal proportion is generally about one-third—of the juice of the white grapes grown in the winefield that produces, in conjunction with "body", the fragrance, the brightness of champagne.

The art of blending champagne, however, is not just a matter of choosing the right proportion of juice derived from red and white grapes; selecting the vineyards from which the grapes come is of equal importance. A bottle of the best champagne may contain the juice of fifteen different vineyards, and some excellent champagnes are composed of juice obtained from over thirty different vineyards.

Now this is matter to reflect upon, because the wine of very great vineyards in other winefields is never blended. There would be a fear- ful outcry if, say, the wine-makers of Bordeaux suddenly started blending together such wines as Château Lafite and Château Margaux. In the Bordeaux, Burgundy, Rhine and Moselle winefields each vineyard has its own entity, its own special qualities or defects, and the purchaser is encouraged to choose the wine of whichever one best suits his fancy or his pocket, in the certain knowledge (this, at least, is the theory) that he is paying for the pure produce of that vineyard. In the Champagne district the situation is quite different. Here each vineyard does, of course, have its own entity and its own qualities and defects too, but, on account of the blending, few people apart from the Champenois themselves are familiar with the characteristics of the individual vineyards. Which leads to the question: why do the Champenois make such extensive use of blending when makers of other great wines do not?

They do so for two good reasons. The first is simply that long experience has proved that as a general rule a far finer champagne is achieved from a blending of the produce of several vineyards than from that of a single red-grape one and a single white-grape one. Why exactly this should be so nobody, not even a Champenois, knows.

The other reason has to do with the northern climate of the Falaises. It would cause a great deal of disappointment in the world if, as a result of a series of calamities that befell the crop, the Champenois announced, "We're awfully sorry, but we're making no champagne this year, and probably none next year either". As it is, they avoid having to do so by making two distinct types of blend: one which they call *millésimé* and we call "vintage", another which they call *sans année* and we call "non-vintage".

Vintage champagne is a blend of the wines of one exceptionally good year. The year in question (the year the grapes were picked) is indicated on the label.* The amount of vintage champagne made is never very great. This is because, even in an exceptionally good year, a large proportion of that year's wine is taken down to the cellars and stored there in magnums, casks or vats until such time as it is needed to make non-vintage champagne. For non-vintage champagne is a blend not only of the wines of different vineyards but of different years as well. Thanks to this arrangement, no matter what sort of disaster may

---

* During the hundred years that preceded the Second World War, the greatest vintage years were 1846, 1857, 1865, 1868, 1870, 1874, 1880, 1892, 1893, 1900, 1904, 1906, 1911, 1914, 1919, 1920, 1921, 1923, 1926, 1928, 1929, 1933, 1934, and 1937. The wartime and post-war vintages that are generally accepted as having potential greatness are 1941, 1943, 1945, 1947, 1949, 1952, 1953, 1955, 1959 and 1961 (the last to have been declared when this book went to press); but it is still too early to make the final evaluation.

have befallen the vines in the previous spring, summer or autumn, the champagne-maker always has at his disposal, deep in his cellars, reserves of wine of preceding years which he can blend and bottle.

That stern guardian of quality, the law of France, insists that a vintage champagne may not be sold until three years have elapsed since the grapes were picked, and that a non-vintage champagne may not be sold until one year has gone by since it was bottled. In reality, the only non-vintage champagne that is aged for such a short time is the type you might be offered at a booth at a summer fair in a village on the Falaises. You would spot the lack of maturity straight away; there would be a harshness to the champagne to which you were not accustomed, and you would certainly dislike it. Any champagne-maker worth his salt ages his non-vintage champagne for about three years and his vintage champagne for about five years. Vintage champagne, having only the wine of an exceptionally good year in it, is normally, of course, the superior product; on the other hand, the non-vintage variety has the delightful advantage of being the cheaper of the two.

A person or a firm whose main professional activity is the making and selling of champagne, as opposed to that of vine-growing, is known in France as a *négociant en vin de champagne* or as a *négociant-manipulant en vin de champagne*. Altogether 144 such *négociants* exist in the Champagne district (by law, the profession may only be exercised within the confines of *Champagne viticole*), but the majority of them have very small businesses and no export trade. About 65 per cent of the champagne sold each year is made by the following eighteen firms:

AYALA, *Ay*
BOLLINGER, *Ay*
Veuve CLICQUOT-PONSARDIN, *Rheims*
HEIDSIECK Monopole, *Rheims*
Charles HEIDSIECK, *Rheims*
IRROY, *Rheims*
KRUG, *Rheims*
LANSON, *Rheims*
MERCIER, *Epernay*
MOËT & CHANDON, *Epernay*
G. H. MUMM, *Rheims*
PERRIER-JOUËT, *Epernay*

PIPER HEIDSIECK, *Rheims*
POL ROGER, *Epernay*
POMMERY & GRENO, *Rheims*
ROEDERER, *Rheims*
RUINART, *Rheims*
TAITTINGER, *Rheims*

There are several reasons why the profession of champagne-making is mainly concentrated in the hands of a few large firms. One is that the manufacture of champagne is so complicated and costly a process that the average vineyard proprietor feels no inclination to undertake it himself: he much prefers to sell his grapes—or his still wine—to the specialist in the field. Another is that the production, year in, year out, of champagne of uniform quality and taste presupposes the possession fo vast reserves of still champagne wine, and the accumulation and financing of these reserves is a burden which a large firm is better able to assume than a small one. Yet another has to do with the fact that, being a blended wine, champagne—like port and cognac, which are also blended—is always sold under the label of the firm that makes it, never under the name of a vineyard, as is the case with burgundies and bordeaux: to succeed in getting the name of a firm known throughout the world requires such a huge outlay of capital and effort over such a long period of time that newcomers to the profession, faced with the competition of the established firms, nowadays seldom consider the attempt worth-while.

A person whose main professional activity is vine-growing, but who also makes champagne, is known as a *récoltant-manipulant*; altogether there are about 1,500 such persons in the Champagne district today. There are also a few firms or persons who are content to sell under their own name—or a brand name patented by them—champagnes made by another firm or by a *récoltant-manipulant*. They are known as *négociants-non-manipulants*.

The great champagne firms are known as *"Les Grandes Marques"*. Ian Maxwell Campbell described them as "the dozen or so Crowned Heads of Champagne". Some of them were founded in the eighteenth century, nearly all are over a century old,* and most of them are still owned and run by the descendants or the descendants by marriage of their founders. Several other firms produce as good a champagne as

* The record is remarkable, but not as remarkable as that of some of the big Bavarian breweries: the Spatenbräu brewery in Munich has been making and selling beer since 1397.

they, but none produces better. Each of the firms which I write about in Part VIII is considered by the Champenois to be a "*Grande Marque*".

The ownership of the vineyards in the Champagne district is split between a greater number of people than is the case in any of the other great French winefields. There are no less than 16,250 proprietors of the 44,478 acres planted with vines. Only 14 per cent of the vineyards (6,000 acres) belong to the *négociants en vin de champagne*; several champagne firms whose names are known throughout the civilized world do not own a single vine.

Two factors are responsible for this extraordinary state of affairs. One is the clause in the Code Napoléon concerning inheritance, which stipulates that most of a deceased person's property must be divided equally between his progeny. The other is the reluctance of the Champenois to sell a square inch of vineyard if they can possibly help it. How deep-rooted this reluctance is I learnt the hard way. Wishing to see for myself how vines are uprooted, in order to write the description of the process which appears later in this book, I made an appointment with a *maître-vigneron* of one of the great Houses. Just before I was to leave for the vineyard concerned, I received a phone call to say that the uprooting had been unavoidably postponed for a week; for several weeks running the same thing happened—by which time the uprooting season had ended, and I had to wait a whole year before it came round again. Eventually I discovered the cause of the delay; the vineyard in question was the last bit of vineyard property that belonged personally to the wife of the chairman of the House, who, unlike her husband, was a Champenois born and bred; all the rest she had already transferred to the House. She had agreed to the transfer of this vineyard too, and at the time when I made the first appointment with the *maître-vigneron* the papers were on her desk awaiting signature; but each time she sat down to sign them, after reminders and prods from her exasperated husband, something held her back, and she was still the proud owner of the plot. For all I know she still is; and if she is, I am sure it is not for sentimental reasons alone. For deep in the hearts of all true Champenois lies a sixth sense which tells them that in times of financial crisis as much as in times of prosperity it is best to hang on to vineyard property, because—who knows?—war may bring ruin to Champagne once again, as it has so regularly in the past, in which case the same old thing will happen: stocks and shares and money in the bank will become worthless overnight, real estate will be demolished or its contents looted; whereas, if they own a vineyard, *that* at least will go on and keep the wolf from the door until normalcy returns.

Indeed, in view of the tenacity with which the Champenois cling to their vineyards, what is surprising is that the ownership of the holdings is not still further split up, and that the *négociants* have succeeded in acquiring as much of the winefield as they have. For most of the big Houses would nowadays much prefer to own more vineyards—more high-class vineyards especially—and work them themselves with salaried workers, rather than, as they have to now, buy the majority of the grapes they need from the small proprietors. The figures below illustrate the situation:

THE MOUNTAIN OF RHEIMS

Growth	Total area (in acres)	Area owned by Négociants	Area owned by Vignerons
Ay	652	321	331
Bouzy	686	145	540
Verzenay	975	350	624
All the red-grape *grands crus*	10,316	2,440	7,874

THE CÔTE DES BLANCS

Cramant	913	247	666
Le Mesnil	1,049	138	909
All the white-grape *grands crus*	5,287	1,052	4,232

As there are over 16,250 vineyard proprietors in the Champagne district, the size of the majority of the holdings is naturally exceptionally small. There are believed to be only nine holdings in the whole region that cover an area of more than 123 acres. The broad picture is as follows:

Vignerons' Holdings

Less than $\frac{1}{4}$ of an acre	1,988
$\frac{1}{4}$ to $\frac{1}{2}$ of an acre	2,546
$\frac{1}{2}$ to $\frac{3}{4}$ of an acre	1,924
$\frac{3}{4}$ to 1 acre	1,454
1 acre to $1\frac{1}{4}$ acres	1,138
$1\frac{1}{4}$ to $1\frac{1}{2}$ acres	880
$1\frac{1}{2}$ to $1\frac{3}{4}$ acres	735
$1\frac{3}{4}$ to 2 acres	634
2 to $2\frac{1}{4}$ acres	553

$2\frac{1}{4}$ to $2\frac{1}{2}$ acres	461
$2\frac{1}{2}$ to $7\frac{1}{2}$ acres	2,440
$7\frac{1}{2}$ to $12\frac{1}{4}$ acres	148
$12\frac{1}{4}$ to $24\frac{1}{2}$ acres	39
$24\frac{1}{2}$ to $49\frac{1}{2}$ acres	6

Négociants' Holdings

Less than $2\frac{1}{2}$ acres	17
$2\frac{1}{2}$ to $7\frac{1}{2}$ acres	21
$7\frac{1}{2}$ to $12\frac{1}{4}$ acres	9
$12\frac{1}{4}$ to $24\frac{1}{2}$ acres	20
$24\frac{1}{2}$ to $49\frac{1}{2}$ acres	24
$49\frac{1}{2}$ acres or more	32

Remarkable as these figures are, they do not show something even more remarkable still: the minute size of the majority of the individual plots of vines. Partly as a result of the Code Napoléon and partly because everyone who makes champagne prefers to have several parcels of vines rather than one big one, in order to have a choice of grapes for the *cuvée*, the average champagne vineyard is probably about the area of a soccer field; some are no bigger than tennis-courts. Stones, carved with the initials of the proprietor, indicate the boundaries of the respective properties and are often encountered every ten yards or so. Each property is further distinguishable because the rows of vines are generally set at a slightly different angle to those in the next property. In areas where innumerable individual vineyard properties are joined together, this difference in angles creates the appearance of a patchwork quilt.

The sub-division of the winefield into such a multitude of parcels inevitably gives rise to problems in today's economic conditions. Often ground that could be planted with vines is taken up by paths, to enable individual proprietors to reach their properties; many a road in the vineyards is badly placed, from the point of view of affording tractors easy access to the vines, but nothing has been done about it because it cuts across several property boundaries. Since the Second World War what are known as *Commissions locales de la Reconstitution* have been operating in each *commune* with the main aim of persuading and helping owners to swap parcels of vines, so that bigger and more economic units are created and access to them is facilitated. On a hill-side behind Ay I recently saw the result of one such exchange between two big vineyard proprietors. What had formerly been a precipitous gully with a track but not a single vine in it was now completely filled with earth, flattened, walled up where necessary, and planted. A huge pipe had been installed below ground to carry off the water that formerly flowed down the gully. A few hundred yards away, as the result of another exchange, bulldozers were literally chopping off the crown of a hill, in order to weaken the gradient and render unused ground cultivable. The *maître-vigneron* in charge of the operation, eyeing the piles of chalk that were mounting up as the bulldozer worked, asked me jokingly if I could do with some. He was going to see the Town Council of Ay the next day to try to persuade them to cart it away to fill up holes in the banks of the Marne, but as he observed, "Champagne's no place to peddle chalk!".

There can be no doubt that in one sense the degree to which the winefield is split up is healthy. As the majority of the holdings are so small and as the vine (unlike livestock) does not require daily attention except at certain critical periods, the average Champenois vineyard proprietor does not depend for his livelihood on his vines. He may work on them in the early morning, in the evening and at weekends, but during the week his wife or his father-in-law looks after them and he is free to take a full-time job elsewhere. Being financially independent of his vines he has been able in the past, and will no doubt be able in future, to weather the buffets of war and economic depression much more successfully than he could have done had his holding been his main source of income.

The labour force in the vineyards amounts to approximately eighteen thousand hands, split up as follows:

Vineyard proprietors	15,500
Employees (who do not own vines)	2,500

About a thousand vineyard proprietors work as employees for other proprietors. Some *vignerons* have *métayage* arrangements with the proprietor of the vineyard: the proprietor provides the plants, ferti-lizers, etc., and the *vigneron* receives part (usually half) of the crop of grapes in lieu of wages.

It is estimated that in the Champagne district a family needs 6 to $7\frac{1}{2}$ acres of vines to live off them exclusively. Less than 200 Champenois families possess holdings as large as that. This, coupled with the fact that the process of champagne-making is a complicated one and has thus become concentrated in a few specialist hands, probably explains why there exists a much greater difference in class distinction between *négociant* and *vigneron* in the Champagne district than in other French winefields (with the possible exception of Cognac, where the majority of the vineyards are also in the possession of small proprietors). In Burgundy and the Bordelais, more so still in other winefields, the average wine-maker may not actually wear tweeds like the English countryman, but he strikes one as a "tweedy" person who is more at home with mud on his boots and his nose in his vines than in his office, much more at home in the country than the town. The average champagne-maker is a more metropolitan fellow. Even if he does not belong to one of the great aristocratic champagne families who made their fortunes in late Victorian and Edwardian times, and whose daughters—known as "the champagne girls"—were the great "catches" of the Paris season of those days, he still gives the impression that he would be just as much at ease in a Paris salon as at his desk in Rheims or Epernay, and that he has no particular desire to rush out and prune a vine. My vision of a mid-twentieth-century champagne-maker is of a cultivated, highly intelligent, affable and well-dressed man directing his concern with a light touch from an office furnished with a pale ginger carpet, beige curtains, lots of comfortable leather chairs and an elegant marquetry desk, who spends his holidays skiing, yachting in the Mediterranean, or shooting bears in the Tatras.

PART II

THE LAND

CHAPTER 4

RHEIMS

Rheims has roots that lie deeper in history than those of any other town in France outside the Midi. For centuries before Caesar conquered Gaul in 57 B.C., it was the capital of a Gallic tribe, the Remi; during the Roman occupation, when Paris was little more than an overgrown village, it was the chief city of Belgian Gaul, with a population of between 80,000 and 100,000.

The Romans called the city Durocortorum. Most historians say that it was later renamed Rheims as a tribute to its original inhabitants; but the present-day Rémois believe that the town owes its name to a different circumstance. They assert that, while Romulus was tracing the future ramparts of Rome, Remus was founding its transalpine counterpart, Rheims. As the words Remus and Rheims are so alike, and as there is a scene depicting Romulus and Remus being given milk by the wolf on the Porte Mars, a Roman triumphal arch which still survives in Rheims, they may well be right.

In the late eighteenth century the French, who have always pronounced the city's name "Rr-ăns", started spelling the word without an "h"; the champagne firm of Ruinart Père et Fils, however, still uses the old spelling on its stationery and labels, and the English have remained faithful to it also.

The mainstay of Rheims's prosperity during the Roman occupation was the wool trade; the city produced "*cuculles*"—hooded coats, like djellabas—that were sold throughout the empire. Its leather-work, pottery, glass and silverware were also much in demand. In the footsteps of economic prosperity came artistic expression. Finding in the Champenois subsoil all the primary materials needed for building—stone, lime, earth for bricks and tiles, slate for roofs—the Gallo-Romans adorned Rheims with many beautiful palaces, arenas, baths and monuments. They also built numerous schools, and the city soon became an intellectual centre. The Emperor Hadrian once referred to it as the Athens of Gaul.

The vitality which Rheims displayed under Roman rule remained strongly in evidence during the next 1,500 years, despite the fact that, after the complete destruction of the city by the Vandals in December 406, the population fell to 4,000, and had only climbed back to 20,000 when the French Revolution broke out.

The history of France may truly be said to have begun in Rheims with
the baptism of Clovis by St. Remi in the year 496. In succeeding centuries
the tradition grew that Rheims should be the chosen city for the coronation of the Kings of France. The germ of the idea that the Archbishops
of Rheims were king-makers sprang from an incident that was supposed
to have occurred during the baptism of Clovis. So great was the crowd
in the church that the priest whose duty it was to hand St. Remi the oil
to anoint Clovis was unable to do so. The saint addressed a silent prayer
to God, and, miraculously, there appeared from heaven a white dove
carrying in its beak a small crystal ampulla filled with holy oil; with this
oil St. Remi proceeded to anoint the King. Whatever the truth of this legend, it gave rise to another one: the suggestion that St. Remi had not just
baptized Clovis but had crowned him as well, the most solemn moment
of the coronation having been the anointing with the miraculous oil.

It seems most unlikely that St. Remi did in fact crown Clovis,
despite a remark in his will that can be interpreted as a claim that he did.
For fifteen years Clovis had been the uncontested ruler of a pagan
people, in whose eyes a Christian coronation ceremony would in no
way have enhanced his prestige. But, as the centuries flew by, two
powers in the land saw that it would be to their mutual interest to
revise faith in the legend and authenticate it—the archdiocese of
Rheims and the French monarchy. If the Archbishops of Rheims
could gain for themselves the right to crown French Kings, they
would become the most important ecclesiastical authority in France;
and if the French Kings could establish the tradition of their coronations
as dating back to the fifth century, and add to the divine nature of the
ceremony by anointment with oil from the Holy Ampulla itself, the
power of their dynasty would be immeasurably strengthened.

The first full-dress coronation to take place at Rheims was that of
Charlemagne's son, Louis the Pious, in 816; but not till 987, when
Hughes Capet was crowned there by the Archbishop and anointed
with oil from the Holy Ampulla, was the episcopacy of Rheims able
to establish a definite ascendancy over the other great towns of France
which also laid claim to the honour. Thereafter Rheims was destined
to be the scene of a French King's coronation and Saint-Denis his last
resting-place. How deeply the sanctity of the city became imprinted on
the minds of the people can be judged from a remark attributed to
Joan of Arc 400 years later.

"Where shall we go?" asked Charles VII at Chinon, secretly counting
on flight to the Dauphiné.

"To Rheims, Sire," replied Joan of Arc. "There lies the salvation of France."

"But I was crowned at Poitiers!"

"Poitiers can only crown the Kings of Bourges," replied the Maid. *"Kings of France are made at Rheims."*

Altogether thirty-seven Kings and eleven Queens and Regents of France came to Rheims to be "made". The last of them was Charles X, who was crowned in the cathedral in 1825. It has been recorded, incidentally, that the people of Rheims did not greet the news of a forthcoming coronation with quite the same enthusiasm as did their Archbishop, for they had to pay for the lavish decorations and for the wines and meats for the receptions.

Rheims today is a thriving, bustling city of 121,000 inhabitants, one of the great provincial towns of France. Big shops, fashionable cafés galore, a university, one of the best children's hospitals in France (given to Rheims by the Americans after the First World War), theatres, concerts, a golf course, a *stade-vélodrome* for bicycle races, a gliding club, a flying club, a football team of world renown, champion boxers, a smart annual horse-show, weekly wrestling matches, the Parc Pommery with its running-tracks, tennis-courts and ultra-modern outdoor swimming-pool (in the shallow end there are always a surprising number of grown-ups wearing life-belts, who bear witness to the fact that Champagne is a land-locked province), a motor-racing circuit where, during the first weekend in July, two important inter-national events, the Rheims Grand Prix and the twelve-hour Rheims International, are staged (the prizes—crates of champagne): all this, and more, Rheims possesses, making Châlons-sur-Marne and Epernay seem like sluggish backwaters in comparison.

Up to about a hundred years ago the two staple trades of Rheims were wine and textiles. Of the two, the latter was not only the more important but the older: to this day members of the traditional woollen families of Rheims tend to look upon champagne magnates as parvenus, no matter how illustrious the titles they bear. Rheims was the southern-most centre of the great textile area of Flanders, as renowned for its cloth, carpets and blankets as it had been for its *"cuculles"* in Roman times; it was an association of dyers in Rheims, known as the Gobelins, who in the fifteenth century founded the famous Gobelins tapestry works, which were later acquired by Louis XIV and transferred to Paris. Soon after the Franco-Prussian war, however, a decline in

Rheims's textile trade set in. During the 1914 war the factories that
had not closed down for lack of orders were destroyed by shell-fire,
and for a time it looked as if Rheims's position in the textile world was
lost for ever; but in the 'twenties new factories were built and equipped
with modern tools, and today they employ 5,000 skilled workers.

This is small beer compared to former glories, but on the other
hand Rheims's other staple trade—champagne-making—has gone from
strength to strength; thirty-seven champagne firms have Rheims
addresses today. And a new source of employment has presented itself
to the Rémois: three giant French grocery firms have made the city
a central depot from which they supply thousands of their shops
scattered over a dozen neighbouring *départements*. Biscuit-making,
metallurgy, glass-making, the production of sugar and the manufacture
of linoleum are the other principal occupations of the Rémois.

But it was not of looms and how-you-earn-your-bread-and-butter
that La Fontaine was thinking when he wrote:

> *Il n'est cité que je préfère à Reims,*
> *C'est l'ornement et l'honneur de la France;*
> *Car, sans compter l'ampoule et les bons vins,*
> *Charmants objets y sont en abondance.*

Whether the *"charmants objets"* he had in mind were pretty Rémoises
or Rheims's artistic treasures is anybody's guess; both still abound,
but it is the latter that concern us now.

Most glorious of them all is the cathedral. It stands on the site of
the original building, which was erected by Bishop Nicasius as the end
of the fourth century. During the next 800 years it suffered many
vicissitudes: it was partially burnt down, rebuilt, enlarged, embellished,
pulled down and rebuilt again; and in 1210 it was completely destroyed
by fire.

At the time, no doubt, the loss of their cathedral struck the Rémois
as starkest tragedy. We, however, able to view the event in the
perspective of history, can see that the fire was the luckiest thing that
ever happened to Rheims. For it occurred at a moment when the long
darkness that had overhung Europe since the fall of the Roman
Empire had given way to a prodigious renaissance of the arts: at that
very moment, in the Ile-de-France and its environs (which included
north-west Champagne), a revolutionary and, as it turned out, superlatively beautiful style of church architecture—what we today call
the Gothic style—was on the point of reaching its highest development.

To build their new cathedral the Rémois were able to call upon local architects, sculptors and craftsmen possessed of talent and enthusiasm of a unique order. And they were further inspired by the vision of Rheims Cathedral as the setting for the coronation of the Kings of France.

Those two considerations—the existence of strictly local schools of architecture and sculpture, positively bursting with the desire for self-expression, and the challenge of creating a structure worthy of the most solemn and splendid moment in the monarch's and the nation's life—explain much of the magnificence of Rheims Cathedral. For one thing, it was possible for the greater part of the building to be finished in the space of a century, thus achieving one of the cathedral's most striking features—its unity, the impression it gives of having all been built at the same time. Besides, only local craftsmen, working in their own homes close to the building site, in day-to-day touch with what was going on and what was needed, incessantly spurred on to greater efforts by the sense of partaking in a great local enterprise, could have produced such a wealth and variety of decoration, such good taste, serenity and simplicity. And, had the necessity of providing a fitting background for the pomp and pageantry of coronations been absent, it is probable that the Rémois would have been content with a more modest edifice, something more on the lines of the cathedrals at Sens, Langres, Châlons-sur-Marne or Troyes, all of which are products of the Champagne school of Gothic architecture. As it was, they commissioned one of the biggest churches that have ever been built in Christendom, 452 feet in length (longer than Notre-Dame-de-Paris), 103 feet across at the transept, 118 feet tall at the highest point of the nave.

The master-mind behind the enterprise, Jean d'Orbais, was truly a son of Champagne, as we can tell if we pass through his native village, Orbais-l'Abbaye, which is between Montmirail and Epernay on the Paris road. It is at once apparent that life in this deep, narrow, tree-lined valley has been lived at the same stubborn pastoral rhythm, undisturbed by alien influences, for centuries; and the village church, built when Jean d'Orbais was a boy, displays in miniature the traditional Gothic lay-out which he adapted and improved upon when the time came for him to build the cathedral. He did not live to see the day in 1311 when the building was more or less complete, a hundred years after the foundation stone was laid. He began it (placing the High Altar on the exact spot upon which the High Altar of the fourth-century cathedral had stood) and worked on it for twenty years; others were responsible for the portals, the vaulting of the nave, the

Grande Rose and the finishing touches (except for the upper parts of the towers, which were added in 1428); but the main design was Jean d'Orbais', and his successors faithfully stuck to it.

As long as the great Gothic cathedrals of France survive, the argument will continue as to which is the most perfect. Some will claim the honour for Chartres, because of the incomparable beauty of its stained glass; some will award it to Bourges on account of its supremely elegant façade and the delicious airiness of its interior; others will cast their vote for Strasbourg because they have fallen in love with its pink stone, or give it to Laon because of its stupendous height. But there will always be those who think Rheims is the most perfect of them all, and who will claim that everything which Gothic art had to offer is expressed at Rheims with a simplicity, a purity, a harmony and a force excelled nowhere else.

Apart from her cathedral, Rheims's greatest treasure is the Basilica of Saint-Remi. Within its portals was buried in 533 the saint and Archbishop of Rheims who baptized Clovis and thus gave France her first Christian king. Begun early in the eleventh century, the present Basilica is the oldest church in Rheims, and one of the loveliest and most venerable in France. It was badly damaged in the First World War, and when the Second World War broke out the restoration work was still not complete; it was not until October 1959 that the church was reopened for worship. Most of the precious twelfth- and thirteenth-century stained glass in the tall windows of the chancel had been destroyed, but the new glass accords unbelievably well with what remains of the old; it was worked by M. Jacques Simon of Rheims, a descendant of a long line of stained-glass artists.

The toll which wars and invasions have exacted from Rheims's other treasures is heavy indeed, but enough has survived to provide the visitor, as he strolls through the streets and surveys the lovely buildings —from the Porte Mars, souvenir of the Roman occupation, to the schoolroom where General Eisenhower received the German officers who signed the document that ended the Second World War—with a vivid glimpse into the city's long history.

One curiosity which did not survive the war was the Palais Oriental. Known as the "P.O.", many a gay blade learnt there the truth of the saying, "Champagne is the wine a young man drinks on the evening of his first mistake". Between the wars there was a famous occasion when the then doyen of champagne-makers invited all Rheims and Epernay to a glittering reception during which he showed—to the horror of the ladies—*films bleus* borrowed from the P.O.

CHAPTER 5

ÉPERNAY AND OTHER LANDMARKS

Epernay, a town of some 21,000 inhabitants, is situated on the left bank of the Marne at the point where that river is joined by the Cubry. As a precaution against flooding, the bulk of the town is built well back from the Marne on high ground, at the base of a 650-foot hill called Mont Bernon. On the right bank of the Marne, directly opposite Epernay, lie two suburbs of the town, Magenta and La Villa-d'Ay.

Epernay makes almost as many bottles of champagne each year as Rheims does—by devoting 80 per cent, rather than 30 per cent, of its energies to champagne-making. For this reason, and also because it is situated slap in the middle of the wine district, Epernay tends more and more to be considered the chief centre of the champagne trade. The governing body of the trade, the Comité Interprofessionel du Vin de Champagne, has its offices there; so do the two largest champagne firms, Moët & Chandon and Mercier. Altogether thirty-seven champagne firms have Epernay addresses; the best known, apart from the two giants, are Perrier-Jouët and Pol Roger. *"Epernay c'est la ville de Champagne. Rien de plus, rien de moins,"* wrote Victor Hugo. In April 1963, during an official visit to the winefield, President de Gaulle paid Epernay an even handsomer compliment: *"C'est la capitale de la Champagne"*. The Rémois were not amused, nor for that matter were the citizens of Troyes (the traditional capital of the province), any more than they had been in the Second World War when the Germans proclaimed Rheims to be the capital.

From time immemorial the valley and hills around Epernay have been inhabited. The town museum possesses a particularly fine collection of local Stone, Bronze and Iron Age relics. Five centuries before Christ two tribes, of particular interest because they were entirely different in their origins and customs, lived in the area. No less than 500 tombs of this period have been found, and from their contents—arms, tools and jewels of amber—it has been possible to tell which tombs belonged to which tribe, their differences having endured even beyond the grave.

The Romans appear to have paid scant attention to the locality, although they were undoubtedly responsible for Epernay's name. Until the Revolution "Espernay" was the more usual rendering, and one historian suggests that the word derives from "Aixperne", derived in turn from "Aquae-Perennes", meaning "Never-failing Waters". The more likely explanation is that the Gallic tribe which lived on Mont Bernon adopted the name of Sparnacum after a Roman officer called Sparnacus: to this day the inhabitants of Epernay are referred to as "Sparnaciens".

It was not, however, until A.D. 460 that Epernay itself became the centre of a community. Its earliest members were vine-growers and tanners. The latter found the pure waters of the Cubry that dash down to the Marne ideal for curing hides. Over 1,500 years later, a rue des Tanneurs still exists in Epernay.

Epernay has had a chequered history, having been passed or sold to one overlord after another. Clovis gave it to St. Remi, who, like his successors, used to spend his summers there. Four hundred years later it was sold to the Count of Champagne, and in 1285 it became part of the Crown Lands of France. Among its many royal owners was Mary, Queen of Scots, who, it may be assumed, used its revenues to finance her attempt to win the English crown.

It was at one time in the possession of Louis XIV, who gave it to the Duc de Bouillon. The Duke had been imprisoned by Richelieu and, to save his life, had renounced sovereignty over his principality of Sedan, an act which gave rise to the pun: "*Il a donné ses dents, pour sauver sa tête.*" The gift of Epernay was to compensate him for this loss. The Sparnaciens lost no time in coining a second pun: "*Nous mangions bien la soupe sans Bouillon.*"

It would be logical to assume that, as a result of its close association with so many leading figures of the French nation, Epernay today must abound in monuments to delight the student of history. Unfortunately this is not the case. The very circumstance which throughout history made the town strategically important—its commanding position at the eastern end of a great valley leading directly to Paris—ensured that no sooner did one generation place its mark on the town than an invader proceeded to obliterate it. Since its first sacking in 533, Epernay has seldom escaped involvement in France's wars; it has been burnt, pillaged or sacked on no less than twenty-five occasions. But what Epernay lacks in visible evidence of its antiquity it makes up for by possessing the Avenue de Champagne, which must be the most incongruous and bizarre main street of any small provincial town in the world.

The Avenue starts at the Place de la République and proceeds eastwards in a straight line up the hill, in the stately manner of the Champs-

Elysées from the Rond Point onwards (but there the resemblance ends). On the right side the fun begins at once, in the form of a very big, very tall house (now a bank) whose first three stories are conventional but whose upper parts are composed of an indescribable collection of soaring turrets, towers and gables reminiscent of the adornments on the hats of late Victorian matrons. A little farther up there is a vast modern yellow brick building whose forecourt, enclosed by tall iron railings, is also so vast that it would allow ample room for the Changing of the Guard: this is the headquarters of Moët & Chandon. The next hundred yards or so of the Avenue are taken up by more modest buildings, each with its little forecourt and tall iron gates, connected mainly with the affairs of Pol Roger and Perrier-Jouët (the long windows and the mellow brick walls of the latter's establishment are particularly attractive); then elegant town houses give way to a succession of Victorian villas.

The first notable building on the left side of the Avenue is the Hôtel de Ville. It is set back from the road in a small public park containing many fine old trees and a not-too-formal garden which, from May to September, is a delight. Next comes one of the present-day residences of the Moët & Chandon family: two identical sugar-white buildings of early nineteenth-century design, separated by a large courtyard. Behind the courtyard, just visible from the Avenue, lies a beautiful sunken garden, with a long rectangular pool in the centre; the farther side of the pool is flanked by a gem of an orangery designed by Isabey, the French miniaturist. And then, thirty yards higher up, stands the Avenue de Champagne's pièce de résistance, the colossal pseudo-Renaissance château Perrier, built in 1863 by the son of the founder of Perrier-Jouët and reputed to have cost £80,000. Today it houses the town's library and museum. The Avenue derives its final touch of fantasy on the left-hand side—after more elegant town houses and more not-so-elegant villas—from a house of many turrets called the château de Pékin, which is the home of the Mercier family; then it peters out into farmland.

Epernay is seen to best advantage from the vine-clad hills west of the Cubry at dusk on a summer's evening. At that hour the ochre-red of the tiles and the bluey-grey of the slates on its roofs blend together in subtle harmony; the overpowering green of its surroundings—vineyards, woods, fields, the Marne—is subdued; the magic softness of the light is a reminder that this is the hinterland of the Ile-de-France; the thought is father to the wish that Monet, armed with easel and brushes, might be at hand to portray the scene on canvas.

Châlons-sur-Marne

The controlling factor in Châlons' destiny always has been and always will be its geographical position: it lies exactly halfway between the Channel ports and Switzerland, and on the direct route from Paris to the Rhine Basin. If the plans made at the Geneva Road Convention of 1950 materialize, Châlons will be the meeting-point of the projected highways Paris–Prague–Warsaw–Moscow and London–Brindizi (via Calais).

The Romans were the earliest to make full use of the site on which the town now stands: in the first century of our era they built a bridge across the Marne there, detailed a garrison to protect it and called the encampment Catalaunum, whence the name Châlons emerged. Catalaunum became an important stage-post on the Langres–Boulogne road and on the road leading out from the centre of Gaul via Autun and Troyes. In the third century the Romans surrounded the town with powerful walls, and it became the pivot of their defences against the Barbarians between Rheims and Troyes. Christianity reached Châlons in the fourth century, and soon the citizens started to enrich the town with remarkable churches. In the eighth century it became the capital of a county which was later incorporated in the County of Champagne. During the Middle Ages the town was an important centre of the wool trade: Chaucer mentioned the woollen cloth made there, calling it "Chalouns"; Dean Swift referred to it as "Shaloons".

In the nineteenth century, when Rheims and Epernay were making a mint of money out of champagne, the Châlonnais decided to try their hand at the game too. But champagne-making so far from the main vineyard area proved to be a difficult undertaking, and, of the five Châlons champagne firms which exist today, only one—Joseph Perrier—has an international reputation. In fact Châlons is really more renowned for its beer than its champagne: the barley grown in the neighbourhood is ideally suited to malting, and there is particularly pure water at hand. The Brasserie de la Comète, founded in 1882, has succeeded in producing a de luxe beer, La Slavia, which is exported all over the world. Châlons is also famous for its carrots and for a substance known as *Blanc de Champagne*. "Champagne Whiting" (as it is called in English) is an extract in powdered form of the carbonate of calcium found in the subsoil around Châlons. Because of its exceptional purity, it is sought after by many different industries in France and abroad.

Five wonderful examples of the Châlonnais' talent for ecclesiastical architecture survive. The most imposing of them is the long, spireless

Cathedral of Saint-Etienne, which was consecrated by Pope Eugenius III in 1147. There are some notable secular buildings also, one of the most interesting, from the point of view of history, being the Porte Sainte-Croix, known formerly as the Porte Dauphine, a triumphal arch which was erected in honour of Marie-Antoinette when she passed through Châlons in 1770 on her way to her marriage. There is irony in the fact that the Châlons library today possesses the Queen's Book of Hours in which, on the morning of her execution, she wrote her last farewells to her children.

Sandwiched between the Marne and the town's numerous canals (which give it a little of the atmosphere of Bruges) lies Châlons' Jard* —a network of gardens, parks and tree-lined paths. As early as 1680 the *Mercure Galant* was writing, "Few public places in France are more agreeable". I think it must have been her walks on the Jard (and perhaps the champagne or the beautiful churches, for she was a very religious woman) that rendered tolerable the long winter which Mme Récamier spent in Châlons when Napoleon exiled her from Paris. She chose Châlons as her retreat because it lay just beyond the forty-league limit imposed, but her friends found the choice odd. Oh, but she must be so bored stuck in the middle of Champagne, wrote Mme de Staël, her best friend, in letter after letter; why didn't she come to Coppet or go to Geneva or to London? But the beautiful Juliette, like so many Parisians, felt that the next best thing to Paris was being as near to Paris as possible, and, serene as ever, she remained in Châlons until the odious order was lifted.

Ay

Ay (pronounced Eye-ee—it used to be spelt Aï) lies a mere two-and-a-half miles north-east of Epernay, and a direct road joins the two towns; but if one approaches it from the direction of Dizy, on the main Epernay–Rheims road, it is not difficult to grasp why this little town of 7,000 inhabitants has throughout Champagne's history enjoyed prestige quite out of proportion to its size. As the tall, tapering spire of the church and the red roofs of its houses come into view, sandwiched between the towering slopes of the Mountain of Rheims and the poplar-lined Marne, it can be seen that Ay guards the entrance to the Marne valley; one can well believe that for most of its history it has been a *ville forte* and that here, time and time again, invaders who have

* All the towns and villages on the Marne have their Jard, constructed from river gravel (which is what the word means). Here, in spring, summer and autumn, are set up the travelling fairs so dear to the hearts of the Champenois.

swept westwards across the plain without encountering much resistance have had the tempo of their dash to Paris, if not halted, at least momentarily slowed down.

One look at the lush vineyards on the left of the road, facing due south, clambering up the steep hill-side to the tree-line and way off into the distance, is enough to show that this is a very special wine-growing area. It is hardly a surprise to learn that a vineyard of Ay, called Le Léon, is believed to be the one from which Pope Leo the Magnificent—the patron of Michelangelo, Raphael and Leonardo da Vinci—drew his supplies of wine; or that, at the junction of the rues Saint-Vincent and Henri IV, a quaint old house still exists which is believed to have contained the presses that turned out Ay wine for Henri IV; or that Henry VIII of England kept a special commissioner at Ay to provide him with wine; or that Ay wine, which has a faint flavour of peaches, used to be referred to as *Vinum Dei* and *Vin du Roi* (Alfred de Vigny once wrote: *"Dans la mousse d'Ay luit l'éclair d'un bonheur"*). And as soon as the concrete air-ducts of Ay's cellars come into view, peeping forth among the vines (the cellars burrow deep into the hill-side), one understands why it is said that the Agéens do not have to lift a finger to make wine: the grape-juice—so the story goes—just filters through the chalk to the cellars and makes itself.

Today, virtually all the wine of Ay goes into the blends that compose our champagne, so the town is less well known to wine-lovers than it was 200 years ago, when still wines were the fashion; but Ay/Champagne (as it is usually referred to on printed stationery and on the labels of champagne bottles, to emphasize the fact that the town's fame is nowadays indissolubly linked with that of champagne) is still the third biggest producer of wine (after Rheims and Epernay) in the winefield. Eighteen champagne Houses have their headquarters there; among the best known are Ayala and Deutz & Gelderman; the best known of all is Bollinger.

Writing of Ay in 1868 Victor Fievet commented:

"The people there are hard-working, thrifty, placid and docile, but above all remarkable for their love of and concern with revolution. It is certain that no commune of the Republic has been more subjected to laws, nor displays more zeal for the exact observance of decadal and republican anniversaries."

The Agéens' propensity for revolution was to manifest itself, fifty years after those remarks were written, in a disturbance known as the

Rheims Cathedral

The château de Brugny

Ay Riots, an account of which appears later in this book. Perhaps their hot blood is the fuel that stokes the Agéens' genius for wine-making. Perhaps it was responsible, too, for another type of genius which they have produced: Lalique, the artist in glass, was born in Ay.

The Vineyard Villages

A village in the Champagne district nearly always gives the impression of having matured slowly. It seems to be standing back in its own little world, a world dedicated exclusively, as it has been for centuries, to grapes and wine. The weather-browned faces of the men, their sturdy frames, their mud-and-dust-covered blue overalls, the rubber boots they appear never to take off, all bespeak a life that is active and healthy; so do the rosy cheeks, the strong arms and the well-worn pale blue aprons of their women; but, plainly, bustle in that life is reserved for such great events as the vintage or a family wedding.

The majority of the villages look neat, well-to-do and fairly clean; most of them possess a gem of a little church★ (often the vineyard scenes portrayed in the stonework emphazise the place that the cultivation of the vine has long occupied in the lives of the inhabitants); a great many of them, like Cramant and Verzenay, are situated in such splendid positions on the vineyard slopes that they delight the eye from a distance and themselves have thrilling views; yet one cannot say that as a general rule the vineyard villages are pretty or even picturesque. There are several reasons why this is so. One is that village architecture in the Champagne district appears to have little or no artistic heritage. It is singularly lacking in those salient traits and curiosities of style that impart so much personality to villages in many other regions of France: simplicity, a total absence of ostentation (even in an exceptionally rich village such as Cramant, ostentation is reserved for the cemetery), and a strictly functional approach to architecture are the general rule.

Another reason why the villages tend to look somewhat drab is that the rough plaster covering the rag-stone with which most of the houses are built is more often than not left grey; before 1918, when the roofs were covered with blue slate rather than the red tiles of recent years, the general impression of chilliness must have been still more marked.

★ First things come first in the estimation of the villagers, however. The approach signs to a village in the valley of the Livre read:

AVENAY-VAL-d'OR
Son Champagne
Son Eglise Historique

Of course, the lack of paint or whitewash on so many of the houses is by no means a peculiarity of the Champagne district: a foreigner visiting France for the first time is always amazed that a nation as gifted with the paint-brush as the French should be so sparing in its use on the outsides of their houses. Often, it is true, initial bewilderment develops into admiration for the innate good taste of the nation, when on a summer's day the play of sun and shadow reveals textures and subtle tones in the building materials which paint would have hidden; but there is no denying that, in winter and on rainy days, the greyness of the walls and doors and window-frames of a village in the Champagne district is infinitely depressing.

Yet another reason why the villages strike the visitor as being some-what severe is that the individual houses have few windows overlooking the streets, sometimes none at all; the life of the house is nearly always directed inwards, towards a central courtyard, access to which is gained by a stone gateway equipped with wooden gates. Some householders, but by no means the majority, keep the gates open in daytime, and in that case a passer-by is often astonished to see that what from the street looks like an extremely modest village house is in fact an establishment of considerable consequence: an elegant, possibly luxurious, two-storied house may take up one side of the courtyard, contrasting strangely with the wing overlooking the street; the other sides of the courtyard may comprise a stable (housing a tractor), a garage (housing, perhaps, a smart new car), potting-sheds, hen-houses and a rabbit-hutch. There may even be quite an elaborate garden and a little lawn in the courtyard. This inclination of the villagers to keep hidden from public view the true surroundings in which they live probably stems from two causes: the frequency of the invasions with which Champagne has been afflicted, and that curious French tax levied on *signes extérieurs de richesse*; both discourage wise householders from displaying their worldly goods in their front windows, so to speak.

But, despite their austere and rather ordinary appearance, the villages in the Champagne district are by no means totally devoid of charm. Usually the charm is discreet, but often it is very real. The wooden gates, hiding the view to the inner sanctum, impart a definite aura of mystery to the village. The lack of colour on the fabrics of the houses themselves is often compensated for by the gaiety of vines scrambling up outside walls and, in summer, by riotous displays of roses, gladioli, dahlias, begonias and giant hollyhocks. (The villagers of the Champagne district are more imaginative gardeners than the

bourgeoisie.) In some villages, the way the streets snake up and down
the slopes and the manner in which the houses on them are squeezed
together like spectators at a Cup Tie (in order that every inch of soil
may be spared for vines) gives character that might otherwise be
absent. And two peculiarities of villages in the Champagne district
never fail to arouse the interest of visitors from other lands: the
minuteness of so many of the new houses being built (there is one such
doll's house on the outskirts of Cramant, where land is particularly
precious, which has the engaging name of *Notre Vie-là*), and the
fantastic number of *chien méchant* signs in evidence. They discourage
gypsy prowlers at the time of the vintage, one villager told me, with
a wry smile on his face, which seemed to indicate that their true
purpose was to ward off Nosy Parkers, in particular the neighbours.

The Châteaux

There is no danger in this book, as there would be, for instance, in one
about the wine-districts of Anjou, Bordeaux, Burgundy or Touraine,
of that irresistible hussy, the French château, gobbling up undue space
in the narrative. Wars, invasions and the Revolution have taken a
terrible toll, and only four notable châteaux survive: Montmort,
Brugny, Mareuil and Louvois.

Montmort, situated in the village of that name ten miles south of
Epernay on the road to Sézanne, is by far the largest of the four. Built
in the sixteenth century, of red brick, it is enclosed by a moat; to the
west extends a splendid park in which an annual horse-show is held.
The central tower contains a wide spiral staircase up which a man can
ride a horse. Victor Hugo mentioned it in *Le Rhin*: 'All of a sudden,
as one emerges from the forest, one catches sight of an entrancing
confusion of turrets, weathercocks, gables, dormer windows and
chimneys. It is the château de Montmort." The castle—for that is the
name it deserves—belongs to M. François Crombez de Montmort.

Brugny lies cuddled on a hillside, surrounded by woods, five miles
south of Epernay on the Sézanne road. The main building, of
bricks that have mellowed to a delicate shade of pink, is rectangular
and has two stories; at either end there are round stone towers.
Opposite, beyond an expanse of lawn and gravel, stands another
building, of similar design and shape but of less refinement. The two
are connected by a crescent-shaped moat. Brugny is the Francophile's
dream of a medium-size country home near Paris come true. It belongs
to Comte Jean d'Eudeville.

The little eighteenth-century château de Mareuil stands in the centre of Mareuil-sur-Ay, the vineyard village on the right bank of the Marne a mile and a half east of Ay. The village is nicknamed "Mareuil-la-Bouteille" because, seen from the Epernay–Châlons road on the other side of the Marne, the oblong, vine-clad hill that rises abruptly behind it looks uncommonly like a champagne bottle lying on its side. The château is intimately connected with champagne-making. It belonged originally to the Orléans family (their arms can still be seen above the main entrance); in 1792 (the year before he died on the guillotine) Philippe-Egalité sold it to the Marquis de Pange. In 1830 it was sold again, this time to the Duc de Montebello, the eldest son of Maréchal Lannes, of Napoleonic fame. The reason the Duc de Montebello acquired the property, it is said, was that he wanted a place near his sister's estate at Etoges, fifteen miles south of Epernay; but no sooner had he done so than he decided to found a champagne firm. Judging by the complimentary remarks about Montebello champagne that one finds in books and articles on the Champagne district written during the nineteenth century, his success as a champagne-maker was by no means eclipsed by his distinguished career as an Ambassador, Minister of the Marine and Minister of Foreign Affairs during the reigns of Louis-Philippe and Napoleon III.

The firm of Montebello still exists, but today it belongs, as does the château de Mareuil, to M. René Chayoux, the owner of a chain of small champagne Houses. Mme Chayoux is a gardener of courage and imagination, qualities which are sorely needed by anyone who tries to garden in the chalky soil of the Champagne district. Most people make do with displays of the small pink begonia (*Begonia semperflorens*), that pomade, perfect in itself, which the French cheapen by smearing it with outrageous abandon on their country's fair face. Not Mme Chayoux, however. Each summer she keeps the flower-beds in front of the château and in the walled garden opposite (all visible from the road) resplendent with variety and colour, and a glimpse of them is balm to eyes surfeited with pink begonias.

The château de Louvois stands at the head of the lush, winding valley of the Livre, on the eastern edge of the vineyard village of Louvois. In 1680 a ruined château that stood on the site of the present one was acquired by Michel Le Tellier, Louis XIV's War Minister, as was the accompanying marquisate (hence the title, Marquis de Louvois, that Le Tellier bore for the rest of his life). Having demolished the ruined château the new Marquis erected another one, of classical seventeenth-century design. He engaged Le Nôtre to lay out a *jardin français*; it contained six pools, the water for which descended by gravity from a spring on a hill a mile away, through a canal system similar to that installed by Le Nôtre to fill the pools at Versailles. Historians tell of the sumptuous fêtes held at the château during Louvois' lifetime. Subsequently the estate experienced many vicissitudes. In the Revolution the château was partially burnt down, and ownership of the property passed to the State. During the First Empire a rich protestant banker bought it, reconstructed the central block and demolished the two wings. In the middle of the nineteenth century the estate was again sold, this time to a Baron de la Charmoye. He completed the restoration of the central block of the château, placed his arms over the main entrance (where they remain today) and renewed the canalization of the pools. Towards the end of the century Comte Frédéric Chandon de Briailles bought Louvois, and today it belongs to his grandson and namesake.

In the late 1950s the present owner repaired the serious damage the property had suffered in the two World Wars: he restored the exterior of the château, did up the interior, restocked the park with deer, and laid out the garden at the back of the house on the lines of Le Nôtre's original plan. The supremely elegant building—two-storied, chalk-white, with a slanting grey roof—and its two little matching pavilions are visible from the road, through cast-iron gates of massive proportions that guard the entrance to the drive; but all that remains visible, from without or from within, of Le Tellier's epoch are the walls of the central building, the orangery, the moats and vestiges of Le Nôtre's canal system.

CHAPTER 6

SUBTERRANEAN CHAMPAGNE: THE CELLARS

THERE IS NOTHING above the ground in the Champagne district that compares in interest with what lies underneath it. Cathedrals comparable to Rheims exist elsewhere; the cellars of Champagne are unique.

It is well that they are so special, because if they were not champagne itself would not be quite so special. Those who make sparkling wines by the *méthode champenoise* in other regions of France and in other parts of the world are painfully aware of this fact. For such wines confront their makers with problems regarding cellarage which do not arise in the case of the manufacture of still wine. The ageing of a still wine must take place in cool surroundings, away from noise, draughts and bright light. The same is true of a sparkling wine made by the *méthode champenoise*, with these additional requirements. In the first place, the cellars must be abnormally cool: the latent possibilities of a sparkling wine are never exploited to the full unless the ageing in bottle takes place very slowly, at a very low temperature. In the second place, there must be no—or very little—variation in the temperature of the cellars: abrupt changes of temperature may cause bottles of sparkling wine that are still undergoing their second fermentation to explode. In the third place, the cellars must be exceptionally large, for wine matured in bottle takes up much more room than wine matured in cask.

A low, constant temperature can be achieved quite simply if a system of air-conditioning is installed. But the cost of installing and running the system in an exceptionally large cellar would make the price of the sparkling wine prohibitive. Many manufacturers of sparkling wine have to make do with cellarage that is far from ideal, and their products suffer in quality accordingly (I have been told of one so-called "champagne cellar" in Australia where in high summer the heat is positively stifling). The Champenois, however, possess something that provides them with ideal cellarage at a fraction of the cost of an air-conditioning system: that something is the thousand-foot-deep seam of *Belimnita quadrata* chalk. The chalk is simple and inexpensive to hew out; yet it is sufficiently strong for the cellars, once they have been made, to support themselves—pit-props or vaulting are unnecessary. The temperature obtained is abnormally low: 12°C. forty feet down, 10°C. a hundred and twenty feet down. And the temperature remains absolutely constant: on the hottest day of summer it is the same as on the coldest day of winter.

The Champenois made good use of God's gift of the *Belimnita quadrata* chalk for storing wine long before champagne sparkled. Every monastery, convent, clerical abode and wine-making establishment in the region had a cellar, and some of them are known to have been spacious.* But as the vogue for sparkling champagne increased it became necessary—because champagne matures in bottle—to expand the existing cellarage to an extent undreamt of in any other wine district of the world. From the end of the eighteenth century right up to the outbreak of the First World War the digging deeper and deeper into the chalk, and the spreading farther and farther outward, continued almost without stop. Sometimes "open-cast" mining methods were used, but as chalk cracks and crumbles when exposed to rain and frost, and as many of the cellars being constructed were to have two or even three levels, more often than not a deep hole was sunk in the chalk and the workmen then proceeded to hew out the tunnels and galleries with pickaxes like rabbits burrowing. Once the tunnels and galleries had been excavated, such matters as ventilation shafts, water pipes and drainage systems had to be attended to—ventilating shafts to permit air to circulate and to allow the temperature to be regulated to some small extent; water pipes to enable the cellars to be kept clean; drainage systems to carry off the water used for cleaning and the champagne from broken bottles. Next, to facilitate the movement of the bottles from one part of the cellars to another, the tunnels had to be paved or cemented, staircases and ramps built and—in later times—lifts installed. Then the question of lighting had to be solved: at first candles were used (in the mid-nineteenth century 60,000 lb. of candles a year were consumed in the cellars of one Epernay firm alone), then gas, and finally electricity.

* *Cavées* were held in the bigger cellars. They took place on winter evenings, and originated as hen parties. Each woman brought her footwarmer and a log for the fire. The time was whiled away with knitting, sewing, the peeling of vegetables, singsongs, parlour games and . . . gossip; sometimes the evenings ended with the cooking of pancakes and fritters over the fire. All went well until men, in particular young men, started joining the ladies, for then there occurred a lamentable drop in the moral tone of the *cavées*, and in 1588 the Archbishop of Rheims felt prevailed upon to issue an ordinance forbidding them. A similar ordinance was issued in 1661 by the Bishop of Châlons-sur-Marne, but the *cavées*—and male attendance—continued until long after the Revolution.

As a result of all this activity there came into being the most elaborate
and perfect network of cellarage to be found anywhere in the world,
estimated to be between 200 and 300 miles in length, sufficient to store
upwards of 250 million bottles of champagne. Underneath Rheims
(120 miles of cellars) and Epernay (sixty miles of cellars) what can only
be described as subterranean cities were created, with main galleries
the length of avenues, transverse galleries the size of streets, and
passages, open spaces and cross-roads of equally metropolitan grandeur.
One cellar, Moët & Chandon's, became (and remains) the world's
largest individual cellar: to explore every corner of it, one would have
to walk fifteen-and-a-half miles—much farther than in the celebrated
Casemates of Luxembourg or Gibraltar.

Underneath the small towns and villages of the Champagne district,
underneath Epernay, Châlons-sur-Marne and Ay, and underneath the
centre of Rheims, what is so staggering about the cellars is, mainly,
their size: their shape conforms with one's preconceived idea of a
cellar. Underneath the south-eastern outskirts of Rheims, however,
there exist cellars remarkable not only on account of their size but
because of their unconventional shape as well.

What happened was this. Towards the end of the eighteenth
century Claude Ruinart, the grandson of the founder of the champagne
firm of Ruinart Père et Fils, made up his mind to move the firm from
Epernay to Rheims. Foreseeing a problem that was to bother many of
the Rheims champagne firms when they wished to expand their
cellarage in the nineteenth century—namely, the tendency of the
Vesle to overflow its banks and thus render necessary the installation
of expensive pumping apparatus in cellars excavated in its vicinity*—
he decided to move the firm not to Rheims itself but to a hill called
the Butte Saint Nicaise situated half a mile south-east of the city
ramparts. Known to him but not to all and sundry, there already
existed underneath the Butte a series of chalk-pits, pyramidal in shape,
which could be converted into champagne cellars, if not for a song, at
least for a sum considerably below what it would have cost to hew out
a conventional cellar.

The chalk-pits, or *crayères*, as they are called in French, were curiosities with a somewhat macabre history: they had been quarried by
Roman slave gangs to provide blocks of chalk for the building of
Durocortorum, and therein lay the explanation of their strange shape—
square or rectangular at the base, with sides tapering upwards to form

* Many cellars over ninety feet deep in Epernay also need pumping out when
the Marne rises.

a pyramid whose summit lay at ground level. For, as I have already mentioned, chalk crumbles and cracks when exposed to heavy rain and frost. Rather than use unsatisfactory "open-cast" mining methods, the Romans very wisely adopted the following procedure: an opening no bigger than a coffin was dug at the surface; the slave gangs then dug downwards to a depth of about sixty feet and outwards until the base of the pyramid was formed. As they dug downwards they were lowered and raised—and the blocks of chalks were raised—by cranes; but, once a number of pyramids had been excavated, connecting tunnels were hewn out at the base of each pyramid, and ultimately staircases were cut to the surface. The beauty of the arrangement was that the opening at ground level could be covered by a stone slab at night and in inclement weather.

Some of the chalk-pits are believed to have been used as hide-outs by the followers of St. Sixtus at the time when the Roman catacombs were being used for the same purpose by the early Christians of Rome. A number of them served as refuges for the Protestants of Rheims after the Revocation of the Edict of Nantes. Others are known to have been reopened on the numerous occasions when Rheims has required re-building after being razed to the ground by the invader. (Only since 1919 have hard stone and reinforced concrete been used extensively for building purposes in Rheims, thus permitting the construction of tall houses. A large part of the cost of the construction of the older, conventionally shaped cellars in the Champagne district was defrayed by instructing the workmen to cut the chalk in blocks, which could be sold for building purposes. Houses built of blocks of chalk are still standing in Rheims: there is one, complete with the customary over-hanging roof to protect the chalk from rain, facing the north-east corner of the Basilica of Saint-Remi.) But the great majority of the 250-odd chalk-pits on the Butte Saint Nicaise had not been reopened since Roman times when Claude Ruinart acquired them.

He decided to concentrate his conversion work on the forty-five or so pits that lay on the northern slopes of the Butte. First, he levelled each pit to an average depths of a hundred feet. Next, he either excavated new tunnels between the pits or repaired the existing ones. Then up to the level where his bottles were to lie, and sometimes above that level, he worked the walls of the pits as smooth and regular as finished masonry. Finally he (or his descendants) substituted blocks of glass tiles for the slabs of stone that had closed the tapering summits of the pits.

The latter refinement is what gives life to the Ruinart *crayères* and renders them so remarkable that they are officially classed as an Historic Monument. For through the glass there filters light, which floods the chalk-pits and confounds the visitor. Is he in a champagne cellar or in the nave of some Gothic church built of chalk? In a sanctuary dedicated to some pagan divinity of ancient Greece, in a virgin's sepulchre, or in a subterranean Egyptian pyramid? At one point, where a staircase is collapsing and is being left to do so behind barriers, he half believes he is inside a wedding-cake whose icing is peeling off. And the visitor's wonder may continue for five miles, for that is the total length of the connecting tunnels.

It was evidently Claude Ruinart's hope that in the decades or centuries to come his firm would convert the rest of the chalk-pits into cellars, and so it might have done had not Mme Pommery, the widow of the founder of Pommery & Greno, been the type of woman men find impossible to refuse when she asks a favour. Just under a hundred years ago, finding that she was running short of cellar space in Rheims itself, she persuaded a descendant of Claude Ruinart's to sell her the whole of the southern portion of the Butte Saint Nicaise; and she then proceeded to convert the 120 chalk-pits underneath it into what are perhaps the most spectacular cellars in all Champagne. Not content with connecting galleries that took the breath away on account of their seemingly never-ending length, she increased their singularity by arching them in different styles—Roman, Norman, Gothic—and naming them after the great champagne cities of the world—London, New York, Rome, Montreal, Stockholm, Buenos Aires, etc. Then she commissioned a Champenois artist of the time, Navlet by name, to carve huge bas-reliefs on the walls. The chalk proved a remarkably successful medium for the sculptor's chisel, and the bas-reliefs—none more so than *Le Champagne au XVIIIe Siècle*, which depicts a rollicking Regency dinner-party, and *Fête de Bacchus*, a hymn of praise to the God of wine—remain as striking today as when they were executed. Her final flourish was to construct a triumphal staircase down to the depth, twelve feet wide, with 116 steps.

Several other champagne firms own chalk-pits. The forty-five that belong to Charles Heidsieck were discovered by builders digging foundations at the time when Rheims was spreading out to the Butte Saint Nicaise. They were used at first by mushroom growers, whose biggest market was the United States, and it was only when that market collapsed that they were sold to the present owners.

Few of the big champagne firms advertise to any great extent in France (Mercier is an exception): they prefer to keep in touch with the public by welcoming visitors to their cellars, arranging conducted tours for them and extending liberal offerings of champagne afterwards. Hundreds of thousands of people from all over the world avail themselves of this red carpet treatment each year—none more eagerly than the Parisians, for whom it makes a nice Sunday outing in summer —with the result that the cellars of Champagne are said to have become the third biggest tourist attraction in France, eclipsed in popularity only by the château de Versailles and the Eiffel Tower.

PART III

THE HISTORICAL PERSPECTIVE

CHAPTER 7

THE FOUNDATION OF THE WINEFIELD
AND ITS EARLY HISTORY

IT IS GENERALLY agreed that the oldest vineyards in France are those of Provence, founded by the Phoenicians around 600 B.C. As far as is known, until the Romans arrived the northward extension of the vine was very slow: Marseilles, Narbonne and Vienne, on the Rhone, are the only wine-producing regions mentioned by B.C. Roman writers. The first important vineyards in France to have been planted by the Romans are believed to be those of Burgundy, which probably came into existence somewhere around A.D. 45. The next to appear—in what order nobody can be sure—were Bordeaux, Alsace and Champagne. But since Champagne borders on Burgundy, it seems unlikely that a long interval separated the planting of vines in the two provinces. The great quantities of early Gallo-Roman pottery, vases, glasses and coins bearing the vine motif which have been found in the soil of the Champagne district suggest that vines must have been growing in Champagne in the middle of the first century A.D.

Some historians, however, maintain that the Champenois were making their own wine long before the Roman invasion of Gaul. It is known, they state, that wine flowed freely at Druid fêtes held in honour of the goddess of childbirth, near Châlons-sur-Marne, and that the tribes of Gaul were consumers of wine a considerable time before the Romans arrived: where, except from local vineyards, could the wine have come from in that era of appallingly bad communications? In any case, they continue, a visit to the show-cases of the Laboratoire de Géologie of the Sorbonne provides incontrovertible proof that vines have been growing in Champagne since prehistoric times, for there the impressions are on view of the perfectly preserved fossilized vine-leaves which, in November 1842, were found embedded in chalk of the Tertiary period at the Cavités du Travertin near Sézanne, less than thirty miles from Epernay. Finally, they quote from Pliny the Elder, who died in A.D. 79, "*Caetera Galliae vina, sunt Regalibus menses expedita e Campania Remense et quod vin d'Ai vocant*", which means, "Are not the other wines of Gaul, chosen for the king's table, in fact those of the Campaign of Rheims, and that called the wine of Ay?".

There are three weaknesses in this argument, however. The first is the assumption that, before the Romans covered Europe with a network of roads, transcontinental trade hardly existed. As recently as 1952 a discovery of the most startling nature was made at Châtillon-sur-Seine, on the border of Champagne and Burgundy, which demonstrated once and for all the folly of any such supposition. In the tomb of a Gallic princess who died around B.C. 1500 there was found a Greek—or, conceivably, an Etruscan—bronze wine-vase, as tall as a large man, weighing 450 pounds and of quite exceptional beauty. In the opinion of the archaeologist who unearthed the vase, it was being taken by Greek or Etruscan merchants to Cornwall to be exchanged for tin when the Gallic princess dispossessed them of it. That such a huge vessel could have been hauled across Europe a millennium and a half before the Romans reached Gaul is proof enough that the importation of wine from the Mediterranean littoral can have confronted the Gauls with no great problem.

The second weakness in the argument is the assumption that the prehistoric vines at Sézanne bore grapes which could be used for wine-making. Modern vine experts who have examined the impressions in the Sorbonne agree unanimously that the vine concerned, which they have named *Vitis sezannensis*, was not of the wine-producing type. They believe that it was one of the many species of sour-graped wild vine which existed in such scattered parts of the globe as Iceland, Devonshire, Silesia, Switzerland and America long before man or the first mammals made their appearance, and which more or less disappeared when the warm equable temperatures of the Tertiary period gave way to a colder climate. One of the few places where this type of wild vine has survived is in America, and one of its species, the *Vitis rotundifolia*, curiously resembles the *Vitis sezannensis*.

Thirdly, the quotation from Pliny is a bogus one. In his *Natural History* Pliny did mention Gallic wines briefly (and not very complimentarily), but in none of his works can I find a single reference to the wines of the Remi.

Yet another reason for doubting that vineyards existed in Champagne at the time of the Roman invasion is the failure of Julius Caesar to have mentioned them: had they existed, he would surely have recorded the fact.

No, the middle of the first century A.D. is the earliest probable date when vines could have been planted in the Champagne district for wine-making purposes. Furthermore, many decades must have passed before the quantity of wine produced in the new winefield became at all considerable. For a multitude of problems confronted the early vine-growers: the choice of suitable sites for the vineyards, the clearing of the thick forests, the breaking of the virgin ground, the selection of species of vines which would flourish in so northern a climate, and the development of the proper methods of culture. And in A.D. 92, when they must have just been beginning to solve them, the Emperor issued an edict that the vineyards of Gaul were to be uprooted.

No one is sure what prompted him.* All that is certain is that the ban on viticulture was exceedingly unpopular and that it was not lifted until A.D. 282, by Emperor Probus—appropriately a gardener's son. Aided, we are told, by troops placed at their disposal by Probus, the Champenois set to work to restore their vines with joy in their hearts. In Rheims a Temple of Bacchus was erected, and in the vineyards many a smaller temple to the god of wine sprang up. It has even been suggested that Rheims's Porte Mars may have been erected in Probus's honour by the grateful Champenois: on one of its columns, now destroyed, there is known to have been an animated vintage scene.

The decades that followed were probably among the most serene in the history of the Champagne vineyards, protected as they were by the might of Rome, and with a ready market in the south. It is not known when the first supplies of wine from Champagne reached Rome, but, in view of what is known about the making of wine in the capital of the Empire, we are entitled to imagine that they created a most favourable impression. It was not unusual for Roman wine-makers to add substances such as sea-water, pitch, resin, pine-needles, myrtle berries, bitter almonds, spikenard, myrrh and poppy seeds to their produce, or for wine to be evaporated in smoke to a solid state and then dissolved in hot water just before it was drunk. How fresh and delicious, in comparison with such potions, must the new wines from the north have seemed. Having a lower alcholic content than Italian wines, they were probably drunk younger, and did not, in consequence, produce that heaviness in the stomach of which many Roman gourmets complained after drinking their own wines.

The inventive genius of the Gaul also manifested itself in the development of a new wine-vessel, the cask, which was far more satisfactory

* Whatever the motive, the edict was the forerunner of much similar legislation. In 1567 the French King, finding that the price of corn was rising on account of the number of new vineyards that were being planted in Champagne and other wine regions, ordered certain vineyards to be uprooted and forbade new plantations. A similar order was issued by Louis XV in 1627. Today the French Government tries to persuade vineyard owners in certain parts of the Midi to switch to other crops by offering them capital sums if they do so.

for the conveyance of wine in northern climates than the Roman
amphora. Because no specimens of these casks have survived, whereas
the more strongly constituted amphora is dragged up in perfect
condition and in unlimited numbers from the bottom of the Mediterranean by today's underwater swimmers, people tend to forget that
the cask was a Gallo-Roman invention: a sculpture in the museum at
Trier showing a Roman barge of the Rhine fleet loaded with casks is
a reminder of the fact.

Some of the Gallo-Roman glasses that have been found in the soil
of the Champagne district are long and slim and not unlike the present-
day champagne flûte, which invites the tantalizing thought that
perhaps even at that early date the Champenois understood how to
develop a slight sparkle in their wine. Whether they did or not, they
were proving themselves to be among the most professional vine-
growers of the Empire.

Before long the Roman province of which present-day Champagne
formed part became one of the richest of the Empire. But dark clouds
were gathering on the horizon. The power of Rome was dwindling;
the Barbarians of central and northern Europe were conscious of the
riches which invasion might procure them; and Champagne, possessed
of no effective natural defences, was particularly vulnerable to their
attack. Already bands of Alamans and Franks had swept across the
countryside in search of loot, but they had been repelled without much
difficulty by the Romans. Soon after Probus had allowed the restoration
of the vineyards the raids had started again. It has been suggested that,
despite the rigid enforcement of the law which forbade the sale of wine
to the Barbarians, the craving for wine was a contributory cause of
these forays.

In 355 the Alamans raided Rheims and burnt it to the ground before
they were driven away. Ten years later Consul Jovinus, after surprising
the Alamans bathing their large limbs, combing their long flaxen hair
and—according to Gibbon—"swallowing huge draughts of rich,
delicious wine" on the banks of the Moselle, lured them back to the
plain surrounding Châlons-sur-Marne and fought a victorious battle
against them, lasting an entire summer's day. After this the Champagne
district enjoyed a short period of peace and prosperity, but in 406 the
Barbarians returned again. Rheims was sacked and the vineyards were
ravaged. For months the rural population lived in the caves and subterranean passages of the Mountain of Rheims and the Côte des Blancs.
These trials, however, were merely a foretaste of mightier ones. By

now the Roman Empire was in its death agony. Champagne, like all north-western Gaul, was about to be cut off from the civilizing influence of the south. Already European Barbarians were establishing permanent settlements in Gaul and the Iberian peninsula. But a new and far more terrible threat was arising in the east. A confederation of Asiatic Barbarians was preparing to leap on the tottering Empire, like a tiger on its prey, and the very future of western civilization was at stake. The issue was to be decided within sight of the vineyards of the Champagne district.

The driving force behind the threat from the Orient was Attila, the Hun. He was known to be utterly ruthless, inordinately proud, bloodthirsty to the extent of claiming blood to be his element, super-stitious, drunken, debauched, and to have only one virtue: his word was his bond. "Wherever my horse shall tread, there nothing shall ever grow again"; "the stars fall, the earth trembles, for I am the Hammer of the Universe": such were his sayings; and when they penetrated to Gaul they sent chills darting down the stoutest spines. This was the tyrant, the most redoubtable Barbarian of all, who was determined to inherit the might of the Roman Empire.

To achieve his purpose, he assembled an army of 600,000 warriors (some say 700,000). Everything about them inspired horror: their hideous faces, their cruelty, the rapidity of their movements, their ubiquity. The Great Wall of China had been built to keep them out. Could defenceless Gaul withstand their onslaught?

By the early spring of 451 Attila was across the Rhine. Slav, Scandin-avian, Saxon, Frankish, Burgundian and Alaman tribes had bent to his will like reeds in the wind, and were being absorbed into his army. His hordes swept on into Gaul. One by one the great Roman cities of the Palatinate collapsed in flames: Mainz, Trier, Speyer, Worms, Metz. By May he was in the Champagne district. The defences of Châlons-sur-Marne were in the hands of young Bishop Alpin, who somehow managed to charm the cobra and save the town from destruction, but Rheims was razed to the ground. By June Attila was in front of Orléans. For eight weeks the city held out. At the precise moment when the Huns finally entered, the Roman legions and the hordes of the Visigoths—bitter enemies who had united in the face of a greater peril—were visible on the horizon.

After a fearful battle, which left the streets of Orléans streaming with blood, Attila retired, the first time he had done so since leaving the Danube. A second, indecisive battle was fought at Méry-sur-Seine, after which Attila again retreated, destroying the bridges of the Seine in his wake. Slowly—for Aetius, who led the Roman legions, did not press him hard, hoping that if a major engagement was avoided the Huns would eventually leave Gaul of their own accord—Attila continued to pull back.

On his previous visit to the area he had noticed, eight miles north of Châlons, a colossal circular camp, dating from 600 B.C., 600 yards in diameter, over five acres in area, surrounded by two fifteen-foot banks with a moat between them. Having destroyed the bridges over the Marne, Attila headed for this formidable lair, followed by 500,000 soldiers and chariots stuffed to bursting point with women and loot. Here, amid minor skirmishing, tremendous preparations were carried out on both sides for the titanic encounter that was in the offing.* Aetius's army was about equal in number to Attila's by now, and almost as cosmopolitan. It consisted of his own Gallo-Romans, the Visigoths, Merovians, Franks, Burgundians, blond, handsome Alains, and a host of other tribesmen whose chiefs had rallied to the Roman flag to face the Hun. By the middle of September a million soldiers were concentrated in the Châlons plain, and all was ready for the great encounter between Orient and Occident.

The battle began about midday on 21 September 451, and the main fighting took place a short distance to the north-east of Attila's camp. The struggle was probably the fiercest and bloodiest mankind has ever known. At first the tide of battle flowed in Attila's favour. How close the issue must have been at that point is shown by a sentence of the harangue which Attila gave his troops that has echoed down through the centuries: "One more blow and you will be masters of the entire world." But at sunset the battle was still raging, and Aetius was winning. In the early hours of the morning victory was his. Over 200,000 men had died, representative of every race of Europe and Asia.

After the battle Attila and the battered remnants of his army barricaded themselves in the encampment. They were on the point of starving to death when Aetius relented and escorted them back across the Rhine.

Attila's camp lies within a few yards of N. 394 and within a mile of N. 77, but there is no sign on either road to indicate that the camp is

---

* A considerable body of opinion believes that the entire battle, not just one engagement prior to it, took place at Méry-sur-Seine. I consider that the brilliant exposition of the drama given by Mlle Geneviève Dévignes in her *Ici le Monde Changea de Maître* provides convincing evidence that the battle did take place near the Camp. I have relied heavily on her judgement throughout this chapter.

there. If only the travellers knew, instead of flashing by they could park their cars beside the Noblette, the little river which flows nearby, cross it by the stepping-stones, and settle down for a picnic on the circular banks of the encampment—one of the loveliest and most tranquil spots for a summer picnic imaginable.

Eight years after the defeat of Attila St. Remi, who was then twenty-two, became Bishop of Rheims. The responsibility of such an appointment was great for so young a man, for the situation of the Church was precarious in the extreme and times were hard for Christians. But St. Remi's strength of character and ability were equal to the challenge. "Hardly," as a French writer has put it, "was the pastoral ring on his finger than he started to perform miracles." Most of these had something to do with wine. For, if ever there was a man who loved wine, it was St. Remi. He owned acres of vineyards, one, it is believed, at Rilly, on the northern slopes of the Mountain of Rheims, another at Fleury-la-Rivière, on the Mountain's southern slopes, two more on the Petite Montagne, at Crugny and Germiny, and a fifth within the walls of Rheims itself.

The miracle that impressed itself most on the minds of the Champenois occurred during a visit which the Bishop made to his cousin, St. Cecilia (or Celsa). The poor lady was caught napping: not one drop of wine did she have in the house to offer her distinguished relative. Being a true Champenois, St. Remi was not to be done out of his glass of Champagne wine. He climbed down to the cellar, blessed an empty cask and—hey presto! out came wine. The incident is commemorated in a sculpture on the north doorway of Rheims Cathedral, as well as in a tapestry in his Basilica in Rheims.

But the greatest miracle of St. Remi's career was the conversion of Clovis, King of the Franks, of which mention has already been made. The modern counterpart of the achievement, both in seeming unlikelihood and in far-reaching effect, would be the baptism of the Head of State of Russia or China. For, among the Barbarian leaders fighting for supremacy in the west, Clovis was emerging as the probable winner. He had put an end to the power of Rome in Gaul; Paris, Rheims and Châlons-sur-Marne were already his. Patiently, St. Remi had been encouraging the rough Barbarian to renounce the faith of his ancestors. In 496 he marched off to the Rhineland to take on the most formidable of his rivals, the Alamans; at his side was his fiancée, Clotilde, a Princess of Burgundy and a Christian. When all seemed lost, the pagan King addressed a despairing prayer to Clotilde's and St. Remi's God: immediately his exhausted troops recovered sufficient energy for one last desperate charge, and it succeeded so well that the power of the Alamans as a nation was swept away for ever. In thanksgiving for the aid he had received, Clovis at once returned to Rheims, where, on Christmas Day, he accepted baptism from the hands of St. Remi, together with 3,000 of his warriors.

The ceremony, it is believed, took place in a rough baptistry on the very spot where the cathedral now stands, and to this day French schoolchildren are taught the trenchant words which St. Remi uttered as he made the Sign of the Cross on the King's forehead: "*Courbe ta tête, fier Sicambre,*★ *adore ce que tu as brûlé, brûle ce que tu as adoré.*"†

It is worth while to consider the precise significance of this simple ceremony. First, it meant that, at the very moment when the civilizing influence of Rome was dwindling, the new medium of civilization and progress—the Church—had come to terms with the major threat to its future, the Barbarians. Clovis, in effect, was to become the Constantine of Gaul, the Defender of the Faith for northern Europe. He threw himself into the task with the customary zeal of the convert, and owing to his efforts Gaul was saved from schism and given a spiritual unity which was to endure for centuries.

On the political plain, the conversion had equally happy results. Clovis's victories over the Burgundians and Visigoths, his most powerful rivals, made him master of Gaul. For the first time a Christian Kingdom flourished from the shores of the Mediterranean to those of the English Channel.

To the city of Rheims the conversion brought vast benefits. We have seen that, as a direct result of St. Remi's triumph, the Kings of France in due course came to Rheims to be crowned, and in so doing conferred on the city an importance quite out of proportion to its size, in addition to many other privileges and marks of royal favour.

The fact that Rheims became a city of special importance and the spiritual centre of France reflected favourably on the development of and the demand for the wines of the district. For although Champagne,

---

★ The Sicambri or Salii (they drafted Salic Law) became the most famous of the fluctuating confederacy of tribes on the Weser and Lower Rhine in Westphalia, Hesse and Brunswick, for which the name "Frank" was the common designation.

† According to one school of thought, Clovis's baptism and the defeat of the Alamans took place in 506, not 496, and the scene of the baptism was Tours, not Rheims. The one point upon which historians agree is that St. Remi administered the sacrament.

like the rest of Gaul, was to be the scene of many invasions and annexations during the years to come—Rheims was pillaged, burnt and razed to the ground no less than seven times between the middle of the fifth century and the end of the tenth—the *vignerons* kept on working, and several indirect tributes to Champagne wines during these times have come down to us. We know, for instance, that in the eighth century the rule of the sisters of the Hôtel-Dieu at Rheims stipulated that "*si aucune des sœurs dit parole injurieuse à l'autre ou jure vilainement, ce jour ne boira pas de vin*". And at about the same time the clergy of Châlons-sur-Marne developed such a predilection for the local wine that it was found necessary to limit canons, priests and deacons to three glasses in the morning and two glasses in the evening, sub-deacons being rationed to only two glasses for each meal. By the ninth century there are indications that distinction was already being made between *vins de la rivière* and *vins de la montagne*. And certain growths were already recognized as possessing special distinction: in the ninth century Archbishop Hincmar of Rheims, writing to the Bishop of Laon, who had been ill during a visit to Germany, advised him "to avoid parsley and small fish and [to] drink the wines of Epernay, Mailly and Cormicy".

But perhaps what helped the wines most were the favours that the grateful monarchy heaped upon the monasteries about to be founded near Rheims. For the destiny of Champagne wines was to rest during the next thousand years in the eager and capable hands of monks.

As the monastic movement gained force in the early part of the seventh century, the Champagne district became a positive constellation of monasteries. Between 625 and 664 no less than six were founded in the Diocese of Rheims, including Hautvillers (the scene of Dom Pérignon's discoveries) and Saint-Basle at Verzy, in whose grounds the famous parasol beeches were to be planted. Among the many famous abbeys founded elsewhere in Champagne were Clairvaux; Paraclet, where Héloise and Abélard lived and loved and died; and Notre-Dame-de-Jouarre. The last was founded in 630, and from that day to this nuns of the Benedictine order have been in habitation, except for one bleak period of forty-five years immediately after the Revolution, when they were forced to hide in the homes of Champenois well-wishers. Their seventh-century sanctuary is still intact, the only one of its kind left in France.

Hardly was the first stone of a new monastery laid than the monks snapped up the best sites for vines; and they embarked on the culti-

vation of their vineyards with the same energy and enterprise that they
lavished on the drying up of marshes, the clearance of forests and the
improvement of farmland. Some of their methods may have been
primitive: holy water to cure disease in the vineyards, exorcism to
banish pests, pilgrimages to ward off hail and frost. But before long
they enjoyed the reputation of having the best-kept vineyards in the
region and of producing the best wine. They were expert, too, at
spreading the fame of their wines abroad.

They had a variety of motives for their preoccupation with viticulture. Foremost, no doubt, was their desire to have first-class wine
for their tables; even in the stricter orders teetotalism was seldom
associated with godliness. Why should it have been, when wine played
as important a part as bread in the celebration of the most solemn
sacrament of the Church? Indeed, at the very root of the monks' and
the priests' interest in the vineyard lay the necessity of providing wine
for the Eucharist. The monks, it should be remembered, also needed
wine for their guests. Many centuries were to elapse before taverns
and hotels existed, and until they did the traveller relied on the
monastery for shelter and food: not to offer wine to a traveller—be
he king or pauper—would have been considered a gross breach of
hospitality. Finally, the monks grew vines to make money: to run
their establishments, to provide for the sick and the poor, and, the
cynic will add, to line their own pockets.

Documents that have survived from the ninth century show how
important the monastic vineyards had become by that time. In a letter
which Archbishop Hincmar wrote to Charles the Bold of Burgundy,
protesting against the arbitrary confiscation of Church property, the
monastic vineyards listed run into hundreds. Other ninth-century
documents show that, like the champagne Houses today, the monks
were busily shipping Champagne wines to kings, bishops and peers
of the realm.

As the monasteries grew, so did their responsibilities towards the
poor. In order to help the religious orders to carry out their charitable
works, the rich started to bequeath them money, land, and often
vineyards. To this day the nuns of the Hospice de Beaune in Burgundy
run a great hospital and carry out innumerable charitable duties with
money raised from the sale of wine from vineyards in Burgundy which
were bequeathed to them (as others still are today). The monasteries
of Champagne acquired vast vineyard properties in this way during
the Crusades: it was an almost universal custom for the Lord and
Knight to transfer his property to the Church before setting off for

Palestine. At the outbreak of the French Revolution, at least half of the really great vineyards in the Champagne district were in the hands of monks.

In recognition of the valuable services which the monasteries rendered the local population, the monks were excused payment of tax on the wines they sold: in addition to being usually the best available the monastic wines were generally, therefore, the cheapest as well (but not always: Dom Pérignon's wines, as we shall see, cost the earth). This situation naturally exasperated the nobles: time and time again, despite papal bulls and archbishoprical warrants forbidding the levying of the *droit de vinage* on wine produced by religious communities, the nobles endeavoured to extort it. Moreover, the privileged tax position of the monasteries often spelled ruin for the ordinary vine-grower. For not only did a law called the *droit de banvin* forbid the commoner to sell his crop of grapes until the seigneurs and the monks had sold theirs; it also required him to pay a tithe to the Church on his crop. We know exactly how much this tithe amounted to in three villages of the Champagne district at the time of the Revolution: at Hautvillers one-eleventh of the crop, at Dizy one-twelfth, at Pierry one-twentieth. What had originated as a perfectly fair dispensation to those who were helping the poor had gradually become an unwarranted abuse. It is hardly surprising that when the Revolution broke out one of the main charges levelled against the monasteries was the excessive amount of revenue which they derived directly and indirectly from the vineyards of the district.

But, despite the wrongs and abuses that undoubtedly existed, we who enjoy champagne today owe a great debt of gratitude to the monastic orders. Had it not been for the monks, the vineyards of the Champagne district would have gone to pieces in the Dark and Middle Ages. Indeed, the influence of the monks and of their Church was as beneficial to the culture of the vine as it was to the development of art and literature during that long period, from the fifth to the sixteenth century, when the Catholic Church dominated Europe.

CHAPTER 8

THE DARK AGES AND THE MIDDLE AGES

THE CENTURIES FROM the tenth to the thirteenth were an oasis of peace for Champagne. It was a little *belle époque* during which the culture of the vine went from strength to strength. In 1088 an undreamt of honour was conferred on the vineyard village of Châtillon-sur-Marne: one of its sons was elected to the papacy, assuming the name of Urban II. The Pope did much to publicize the wines of his native land, letting it be known that he preferred them to all others; a pilgrim to Rome, it was said, could be sure of a warm welcome if he arrived armed with a supply of the Pope's favourite vintage. The Pope's connection with Champagne undoubtedly explained why the Champenois nobles responded in such particularly large numbers to his appeal for the Second Crusade. They also played an important part in the Fourth Crusade. And the Knights Templar originated in Champagne, where they owned vines and a Commanderie at Rheims. North of Châlons-sur-Marne, near Attila's camp, the hide-outs which they used while they were being persecuted can still be seen.

But, from the winefield's point of view, probably the most advantageous circumstance of these happy times was the institution of the Champagne Fairs. Situated at the southern limit of the great textile region of Flanders and the north of France, Champagne was an obvious point of contact between that region and the commerce of the Mediterranean; and from the latter part of the eleventh century until the end of the thirteenth virtually all the exchanges between the two trading areas took place in Champagne.

The merchants sometimes met at Rheims and Château-Thierry, but the most important Fairs took place at Troyes, Lagny, Bar-sur-Aube and Provins. The visitors were housed at first in tents beneath the walls, but permanent lodgings and markets were soon erected, many of which survive to this day, the most interesting being *La Grange aux Dimes* at Provins. There were few weeks in the year when trading was not taking place at one of the four towns, and all of them prospered greatly. The trade was not *de luxe*, and the articles exchanged were mostly the homely necessities of life. From the north came blankets: top quality scarlet blankets from Ypres, Bruges, Brussels and Louvain; much prized blue blankets, others of "good colour" and common undyed ones from Lille, Cambrai, Douai, Tournai, Rheims and Ghent. Also offered for sale were leathers, pelts and all kinds of haberdashery. Much of the last came from Champagne: linens from Rheims and cotton bonnets from Troyes. Later, blankets from Catalonia, Swabia and Basle, velvets from Toledo and linens from Constance were also exchanged. On the Mediterranean side the trade was mostly conducted by Genoese merchants. To pay for their purchases they brought spices from Zanzibar, Venice treacle (orvietam), silks, alums, dyes and other products of the mysterious Orient.

All this activity was of immense advantage to the wine-makers of Champagne. Quite apart from the great quantities of wine consumed by the merchants, the Fairs were a heaven-sent opportunity for spreading the fame of the vineyards abroad. Before long wine merchants from Spain, Italy, Montpellier and Germany began attending them. But they were destined to have a short existence. Europe was giving birth to great maritime nations, and by the end of the thirteenth century commerce between north and south was being transacted via the Straits of Gibraltar.

Soon a worse blow was to befall Champagne: it was to become one of the principal battlegrounds of the Hundred Years' War. By 1358 the English invasions had caused such misery that in May of that year the peasants (or "Jacques") of Brie revolted, the first of many uprisings which came to be known as "Jacqueries", and which the nobility suppressed with varying degrees of success but with sustained ruthlessness.

On the wet St. Andrew's Day of 1359 Edward III of England arrived under the walls of Rheims, intent on having himself crowned King of France in the traditional manner. The Rémois would have none of it. They resisted furiously, and throughout the winter Edward's half-starved, shivering army besieged the city. The capture of 3,000 barrels of wine consoled the soldiers and perhaps made Edward the first English monarch to taste the wines of Champagne;* but they failed to give his troops the necessary impetus to win, and in the spring Edward retired, bitterly disappointed. The treaty of 1360 brought

* During the campaign the English played a dirty trick on the French. Besieged in Epernay, they sent off a wagon-load of wine towards Châlons under the protection of an inadequate escort; the French swooped down on it; the English retreated; the French got drunk; whereupon the English sallied forth again and gave the French a good thrashing. The incident is of interest in that it is one of the rare examples in Champagne's history of French soldiers succumbing to the temptations offered by the winefield's produce: generally, it was the invading forces to whom this happened.

about a respite in the war, but in 1369 the English raids across France started again. The resistance of the Champenois prompted the English to institute a "scorched earth" policy. As was to happen time and time again in the history of the Champagne district, the inhabitants took refuge in the caves of the Mountain of Rheims and the Côte des Blancs.

From 1386 to 1417 there was another respite in the war, but in 1417 the Duke of Burgundy, who had inherited Flanders from his father-in-law, decided to annex Champagne. A Burgundy stretching from the North Sea to Dijon in no way suited the English. Fighting broke out again, and village after village disappeared in a sheet of flame. The population, unable to tend their vines or gain their living in other ways, started to thin out alarmingly. France, but above all Champagne, was in the grip of a cruel, disastrous struggle which seemed eternal. And then in 1429, when the French forces, the party of the Dauphin, were about to surrender, the miracle happened. Joan of Arc, the peasant girl whose home at Domremy was on Champagne's eastern border, breathed fire into the nation's flagging spirits and dragged Charles to Rheims to be crowned. Champagne was reconquered. The coronation took place on 17 July while the English fled, taking with them, it is said, as many wagon-loads of the wines of Champagne as they could lay their hands on. But another fifteen years passed before the English and the Burgundians were finally expelled.

Since the products of the wine-maker's art are ephemeral, with a lifetime measured in decades, it is extremely difficult, if not impossible, to form an accurate impression of what sort of wine a winefield was producing at any given moment of history. At the stage of Champagne's development which we have now reached there are definite indications that, according to the standards of the day, the quality of the wine was outstanding: in 1410, for instance, Emperor Sigismond of the House of Luxembourg made a detour during a visit to France in order to drink the wine of Ay on the spot; and a song composed for Charles VII's coronation states that the growths of Ay and Epernay were among the best in the kingdom. On the other hand, there are also indications that, judged by our standards, the wine might not have met with much approval. It was apparently the custom to dilute it with water; though Thibault IV, a thirteenth-century Count of Champagne, consumed his Champagne wine warm and neat, on account, he explained, of "his large head and cold stomach". Indeed, so rough and strong may much of the wine have been that the careless drinker risked a fate like that which befell Wenceslas, King of Bohemia and

Emperor of the Holy Roman Empire, during a visit to Rheims in 1397 to discuss with Charles VI the schism that was then splitting the church. He got so royally drunk that, when the Dukes of Berry and Bourbon arrived at the monastery of Saint-Remi to escort him to their sovereign, he was incapable of walking, and the meeting had to be postponed. This state of affairs lasted several days until, still bemused, he signed all the documents placed before him without even glancing at them, and departed.

It is almost impossible, too, to gauge with any accuracy the size of the winefield in those far-off days. Up to the thirteenth century we can be reasonably sure that production was not sufficient to quench the thirst of the ordinary Champenois; except at coronation time he had to be satisfied with cervisia, the beer of ancient Gaul; wine was still only for the rich. But before the Hundred Years' War broke out it is certain that the vineyards had already greatly expanded, and that the expansion continued at a definite rhythm from then on, whenever peace allowed: it is probable that by the end of the fourteenth century the majority of the population of Champagne were wine-drinkers. By 1412 wine was Rheims's chief trade, according to a charter granted to the town by Charles VI. And at about the same time *courtiers de vin*, or wine-brokers, are first mentioned. All of which indicates that viticulture and wine-making made much progress in Champagne in the fifteenth century. But both trades still required the patience of Job: when Henry VII landed in France in 1495, *vignerons* near Rheims were ordered to pull up their vine-stakes for fear the English might use them for cooking or for filling up moats to scale the city ramparts.

During the first half of the sixteenth century the winefield flourished, largely owing to François I's thoughtfulness—as a Champenois historian has put it—in waging his wars a long way from Champagne. The most intriguing facet of these decades is the magnetic appeal which the vineyards of Ay exercised on Europe's leaders. François I, Pope Leo X, Charles V of Spain and Henry VIII of England all bought vineyards there; and such was their passion for the wine that they maintained their own presses and resident superintendents, to make sure they were not cheated.

In 1552, during the Wars of Religion, the vine growers were once again ordered to pull up their vine-stakes—this time to prevent them from falling into the hands of the advancing Germans; but, in general, the latter half of the sixteenth century was as happy a period as the first half. It produced an amazing royal testimonial: Henri IV (who owned vineyards at Ay) was one day receiving the Spanish Ambassador, whose habit of reeling off the full list of his sovereign's titles before getting down to business invariably annoyed the French monarch. On this occasion his patience deserted him and he interrupted the Ambassador in full flow, saying: "You can tell His Most Catholic Majesty the King of Spain, Castile, Aragon, etc., etc., etc., that Henri, Lord of Ay . . .". And that happy half-century produced a dramatic rise in the prices paid for the winefield's produce. At the coronation of François II, in 1559, a *queue** of Champagne wine fetched 14, 17 and 19 livres; at Charles IX's, in 1561, 28 to 34 livres; at Henri III's, in 1575, 54 to 75 livres; and at Louis XIII's, in 1610, no less than 175 livres. The records of the coronation celebrations provide yet further evidence of the progress the region's wines were making at this time: at Charles IV's coronation, in 1322, the wines served had included *vins de Bianne* (Beaune) and *vins de rivière* (Marne valley wines); at Philip IV of Valois', in 1328, the main offerings had been from Beaune, St. Pourçain and the Marne; but at the banquets for Henri III in 1575 and Louis XIII in 1610 the only wines to be served at the royal tables were those of the Champagne district.

The twenty-year civil war known as the Fronde, which took place during Louis XIV's minority, brought destruction and misery once again to the Champagne district, but as soon as the King attained his majority and was on the throne the winefield enjoyed a period of great prosperity. This was in some measure due to the King's own patronage of Champagne wines. He took a liking to them at his coronation in 1666, and apart from one short period at the end of his life, when his doctor insisted that he should drink burgundy for health reasons, he rarely drank anything else. Saint-Simon in his *Mémoires* states that the King's particular favourite was the red wine of Bouzy, and it is known that he ordered it from an Ay wine-maker called Rémy Berthauld. The accounts of the King's coronation show that the Rémois had already developed that publicity sense of which no one would deny they are the masters today. The head of the reception committee merely said: "Sire, we offer you our wines, our pears, our gingerbreads, our biscuits and our hearts",† to which the King replied: "That, gentlemen, is the kind of speech I like."

---

* About 400 litres (88 gallons).

† A guild of gingerbread-makers was established in Rheims in the sixteenth century. Sieur de la Framboisière, *doyen* of the Rheims faculty in 1586, attributed the "good complexion and the robust, succulent body of the Rémoise" to the gingerbread.

But the Champagne district owed its prosperity during the King's reign to an even greater extent to the activities of a group of young noblemen, most of them property-owners in Champagne, who banded together at the time of the coronation and decided to do everything in their power to popularize the winefield's produce. The original members of the group are thought to have been Commandeur de Souvré, the Marquis de Sillery, the Duc de Mortemart, the Marquis de Saint-Evremond, the Comte d'Olonne and the Marquis de Bois-Dauphin; it was the last three who were responsible for the curious name by which the group came to be known. Soon after the coronation they dined with the Bishop of Le Mans, and so horrified the old man with their fastidiousness in matters of food and wine that he went about Paris afterwards saying: "These gentlemen, in seeking refinement in everything, go to extremes: they can only eat Normandy veal; their partridges must come from Auvergne, and their rabbits from La Roche-sur-Yon; they are no less particular as regards fruit; and, as to wine, they can only drink that of the good *coteaux* of Ay, Hautvillers and Avenay." Their friends, who thought this a huge joke, started calling them the *Trois Coteaux*, and before long the whole group became known as the *Ordre des Coteaux*.

It was easy to poke fun at the *Ordre des Coteaux*, but they did an excellent job for the winefield. At the very outset of the reign they succeeded in making the wine of Champagne all the rage at Court, and, what was more difficult, they maintained its position as the wine of fashion at Versailles. In effect, they were the forerunners of champagne's present-day publicity agents. There can have been few moments in the winefield's destiny when it stood in greater need of such services. For under Louis XIV France, for the first time in its history, had a really strong central government; the Court was the sole arbiter of fashion; and every French winefield was engaging in cut-throat competition to gain Court favour for its products. If the Champagne district had not had the support at Versailles of the *Ordre des Coteaux*, who knows whether all the good work in the technical field which Dom Pérignon was quietly accomplishing at Hautvillers, more or less at the same time, would in the end have laid such an outsize golden egg?

The *Ordre des Coteaux* did not confine their activities to France. In 1662 one of their founder members, the Marquis de Saint-Evremond, fell into disgrace at Court and took refuge in England, where he at once proceeded to reintroduce the English to the delights of Champagne wine, which they appear to have been deprived of since the reign of Henry VIII. In fact, he may properly be described as the winefield's first foreign agent. His friendship with Charles II, the wide range of his acquaintance among the aristocracy, and the craze for everything French which lingered on at the Court as an aftermath of the King's exile in France greatly facilitated his task; and it was not long before the wines of Champagne were enjoying the same vogue at Whitehall as they were at Versailles. Indeed, if the frequency with which the Restoration playwrights and poets mentioned "Champaign" is any guide, it would seem that the English quickly developed a passion for the winefield's produce similar to that which their descendants display today. Every modern Englishman would applaud the lover who in Sir George Etherage's comedy, *She Would If She Could*, first performed in 1668, remarks:

> "She's no mistress of mine
> That drinks not her wine,
> Or frowns at my friends' drinking notions;
> If my heart thou wouldst gain,
> Drink thy flask of Champaign;
> Twill serve thee for paint and love-potions."

And many a modern Englishman must at some time or another have been submitted to a lecture like the one in Sir Charles Sedley's poem, *The Doctor and the Patients*:

> "One day he called 'em all together,
> And, one by one, he asked 'em whether
> It were not better by good diet
> To keep the blood and humours quiet,
> With toast and ale to cool their brains
> Than nightly fire 'em with Champaigns."

CHAPTER 9

THE ABBEY OF HAUTVILLERS

ONE HOT SUMMER'S day in 650 St. Nivard, twenty-fifth archbishop of Rheims, left his domain of Epernay to make his way back to Rheims on foot. He was accompanied by his nephew and disciple, St. Berchaire. The two men crossed the Marne and climbed slowly up the steep, vine-clad slopes of the Mountain of Rheims. The ascent tired the ageing prelate and, just before he reached the point where the slopes flatten out, he lay down in a meadow under the shade of an oak to rest. Soothed, perhaps, by the gentle trickle of water from a nearby spring, which is known today as the Fontaine Saint-Nivard, he fell asleep. While he slept, he had a dream. In his dream he beheld a snow-white dove (the same dove, believers later suggested, that had brought down the holy oil for the anointment of Clovis). Three times this dove, enveloped in a brilliant light, circled the oak above St. Nivard, and three times it alighted on the tree; then suddenly it soared up to heaven.

When St. Nivard awoke he found that St. Berchaire, who had never closed his eyelids, had shared the same vision. For many moments the two saints stared in wonderment across the glorious valley beneath them. Soon St. Nivard's eyes focused on the spot beside the Marne where he had founded the monastery of Villers, which barbarians had since twice destroyed. There and then, he decided that on the exact spot where the tree stood upon which the snow-white dove had alighted a new monastery should arise, to be called Hautvillers. Such is the sublime origin of the Abbaye de Saint-Pierre d'Hautvillers, of which, almost exactly 1,000 years later, Dom Pérignon was to be appointed cellarer.

St. Nivard made arrangements to buy the necessary land, trees were felled, masons were engaged, and before long the buildings were complete. In memory of the snow-white dove, part of the trunk of the oak-tree on which it had alighted was left embedded in the stone altar of the new church. The abbey was placed under the special protection of the archbishopric of Rheims, and St. Berchaire is believed to have been the first abbot. St. Nivard spent part of each year at Hautvillers, and it was there that he died; he was buried at Rheims, but his relics were later returned to the abbey, where they can be seen today in the church.

From the very beginning Hautvillers seems to have had an extraordinary appeal for the faithful. Young men flocked there to become monks; old men came there to die. Perhaps the abbey's immediate and enduring popularity was explained by the perfection of its site. Facing due south, protected from north, east and west winds by the Mountain of Rheims, blessed all the year round with what can only be described as champagne air, it is impossible to imagine a spot more conducive to the contemplation of celestial matters and to the turning of man's mind towards love of his creator. In the ninth century a learned monk called Almanne described the site as fit "to delight every eye, satisfy every desire and charm every heart", and among the attractions of the surroundings he specially mentioned the thick foliage of the nearby forests, the abundance of fruit trees, the rich harvests of the fields, the greenness of the pastures, the gardens fragrant with the scent of every variety of flower, and the vines laden with grapes whose juice "causes the cup to gleam with the brightness of pearls" (a remark which could be taken as a reference to the tendency of the wine to sparkle).

For over twelve centuries Hautvillers was one of the most famous of all French monasteries. It was the proud boast of the brotherhood that it had produced nine archbishops for the see of Rheims, twenty-two abbots for various celebrated monasteries and many a recruit for the sacred college. Several of its abbots came from the great families of France.

For many centuries the monks of Hautvillers followed the rule of Columban, which, with its emphasis on obedience, silence, humility, fasting, prayer, solitude and work, was very similar to that of St. Benedict; and eventually the two rules merged. The life of a Hautvillers monk was moderately austere. Much of his day was taken up with teaching: showing people how to make the best use of their land and how to build houses, and instructing them in the faith. Before the invention of printing another important activity of the monastery was that of copying manuscripts. At this the monks of Hautvillers particularly excelled. Their abbey became the brightest ornament of a school of manuscript copying, known to experts as the School of Rheims, which, together with the schools of Tours and Corbie (near Amiens), produced the finest bibles, prayer-books and psalters of the Carolingian period. A magnificent example of their work in a perfect state of conservation—known as the Ebbon Manuscript because it was dedicated to the Archbishop of Rheims of that name—is now in the possession of the town library of Epernay. It is a ninth-century gospel, worked from beginning to end in gold letters on the richest vellum. People come from the four corners of the earth to look at it, and often they go away disappointed, because the manuscript is in such constant demand for exhibitions that it seldom seems to spend much time at Epernay.

That the Ebbon Manuscript is still in almost as perfect condition as when it was so lovingly transcribed is little short of a miracle, in view of the never-ending depredations that the abbey has suffered in the course of its history. Four times, between 882 and 1562, it was burned to the ground. Each time, with their customary patience, the monks set about the task of rebuilding, and for two centuries the new buildings suffered no damage from war. But this turned out to be merely the calm before the storm. One of the first laws passed by the Revolutionaries called for the suppression of the monasteries and the sale of all Church property. By July 1790 the entire brotherhood of Hautvillers had scattered to oblivion or to a meagre state pension; and from that day to this no monk has resided at Hautvillers.

In 1814 the abbey was pillaged by 700 Russian troops stationed nearby. In 1825, what was left of it was acquired by Comte Pierre-Gabriel Chandon de Briailles, the son-in-law of Jean-Remy Moët, the grandson of the founder of Moët & Chandon. By then the right to worship had long been restored, and the new owner presented the abbey church to the villagers of Hautvillers as a replacement for their own ninth-century church, which had been sold and pulled down at the height of the revolutionary fervour. He and his descendants lavished care on the property, but they could not protect it from the scourge of war. In 1870 it was requisitioned by German troops; during the First World War it was for a time the headquarters of the Italian general Albricci; and in 1940, during the German invasion, the manor house which the Chandons had erected on the site of the abbot's house was burnt to the ground. After that the abbey—and its vineyards—passed into the possession of Moët & Chandon.

A visit to the grounds of Hautvillers and to the abbey church is still a most rewarding experience. On that hallowed ground the sensitive observer feels in closer contact with the forces that have shaped the destiny of Champagne wines than he does anywhere else in the countryside. That is why, since October 1924, the entire property has been classed as an Historic Monument, and not a stone may be touched or any alteration made without the prior approval of the Ministry of Fine Arts in Paris.

The three-mile drive to Hautvillers from Epernay is rewarding in itself. If the approach is made via the little riverside village of Damery, along the narrow road that twists obliquely up the southern slopes of the Mountain of Rheims towards Hautvillers, one of the loveliest views in all Champagne is obtained. Hedged in by vines, the visitor looks down upon the Marne curving gracefully into the valley out of the flat plain of *Champagne pouilleuse*, and he does not need to be a field-marshal to see why throughout history the Marne valley has been one of the traditional gateways through which the nations of the east have passed in their greedy haste to reach Paris. If the approach is made along the main road from Epernay to Fismes, Hautvillers becomes visible soon after the Marne is crossed, and a better idea is obtained of the village's splendid position, perched just below the tree-line, over-hanging a vast amphitheatre of vineyards. On certain summer days a trick of the light, aided by the red tiles of the roof-tops and the honey-coloured walls of the houses, imparts the impression that a hill-top village in Provence is being approached. And when the day is still and the sun is strong, only the tiniest effort of the imagination is required to picture the stillness of that amphitheatre being disturbed by the bent backs of the monks.

The entrance to the grounds of the abbey is through an ancient gateway connected to the south transept of the church. As likely as not, the first thing a visitor encounters is a barking dog, a white rabbit, some hens or an antiquated car belonging to the concierge, which comes as rather a shock if his expectations were on a higher plane. But he must be patient: only the shadow of this once great abbey remains; its image is fragile, more vividly revealed by atmosphere than by anything else, and the farmyard welcome is part of that atmosphere. On the left stands a small two-storied building in which are incor-porated a quantity of mellow stones and bricks rescued from the abbey ruins. It houses a small village convent school, and the un-obtrusive comings-and-goings of the brown-habited nuns proclaim the enduring sanctity of the spot. On the right, attached to the church wall by strong buttresses, is the only one of the four original cloisters of the abbey that remains. It was restored in 1932; into the wall is sunk a full-length statue in relief of Dom Pérignon, with the cloister itself, which he must have known so well, depicted in the background. Facing the cloister, beyond an open space which was formerly the quadrangle, lie the lawns and groves where the monks strolled and read their breviaries. Here wars and time have wrought no vengeance. Two superb trees which the monks planted, a Spanish fir and a blue cedar, still shade the lawns. Nearby lie the vegetable garden and the fishpond which once supplied the monks' tables; both are still in use. And beyond the vegetable garden stretches the stupendous view which is the soul of Hautvillers. Vines galore in the foreground; golden wheat-fields, the glittering Marne and delicate poplar brakes in the middle distance; Epernay and its backdrop of gentle forest-capped hills beyond; off to the left the plain of Châlons: the combination is breath-taking at any time, and on a hazy summer's day recalls the view from that other monastery at Fiesole, looking down upon Florence.

The church has two great treasures. The first of them is the St. Helena reliquary, which stands upon a shelf attached to a wall of the eastern side aisle. It is a brass tabernacle, lavishly engraved; the only clue to what it contains is a notice which reads: "Relics of St. Helena, mother of Emperor Constantine, A.D. 230–301".* There is nothing to indicate that a strange tale surrounds the presence of these relics at Hautvillers today.

It all began in 841. In that year a priest from Rheims called Teutgise, who was attached to the monastery of Hautvillers, decided to visit Rome. He had been ill for many years, and in the Eternal City he hoped to achieve a miraculous cure for his malady. He prayed at many shrines, and finally, through the intercession of St. Helena, his prayers were answered. When at last he left Rome to return home, he calmly removed St. Helena's mummified body from the porphyry urn in which it lay, and spirited it out of the city. So great was his adoration for the saint—who was venerated, not only as the mother of the Emperor Constantine and for her piety and kindness to the poor, but for the great part which she had played in saving Jerusalem from the pagans—that he had determined never to be separated from her remains.

Wherever he stopped, on his journey back to Hautvillers, people enquired what the object in his wagon was that he treated with such reverence. When he revealed the truth, the sick flocked to touch the precious relic. Many miraculous cures were effected, the details of which Teutgise methodically recorded, so that it is known today exactly where and when they took place, and from what illness the person restored to health was suffering.

After many months he arrived at Hautvillers. The reception he received was a great disappointment to him. The monks, the abbot, above all Archbishop Hincmar, were scandalized that a priest should

* In reality, neither the date of St. Helena's birth nor that of her death is known for certain, but it is now believed that she was still alive in 325.

have stolen a saintly relic from under the very nose of the Pope; and they scoffed at the miraculous cures that Teutgise claimed had taken place on his journey. As for the local Champenois, nothing would persuade them that the relics were genuine. Teutgise, however, was a man with a will, and he wasted no time in showing that the relics had miraculous powers. The vines were suffering from drought; he persuaded the vineyard owners to fast for three days and to pray to St. Helena: the rains came. Shortly afterwards, a party of fishermen spent an entire night fishing the Marne without catching a thing. As dawn broke, it occurred to one of them to pray to St. Helena. Immediately they landed two big fish; but one of them jumped back into the river. More prayers. Miraculously, the same fish leapt out of the water, caught hold of the bait and refused to let go!

These signs completely vanquished the doubts of the common people; even the religious authorities began to wonder if Teutgise had not been telling the truth. Eventually Hincmar dispatched a delegation to Rome, entrusted with the delicate mission of persuading the Pope to allow St. Helena's body to remain at Hautvillers. Somewhat surprisingly, the Pope gave his permission, and even pardoned Teutgise for his crime, on the pretext that, judging by the miracles which had occurred since the theft, St. Helena herself appeared to have pardoned him. It was whispered that the Pope wished at all costs to avoid a scandal.

For the abbey, for the see of Rheims, indeed, for France itself, the acquisition was a matter of the highest import. In fact, it could soon be claimed that Rheims and the neighbourhood were the very fount of royal and spiritual power. Here Clovis had been baptized. Here French Kings came to be crowned. Here Kings could be anointed with an ointment sent specially from heaven (a service no other church could provide for no other monarchy). Here were the relics of St. Marcoul, which could cure scrofula.* And here were the mortal remains of the mother of the first Christian Emperor, of the discoverer of the True Cross. Such riches, such power, swelled the pride of the Arch-

---

* Up to comparatively recent times, a Frenchman who contracted this terrible disease believed he had three chances of being cured: by being touched by the King's hands; through the intercession of the sixth-century saint, Marcoul, who was born at Bayeux and whose relics lay at the Abbey of Corbeny, near Rheims; and by being touched by the seventh son of a marriage which had produced no daughter in between. The Church, of course, denied the efficacy of the touch of a seventh son, but encouraged belief in the miraculous powers of the Royal Touch, and continued to do so until the last application by Charles X on 31 March 1825.

bishops of Rheims; it dazzled the ordinary believer, and the faithful of all classes began to flock to the abbey.

It would not be much of an exaggeration to state that, until the Revolution, Hautvillers held a position not far removed from that which Lourdes holds today in the eyes of the Catholic believer. As at Lourdes, the miraculous cures effected by the relics were witnessed and attested; and the record was formidable. But what concerns us particularly is to see the effect that the new acquisition had on the Champagne district. St. Helena, of course, soon became the patron saint of the Champagne vineyard worker, which she remains today. Whenever drought or pestilence or some other calamity overtook the vineyards, it was to her that the vineyard workers appealed. And even today her protection is sought. In the church at Hautvillers, a few feet away from the reliquary, there is a little seventeenth-century rococo altar with a statue of the saint in the centre; it is still the custom for the first bunch of grapes picked in the Hautvillers vineyards to be entwined round the statue. But perhaps the greatest aid which the relics afforded the winefield was the steady flow of influential visitors that they attracted.

When the Revolution broke out, St. Helena's body was secretly removed from the abbey by a monk called Dom Grossart and taken to Montier-en-Der in Haute Marne, where it remained hidden for many years. After the Concordat Dom Grossart contacted Monseigneur de Talleyrand, the Archbishop of Rheims, and expressed his willingness to return the relics to Hautvillers. To Dom Grossart's indignation he was told that, as the church at Hautvillers was now only a parish church, a more important resting-place for the relics must be found. Dom Grossart refused point-blank to agree to this; he hung on to the relics and declined to reveal the hiding-place. Eventually, after protracted negotiations, he gave in, and in 1826 the coffin was opened and the relic was divided into three parts. The greater share was retained by the church of Saint-Leu in Paris; a second lot was handed to the Archbishop of Toulouse for one of the parishes in his diocese; and St. Helena's tibia, fourteen inches long, was given to the village church of Hautvillers. It is this somewhat meagre allotment, wrapped in silk and then in golden cloth, that rests today beside the St. Helena altar at Hautvillers.

The second great treasure of Hautvillers church, the tomb of Dom Pérignon, lies in the chancel at the foot of the altar steps. It is covered by a black marble slab on which is recorded the following inscription:

D . O . M .

HIC JACET DOM.

PETRUS PERIGNON

HUJUS MŇRII PER

ANNOS QUADGIN-

TA SEPTEM CELLE-

RARIUS QUI RE FA-

MILLIARI SUMMA CUM

LAUDE ADMINIS-

TRATA VIRTUTIBUS

PLENUS PATERNO

QUE JMPRIMIS IN

PAUPERIS AMORE

OBIIT AETATIS 77°

ANNO 1715

REQUIESCAT IN PACE

AMEN

According to classical scholars, the wording suggests that the abbey's Latin was by no means as good as its wine. The meaning is:

Here lies
Dom Peter Pérignon,
for 47 years
cellarer of this monastery, who,
having administered the affairs
of our community
with praiseworthy care,
full of virtue,
above all in his fatherly love
for the poor,
died
at the age of 77
in 1715
Rest in Peace.

CHAPTER 10

DOM PÉRIGNON: THE LEGEND AND THE TRUTH

Soon after the Second World War, the citizens of Sainte-Ménehould in eastern Champagne became aware of an odd situation. The world whole seemed to know about Dom Pérignon; wine-lovers everywhere held him in the highest esteem as the "inventor" of sparkling champagne; yet in Sainte-Ménehould itself there was absolutely nothing to indicate that this was where he had been born. An agitation arose; purse strings were untied; and it was decided to erect a statue to the town's most famous son. The choice of the sculptor was carefully considered. It was agreed that a copy of the statue by Chavillaud, which stands in the courtyard of Moët & Chandon and reproductions of which are to be seen in every nook and cranny of the Champagne district, would be unworthy of Sainte-Ménehould, and eventually the choice fell on a sculptor of local fame. On the day of the unveiling the Ménehouldiens donned their best bib and tucker and attended the ceremony in force. When the drapings were removed, they received the shock of their lives. Instead of a tall, stately monk, which was the way the statue by Chavillaud had taught them to think of Dom Pérignon, they beheld . . .

Well, let me explain. The sculptor had decided to have a little fun. It is a well-known fact that in parts of Champagne Asiatic barbarians were so smitten with the local girls that today, over a thousand years later, it is not at all uncommon to come across whole families with marked Mongolian features.* Since no one really knows what Dom Pérignon looked like, why not, the sculptor said to himself, let the statue bear the imprint of this local peculiarity? So, using white stone, he made it as small and frisky as a pony from the Asian steppes. He depicted Dom Pérignon with his left hand clapped across his mouth, as if he had just committed some frightful *faux pas*; and all he left visible of the poor monk's face were the forehead and the eyes, mere slits below ponderous lids, as slinky as his chisel could make them. Needless to say, there was an immediate outcry, echoes of which

---

* Once, at Ay, I observed a vineyard-worker whose weatherbeaten face was pure Mongolian. Mongolian features are one a penny in Courtisols, the longest village in France, which lies a couple of miles east of Châlons-sur-Marne, on the way to Sainte-Ménehould.

linger on; but the statue is still on its pedestal, and can be seen by anyone who is driving along the main road from Paris to the Palatinate.

It is not only Dom Pérignon's appearance that is a mystery. Little is known, either, of his life and achievements. Some Frenchmen even pretend that all the fuss about him is cooked up for tourists; the evolution of champagne from a still to a sparkling wine, they are apt to say, was a perfectly natural process with which Dom Pérignon had little to do. I have even been told in all solemnity by a Frenchman that Dom Pérignon never existed. The time has come to try to sift the truth from the legend.

The main reason why so little is known about him is that virtually all his papers disappeared from Hautvillers when the monks fled in 1790. Exactly what these documents comprised, and whether they were burnt or destroyed or smuggled away to a secret hiding-place, so that they may still turn up one day, no one knows. But I often wonder whether there may not be a more fundamental reason why more is not known about Dom Pérignon. A monk, after all, is barred by the very nature of his calling from seeking worldly fame. Indeed, he must take precautions to avoid it, because a surfeit of it would compromise his position within his community. If this factor is taken into consideration, perhaps a surprising amount is known about Dom Pérignon—and it is of the greatest possible interest.

It was probably late in 1638 that Pierre Pérignon was born, because the municipal archives of Sainte-Ménehould record his baptism as having taken place on 5 January 1639. The father's position is given as *greffier en provoste*, a judge's clerk. The Pérignon family had been long established on the Champagne–Lorraine border and were people of quality. Many of the male members of the family took holy orders, but their traditional occupation seems to have been the law: there is frequent mention of Pérignons as lawyers, notaries and tax-collectors in the local records of the *ancien régime*.

It is known that Dom Pérignon had a brother and a sister, as their christenings are recorded, but there is a complete blank regarding his childhood and education. On 3 July 1658, when he was only nineteen, he entered the Abbey of Saint-Vannes at Verdun. After that, there is another blank until he became cellarer at Hautvillers. The date of his appointment is given in some records as 1668, in others as 1670. It is safe to assume that his superiors must have thought highly of him to have appointed him at the age of twenty-eight or thirty, for the job carried many more responsibilities than its title suggests. In addition to the administration of the abbey's vineyards and the making and selling of the wine, he was responsible for the cutting and sale of wood; the purchase and distribution of all the abbey's requirements in the way of provisions, clothing and implements; the maintenance and repair of the buildings; the dispensing of charity and the handling of the abbey's finances. Apart from the abbot, he was the most important monk in the monastery. If he fulfilled his duties efficiently, the abbey would thrive; if he failed in them, he could lead the brotherhood towards ruin.

Dom Pérignon remained the cellarer of Hautvillers until his death, aged seventy-seven, in 1715. He was said to be learned, intelligent, amiable, charitable, and as scrupulous in the performance of his religious duties as in the discharge of his temporal ones. A small but, I think, revealing indication of his popularity is the fact that his name was inscribed on the biggest of a set of eight bells which was installed at Hautvillers church in 1706. It has always been a practice in the Catholic Church to inscribe on new bells the date of their baptism, the name of the officiating bishop and the names of two sponsors. Dom Pérignon would not have been chosen as a sponsor for the biggest bell if he had not been greatly respected.

So much for the man and the monk. It is now time to try and size him up as a wine-maker. Perhaps the best way to begin is to take a look at the comparative prices being paid for the wines of Champagne during his tenure of office. In those days, as they do today, the best wines commanded the highest prices, so Hautvillers' position on the seventeenth-century wine list, so to speak, should give a fair indication of the quality of the abbey's wine. What do we find? In a letter dated 10 November 1700 from Bertin de Rocheret, an Epernay wine-maker, to a Lieut.-General of the King's Army called d'Artagnan, it is stated that whereas a mediocre wine of Champagne cost 200 livres the *queue* and a good one 400 and 500 livres, the wines of Hautvillers fetched 800 to 900 livres a *queue*. And it is known that in at least one year Hautvillers wines fetched an even higher price: the old press-house there, now destroyed, bore the following inscription: "In 1694, the wine of Hautvillers was sold by the abbot for 1,000 livres the *queue*."

But I can imagine a sceptic saying: "This certainly proves that Hautvillers turned out good wine, but how do we know that Hautvillers did not always turn out good wine and that Dom Pérignon was not merely carrying on a tradition?" Well, that doubt is easily settled. For instance, there is the letter which the Marquis de Puisieulx, a Champenois by birth and the French Ambassador to Naples at the time, wrote to Bertin de Rocheret on 23 September 1690:

"I should also like two excellent *pièces* of river wine. I think it would be best to get them from Hautvillers rather than anywhere else . . . Please approach the Abbot of Hautvillers and the Abbey's cellarer, Dom Pierre Pérignon, on my behalf and give them my best wishes."

And the letter which d'Artagnan wrote to Bertin de Rocheret on 9 November 1715:

"The Marquis de Puisieulx, who arrived yesterday, told me that Father Pierre Pérignon is dead. He certainly attracted much attention to himself during his life. I wish you would keep me in mind for the next lot of wine from that Abbey; for, frankly, they are the best."

And the sentence, in a pamphlet on the culture of the vine in Champagne by Brother Pierre, Dom Pérignon's immediate successor as cellarer of Hautvillers, in which he wrote:

"The Reverend Father Pérignon achieved the glory of giving the wines of Hautvillers the high reputation they enjoy from Pole to Pole."

But, if a sceptic still has doubts, here are two curious facts that must clear them up. During Dom Pérignon's lifetime people often referred to the wines of the abbey, not as Hautvillers wines, but as "*vins de Pérignon*". For example, in a letter dated 28 November 1712, Bertin de Rocheret informs d'Artagnan that he has sent him bottles of the *bon vin de Pierry* sealed with two stars and bottles of Father Pérignon's wine sealed with a cross. Secondly, there is evidence that, by the time Dom Pérignon died, his name had become so closely associated with the excellence of Hautvillers wines that people got mixed up and imagined Pérignon was the name of a vineyard. There are many instances of this, but I will give just one: in 1716, when editing the works of his friend Boileau, Boisette mentions Pérignon as a *coteau*, a hillside. If that is not glory for a wine-maker, I do not know what is.

But was Dom Pérignon just a very skilful manipulator of wine or was he genuinely creative, an originator, in the realms of wine? Was the influence of his life's work ephemeral or can he be regarded as the founding father of the present-day champagne trade? I believe myself that he had an innate instinct for growing grapes and making wine that probably amounted to genius; that he penetrated into the tiniest details of his art with the intuition and the determination of a really great man; that he laid down the basic principles which are still in use today, because nothing fundamentally new has been invented since his time and scientific research has only tended to confirm his deductions; and that he prepared the way for the present high fortunes of the champagne trade by conferring on the wines of Champagne, without in any way altering their delicate properties, new qualities which turned a fundamental weakness into a towering strength. Moreover, having previously laid on a non-stop supply of champagne to help me, I intend to undertake the formidable task of trying to prove that my suppositions are correct.

It cannot be too strongly emphasized that at the heart of a really good bottle of wine lies the skill with which the grapes were grown. It is perfectly possible to make bad wine from good grapes, but only an exceptionally gifted wine-maker can make good wine from poor grapes. In no wine region in the world, except that of the Rhine–Moselle valleys, does this fundamental truth apply more forcibly than in Champagne, because the northern climate presents the skill, ingenuity, determination and patience of the vine-grower with a supreme challenge. We know that for nearly 2,000 years the vine-growers of Champagne have been responding to the challenge with marvellous success, but it would be interesting to discover whether the art of viticulture has been perfected gradually in Champagne, or whether there was ever a time when a superior mind made a searching examination of ancient methods, breathed new life into the art and coerced the ultra-conservative vine-grower into new and more efficient ways. In a moment I shall explain why I believe that such a superior mind, in the person of Dom Pérignon, did come to the help of the Champagne vine-grower; but first it is necessary to take stock of the progress which viticulture had already made before he arrived at Hautvillers. Unfortunately, this is exceedingly hard to do because of the paucity of reliable information. How much attention should be paid, for instance, to the indications that the wines of Champagne were rough and strong in the Middle Ages—such as St. Louis' shocked disapproval of Thibaut IV's habit of drinking Champagne wines neat, and the order which Henry V is supposed to have issued to the English army at Agincourt always to drink them diluted with water? The most likely explanation of their strength is that some sort of spirit, or wine from the sunny south, was added to them, because, except in outstanding years, the climate of Champagne prevents grapes grown there from manufacturing enough sugar for a really strong wine to be produced. Were they rough because the grapes were undistinguished, because they were poorly made, or because they were imperfectly fermented? There is no possible way of telling.

What is certain, however, is that at least a century before Dom Pérignon's birth the wines of Champagne improved greatly in quality; otherwise men like Henry VIII and Pope Leo X would not have gone to such an immense amount of trouble to obtain them. This quality can only have been achieved by the care with which the grapes were pressed, the skill with which the grape-juice was handled, and above all the flair and industry of the vine-growers. We can be pretty sure, therefore, that by the time Dom Pérignon appeared on the scene in the middle of the seventeenth century the art of viticulture in Champagne had attained a standard that equalled, if it did not excel, that of any other wine district in France.

What prompts me to believe that during Dom Pérignon's lifetime it reached an even higher standard is the little pamphlet from which I have already quoted, the *Traité de la Culture des Vignes de Champagne* by Brother Pierre, Dom Pérignon's immediate successor at Hautvillers. By a singular stroke of good fortune this pamphlet, which is written in beautiful script on vellum paper, having apparently been lost during the Revolution, turned up among the papers of the Marquis de Créqui. It was immediately acquired by the Chandon de Briailles family, and they later presented it to the Epernay library, where it now rests. In 1931 the late Comte Chandon-Moët deciphered the text and had it printed, a labour for which anyone interested in champagne must be profoundly grateful, because it is a document of the greatest possible interest. It covers every one of the basic principles of the culture of a Champagne vine, from the time it is planted to the time it has outlived its usefulness and must be pulled up; indeed, so complete is the exposition that it enables a detailed comparison to be made of the viticultural methods used in Champagne in the early eighteenth century and those in use today. And what does such a comparison reveal? It shows that, apart from one major change of method which the phylloxera invasion of the late nineteenth century entailed (a subject which will be dealt with later), nothing fundamentally new has been introduced into viticulture in Champagne since Dom Pierre wrote the pamphlet. This becomes of double interest when it is considered in conjunction with the sub-title: "Principles presented by Brother Pierre, pupil and successor of the Reverend Father Pérignon, monk of Hautvillers Abbey, to whom is due the reputation of the wines of that Abbey", and with a sentence from the nineteenth chapter of the pamphlet: "The Reverend Father Pérignon, scrupulously concerned with details that to others appeared insignificant . . ." The substance of this tribute is reiterated in the twenty-sixth chapter, when Brother Pierre stresses that Dom Pérignon invariably took the trouble to perform a certain task which other vine-growers considered "impossible, even ridiculous". This seems to make incontrovertible the claim that Dom Pérignon's influence on the art of viticulture in Champagne must have been very considerable indeed.

In the century and a half before his arrival at Hautvillers, the following minor improvements are known to have been made to the wine-making installations at the abbey: in 1508 a small cellar was built; in 1650 the press-house was enlarged; in 1661 a large vaulted *cellier* was built.*

In 1673, a few years after Dom Pérignon came to Hautvillers, a major improvement was undertaken. With money provided by "benefactors of the abbey and the economies of the monks", a really large cellar was hewn out of the chalk subsoil underneath the abbey grounds, and named the Biscornettes cellar. Was this the forerunner of the gigantic cellars that the Champenois hewed out of the chalk in the eighteenth and nineteenth centuries? Was Dom Pérignon the first to realize that, to mature properly, champagne requires several years in a low and constant temperature, and the first to appreciate that in the soft chalk beneath the Champagne district huge tunnels could be excavated at a comparatively small expenditure of money and effort? As the first major cellars which Hautvillers possessed were constructed so soon after Dom Pérignon took over as cellarer, there seems to be at least a possibility that he, before anybody else, realized that first-class champagne cannot be made without first-class cellarage.

Several wine historians have stated that white grape vineyards hardly existed in the Champagne district prior to the eighteenth century. Yet Brother Pierre devoted a whole chapter of his pamphlet on viticulture to "The way to make white wine with the white grapes of the district, known as Fromantins, Mauribards and Genests", and claimed that: "When white wine from white grapes is made well and the grapes are

* There is no exact English equivalent of the word *cellier*. *Celliers* often resemble cellars in appearance, but they are always situated at ground level. They are used principally for the storage of casks and equipment; low quality champagnes undergo their second fermentation in them.

really ripe, it is a wine that has much merit, not only because it is agreeable but also because of its medicinal qualities." (For stomach pains, chest troubles and stones in the kidneys, he recommended a good glassful each morning upon rising.) He admitted, however, that these white grape wines of Champagne had a definite tendency to "turn" and fall into a decline, and in view of this failing we may be sure of two things: first, that in ancient times the white wines of Champagne, like so many delicious but delicate white wines made in France today, were for the most part consumed locally and seldom exported; secondly, that throughout the history of the Champagne district at least three-quarters of the wine made there has been the produce of red grapes. Yet it can be stated with equal certainty that until Dom Pérignon arrived at Hautvillers these red grapes had never been made to produce a real red wine. Doctor Plot wrote in his History of Staffordshire (1679): "Champagne has a faint reddish colour." And Brother Pierre stated: "It was only about fifty years ago that certain distinguished persons made a study of how to make red wine . . . in past centuries only so-called red wines were made in this district, by which I mean that they were either grey in colour or the colour of a partridge's eye; it was mostly hazard that decided the nuance in the variations of colour." Other sources tell us what these nuances might be: the colour of straw, of a lion's mane (*fauvelet*), of a cherry (*clairet*), of honey, vermilion, even black, but never, never a true red.

It sounds fantastic that the Champenois could not make red wine out of their red grapes. But it was in fact perfectly logical—in a climate as northern as Champagne's. In a normal year there just is not enough sun to cause a vine to bear grapes whose skins are so richly red that, when pressed, they permeate the juice with sufficient redness for that juice to become a red wine. The situation is much the same as that which occurs with human skin: a man who spends all summer in Italy, in Spain, in Bordeaux, even in Burgundy, is likely by the autumn to have acquired a heavy, healthy tan; whereas if he spends the summer in Champagne, although he will certainly enjoy many sunny days and a few scorchers, the chances are very much against the cumulative effect of the sun having been sufficient to give him the complexion of an Australian life-guard. Then how *did* Dom Pérignon succeed in making a truly red wine (for we need not doubt that the "distinguished persons" referred to in Dom Pierre's pamphlet were Dom Pérignon and his aides)? Dom Pierre devotes no less than three chapters to the process, and the basic principles are the same today as they were then: the grapes must have enjoyed exceptional warmth during the summer; they must be the produce of old vines, which produce grapes whose skins are more fragile than those borne by young vines, and impart more colouring matter to the juice; grapes that have not matured thoroughly must be picked off the bunches; fermentation must take place with the skins in contact with the grape-juice (see Chapter 35).

If one takes stock of the situation in Champagne at this particular moment in its history, one is left with the impression that its future as an important wine-producing region did not look very hopeful. It was capable of producing an excellent white wine with white grapes, but only in small quantities, because, as Dom Pierre pointed out, high quality could only be achieved when the grapes were exceptionally ripe—a condition fulfilled, on average, three or four times a decade. It was capable, thanks to Dom Pérignon, of producing an excellent truly red wine, but, again, only in exceptionally favourable years. By far the greater part of its production was bound to be in the form of a wine that was neither white nor red, but of a nuance (to use Dom Pierre's words) between the two: what was called then—and is still called today—*vin gris*. In the centuries to come, with competition between winefields ever stiffening, it seems most unlikely that champenois *vin gris* could ever have provided its makers with a decent livelihood. Besides, if a product is to enjoy huge sales, uniformity, year in, year out, is essential: a wine that varied between vermilion and the colour of a lion's mane, depending on the climatic conditions and the vineyard from which the grapes came, could never have fulfilled that condition. Happily, the genius of Dom Pérignon was to save the situation.

In a letter dated 25 October 1821 Dom Grossard, the Hautvillers monk who saved the relics of St. Helena, informed the deputy mayor of Ay: "It was Dom Pérignon who discovered the secret of making . . . still white wine. . . . Before him, people only knew how to make a grey wine or one that was the colour of straw." The statement, it seems to me, makes it virtually certain that it was Dom Pérignon who worked out the method of pressing—which is used today in the Champagne district—to produce white wine from red grapes. This was a tremendous step forward. It meant that, no matter what the weather had been like in the course of the summer and no matter which vineyards the grapes came from, the Champenois could offer their customers a wine that was consistently the same colour—and a very beautiful colour at that: golden is a better word than white to describe the resulting tint. But, before a new future could open up, yet another difficulty had to be overcome. This was the extraordinary individuality of Champagne wines. By making a white wine out of red grapes, Dom Pérignon had achieved uniformity of colour; but the personality imparted to each vineyard (even, sometimes, to different sections of a vineyard) by the soil, the aspect and the behaviour of the weather in that particular spot still manifested itself in the wines as strongly as ever.

It was no doubt in an attempt to tone down the individual personalities of his wines, and to give them a more uniform character, year in, year out, that Dom Pérignon stumbled upon the second of his great innovations: the practice of blending. I say "stumbled" because, although there was presumably nothing new in the actual act of blending two or more wines together, what must have been totally unexpected was the way in which the wines of Champagne reacted to skilful blending. In Champagne, *mirabile dictu*, blending (always with the proviso that it is done skilfully) actually enhances the qualities of each wine and produces a resulting harmony which not only is distinctive in itself but surpasses in excellence many of its component parts.

There is no proof that it was Dom Pérignon who was responsible for this innovation: on the other hand, the fact that there is no reference to the wines of Champagne having been blended hitherto, coupled with the fact that both Dom Grossard and Brother Pierre considered it worth while to record for posterity—in considerable detail—how Dom Pérignon set about blending, suggests it. Dom Grossard wrote:

"When the vintage approached, Dom Pérignon would say to Brother Philippe: 'Go and fetch me grapes from Prières, Côtes-à-bras, Barillets, Quartiers or Clos Sainte-Hélène.' He could tell at once, without being told, which grapes came from which vineyard, and he would say, 'The wine of that vineyard must be married with the wine of that one,' and never did make a mistake."

This is what Dom Pierre wrote:

"Father Pérignon did not taste the grapes in the vineyards, although he went out almost every day to inspect them as they approached maturity, but he arranged for samples to be brought to him and tasted them the next morning before breakfast, after they had spent the night on his window-ledge. He composed his blends not only according to the flavour of the juice but also according to what the weather had been like that year—an early or late development, depending on the amount of cold or rain there had been—and according to whether the vines had grown a rich or a mediocre foliage. All these factors served him for rules as to the composition of his blends."

There are two probable explanations of Dom Pérignon's skill as a blender. The first is the rich variety of wines that were at his disposal to experiment with. It is known that in 1636 the Abbey of Hautvillers owned 100 *arpents* of vineyard (the *arpent* is the equivalent of the acre), which is considerably more than even some of the bigger champagne firms own today; and during his lifetime this acreage was almost certainly increased. Then there was the wine which the Abbey received by way of tithes. Altogether, Hautvillers probably had a greater variety of grapes to blend with than any other wine-making establishment in the district.

The second is his blindness. By the end of his days Dom Pérignon was totally blind. No doubt, as so often happens when a person has lost one sense, another of his senses developed unusual powers to redress the balance—in this case, his palate.

Uniformity of colour, uniformity of character—having achieved these, Dom Pérignon now had the wherewithal to turn them into a product as desirable as still *vin gris* was not: sparkling champagne. Was he, or was he not, the man whose genius was responsible for this metamorphosis? That is the $64,000 question. According to Dom Grossard, Dom Pérignon definitely did "invent" sparkling champagne. "As you know, Monsieur," he wrote to the deputy-mayor of Ay, "it was the celebrated Dom Pérignon . . . who found the secret of making white sparkling wine." By his own admission, however, Dom Grossard was old and doddery when he wrote the letter; and he was in any case born several decades after Dom Pérignon's death. The truth is far more likely to emerge if all the facts that throw light on the subject are marshalled and calmly reviewed.

First let us examine the evidence to support the theory that sparkling wine had existed long before Dom Pérignon's time. The most important items are these:

1. The sentence in the thirty-first verse of the twenty-third chapter of the Book of Proverbs: "Look not upon the wine when it is red, when it giveth his colour in the cup, when it moveth itself aright." A wine that "moveth itself", it is suggested, is surely an effervescent wine.

2. The seventeenth verse of the ninth chapter of the Gospel of St.

Matthew: "Neither do men put new wine into old bottles; else the bottles break, and the wine runneth out, and the bottles perish: but they put new wine into new bottles, and both are preserved." Only someone, it is claimed, who had had experience of sparkling wines would have written this, because only a sparkling wine exerts pressure on the surface of the bottle, distorts it and renders its subsequent use for a sparkling wine undesirable.

3. Lines 738–9 of Book I of Virgil's *Aeneid*: "*Ille impiger hausit spumantem pateram*" ("He drank the brisk cup without faltering").

4. The Romans, it is said, built their cellars with sloping floors, in order to save the bubbling wine which poured forth from the amphorae when the pressure inside, whipped up by secondary fermentation, became too great and caused them to burst.

5. It is claimed that a century or more before Dom Pérignon the Italian wines Refesco and Moscato were sold "spumante", or "sparkling".

6. Baccius, physician to Pope Sixtus V, writing in 1596, mentions wines of France which "bubble out of the glass".

In examining this evidence, it must be remembered that natural effervescence in wine is by no means restricted to the Champagne district. It manifests itself more powerfully there than anywhere else in the world because of the northern climate, and perhaps because of certain properties imparted to the wine by the chalk; but, provided three conditions are fulfilled, the phenomenon can occur in wine made anywhere in the world. First, the cold of winter must follow so quickly upon the gathering and pressing of the grapes that the yeasts do not have time to finish converting the sugar in the grape-juice into alcohol and carbonic acid gas before the cold lulls them into temporary inactivity. Secondly, in the spring, when warmer weather returns and stirs the yeasts to action again, the wine must be placed in a vessel of sufficient strength to withstand the pressure that builds up inside it as soon as carbonic acid gas is released during the break-down of the unconverted sugar by the yeasts. Thirdly, a stopper must be available to seal the vessel hermetically without imparting an unpleasant taste to the wine.

It would be wrong to minimize the difficulties presented by the first condition. In by far the greater part of the wine-producing area of the world, the warmth of the autumn is such that all the sugar in the wine is converted by the yeasts long before winter comes along. On the other hand, most wine-producing countries do contain regions where, at least in certain years, the autumn is sufficiently cool and the winter sufficiently early for there still to be unconverted sugar in the wine in the spring. So we are justified, I think, in assuming that from this point of view there was no reason why the ancients should not have made a sparkling wine occasionally. There is always the possibility, too, that they had grasped the fact that, if all the natural sugar of the grape had been converted, the addition of a little sugar at the time the wine was placed in a closed vessel in the spring would cause the wine to effervesce.

The ancient world also appears to have been perfectly adequately equipped to fulfil the second condition. The ancient Egyptians, the Greeks and the Romans all used amphorae to conserve and transport their wine. Although it is most unlikely that the shape and strength of the amphora would ever have enabled it to withstand the pressure which a fully sparkling champagne imposes on the modern champagne bottle, it could certainly have withstood a smaller internal pressure, one sufficient, probably, to produce what the French call today a *vin perlé*, perhaps even a *vin pétillant*. The Romans, it should be recalled, were also excellent craftsmen in glass. Several Roman bottles I have seen—at the museums at Rheims, Worms and Tetuan, and at the Victoria and Albert Museum in London—look nearly as strong as eighteenth-century champagne bottles.

What about the question of a suitable stopper? No evidence has yet come to light revealing that the ancient Egyptians or the ancient Greeks used cork, but the Romans certainly did. Corks have been found in Roman amphorae dating from the fifth century B.C. to the fourth century A.D. And recent excavations undertaken at the submerged Roman port at Fos-sur-Mer near Marseilles have revealed how neatly the corkage was arranged from the second century B.C. onwards: after the cork had been inserted a small stopper, made from pozzolana (volcanic ash from Pozzoli) and stamped with the maker's mark, was inserted above it.

As the Romans loved wine and were dedicated wine-makers, there is no possible reason, therefore, for assuming that they did not make sparkling wine from time to time, particularly in view of Virgil's remark about the foaming cup. Perhaps their garrisons in Palestine made it with local grapes: in that case St. Matthew's remark about putting new wine in new bottles has just as much meaning in a literal sense as in a symbolical one. Perhaps the Romans made a sparkling wine in the Champagne district itself. It is perfectly possible that they did, but there can be no certainty. What is certain, however, is that, if the Romans did make sparkling wines, they bore about as much resemblance to champagne as we know it today as fish and chips served at Clacton does to *sole à la normande* prepared by Maxim's in the rue Royale. Most wines do not take kindly to a second fermentation, for carbonic acid gas more often lowers than heightens their quality, and there were few thoroughbred Pinot Noir or Chardonnay grapes in those days to impart a flavour like champagne's. Such vital matters as pressing, fining, blending, the removal of the sediment or ageing in a cool, even temperature had certainly not been reduced to the fine art they have reached today: otherwise Pliny or Virgil would have written about them. A sparkling wine in the ancient world, if it did exist, was probably not even as good or as lively as the *pétillant* wines of Neuchâtel today, which have to be poured from a considerable height for bubbles to appear in the glass. A fully sparkling wine like champagne is a modern French miracle, and there is no escaping that fact.

Moreover, from the moment when Rome ceased to exert her influence, that is to say, during the fifth century A.D., the amphora and the bottle went completely out of fashion and the cork disappeared from circulation with them. Instead, people took to casks to transport and store their wine. The cask was far handier than the amphora to convey on mules and chariots, and in general it saved a lot of bother. When a person bought wine, he bought it in cask and stored the cask in his home; when he wished to serve the wine, he had it brought to the table direct from the cask in a special receptacle made of wood, stoneware, metal, pottery or glass.

The cask, of course, is a vessel completely unsuited to the making of sparkling wine: the joins in the wood would "give" the moment the pressure of the carbonic acid gas started building up, and there would be an almighty explosion. So it may be stated with assurance that, so long as the cask held solitary sway as a wine-vessel, the conditions necessary for the making of sparkling wine did not exist. And this state of affairs lasted for approximately 1,300 years, up to, but not beyond, the period when Dom Pérignon was cellarer of Hautvillers Abbey.

Bottles did, of course, exist long before this. But they were made of very thin glass, and were used simply as receptacles to carry wine from the cask to the table. It is these that can be seen in paintings of the fifteenth and sixteenth centuries, and that one assumes to be wine-bottles. Read what M. James Barrelet, the great French expert on glass, has to say in his book, *La Verrerie en France*:

"Up to the end of the seventeenth century in France the word bottle was freely used to describe what we today call a flagon, a flask, a phial, a carafe or a decanter. This recipient had neither the form nor the economic role the bottle has today. Its shape was stumpy and, so fragile was the glass, it was nearly always covered in a wicker envelope. It was used neither as a receptacle for storing wine, nor for the transport of wine for any distance. It was used only to bring wine to table from the cask and sometimes as a carafe."

The wine-bottle, or, shall we say, a bottle strong enough to be of service to wine, is an English invention. It owed its life to a new technique in glass-blowing which produced a dark green or dark brown glass thicker and more resistant to strain than any made hitherto. The precise date when this type of glass was first used for bottles in England is not known, but it is thought to have been between 1660 and 1670. Nor is it known precisely when the first consignment of the new bottles—or the secret of how to make them—reached France. But certainly this revolutionary form of wine-vessel became available for the first time during Dom Pérignon's term of office. This fact has tremendous significance in the history of champagne. It explains why sparkling champagne was not made earlier. It means that, the closer we can come to establishing the date when bottles made of *verre anglais* (or, as it is often somewhat misleadingly called, *verre noir*) appeared in Champagne, the closer we can pinpoint the début of sparkling champagne. It could mean that Dom Grossard's claim that Dom Pérignon was the first person to make a sparkling champagne is almost certainly true. And it could also mean that Dom Pérignon initiated the practice of ageing, conserving and transporting wine in bottles. I hasten to add that this last possibility, that Dom Pérignon may have been, so to speak, the "Father of the Wine-Bottle", is mainly (but not entirely) my own deduction. No Champenois historian has specifically claimed this honour for him, and in *La Verrerie en France* M. Barrelet goes no further than to state that "it was to this type of bottle that sparkling wine owes its existence".

Before discussing the matter further, it is necessary to say a little about the important subject of corks, because the cork joined forces with the bottle to act as midwife at the birth of sparkling champagne.

Once again I shall begin by quoting from Dom Grossard's letter to the Mayor of Ay. Before Dom Pérignon's time, he wrote, "instead of corks, they used hemp soaked in oil". His description is not quite accurate: the historians of cork state that the stoppers consisted of a piece of wood with hemp wound round it which, before being inserted, was dipped in olive oil. All cork historians are agreed that, from the Roman decline in the fifth century until the late seventeenth century, the cork was not used in France for sealing wine vessels. What earthly use would it have been during the hegemony of the cask? The bung-hole was plugged, as it is today, with a wooden stopper. If a glass bottle *was* used to store wine for a month or two, the bottle had to be kept standing upright on account of its fragility, and thus a wooden stopper surrounded by hemp was entirely adequate. In actual fact, most people probably did not even bother with wooden stoppers: they just poured a drop of oil on the wine, in order to prevent it from coming into contact with the air. This simple device is still used by peasant families in Italy and Spain to keep air away from wine stored in demijohns; it is said, incidentally, to have given rise to the custom of pouring a few drops of wine into the host's glass before the guests are served—to ensure that no oil remains in the wine that the guests drink.

It has always been accepted in Champagne that it was Dom Pérignon who initiated the practice of sealing wine-bottles with cork. One day, the story goes, two Spanish monks, passing through Champagne on their way to Sweden, were put up for the night at the Abbey of Hautvillers. Their hosts noticed that their water-gourds were stopped with something peculiar, and asked what the substance was. "Why, the stopper is made of the bark of the cork-oak tree," replied the Spaniards, and without further prompting launched into a panegyric concerning cork and cork-oak trees. Dom Pérignon's aides rushed off to tell their blind master what they had learnt, whereupon Dom Pérignon ordered a consignment of Spanish cork-bark to be sent to him. And so successful did it prove as a material for stopping bottles that from that day to this, the story ends, cork has been the substance most commonly used by wine-makers all over the world for sealing their products.

If one accepts that Dom Pérignon was trying to find a way of capturing the natural sparkle of Champagne wine, it follows that in all probability he was the first modern wine-maker to use cork, because in no circumstances can hemp-surrounded wooden stoppers be made to act as hermetic seals. For that reason alone the story of the Spanish monks rings true. And there are other reasons for not dismissing it out of hand as legend. One is that it was the invariable rule in Benedictine monasteries that travellers should be put up for the night. Another is that most of the cork used in Champagne today does come from Spain, because Spain produces the best cork in the

world and modern sparkling champagne has need of the best available.*
All the same, the story is based purely on oral tradition, and I have
always felt that further enquiries were essential before it could be
accepted. For this reason I decided to visit Spain and see what I could
find out there. I left with two objects in mind: first, to try to discover
when the earliest shipments of cork were made to Champagne or, for
that matter, to any other wine district in France; secondly, to discover
whether the Spaniards believed in the story of the monks and their
water-gourds, or whether they had another explanation for the early
marriage between cork and sparkling champagne.

The first part of my mission became a complete wild-goose chase.
I spent long hours looking through the archives of libraries in Barcelona
without finding anything whatsoever of the slightest relevance. In
fact, the archives of Champagne prove more revealing in this respect,
for at least they record that Spanish corks had reached Epernay by
1717 (two years after Dom Pérignon's death). In a letter dated that
year Bertin de Rocheret, the Epernay wine-maker, thanked d'Artagnan
for sending him some. And a year or two later Father Jean, director of
the Clos Saint-Pierre at Pierry, a wine-making establishment which
belonged to the monastery of Saint-Pierre at Châlons-sur-Marne,
wrote to Hautvillers itself to order Spanish corks.

However, my visits to Gerona and Figueras in northern Catalonia,
which are to cork what Rheims and Epernay are to champagne, were
more rewarding. Talking to cork-manufacturers, many of whom came
from families that had been connected with the trade for over a century,
I at once discovered that Dom Pérignon is every bit as much a "hero"
to the Catalans as he is to the Champenois. When I asked whether, in
their opinion, Dom Pérignon had been the first wine-maker to use
corks, they replied, "Of course". They showed me several trade books

* There is yet another reason for supposing that there may have been a coming-
and-going between Spain and Hautvillers in the seventeenth century. Shortly
before the Second World War Mme Mélanie de Vilmorin, a member of France's
leading horticultural family and the mother of Louise de Vilmorin, the well-
known authoress, arrived to lunch with Comte and Comtesse Chandon-Moët
at their house in the grounds of the Abbey. Upon alighting from her car she
spotted the giant Spanish fir (which I mentioned in the preceding chapter), and
exclaimed, "What's that doing there? It's not mentioned in Napoleon's Index of
the great trees of France—and it looks much older than my Spanish fir, which I
thought was the oldest in France!" The Spanish fir only flourishes on chalky
soil, is a native of Spain, and can live for 400 years: if the Hautvillers Spanish fir
really is the oldest one in France, the assumption is permissible that there was a
very early link between Hautvillers and Spain.

and pamphlets in which his name is mentioned in this connection, and referred me to the following paragraph in the *Enciclopedia Universal Illustrada*, the Spanish equivalent of the *Encyclopædia Britannica*, a publication no more given to the recording of fancy than its Anglo-Saxon counterpart:

"The use of cork as an hermetic seal for wine-bottles is attributed to Dom Pérignon, the monk in charge of the cellars at Hautvillers Abbey between 1670 and 1715."

Everywhere I went I found it generally accepted that it was the demand for champagne corks which had been responsible for the foundation of the cork industry in Catalonia.

Next, I enquired how they thought cork had come to the notice of Dom Pérignon. They all knew the story of the Spanish monks and their water-gourds, but they offered two other possible explanations. Local tradition in Estremadura, they said, maintained that Dom Pérignon had spent several years at the Benedictine monastery at Alcántara, on the Portuguese border, and had worked in the vast forests of cork-oak trees in the neighbourhood. If this were true, it would explain the complete blank in our knowledge of Dom Pérignon's movements between the time he took his vows at Verdun and his arrival at Hautvillers; it would also add zest to his story, because it is from these Estremaduran forests that much of the cork for champagne bottles comes today, via Catalonia, where it is processed.* The other explanation they offered, and the one they set most store by, was that the wine-makers of Hautvillers and the cork-makers of Agullana and Darnius—two villages near Massenet in northern Catalonia in which the cork industry is known to have started—first made contact when they came to sell their respective wares at the annual fair held at Beaucaire near Nîmes. Agullana and Darnius are situated close to forests of cork-oak trees whose bark has long been recognized as the "hardest" and finest in the world. In the late seventeenth century,

---

* On a subsequent trip to Spain I visited Alcántara, in the hope of finding confirmation of Dom Pérignon's sojourn in the monastery. No one I approached had even heard of him. In nearby Carcares Don Miguel Muñoz de San Pedro, Conde de Canilleros y de San Miguel, the historian of Estremadura, kindly allowed me to consult one of the treasures in his fabulous library, the full list of the Knights and Monks of the Order of "San Benito de Alcántara", but Dom Pérignon's name was not in it. Don Miguel assured me, however, that this in no way detracts from the possibility that Dom Pérignon did spend some time there; he considers it unlikely that the name of a visiting foreign monk, and a commoner, would have been included in the list.

it seems, the inhabitants, desperately poor and convinced that a few pennies might be made from cork-bark, started cutting it up into rough oblongs for sale; and as they could find no market for their new product in Spain they set off for Beaucaire to try their luck there.

Señor Perxés, a cork-manufacturer in Palafrugell, told me that little had changed in these villages since Dom Pérignon's time, and he kindly arranged for me to visit Agullana with one of his agents. It was a memorable experience. About ten miles south of the French border we swung off the main Barcelona–Perpignan road and entered the gloomy cork-forest. To the untrained eye individual cork-oak trees look like large olive trees; en masse, they are macabre and harbour witches, I am sure. For what our spines told us was an age we crashed along the most appalling tracks, climbing steadily into the southern foothills of the Pyrenees. And then the little village appeared, forlorn and ghostlike on top of a ridge. It was four p.m. when we arrived, but there was none of the bustle and animation normally apparent in a Spanish village at such an hour. Hardly a soul or a cat was about. My escort stopped the car, and we made our way up broken-down steps to a small two-storied house. Here we were greeted by an elderly cork-maker, wearing a blue shirt, a beret and *two* pairs of trousers, one in the normal position, the other wrapped around his hips to perform the function of an apron. He led us into his ground-floor workroom, swishing aside a fly-curtain made of roundlets of cork, selected a strip of cork-bark from a basket made of cork, and proceeded to give us a demonstration of his art. He took up a position in front of a barrel which had an attachment on top to hold the bark firmly in place; then he picked up a murderous-looking instrument, akin to a butcher's hatchet, with which he lashed into the cork-bark with swift, sharp blows. When he cut close to the outside of the bark, where the cork is soft, it was as though he was slicing cake; when he attacked the inside of the bark, which is old and hard, he had to exert pressure with both hands. But in less than a minute he had cut out and trimmed what is called a *trefinos*, a rough oblong of cork which, later, is trimmed again to fit a champagne bottle.

Two things are certain. First, whether it was through the intermediary of itinerant monks, a sojour in Estremadura or a meeting at Beaucaire, it was oblong *trefinos* such as these, cut in a similar manner in some poverty-stricken Spanish village like Agullana, that first gave Dom Pérignon the idea of using cork for his wines and thus made sparkling champagne possible. Secondly, *trefinos* may have saved the villagers of Agullana from starvation in the seventeenth century, but

they have brought to their descendants, not riches, but a legacy of
scars, thick and terrible, across the back of the hand and along the
finger (if the finger was not severed altogether), inflicted, in a moment
of inattention, by that merciless hatchet.

Before branching off to investigate the début of corks, I left hanging
in mid-air the somewhat daring suggestion that Dom Pérignon was
not only the Father of Sparkling Champagne but also responsible for
the practice of conserving wine in bottles. I am not entirely un-
supported in this surmise. In his erudite book on cork, *Le Liège et les
Industries de Liège*, published in 1957, M. Charles Pouillaude states:

"By using the glass bottle and the cork to make sparkling champagne,
Dom Pérignon instituted the use of glass bottles and cork for the
conservation of wine."

Now, if Dom Pérignon did initiate the practice of storing wine in
bottles, it should be possible to establish that *verre anglais* bottles were
being made in France during his stewardship at Hautvillers, and that
they were being manufactured fairly close to Hautvillers, as it is
unlikely that he could have made extensive use of them if, to obtain
supplies, he had to send a long distance away.

There can be no doubt that the *verre anglais* bottle was being manufactured extensively in France while Dom Pérignon was at Hautvillers.
In 1723, only eight years after his death, Savary des Brulons was writing:
"Certain glass-works only make heavy glass bottles which have been
in great demand ever since it was discovered that the best wines conserve better in bottle than on their lees." It is even conceivable that the
verre anglais bottle was being made in France prior to Dom Pérignon's
arrival at Hautvillers. What is believed to be the earliest surviving
example of this type of bottle in France can be seen today in a show-
case at the Musée du Vin at Beaune, with a label (authenticated by M.
Barrelet, the historian of glass, and by M. Henri Rivière, *conservateur
en chef* of the Musée des Arts et Traditions Populaires in Paris) attributing to it the date "1660–1670". But, as there is no guarantee that this
particular bottle was not made in England for export to France, we
are on safer ground if we refrain from trying to give such an early
date to an extensive adoption of the *verre anglais* bottle by French
glass-makers, and content ourselves with the opinion expressed by
most historians that French glass-makers began manufacturing it
extensively "around 1700". That opinion is based largely on a fact

which they have proved to their satisfaction: the manufacture of wicker-enveloped bottles practically ceased in France around that date.

It seems equally certain that Dom Pérignon did not have to go far afield to procure his *verre anglais* bottles. There is even a faint possibility that, in the beginning, he made them himself at Hautvillers: a late nineteenth-century Champenois stated in a pamphlet that the ruins of a glass-works had recently been found at the abbey. No one knows anything about these ruins today, however, and, although it is immensely intriguing, I think the suggestion that Dom Pérignon included the role of glass-maker among his many accomplishments is a little far-fetched. Probably the first champagne bottles came either from the glass-works at Quiquengorgne in Aisne (near the present-day mammoth Saint-Gobain glass-works) or from those of the Argonne forest, in the extreme west of Marne, both a mere fifty-odd miles from Hautvillers.

Of the two regions, I count that of the Argonne as being by far the most likely source of supply, mainly because we know for certain that, by the middle of the eighteenth century, it was these glass-works that were supplying virtually all the bottles for champagne. In 1747 no less than eleven furnaces were in operation there, all turning out *verre anglais* bottles for champagne. We are in possession of this useful piece of information for a curious reason—the vociferous complaints of infuriated champagne-makers about the quality of the bottles the Argonne glass-makers were producing. In a paper read at the Academy of Sciences in Paris on 17 January 1748, it was specified that many Argonne bottles arrived broken, others broke while being washed with water, and none compared in strength with similar bottles made in England. The reason for this sorry state of affairs was given as follows:

"Formerly, only lye-ash . . . and sand from the Argonne forest was used. . . . As only very little azure was added, the glass was yellow. . . . Recently, it has been necessary to add a greater quantity of azure to make them green or at least less yellow, which has resulted in weaker glass."

It is specifically stated that champagne-makers were forced to rely on this source of supply for their requirements. No mention is made of Quiquengorgne.

Now, if it was in the Argonne that the first champagne bottles were made, we are hard on the scent of the clue which throws Dom Pérignon's entire life-work into focus. The Argonne glass-works were founded, while Dom Pérignon was still a young man, by Colbert, as part of a nationwide attempt to create employment in districts where the standard of living of the inhabitants was particularly low. They came to be known as the *verreries de Sainte-Ménehould* because they were situated in two villages, Beaulieu and Clermont, which lie less than five miles as the crow flies from the town of Sainte-Ménehould —the birthplace of Dom Pérignon, the town where his family had lived for generations. As the Pérignons were local gentry, and as glass-making was a gentleman's profession (glass-makers in those days were known as *gentilhommes-verriers*), what could have been more natural than that the Pérignons and their neighbours the glass-makers were on friendly terms? Although it is pure conjecture, I feel in my bones that it is more than a coincidence that Dom Pérignon was a Ménehouldien, and that Sainte-Ménehould was the chief centre of the first champagne bottle industry.

This, I think, is what happened. When Dom Pérignon arrived at Hautvillers, he first of all made a careful study of the wines of Champagne and the methods used to make them. He then set about reforming. He rationalized viticulture and improved the existing facilities for maturing the winefield's produce by forging great galleries out of the chalk. He then applied his mind to a major problem: how to produce a wine that had an attractive and consistent colour despite the vagaries of the climate. The result was a white wine made from red grapes. Then he determined to produce a white wine year in, year out, that had a uniform character. The secret of success, he found, was blending. The next thing that happened, I think, was that he became disenchanted with the cask, for one of two reasons: either because he found that the character and the colour of his blended wine were being altered by the casks; or because he wanted not only to sustain but to develop the natural sparkle of Champagne wines, and he knew that the cask was totally unsuitable for the purpose. Casting about in his mind for a solution to this problem, he suddenly remembered having been told by his family that their friends, the *gentilhommes-verriers* of Sainte-Ménehould, were raving about a remarkable new type of glass invented in England. He went to them, in much the same way as a modern businessman approaches a factory which is turning out a new type of alloy or plastic, and said: "Look, I'm fed up with the cask. Can you make me a glass bottle, strong enough to withstand considerable internal pressure and of a shape convenient for bulk shipment?" They set to work, and a few weeks later they sent Dom Pérignon a yellow bottle, about ten inches high and as corpulent as an onion. Dom

Pérignon tried it out and very soon became convinced that his hunch had been correct, that glass was an ideal substance in which to store wine. So he ordered a further supply, thus laying the foundations of a whole new industry, the wine-bottle industry. Finally, ever restive, ever inventive, he applied his genius to the only remaining problem: how to hold the sparkle in his new toy. Here, either a memory from his early manhood in Estremadura, an encounter with an itinerant Spanish monk with a water-gourd at his hip, or a suggestion from a Hautvillers monk who had been selling the abbey's wine at Beaucaire came to his rescue. Now all he had to do was to tie down the cork-bark in the neck of his bottle with string and sealing wax, so that the captured sparkle did not catapult the stopper out—and he had earned the gratitude of mankind for ever.

That, for what it is worth, is my interpretation of Dom Pérignon's life-work, in the light of the slender evidence available. Perhaps, one day, the Hautvillers archives that were lost during the Revolution will turn up in some dusty attic and help to disentangle truth from legend. If that day should come, I am confident that it will be found that Dom Pérignon deserves an even higher place in the esteem of wine-lovers than he enjoys already.

But I must now explain something that could be said to detract from Dom Pérignon's achievement: it seems pretty certain that the answer to the question, "Was it Dom Pérignon who produced the first bottle of sparkling champagne?" is in the negative. He almost certainly *was* the first man to produce sparkling champagne *in France*, but, astounding as it appears at first sight, it is almost equally certain that the English were quietly making sparkling champagne for themselves nearly a decade before he took up residence at Hautvillers. For, whereas no mention of sparkling champagne is made in French literature or in the archives of the Champagne district until around 1700, there is one probable and one definite reference to it in English Restoration comedies. The probable reference—the actual allusion is to champagne being "brisk"—is to be found in Butler's *Hudibras*, which was first performed in 1666:

> "The sun shall no more dispense
> His own, but your bright influence;
> I'll carve your name on barks of trees
> With True-Love-Knots, and flourishes,
> That shall infuse eternal spring
> And everlasting flourishing,

Drink every letter I'it in stum,[*]
And make it brisk Champaign become."

The definite reference is in Sir George Etherege's *The Man and the Mode*, which had its opening night in 1676:

To the Mall and the Park
Where we love till 'tis dark,
Then sparkling Champaign
Puts an end to their reign;
It quickly recovers
Poor languishing lovers,
Makes us frolic and gay, and drowns all sorrow;
But alas we relapse again on the morrow.

    As I said, at first sight the situation seems astounding; but, if reflected upon, it ceases to be so. What are the two articles indispensable to the making of a sparkling champagne? Strong bottles, and corks. Now the English, as I have already related, invented the heavy glass bottle around 1660, so from that date onwards they were in possession of the first requisite for the making of sparkling champagne. And, since they were a maritime nation in frequent contact with Spain, they had been in possession of cork long before it came to the notice of the land-locked Champenois. There is a reference to corks in Shakespeare's *As You Like It*, when Rosalind says to Celia:

"I would thou wouldst stammer, that thou mightest pour this concealed man out of thy mouth, as wine comes out of a narrow-mouth'd bottle—either too much at once, or none at all. I prythee, take the cork out of thy mouth, that I may drink thy tidings."

And in the Woburn Abbey archives there is an account book for 1665 in which is recorded the purchase of two dozen corks for the fifth Earl of Bedford.

    From about 1660 onwards, therefore, there was nothing to prevent the English from having still champagne sent over in cask during its first winter of life and bottling it in England in the spring, so that the remainder of the fermentation took place inside the bottle, thus producing a slight sparkle. That is almost certainly what they did. Furthermore, the English appear by this time to have been fully aware

[*] Still wine.

that the addition of sugar at the time of bottling would produce a stronger sparkle. In *Some Observations concerning the producing of wines*, read before the Royal Society on 26 November 1662, Dr Merret stated that "our wine-coopers of recent times use vast quantities of Sugar Molasses to all sorts of wines to make them drink brisk and sparkling and to give them Spirits". From which we may deduce three things: that the "brisk Champaign" alluded to in Butler's *Hudibras* was sparkling, in which case this really is the very first reference to sparkling champagne; that it was not only the wine of Champagne that the English were in the habit at this time of rendering sparkling; and that the sparkle produced may have been not just slight but of considerable force. Club's final words in this conversation from Farquar's play *Love and the Bottle*, produced in the last decade of the seventeenth century, would seem to lend credence to this last suggestion:

"B. You're clear out, Sir, clear out. Champaigne is a fine liquor, which all great beaux drink to make 'em witty.

"M. Witty! Oh, by the Universe, I must be witty. I'll drink nothing else; I never was witty in all my life. I love jokes dearly. Here, Club, bring us a bottle of what d'ye call it; the witty liquor.

(Club, his servant, having brought in a bottle of Champagne)

"Club. Egad, Master, I think 'tis a very good jest.

"M. What?

"Club. What! Why, drinking. You'll find, Master, that this same Will-o'-th'-Wisp is a wit at the bottom. (Fills the glasses) Here, here, Master, how it puns and quibbles in the glass!"

Of course, this seventeenth-century English champagne must have been primitive in the extreme. It was almost certainly made entirely from *vin gris* and was not therefore golden in colour; if it was aged at all, which is extremely doubtful, it certainly never enjoyed a long sojourn in a champagne cellar, so it was probably very rough, lacking all finesse. However, the fact remains—and what a curious footnote it makes to the story of Dom Pérignon!—that the basic principle of the manufacture of sparkling champagne, which Dom Pérignon worked out for himself at Hautvillers, had, without his knowledge, already been discovered and applied by the English.

CHAPTER 11

THE DÉBUT OF SPARKLING CHAMPAGNE

Brother Pierre, in his pamphlet—which was published in 1718—stated that "the French took to sparkling champagne more than twenty years ago", adding: "They developed a positive mania for it." This suggests that Dom Pérignon's sparkling champagne first became available around 1690, which is roughly the date when our own studies of Dom Pérignon show the event to have most probably occurred. But, if it really did make such an immediate hit in France, the writers of the period certainly kept very quiet about it: so far as I am aware, it was not mentioned in French literature before 1712. In that year Charles Coffin, a Rheims poet who taught at Beauvais College, published a delightful poem entitled *Champagne Avenged* which contains, I believe, the first detailed description of a glass of sparkling champagne. The poet describes it thus:

> "*D'abord à petits bonds une mousse argentine*
> *Etincelle, pétille, et bout de toutes parts;*
> *Un éclat plus tranquille offre ensuite aux regards*
> *D'un liquide miroir la glace crystalline.*"

But his approval was not echoed by his fellow-countrymen. The French, in fact, appear to have been exceedingly reluctant to show favour to the revolutionary new wine, and even the Champenois were slow to realize what a gold-mine Dom Pérignon had presented them with. When supplying the Maréchal de Montesquieu with an excellent Ay wine in 1711, Bertin de Rocheret strongly advised against its being rendered sparkling, and suggested a much cheaper wine for that purpose. Two years later, in a letter to d'Artagnan, he refers to sparkling champagne as "*cette abominable boisson . . .* which destroys the flavour of the individual growths", and he maintains that "effervescence is only a merit in a *petit vin* and belongs rightly to beer, chocolate and whipped cream". Sparkling champagne was frequently referred to at this time as "devil's wine" or "cork-jumper", and the phenomenon of effervescence was ascribed to such fantastic causes as the addition of alum and pigeons' excrement at the moment of bottling.

It is hardly surprising that the new drink had a somewhat tepid reception in France; the sunset of Louis XIV's reign was hardly a propitious moment to launch a novelty that was bright, sparkling and gay. The splendour of Versailles was on the wane; the popping of champagne corks would have scandalized the ailing king and his pious mistress, Mme de Maintenon. But the new wine did not have to wait long before the mood of France changed. On Louis XIV's death in 1715 his nephew Philippe, Duc d'Orléans, became Regent of France, Louis XV being then only five years old; and the country at once embarked upon one of the most frivolous, extravagant, rip-roaring decades in its history.

The orgies of the Palais Royal, where the Regent lived surrounded by gay roués and fast young women, were an open secret in Paris, and the pursuit of pleasure was the main aim of all classes of society. This was the era of gallant abbés, of powdered dandies, of Boucher's pink-and-gold goddesses rustling in silks and taffetas, of fortunes won and lost at cards overnight, of gourmets and heavy drinkers, above all of the *petit souper*. And what finer springboard to fame could sparkling champagne have wished for than the candle-lit *petits soupers* of the Regency? At one of the earliest, given by the Duc de Vendôme at Anet, his country home near Paris, twelve luscious girls, scantily dressed as Bacchantes, each carrying a basket of flowers on her arm, suddenly made an appearance, and at a signal from the Marquis de Sillery, who owned vineyards in Champagne, plunged their hands into the baskets and presented each guest with—according to Saint-Simon —"a pear-shaped bottle of champagne, ten inches high, including the four or five inches of the neck, stamped with the Sillery arms and secured with sealing-wax". By the end of that supper, the success of sparkling champagne in France was assured. "Hardly did it appear," wrote the Abbé de Chaulieu, "than from my mouth it passed into my heart." As for the Regent, his passion for it, if we are to believe his mother, Princess Charlotte-Elizabeth of Bavaria, was in keeping with the times: "When my son gets tipsy," she wrote in a letter dated 13 August 1716, "it is not on strong drinks or spirituous liquors, but on the pure wine of Champagne."

But, although sparkling champagne was the talk of the town throughout the Regency, most people at that time had no alternative but to offer their guests a very inferior type, bottled in Paris from casks sent up from the Champagne district, identical in every respect with what one might describe as the home-made brew the English had been concocting since the Restoration. Only Royalty and people of exceptional influence could procure the real stuff, bottled and aged in the winefield and dispatched thence to Paris. This was because the law, to hinder tax evasion, forbade the transport of wine in bottle. In 1724 the citizens of Rheims petitioned Louis XV, now King Regnant, to alter the law. They pointed out that of late the trade in the wines of Champagne had greatly increased, as a result of their being bottled locally "during the first new moon of March" so that a sparkle was produced; that lovers of Champagne wines preferred those that sparkled to the still variety; and that, as sparkling champagne could not be made in casks, it was essential for the prosperity of the winefield that new legislation should be produced immediately. On 25 May 1728 the King in Council announced himself "*pénétré de ces raisons*", and thenceforward the transport of champagne in bottles was permitted, but, when destined for consumption within the kingdom, in cases containing a hundred bottles and, for export, in cases of fifty or a hundred bottles. The proviso regarding the size of the cases—imposed, once again, to hinder tax evasion—was a grave disappointment to the Champenois, and as late as 1780 they were unsuccessfully petitioning Necker, Louis XVI's Finance Minister, to have it removed. Nevertheless, they had gained their main point, and the commercial exploitation of sparkling champagne could begin in earnest.

Hitherto *négociants en vin de champagne*, as families or firms specializing in the making and sale of the wine of Champagne district are known today, had not existed. Neither the small vineyard proprietors, nor the monks, nor the nobles, nor the bourgeois families who owned extensive vineyard properties, had made this their principal activity: much of their output they disposed of among friends and relations in Champagne and the rest of France; any surplus was sold in bulk to *courtiers de vin* in Rheims and Paris.

The office of *courtier de vin* is a very ancient one, dating back to the thirteenth century or earlier. Originally it was a Crown appointment, held exclusively by nobles and landed gentry who purchased the necessary licence from the King and then became entitled to the considerable revenue in the form of commission that accrued from the office. Gradually, however, the monarchy had conferred the right of making new appointments on municipal authorities—in the case of Rheims, on the sheriff—and thereafter *courtiers de vin* were recruited mainly from the merchant class.

This system, whereby the vineyard owner made the wine and the *courtier de vin* sold for him any of his output which he could not sell to friends and relatives, seems to have worked fairly well. But in the 1720s it became clear that the system was outdated. Now that the making of Champagne wine was so much more complicated than it had been before, the *courtiers de vin* felt they could no longer rely on peasants to make it for them, and decided to branch out as wine-makers; while the more intelligent vineyard owners saw no reason why the *courtiers de vin* should be the main beneficiaries of the winefield's expansion, and determined in future to sell all their wine themselves, either direct to the public or through the intermediary of wine merchants. Neither party, it seems, was entitled by law to engage in the other's activity, but, with that fine disregard for authority which Frenchmen display when it suits them, both did so; the result was that in 1776, when the commerce of wine was freed from all restrictions, a situation that had long existed was merely legalized. *Courtiers de vin* who owned vineyards and engaged in wine-making were indistinguishable from vineyard owners who made and sold their own wine; both had become *négociants en vins de champagne*, the forerunners, and in some cases the ancestors, of the great champagne families of today.

One of the most successful of them was Philippe-Valentin Bertin de Rocheret, the son of the man who described sparkling champagne as "*cette abominable boisson*". As much aware of the new wine's destiny as his father was not, he "pushed" it for all he was worth. In 1729 Nicholas Ruinart, an Epernay textile merchant, founded what was to become, it is believed, the first firm exclusively devoted to champagne-making. His lead was followed in 1730 by a M. Chanoine of Epernay, and in 1734 by M. Jacques Fourneaux of Rheims. The first and the last are still flourishing concerns (control of the Fourneaux firm was acquired by the Taittinger family in 1932, since when it has traded under their name), although neither of them is quite so well known as the firm founded in Epernay by M. Claude Moët at about the same time (now Moët & Chandon).

Since the turn of the century the district's cellarage had evidently been substantial, for Brother Pierre proudly stated in his pamphlet that "nowhere in the world are such good cellars to be found as in Champagne". But they were quite inadequate for the needs and ambitions of the budding champagne magnates, who now set about the Herculean task—which their nineteenth-century successors completed—of hewing out of the chalk subsoil the vast underground network of cellars that exists today. Also, to cope with the growing popularity of sparkling champagne, they began to plant on the Côte des Blancs more and more Chardonnay and Fromentin white grape-bearing vines; by the middle of the eighteenth century, it is believed, white grapes had become predominant there.

Another step taken at this time which helped to set the new industry on its feet was the passing of legislation to control the size of the champagne bottle. On 8 March 1735 the King stipulated that it must in future weigh twenty-five ounces (quarter-bottles, half-bottles, and magnums in proportion), contain exactly one Paris pint (about 1·6 British pints), and be tied down "with three-threaded string, well twisted and knotted in the form of a cross over the cork". From then on, the bottles delivered by the Argonne bottle-makers became slightly more uniform in size; but one gathers from the champagne-makers' complaints that until the bottles started to be made by machine at the end of the nineteenth century, instead of by hand, uniformity was the exception rather than the rule (a situation which was certainly not confined to champagne, since not so long ago a member of the Irish Dail proposed "that every quart bottle should hold a quart"). The bottles were already becoming slightly less corpulent; they were beginning to resemble the present-day Benedictine bottle rather than the present-day armagnac bottle, as they did in Dom Pérignon's time, and this remained their form until the end of the eighteenth century.

The decade between 1725 and 1735 must have been a stimulating one in the Champagne district. In the course of it, the Champenois appear to have woken up at last to the almost unlimited benefits which sparkling champagne might bring them, and to have set about energetically adjusting themselves to the new situation. By 1735 they had so arranged matters that they were in a position to deliver what one might call Champenois sparkling champagne—the genuine article, bottled and aged in the cellars of the Champagne district—anywhere in France; and they had supplies available to meet a much greater demand. From now onwards, every Frenchman who had a sou or two to spare was a potential customer; but he still needed wooing. Just the fillip which was needed was given by Voltaire, who paid a visit to Epernay in May of that year—perhaps at the pressing invitation of his friend Philippe-Valentin Bertin de Rocheret. For Voltaire was the one man in France to whom the whole nation could be counted on to listen, and within a year he published in Le Mondain a couplet which gave sparkling champagne a splendid boost:

"De ce vin frais l'écume pétillante
De nos Français est l'image brillante."

The French were quick to take the hint, and by 1737 sparkling champagne had invaded the cabarets. We know this because a description has come down to us of a party held on a November evening of that year at a cabaret called Au Caveau, situated at the carrefour de

Bussy in the heart of the Faubourg St. Germain, at which Helvétius, Rameau and Boucher were among the poets, singers and artists present. When the dinner was over, four bottles of sparkling champagne were produced. A footman was about to open the first one when a guest rose to his feet and called for silence. "I propose," he said, "that we drink to that man of genius, that benefactor of humanity, who, by a procedure evidently inspired by the gods, has turned champagne into this sparkling nectar. . . . Gentlemen, let us drink to Dom Pérignon!" The toast was drunk, and it was agreed that to the next dinner each guest should bring a tribute to sparkling champagne. Boucher promised an allegorical sketch, "*La Réception de Dom Pérignon au Caveau*", and Rameau a suitable melody. (Whether they fulfilled their promises I have not, alas, been able to ascertain.) By 1739 the popping of champagne corks was already considered indispensable to the success of a ball: when the city of Paris held one on 30 August of that year, which Louis XV attended masked and incognito, no less than 1,800 bottles of *mousseux* were consumed.

In the 1740s sparkling champagne brought off what was perhaps the greatest triumph of its career to date: it won the favour of the gorgeous marquises whose taste and intelligence were turning Louis XV's Court into one of the most civilized societies the world has ever known. The foaming liquid was so deliciously feminine: "It gives brilliance to the eyes without flushing the face," said Mme de Parabère, and, "Champagne," Mme de Pompadour used to remark, "is the only wine that leaves a woman beautiful after drinking it".* The lovely women of the Court used the gentle effervescence of champagne as counterpoint to their amatory adventures:

* Any lady who pays a visit to the Champagne district has Mme de Pompadour's remark quoted to her by a Champenois within five minutes of her arrival; and the recital is enlivened by a graphic description of the dreadful things that happen to her if she is unwise enough to drink red wines, particularly heavy burgundy: she goes puce in the face, she gets all hot and bothered. This annoys the Burgundians. At a Tastevin dinner which I attended at the château de Clos Vougeot, a Burgundian speaker went so far as to attribute the remark to pique. "Mme de Pompadour was really a lover of burgundy," he said, "and so great was her love that she decided to buy a property at Romanée; but at the last minute the Prince de Conti outbid her, and she was so annoyed that she went over to the Champenois camp." It may be true that Mme de Pompadour once considered buying an estate in Burgundy, but from the day she was born to the day she died she had ties with Champagne which she treasured. Her father owned a house a few miles south-west of Château-Thierry; after her father's death Louis XV presented her brother with an estate in the same neighbourhood, near the village of Marigny; and it was as Marquis de Marigny that he was elevated to

"Ta mousse se posant aux lèvres des marquises
A leur poudre argentée a mêlé ton argent;
Tu fus le conseiller d'aventures exquises . . ."

Besides, it was a well-known fact that the King was prepared to accept invitations to *fêtes champêtres* if a generous supply of sparkling champagne was provided. When the Pompadour died in 1764, it was to champagne suppers that he turned for consolation. It was the custom, on these occasions, to choose a theme and toast it in impromptu verse. Once, the Duc de Nivernais proposed "Adam":

"Il buvait de l'eau tristement
Auprès de sa compagne,
Nous autres, nous chantons gaiement
En sablant le Champagne."

To which the bereaved King replied:

Il n'eut qu'une femme avec lui:
Encor, c'était la sienne.
Ici je vois celle d'autrui,
Et n'y vois pas la mienne."

Such was the impact which sparkling champagne was making in France as the years of revolution approached. The vogue for it, ever increasing, resulted in the foundation of several new firms, four of which were to make the names of Lanson, Roederer, Clicquot and Heidsieck famous throughout the world. For already sparkling champagne was enjoying sensational successes abroad. Ex-King Stanislas of Poland, busy turning his new capital of Nancy into an architectural poem, was now a faithful client. So was Frederick the Great of Prussia. The effervescence intrigued him so much that he submitted the following question to the Berlin Academy: "Why does champagne sparkle?" He never received an answer, because the astute Academicians asked for forty bottles to experiment on, and the King was too stingy to provide them.

The warmest support for the new wine, however, was coming from across the Channel. Here, after the initial vogue for home-made

the peerage. In order to facilitate the Pompadour's journeys to her brother's house, Louis XV rerouted N. 3 through the heart of Château-Thierry (previously it had run just south of the town). His action brought—and continues to bring— much prosperity to the town, and to this day a pageant is held there each summer in the Pompadour's honour.

sparkling champagne at a time when such a drink was unknown in France, the situation had been gloomy. No sooner had the English taken a fancy to sparkling champagne than Charles II and William III successively introduced all manner of vexatious regulations, such as restrictions on imports and crushing duties, which made it at times impossible, and invariably expensive, for the English to satisfy their thirst for champagne. A further blow followed with the Methuen Treaty, which the Government of Queen Anne signed with Portugal in 1703. This laid down that the wines of Portugal might henceforward enter England on payment of a duty of only £7 per tun; at the same time the duty on French wines was raised to £55 the tun. Thus port suddenly became dirt cheap and French wines inordinately expensive. As Marlborough's armies were at that moment engaged in a titanic struggle to break the power of Louis XIV on the Continent, the Treaty had the full support of the man-in-the-street, who was a beer-drinker anyway. Swift undoubtedly reflected popular sentiment when he wrote:

> "Be sometimes to your country true,
> Have once the public good in view,
> Bravely despise Champagne at Court,
> And choose to dine at home with Port."

But once Louis XIV had been brought to heel and the need to cripple French trade in wine to such a drastic extent no longer existed, there were a great many Englishmen who bitterly resented this interference with their drinking habits. In 1716 Matt Prior, a great champagne-lover (he made one of his heroes "from this world retreat, as full of Champaign as an egg's full of meat"), lamented:

> "By nerves about our palates placed,
> She likewise judges of the taste,
> Else (dismal thought!) our warlike men
> Might drink thick Port for fine Champagne."

And Shenstone, in *Verses written at a Tavern at Henley* (he scratched them on a window-pane), gave vent to similar feelings:

> "Tis here with boundless power I reign
> And every health which I begin
> Converts dull Port to bright Champagne;
> Such freedom crowns it at an inn."

The authorities, however, remained unmoved, and on 28 May 1728, precisely three days after Louis XV signed the Order in Council allowing champagne to be exported in bottle, a second blow fell: George II gave the Royal Assent to a Bill forbidding the import into England of wine in bottle. The official justification, of course, was the ease with which wine in bottle could be smuggled into the country without payment of duty; but in view of the lightning speed with which the Government reacted to the French Government's shot-in-the-arm to the budding sparkling champagne industry, one cannot help feeling that their motive was more perverse. And in 1763 came the third shock: the duty on French wines was raised to £73, which meant that from then on only the very rich could afford champagne or, indeed, any other French wine.

Not until 1786 did the position improve. In that year a commercial treaty, sponsored by Pitt, was signed with France, the first article of which stipulated that the wines of France imported directly from that country into Great Britain should never have levied upon them a higher duty than that imposed on the wines of Portugal. It is ironic, on the face of it, that Pitt, the stalwart champion of port (it is said that, while studying French in Rheims, he complained of having nothing to drink), should have been the driving force behind a treaty which ended the hegemony of Portuguese wines in England; but we know he did sometimes drink champagne. Once, after partaking of it unwisely at a dinner given at Addiscombe by his friend Jenkinson, he galloped through a turnpike gateway without paying the toll, whereupon the keeper fired a blunderbuss at him, an incident which gave rise to the following rhyme:

> "How as Pitt wandered darkling o'er the plain,
> His reason drowned in Jenkinson's Champaign,
> A rustic's hand, but righteous fate withstood,
> Has shed a Premier's for a robber's blood."

The effect that all this hostile legislation had on the wine trade between France and England is revealed at a glance by the Customs and Excise figures for the period. In 1688, 20,000 tuns of French wine were imported into England; in 1701, 2,051 tuns; in 1786, the last year in which the Methuen Treaty regulations applied, 476 tuns. After Pitt's Treaty, imports from France jumped up again to an average level of 2,000 tuns a year.

Yet, throughout the eighteenth century, the supplies of sparkling champagne that reached England were in all probability considerably larger than such statistics would suggest. The law against the importation of wine in bottle was waived when the wine was destined for the Royal Household, foreign Embassies and certain Ministers of State; and rich and well-connected people could always get round the law— and the duty—either by arranging with a friend to buy a few cases in France and engage smugglers to bring them in via Dunkirk or a Dutch port, or by persuading an Ambassador to do the importing for them. There were surprisingly many people in the eighteenth century who, having what Mrs. Centilever, in her play *A Bolde Stroke for a Wife*, described as "a good champagne stomach", succeeded, by fair means or foul, in satisfying it.

George II was partial to it; he shared a *cuvée* of the 1753 vintage with ex-King Stanislas of Poland. So was Lord Chesterfield, the Steward of George II's Household and the most perfect host of the day. The wine inspired him to many a gallant toast. On one occasion he roared out,

> "Give me Champaign, and fill it to the brim,
> I'll toast in bumpers ev'ry lovely limb."

By 1762, we know, sparkling champagne was on sale at the Pleasure Gardens; at Vauxhall, that year, it cost 8s. a bottle, while the price of a bottle of port was listed at a mere 2s. City businessmen, it seems, found this too expensive: in Colman and Garrick's play *Clandestine Marriage*, produced in 1766, an ambition of a merchant is described as that of being able to offer "such a glass of Champagne as they never drank in their lives; no, not at a duke's table". At Bath and Tunbridge Wells, the willingness of rich invalids to spend money on champagne and their habit of drinking it instead of the waters was exasperating the doctors. Foote, in *The Fair Maid of Bath*, produced in 1771, makes the hero remark: "My dear Sir Kit, how often has Doctor Carawitchet told you that your rich food and Champaigne would produce nothing but poor health and real pain?"

One could go on indefinitely describing the fondness of eighteenth-century English for champagne, but I have written enough, I hope, for the reader to realize the promising state of the market when Pitt's treaty with France at last made it possible for the wine to be sold in England at a reasonable price. Thereafter, sales should have soared, and the budding champagne magnates were determined to make them do so. But the French Revolution played havoc with their plans.

CHAPTER 12

REVOLUTION AND WAR

THE SOCIAL UPHEAVALS caused by the French Revolution in no way interfered with the status which champagne had won in its native land. All except the most bloodthirsty revolutionaries saw nothing unfitting in giving their patronage to what had become one of the symbols of the love of luxury and the frivolity of the *ancien régime*. Danton took a bath in it; and a few minutes before he and Camille Desmoulins were taken to the guillotine in the Place de la Concorde they were drinking Ay *pétillant* and singing "*Vive l'Ay et la liberté*". As for Mirabeau's brother, he was credited with the consumption of two bottles of champagne per meal: in a caricature entitled "*Mirabeau Tonneau*" and dated "*An Ier de la liberté*", his torso is shown as a cask and his legs as inverted champagne bottles; in his left hand he holds a foam-crowned *flûte*, in his right hand a bottle to refill it.

For the average Champenois, however, the immediate effects of the Revolution were disastrous. It so happened that the 1789 crop of grapes was a twelfth of its normal size, and this, coupled with the general breakdown in food distribution, led to famine and misery. True, the vineyard-owner was now free to increase the extent of his holdings: the law which forbade him to do so under the *ancien régime*—based on the dubious assumption that an increase in viticulture led to a decrease in food production—was one of the first to be repealed by the revolutionaries. But few vineyard owners had the capital to take advantage of the new decree, and even those who were entitled to a small slice of a vineyard recently appropriated from an aristocrat or a monastery derived little comfort from the acquisition when their families were starving.

Somehow or other, however, the majority of the champagne-makers carried on their business during the revolutionary period,* despite the food shortages, the wars, the political unrest and the obligation to sell their wine in bulk at ridiculous prices to representatives of the new order. In a letter to Messrs. Zeltur & Cartier of

---

* In l'an III de la liberté (1793), a M. Boizel of Epernay actually founded a champagne firm. It is still a thriving concern, though very small, and is run by a direct descendant of the founder. It supplied the late Prince Aly Khan with pink champagne.

Solothurn in Switzerland dated 12 December 1795, Jean-Remy Moët makes scathing reference to the last of these trials:

"No wonder there is such a vast quantity of Champagne wine in Switzerland. We have been besieged by speculators, and it is not surprising that, having bought champagne with *assignats** at extremely low prices (for nothing, virtually, in view of the rate of exchange), they find it greatly to their advantage to sell it again in exchange for gold at a rate of as much as twenty-five francs a bottle."

Some of the most dramatic moments of the flight of the Royal family to Varennes in June 1791 were played out in the Champagne district. The royal party set off from Paris in a *berline* along the road which anyone driving from the capital to the Champagne district takes today. At La Ferté-sous-Jouarre they were confronted by the same little problem that faces the modern traveller: whether to fork left and follow the Marne valley to Châlons-sur-Marne, or carry straight on along the more southerly route to Châlons via Montmirail. They chose the latter, for precisely the reason that anyone in a hurry makes the same choice today—the roller-coasterlike bumpiness of part of the valley road.

Twenty-one years before, Marie-Antoinette had passed through Châlons on her way from Austria to be married; now she was a fugitive, and the *berline* spent no longer in Châlons than the time it took to change the horses. When the graceful towers of the Basilica of Notre-Dame-de-l'Epine came into sight, the royal party heaved a sigh of relief. They had only three more miles to go to the posting station at Somme-Vesle, and there the Duc de Choiseul would be waiting with his Huzzars to escort them to Montmédy. But when they arrived there was not a Huzzar to be seen. By an extraordinary stroke of bad luck some peasants in the neighbourhood, who had refused to pay their taxes and had been threatened with punishment, had assumed that the Duke had arrived for the purpose of administering it, and had sounded the tocsin; whereupon Choiseul, wishing at all costs to avoid a disturbance, had withdrawn his Huzzars and was now making his way back to Varennes. Of this circumstance the royal family were entirely in ignorance.

Return was out of the question; so on they went to Sainte-Ménehould, birthplace of Dom Pérignon, and there, as every schoolchild knows, they were recognized by the *maître de poste*, Drouet, who

* The paper money of the Revolution, in circulation from 1789–97.

followed them to Varennes and raised the alarm. Today, if one visits the sleepy little Argonne town, one can see the inn where the arrest took place, and also, on a patch of bare ground nearby, a stone wall with a plaque set in it, recording this historic occasion:

"Ici s'élevait la maison de l'épicier Sauce . . . C'est dans cette maison au Ier étage que Louis XVI, la Reine, et la Famille Royale après leur arrestation passèrent la nuit du 21 au 22 Juin 1791 . . . après avoir formé d'inutiles projets d'évasions et attendu vainement l'arrivée des troupes du Général de Bouillé."

During the Directoire things began to look up for the champagne-makers, and they were joined by a new recruit, M. Jacquesson; his firm, which was to become an important one and which still exists, was established at first at Châlons-sur-Marne, but later moved to Rheims. One or two houses even managed to get champagne through to England, where, according to *The Original*, it was doled out like drops of blood.

It was lucky for champagne that export to England was becoming possible again, for soon afterwards legislation of vast importance to Rheims and Epernay was introduced. In 1800 George III gave his assent to an Act allowing French wines to be imported in bottle if shipped via the Channel Islands; and two years later another Act was passed permitting importation direct from France as long as each case contained at least six dozen bottles (this to hinder the evasion of customs duties). For the first time since champagne-making had established itself on a commercial footing, the requirements of the English market could be met without resort to special licences or smuggling. An inkling of how great these requirements were likely to become was given in a letter dated 18 March 1806 from Carlton House to M. Jean-Remy Moët, informing him that the Prince Regent had recently tasted his wines and desired 2,000 bottles of Sillery 1802 to be sent to him at once, some of it to Brighton. Most of this consignment was probably used to make the purchaser's favourite beverage, a highly alcoholic concoction known as Regent's Punch, of which this was the recipe: three bottles of champagne, two of Madeira, one of hock, one of Curaçao, one quart of brandy, one pint of rum and two bottles of seltzer-water, flavoured with four lb. of bloom raisins, Seville oranges, lemons and white candy-sugar, and diluted with green tea.

The charms of champagne were celebrated by many of the famous

men of the day, including Sheridan and Byron, and at Crockford's the
pop of champagne corks almost drowned the rattle of the dice:

> "While Champagne in close array,
> Pride of Rheims and Epernay,
> Not in bottles but in dozens,
> (Think of that, ye country cousins!)
> Stood, of every growth and price,
> Peeping forth in tubs of ice."

The English, when abroad, continued to indulge their passion for the
wine. In her *Sojourn amongst the German Courts* Mrs. St. George records
that in 1800 Nelson, together with Sir William and Lady Hamilton,
was a guest of the British Resident at Dresden. At dinner Lady
Hamilton drank more champagne than Mrs. St. George imagined a
woman was capable of consuming, and afterwards proceeded to entertain the company with her imitations of classical statuary. Nelson
thereupon became uproarious and continued to empty bumper after
bumper of champagne in honour of the fair Emma, swearing she was
better than Mrs. Siddons. The host kept trying "to prevent the further
effusion of champagne" but did not succeed until Sir William "lay
down on his back, with his arms and legs in the air, and in this position
bounded all round the room like a ball, with his stars and ribbons
flying around him".

Yet in his *Letter*, Prince Puckler Muskau mentioned that by 1814
"your bottle of champagne cost you a guinea"—very nearly the
equivalent of a fiver today. No wonder Beau Brummel, when asked
by a young man where he got the blacking for his boots, replied, "My
blacking positively ruins me", for it was made, he went on to explain,
with the finest champagne.

The advent to power of Napoleon (who is credited with the remark
"champagne banishes etiquette") ushered in a period of real prosperity
for the champagne-makers. Wherever French troops were to be found
—in Germany, Poland, Moravia—a Heidsieck, a Ruinart, a Jacquesson
or an agent of one of the other firms was never far behind. As soon as a
battle was won, up they would move their supplies for the victory
celebration, and quickly establish a sales organisation in the invaded
territory. Two of the present-day champagne firms were founded
during the Napoleonic period: Henriot of Rheims (1808) and Perrier-
Jouët of Epernay (1811).

But the Napoleonic era did not only bring gain. Once more the

Champagne district became a battleground, for it was here that the Emperor fought the final series of delaying actions which preceded his abdication at Fontainebleau and his subsequent exile in Elba.

The armies of Russia, Prussia and Austria invaded eastern France early in January 1814. According to Kopisch's poem *Blücher am Rhein*, the thought that he was soon to traverse the Champagne district was already causing the mouth of the Prussian commander to water:

> *Nun schlagt die Brücken übern Rhein!*
> *Ich denke, der Champagnerwein*
> *Wird, wo er wächst, am besten sein!*★

Blücher did not have to wait long to quench his thirst. By the night of 18 January Napoleon had pulled back his headquarters to Châlons-sur-Marne, and soon he had to retreat again.

To the inhabitants of the Champagne district, the prospect of being overrun by Prussian and Austrian troops was alarming enough, but the thought of Cossacks and Kalmucks filled them with holy terror. They reacted in exactly the same way as their ancestors had done in the face of Mongol invasions: they fled to the forests, or took refuge in the bowels of Mont Aimé, a huge mound, blessed with innumerable springs for drinking water, just to the south of the southermost point of the Côte des Blancs, near Bergères-les-Vertus. The great stone that barred the long passage leading into the mound was removed, and in trooped nearly a thousand Champenois from the surrounding villages, carrying with them bedding, food and their most precious possessions. Each family formed its own little circle; someone who was present described how picturesque the small groups looked, squatting round pale lamps in the huge, dark cavern. A sentinel was posted at the entrance to keep watch on the plain. To his horror, this sentinel suddenly espied a band of 9,000 Russian Grenadiers passing by the foot of the mound, bound for Paris. And a few hours later news arrived that Blücher had established his headquarters less than half a mile from Mont Aimé. If the Prussians discovered their hiding-place and blocked up the entrance, they would all die of asphyxia: nearly everyone left that night. In reality, however, Napoleon was proving far too redoubtable an adversary for the Allies to give a thought to the refugees in Mont Aimé. He fought like a wounded tiger, and according to many military historians these were the most brilliantly executed actions of his entire career.

★ "Up with the bridges over the Rhine: I think champagne is at its best where it is produced!"

Thus far he had kept the invaders south of the Marne, but four battles in four days had exhausted him, and he could not prevent a party of Cossacks from entering Rheims on 16 February. The humiliation of losing France's Coronation city soon restored his pugnacity, however. By 5 March Rheims was in French hands again, but a week later it was retaken. Napoleon rushed to the rescue, and finally the Russians were chased away. He remained in Rheims until 17 March, staying at the home of the Veuve Clicquot's brother, M. Ponsardin. From here he wrote to his brother, King Joseph:

"Whatever happens you must prevent the Empress and the King of Rome from falling into enemy hands. Do not desert my son, and remember that I would rather he was in the Seine than in the hands of the enemies of France."

Meanwhile, the Allies had been forced to withdraw from Epernay and thither, on the 17th, Napoleon proceeded, entering the town at the head of the 40,000 men of his Guard. That night, which he spent at the home of M. Jean-Remy Moët, the Mayor, news reached him that the English had entered Bordeaux. M. Moët had been away when the Emperor arrived, and did not return until after midnight. At daybreak, hearing that Napoleon had ordered consommé from the kitchens, M. Moët took it up himself; as he entered the room, Napoleon was consulting a map with an aide-de-camp.

" 'Well, all is not lost; France isn't in Russian hands yet, my dear M. Moët,' exclaimed the Emperor as they shook hands."

He then described his plan for cutting the Allied communications.

" 'If I should fail,' he said, 'within a month I shall either be dead or dethroned. So I want to reward you now for the admirable way you have built up your business and all you have done for our wines abroad.' "*

Removing his own Chevalier's cross of the Legion of Honour from his uniform, he pinned it on M. Moët's chest, adding: "My Chancellery will shortly regularize the brevet. Don't thank me, I give you what you deserve."

Two days later he was gone. Within hours of his departure Rheims

* *J.-R. Moët* by Victor Fiévet, page 91.

fell for the third time to the Russians and Prussians, and soon Epernay was in enemy hands too.

The months that followed Napoleon's abdication were painful ones. The occupying forces imposed enormous fines, in retaliation for similar levies that the Napoleonic Armies had raised from one end of Europe to another; there were crushing requisitions and, of course, looting.

Thanks to its Russian commandant, Prince Wolkonski, Rheims had an easier time than the rest of the winefield. Not a single bottle of champagne was forcibly removed from the Veuve Clicquot's cellars. "I was spared, thank Heaven," she wrote. "I suffered no loss whatsoever." When a Prussian official demanded a large sum of money and supplies in kind from the Rémois, and threatened to obtain them by force if necessary, Wolkonski told him: "I have orders from the Tsar to requisition nothing from the townspeople, and as to your insolent threat of sending troops to Rheims, I have plenty of Cossacks here to receive them." Small wonder that, when the handsome Russian left Rheims, the municipality presented him with a diamond-studded box, and that his portrait hangs in the museum.

And another glint of sunshine penetrated the dark clouds overhanging the district. There is a French saying "*Qui a bu, boira*" ("He who has drunk once will drink again"). Of the truth of this M. Moët, who most people thought had been virtually ruined by the looting, remained stubbornly convinced; according to local tradition he actually encouraged the occupying forces to take his wine, murmuring to friends as they did so, "I'm letting them have all they want—they'll pay later". Gradually it dawned on champagne-makers who lacked his sang-froid and vision that perhaps he was right. Whenever again would such an opportunity occur of converting the Russians, Prussians and Austrians into champagne drinkers? With a little persuading, in the form of free or cost price champagne for their messes, these foreign officers stationed in the district might be made to serve the winefield's interests, when they returned home, more effectively than a battalion of commercial travellers. When, therefore, early in July 1815, a fortnight after the battle of Waterloo, it was announced that the occupation period was to be extended to five years, certain Champenois greeted the news with satisfaction.

Fate had up her sleeve, however, an incident which was to provide the local Champenois with an even better opportunity of making the Russians aware of the charm of their wine, and bring immense publicity to the Champagne district.

It all came about because of the concern of the Allies to maintain the balance of power in Europe. At the opening of the Congress of Vienna in 1814, they had been in more or less unanimous agreement that France must at all costs be kept weak. But by the summer of 1815 grave doubts as to the wisdom of this policy—doubts that were being skilfully fanned by Talleyrand—had arisen in the minds of Tsar Alexander of Russia and the English Cabinet. What worried them were the extravagant demands of Prussia, backed by Austria, for French territory. The Tsar therefore informed his *chers frères*, the King of Prussia and the Emperor of Austria, that he disapproved of their plans for the division of France and wished them to moderate their ambitions; and, to show he meant business and had the power to enforce his will, he decided to stage a great review of Russian armed might, and to invite the Allied sovereigns to attend it.

The question immediately arose as to where the review should be held. The entire Russian forces in Europe, amounting to some 295,000 men, were to be on parade, and civilian employees and spectators were expected to account for another 150,000 persons. The site chosen, therefore, would have to be capable of accommodating nearly half a million people. It was eventually decided that the ideal spot for the purpose was none other than Mont Aimé. It was conveniently close to Paris; the Tsar and his guests would be able to watch the review from a balustrade to be specially erected on top of the mound; and the plain beneath would afford ample room for the soldiers of All the Russias to display themselves in dread array.

News of the decision was conveyed to the préfecture in Châlons by the Russian authorities early in August 1815. The Préfet and every other official of the *département* of Marne nearly died of heart-failure on the spot. The *département* was still licking the wounds it had received during the 1814 campaign; it was committed to supporting 20,000 occupation troops for the next five years: how could it possibly be expected to undertake the stage-management of a military pageant of unprecedented proportions, involving the feeding and housing of this vast concourse of people? The Préfet tried desperately to get the site of the parade changed, but the Tsar's mind was made up.

In the Municipal Archives of Châlons one can inspect the pieces of paper, now yellow with age, on which the orders and requisitions imposed on the Champenois during the next five weeks were recorded. The mind boggles at their variety and extent. One demand was for 100,000 horseshoes, another was for 295,000 poles, each six feet high and an inch in circumference, for the bivouacs; others, all on much the same scale, were for grease to oil wagon-wheels, coal, bread, brandy, cattle, sheep, hay, wheat, straw, carriages, wheelbarrows, rakes, buckets and brooms. Hundreds of obscure Champenois—foresters, vineyard workers, farmers (who were desperately trying to get their harvests in before the Russians arrived), lawyers, clerks—were conscripted into working parties.

But, of all the Champenois whose lives were upset by the Tsar's whim, one cannot help singling out for special sympathy—particularly as we are informed that he loved "peace and tranquillity"—Picard de Flavigny, the Mayor of Vertus, the little town in the vineyards near Mont Aimé, who suddenly found himself invested with supreme powers and with responsibilities worthy of a Prime Minister, and at the receiving end of a non-stop barrage of Russian orders, threats and reproaches. On him fell the burden of converting the local doctor's house into an abode fit for the Tsar; of distributing seven Russian Army Corps, amounting to 295,000 men, between Vertus and seven surrounding villages, and of finding provisions for them; and of building the platform on Mont Aimé, which involved levelling the top of the mound, banking it up into the shape of an amphitheatre and surrounding it with a wooden fence as a security measure against accidents.

Somehow or other it was achieved. At four o'clock on the morning of 10 September the first part of what must have been one of the most complicated sets of orders in the history of military ceremonial was executed, and three hours later the 295,000 soldiers of the Tsar were in their allotted positions on the plain below Mont Aimé. At eight a.m. the Sovereigns rode in procession to the summit of the mound and occupied the amphitheatre—on the Tsar's right the Emperor of Austria and the King of Prussia, on his left the Prince of Wrede, the Duke of Wellington and the Prince Royal of Bavaria. At a signal given by the Tsar the mighty phalanxes carried out manœuvres and then formed themselves into a huge square to be inspected by the Sovereigns on horseback. The next day a second parade was held in the plain behind Mont Aimé to celebrate the Tsar's birthday. The Emperor of Austria left that night, the King of Prussia the following morning—both intensely aware of the indirect warning they had been given. The Tsar stayed on until the 13th. Throughout his visit he regularly gave banquets for 300 covers.

It was not long before the review proved to have served its purpose: the demands of Prussia and Austria for French territory gradually dwindled, and France was given back the frontier of the Rhine.. And the Champenois, who had been singing:

> "*Buveurs de la Moscovie,*
>   *Quand partirez-vous enfin?*
>   *Avez-vous encore envie*
>   *D'avaler tout notre vin?*"

soon found that the sufferings they had endured on the review's account were paying dividends. When they returned to their homeland many of the Russian officers who had been present at Mont Aimé started sending in orders for champagne, which helped Russia to become, as she remained until the 1917 Revolution, champagne's greatest export market, with the sole exception of Great Britain.

CHAPTER 13

A CENTURY OF ACHIEVEMENT

THE CENTURY THAT elapsed between the Battle of Waterloo and the outbreak of the First World War was a momentous one for the Champagne district. It witnessed the virtual withdrawal from the market of the still wines which had produced the winefield's bread-and-butter for close on 1,800 years, and an expansion in the sales of sparkling wines such as Dom Pérignon can hardly have imagined to be within the realms of possibility.

It is impossible to tell at exactly what point the sales of sparkling champagne overtook those of the still wines of the district. For when, according to the statistics, the amount of wine which the winefield produced over a given period greatly exceeded the amount of wine needed to fill the number of bottles of sparkling champagne which were sold during that period, it did not follow that the remainder was sold as still champagne: as the demand for sparkling champagne increased, it became more and more the custom to use only the better still wines available to make sparkling champagne, and to sell the rest in bulk to firms, in France and abroad, which specialized in the sale of anonymous *vins ordinaires*. All that can safely be said is that round about the middle of the nineteenth century the sales of sparkling champagne became greater than those of still champagnes, and that thenceforward less and less still wine was sold, until, by the time the First World War broke out, it had entered the oblivion where it has since remained (apart, as we shall see, from one brief come-back in the 1930s).

Happily, it is possible to be more precise about the actual, as opposed to the relative, sales of sparkling champagne during the greater part of the hundred years in question, as the Champenois started keeping fairly reliable production records from 1844 onwards. One comes across many estimates of the situation previous to 1844, but the only figure upon which I place the smallest reliance is one quoted by M. René Crozet in his *Histoire de Champagne*: he says that in 1785 the sales amounted to 300,000 bottles. This, then, is the picture of sparkling champagne's staggering triumphs between 1785 and the First World War:

Year	Bottles sold
1785	300,000
1844	6½ million
1853	10 million
1868	15 million
1871	20 million
1890	25½ million
1902	31½ million
1905	35½ million
1909	39 million*

What happened? What prompted the Champenois suddenly to give up making the still wines that generation after generation of wine-lovers had drunk with so much pleasure? And how did they manage to be making and selling about 130 times the amount of sparkling champagne in the Edwardian era that they were producing in the reign of George III?

The answer to the first question can be given in a single sentence: the profit to be made on a bottle of sparkling champagne is so much greater than the profit to be made on a bottle of still champagne that it became—and remains—to the advantage of the Champenois to devote the entire resources of the vineyards to the making of sparkling champagne.

The second question is far more complicated.

One of the main reasons why sparkling champagne made such gargantuan strides during the nineteenth century was, of course, that the period was one of relative peace and unprecedented prosperity. It would have been surprising if the sales of the wine had not leapt forward in tune with the wealth being created by the industrial revolution. But it would be wrong, I think, to lay too much stress on the favour of circumstances; it was the imaginative use which people in Rheims and Epernay made of the opportunities they were offered that was responsible for the extent of the triumph.

It was fortunate that, by the middle of the nineteenth century, the champagne-makers had got themselves organized on much the same basis as they are today, for it was in the second half of the century, when the wealth created by the industrial revolution came into circulation and a tremendous improvement took place in transport facilities, that the golden opportunities for sparkling champagne presented themselves. Irroy was founded in 1820, Joseph Perrier in 1825, Mumm in

* A figure not to be equalled or exceeded until 1937.

1827, Bollinger in 1829, Pommery & Greno and Deutz & Gelderman in 1836, Krug in 1843, Pol Roger in 1849 and Mercier in 1858. All this new blood broke down the virtual monopoly in champagne-making that the Ruinarts, the Moëts, the Jacquessons and the Veuve Clicquot had enjoyed since the suppression of the monasteries; it acted as a spur to competition, and it ensured that the trade embarked on perhaps the most important half-century of its existence in vigorous condition.

For the problems that had to be solved before really big sales of sparkling champagne could be achieved were complex in the extreme. The one which caused the greatest worry and proved the most difficult to solve was the appalling extent of the breakages that occurred among the bottles when the wine was undergoing its second fermentation in the cellars. Ever since the winefield had started to make sparkling wine, there had never been a year when fewer than 4 per cent of the bottles containing new wine had burst. Ten per cent breakages was considered normal, and breakages amounting to between 30 per cent and 40 per cent were by no means exceptional. In 1776 one champagne-maker preserved only 120 out of 6,000 bottles; the loss in 1833 in another cellar amounted to 35 per cent; and in his *Facts about Champagne*, written in 1871, Henry Vizetelly states that: "It is not long since that 120,000 out of 200,000 bottles were destroyed in a well-known firm."

No wonder the *cuvées* in the eighteenth century were small: when M. Moët bottled 50,000 bottles in 1780, it was considered an act bordering on lunacy. And no wonder the Champenois sometimes succumbed to despair: local tradition tells of one champagne-maker who, seeing his bottles exploding and the wine streaming through his cellars, so far lost control of himself as to start beating the remainder of the pile with his stick, shouting "*Eh, casse donc aussi, toi!*" In the months of July and August, when breakages were most to be feared, as the second fermentation was then in full swing, the cellar-workers invariably wore iron masks to protect their faces. So did visitors. "*Il n'est pas prudent,*" wrote Victor Hugo's son, Abel, about his visit to a champagne cellar, "*de traverser alors une cave sans être garanti par un masque en fil de fer.*" Despite these precautions it was not infrequent for a cellarman to lose an eye. Up to the Revolution, as a form of compensation for the risks they took, the broken glass was given to the workmen to sell.

Long and bitter experience of the bottle-breaking nightmare had taught the champagne-makers one or two tricks which sometimes reduced their losses. They had realized, for instance, that, once breakages set in on a large scale, the temperature of the cellar was raised by the volume of carbonic acid gas let loose, which was not without its effect on the remaining bottles: so, if they had time and the space available, they would quickly remove the unbroken bottles to a cellar where the temperature was lower. When this was not possible they would hose cold water on to the pile, to prevent the wine remaining in the broken bottles from fermenting and filling the cellar with a dangerous quantity of carbonic acid gas. For this reason the floor between two piles was always built to slope slightly towards a narrow gutter in the centre, along which the wine and water would pass to a reservoir. Many of these gutters are still visible in the cellars, and the story still circulates that the head of one Epernay firm used to insist that the fluid rescued from his reservoir should be used for cooking in his home.

In the early nineteenth century an immense iron vat, known as a *paracasse*, was invented, in which thousands of bottles could be placed during the second fermentation, the theory being that, as the *paracasse* could withstand a pressure of seven atmospheres, the pressure of the gas inside the bottles would be neutralized; but it was never very successful and was soon discarded. Hopes were raised again in 1836, when a chemist from Châlons-sur-Marne, M. François by name, invented an apparatus known as a *sucre-œnomètre*, which made it possible to measure fairly accurately the amount of sugar left over in the wine after the first fermentation. Thenceforward, a champagne-maker could gauge with greater accuracy the amount of sugar he should add to the wine at the time of the bottling, so that, in the course of the second fermentation, enough carbonic acid gas was produced to give the wine a nice sparkle but not so much that it imposed an unbearable strain on the bottle.

But although the *sucre-œnomètre* did help—by 1842, according to a report of the Rheims Academy, breakages amounted on average to 10 per cent—the champagne-makers were well aware that the breakages would never be cured completely until the bottle-makers found a way of making stronger bottles and the scientists unravelled the mysteries of alcoholic fermentation. By the mid-1850s the bottle-makers, who had been submitted to a ceaseless barrage of threats and entreaties by the champagne-makers, did finally produce a bottle capable of withstanding an internal pressure of six atmospheres or more; but science was much slower in throwing light on the process of fermentation.

For centuries, perhaps for millennia, the fermentation of grape-juice had intrigued scientific minds. Mediaeval alchemists had likened it to the effervescence produced by the action of vinegar on chalk: they believed that the crushing of the grape set certain bodies at liberty, whose reaction upon one another engendered effervescence. In the early seventeenth century, van Helmont recognised that a special kind of gas was discharged during the fermentation of grape-juice, but he asserted erroneously that it was the same as that exuded by the earth in the Grotta del Cane near Naples, and as the lethal gas produced during the burning of coal.* The first man to grasp the true nature of the chemical reaction was Lavoisier. In 1776 he named the type of gas produced in the course of fermentation "carbonic acid gas", but he failed to fathom the cause of its production. In 1836 Cagniard de Latour came close to unveiling the secret: he proved that fermenting liquids contained round cells which reproduced themselves by budding. But it was left to Pasteur to discover the real cause. In 1859, after extending to wine the studies which he had already made of beer and milk, he informed wine-makers that the agents which so miraculously transformed the juice of the grape into wine were organisms called yeasts, or, as he named them, saccharomyces. These yeasts, he explained, attacked the sugar in grape-juice and broke it down into two things: alcohol, which combined with the grape-juice and converted it into wine, and carbonic acid gas, which, in the case of a wine put through one fermentation only, vanished into the air, and, in the case of a wine put through a second fermentation in a closed vessel, remained suspended in the wine until such time as the vessel was opened and it could escape, leaving a trail of effervescence in its wake.

Pasteur's revelations were of capital importance to champagne-makers, as they were to wine-makers everywhere; but much study was still required before champagne could be made with scientific precision. This work was accomplished by such men as Professor Robinet of Epernay, who in 1877 published the first book on champagne-making to deal fully with the question of yeasts; Professor Salleron, who published an important paper in 1889; the German scientist Büchner, who in 1897 revealed that the decomposition of sugar during the alcoholic fermentation was not in fact caused by the yeasts themselves but by substances secreted by them, called enzymes; above all by Monsieur H. E. Manceau, a Champenois, who in 1900 perfected a far more scientific method of measuring the quantity of sugar which the wine requires at the time of the bottling. Thanks to these men (and to the bottle-makers), not only were the average breakages reduced to

* Both of these contain carbonic acid gas, but neither is uniquely composed of it.

their present proportions of about ¼ per cent (one is still unwise to go poking one's nose into a pile of bottles in the cellars while the second fermentation is in progress), but the element of uncertainty in champagne-making was almost entirely removed. From 1900 onwards the intelligent champagne-maker no longer had to fear such unpleasant surprises as finding that the "take" of the effervescence in one pile was so feeble that the contents could not possibly be sold as a sparkling champagne; no longer did he run the risk of finding the bottles in another pile half evaporated, or those of a third pile to have turned to vinegar.

Several other techniques in the champagne-making process were streamlined by the nineteenth-century champagne-makers themselves. Throughout the previous century, the accepted method of clearing a bottle of champagne of sediment prior to its sale had been to decant the wine into a new bottle: the Veuve Clicquot, so the story goes, became so exasperated with the time this took and with the loss of effervescence which it occasioned that she spent whole nights in her cellars making secret experiments, and eventually worked out the system of *remuage* which is used today.* In 1836 the House of Mumm imported from the Palatinate some colossal 12,000-litre tuns in which to carry out the first fermentation of the wine. These helped to give their champagnes a more consistent and uniform character than had been possible with smaller casks. The idea was soon taken up by other firms, and led to the huge blends of the modern vat—a trend, incidentally, which finds no favour with the older generation of champagne-lovers, who complain that all champagnes taste and look alike nowadays, and hanker after the "mahogany streak" of the 1874s or the "green-gold sheen" of the 1889s.

It was innovations such as these that made it possible for the Victorian champagne-makers to turn out more and more champagne each year, steadily to improve its quality and its attraction, and to reduce its selling price. The combination of these circumstances paved the way for what was perhaps the winefield's greatest achievement in the nineteenth century: the conquest of world markets.

Throughout the Victorian and Edwardian eras the export of champagne underwent a phenomenal expansion:

---

* It would have been thoroughly in character for the Veuve Clicquot to have taken such forceful steps to solve a problem. Confirmation that *remuage* was practised in her cellars in 1815 is provided by Mr. J. MacCullough, the author of *Remarks on the Art of Making Wine*, who visited Champagne that year.

Year	Bottles sold abroad
1844	4 million
1865	10 million
1871	17 million
1890	21 million
1909	26 million

The last figure remains the highest ever recorded.

Meanwhile, the poor French hardly had a look-in: in 1844, half the champagne being produced was consumed abroad; in 1853, about 65 per cent; in 1868, 75 per cent; in 1876, 80 per cent. Throughout the 1880s foreigners continued to consume about 80 per cent of the production, and from 1890 until the First World War they invariably drank between half and two-thirds of the supply. Not until the 1930s did Frenchmen attain the enviable position, which they still enjoy today, of being the imbibers of more champagne than the rest of the world put together.

There were several reasons why the expansion in home sales proceeded at such a sedate pace. One was that during the early part of the century a heavy tax was levied on all wine entering Paris in bottle. Another was that the average Frenchman was slow to prefer sparkling champagne to the district's still wines. But the main reason was undoubtedly that France's finances had been drained to such an extent by the Revolutionary and Napoleonic wars that for many decades only the very rich could afford sparkling champagne. Where there was money during the nineteenth century, there was champagne.

The brains behind the tremendous export drive were the heads of about ten, at the most a dozen, great firms, among which Clicquot, Moët & Chandon, Mumm and Pommery were the leaders. The vast sums which they expended on intelligent publicity and advertising, and the ingenuity of their agents, created or expanded the demand for champagne in all five continents, and made their names known to wine-loving households throughout the world; their achievement was all the greater in so far as exporting on a big scale cannot have seemed quite as natural an enterprise to the land-locked Champenois as it must have done to the inhabitants of other great European winefields, who all, except the Burgundians, had harbours on their doorsteps (Bordeaux, Jerez, Oporto) or direct access to the sea via a major waterway (Moselle, Rhine). Australia and South America were two important markets which they pioneered: at the outbreak of the First World War Chile, with its nitrate fortunes, was the country that consumed the most champagne per head of population in the world, a position now held by Belgium. The first large shipments of champagne to the United States were made in the late 1830s. By 1877 annual sales there, backed by a vast advertisement campaign, had risen to over a million and three-quarter bottles (not far off what they amount to today). Nearly half this total was supplied by Mumm, a House which ever since its foundation had made a speciality of the American market. In 1902 George Kessler, Moët & Chandon's agent in the U.S., brought off a coup which was to have international repercussions: somehow or other, at the launching in a New York dockyard of the German Emperor's yacht, *Meteor*, he succeeded in substituting a bottle of Moët for the bottle of German sparkling wine that had been provided, and in having Moët in magnums served at the luncheon after the ceremony, which was attended by the American President and Prince Henry of Prussia. The resulting publicity for champagne so infuriated the Kaiser that he recalled the German Ambassador from Washington. In 1906 Kessler caused a further stir by presenting a whole railway carriage of champagne to the victims of the San Francisco earthquake.

The amount of champagne consumed by the Americans in the nineteenth century, however, was small compared to Russian consumption. In *The Snow Plough* Pushkin gives a delightful account of Russia's mood shortly after the parade at Mont Aimé, a mood perfectly attuned to a champagne whirl: "The war had ended gloriously. Our regiments were back from abroad. The people rushed forward to greet them. Foreign airs were all the rage: *Vive Henri Quatre*, Tyrolese waltzes and snatches of *La Gioconda*. Officers, who had left for the campaign almost adolescent, returned mature and covered with decorations. An unforgettable period, a period of glory and enthusiasm! . . . The women, Russian women, were incomparable then. They had discarded their normal coldness." Soon Russian literature became peppered with references to champagne. In *The Shot* Pushkin's hero, Silvio, dines off "two or three dishes prepared by a retired soldier, but the champagne flowed like water"; in Lermontov's *Hero of Our Time* Petchorin complains that his villa on the Black Sea is overcrowded with people: "We lunch there, we dine there, we play cards there, and my champagne, alas, proves an even more magnetic attraction than [his girl friend's] pretty eyes."

Evidently Russian aristocrats were very much aware of the difference between champagne and their own sparkling wines: in Pushkin's *Dubrovsky*, the fabulously rich Troyekurov gives a party at which "several bottles of Gorskoye and Tsimlyanskoye were noisily uncorked and generously accepted as champagne". But although the Russians were crazy about all champagnes the one they preferred, if they could get it, was the very sweet brew specially prepared for them by the Widow Clicquot, which, according to Mérimée, they called "*Klikoskoe*". Pushkin compared the Veuve Clicquot's wines to the fountain of Hippocrene to which poets turn for inspiration. Today, when hardly a drop of champagne penetrates the Iron Curtain, Frenchmen in a position to do so seldom miss an opportunity of gently reminding the Russians of their former feelings for the Veuve Clicquot, as is shown by this report in the *Figaro* of a luncheon given by the French Foreign Minister for Mr. Gromyko at Geneva in the summer of 1959:

"*M. Couve de Murville avait tenu à faire figurer au menu, qui comportait Suprême de Sole à la Cherbourg, Agneau aux haricots verts, fromages et méringue glacée, un champagne Veuve Clicquot qui occupe une certaine place dans la littérature russe et notamment dans l'œuvre de Pouchkine.*"

Great though it was, the Russian bear's capacity for champagne-drinking was no match for that of the British lion. Rich from the profits which she had made during the Napoleonic Wars, when practically the whole of the trade of Europe was in her hands, becoming richer every day as she industrialized herself, Britain demanded, and got (as she still does), the best champagnes that Rheims and Epernay could produce. During the early part of the century, however, champagne was still very expensive in England, and, according to the 2 September 1835 issue of the *Original*, was seldom doled out liberally:

"Perhaps the most distressing incident in a grand dinner is to be asked to take champagne, and, after much delay, to see the butler extract the bottle from the cooler, and hold it practically parallel to the horizon, in order to calculate how much he is to put into the first glass to leave any for the second."

It remained expensive in England until 1861. In that year the Chancellor of the Exchequer, Mr. Gladstone (who once remarked that if he found himself with an old volume and a bottle of old wine close by the situation was irresistible), negotiated a trade treaty with France which reduced duties on French wine in such a sensational manner that an English restaurateur could thenceforward offer his clients a bottle of good claret for 1s., a passably good bottle of champagne for 5s., and a really good bottle of champagne for between 13s. and 18s. Members of Parliament, thinking no doubt of their own pockets as much as the true aim of the treaty, which was to woo the man-in-the-street away from his excesses with gin, greeted Mr. Gladstone's announcement with resounding applause. What turned out to be most remarkable about the new treaty was that its provisions remained in force, impervious to the greed of subsequent Chancellors, right up to the 1920s: between 1862 and 1919 the rate of duty on champagne never varied more than $2\frac{1}{2}d.$ a bottle. In 1867 the trade was given a further fillip when the restrictions on the number of bottles any one case might contain were removed altogether.

Mr. Gladstone was not the only Englishman in that decade who deserved to have a statue erected to him in the Champagne district: a million pounds spent on advertising would not have been as effective in popularizing champagne as was George Leybourne's music-hall song "Champagne Charlie", which was the smash-hit of 1869. "The song swept through London like wildfire," wrote W. Macqueen-Pope in *The Melodies Linger on.* "Most people believed that the *jeunesse dorée* had nothing else to do but stop up all night, spend money like water and drink champagne. Some actually did; but those who liked the song best had never tasted champagne and therefore got a tremendous kick out of singing about it." In actual fact, the title of the song (with its Cockney spelling) was *Moet and Shandon for me*, and the chorus, which was the making of the song and of George Leybourne himself, was more in the nature of a tribute to Moët than to champagne in general. It ran:

> "Champagne Charlie was my name,
> Champagne drinking gain'd my fame,
> So as of old when on the spree,
> Moet and Shandon's the wine for me."

The song's fantastic success naturally mortified the other big champagne makers, and George Leybourne's colleagues in the music-hall fraternity suddenly found they could hardly get into their dressing-rooms, such was the deluge of champagne showered upon them by Moët's competitors. The first to respond to this treatment was the Great Vance; he challenged Leybourne to a singing-drinking duel, which resulted in Leybourne singing "Champagne Charlie" from one end of the stage while at the other Vance sang:

> "Clicquot! Clicquot! That's the stuff to make you jolly,
> Clicquot! Clicquot! Soon will banish melancholy.

Clicquot! Clicquot! Drinking other wine is folly.
Clicquot! Clicquot! That's the drink for me."

Their fans thought this a huge joke and clamoured for an extension of
the combat; thus it came about that songs plugging several other of the
great firms were composed and sung, and this is why for the rest of
his life George Leybourne was known as "Champagne Charlie".

During the next few decades the sales of champagne in the British
Isles never ceased to rise; in 1897 they amounted to 9½ million bottles,
a record figure for all time, and nearly twice the quantity that is
consumed annually in Great Britain today. The Naughty Nineties was
the golden age of champagne in Britain. Chorus girls drank it from
slippers, connoisseurs wrote poems about their favourite vintages.
This is the final verse of an *Ode to Pommery 1874* (to be sung to the air
of Old Lang Syne), which appeared in *Vanity Fair* in December 1894:

"Farewell, then, Pommery Seventy-Four,
   With reverential sips
   We part, and grieve that never more
   Such wine may pass our lips."

The new century placed an ardent champagne-lover on the throne.
At shooting-parties the King used to be followed by a boy carrying a
basket of champagne bottles, and when he was thirsty he would call
up "the Boy": hence "a bottle of the Boy" became as familiar an
expression to Edwardian ears as "a bottle of Bubbly" is to ours. The
King's pronounced Francophilia, the Entente Cordiale and the Franco-
British Exhibition of 1908 all helped to keep champagne on the
pinnacle of popularity epitomized for ever by one sentence in Evelyn
Waugh's *Vile Bodies*: "Unless specified in detail, all drinks are champagne in Lottie Crump's parlour at Shepheard's Hotel."*

* "Wine", according to Jelly Roll Morton, had the same meaning at this time
in the plush brothels of Storyville, New Orleans, where Creole musicians
engaged to entertain the customers were hammering out the first jazz tunes. In
Mister Jelly Roll by Alan Lomax, Jelly Roll describes how at Hilma Burt's place
on the corner of Custom House and Basin Street, where he was the pianist,
"Wine flowed much more than water—the kind of wine I'm speaking about I
don't mean sauterne or nothing like that, I mean champagne, such as Clicquot
or Mumm's Extra Dry". "When the place was closing down," he continues,
"it was my habit to pour these partly finished bottles of wine together and make
up a new bottle from the mixture. That fine drink gave me a name (Wining

Grafted vine stocks
ready for planting

A one-year-old
grafted vine

Ungrafted vines planted *en foule* near Bouzy

Laying new earth

Pol Roger 1892 in magnums was served at the dinner given at Marlborough House by King George V for the seven reigning monarchs attending his father's funeral.

Great fortunes were made by the more enterprising champagne-makers in these lush late-Victorian and Edwardian years. Great, also, was the legacy of charitable and social work which many of them left behind. M. Emile Mercier founded and endowed the "Cercle de l'Abbé de l'Epée" in Rheims, France's first asylum for the deaf-and-dumb. M. Aubon-Moët gave Epernay its present hospital, which bears his name. Mme Pommery devoted much time and money to welfare work for children in Rheims. The Roederer family gave a chocolate factory—and much else—to the twelfth-century Abbey of Igny, near Fismes, where twenty-three monks were struggling to refound a community in the late eighteen-seventies.*

Shortly after "Champagne Charlie" and the Great Vance engaged in their singing duels, champagne became the subject of another controversy in Great Britain. The outcome largely explains the size of the sales which champagne enjoyed here during the late Victorian and Edwardian periods.

The seeds of the battle were sown way back in 1848 when an enter-prising London wine merchant, Mr. Burnes, having tasted Perrier-Jouët's 1846 *cuvée* at Epernay in its natural state, asked the firm to let him have some as it was, without a *dosage* of sugar. The idea struck Perrier-Jouët as tantamount to heresy. For as long as people could remember, possibly since its first appearance on the market, sparkling champagne had been artificially sweetened just before it was shipped. True, the quantity of sugar added depended on the wine's destination:

Boy) and from that I made a tune that was very, very popular in those days . . .

> 'I'm a wining boy, don't deny my name,
> I'm a wining boy, don't deny my name,
> I'm a wining boy, don't deny my name,
> Pick it up and shake it like Stavin Chain,
> I'm a wining boy, don't deny my doggone name. . . .' "

Thus, champagne may be said to have assisted at the birth of jazz.

* The enchanted soft-lined valley in which Igny lies was in the front line throughout the First World War and all the buildings were destroyed. Today, rebuilt, Igny is a convent. The nuns make an admirable cheese called "Igny". To purchase it, one rings a bell beside a grid in the entrance hall; a nun's voice is heard to say "*Benedicamus Domino*"; one replies, "*Deo Gratias*", and puts the money on a tray below the grid. The tray spins, and round comes the cheese.

to cater for the sweet tooth of the Russians, for instance, the *dosage* was considerable, whereas for the English it was much smaller; but to eradicate the *dosage* almost completely and expect people to drink champagne "dry" would, they felt, be courting disaster. In their eyes it was like inviting the owner of a fashionable tea-shop on the rue de Rivoli suddenly to stop serving sugar with hot chocolate and whipped cream. Besides, it would be mightily inconvenient for all champagne-makers if the crazy English did develop a passion for "dry" champagne. The sugar masked the tartness of a young champagne and enabled the makers to sell the majority of their wines two years, sometimes one year, after they were made; a "dry" champagne would need to age for at least three years in the cellars before its rough edges were rounded off, and this would involve an increase not only in the size of the cellars but in overheads and locked-up capital as well.

Mr. Burnes, however, had built up a formidable argument to support his proposition. He pointed out that, as long as the makers insisted on sweetening champagne (which is by nature one of the driest wines in existence), the majority of English people would only drink it as a dessert wine, at the end of a meal; and that, as Englishmen already had a dessert wine, port, to which they were inordinately attached (not to mention the sweet after-dinner sherries and Madeiras then in vogue), it was pure wishful thinking to imagine that really large sales of sweet champagne could ever be achieved. If, on the other hand, champagne was sold to English wine merchants unsweetened, they stood a fair chance of persuading their customers to drink it as a table wine, right through the meal, with fish and game and meat, in which case sales might be increased enormously.

To their credit, Perrier-Jouët overcame their misgivings to the extent of letting Mr. Burnes test out his theories, and a small shipment of their 1846 vintage was dispatched to him in its natural state. Mr. Burnes chose as his guinea-pigs the members of a well-known military club in London; the experiment was a complete flop and Mr. Burnes suffered the embarrassment of having to take back his dry champagne and replace it with a sweet one. Two years later, undaunted by the failure of his experiment, he asked Louis Roederer to let him have some dry champagne: they turned down his request point-blank, affirming that the export of unsweetened champagne might injure the reputation of their House.

There the matter rested until 1860, when several firms, among them Clicquot, sent the English some champagnes of the 1857 vintage that were drier and more mature than usual: some of these were actually labelled "dry", but the majority of makers supported Louis Roederer's attitude, and the dryness was in reality far from complete. The English reacted favourably to these wines, and in response to pressing demands from English wine merchants Ayala, Bollinger, Clicquot and Pommery, among others, decided to take the plunge with their 1865 vintages: they reduced the *dosage* to an infinitesimal amount and marked the labels "Very Dry". These proved extremely popular, especially the Ayala, to which the Prince of Wales is said to have taken a fancy at the Oxford Bullingdon Club; but it was not until the time came for the famous vintage of 1874 to be shipped that the resistance of the majority of the makers to dry champagne was finally overcome: nearly all the champagnes of that vintage were shipped really dry, and for the first time an Englishman could decide for himself the relative merits of the two types of champagne without deserting his favourite brand. Whether he was in the sweet camp or the dry one rapidly became a matter of considerable interest to a man's friends. Supporters of dry champagne dubbed the sweet variety "gooseberry juice" or "chorus girl's mixture"; supporters of the sweet variety coined the phrase "A man who would say he likes dry champagne" to describe someone they despised. *Punch* published a John Leech drawing depicting a dinner-party at which a schoolboy is thus addressed by his father:

"Now, George, my boy, there's a glass of champagne for you. Don't get such stuff at school, eh?"

"H'm!" George answers. "Awfully sweet. Very good for ladies. But I've arrived at a time of life when I confess I like my wine dry."

A couplet about Gladstone, written by Lord Houghton, announced which side he and the Grand Old Man were on:

"Trace we the workings of that wondrous brain,
        Warmed by one bottle of our dry Champagne."

By the early 1880s devotees of the sweet variety had to admit defeat; the vast majority of English champagne-lovers had realized by then how infinitely the more desirable dry champagne was of the two. Not only could it be drunk with pleasure right through a meal, as well as at weddings and balls, but the absence of sugar allowed the true character of the wine to emerge in all its pristine purity and made it practically impossible for the champagne-maker to cover up any deficiencies his wine might have. From that day to this nearly all the champagne shipped to England or destined for the English-speaking world has been dry, although for many years some champagne-makers added a small label to bottles in their English consignments, which stated that they had been "specially selected" by the wine merchant concerned, as they could not quite believe that the English really did want dry champagne and wished to disown responsibility for the lack of sugar in the contents.

For the French exhibited an exclusive preference for sweet champagne right up to the First World War; and even today the majority of the champagne drunk in France is sweet. If one was invited to the wedding reception of Adèle Dupont, the farmer's daughter, in the village of Fouilly-les-Oies, one could safely bet one's bottom dollar that the champagne would be sweet; but if one was dining with the Duchesse de X in her Paris hôtel, one could be equally certain that the champagne would be dry. There is a continued (though lessening) allegiance of the French people, apart from the connoisseur and the upper classes, to sweet champagne. A French meal consists of (at least!) four courses, of which the last two are invariably cheese and a sweet (in that order). A Frenchman dislikes eating cheese without a red wine to accompany it; he therefore tends to drink a red wine during the first three courses and to keep his champagne (which is much too delicate a wine to drink with most cheeses) for the sweet. Now, if the occasion is sufficiently noteworthy for him to be drinking champagne at all, it is extremely unlikely, indeed unthinkable, that the sweet will be blancmange or junket; it is more likely to be some concoction fit for a goddess, containing cream, perhaps a touch of a sweet liqueur and lots and lots of sugar; and, quite logically, he likes the champagne that he drinks with it to be sweet. Similarly, if his wife is entertaining some ladies of her acquaintance to tea (or, as she would put it, to a goûter) she either makes, or buys at the pâtisserie, a great selection of fabulously rich cakes; it follows that when she offers her guests the choice between tea and champagne, and they all politely refuse tea, she and they infinitely prefer to wash down the cakes with the sweet, rather than the dry, variety.

It is not, therefore, an exaggeration to state that dry champagne is a British invention (as are port, whisky and, to a large extent, sherry). Champagne-makers acknowledge the fact with gratitude, knowing that the innovation was largely responsible for the huge sales which champagne has enjoyed in England ever since.

The rising export sales were achieved in the face of great difficulties. First there was the Franco-Prussian war, which was largely fought in

Champagne and which resulted in a two-year occupation (and also, with the loss of Alsace and Lorraine, in Champagne becoming a frontier province for the next forty-eight years, and Rheims and Epernay garrison towns). To make matters worse, the vintages of 1871, 1872 and 1873 were all poor ones; sunshine did not return until the magnificent vintage of 1874.

Worst of all, the Champenois were threatened by a far more formidable enemy than Hun, Cossack or Tartar, an invader capable of wiping out the vineyards and of reducing to penury everyone who depended upon them for their livelihood. The name of the enemy was Phylloxera; it is a yellow aphis or plant-louse, so small that it is invisible without a microscope, belonging to the same family of insects as the green-fly. The mortal danger lies in its habit of sinking its snout into vine-roots to suck out the sap, and in so doing secreting a poisonous saliva which infects the wound, prevents it from healing, and thereby causes the vine to wither and die.

Phylloxera was first identified in 1854 by an American entomologist, Asa Fitch, among the wild vines of the Mississippi valley. Mr. Fitch's discovery caused no stir in the entomological or viticultural worlds at the time, because the louse appeared to be perfectly harmless and to have been living peacefully in the neighbourhood of vines for thousands of years. In 1863, however, a colony of phylloxera suddenly crossed the Atlantic (exactly how nobody knows—perhaps on bunches of table-grapes) and installed itself in a vineyard near Nîmes in Provence. It at once became apparent not only that the bug's bite was lethal when inflicted upon the more tender roots of European vines, but also that the nourishment it derived from them was causing it to reproduce at lightning speed.

During the next thirty years phylloxera invaded practically every important vineyard area in the world: Bordeaux and Portugal in 1869, Beaujolais and the Rhone Valley in 1870, California in 1873, Australia in 1874, Burgundy in 1878, Algeria and South Africa in 1887, Italy in 1888. Vineyards in their thousands were destroyed; terrible were the tales of woe and misery and starvation and bankruptcy among the vine-growers. By the late 1880s virtually the only winefields that had not been attacked were those of Champagne, the Rhine and the Moselle, and it was beginning to look as though the climate in those regions was too rigorous for phylloxera to operate. In 1890, however, such optimism was confounded: a report came in that phylloxera had been discovered in a vineyard a few yards from the Marne, near the hamlet of Tréloup in Aisne. Moët & Chandon immediately bought the affected area and burnt every vine in it, hoping thus to nip the invasion in the bud. In 1892 four acres of vineyard in Marne were attacked. This time the champagne-makers' trade association, the Syndicat du Commerce des Vins de Champagne, gave 20,000 francs to have the vines destroyed; but when, in 1894, another ten acres of vineyards in Marne were invaded, it was realized that destroying the vines did little good and that the money would be better spent in fighting the louse in other ways.

For the previous thirty years, ever since phylloxera had first appeared in Europe, entomologists, chemists and viticulturists had been struggling to find an effective way of combating the louse. It was recognised early on that spraying the vines with insecticide would be useless, because, although the insect often elects to live and breed on vine-leaves, especially in a warm climate, it does so equally happily on the roots, where no spray can reach it. In 1873 a mite that was known to prey on phylloxera was imported from America and let loose in infested vineyards, but its pugnacity vanished in Europe's milder climate, and it left the phylloxera in peace. In despair, some vine-growers resorted to the drastic expedient of flooding their vineyards, but submersion for five weeks killed only two out of every three bugs, and the soil suffered severe impoverishment in the process. In any case, this could never have been a final solution to the problem, as most of the world's great vineyards lie on hills, where flooding is impractical. At the time when phylloxera reached the Champagne district, vine-growers everywhere were waging war on the bug with a solution of carbon disulphide. Heavier than air, highly inflammable, poisonous to human beings and a foul colour, the gas was unbelievably unpleasant to handle; but when injected into holes between a row of vines it did succeed in killing a fair number of phylloxera in the vicinity.

Carbon disulphide, however, was extremely expensive. As early as 18 June 1891 the Préfet of the Marne had summoned all vineyard owners to a conference at Epernay to discuss ways and means of helping the poorer vine-grower should its use become necessary. At this meeting it was agreed that a combined operation was essential. A fund was started into which the State, the Chamber of Commerce of Rheims, the big champagne firms and many private individuals poured money, to ensure that ample supplies of carbon disulphide would be available to all. A combined operation, however, was an unfamiliar method of procedure to the Champagne vine-grower, who had been used for centuries to fighting his battles alone: all his innate suspicion of authority, of the big Houses in particular, flared up and was cunningly fanned by a newspaper, founded for the purpose, called *La Révolution Champenoise*. When the time came to use carbon disulphide, only 17,000 of the 25,000 vineyard proprietors of the district agreed to do so. The remainder refused to make any contribution to the central fund, and proclaimed that their property rights were being interfered with. The venerable professor who had been engaged to conduct the combined operation had rotten eggs thrown at him, and eventually it fizzled out, although individual activity continued.

Meanwhile phylloxera encroached upon the winefield, happily for the Champenois at a somewhat slower rate than in other parts of France, owing to the colder climate. By 1897 thirteen acres of vineyard were affected, by 1898 ninety acres, by 1899 237 acres, while the hot summer of 1900 increased the extent of the ravaged area to 1,581 acres. Vineyards in the Marne valley suffered most because there the roads and the railway facilitated the bug's passage. At the end of the first year of the new century phylloxera was estimated to be costing French winegrowers £50 million annually, yet still no fully effective method had been found of combating it.

It was at this stage that vinegrowers the world over had to reconcile themselves to the fact that phylloxera might never be driven from the vineyards, and that their one hope of salvation lay in America's and Canada's sixteen species of native vine, whose roots are tough and fibrous enough to heal after the phylloxera has bitten. No single North American species proved capable of producing good wine in European soils; but experiments showed that, if a cutting of a European vine was grafted on to a cutting taken from certain American vines, and the grafted cutting was then planted in such a way that the roots formed on the American half, not only was the resulting vine immune to phylloxera but the top half—and the grapes—assumed the characteristics of its European forebears. In other words the *Vitis vinifera*, which had been cultivated in Europe since the days of the Phoenicians and whose thousands of sub-species produced all French wine, and all really good wine elsewhere, including that of California, Australia, South America and South Africa, would have to be pulled up, and virtually every vineyard in the world would have to be replanted. The task would be a stupendous one, but there was no alternative. America, christened Vineland by the Vikings, responsible for the most terrible scourge in the history of viticulture, was about to atone: in future burgundies, bordeaux, champagnes and all other great wines would, in a sense, be partly American.

Up to the outbreak of the First World War lavish use continued to be made of carbon disulphide, but, concurrently, each winefield set about the soul-destroying business of replanting. Viticulturists had recognized early on that grafting would present special problems in the Champagne district's climate; doubts were even expressed as to the feasibility of getting grafts to "take" successfully so far north. Defeatism, however, was not the attitude of the personnel working at the Station expérimentale de Viticulture et d'Oenologie du Fort Chabrol on the outskirts of Epernay. This organization, the first research and experimental station which the winefield had ever had, was founded in 1890 by Moët & Chandon with the primary object of defeating phylloxera. It was an entirely private institution, supported by the firm's money and endowed with several acres of the firm's vineyards, but the outcome of its research was always freely made available to all. There, under the direction of Monsieur E. Manceau, chemists and viticulturists were vigorously tackling the problems set by the forthcoming Franco-American marriage.

The problem of forcing the grafted cuttings to "take" proved to be soluble. A procedure was fairly quickly worked out, involving the use of hothouses and nurseries, which, though expensive and time-consuming, ensured a satisfactory join. It is still in use today, and a description of it will be found in Chapter 18. Much more complicated was the question of selecting the American vines that were best suited to each of the Champagne district's many soils. Three were found; but it had taken hundreds of years to find sub-species of *Vitis vinifera* that were perfectly adapted to the soil conditions of each district, and the search for the most suitable American sub-species and hybrids still goes on, having become almost a science in itself, in which such matters have to be taken into consideration as the quality of the wine produced, the regularity of the vine's production, the age it will live to, the degree of its resistance to phylloxera and to other pests and diseases, its vigour, its fertility and its affinity with the soil.

Before replanting with Franco-American stocks could begin in earnest, many other difficulties had to be overcome. The existing law, which forbade new species of vines from entering the Champagne district, had to be altered. Certain champagne firms insisted that the vineyards could be saved without resort to grafting; others refused, for a time, to accept grapes from grafted vines, maintaining that they lacked quality. The financing of the undertaking was another headache. This was shouldered to a large extent by an organization known as the Association Viticole Champenoise, founded in 1898 by twenty-four great firms after the earlier attempt to get the vine-growers to pull together had ended in fiasco. Each firm paid a contribution in proportion to the number of bottles it sold annually, and the money thus raised was used for the benefit of the entire winefield. The A.V.C. bought the American roots in bulk, distributed them to the vine-grower, and allowed him to postpone paying for them until the grafted vines were earning money. It opened a grafting establishment at Ay, established nurseries at Epernay and Châlons, subsidized the erection of communal hothouses, and issued large quantities of carbon disulphide free. Later, sub-associations of the organization were started in the vineyard villages, and the vine-grower was invited to join them: at these, technical advice of the highest calibre was to be had for the asking. But the attitude of the vine-grower to communal effort remained lukewarm: by 1912, only 11,000 of the 25,000 vineyard proprietors had enrolled.

The bulk of the replanting was not done until after the First World War, but the following figures show the progress that was made before 1914:

Year	Acres planted with grafted vines
1900	427
1905	1,944
1910	4,800
1913	6,043

During those pre-war years, it was mainly secondary growths that were restocked, for hopes were still entertained that it might be possible to avoid the changeover in the great growths. But in 1904 phylloxera obtained a foothold in the vineyards of the Mountain of Rheims, and thereafter, as the figures below demonstrate, the rate at which it spread dashed such hopes to the ground:

Year	Acres ravaged
1905	7,960
1906	10,413
1907	11,958
1908	13,346
1909	14,366
1910	15,636

Before the war broke out, a fairly clear picture was emerging of the consequences of the phylloxera blight throughout France. Altogether,

2 million acres of vineyards were ravaged, and the cost to the country was estimated at £500 million. As far as the Champagne district was concerned, there was much to regret, but much to be thankful for. The winefield had been fantastically lucky to be attacked so late in the day: if the bug had appeared twenty years earlier, it is extremely doubtful whether the vineyards would have been producing enough wine to make the huge sales of the 1890s and the Edwardian era possible. It was also to benefit, decades hence, from the revolution in viticultural methods which the switch to grafted vines provoked.

The phylloxera crisis had revealed a deplorable lack of confidence between the vine-growers and the champagne-makers. Men who work on the soil may be stubborn, conservative, unreceptive to new ideas; Frenchmen may be unduly suspicious of the motives of their fellow-beings, too fiery in temperament to take easily to discipline; but a situation like the one that arose during the phylloxera invasion, with vine-growers refusing to make a concerted stand against a deadly enemy threatening their livelihoods, was almost incredible, and would never have occurred had all been well in the kingdom of Champagne.

The root of the trouble lay in the fact that champagne-making had suddenly, in the course of less than half a century, become Big Business, whereas the laws and safeguards with which Big Business needs to be surrounded if harmony is to exist within it had as yet to be formulated. Most of the big firms, as any elderly Champenois will confirm, bent over backwards to see that the vine-grower got a fair deal; but there were others who cared not a hoot whether he obtained a living wage or not. In years when grapes were plentiful they paid absurdly low prices for them, knowing full well that the grower could not dispose of them more profitably elsewhere and that, owing to the complexity of champagne-making, he could not undertake the vinification himself.

The vine-grower's resentment at this state of affairs had been smouldering quietly throughout the latter decades of the nineteenth century. At the very end of the century, fire was added to it by the rapid extension of the vineyards that was taking place in the outlying districts of the province. The wine these vineyards produced was nearly always inferior to, and often of a completely different character from, the wines of Marne; yet, even in years when there was plenty of Marne wine available, certain champagne-makers were buying great quantities of the inferior product, attracted by its cheapness, and only accepting Marne wine at scandalously low prices.

Early in the 1900s the vine-grower's resentment turned to fury: the secret got out that certain unscrupulous firms, determined to make hay while the Edwardian sun shone, were succumbing to the temptation of importing wine from beyond the boundaries of the province and incorporating it in *cuvées* destined to be sold as champagne. How prevalent this practice became it is impossible to gauge with any accuracy; though it has been estimated that, on average, 12 million bottles were being sold each year in excess of the winefield's production of grapes. In London the rumour got about that Rheims and Epernay were buying rhubarb from Nottinghamshire to turn into champagne. That, we may be sure, was sheer fantasy; but in his *Notes on a Cellar Book* George Saintsbury remarked that before the First World War no wine needed greater care in buying than champagne, which shows how harmful for the winefield's reputation the greed of certain firms had become.

In 1904 the Syndicat Général des Vignerons was founded, with the declared object of putting a stop to the abuses which were preventing the vine-grower from receiving a fair price for his grapes. The honest champagne Houses, as much outraged as the vine-growers at what was going on, supported this organization in an attempt to force the Government to promote legislation designed to protect both vine-grower and consumer. It was obvious that, as a first step, legal definition must be given to the boundaries of the vineyard area whose products were entitled to the name "champagne". The question, however, was an exceedingly thorny one, and in a decree concerning the repression of fraud, promulgated on 1 August 1905, the Government neatly side-stepped it: all decisions concerning the boundaries of winefields and the names of wines, the decree stated, must be decided by administrative order.

During the next couple of years the issues at stake were further complicated by growing dissension among the vine-growers themselves. In one camp were the supporters of the Fédération des Vignerons de l'Aube. They wanted the Aube vineyards to be included in any delimitation of the Champagne district that might take place, on the grounds that the *département* of Aube had always formed part of the ancient province of Champagne and that the *département*'s chief town, Troyes, was its capital. In the opposing camp were supporters of the Fédération des Vignerons de la Marne. They argued that *la Champagne* and *le Champagne* had always been essentially different; that the fame of champagne derived solely from the vineyards of Marne; that it would be iniquitous to include in *Champagne viticole* the whole of the huge province, where widely different soil conditions existed, and whose limits had always varied; and that besides, until very recent times, no champagne-maker had dreamt of incorporating the produce of the great majority of the Aube vineyards in his *cuvées*, which last statement they proved with figures. To complicate matters still further, vine-growers and politicians from the *département* of Aisne also started agitating to have their vineyards included in any delimitation proposals, basing their claim, as the Aubois were doing, on the fact that the vine-yard area of the *département* had once formed part of the province of Champagne.

The rivalry was becoming so bitter that the Government finally decided to intervene. On 17 December 1908 a bill was passed which stipulated that henceforward only grapes grown in the following area might be used for champagne-making:

The Marne département: all communes of the arrondissements of Rheims, Epernay and Châlons-sur-Marne, plus thirty-five communes of the arrondissement of Vitry-le-François;

The Aisne département: forty-six communes of the arrondissement of Château-Thierry and thirty-six communes of the arrondissement of Soissons.

The Aube *département* was entirely excluded.

The Aubois, naturally, were furious. The Marne vine-growers were not particularly pleased either: although they had more or less gained their point they were insulted by the ranking, in a class with their own "*bons vins*", of what they dubbed "*la purée de haricots*" of Aisne. Besides, the new law was singularly lacking in provisions for its enforcement. It was common knowledge that wine from Aube and goodness knows where else was continuing to find its way into the cellars of certain firms.

Fate chose this moment to inflict on the Champenois a sequence of poor harvests such as they had seldom experienced in their history. 1907, 1908 and 1909 were bad enough; as to 1910, it was a complete disaster, largely owing to attacks of mildew, an affliction which the vine-grower was still a novice at handling. Many vineyards produced not a single bunch of grapes worth picking. The plight of the vine-grower became really desperate. In certain localities more than two-thirds of the vineyards were mortgaged; and what made the present situation all the harder for the vine-grower to bear was the contrast it afforded with the prosperity which he had enjoyed during the late nineteenth century. In *Wines of France* H. Warner Allen, who visited the Champagne district in early 1911, wrote:

"The contents of their houses showed how prosperous they had been. After a bumper year they were regularly victimized by ingenious commercial travellers, who persuaded them to buy pianos which neither they nor their families could play, clocks to the extent of three or four per mantelpiece, and enormous safes more suitable for the millionaire than the small-holder. But in 1911 they were faced with bankruptcy."

The Champagne district was becoming a powder-keg which might explode at any minute. Once again the Government was forced to take action. On 11 February 1911 a bill was passed which it was hoped would prevent champagne-makers from using imported wine in their *cuvées* of champagne. In future, firms that manufactured both genuine champagne and sparkling wines made with imported wine would have to do so in establishments at least the width of a street apart; the two types of wine would have to be entered separately on the *acquit* of the Régie,* and a champagne-maker would be fined if he failed to put the word "champagne" on the cork and label of a bottle of genuine champagne, or if he mentioned the word on bottles which did not contain genuine champagne. But, to the exasperation of the Aubois, once again the bill contained no proposals for the inclusion of their vineyards in *Champagne viticole*. This time they turned militant. In Troyes there were processions, huge demonstrations and disorders of a grave nature, including the public burning of tax papers; Bar-sur-Aube, in the heart of the vineyard district, hung out red flags and

---

* In France, wine or spirits being moved in bulk or bottle from place to place must be accompanied by a document issued by the "Régie", which is a department of the Ministry of Finance. This *titre de mouvement* is called a *congé* if the tax on the wine or spirits has been paid (nowadays it amounts to roughly 1 F. on a bottle of champagne), and an *acquit*, if it has not been paid. In the latter case, the Régie keeps track of the consignment from bonded warehouses to bonded warehouse until the tax has been paid or the consignment leaves the country.

Woe betide any traveller in France, from truck driver transporting casks of wine to tourist with more than the odd bottle or two in his car, who cannot produce the document of the Régie. The French police are renowned for their skill in detecting bottles in the vehicles they stop, and there is hell to pay if the right papers are not produced. Rightly so, in that the tax on wine and spirits is not levied until it leaves the maker's cellars, and the *congé* is proof that it has been paid.

In effect, the cellars of Champagne are one vast bond.

chanted the Internationale. Thoroughly alarmed, the Government prepared to give in; on 11 April the Senate was persuaded to pass a resolution recommending that the law of 17 December 1908, which had delimited the Champagne district, should be annulled forthwith.

A telegram describing the Senate's recommendations reached the nerve-centre of the Fédération des Vignerons de la Marne in Epernay at five o'clock that evening. That night a sound all too familiar to French ears reverberated through the vineyards on the right bank of the Marne below Hautvillers: the beat of the tocsin. Rockets zoomed across the sky, bugles blared, and in several riverside villages strange figures were to be seen lurking in the shadows of houses. Around two o'clock in the morning these figures converged on the cellars of a champagne-maker in Damery and one in Cumières, both suspected of having imported wine from the Midi to sell as champagne. Doors were forced open, and in a matter of minutes both cellars were completely ransacked.

At dawn, vine-growers armed with vine-stakes and mattocks poured into Ay, and there all hell broke loose. Systematically, the cellars of every firm suspected of using grapes from outside the district were smashed up: casks were unbunged, bottles broken, machines sabotaged, ledgers torn up. By midday rivers of wine were flowing through the streets; the gutters choked and, it is said, the Marne drank champagne that morning. Dragoons, summoned hastily from Epernay, barricaded the streets, but vine-growers continued to slip in from the hills and vineyards, 5,000 to 6,000 in all, it was estimated, the representatives of over forty growths. The authorities had been caught napping; clear orders had not been given to the troops and, although there was some fighting, most of the time they stood helplessly by as the pillage continued. In the afternoon the rioters, a red flag ahoist, switched their attention to the homes of certain champagne-makers: pictures were torn from the walls and strong-boxes emptied, and, while furniture and bric-à-brac cascaded out of the windows to the applause of spectators, the occupants fled for their lives. When dusk fell several buildings were drenched with petrol or with the carbon disulphide used to fight phylloxera, and set alight; flames leapt into the sky, and that night Ay was shrouded in a blanket of smoke. There was smoke over the vineyards, too, for the rioters had ignited the straw which, as a protection against frost, was covering the vines belonging to a well-known Epernay firm. And hundreds of vines were trampled underfoot. Before order was established on the evening of the 13th the rioting had spread to the outskirts of Epernay, but the town's garrison kept it in hand, and only one or two small cellars were ransacked. In Ay the total damage amounted to forty-one buildings and warehouses sacked or burnt.

France was stunned by the viciousness of the Ay Riots. No one had foreseen that the Champagne vine-grower, normally so reserved, so good-humoured, so law-abiding, would act, all of a sudden, with such violence. In his defence, the vine-grower pointed out that firms which had not imported wine from other districts had been left alone. This was true as far as Bollinger was concerned (years later, standing near a window of her home in Ay, Mme Jacques Bollinger heard a passer-by say to another, "That's the Maison Bollinger, you know—we didn't touch it during the riots—in fact, we lowered the red flag as we passed!"); but it was not the full truth, as both Ayala's and Bissinger's premises had been set on fire, and neither firm was on the black list. Besides, there was the damage to the vines to explain; many people believed that the culprits were professional agitators sent down from Paris by the General Federation of Labour. There is no simple explanation of what happened. Maurice Crabellier and Charles Julliard, in their recent history of Champagne, probably came as close to the truth as it is possible to get by attributing responsibility to "a mixture of mediaeval-type hatred of the *seigneur*, of socialism, even of anarchism, with undercurrents of boulangism thrown in", and by stating that the riots "expressed confusedly a craving for a society which would guarantee the vine-grower a fair wage and cut down the businessman's share of the profits".

An immediate effect of the riots was that the Government turned the Champagne district into an armed camp. "*Plus de soldats que de vignerons en Champagne*" ran a banner headline in *l'Humanité*. Altogether 40,000 soldiers were moved in; each village had a squadron of cavalry or a company of infantry billeted in it; and the troops were not moved out—many a village lass shed tears as they left, it is said—until the autumn, when the billets were required for the grape-pickers.

A happier effect of the riots was that the Government decided to ignore the Senate's recommendations, and on 7 June produced a bill of its own. This recognized four types of sparkling wine:

1. *Champagne*. This name was to belong exclusively to wine produced from grapes grown in the arrondissements and communes of Marne mentioned in the decree of 17 December 1908 and in a few communes of Aisne.

2. *Champagne Deuxième Zone*. This name was to be borne by wine

produced from grapes grown in the communes of Marne excluded by the decree of 17 December 1908, in a great many communes of Aube, in the arrondissements of Wassy in Haute-Marne and in two communes of Seine-et-Marne.

3. *Vin Mousseux*. This was to be the name by which a sparkling wine produced with grapes grown in other wine districts of France was to be known.

4. *Vin Gazéifié*. This was to be the name by which a sparkling wine whose sparkle was produced artificially was to be known.

The bill also contained a clause to the effect that a firm engaged in the manufacture of both champagne and *vin mousseux* must in future conduct the two businesses in premises at least the width of a street apart. This, it was hoped—over-optimistically, as it turned out—would finally put a stop to the practice which had been the principal source of the vine-growers' grievances.

There were obvious drawbacks to the bill—notably, the cumbersome name allotted to champagne made with Aube grapes, and the dire confusion that would inevitably result from the existence of two types of champagne—but at least the Marne vineyards had been recognized as the fount of all true champagne, which every reasonable person who knew anything about the subject believed them to be. The Marne vine-growers were jubilant over this victory, and claimed that they could never have achieved it by constitutional means (which was almost certainly true); but, as it turned out, so far they had only won a victory on paper: it was two years before the law was passed by the Lower Chamber, and it had not come up for discussion in the Senate before war was declared.

CHAPTER 14

THE FIRST WORLD WAR

On 3 September 1914 the Prussian Guards swept into Rheims, which was not defended. South of the city the advance continued, and by 6 September Epernay and Château-Thierry had been evacuated. The next day the Germans crossed the Marne. They now had only thirty miles to go before they reached the Seine; and once they were across that river the fall of Paris was inevitable.

But they never did reach the Seine. When they got as far as the main road running from Montmirail to Châlons-sur-Marne they paused, for two good reasons. One was that they were exhausted by their long, bitterly-resisted advance, and needed to recover strength for the final push to the Seine. The other was that a mile or two south of the main road lies a great belt of marshland, known as the Marais de Saint-Gond; throughout French history it has proved an obstacle to invaders, as it was to do on this occasion also. The Germans did succeed in getting across the marshes to the hamlet of Mondement, but Moroccan troops pushed them back into the marshland, and Joffre issued his famous Order of the Day that resulted in the Battle of the Marne.

Thus, for the second time in history, the Champagne district became the setting of one of the dozen or so decisive battles of the world. This time the bulk of the fighting actually took place in the vineyards; and once again the vines were laden with fruit. As usual, the invader's fondness for the district's wine proved helpful to the French: the advancing poilus found countless lorries abandoned because the tyres had been ripped by the crunched glass of discarded champagne bottles, and they took prisoner many German soldiers paralysed not so much by fear as by an overdose of champagne. Nevertheless, when the battle was over, and Epernay and the whole south bank of the Marne had been liberated, victory was still a long way off. The French re-occupied Rheims on 13 September, but their energy was spent, and for nearly four years the front line formed a three-sided buckle round the city, extending westwards along the Aisne canal, eastwards along the Rheims-Châlons road at the very foot of the Mountain vineyards.

Whole books have been written about that four-year nightmare which descended on the Champagne district. All I can do here is to try to give the reader an inkling of what it meant to the three groups of people most intimately involved: the soldiers, the Rémois and the makers of champagne.

The Soldiers' War

If you ask a man who fought in Champagne what is his most vivid memory of the campaign, he replies, "The Chalk": the chalk that in summer lay like virgin snow on hill and plain, ready at a whisper from the wind or a flicker of human movement to rise up in furious puffs and shroud man, beast and vehicle in ghostly whiteness (the big guns had leather over their mouths to prevent it from getting down their throats); the chalk that in winter became a hell of grey, clinging mud; the chalk that all the year round was lanced with zigzag trenches, pocked with shell-holes and mines. "The chalk—and," the veteran adds, "the waiting." For the war in Champagne, as elsewhere along the front, was mostly static, that atrocious thing known as a "war of positions"; a succession of intervals, seeming eternities, between the offensives wherein resided the only hope of bringing the screaming nightmare to an end.

And so it lasted from the winter of 1914 until 18 July 1918, when a great Allied counter-attack was launched which developed into the Second Battle of the Marne. This proved to be the prelude to victory. In late September another great Allied attack took place: British, French and Italian troops brought deliverance to the Rheims area, and by the end of the first week of October the whole of Champagne had been reconquered.

Flesh and life, colour and glory, are brought to the bare bones of the story by the magic pen of Alan Seeger, America's Rupert Brooke, who was killed in Champagne in 1916, aged twenty-eight, while serving with the French Foreign Legion. Seeger arrived in Champagne shortly after the Battle of the Marne and was stationed for a while between Troyes and Châlons-sur-Marne. That autumn he wrote home:

"How beautiful the view is here, over the sunny vineyards! And what a curious anomaly. On this slope the grape-pickers are singing merrily at their work, on the other the batteries are roaring. Boom! Boom! ... The yellow afternoon sunlight is sloping gloriously across this beautiful valley of Champagne."

The following July he wrote his masterpiece, a poem entitled *Champagne (1914–15)*, which not only crystallizes the hopes and fears of all those who fought in Champagne but also, with its subtle injunc-

tion to future generations of champagne-lovers, introduces a mystical
element into champagne-drinking for all time:

"In the glad revels, in the happy fêtes,
   When cheeks are flushed, and glasses gilt and pearled
With the sweet wine of France that concentrates
   The sunshine and the beauty of the world,

"Drink sometimes, you whose footsteps yet may tread
   The undisturbed, delightful paths of Earth,
To those whose blood, in pious duty shed,
   Hallows the soil where that same wine had birth.

"Here, by devoted comrades laid away,
   Along our lines they slumber where they fell,
Beside the crater at the Ferme d'Alger
   And up the bloody slopes of La Pompelle.*

"And round the city whose cathedral towers
   The enemies of Beauty dared profane,
And in the mat of multicoloured flowers
   That clothe the sunny chalk-fields of Champagne,

Under the little crosses where they rise
   The soldier rests. Now round him undismayed
The cannon thunders, and at night he lies
   At peace beneath the eternal fusillade . . .

"That other generations might possess—
   From shame and menace free in years to come—
A richer heritage of happiness,
   He marched to that heroic martyrdom.

"Esteeming less the forfeit that he paid
   Than dishonoured that his flag might float
Over the towers of liberty, he made
   His breast the bulwark and his blood the moat.

* Mont de la Pompelle lies 3 miles beyond the outskirts of Rheims on the
Châlons-sur-Marne road. The first Christians of Rheims suffered martyrdom on
it; there, in 1657, the Rémois scored a thumping victory over Spaniards who were
ravaging the nearby vineyards; and in the First World War the fort erected on it
became a key point in the defences of Rheims and changed hands frequently,
always at a fearful cost in human lives. Today tourists stop to inspect the remains
of the fort, despite the notices stating that unexploded shells still lie buried in the
earthworks.

"Obscurely sacrificed, his nameless tomb,
　Bare of the sculptor's art, the poet's lines,
Summer shall flush with poppy-fields in bloom,
　And Autumn yellow with maturing vines.

"There the grape-pickers at their harvesting
　Shall lightly tread and load their wicker trays,
Blessing his memory as they toil and sing
　In the slant sunshine of October days . . .

"I love to think that if my blood should be
　So privileged to sink where his has sunk,
I shall not pass from Earth entirely,
　But when the banquet rings, when healths are drunk,

And faces that the joys of living fill
　Glow radiant with laughter and good cheer,
In beaming cups some spark of me shall still
　Brim towards the lips that once I held so dear . . ."*

The Rémois' War

19 September 1914 is a date for ever solemn in the history of Rheims: on that day "the enemies of Beauty", as Alan Seeger put it, "dared profane" the cathedral, the city's soul. The German bombardments had started on 14 September, and during the morning of the 18th the cathedral was hit several times. The first shell killed a beggar who, for as long as people could remember, had squatted on the cathedral steps, holding out his hand to the faithful; shortly afterwards the Smiling Angel of Rheims was decapitated. Later, falling masonry killed a French policeman and two of the 150 wounded German soldiers who had been put in the cathedral. Their death caused panic to break out among the survivors, many of whom were being wounded afresh by the falling masonry, and the German doctor begged to be allowed to go through the lines to stop the shelling. Permission was refused, but in the afternoon, while the bombardment was still in progress, Abbé Thinot climbed up the north tower of the cathedral and hoisted a Red Cross flag. He reported that the noise was fantastic: it seemed to him that "the great homogeneous mass of stones was shuddering and trembling with rage".

* A passage from *A Thousand Days* by Arthur M. Schlesinger bears witness to President Kennedy's admiration for this young poet: "On Cape Cod in October 1953, when he returned from his wedding trip, he had read his young wife what he said was his favourite poem. She learned it for him by heart, and he used to love to have her say it. It was Alan Seeger's *I Have a Rendezvous with Death*."

The shelling began again at eight a.m. the next morning. Abbé Laudrieux was saying Mass, but he continued his ministering throughout the morning, although the violence of the bombardment ever increased. At about three p.m. a shell hit the scaffolding which had been erected on the north tower in 1913 by workmen engaged in restoring the masonry. It caught fire, as did the Red Cross flag, and within minutes the flames had spread to the cathedral roof. The roof was 430 years old, composed of enormous oak beams sufficient, it is said, to fill 180 wagons with ten-ton loads, and it supported a coating of lead weighing a further three-and-a-half tons. Suddenly, as flames shot into the sky, the tremendous construction burst asunder, emitting heat of fabulous intensity and discharging into the nave a torrent of molten lead and a cascade of crackling beams. The clergy, aided by some of the wounded German prisoners, tried desperately to remove the cathedral's precious treasures, but soon the stalls and doors, and the 15,000 palliasses in the nave, caught fire, half the Rose Window blew out and the heat became intolerable. The clergy fled. So would have those among the German wounded who could walk or crawl, but the guards refused to let them out, fearing they would be massacred by the vast and angry crowd which had assembled in the cathedral square. Luckily, at three-thirty the German battery commanders, having guessed what had happened, ceased fire; this quietened down the crowd to some extent, and the guards were able to whisk the majority of the prisoners, and three German nuns who were looking after them, to the Printing Office. But meanwhile the wind had risen and was fanning the flames, and before dusk 400 houses in the immediate vicinity were on fire. The cathedral burnt on through the night; by morning there was hardly a gargoyle, a sculpture, or a flying buttress that was not plastered with hideous blobs and stalactites of molten lead.

For those who lived through the Second World War, when the overnight destruction of an entire city was a common occurrence, it is difficult to appreciate the revulsion which the shelling of Rheims Cathedral inspired. It caused a world outcry which proved as detrimental to German prestige as the sinking of the *Lusitania*. While flames were still licking the cathedral Cardinal Luçon had written to the Pope, imploring him to denounce the German action and to use his influence to prevent a repetition of it. The Pope's reply was non-committal, for the Germans had succeeded in convincing the Vatican that the French had been using the cathedral for military purposes, and for the rest of the war correspondence passed between the Cardinal, the Pope and the Kaiser on the subject of the cathedral; almost without

exception, the Pope's letters to the Kaiser were friendlier in tone than
those he wrote to Cardinal Luçon.

Whatever the rights or the wrongs of the case, the Germans clung
to the belief that the French were using the towers as observation posts,
despite Cardinal Luçon's repeated assurances that the keys to every
entrance were kept in his pockets, and on 24 April 1917 they bombarded the cathedral systematically for three-quarters-of-an-hour with
big calibre shells. The apse was torn to pieces, the towers were seriously
damaged and three flying buttresses were broken. It was feared that the
immensely thick walls had been permanently weakened. But, although
the building is estimated to have been the victim of a greater volume
of shell-fire than certain Verdun forts specially designed to withstand
bombardment, it is still magnificently alive, as everybody knows. And
much more of its famous glass may yet be in existence than is realized,
as many a fragment, set in aluminium rings made in the trenches from
German fuses, passed to souvenir-hunters; according to Lord Northcliffe, the blue fragments were difficult to distinguish from sapphires.

The Rémois lived through a total of 1,051 days of bombardment.
Indeed, the attacks occurred with such persistent regularity that after
a time the French communiqués ceased to report them. As time went
on the main activities of the city were transferred to the cellars. They
were bomb-proof (not a single bottle of champagne was broken on
account of enemy action throughout the war) and, when warmed with
electric or fuel stoves, proved by no means uncomfortable to live in.
People slept on mattresses beside the stacks of bottles, and as holes had
been cut in the chalk walls between the cellars bread-winners could go
to work, children to school, patients to hospital, worshippers to a
church service (at which they sat, gas-mask in hand, on banked-up
champagne cases) without once setting foot above ground. Concerts
frequently took place underground; once a whole opera was performed
in Roederer's cellars. There was little illness, even when the pumps
were put out of action and it became impossible to drain the cellars;
in fact, many people were so content underground that they did not
come up for months at a time, in certain cases for as long as two years.

From November 1915 onwards the cellars played an important
part in the defence of the city. That winter the army cut connecting
passages, broad enough for a double line of soldiers to pass along them,
in cellars belonging to Pommery & Greno, Mumm, Ruinart, Goulet
and Veuve Clicquot-Ponsardin. Pommery's cellars, which projected
into no-man's-land, were of particularly strategic value. In addition to
the families of 400 of the workers, several battalions of front-line

replacement troops were permanently stationed in them. One of the principal galleries could hold 1,500 men; the seating arrangements extended for over a kilometre; thirty hundred-litre casks provided water for washing and a 200-foot well produced water for drinking; sixty *chaises percées* took care of another need, *"car il fallait penser à tout!"*. By March 1916 it was estimated that thirty-four battalions, say 50,000 men, could be quartered in the city's cellars; a secret report submitted to the French cabinet stated that the cellars were so powerfully armed that they were capable of withstanding as long a siege as the forts of Verdun.

Life in Rheims became so strange that journalists, politicians and foreign V.I.P.s badgered the High Command for permission to visit the city. The President of the Republic popped down several times a year; other prominent visitors included the King of Italy, the Queen of Portugal, the American Ambassador and Gabriel d'Annunzio. Reading between the lines, one gathers that it was more on account of the inconvenience which these visits caused than because of any real necessity that on 25 March 1918 the military authorities finally ordered all civilians to leave the city, because by that time only 5,000 Rémois, out of the pre-war population of 120,000, remained, the majority of them women engaged on important war work. It proved easier, however, to issue the order than execute it. Dr. Langlet, the Mayor, who had done wonders for the past four years to bolster Rémois morale, refused point blank to leave unless Cardinal Luçon, his rival in the esteem of the populace, left at precisely the same moment, and many a householder applied for permission to stay because the hens or the rabbits—even the roses—needed looking after, and, when his request was refused, placed barbed-wire across the front door to prevent the police from entering. But eventually the authorities had their way, and by the middle of April 1918 only about a hundred civilians were left.

By the time war ended Rheims was a martyred city. Eight hundred of her citizens had been killed. Not one of her 14,000 houses had escaped damage, and 12,000 of them were total ruins. The Archbishop's Palace, Lord Northcliffe wrote, looked like a house in Pompeii.

Compared to beleaguered Rheims, Epernay and Châlons-sur-Marne had a somewhat easier war, but they too suffered considerable material damage and no small loss in human life from air attack and shelling.

The Champagne-Makers' War

The vineyards emerged relatively unscathed from the ten days of enemy occupation in September 1914; even in the course of the heavy fighting that took place among them during the Battle of the Marne they came to no irreparable harm. Their real sufferings began only when the front line stuck in the valley of the Vesle. The brunt of those sufferings was borne by the vineyards on the northern slopes of the Mountain of Rheims that extend down almost to the Vesle itself; they had impaled upon them for the next four years a gruesome network of trenches, and there was hardly a day during that period when they and the *poilus* in their midst were not molested by shells, machine-gun fire or poison gas.

Yet—and this is what is truly amazing—until March 1918, when all civilians were ordered out of the area, the vines in those vineyards continued to be tended. Many growers needed a military permit to get to their plots; many found that shells rained down on them the moment they showed themselves among the rows; but so great was their love of the vine, so strong their determination to save something for those who returned, that day in, day out, they risked—and sometimes gave—their lives for the vines.

Perhaps the most remarkable example of the vineyard worker's dedication centred round two vineyards belonging to Pommery & Greno, the Clos de la Pompadour and the Clos du Moulin de la Housse. Both lay within a few hundred yards of no-man's-land; both had a battery of heavy artillery dug in on them; more than fifty French soldiers were killed within their boundaries; yet throughout the war Chef Vigneron Corpart, aided by a small group of volunteers, looked after them, crawling among the vines whenever mist or fog or hazy moonlight allowed. Each autumn, when the time came for the grapes to be picked, courage of an almost equal order was needed. Over twenty children—nobody is quite sure how many adults—were killed during the 1914 vintage; two little girls (aged twelve and fifteen), several *poilus* who were lending a hand, and many other adults received wounds while picking the 1915 one. Both vintages were blessed by heaven; both are still drunk on very special occasions in the Champagne district today; both may be said to have the blood of France running through them.

The professional vine-grower's courage and, one must not forget, the hard work of many an amateur—for the vineyards well behind the front line were tended for the most part by women, children and old men, often with inadequate tools, invariably without proper supplies of chemicals and fertilizers—these kept the champagne firms supplied with grapes and enabled champagne-making to continue throughout the war. Even in Rheims the majority of firms kept going, turning out approximately half their pre-war production; after the evacuation of the city in April 1918 they continued to operate through their Paris offices. Never, to quote Mr. Maurice Healy, were wines so gallantly made. At Heidsieck Monopole's two *chefs de caves* lost their lives; at Pommery & Greno's seventeen workers were killed, several of them women; as the men were called to the colours women took over more and more cellar jobs, including that of *remuage*. Over half a million cases of champagne destined for export left Rheims between September 1914 and April 1918.

One of the difficulties with which the Rheims champagne-makers had to contend was the temptation that the stocks of champagne offered the troops billeted in the cellars. At Mumm's holes were found to have been bored in the back of the huge casks which the firm had imported from the Rhineland in 1836: soldiers, it transpired, had been surreptitiously filling up their gourds from them for weeks. At another cellar the frequency with which a coffin, apparently of enormous weight, was seen being carried backwards and forwards between the galleries aroused suspicions which enquiry most definitely confirmed. At Mumm's again, when the time came to dispatch a quantity of cases which had been used as seats during Mass, every bottle was found to be empty. The flooding of the cellars that followed the destruction of the pumps was another perplexing problem with which the champagne-makers were faced. At a time when the lower cellars at Veuve Clicquot-Ponsardin's were flooded to a depth of six feet Comte Bertrand de Mun, the head of the firm, decided to give a party to boost the morale of his fifty remaining workmen: he seriously considered giving a *fête vénitienne*.

When finally the Rheims champagne-makers did have to evacuate the city, they were forced to leave their stocks behind. It was a good thing they did because, when the city was all but lost in May 1918, the thought of all that precious wine falling into enemy hands prompted a soldier of the colonial infantry to say: "*Mon vieux, tant qu'il y a du champagne à Reims, nous nous chargerons de sa défense*", a resolve in which his comrades discerned such wisdom that, with a champagne bottle in one hand and a rifle in the other, they held on grimly and saved Rheims.

Remembrance

Memories of the First World War die hard in the Champagne district. Recently, near Faverolles on the Epernay-Hautvilliers-Fismes road, a farmer ploughed up the corpse of a German soldier; in the hamlet of

La Chappe, within a stone's throw of Attila's camp, a faded sign over
the door of a farmhouse still reads:

Popote★	I
Hommes	60
Chevaux	10

And then there are the war cemeteries and the monuments.

The pilgrim to these shrines finds much of interest, much to ponder
over. The diversity of the stelae erected by the different nations in their
cemeteries, for instance: the French crosses, mostly wooden, with the
names carved directly on them, so that in too many cases both the
cross and the inscription are disintegrating; the Italian crosses (at
Bligny, on the Rheims-Dormans road), wooden too, but with the
names of the fallen attached to them on punched rust-proof metal
strips, so that at least the incriptions are surviving; the British
Commonwealth rectangles of Portland stone, seemingly more
generous, but also with many an inscription obliterated by the weather;
finally, the luxurious American crosses and stars of David, of milk-
white Italian marble veined with quartz and feldspar, which, with their
inscriptions, look as though they will endure for ever. And, in high
summer, the pilgrim finds much to delight the eye. The Commonwealth cemeteries, nearly all small in Champagne, and for the most
part hidden behind grey stone walls in secluded woods or on lonely
belts of farmland, are havens of quiet beauty at that season: as one
opens the little safe in the wall to read the register of the fallen and a
short description of the battle, as one signs the visitors' books (even in
the remotest spots these have to be continually renewed, so quickly
are they filled with English and French signatures, the latter often
followed by a handsome tribute such as "*Hommage aux braves soldats
britanniques*"), as one counts the number of headstones marked "Known
unto God", the sweet scent of English flowers—roses, lavender and
stocks—kisses the air. The hand that tends the flowers is probably
English, for the majority of the gardeners are veterans of the B.E.F.
who married French girls and stayed.

The most beautiful of the Champagne cemeteries is the one which
the Americans built at the Bois de Belleau, three miles north-west of
Château-Thierry; there, in 1917, very "green" but very brave
American troops, commanded by General Pershing, fought their first

★ Field-mess.

battle of the war, incurring terrible casualties, but in so doing prevented the enemy from crossing the Marne again and relieved pressure on the exhausted Allies at a crucial moment. An avenue of trees leads up to a small white chapel with an observation platform on top; from there one looks down upon gracefully curving rows of white marble headstones, arranged by some trick of geometry to form further graceful curves in the vertical plane. Well-kept lawns, gay beds of flowers, paddocks and spinneys superimpose on Champagne the enchantment of Virginia, and banish all oppression. High up on an escarpment overlooking Château-Thierry itself, the Americans erected a Parthenon in memory of those who fell at Belleau Wood (and in other parts of Aisne); the surrounding land, affording glorious views over the Marne valley, is maintained by the Americans as a park for the enjoyment of the people of Château-Thierry.

Twelve miles south-west of the Bois de Belleau, in La Ferté-sous-Jouarre, on the exact spot where the British crossed the river in the opening offensive of the Battle of the Marne, stands the British Marne Memorial, a rectangular block of Vaurion Marbrier stone on which are recorded the names of 3,888 officers and men who fell in the retreat from Mons and the advance to the Aisne in 1914 and who have no known graves. In the woods near Perrouse, three miles to the south, where lie buried 150 British soldiers killed in the Battle of the Marne, all is perfection. The little cemetery is bright with flowers and a fig-tree clambers along its eastern wall. The average age of the men buried there was twenty-seven, which reveals an interesting fact; the Battle of the Marne was the last great engagement of the professional British Army; thereafter, conscription and the short-term engagement provided the majority of recruits.

The French memorials are rather austere, no doubt partly because the Frenchman's attitude to death is more solemn that the Anglo-Saxon's, partly because they commemorate the ruin of a homeland as well as loss of human life. The Chapelle de la Marne at Dormans, which was erected in tribute to all who fell in the fighting on the Marne— irrespective of nationality—and which harbours an ossuary containing the bones of 1,500 unknown Frenchmen, is an architectural horror, but its site is hallowed, for the trench-torn vineyards thereabouts are soaked with the blood of thousands of French soldiers. Half-a-mile south of Suippes, on N. 77, beside a gigantic cemetery, a small marble column set on a stone pedestal marks the area where the villages of Tahure, Mesnil-les Hurlus, Perthes-les Hurlus, Hurlus and Ripont once stood, an area that was so badly mauled during the 1914–15 offensives that no attempt was made to rebuild, and it was handed over to the Army for use as a firing-range. Further north, just beyond Souain, stands the Monument de la Ferme de Navarin, commemorative of all the battles fought in Champagne between 1914 and 1918, its setting as bleak and lonely as any of this planet, symbolic for that very reason of all the cold misery of war. Between Navarin and Rheims many of the famous Monts de Champagne still contain weed-covered, half-collapsed trenches: as at Verdun, interminable shell-fire played such havoc with the soil that reclamation was deemed impracticable, and still is.

The two most remarkable First World War monuments in Champagne are the least known to visitors, because both are far, far off the beaten track. The first is at Mondement, the hamlet on the southern banks of the Marais de Saint-Gond, which was the southern-most point reached by the Germans in September 1914. It stands on the grass hillock that acts as village green, a colossal chunk of what appears to be pink sandstone, at least 150 feet high, looking, I swear, un-commonly like a pink whale that has lost its flukes and back-dived on to dry land. Closer inspection reveals the whale's stomach to be inscribed with what at first sight appear to be hieroglyphs, but turn out to be the names of every French and British unit that fought in the Battle of the Marne, together with the names of their commanders —French, Haig, Lomax and Smith-Dorien, of course, included. Still closer inspection reveals the leviathan's hind-quarters, facing the marshes, to contain over-lifesize bas-reliefs of about a dozen generals— Joffre, larger than the others, looming forwards in the centre, French squeezed in between two gallic generals and looking decidedly uncom-fortable. Above them—it took me a quarter-of-an-hour to decipher the hieroglyphs—is the following sentence, unpunctuated:

"*A la voix de Joffre l'armée française en pleine retraite s'arrêta et fit face à l'ennemi alors se déchaina la bataille de la Marne sur un front de soixante ligues de Verdun aux portes de Paris après plusieurs jours de luttes héroïques l'ennemi de toutes parts battait en retraite et sur toute l'étendue du front la Victoire.*"

Prolonged enquiry has unearthed the following facts: the monument is made of pink cement; the cement is pink in honour of the Moroccan troops who shoved the Germans back into the marshes (Marrakesh, rather than Virginia, superimposed on Champagne this time); the hieroglyphs are supposed to resemble the Arabic script; the unveiling was performed by President Lebrun in the summer of 1939—less than a year before the Germans reappeared in Champagne.

The second is at . . . well, it isn't *at* any place, in fact it is so far from anywhere that, even if you ask the way of a Champenois who knows the countryside like the back of his hand, he utters so many "Ums" and "Ahs" and issues so many confusing directions that you get lost; but to go there—and you should—buy the Michelin Paris–Rheims map (No. 56), find Châlons-sur-Marne on it, run your finger due north until it alights on the town of Mourmelon-le-Grand, and then run it one centimetre north-west along D. 19 to where D. 21 forks off to the left. Precisely one more centimetre along D. 21 is the objective, marked on the map with a circle topped by a cross and a rectangle with another cross in it, the map-maker's symbols for a church and a cemetery. Both are very, very special: they are Russian. The church or chapel (that is what it really it) is as white as Siberian snow. It is built (I quote from the brochure I bought there) "in the spirit of the Novgorodian style of the fifteenth century"; it sports two onions, one small, slender and golden, the other much bigger, more bulbous and bright blue; the interior is a riot of garish frescoes and icons. It's delightful in every way; but it's about the most improbable edifice one would expect to find in this—one had thought—God-forsaken flat-land of *Champagne pouilleuse*. Improbable, that is, until one brushes up one's history and recalls to mind that the Russians sent an expeditionary force to Champagne in 1916, that once again Cossack uniforms set the hearts of Rémoises and Sparnaciennes a-flutter, that many a son of All the Russias breathed his last in Champagne and that, of course, there must be a Russian cemetery here, just as there are French ones and American and British and Italian ones. But why right here in the barren chalk-land; why not near Rheims or Epernay or beside the green waters of the Marne? That was the whim of the White Russian refugees, many of them aristocrats turned Parisian taxi-drivers, who clubbed together and by 1936 had raised a sufficient sum to build the chapel. The bleakness, the loneliness, appealed to them; it also appealed to the monk who was to chant prayers daily beside the graves marked "*Mort pour la France*"—not "*Mort pour la Russie*"—and in his spare time run an Orthodox monastery. The monastery still exists—comprising a two-roomed cottage crammed full with icons, and a few square yards of vegetable garden—but it has a brotherhood of one; the monk lives there alone now with his chickens, his bees, his *chien méchant* and his beard.

CHAPTER 15

THE ISTHMUS YEARS OF PEACE

AFTER THE ARMISTICE the Champenois were confronted by a bed of nettles. The Russian market, which for half a century had been taking about 10 per cent of the winefield's production, had vanished in the smoke of the October 1917 Revolution. Germany and the former Austro-Hungarian Empire were bankrupt, unlikely to be able to afford champagne for at least a decade. The Americans, who, according to the French Chamber of Commerce in New York, had imported close on 3 million bottles of champagne in 1913, were about to slam their doors on Bacchus.* The Scandinavians also were flirting with Prohibition, and were soon to succumb. Rheims needed to be entirely rebuilt, as did almost all the villages that look down on her from the northern slopes of the Mountain. The vineyards were in a deplorable state. Over half of those on the Mountain of Rheims, among the very best in the winefield, had been torn to shreds during the fighting in the last months of the war. Phylloxera was now firmly entrenched in the

* The Prohibition Bill became law on 30 January 1920, and a mere trickle of champagne cases stamped with an American address left Rheims or Epernay between 1920 and 1939; yet, thanks to the bootleggers, 71 million bottles of champagne, it is estimated, entered the U.S. during the period. At the outset the supplies were funnelled through the French islands of Saint-Pierre and Miquelon in the Gulf of St. Lawrence; but soon a chain of distribution centres sprang up around the North American continent.

At the maritime distribution centres, the cases were loaded on to ships which sailed to a point just outside the three-mile limit; there they were transferred to smaller craft and dumped on a sandbank. Bootleggers ashore drove on to the sandbank and recovered them. If the Coast Guard arrived before the dumping was accomplished, the sailors would hasten off to sea and jettison the telltale cargo. Sometimes, however, the cases were carried shorewards in the nets of fishing-boats and dumped in the sea, there to be retrieved by the bootleggers. When such a course was envisaged, the co-operation of Rheims and Epernay was necessary: each case would be wrapped in canvas that had been soaked in tar, to keep out the sea-water, and then fitted into another case, which bore no markings. After a winter storm, the ocean depths around America still occasionally regurgitate what the bootleggers missed. In the spring of 1959, a young couple raking for clams on a Cape Cod beach noticed nine well-corked bottles bobbing in the water. They fished one out and found it contained champagne—a trifle *madérisé*, but perfectly sparkling. They took the lot to a nearby inn and threw a party. There were no labels, but someone had a brain-wave and looked at a cork. It read: "Charles Heidsieck. Extra Dry. 1920".

remainder of the Marne vineyards. Of the 27,600 acres in production in 1913, only 16,500 acres were considered likely to bear a reasonable crop of grapes in 1919. And it was obvious, now, that further treatment with carbon disulphide would be a waste of time and money. The only sensible course was to proceed to a complete reconstitution of the winefield with grafted vines. The operation would take at least ten years to complete, and might well cause a desperate shortage of wine in the intervening period.

But there were a few roses sprouting in the nettle-bed. Surprisingly, stock-taking revealed that the cellars of Champagne contained more wine awaiting shipment than had ever been the case before the war. Frequent bans on export had caused the war vintages to accumulate, and the stocks of firms owned by enemy aliens, which had been confiscated by the French Government, were now available for sale, as were those of firms which had been unable to keep going during the war. A quick fortune could be made if buyers were forthcoming; and forthcoming they were. In France, England and Belgium people were in the mood for a champagne splurge: everyone wanted to blot out the nightmare of the daily casualty lists, war-profiteers had money to burn, demobilized soldiers had girl-friends to woo or wives to woo back. Besides, in England many returning soldiers, having grown accustomed to drinking wine during their service in France, were determined to retain the habit, and the same was true of many a civilian who had taken to wine because of the shortage of spirits. The demand was huge and the champagne excellent, particularly the 1911s and the 1914s. English wine merchants noted that their post-war clientele lacked discrimination—fancy calling champagne "Fiz" or "Giggle Water"!—and they foresaw great changes in the champagne trade now that the big private cellars were clearly a thing of the past; but with sales booming it was no time to shed tears of regret.

The boom, however, did not last. In England it was scotched by, of all people, that mighty champagne-lover, Mr. Winston Churchill, then Chancellor of the Exchequer. Against the advice of the Customs Commissioners, it is said, he decided to burden champagne with a special tax, which caused imports to fall by half. In *Wayward Tendrils of the Vine* Ian Maxwell Campbell relates how, as a member of a deputation concerned with this tax, he asked the Chancellor, "What did Mr. Gladstone do in 1860–61?", and how Churchill turned to him, took the cigar out of his mouth and replied with the most engaging simplicity: "Ah, you must remember that Mr. Gladstone was a very great man dealing with comparatively small figures, whereas I am a

small man dealing with gigantic figures." In France, and in many
other countries, the boom was scotched by a general tightening of belts
after the midsummer madness of immediate post-war spending. The
result was that in 1921 and 1922 sales were the lowest ever recorded
in peace-time between the 1860s and the present day.

During the next four years things looked up again (Mr. Churchill's
tax lasted only a year): in 1926 a total of 37 million bottles was sold,
a figure only 2 million below that recorded in 1909, champagne's
record year so far, and not to be appreciably exceeded until 1956. The
wine that made these sales possible came mostly from the three small
but excellent harvests with which the Champagne district was blessed
after the Armistice, 1919, 1920 and 1921. The vineyards were getting
into much better shape, too. Vineyard owners whose vines had suffered
damage or destruction had been heavily and swiftly compensated. In
many completely destroyed villages the first building to be erected
had been a hothouse for grafts, and an average of 2,000 acres a year had
been replanted with Franco-American stocks; by 1926, little more than
2,500 acres of vineyard vulnerable to attack by phylloxera remained.
The day was not far off when, for the first time since the beginning of
the century, the Champagne vineyards would be in a perfectly healthy
state; what remained to be seen was whether the winefield in full
production would be capable of selling all it produced.

It was extraordinarily bad luck that, at this crucial moment in the
Champagne district's history, when the ravages of war and of phylloxera were on the point of being fully repaired and the winefield
seemed destined to go forward from strength to strength, there should
have occurred a world-wide economic crisis of unprecedented proportions. The first sign that there was trouble ahead came in 1927, when the
sales of champagne in France, which had averaged 14 million in the
preceding four years, nose-dived to a meagre 8 million bottles; but
the full effect of the crisis was not felt until the autumn of 1929, when
the panic on Wall Street plunged the West's economy into depression.
In 1930, the year in which the reconstitution of the vineyards was finally
completed, the price of grapes fell to half, in some cases even to a
quarter, of what they had fetched in 1913, and the shipping depart-
ments of many firms were put on a half-time basis. In 1931, when
England went off the Gold Standard and the champagne-makers
suddenly found themselves receiving 420 francs instead of 620 francs
for each £5 of wine sold, the purchase of grapes had to be practically
suspended. The worst years of all, however, were 1932 (when, with
close on 150 million bottles in the cellars, only 4½ million were sold

A Champenoise in a *bagnolet* pruning a vine

Vines near Verzenay being attached to the wires as spring returns

Vines being banked up with the aid of a winch

Champagne vine in flower

abroad) and 1934 (when the huge crop, the first really big one since the reconstitution of the vineyards, remained largely unsold, despite the fact that grapes from some of the best growths were being offered at fifty centimes the kilo). These were evil days indeed for vine-grower and champagne-maker alike, as bad as any in the winefield's history. And, as more and more countries were switching from a free-trade policy to a Protectionist one, it would have been folly to expect the situation rapidly to improve.

As a stop-gap measure, some champagne-makers unloaded their excess wine on the market by offering it at absurdly low prices, often (to hide the shame) in bottles labelled with the name of a fictitious firm. As a long-term policy, they started to woo the home market, having realized almost too late that the industry's security would always be at the mercy of foreign tariff fluctuations unless a solid and permanent basis of sales could be established in France itself. In this endeavour they had to spend a fortune in advertising, and for many years they were forced to accept very low profit margins, but increase their French sales they did, in a spectacular manner. By 1933 sales in France had reached the 20 million mark (three times what they were at the beginning of the century), and ever since they have greatly exceeded sales abroad.

The vineyard owners, for their part, were also forced to take drastic action to save themselves from starvation. As they could not sell their grapes to the champagne firms, many of them turned the grapes into still wines of their own accord, took the train to Paris and went from restaurant to restaurant offering them for sale. The sudden reappearance on Parisian wine-lists of the still wines of Champagne caused a minor sensation. The Parisians liked them; they were light, fresh and relatively cheap; they rapidly became the fashion. But the first consignments were mostly from the famous vintages of 1928 and 1929, and when the 1930s, 1931s and 1932s, which were rather undistinguished years in Champagne, came along they did not enjoy the same popularity.

Other vineyard owners went the whole hog and started turning their grapes into sparkling champagne themselves. But the process is so complicated, the need for capital so great, that few of them had much success.

Yet other vineyard owners formed themselves into co-operatives, marketing a champagne under the name of a village and adopting the motto, "Let the growth in Champagne replace the brand". All winter long, when their work in the vineyards was finished, they dug out cellars, progressing a yard a night, and with their savings built *vendangeoirs*. Many a famous champagne firm lent them casks and equipment. But the going was tough, with so little capital, with no known "name", with no possibility of achieving a blend.

By such devices, and others which will shortly be related, the winefield hauled itself out of the morass into which it had fallen. By 1937 the worst was over: 37 million bottles were sold that year, including 12 million for export.

The struggle during the inter-war period to put the business of champagne-making on a sounder footing was helped immeasurably by the steps that were taken to define and legalize the status of Champagne as a winefield and a wine. During the 1930s the law of France went to great lengths to try to prevent confusion in the public mind between genuine champagne and other sparkling wines, the reason being that ever since sparkling champagne first came on to the market people had been trying to imitate it—as they still are. At first this was only done on a small scale; around 1860, however, when sales were rising fast and the wine was beginning to enjoy world-wide popularity, imitating champagne ceased to be a pastime of amateurs and became the full-time occupation of professional wine-makers the world over. Many of these professionals were motivated by the perfectly honourable ambition of turning out as good a sparkling wine as the soil and climatic conditions of their vineyards allowed and of selling it to a clientele that wanted a sparkling wine but could not afford champagne. Many others, however, could not have cared less about the quality of the sparkling wine they were launching out with, but were only concerned to produce at the smallest possible cost a sparkling wine that behaved and looked like champagne. Two factors aided them. The first was the colossal success which champagne itself enjoyed in the late Victorian and Edwardian eras; the second was the perfecting of two methods whereby a sparkling wine could be produced much more cheaply than by the Champenois method.

The first of them to be widely used is now generally known as the Tank or Charmat method, although the main credit for its invention belonged to a French chemist called Maumené. Its great advantage over the *méthode champenoise* is that the expensive and complicated procedures of *remuage* and *dégorgement* are avoided by putting the wine through its second fermentation in large enamelled steel tanks instead of in individual bottles. The tanks are hermetically sealed so that the carbonic acid gas produced by the second fermentation cannot escape.

As soon as the second fermentation is complete and the sediment in the wine has fallen to the bottom of the tank, the wine is filtered off under pressure through a hole above the sediment into another tank, and then bottled. As the carbonic acid gas which produces the bubbles when the bottles are opened is generated by the wine itself, sparkling wines so made are claimed to be naturally sparkling. The Champenois would have made immediate use of the Tank method to make champagne if they had believed that it was possible to produce by it a sparkling wine that even remotely approached in quality one made by the *méthode champenoise*. Being firmly convinced that this is not possible they have never done so, and in all probability never will.

The other method cannot by the remotest stretch of the imagination be considered to have anything natural about it. The principle used is precisely the same as that employed by makers of aerated waters. A quantity of carbonic acid gas is pumped into a tank containing wine that has been cooled, the resulting mixture is allowed to warm to room temperature so that the pressure of the gas increases, and it is then bottled. Known as the Aerated or Impregnation method, it enables sparkling wines to be produced even more cheaply and easily than by the Tank method. Its major drawback is that the bubbles disappear much more rapidly than is the case with wines made by the Tank method or the *méthode champenoise*.

In no country did the mania to imitate champagne produce more surprising results than in France itself. For almost as long as it had had sparkling champagne, France had had other wines which had a natural tendency to sparkle, such as St. Péray from the Rhone, Seyssel from Savoy, Vouvray and Saumur from the Loire. Many of them were only *pétillant* or at the most *crémant*, but they were pleasant and cheap, one reason for their low price being that they were unpretentiously attired—a cork only a trifle stouter than those used for still wines, string to hold it on, light silver paper round the neck of the bottle, a modest label. All of a sudden the majority of these wines could only be obtained in a fully sparkling state, in green bottles tarted up with mushroom corks, cat's cradle wiring, rich gold foil, labels emblazoned with armorial bearings, etc., and at a price which their devotees found absurd.

Not to be outdone, other minor French winefields, most of which had never produced a drop of sparkling wine before, started effervescing: to the astonishment of late Victorian wine-lovers it became possible to buy *mousseux* from Provence, *mousseux* from Hermitage, *mousseux* from Alsace, *mousseux* from Gaillac. But the event that gave connoisseurs of wine the greatest shock was when those two bastions of conservative wine practice, Bordeaux and Beaune, succumbed to the craze for bubbles. In the 1870s a sparkling Sauterne appeared on the market, followed soon after by Royal Médoc Mousseux. From Burgundy came sparkling Meursault (white), sparkling Clos Vougeot, sparkling Chambertin and sparkling Pommard (all red), but, probably because these venerable names meant nothing to the type of person who bought *mousseux*, whereas the word "Burgundy" did mean something to them (vaguely), the new Burgundian product that enjoyed the greatest success was a red one christened (simply) Sparkling Burgundy. By the time the First World War broke out, virtually the only important French winefield that had resisted the temptation to produce a sparkling wine was Cognac.

The same metamorphosis took place, too, in other parts of the world. The winefields that produce port, Marsala, sherry and Madeira remained as still as Cognac, but elsewhere the conquest of bubbles was complete. A sparkling wine industry had been started in Würtemberg and Silesia as early as 1826; during the rest of the century it grew enormously, and as it grew the main centre of its activity became concentrated on the banks of the Rhine, the Moselle and the Main. Even such a hallowed growth as Schloss Johannisberg started to effervesce. As late as the 1930s the Germans would buy by the train-load still wine that the vine-growers of Champagne had been unable to sell to the champagne Houses and turn it into sparkling wine, having often, it is said, blended it first with apple-juice. In Italy, many a winefield like Asti and Alba that had previously turned out *pétillant* or *crémant* wines—and many a winefield that had never even done that—blossomed forth with fully sparkling wines decked out to kill.

Other lands that founded sparkling wine industries were Switzerland, Portugal, Spain, Rumania, Hungary, Algeria, Cyprus, Palestine, South Africa, Argentina, Chile, Canada and Australia. The two countries, however, in which the making of sparkling wine was destined to become really big business were Russia and the United States. In Russia the new industry took root in the winefields of the Ukraine, the Crimea, Moldavia, Uzbekistan and Alma-Ata, the home of the Cossacks. In America the main centres of production came to be situated in California, Ohio and the Finger Lakes Region of New York State on the shores of Lake Erie.

Although there is not a shred of doubt that the driving force behind the surging rise of sparkling wine industries the world over was the desire to imitate champagne and cash in on its popularity—the fact that almost without exception the new sparkling wines were dressed up to resemble champagne is sufficient proof of that—it must not be imagined that the Champenois viewed the new development with hostility or even with particular alarm. In many cases, notably in Russia and the United States, the new industries were set on their feet by hired Champenois technicians. Having developed the world's taste for sparkling wine, the Champenois were fully aware that they could never hope to produce enough champagne to satisfy it. Their product, they realized, was a luxury one, which would always have a restricted market; they saw no reason to dread competition from those who were catering for a clientele that lacked either the money or the appreciation to buy champagne. Indeed, in one way they welcomed the competition, for there is a proven axiom in commerce that once people have developed a taste for a product they nearly always end up wanting and, if they can afford it, procuring the best example of that product available. Thus, to Rheims and Epernay everyone who bought a bottle of the new sparkling wines appeared as a potential customer of champagne.

There were, however, two aspects of the situation, both resulting from the fact that the new sparkling wines were direct imitations of champagne, that sent the Champenois into paroxysms of rage. The first was the downright commercial dishonesty of certain makers of the new wines. During the 1870 war, unscrupulous German firms sold thousands of bottles of sparkling wine of German origin with corks and labels that had been branded and printed with the names and insignias of great champagne firms. A decade or so later the Americans embarked on similar villainy, all the more disturbing in that it was perfectly legal. For example, a town in the Finger Lakes district was re-christened Rheims; and an elderly French widow who had been a cook, but who happened to possess the magic name of Mme Veuve Pommery, was paid a large sum of money by an American sparkling wine company to cross the Atlantic and become the founder of a brand of American Bubbly called "Mme Veuvé Pommery". The second circumstance that made Champenois blood boil was the assumption of the great majority of the foreign makers of the new sparkling wines that they had the right to name their products "champagne".

Dishonest competition has of course been a problem with which merchants have been confronted since trade began: the reference in Fielding's *Tom Jones* (1748) to cider being sold in taverns as champagne is just one example among many that could be quoted. Distressing as dishonest competition is, the victim does at least enjoy the sympathy of all right-minded people, the right to litigate, and, if the law as it stands is of no help to him, the comfort of knowing that one day it may be changed in his favour. Precisely such a tightening up of the law regarding blatant commercial plagiarism did occur in the majority of the countries where large quantities of champagne have been sold since the First World War, and such bugbears as forged labels and corks with famous champagne names on them no longer cause the Champenois loss of sleep. However, the name by which other sparkling wines should be known is a problem of quite another sort. In many countries both producers and consumers of sparkling wines saw—and still see— no reason why the sparkling wines of Rheims and Epernay should alone be entitled to the name "champagne", and in this opinion they were— and in many cases still are—supported by the laws of their lands. So complicated are the issues involved that wine-producers, wine-lovers and jurists are likely to be debating them for centuries to come.

Stated in broad terms, the Champenois argument may be said to run as follows:

1. The word "champagne" means wine made in and exported from the confines of the Champagne district, wherein soil and climatic conditions, the type of vines grown and traditional wine-making methods combine to render possible the production of a wine of unique character and inimitable quality.

2. The word means no other wine and does not mean a type of wine.

3. To sell other wines under the name "champagne" is misleading, and whoever does so is trading upon the stupendous prestige which Champenois vine-growers and wine-makers have built up for their wine by their skill and hard work over many centuries.

4. The inevitable consequence of the word "champagne" being used to describe other wines is that an order for champagne becomes ambiguous and detracts from the glamour rightfully attaching to the genuine product.

5. It is thus as much in the interest of the public, particularly of the less educated part of it, as of the producer that the word "champagne" should belong exclusively to the wines of the Champagne district.

The argument of the makers of other sparkling wines runs something like this:

1. The fact that the Champenois use the word "champagne" to describe the wine produced in only one small section of the ancient

province of Champagne and do not use it to describe wine produced in the remainder of the province is proof that even the Champenois themselves attach no geographical significance to the word.

2. Champagne is a generic term which may properly be used to describe all wines resembling those produced in the Rheims-Epernay area no matter where they are made, just as the term eau-de-cologne may properly be used to describe toilet waters of a particular character no matter where they are made.

3. Granted that sparkling wine produced in the Champagne district is of exceptional quality, but the difference in quality between it and good sparkling wine produced elsewhere is so slight that for the Champenois to maintain that theirs is exclusively entitled to the name "champagne" is absurd.

4. Quite apart from these considerations, the producers of the sparkling wine of the Champagne district reap enormous advantage from the word "champagne" being used to describe other sparkling wines. Every time the word is mentioned in connection with other sparkling wines—on wine-lists, in advertisements, in conversation— the produce of the Rheims-Epernay area is given free indirect publicity. This publicity, far from detracting from the glamour that surrounds the sparkling wine of the Champagne district, in fact helped to establish it and continually enhances it.

Some Champenois agree with this last point, and for that reason they suffer only slight rise of blood pressure at the mention of "American champagne" or "Australian champagne". But no one in Champagne accepts the remainder of the argument. There is, in fact, one flaw in it so glaring and of such importance that it may be said to take the bottom out of the entire case. It is simply not true to say that because the Champenois do not call all wine made in the ancient province of Champagne by the province's name the word has no geographical significance. Up to the end of the sixteenth century, the vineyards in the Rheims–Epernay area formed part of a viticultural area called "France" which more or less corresponded with that part of the Parisian tertiary mass which today stretches from Mantes, just north of Beauce,* to the Mountain of Rheims; it included the hillsides round Laon and Soissons but did not include any vineyards south of the Rheims–Epernay area. Late in the sixteenth century those vineyards of "France" which lay in the province of Champagne—i.e. the vineyards

* The ancient name of the area of flat land, famous for the fertility of its wheat-fields, of which Chartres was formerly the capital.

in the Rheims–Epernay area—broke away from the viticultural area of "France" and began to style their wine "*vin de Champagne*". The earliest known reference to the split is in a document dated 1 January 1600 addressed to Henri IV in which La Framboisière wrote: "Among all the wines of Champagne, those of Aï hold first rank in excellence and perfection." "Vins de Champagne" are subsequently mentioned in Acts of Parliament dated 1651, 1652, 1661.* In other words, when it was first used in connection with wine the word "Champagne" had immense geographical significance, as much geographical significance as it has when correctly used today: it meant —and means—a wine produced in the Rheims–Epernay area of the French province of Champagne.

In the final analysis, however, most reasonable people would agree that the Champenois' claim to a proprietary right in the name "champagne" must be judged on a single point: whether or not the sparkling wines of the Champagne district are—and are likely to remain—in a class by themselves as regards quality and perfection. There are many references in the literature of wine to show that connoisseurs in the past have regarded them as such, and a host of anecdotes and stories, of which I will quote only one, which is irresistible. It is said that dining one night at Potsdam with Wilhelm II Bismarck was served German "champagne" or Sekt. He tasted it—and put down his glass. The Kaiser looked at him enquiringly. "Your Majesty," said Bismarck, "I cannot drink German champagne." Wilhelm explained that he had decided to serve Sekt rather than the Chancellor's beloved Heidsieck, not only for reasons of economy, but as a patriotic gesture. "Your Majesty," said Bismarck simply, "I am extremely sorry; my patriotism stops short of my stomach."

Such anecdotes, however entertaining, are in my opinion in many

---

* M. Robert Dion, to whose *Histoire de la vigne et du vin de France*, the most erudite and up-to-date history of French viticulture in existence, I am indebted for the information in the above paragraph, suggests in the same book that the vine-growers of Champagne would never have allowed their wines to be called "*vins de Champagne*" if the custom of blending had not been in common usage at that time, a suggestion which casts doubt on the theory that Dom Pérignon was the first wine-maker in Champagne to blend extensively. It seems to me that it was in the interest of the vine-growers of Champagne to break away from the viticultural area of "France" whether their wines were blended or not, for the simple reason that their wines must have been so much better than those produced elsewhere in the area, and I do not see that the fact that the split took place before Dom Pérignon's time can be used as evidence to show that Dom Pérignon was not the initiator of blending in Champagne.

cases unjustly disparaging to the wines concerned. If you have spent long periods without money to burn, as I have, in countries such as the United States and Germany, which produce their own sparkling wines, venomous references to the failings of such wines seem to indicate a certain lack of sense of proportion in the people who make them. Far better, it seems to me, to cut out the brick-bats and instead record one's own experience of sparkling wines, to compare one's own experience with that of wine-lovers in whose opinion one has confidence, and then to mention one or two technical points that bear upon the quality of sparkling wines.

In the course of my travels I have drunk a great number of sparkling wines. A very few I found really nasty, a few I found very good. The best I have tasted so far was a sparkling wine from the Moselle: it had an excellent bouquet, small lively bubbles and a true golden colour, and its taste was both pleasant and clean. The next best was a *Bourgogne mousseux*, white, of course, and in no way related to purple "Sparkling Burgundy", which is hardly known in France and is sold almost exclusively in the United States and Canada. The third best was a sparkling Vouvray. But much as I enjoyed these three, and many others that I found inferior to them in quality, I missed in them something that is always present in champagne: a delicacy, a roundness, a panache, a touch of aristocratic elegance.

While I have been writing this book, I have had occasion to meet many great connoisseurs of wine whom I have been at pains to question about sparkling wines that I myself have not had the opportunity to sample. All I can say is that, while many of them have told me of sparkling wines which a person with a trained palate can drink with enjoyment, not one of them has wavered from the contention that, as regards quality, champagne stands in a class by itself.

The question remains, "Why is this so?" Of course, the explanation lies largely in the combination of soil and climatic conditions that exists in the Champagne district, and in the care with which the grapes are grown and the wine is made there. All these factors are treated fully elsewhere in this book. Here I merely wish to mention certain other factors relevant to the quality of sparkling wines. It is a curious but incontrovertible fact that, with the sole exception of the wines of the Champagne district, carbonic acid gas has the effect of intensifying a wine's characteristics to that wine's detriment: a poor wine becomes poorer still; the delicate balance of qualities to be found in a perfect wine is upset. For this reason no owner of really great vineyards anywhere in the world would dream of using his grapes to make a spark-

ling wine. Quite apart from the fact that wine-lovers would consider
him a criminal if he did so, he would derive no financial advantage
from the act, the price his wines fetch in a still state being far greater
than anything they would ever fetch in a sparkling state. With the
magnificent exception of champagne, carbonic acid gas may thus be
said to be the enemy of wine. And this fact largely explains why
sparkling wine makers are at a grave disadvantage in their attempts
to rival champagne's perfection. For one thing, their sparkling wines
are nearly always too sweet, either because the grapes that made them
were too sweet in the first place and the carbonic acid gas intensified
that sweetness, or because, in order to cover up the shortcomings of the
sparkling wine which have been intensified by the carbonic acid gas, an
unfortunate amount of sugar had to be added at the last moment. For
another, their sparkling wines are generally bad travellers. Only by
the *méthode champenoise* can carbonic acid gas be incorporated in a wine
successfully enough to enable the sparkle in the wine to survive ocean
journeys and extremes of heat and cold; and when the *méthode
champenoise* is used the difference in price between champagne and
other sparkling wines is negligible, whereas the difference in quality
remains great.

One may safely say, therefore, that sparkling wine manufacturers do
not enjoy the support of the majority of wine-lovers when they claim
that they, too, should be entitled to call their products "champagne".
What the majority of wine-lovers find absurd are claims like the one I
have italicized in this advertisement, which recently graced the pages
of the *New Yorker*:

"Let's face it! This is America's most glorious Champagne. *There's
not a more exciting Champagne on the face of the earth.* A blessed blend of
the world's most exquisite grapes and the infinite patience of man.
Great Western is America's favourite. And the price of this extravagance is the nicest price. For Champagne Party booklet write: Dept.
Y. 10., Great Western Products Inc., Hammondsport, N.Y."

They feel, as the Champenois do, that the only fair solution to the
problem is for the sparkling wines of the Champagne district to be
called "champagne" and for other sparkling wines to be called by a
different name—*vin mousseux*, Sekt, spumante or what have you—just
as the name cognac should by rights only be applied to the distilled
spirit of Cognac wine and not to that of other wines, which can perfectly well be called brandy, Weinbrand, etc. But, however strong this
argument, a long fight was necessary before the Champenois obtained

adequate protection for the name "champagne" in France; while protecting the wine's name abroad has proved—and is proving—an even more formidable undertaking.

The Champenois first went to law on behalf of the name of their wine after a bill was passed by the French Parliament on 28 July 1824 which was designed to prevent the fraudulent misuse of the indications of origin of manufactured products. The suit was brought against a wine-maker who had sold a Vouvray wine as champagne, and judgement was given in favour of the Champenois. Thereafter, French jurisprudence upheld time and time again that only wine composed of the juice of grapes grown in the Champagne district and made there had the right to be called "champagne"; but it was not until 1919 that a French law was drafted dealing specifically with the problems concerning the rightful nomenclature of wines as opposed to those of manufactured products in general.

The reader will recall that in 1911, as a direct result of the Ay riots, the Government had introduced a bill recognizing the existence of four types of sparkling wine—champagne, champagne *deuxième zone*, *vin mousseux* and *vin gazéifié*—but that this bill had not been passed by the Senate when war broke out in 1914. Throughout the First World War, therefore, the legal limits of the Champagne district remained those laid down by the law of December 1908, an area that included all the important Marne vineyards and many unimportant Aisne vineyards, but totally excluded the vineyards of Aube. Hardly had the Armistice been signed than the Government decided to put an end to this anomalous situation: on 27 February 1919 a new bill dealing with the Champagne district's problems was drawn up, and on 6 May it became law.

This law gave prominence to an immensely important and comparatively new phrase in the language of wine. A wine, the law stated, was entitled to an *appellation d'origine*, and the producer of the wine had a right of usage in that *appellation* which could be established and defended in the courts, provided that:

(*a*) factors such as climate, soil and the type of vine traditionally grown in the area where the wine was made played a predominant role in determining the wine's character;

(*b*) these factors allowed an area of production to be defined and limited.

There was never any doubt, of course, about champagne's right to an *appellation d'origine*, but, as the thorny question of the winefield's limits was not settled until some years later, the wine's appellation was still not defined in a sufficiently precise form to enable the Champenois to take effective action against manufacturers of other French sparkling wines who put ambiguous statements on their labels such as "*préparés soigneusement selon les meilleurs procédés champenois*", or Norman cider-makers who gave such names as "Champagne de Pomme" to their products.

The 1919 law contained the same provisions regarding the winefield's limits as the bill drawn up in 1911: there would still be two types of champagne, champagne proper and champagne *deuxième zone*. But the new law contained a proviso which offered the Aubois some hope that the juice of their grapes might one day be allowed to enter a bottle of true champagne again, and would not be for ever condemned to turning out champagne *deuxième zone*. This proviso stated that any person or professional organization which considered that its products were being unfairly deprived of the right to bear the name "champagne" could apply to the Courts for a restitution of that right. In other words, the Government was disclaiming all further responsibility concerning the winefield's limits, and was handing the whole thorny question over to the country's judicial system. This turned out to be remarkably efficacious in bringing about a peaceful and permanent solution of the problem. From 1921 onwards innumerable lawsuits took place between the vine-growers' syndicates of Marne and Aube over the right of Aube grapes to enter into *cuvées* of true champagne, litigation which on 26 May 1925 ended in final judgement being given in favour of the Aube growers.

In 1927 a new law swept away the "champagne *deuxième zone*" designation for good and all. It stipulated that in future only one type of champagne would be made in France and that, subject to certain conditions, the grapes used to make it might come from vineyards situated anywhere in the following area:

Marne Département: all communes of the arrondissements of Rheims, Epernay and Châlons-sur-Marne, plus thirty-five communes of the arrondissement of Vitry-le-François (272 communes in all);

Aisne Département: forty-six communes of the arrondissement of Château-Thierry and thirty-six communes of the arrondissement of Soissons;

Aube Département: seventy communes;

Seine-et-Marne Département: five communes;

Haute-Marne Département: two communes.

The gist of the conditions was that:

(a) Only those vineyards which were already planted with vines at the time the bill became law or which had been planted with vines prior to the phylloxera invasion should be eligible.

(b) The vines in those vineyards should be of one of four types: Pinot, Chardonnay, Arbanne or Petit Meslier. To prevent hardship, a dateline of eighteen years was set before this condition would come into effect.

(c) Local Government-sponsored commissions should be set up immediately within the area to determine the eligibility of individual vineyards; they would be empowered to strike off the list all vineyards situated on flat, clayey ground and on ground overlying micraster chalk, neither of which is suitable for the growing of champagne vines.

Despite the slight cold douche of the conditions (which were directed mainly against them), the vine-growers of Aube, Seine-et-Marne and Haute-Marne naturally hailed this law as a signal triumph. The victory was in fact a real one. The law established the boundaries of the Champagne district almost precisely as they exist today; the only alterations that have been made subsequently have been of a minor character, concerned with the eligibility of vineyards *within* the boundaries laid down in 1927 (the total area eligible is believed to cover between 60,000 and 70,000 acres); and it is unlikely now that the right of vineyards in the outlying areas of the Champagne district to participate in champagne-making will ever be contested again. All the same, a glance at the present-day harvest declarations of these outlying vineyards makes the long struggle and the burning passions it aroused seem a trifle absurd. In 1966 the situation was as follows:

Vineyards in Production

Marne *Département*	33,176 acres·
Aube *Département*	3,709 acres
Aisne *Départment*	1,574 acres*

And, in fact, the contribution of the Aube and Aisne vineyards in recent years was even less than these figures indicate, as a considerable quantity of the harvest declared was not sold to be made into champagne. Time has proved to be correct the contention of the

---

* These figures are lower than the ones given in Chapter 2 as they refer to vineyards in production as opposed to planted vineyards. Of the 44,478 acres of planted vineyards in the winefield only 38,459 acres were producing in 1966.

vine-growers of Marne that their vineyards are the mainstay of the wine-field's fortunes: nowadays their vineyards supply over four-fifths of the grapes that go to make our champagne. Furthermore, within the *département* of Marne the *arrondissements* of Rheims and Epernay reveal them-selves to be the real fount of all Champagne. On average in recent years only communes of the *arrondissement* of Châlons-sur-Marne have de-clared harvests—only one, Vertus, for important quantities; and in the *arrondissement* of Vitry-le-François only two communes have made use of their right to sell their crops to the champagne-makers.

The law of 1927 was merely a beginning. The Government and all thoughtful people in Champagne were aware at the time when the bill became law that defining the winefield's boundaries and controlling the type of vine that could be grown on it, though important steps forward, were not nearly enough; they knew that, if a luxury product like champagne was to survive the economic buffets of the twentieth century, far harsher measures would be necessary. It thus came about that in the ensuing decade Champagne gradually became hemmed in by a positive stockade of special legislation which amounted to what can truly be called a Statute of Champagne, and which made it the most rigorously controlled wine in the world.

In essence, the special legislation had four main aims. The first was to guarantee champagne's purity. As the reader will recall, it was the vine-growers' certain knowledge that unscrupulous firms were import-ing wine from other parts of France to make champagne, at a time when the grapes of the Champagne district were fetching absurdly low prices, that had fanned their smouldering discontent into the flames of the Ay riots. Since then few, if any, firms had dared to import wine from elsewhere expressly for the purpose of making champagne, but, as it was still legally possible to manufacture *vin mousseux* in addi-tion to champagne (as long as the premises where the two types of wine were made were at least the width of a street apart), suspicions naturally lingered that perhaps some of the wine imported to make the *vin mousseux* was finding its way into *cuvées* of champagne. The only possible way of burying such suspicions was to make it illegal not only for *vin mousseux* to be manufactured within the confines of the Cham-pagne district but also for wine to be imported in bulk into the district under any pretext whatsoever; and it was precisely this drastic action that the law took in 1934. The Champagne district thus became—and remains—the only place in the world where the making of *vin mousseux* is forbidden.

The second aim of the special legislation was to ensure that all the champagne sold in the future was of a consistently high standard. An Order in Council dated 28 September 1935 gave legal backing to the old adage that the quality of wine is in inverse proportion to the fecundity of the vine from which it comes. Henceforward all champagne vines would have to be pruned in an approved manner; if they were not, the grapes they produced could not be used to make champagne. To discourage further poor viticultural practice, it was laid down that the juice of only 7,500 kilos of grapes produced by each hectare of vines would have the right to enter a *cuvée* of champagne; any excess would have to be used for distillation purposes or to make *vin ordinaire*. Moreover, only the first 100 litres of juice extracted from each 150 kilos of grapes might be used to make champagne; the rest, being of inferior quality, would have to be consumed as *vin ordinaire* or in a distilled state. The makers were forbidden to sell their champagne for at least a year after the bottling, a restriction which had the effect of ensuring that all the champagne sold in the future would be made with grapes picked at least eighteen months previously. It was also laid down that the minimum alcoholic strength of must to be used for the manufacture of champagne could be fixed each year, just before picking started, by prefectorial decree; this would prevent firms whose concern for the reputation of the wine was nil from incorporating wishy-washy still wines in their blends.*

The third aim was that of endeavouring to bring greater security into the lives of the workers. For decades everyone concerned with the welfare of the industry had recognized that such security would never be achieved without a concerted effort on the part of champagne-maker and vine-grower—and of every other person whose livelihood was connected with champagne—to work together for the common good. But the stumbling block in the way of such co-operation was the incorrigible individualism of the vine-grower; in the post-war period he had proved little more willing to submit to discipline or to work together intelligently with the champagne-maker than he had at the time when phylloxera struck the winefield. In the autumn of 1934, however, even the most thick-headed of the vine-growers had it brought home to them that the existing state of affairs could not continue. For that autumn, as I have related, the huge and excellent crop,

---

* It speaks well for the standards of the profession that seldom has it been found necessary to fix a minimum alcoholic degree. The last occasion was in 1953, when the permitted minimum was 10·5°. In years when no decree is issued, champagne is still bound by the clause in French law which states that a beverage, to qualify as "wine", must possess a minimum alcoholic strength of 8·5°.

the first really big one since the phylloxera invasion, did not sell,
despite the fact that grapes from the *grands crus* were being offered at
fifty centimes a kilo. The cry went up that something must be done
quickly, before the next vintage. Done it was—and in a manner that
proved as efficacious as it was original. The following autumn, eight
days before the vintage began, there assembled in the Champagne
district—and there has assembled at that time of the year ever since—
a committee composed of an equal number of representatives of the
champagne Houses and the vine-growers and one representative of the
Ministry of Agriculture; their mission was to fix the price the grapes
would fetch. The efficaciousness lay (*a*) in the presence of the Third
Man, the Government representative, as in the event of the other
members of the committee failing to agree he was empowered to take
the decision himself; and (*b*) in the ruthlessness inherent in the decision
itself: henceforward, only champagne made from grapes for which the
agreed price had been paid would qualify for the appellation "champagne". The originality lay in the method of compulsion employed—
economic rather than judicial.

The committee was appointed by an organization which was
brought into being at the instigation of the winefield by the Order in
Council of September 1935. The full title of the new organization was
Commission Spéciale de la Champagne Viticole, but it soon became
known as the Commission de Châlons, because its meetings were
held at the Préfecture at Châlons-sur-Marne. It was virtually a little
parliament, composed of representatives of the champagne Houses,
the vineyard owners, the local Chambers of Commerce and local
government officials, the Ministry of Agriculture and the Treasury.
It was the forerunner of the present day Comité Interprofessionel du
Vin de Champagne, of which more anon.

The fourth aim of the special legislation was to prevent the customer
from being defrauded. Henceforward the corks of all champagne
bottles would have to be marked with the word "champagne" on that
part of them actually inserted in the bottle: the purchaser would thus
have only to glance at the cork, after pulling it, to know whether or
not the champagne was genuine. The makers were also placed under
the obligation to print the word "champagne" in prominent characters
both on their labels and on their packing cases. Decrees empowered
champagne-makers to go to law against manufacturers of other
sparkling wines who used in any context whatever such misleading
terms as "champagnisé" and "champagnisation". Champagne-makers
also had the right—and they use it—to litigate against confusing,

ambiguous or impertinent descriptions such as "*Grand Vin récolté hors Champagne*", "*Champagne de Cognac*", "*Sirop de Champagne*", "*Bière-Champagne*", "*Cidre-Champagne*", "*Grenadine-Champagne*", "*Lait-Champagnisé*" (sic), "*Limonade-Champagne*", "*Madère-Champagne*", "*Vermouth-Champagne*" and "*Vichy-Champagne*" (the examples given had all actually been used by some smart alec of a manufacturer or another). And it was laid down that a restaurateur could be prosecuted for listing *vins mousseux* under the heading "champagnes" on his wine-card. Restaurateurs were also constrained to list the still wines of Champagne under a separate heading, "*vin non-mousseux originaire de la Champagne Viticole*",★ to make the distinction perfectly clear.

The law continued to permit champagnes to be sold under the name of fictitious or non-existent firms, titles of nobility, etc., with appropriate crests and mottoes, as long as the labels conformed in other respects with the regulations. Such wines ("Champagne Henri IV", for instance) are made by the smaller firms, never by the Grandes Marques. When their labels bear no indication of who put them on the market, their cheapness is often more remarkable than their quality; when, however, the name of a reputable wine merchant figures on the label below the fictitious one, the wine merchant's reputation is involved, and the respectability of the champagne can be taken on trust. The consumer can always inform himself of the provenance of a champagne by glancing at the "N.M." or "M.A." (followed by a number) which the law requires to be printed in small type at the bottom of the label: the "N.M.", standing for "*Négociant Manipulant*", signifies that the champagne was made by the firm whose name figures on the label; the "M.A.", standing for "*Marque d'Acheteur*", signifies that the name figuring on the label is not that of the firm or person who actually made the champagne. In theory, there is nothing to prevent any champagne-lover from approaching a firm which specializes in the manufacture of Buyer's Own Brand champagne (as such wines are termed in the parlance of the British wine trade) and arranging for a consignment of his chosen champagne to be labelled with his own surname.

An Order in Council dated 30 July 1935 created a new category of French wine, one possessed of an "*appellation d'origine contrôlée*". These were wines, like champagne, whose excellence depended not just on simple factors such as climate and soil and the type of grape grown, as was the case with a wine entitled to a plain *appellation d'origine*, but on

★ Time proved this designation to be excessively cumbersome and the law was modified to allow the still wines of the Champagne district to be labelled "Vin Nature de la Champagne".

far more complicated factors such as the way the wine was made, the manner in which the vines were pruned, the maximum quantity of grapes a vineyard was allowed to yield, and so on—upon precisely that type of refinement which constitutes the Statute of Champagne. The same Order in Council brought into being a Government-backed organization called the Institut National des Appellations d'Origine des Vins et Eaux-de-Vie. Within a few months of its formation the Institute started to determine which of the wines and brandies that already had the *appellation d'origine* were entitled to be *contrôlée*, and to establish the conditions of production that would have to be adhered to in each case; and then it proceeded to see that the regulations were enforced. Later the laws relating to each wine entitled to either an *appellation d'origine* or an *appellation d'origine contrôlée* were codified and issued in a publication called the *Code du Vin*.

One of the most important results of the Institute's work, as far as the Champenois were concerned, was that the many different types of sparkling wine which France produces in addition to champagne were classified, and the designations they must bear were decided upon once and for all. This, briefly, is the situation as it exists today. In a category by themselves stand the sparkling wines that have an *appellation d'origine*. They are:

Bordeaux mousseux

Bourgogne mousseux

Blanquette de Limoux mousseux
Vin de Blanquette
Gaillac mousseux

Anjou mousseux
Montlouis mousseux
Saumur mousseux
Touraine mousseux
Vouvray mousseux

Arbois mousseux
Côtes du Jura mousseux
L'Etoile mousseux

Clairette de Die

Saint-Péray mousseux

Savoie mousseux

Seyssel mousseux.*

With the exception of three of them, the *méthode champenoise* is compulsory.

In another category are the sparkling wines that have no *appellation d'origine*. In all circumstances their labels must carry the words "*vin mousseux*". Finally, there are the slightly sparkling or semi-sparkling wines of France, what the French call *vins perlants* or *vins pétillants*.

As a result of these arrangements, the name of champagne may be said to have been protected completely and for all time in France itself. The position abroad, however, is far less satisfactory.

During the late nineteenth and early twentieth centuries repeated attempts were made, by the various nations concerned, to protect the appellation of their manufactured products by international legislation, but none of it was foolproof. The Treaty of Madrid, signed in 1891, laid down that goods imported under a false appellation should be seized; but several of the signatories—including Great Britain—either failed to ratify it, or did so in such a fashion that its provisions proved useless.

France, with her huge range of wines, cheeses, *pâtés* and the other unique products of her generous soil, probably stood more to gain than any other country from an acceptance on an international basis of the principle of the right of proprietorship in appellations—and more to lose if it was not accepted; and she was not only willing but determined to take swift and effective action to ensure that her appellations conformed with reality. It was to some extent as evidence of this determination that on 6 May 1919 the French Parliament gave its blessing to the law which not only ushered in the concept of *appellations d'origine* for French wines but also dealt with the problem of the delimitation of the Champagne district in such a way that it was finally solved by 1927.

The main reason, however, why the bill was drawn up and passed with such tremendous speed was that the Treaty of Versailles was going to include guarantees concerning appellations, and it was vital that French law should be clear on the subject beforehand. In the Treaty Germany engaged to take the necessary steps to guarantee the products of each Allied nation against all forms of disloyal commercial competition, and undertook to prohibit the import or export of all products and

---

* Only when regulations allow it may *appellation contrôlée* wines be rendered sparkling and sold as such: you can render a Chablis wine sparkling but you may not sell it as Chablis mousseux; you may sell it only as "Bourgogne mousseux", Chablis being a Burgundy wine.

merchandise carrying names and inscriptions which were false indications of the origin, nature or quality of the product. Similar clauses were written into the peace treaties with Austria, Hungary, Bulgaria and Turkey. And never since has the word champagne appeared on a bottle of German, Austrian, Hungarian, Bulgarian or Turkish sparkling wine. German and Austrian sparkling wines have ever since been called "Sekt"; in the other three countries, the equivalent in each country's language of the words "sparkling wine" has been used.

During the twenty years that elapsed between the two World Wars several more nations ratified the Treaty of Madrid, and others signed commercial treaties with France that included guarantees concerning wine appellations. By the time the Second World War broke out more or less adequate protection had been arranged for the name "champagne" in the following countries: Albania, Belgium, Brazil, Bulgaria, Canada, Cuba, Czechoslovakia, Denmark, Finland, Germany, Greece, Guatemala, Holland, Hungary, Ireland, Italy, Lebanon, Luxembourg, Monaco, New Zealand, Norway, Poland, Portugal, Rumania, Spain, Sweden, Switzerland, Syria, Tunisia, Turkey, United Kingdom and Yugoslavia.

This was a considerable step forward; on the other hand, it left much to be desired. Neither the United States nor the U.S.S.R., the two largest producers of sparkling wine in the world, had displayed the slightest willingness to enter into agreements concerning the protection of champagne's name; nor had Australia and South Africa, both of which had flourishing sparkling wine industries; nor had Argentina and Chile, both potentially big producers of sparkling wine. Besides, even in those countries that had ratified the Treaty of Madrid or had signed appellation agreements with France cases of the misuse of the word "champagne" were by no means rare. From 1935 onwards the Champenois—and all makers of *appellation d'origine* wine—had a powerful ally in the Institut National des Appellations d'Origine, because one of the Institute's duties is to be on the outlook for infringements of the rights of French wine appellations in countries where they are protected and to institute proceedings against the offenders. (It is also the Institute's duty, it is well to add, to take action against French firms which misuse foreign wine appellations that are protected in France.) The Institute soon found out, however, what French winemakers had already discovered—that going to law abroad can be a discouraging business, because the laws of other countries, and their attitude towards matters concerning wine and spirits and appellations in general, are often quite different from those of France.

CHAPTER 16

THE SECOND WORLD WAR

IT WAS AS well that such tremendous efforts were made in the 'thirties to settle all these difficulties, for as a result the champagne industry was in a far stronger position to face the ordeals of the next six years. For the outbreak of the Second World War brought the sales of champagne to a grinding halt. Expecting invasion hourly, most firms walled up part of their cellars and hid away their best *cuvées*—plus a car or two. That autumn considerable quantities of champagne were sent off to neutral America and even to Great Britain, but throughout the "phoney" war sales in France remained very quiet.

When the German tanks started to roll, on 10 May 1940, they entered France via Champagne. Nearly all the champagne-makers closed down at once, those in Rheims having no alternative, as the French High Command ordered a total evacuation of the city. Many of the heads of the firms, many of the workers too, left for south-west France, joining that general exodus from Paris and the north which turned out to be the bitter prelude to an even bitterer defeat. Never again, I have heard it said, will a Champenois leave his home when invasion comes, because, although getting away was difficult enough, getting back, without regular train services, without petrol, in many a case without money, proved a positive nightmare. All the champagne-makers experienced the greatest difficulty in regaining possession of their offices and cellars, and weeks went by before the muddle was sorted out.

During the invasion the German armed forces helped themselves to much of the champagne that was ready to drink in the unguarded cellars, but after the surrender the occupation authorities put a stop to all that. They wanted the production of champagne to continue, under their strict control, of course. With this end in view Herr Klaebisch, a member of a Rhineland family long connected with wine, was appointed Führer of Champagne, with offices at Rheims. The news of his appointment was received with a certain relief by most people, for, if you were going to be shoved around, it was better to be shoved around by a wine-maker than by some beer-drinking Nazi lout. But

very soon the reams of paper that issued from the Führer's office foretold how bleak the future was to be. Sales to civilians were forbidden
without authorization. Between 300,000 and 400,000 bottles were to be
dispatched each week to the German armed forces on all fronts,
priority to be given to the demands of the Luftwaffe and the Navy.
All this at a time when the vineyards damaged during the invasion
needed repairing, when there was a serious shortage of manure and
fertilizers, when the labour force both in the vineyards and in the
cellars was greatly reduced.

As the months went by the German demands grew daily more
imperative, and little by little the champagne-makers began to realize
that the only hope of saving their precious stocks lay in facing the
German authorities with a united front. It thus came about that on
12 April 1941, thanks largely to the persuasive influence of Comte
Robert-Jean de Vogüé and M. Maurice Doyard, representing respectively the interests of the champagne-makers and those of the vineyard
owners, the Commission de Châlons was disbanded and its duties were
taken over by a new organization, the Comité Interprofessionel du
Vin de Champagne, with headquarters at Epernay. Precisely how
the C.I.V.C. works I shall explain in the next chapter; suffice it to
say here that the power granted it by champagne-maker and vineyard
owner alike (much greater than that vested in the Commission de
Châlons), and the discipline which it imposed on them, proved during
the days of occupation, as they still do today, to be of immense benefit
to the winefield.

From then on most of the problems that arose were thrashed out
between the Führer's office and the C.I.V.C., and the individual
champagne-maker was to a large extent relieved of day-to-day
wrangles with the Germans. Soon the C.I.V.C. obtained a concession:
permission was granted for about a quarter of the winefield's annual
production to be sold to civilians in France, Belgium, Sweden and
Finland. Concessions were few and far between, however, and the
C.I.V.C. had to act with extreme caution, for if the Germans suspected
that their designs were being resisted, reprisals were swift and severe.
Nevertheless, regardless of the consequences, resistance was mounting
in many firms. It might only take the form of a cheeky remark.
"Remember the Wehrmacht is your best customer," the Führer's
representative would say. "Maybe our biggest, but not our best," the
champagne-maker would answer. Or it might involve risks punishable
by death. Some firms, I am told, when ordered to dispatch a shipment
to, say, Hamburg, used so to arrange matters that it turned up at, say,

Homburg—or got lost altogether; others would purposely put bad corks in the bottles, pretending they had no others; others composed *cuvées* destined for the Wehrmacht with their poorest wines and hid their good ones. When the Germans arrived to investigate a firm suspected of such goings-on the management would be terribly, terribly sorry, but a pipe had burst or the Marne had risen, and, not wishing to mess up their beautiful shiny jack-boots in a flooded cellar, the Germans—with luck—would go away. Not that they ever displayed much enthusiasm for visiting champagne cellars during the occupation; they were afraid of meeting the fate of Fortunato, the hero of Poe's *Cask of the Amontillado*, who was walled up alive in the eerie catacombs of the Montresors.

One day late in 1942 Comte Robert-Jean de Vogüé, the chief delegate of the champagne-makers on the C.I.V.C., accompanied by his young assistant, M. Claude Fourmon (now *directeur commercial* of Moët & Chandon), and his cousin, M. René Sabbe, who was acting as his interpreter, drove from Epernay to Rheims to attend a meeting at the Führer's office. Hardly had the meeting begun than the Führer was called to the telephone. When he returned he said: "I am sorry, gentlemen. That was the Gestapo on the 'phone. You are under arrest." The news of these arrests was received with indignation in Epernay and Rheims, but when it became known that Comte de Vogüé had been condemned to death for obstructing the Germans' demands a wave of revolt swept through the Champagne district. Protests poured into the Führer's office, among them a joint one from sixteen firms— who were fined the equivalent of £100,000 for their trouble. The death sentence was never revoked, but eventually, at the behest of the German military authorities, who dreaded civil unrest in France at a time when every available unit was needed on the Russian front, it was indefinitely deferred. Both Comte de Vogüé and M. Fourmon spent the rest of the war in concentration camps; M. Sabbe was freed after a term of imprisonment.

In the course of the next two years several other chiefs of the champagne Houses and many employees were arrested by the Gestapo on some pretext or other, and deported. In 1944 two of the leading firms—Moët & Chandon and Piper Heidsieck—were heavily fined and their management was taken over by the Germans. In the middle of August 1944 a complete trainload of champagne left Rheims for Germany; had the Liberation been long delayed, and had the supply of bottles improved (the shortage had recently made it impossible for the firms to fulfil all the Germans' compulsory orders), the greater part of the stocks in the cellars, if not the whole lot, would have disappeared to the Reich.

An even worse threat hung over the cellars of Epernay at this time, I am told. The Germans had stored away in the town a great quantity of dynamite, and it was apparently Himmler's intention to give the order for the cellars to be blown up if it became necessary to evacuate Epernay, the motive of his diabolic design being, presumably, to give German Sekt-makers a headstart in the post-war period. When one remembers that it was only through the intervention of the Swedish Consul-General in Paris, Raoul Nordling, and the humanity of General von Choltitz that a similar threat to blow up Notre-Dame, the Sainte-Chapelle, the Invalides and the Bibliothèque Nationale was averted, one can well believe that Epernay escaped this fate by the skin of its teeth. The saviour in Epernay's case was General Patton, whose 3rd Army swept into the town on 28 August 1944, taking the Germans completely by surprise. Epernay will never forget General Patton; it was the hope of the inhabitants that he would return to the town to accept their homage, but before that could be arranged he was involved in a car accident and went to join his fallen comrades-in-arms in the American Military Cemetery at Hamm in Luxembourg.

As soon as the Germans had left, the champagne-makers tore down cellar-walls behind which a surprising quantity of champagne that was ready to be drunk lay hidden, and sent off the wine to bolster the morale of the Allied Armies, whose lightning advance across France and Belgium had been halted, and who were now faced with the prospect of a dreary winter of static warfare on the western banks of the Rhine. That winter of 1944–5 was not an easy one for the Champenois; they were short of food, very short of fuel. It was evident that years would go by before things returned to normal. The province had suffered greater damage during the war than any other French province except Normandy, mainly from bombing.

One of the worst hit spots in Champagne was the military camp at Mailly, situated in the centre of *Champagne pouilleuse*. During the build-up of the Allied forces in Normandy in 1944 two citizens of Epernay—one a massive policeman, the other a diminutive hunchback —bicycled night after night from Epernay to Mailly and back, a total distance of fifty-five miles, in order to keep track of the arrival of the Von Stauffen division, which was concentrating at Mailly before being moved to the Normandy front. As soon as the concentration was complete the news was passed on by the Resistance to London, the camp was solidly bombed for eight hours, and nearly the whole division, 10,000 strong, was wiped out. Another place which suffered badly was the village of Rilly, on the northern slopes of the Mountain of Rheims. Why Rilly, with a population composed almost entirely of vine-growers, suddenly became a target of Allied block-busters was a complete mystery to the majority of its unfortunate inhabitants: only after the Liberation did it become generally known that the Germans had been using the tunnel through the Mountain of Rheims, which the Rheims-Epernay railway enters at Rilly, to store V2 rockets. The proprietors of the Hôtel des Berceaux at Epernay, however, had already guessed that the tunnel was of vital interest to Allied agents. One night, watching the village being bombed from a vantage point on the roof of the hotel, in the company of a French couple who had been their guests for months and who made a habit of going up on the roof to watch bombardments, they heard the husband refer to a cloud as *"une nuage"* instead of *"un nuage"*, a mistake which no Frenchman would have made; later they learnt that their surmise was correct and that he was a British agent married to a Frenchwoman.

During the winter of 1944–5 a great number of Champenois learnt with amazement of the extent to which the resistance movement had developed around them without their knowing much about it, for the need for secrecy had, of course, always been paramount. Many of the stories concerned people connected with the champagne trade; many concerned railway workers in Rheims and Epernay and Châlons-sur-Marne, for, until the fortunes of war turned in the Allies' favour and an invasion of the Continent was imminent, *cheminots* were in a much better position than others to worry the Germans—by blowing bridges, slowing down troop movements, etc. Nowhere in Champagne does more eloquent testimony exist to the price that was paid for this resistance than on the Monument aux Morts which stands today in the Place de la République in Epernay. Embedded in the concrete stele lies a black urn with the words Buchenwald, Dachau, Mauthausen, Auschwitz and Ravensbrück painted on it; listed on the four faces of the stele are the names of 208 citizens of Epernay who gave their lives for their country.

CHAPTER 17

MODERN TIMES

By JULY 1945 the last of the Champenois prisoners-of-war and deportees had come home. That autumn, in time for Christmas, a shipment of 50,000 cases of champagne was sent to England, the first for over five years. By the following spring a semblance of normality had returned to the winefield.

There were people in Champagne, however, who viewed the future with profound pessimism. Looked at purely from the short-term point of view, the situation did indeed seem pretty grim. The finances of a number of champagne firms, even of some of the bigger ones, were in a precarious state. All the firms were desperately short of wine, partly because of the extent of the compulsory sales to Germany (75 million bottles in all, it was reckoned), partly because the crop of 1940 was virtually missing (it would have been a bad year anyway, but the damage which the vines suffered during the invasion, and the trying circumstances in which the picking was conducted, made the situation infinitely worse), partly because hardly any replanting of vines had taken place during the war—and senile vines produce far fewer grapes than vines in their prime. In fact, there was only one aspect of the short-term future that was encouraging. This was that the quality—although not the quantity—of the champagnes made with the 1941, 1942 and 1943 crop of grapes, now quietly ageing in the cellars, was excellent, superlatively so in the case of the 1943s.

But it was not so much the short-term prospects of the winefield that worried people as the long-term ones. The whole of Western Europe had emerged from the war in a desperate economic plight. It was touch-and-go whether France and Italy turned Communist or not; even Great Britain was flirting with Socialism; monarchies were falling like ninepins; an iron curtain was being raised across Central Europe; austerity was the order of the day in nearly every country on the planet. A very different world from the pre-war one was being born, a world in which it seemed unlikely that there would be a place for luxuries like champagne. There appeared to be only one ground for optimism: America had come through the war richer and stronger than ever; she was now "wet" again, and wide open as a market for champagne.

The prophets of doom were confounded, however. In 1950, less than five years after the war, the sales of champagne amounted to over 32½ million bottles, a figure that exceeded the average annual sales of the 'thirties and equalled those of champagne's most triumphant decade previously, 1900–10; in 1954 44 million bottles were sold, 7 million more than in 1937, the record year to date in the wine's history; and in 1966 sales reached the astounding total of 86 million bottles. The post-war years have turned out to be the most prosperous, the balmiest, the winefield has ever known. The figures speak for themselves:

Total Sales of Champagne since the Second World War

Year	Bottles
1945	21,792,376
1946	24,851,092
1947	22,421,696
1948	29,281,056
1949	28,522,898
1950	32,612,196
1951	35,221,667
1952	30,528,561
1953	30,366,899
1954	32,977,780
1955	37,706,826
1956	44,304,197
1957	48,400,000
1958	40,702,291
1959	42,270,073
1960	49,265,501
1961	54,187,849
1962	57,919,726
1963	64,018,259
1964	70,204,695
1965	78,621,036
1966	86,887,944*

* Compared to the 400 million bottles of Scotch whisky and the 400 million bottles (at least) of *vin mousseux* that were sold in the world in 1966, this figure is not very large. Nor can the champagne industry, with recent annual sales valued at around £60 million, be compared with the real giants of the French economic scene. Nevertheless in recent years the value of its sales was greater than those of any other *appellation contrôlée* winefield, including Cognac, over twice those of the perfume industry and over three times those of the Haute Couture industry.

What happened? Why, at the time I write, is the Champagne district selling more wine than ever before in its 2,000 years of history?

Without doubt, the main reason is that the wine-drinking countries of the world are enjoying unprecedented affluence. As the purchasing power of the consumer grows, it is normal for the sales of a luxury product like champagne to rise. Prosperity draws the corks.

Another reason is that far more people are visiting the Champagne district today than ever before. In pre-war days visitors to Moët & Chandon's cellars, for example, numbered roughly 5,000 annually; today they number over 100,000. In this age of cheap and swift communication the winefield's proximity to Paris and to densely populated Belgium, coupled with the fact that it lies on the main roads from the Channel ports to Switzerland and from Germany to Paris, is proving of inestimable advantage in attracting the custom of Frenchmen and foreigners.

Another reason is that the replanting of vineyards which had fallen into disuse has continued apace: over 10,000 acres have been brought back into service since the end of the war.

Yet another reason is that, since the war, the vines have been producing unusually bountiful crops. There have been bad years, of course: 1957, for example, which was so bad that the makers had to cut down on the amount of champagne which they allowed out of their cellars. But there have been superlatively good ones too: 1947, 1949, 1952, 1953, 1955, and then the memorable trio of 1959, 1960, 1961, which in 1961 enabled the makers to do what they had never done before— release for sale over 50 million bottles in a single year. (One firm, in a lyrical publicity hand-out about the 1961 crop, announced that the 270,000 casks which the wine would fill, if placed end to end, would cover the distance from Paris to Brussels.) The 1963 vintage was the largest since 1934. Although the quantity of grapes that the vines produce over a given period always depends primarily on weather conditions, the unusual bounty of the crops in the post-war period is explained to some extent by (a) the fact that, apart from the six years 1934–1939 (I do not include the war years because of the abnormal conditions that prevailed), the decades in question have been the first since the 1890s when the whole winefield has been producing; between the 1890s and the early 1930s there were always some vineyards whose vines were unproductive owing to the ravages of phylloxera or whose normal rhythm of production was interrupted by the switch from non-grafted to grafted wines; (b) the efficiency of modern methods of pest and disease control; (c) the success of the measures taken to protect particularly vulnerable vineyards against spring frosts.

But it would be wrong to attribute the present prosperity of the winefield to external causes alone. Much of the credit belongs to the post-war generation of champagne-makers. When the war ended there were many firms whose cellars and offices, whose sales and production methods, had changed little since the turn of the century (largely, it is only fair to add, because there had hardly been time to recover from the First World War before the economic depression set in, and hardly time to recover from that before the Second World War broke out). The spirit with which some firms set about modernizing themselves—and their ideas—was truly dynamic, and their example, in the main, proved contagious.

A good deal of the phenomenal rise in sales during the post-war years is due to increased consumption at home, as is shown by the figures below:

Sales in France since the Second World War

Year	Bottles
1945	17,000,000
1946	11,000,000
1947	13,000,000
1948	19,000,000
1949	18,240,602
1950	19,439,113
1951	20,750,839
1952	18,651,060
1953	19,477,929
1954	22,153,428
1955	25,773,214
1956	31,278,718
1957	35,705,008
1958	27,587,354
1959	28,731,117
1960	35,356,579
1961	38,659,873
1962	42,484,190
1963	46,831,453
1964	52,050,368
1965	58,192,955
1966	64,847,515

Export figures, however, give the Champenois much less cause for satisfaction. Before 1914 exports represented two-thirds of the total sales, in the 1930–40 decade one-third, and today only a quarter. These are the figures:

Export Sales since the Second World War

Year	Bottles
1945	3,748,215
1946	12,690,500
1947	8,778,595
1948	10,416,834
1949	10,282,296
1950	13,173,083
1951	14,470,828
1952	11,877,501
1953	10,888,970
1954	10,824,352
1955	11,933,612
1956	13,025,479
1957	12,717,111
1958	13,114,937
1959	13,538,956
1960	13,908,922
1961	15,528,976
1962	15,435,536
1963	17,186,806
1964	18,154,327
1965	20,428,081
1966	22,040,429

The table below shows that the Champenois have genuine cause for disappointment as regards many of their export markets: the twelve markets listed take between them three-quarters of the champagne exported:

	1961	1962	1963	1964	1965	1966
Great Britain	4,217,574	4,294,952	4,797,943	5,337,528	5,181,185	5,489,878
U.S.A.	2,706,551	2,802,330	2,708,453	3,084,393	3,478,522	4,122,875
Belgium	1,471,223	1,601,096	1,757,924	1,929,926	2,429,297	2,670,655
Italy	1,155,999	1,516,340	1,906,847	1,280,562	1,617,351	2,206,103
Federal Republic of Germany	731,456	903,874	891,976	964,002	1,201,797	1,108,162
Switzerland	541,497	692,812	646,864	712,639	811,162	856,508
Holland	248,578	277,368	298,755	338,594	370,971	409,897

Canada	243,791	278,105	166,292	292,426	350,623	405,040
Venezuela	176,188	172,188	220,381	297,203	411,720	367,945
Sweden	279,361	265,077	356,500	297,754	362,038	283,018
Denmark	182,794	179,954	155,529	222,917	244,587	244,584
N.A.T.O. Forces in Germany	148,425	169,321	184,738	205,160	232,062	241,129

Great Britain, though still the best export market of all and increasing her purchases yearly, only buys in an average year just over half what she did in 1897 (9½ million bottles).* The United States, the richest country in the world, buys little more annually than the 3 million bottles she took in 1913 (no doubt partly because of the average American's preference for hard liquor, and partly because the country makes its own sparkling wines and therefore imposes a very severe duty on champagne). Neither Canada nor the Scandinavian countries buy as much as their standard of living suggests they could afford. And in many another of the 150 or so countries to which champagne is exported progress is impeded by quotas, luxury taxes or crushing duty. There are even some countries, most of them behind the Iron Curtain, where no champagne is sold at all, and is only to be found in the cellars of the Diplomatic Corps. In fact, just about the only foreign country with whose purchases the Champenois have reason to be entirely satisfied is Belgium. Little Belgium, which developed a love of good wine while linked to Burgundy by the Hapsburg Crown and has never lost it, is now what Chile used to be before the First World War: the country that drinks more champagne per capita than any other in the world.

Quite a large slice of the credit for the present prosperity of the wine trade must be given to the Comité Interprofessionel du Vin de Champagne. This body, it will be recalled, was founded in 1941, at one of the darkest moments in the winefield's history. In the bill which brought it into existence its mission was defined as follows:

(i) To establish and maintain a record of the resources and needs of the winefield.

(ii) To organize and control both the production of champagne and

* By the late 'forties, the duty in Britain on imported table wine had increased to 4s. 2d. In his 1949 Budget Sir Stafford Cripps reduced it to 2s. 2d., but not on wines, like champagne, that are imported in bottle. In his 1960 Budget Mr. Selwyn Lloyd corrected this anomaly, but in 1964 the duty on a bottle of champagne was raised to 4s. 8d., in 1965 to 5s. 2d. and in 1966 to 5s. 8d. In 1967 it was reduced to 5s. 5½d.

its distribution at home and abroad, with the constant aim of ensuring that honest and traditional practices are adhered to and that quality is maintained.

(iii) To organize and discipline the relations between the various professions.

(iv) To take action designed to keep the market supplied in years of under-production and in a healthy state in years of over-production, with a view, as far as possible, to maintaining stability in the price of grapes and of the finished article.

(v) To decide the price to be paid and the method of payment in transactions between growers and producers, also the remuneration of intermediaries.

(vi) To lay down the general conditions that export contracts must fulfil and to control the quality of exports.

(vii) To institute a system of professional licences.

(viii) To draw up each year the budget necessary to the efficient functioning of the organization.

It was not to be expected that every one of these provisions would please the independent-minded Champenois. "What—me, Auguste Dupont, vineyard owner from father to son since 1580, allow myself to be organized and controlled by some official? Never!" "Supply facts and figures about my business—over my dead body!" "Champagne-makers to be licensed? Who do they think we are—brothel-keepers?" But this was 1941, no time for pettiness. And in the immediate post-war years, when the organization might have been expected to fall apart under the strain of the inevitable tug-of-war between *négociant* and *vigneron*, it did not, principally because its architects had invested it with so much real power that its position was impregnable.

The power of the C.I.V.C. derives from the fact that it is a semi-public organization. The twin foundations upon which its administrative structure rests are the Union des Syndicats du Commerce, to which every one of the 144 champagne-making establishments belongs, and the Syndicat Général des Vignerons, whose members represent every shade of opinion among the vineyard owners. Neither Syndicat plays an active role in the organization in a corporate sense, but their two Presidents and the four chosen representatives of each of them (five *négociants* and five *vignerons* in all) constitute what is known as the Commission Consultative of the C.I.V.C. As its name suggests, the function of the Commission Consultative is to express approval or

Spraying the vines with
insecticide

Spraying by motorized
vaporizers

An early morning scene during the picking

The forecourt of a *vendangeoir* at vintage time

disapproval of concrete proposals submitted to it. These proposals may come from three sources: from one of the nine Commissions which are responsible for specialized branches of the winefield's activities and upon which sit representatives of all the professions connected with the winefield;* from the Commission Permanente, which is composed of the two Presidents of the Syndicats (its duty is to deal with routine business and make policy decisions); or from the Commissaire du Gouvernement. He is appointed by the Minister of Agriculture, and in his hands is concentrated the entire executive *power* of the organization. But if the proposals come from this last source it can only mean that the two most important professions represented—*vigneron* and *négociant*—have failed to agree on some major question affecting the winefield. For although the Government Commissioner really is all-powerful, he was never meant to interpret, and never has interpreted, his role to be that of a dictator, but rather as that of an arbitrator and a conciliator in case of need. In fact, as long as everything is going smoothly—and everything, I am assured, has gone smoothly in recent years—he rarely feels compelled even to visit the pleasant offices of the C.I.V.C. in the Maison de Champagne in Epernay's rue Henri Martin. His mere presence in the background of Châlons-sur-Marne is enough to ensure that *vigneron* and *négociant* will find a workable solution to the problems of the winefield.†

The State has a finger in the C.I.V.C.'s financial pie to the extent that the organization is authorized to raise its own revenue, and the sum to be raised figures as a supplementary Estimate in the Government's annual Finance Bill. The two main dues are raised as follows:

1. A tax on the value of the crop of grapes, amounting on average to between 1 per cent and 1·5 per cent, with the burden distributed according to a percentage rating between the vineyard owners and the firms that buy grapes.

* Members of the Commissions include vineyard owners, champagne-makers, owners of pressing establishments, sales agents of the wine, personnel employed by the vineyard owners and champagne Houses, transport agents, glass-makers, case- and carton-makers, makers of straw and papier mâché envelopes, muzzles and tin-foil, and manufacturers of products used in the culture of the vine.

† In the event of an infraction of one of its rulings the C.I.V.C. can impose the following penalties:

(*a*) Fines.

(*b*) Temporary withdrawal of the culprit's *carte professionelle*.

(*c*) Confiscation, to the profit of the State, of all or part of the products or commodities that are the subject of the dispute.

(*d*) The temporary closing down of the culprit's establishment.

2. A tax on the sale of bottles.

Recently, annual receipts from these dues have amounted to between 4 million and 5 million francs. Only a quarter of this sum is required to meet the running expenses of the C.I.V.C. The remainder finances the organization's manifold activities, which cover, broadly speaking, five different spheres: the commercial, legal, social, technical and economic.

In the commercial sphere, the organization's concern is to enter into any course of action that will help the sales of champagne to expand. It studies and reports on export markets, negotiates commercial agree-. ments with foreign countries and is active in the fields of publicity and public relations.

In the social sphere, the C.I.V.C.'s concern is the betterment of the lot of the inhabitants of the winefield. Annual grants are made for such purposes as aid to injured workmen, the granting of scholarships, the support of homes for the sick and elderly and the maintenance of a *colonie de vacances*.

Technically, its responsibility is to see that the winefield's resources are used and developed to the best advantage, and to help *négociant* and *vigneron* to solve all the problems that arise. It passes on to the *vigneron* in the simplest possible form details of new ideas and techniques, organizes and finances co-operatives for grafting and cuttings, drafts and supports plans for the replanting of vineyards that were pulled up during the phylloxera invasion, and gives financial help. In its own experimental vineyards the C.I.V.C. tests new manures, fertilizers, insecticides and fungicides, and is for ever trying to find better methods of combating such enemies of the vine as hail and frost. In its laboratories analyses of grape-juice and wine are made without charge, and research is always going on into such subjects as microbiology and the illnesses of wine. And at Avize, on the Côte des Blancs, there is a school for future *vignerons* and *négociants*.

So far as the law is concerned, the C.I.V.C.'s concern is to defend and strengthen the Statute of Champagne, and in particular to uphold the appellation "champagne" at home and abroad. Since its foundation it has taken six major steps to strengthen the Statute. In 1945 it sponsored a law making it illegal for champagne to pass through the French Customs unless accompanied by a Certificate of Origin; this ensures that foreigners have a formidable additional guarantee that the champagne they buy is the genuine article.

It has also tidied up the vexed question of the Gamay vine. In 1927 vineyard owners in Aube, whose plots were planted with the Gamay, were given until 1945 to switch to the traditional vines of the Champagne district. It was found necessary, on humanitarian grounds, to extend the dateline to 1962, and widows and *mutilés de guerre à plus de 80 pour cent* are still exempted, with typical French magnanimity towards people in straitened circumstances; but apart from this the change-over is already almost complete, and little more than 200 acres of Gamay vineyards remain.

In 1948 a law sponsored by the C.I.V.C. rendered the export of must and of the still white wine of the Champagne district illegal. This was done for one reason and one reason alone: someone, somewhere (no names, no pack-drill), had imported the still white wine of the district, pumped carbonic acid gas into it and sold it as "champagne".

In 1949 a decision of capital importance was taken. A Commission was set up within the C.I.V.C. to guarantee the quality of champagne for export; unless the Commission is satisfied with the quality, they can refuse the Certificate of Origin. This was followed in 1952 by a law which laid down the most stringent regulations as to exactly what was required of a champagne if it was to be sold as a vintage wine.

Finally, in 1955 the C.I.V.C. tightened up the regulations concerning the production of *vin ordinaire* in the winefield. Since kingdom come, there had been nothing to prevent a vineyard owner from cultivating the noble vines of Champagne in part of his plot and pruning them in the correct manner so that their produce was eligible for appellation, while devoting the rest of the plot to plebeian vines which would be consumed by the family or sold as *vin ordinaire*. The law merely constrained him to vinify the grapes of the two varieties of vine separately—a freedom of action that invited sculduggery. Under the new regulations plebeian vines are still permitted (although discouraged) in the winefield,* for the purpose of producing *vin ordinaire*, but no longer may they hob-nob in the same plot with their nobles: a single vine of plebeian origin in a plot of Champagne vines is cause enough for the whole crop to forfeit the right to the appellation. Furthermore, not only must anybody who cultivates both noble and plebeian plots send the two crops to separate press-houses, but the return made out for the crop of the plebeian plot must show it to have been at least 10 per cent more prolific than the noble one, if wine made from the latter is to be granted the appellation. This last proviso ensures that

---

* Certain varieties of vine, however, notably the Noha, the Isabelle, the Jacquez, the Clinton and the Herbemont, are prohibited altogether, on account of the disagreeable "foxy" taste of the wines they produce.

there has been no jiggery-pokery over the pruning of the noble vines, because the latter, pruned correctly, invariably produce a smaller crop than their commoner brethren.

In its task of upholding abroad the appellation "champagne", the the C.I.V.C. works closely with the Institut National des Appellations d'Origine. Since the war there have been many instances in many different lands of the two organizations themselves bringing or helping others to bring court actions against misuses of the appellation,* but none of these attracted a fraction of the publicity that surrounded the "Spanish Champagne Case" in London in the late 'fifties. The plaintiffs were the twelve Houses which were then the leading suppliers of champagne to Great Britain. The defendants were a British firm, the Costa Brava Wine Co., which was selling under the name "Spanish Champagne" a Spanish sparkling wine produced at the castle of Perelada near Figueras. In November 1958, in the Central Criminal Court of the Old Bailey, a jury acquitted the defendants, but two years later the plaintiffs took the case to the High Court, and this time judgement was given in their favour. The Costa Brava Wine Company was restricted by injunction from ever again selling Perelada under a name that included the word "champagne", and was ordered to change its labels within forty-eight hours.

This ruling, delivered as it was in the country that consumes more champagne than any other apart from France itself, is undoubtedly the most important step forward which the winefield has achieved in the post-war era in defence of its appellation. But there remains one gaping lacuna in the protective arrangements: the United States. What is so absurd is that without a shadow of doubt the Champenois *could* have achieved complete protection for their product in the United States at the beginning of the century. In the years 1905–6 the United States Congress made a painstaking study of cognac, which resulted in an definition identical in almost every detail to that given later by French wine law. But at that time the Champenois were at odds among themselves about the definition of the winefield's boundaries—and so the chance of a lifetime was missed.†

---

* The I.N.A.O. has also fought several successful actions in recent years to stop Frenchmen misusing foreign appellations, including that of "Scotch Whisky".

† In addition to helping the C.I.V.C. to protect the appellation abroad, the I.N.A.O. has a further duty towards the winefield. By the late 'forties it had become evident that the settlement, supposedly final, regarding the eligibility of individual vineyards to be included in *Champagne viticole* (see sub-paragraph "c", page 205), had resulted in certain errors, omissions and injustices; and in 1951 a

Finally, we must consider the C.I.V.C.'s concern in the economic sphere. This, in essence, is to maintain stability in the price of grapes in the face of the inevitable instability, as regards quantity and quality, of the vintages. The organization has tackled the problem from five different angles.

First and foremost, it has taken upon itself the responsibility of deciding each year precisely what price the grapes shall fetch. On the eve of the vintage an equal number of delegates of the two main professions, *vigneron* and *négociant*, meet to thrash out the price, and just in case they should end by thrashing each other the Préfet of the Marne, representing the Minister of Agriculture, is there in person to keep the peace and—in extremis—to make the decision himself. The search still goes on for the perfect basis on which to reach agreement, but so far none fairer has been found than that of relating the price to be paid to the current average price of a bottle of champagne. The Champagne district is believed to be the only winefield in the world where a minimum price is fixed by law, and where the right of the grapes to the appellation is dependent on this price being paid.

Secondly (this was done in 1945), the C.I.V.C. has drastically overhauled the traditional classification of the vineyards, on which the price is based. The ingenious point about the classification is that at the time of the vintage only one figure has to be agreed upon, that of the price to be paid for grapes in the *catégorie hors-classe*. The price paid for grapes in the lower categories follows automatically on a percentage basis. Grapes from the *première catégorie*, for instance, are paid for at the rate of between 90 per cent and 100 per cent of the agreed sum, while those from the bottom category fetch only 60 per cent of the agreed sum. (The growths in the first five categories are further sub-divided, allowing for slight variations in price within their percentage ratings.)

law was passed empowering the I.N.A.O. to make the necessary adjustments.

The first thing the I.N.A.O. does, when asked to classify a piece of ground as forming part of *Champagne viticole*, is to call for the most stringent documentary proof of vines having been planted on it prior to 1927; the testimony of other vineyard owners is not accepted as evidence. It then convenes a local commission of enquiry, composed of experts, to report on such factors as aspect, the nature of the soil and the sub-soil, altitude, etc. If this report is favourable, and if the Syndicat Général des Vignerons gives its assent, then, and then only, will the request be granted.

The Champagne district is the only winefield in the world in which the traditional use of a plot of land as a vineyard is the controlling factor in determining the plot's eligibility; the I.N.A.O. fulfills a similar function in all the other major French winefields, but in them factors such as soil and aspect alone count.

These percentage ratings by category explain why the Champenois often refer to a "such-and-such per cent vineyard". What they mean is that the vineyard is in a category rated at, let us say, 75 per cent, and that, if the price of grapes that year is fixed at 3 F. a kilo, the amount per kilo the owner of the vines in that category will receive is 2·25 F. The new classification seems to be generally accepted as fair, and applications for a vineyard to be upgraded are rare.

Thirdly, the C.I.V.C. encourages—and, in a crisis, might compel—*vignerons* and *négociants* to sign long-term sales and purchasing agreements, usually of eight years' duration. In this way the *vigneron* is assured of a sale in a year of overproduction, the *négociant* is assured of being able to procure grapes in a year of underproduction, and neither side has much justification for grumbling if this year's price of grapes is related to last year's price of a bottle. In a year when there is a gross shortage of grapes, the C.I.V.C. institutes a rationing system, allotting each House a quota on the basis of the number of bottles it sold the previous year.

Fourthly, the C.I.V.C. encourages, and if necessary finances, the creation of co-operative stocking establishments (*cuveries*) equipped to receive grapes, put them through the first fermentation and then conserve the still wine until such time as the Houses are in a position to buy. The aim is to give the *vigneron* every possibility of putting into reserve at least half his produce in a year of superabundance, to await sale in the year of paucity that cannot, by the law of averages, be long delayed. Before the war thirty such co-operatives existed: today they number over a hundred.

Lastly, the C.I.V.C. is responsible for an insurance fund which compensates the *vigneron* for any losses he may have sustained through circumstances beyond his control. This fund has enabled many a *vigneron* to repair damage that his property had sustained during the Evacuation, the Occupation and the war; recently it generously compensated those who had suffered the horror of having their year's work rendered profitless by a hail storm.

The founders of the C.I.V.C. considered that the action which the organization would take towards maintaining stability in the price of grapes would be its virtual *raison d'être*. Certainly its work in this direction has already been crowned with enormous success. Where fluctuation, speculation and uncertainty once prevailed, stability is the order of the day. And, what is perhaps most important of all, the *vigneron*—inevitably the weaker of the two principal partners in the champagne-making process—has been given a new deal. Experts consider that a situation like the one in which the *vigneron* found himself in the early 'thirties is practically inconceivable today. The most eloquent testimonials to the success of the C.I.V.C. are the thirty other similar organizations in France for which it has served as a model. They are concerned with a multitude of products ranging from semolina, olive oil, cider, linen and sugar to tartar, perfume, wood and other wines.

Not, I might add, that absolutely everyone is enchanted with the C.I.V.C. all the time. The poor Champenois *vigneron* is now the most regimented of any in France. "Life's impossible," I've heard him say, "what with filling up forms and you can't do this and that . . . high time we had another 1911!" And champagne-makers fret a bit too; now and again they even threaten to resign. The trouble is that they can't resign, unless they have the law changed—and that would take some doing.

What of the future of Champagne—the province and the product? Plans are already afoot to make Rheims a city of a million inhabitants before the close of the century, to meet the crying need for a town of major importance between Paris and the metropolises of the Ruhr; in many other towns in Champagne, too, bright industrial zones are being created to which, it is hoped, Parisians, fed up with the tensions of big city life, will be attracted. The province is also likely to benefit from people's disenchantment with another bugbear of twentieth-century life—overcrowded, soulless holiday resorts—for Champagne is still itself, still truly part of *vieille France*.

As for the winefield, it will surely produce a little more champagne as time goes by, because there are still many thousands of acres where vines once grew and which are thus entitled to the appellation, but which are at present used for other purposes. The expansion will be very slow, though; the *vigneron*, remembering the early 'thirties, wants to be quite sure that he can sell more grapes before he replants, and the *négociant* wants to be quite sure that the resulting grapes are up to standard. Still more champagne could be made if someone discovered a method of stamping out phylloxera—what a challenge for the young entomologist!—because grafting reduces a vineyard's average yield. *Izvestia* recently announced that the Institute of Scientific Experiment for Fertilizers and Insecticides, in collaboration with the University of Moscow, had invented a substance called Perchlordivynil which had kept phylloxera at bay in Moldavia for two years. So perhaps there is hope in this direction. A hint, too, of possibilities to come was given when it was announced that engineers of the Atomic Energy Commission at Peck Rouge are studying the uses of radioactive elements in viticulture.

As for the wine, there is many a market awaiting conquest or reconquest by the champagne-maker of the future who possesses the enterprise of his forebears—Russia, China, Japan, emergent Africa. Two things are certain: no other wine has so consistently preserved its quality in the post-war world, and none is more likely to do so in the future, thanks to the Statute of Champagne. In the ups and downs of their lives, it is a fair bet that our descendants will have champagne exactly as we know it, to sustain them with its immediacy, its brightness, its gentle gaiety.

PART IV

THE CULTURE OF THE VINES

CHAPTER 18

THE CREATION OF A CHAMPAGNE VINE

A VINE CAN, of course, be created by planting a grape-pip in the soil, but this method of reproduction is rarely used in Champagne or anywhere else, for two reasons. First, a grape-pip does not "take" easily. Secondly, a vine raised from a pip seldom resembles the parent vine: it usually takes after some remote, primitive and much inferior ancestor.

From time immemorial the viticulturist has produced new vines either by layering or by planting cuttings removed from the healthiest, most prolific vines in his vineyard. As the reader is already aware, however, the first of these methods is impractical today because phylloxera would irreparably damage the roots thrown out by the branch and cause the new vine to die; and the second method can only be employed if, prior to planting, the cutting is grafted on to another cutting taken from a vine of American ancestry, resistant to phylloxera, so that the roots of the new vine develop from the American half of the plant. In Champagne this grafting operation takes no less than sixteen months.

The so-called *vignes-mères* which provide the cuttings for the roots are no longer of pure American stock: they are almost all Franco-American hybrids. It took nearly forty years of intensive study and experiment to produce them. As soon as it was realized that the native American vine was resistant to phylloxera, French viticulturists and botanists studied all the native vines that were already being cultivated in America, as well as many varieties that lived only in a wild state in the forests. Eventually they singled out three varieties which would live in grafted harmony with French vines in the soils and climates of France, and imported them; these were the *Vitis riparia*, the *Vitis rupestris* and the *Vitis berlandieri*. They then set about producing sub-varieties, by intermarrying the American varieties with certain French ones which were more or less resistant to phylloxera. The result is that the modern viticulturist has literally hundreds of Franco-American hybrids to choose from, and he can select the one most suited to the species of French vine which he grows and to the climate and soil of his vineyard.

In view of the vital role which the Franco-American hybrids play in the creation of modern Champagne vines, I decided to visit one of the centres where they are grown. I timed my visit for December, as that is the month when the cuttings are taken and dispatched to Champagne. The firm to which I was introduced was the Maison Gendre, at Quissac in the *département* of Gard (nearly all the *vignes-méres* vineyards are situated in Southern France). They have been vine suppliers since 1879 and today, in addition to a large clientele in France, they have customers in Switzerland, Germany, Luxembourg, Algeria, Morocco, Lebanon, Syria, Israel, Jordan and the Argentine. Quissac lies in the former silk-producing area of Basse-Cévennes, twenty miles west of Nîmes, thirty miles north of the Mediterranean. The mulberry trees have now entirely disappeared, and today the inhabitants of this gaunt and desolate hill country, with its pale grey villages, orange-roofed houses and blood-red soil, earn their livelihood almost exclusively from the olive tree and the vine. As I drove out from Nîmes, I readily understood why the Champenois like to come here to obtain their *vignes-mère* cuttings: it was mid-December, yet there was a baking sun and the windows in the villages were wide open.

After a short stop at the Maison Gendre's ranch-style offices, I was taken out in a jeep to inspect the vines. My escort was soon pointing out the vineyards to me; but, when I looked in the directions he indicated, all I could perceive were huge areas of stony, barren hillside broken here and there by a white, red-tiled wall, or a single row of cypresses leading to a rustic graveyard. At first I thought I must be misunderstanding his French, so I kept quiet; later I kept quiet because I decided that my companion must be deranged: there simply were not any vineyards where he said there were. Eventually we turned off the road on to a track, in order, my escort insisted, that I should see the vines at close quarters. Not until he stopped the jeep did it dawn on me that we were indeed in a vineyard, that it was I who was the crazy one. For I had been looking out for neat rows of vines raised high off the ground by stakes and wire: it had not occured to me that here, where the vines are grown to produce cuttings, they would be growing in their natural form, with their shoots sprawled across the ground in wild abandon. The dark red shoots, all at least twenty feet long, covered the ground in such profusion that hardly any soil was visible, and they were quivering in the breeze like the tentacles of monstrous octopuses.

We watched the twenty-foot cuttings being taken (the work starts as soon as the leaves have fallen from the vines), and then we drove to a nearby village to see them being prepared for the journey to Champagne. Around three sides of a high-walled farmyard, open sheds with corrugated iron roofs had been built, and in these a regiment of women, wearing scarves on their heads and long dark blue aprons, were nimbly wielding secateurs to cut each shoot into three-foot lengths. Other women were lugging the bundles of twenty-foot shoots off the lorries and dragging them under their arms across the farmyard to the shed: they looked like witches riding colossal broomsticks. On the return journey they carried bundles containing 200 cut-up shoots tied together with leather straps, and deposited them on other lorries waiting to whisk them off to Champagne.

The cuttings spend the winter in storage in Champagne, for the grafting season is not until April. Upon arrival they are soaked in water, as the journey dries them up. Sometimes cellars are used to store them, but any clean place suffices, as long as it is protected from draughts and sheltered from the sun, which in the spring might cause the tissues to dry up. Wherever they are stored, fine sand is placed on top of them to retain the moisture.

In February the vine grower takes from the Champagne vines the cuttings on to which the Franco-American cuttings are to be grafted, and stores them beside the Franco-American cuttings. His choice as to which vines are to provide the cuttings was made the previous autumn, a couple of weeks before the vintage, when, by inspecting the quality and quantity of the grapes, he was able to judge of what stuff each vine was made. He singled out those vines that were yielding the juiciest bunches and, provided their shoots were sufficiently thickened (*aoûté*), indicating that they were well filled with reserve matters, and provided the diameter of the shoots was suitable (between half and three-quarters of an inch), he marked them, either on the stump of the vine or on the shoots themselves, with a blob of paint. Some of the vines he was probably marking for the second or third year running, so persistently excellent had been their performance. Vineyard workers known to be *très sérieux* are always entrusted with the selection in the autumn because it is a highly responsible job and, as a *maître-vigneron* said to me, "*Il ne faut pas regarder les avions*". The actual cutting must always be done in February before the sap has begun to rise in the vine and before the buds have made the slightest movement.

During the last week in March both lots of shoots are removed from storage and transferred to the building where the grafting is to be done. The Franco-American shoots are totally immersed in cold water, to cause the sap in them to rise; the French shoots, whose sap may lie dormant for the time being, are stood in cold water about an inch deep. A few days later the Franco-American shoots are taken out of the water and cut into lengths of just over seven inches, one bud being left at the bottom of each. The French shoots are cut up the day grafting is to take place. Each length must measure approximately two-and-a-half inches, and the cut must be made half an inch below a bud; they are then deposited in a tub of cold water, to remove any dirt that may be clinging to them.

Supplies of each type of cutting are now placed on a table in front of the grafter. He selects a Franco-American shoot and searches in the pile of French shoots until he finds one of precisely the same diameter. Next, with an instrument known as a *greffoir*, which resembles a pocket-knife with a slightly curved blade, he slices off the ends of both shoots at a forty-five degree angle. Then, very carefully, he makes a shallow incision in the sloping ends of each shoot. These incisions are so placed that when he joins the shoots together they dove-tail into each other and become one.

Grafting is a surgical operation which requires much skill. To be considered an expert, the grafter must be able to produce about 1,500 perfect grafts a day. Until comparatively recently women were employed on the work, and the Champenois' innate gallantry makes him a little vague in his explanations as to why today the job is done almost exclusively by men. He points to the weals on the men's fingers, caused by the *greffoir*, but the true explanation, I believe, is that a far higher standard of grafting is required nowadays, and men have been found to be more gifted at the job than women.

At Moët & Chandon's grafting establishment at Fort Chabrol, where the art of grafting the Champagne vine was brought to perfection at the beginning of the century, no less than 860,000 grafts are produced in an average year.

To the naked eye, the join in the graft is invisible; only by exerting pressure on both ends of the graft and feeling the "give" is it possible to tell that a join has been effected. But, firm though it looks, in reality it is just as tender and fragile as a join performed on a human bone. If it is to hold, no time must be lost in forcing the sap in the lower part of the graft to rise up into the upper part so that an indissoluble link of veins and fibres is created between them. Warmth is required, and as this is unavailable in April it must be produced artificially—in a hothouse heated to 30°C. But elaborate precautions must first be taken to ensure that the grafts do not dry up and disintegrate in such heat. They are therefore placed in the hothouse in boxes made of poplar, a wood that is particularly resistant to humidity. The boxes, which hold 1,500 grafts, are packed with the greatest possible care, each layer of grafts being separated by a layer of intensely porous peat that has previously been soaked in water. The peat is imported from Holland, and will hold five times its own weight in water. As a further precaution against drying-out some very fine oak sawdust, which has been dampened, is placed over the join in each graft before the peat is applied; and when the box is full a thick layer of the same sawdust is spread over the top so that the grafts are completely covered up. When the box is carried into the hothouse, to be placed on a shelf there, it looks like a small coffin.

The boxes remain in the hothouse for ten days. The covering of sawdust is then removed, and it can be seen at once how many of the grafts have "taken": there sticks out of the peat, from each healthy graft, a tiny white leaf. What the grafts need now is sun and rain and fresh air, to fill them out and make them grow and turn their leaves green, but if they were put out in the open straight away they would die of cold. So the boxes spend five to six days in a greenhouse heated to 25°C., and a further week in an unheated greenhouse. Just over three weeks elapse, therefore, between the arrival of the shoots at the grafting establishment and their departure as grafts.

They are bedded out some time between 1 May and 15 June, ideally after 15 May, by which time the danger of spring frosts is over.

Many small vineyard owners use their back gardens for the purpose, but the big champagne Houses maintain special nurseries. These are always situated near a little river or brook, as the grafts need plenty of damp to quench their thirst. They have healthy appetites, too, so the nurseries are generally on flat ground, where the soil is richer than on a slope. In the weeks that precede the bedding out the nursery is ploughed, then toned up with manure, phosphatic fertilizer and if necessary fresh earth.

On the day the bedding out is to take place the grafts are removed with great care from the peat-filled boxes, placed in small wooden cases designed to hold between 200 and 300 at a time, and transported to the nursery by lorry. Awaiting their arrival at the nursery which I visited near Epernay were about thirty temporary workers—middle-aged men in overalls, young girls sporting yellow coolie hats and teenage youth in dungarees—all set to earn a few extra sous by planting. A warm spring sun was shining brightly, and as the work got under way the scene took on an animation reminiscent of the vintage: temporary workers always indulge in non-stop cheerful banter which contrasts markedly with the more stately comportment of the professional vineyard worker.

Meanwhile, the preparation of the nursery has been going on. The soil has been loosened by a fuel-powered rotavator which somewhat resembles the old-fashioned type of carpet sweeper. The operator propels it up and down the length of the nursery, and, provided he exerts considerable pressure on the shaft handle, a very fine tilth is obtained.

The day before bedding out is to take place, six-inch-tall wooden stakes are inserted two feet apart at the top and bottom of the nursery, to mark the intervals between the rows to be planted. As soon as the rotavator has passed by, string is attached to the stakes, and, guided by these, men armed with forks proceed to excavate little trenches two inches deep beside them. The trenches are then generously watered.

And now, kneeling on wooden boards laid beside the trenches, the workers proceed to stick the grafts into the soil. Hardly more than the width of a man's finger is left between each graft. Another watering is immediately administered, this time from a watering-can, as a more powerful jet might injure the grafts. Finally a man hoes each side of the row to bank up the soil against the grafts. He finishes the job with his hands. All that remains visible of the graft is the wisp of foliage.

Ramrod straight, packed close together in an alignment which would do credit to a Guards regiment, with their brace of miniature leaves sprouting gaily above them like little hats, the grafts suddenly assume a cocky air, and it no longer seems incredible that these small pieces of wood, which before they were planted looked rather like long thick pieces of brown asparagus, will one day turn into great vines.

All summer long the grafts remain in the quiet meadow or the vine grower's back garden, gaining in strength and vigour. They are particularly susceptible to mildew and other ills, so in humid summers they may have to be sprayed with copper compounds every day; in a normal summer spraying once or twice a week suffices. The vine grower also has to water them frequently and remove all weeds the instant they appear. In July, by which time the grafts are perhaps a foot tall and possessed of considerable foliage, he proceeds to what is known as a *sevrage*: this consists of removing any little radicles that may have grown on the upper half of the graft near the join; if allowed to develop they would prevent the graft from devoting all its resources to strengthening the join.

The grafts are left undisturbed until their leaves fall off in the autumn. In some years this does not happen until late November, when a hard frost can make it practically impossible to uproot the grafts. In any year this is a very tricky job, requiring much patience and careful handling; sufferers from lumbago avoid it like the plague. Thick corduroy trousers and woollen mufflers are always much in evidence.

The uprooting process is begun with a specially designed plough which has two prongs that cut into the ground about six inches deep on either side of the grafts. The plough is pulled by a cable attached to a winch, but a horse waits patiently at the end of the meadow to return it to the starting-point. The function of the prongs is to cut the roots of the grafts; if they were not cut, they would be too firmly entrenched to render possible the removal of the grafts. Next a man goes along the row, putting his fork firmly but carefully into the ground beside the graft to loosen the soil. He is followed by a colleague who grasps the graft firmly below the join and pulls it gently out of the ground. He puts the grafts that have "taken" on one pile; those that are dead, just dried up pieces of wood, he places on another pile.

After the uprooting the grafts, which are now known as plants, are tied together in bundles and taken to a workroom for sorting. Most of them have by this time grown to a foot in length, some to over two feet. The top (French) halves are swishy, elastic; the bottom (Franco-American) halves are slightly thicker and straighter, and end in bulbous stumps from which the rootlets hang down.

The sorting, on the grey November day when I watched it, took place in an outhouse of a farm in Grauves. We made our way to the building past rows of rabbit hutches, through an army of clucking hens and on through the farmhouse kitchen where a huge and welcome log fire was blazing. The main object of the sorting is to ensure that the join in the plant is good and firm. Sitting in front of low wooden trestle tables, the workmen were exerting pressure on each join with their fingers; if it resisted and remained firm under the pressure, the plant was passed as fit; if it fell apart, the plant was discarded and used as firewood.

It is considered satisfactory if, out of every hundred grafts that are bedded out in a nursery each spring, thirty are in fit condition to be planted in a vineyard the following spring; in a bad year the number may be as low as twenty-five; seldom does it exceed forty. Which goes to show how terribly difficult it is to graft a vine successfully in a northern climate.

After any small shoots that have grown above the join have been removed, the accepted plants are collected together in bunches of fifty, secured top and bottom with wire, and sent away to await planting in the spring. Since the new vineyard cannot be planted until April, the plants are meanwhile bedded out in a thin soil at some convenient spot where they are well protected from winds and frost. Just before planting takes place they are inspected once more, the join is tested and the roots are trimmed.

That is how a champagne vine is created today. Sixteen months have gone by since the cuttings for the roots were taken in the Midi, and the attention lavished on the grafts has cost many thousands of man-hours of labour, many a chill and many a sore back. All this on account of a louse that somehow or other ferried itself across the Atlantic in the 1860s.

CHAPTER 19

THE NEW PLANTATION

IN THE CHAMPAGNE district, where the vine only flourishes in a strictly limited number of localities, the rotation of crops is out of the question. Vine succeeds vine in a Champagne vineyard, and has done so for centuries. The vine grower cannot, however, just pull up a senile vine and plant a new one in its place; he has to let the ground rest in between plantations, and during this rest period he must do everything in his power to instil new life into the soil.

The vine is capable of attaining an age equal at least to that of the oak. Pliny mentions one that lived for 600 years, and there are stories in both Champagne and Burgundy of vines that lived for 400 years. Today, however, the average vine in Champagne has outlived its usefulness after twenty-five to thirty-five years. The main cause of this short life-span is the grafting operation necessitated by the presence of phylloxera in the vineyards; however skilfully the grafting is done, the scar prevents the sap from mounting perfectly, and this results in the premature enfeeblement of the vine. Another cause is the mechanical plough: the vine is submitted to shocks it never had to suffer in the olden days, and often the roots are cut or damaged. The old French vines used to live for at least sixty years, frequently for much longer.

Once it has been decided that a vineyard needs renewing, the vine grower's first task is to remove the stumps of the old vines and as many of the roots as will yield to pressure. He does this as soon as he can after the vines have produced their last crop of grapes, usually in October, November or early December: later in the winter the hardness of the ground would render the job practically impossible. Even in the late autumn the job is no sinecure. When a vine has been in the ground for between twenty-five and thirty-five years, its roots are embedded in the soil and subsoil with a vicelike grip, and enormous strength is required to uproot the stump. The usual procedure is, first, to scoop out a great hole round the stump with pickaxes and crowbars, and then to haul out the stump with a chain harnessed to a horse or a winch. Even when a winch is used there is always a mighty tug-of-war before the roots snap or yield, and sometimes several hours of intense effort are required to uproot a single stump.

No matter how carefully the stump is removed a certain number of roots invariably remain in the ground, and this fact has a bearing on the length of time a vineyard must rest. For, since they are covered with thick protective tissues and are rich in reserves of sap, the roots go on living long after the stump is removed: in chalky soil they continue to live for between five and six years, in a clayey soil for between eight and ten years. And as long as they remain alive they attract to themselves fungi and bugs which are injurious to the soil and would soon kill a fragile young vine.

Twenty years ago no satisfactory method existed of hastening the death of the old roots, so it was not unusual for ten years to elapse between the pulling-up of the old vines and the planting of new ones. Today, however, chemicals specially developed for the purpose enable the vine grower to kill off the old roots prematurely, and as a result the rest period which a vineyard requires has been reduced, on an average, to three or four years. The best months for the injections to be administered are September and October, which generally means that they have to be postponed until the autumn following the removal of the stumps, the vine grower being too busy in September and October with his newly-made wine to cope with the removal of the old vines and the injections as well.

In the days when a vineyard had to rest for nearly a decade between plantations, it was customary to grow clover, oats, lucerne or even, sometimes, potatoes in it during that period. Now that the rest period is much shorter, and because the cost of labour is so high, the planting of such crops is seldom considered worth while. The ground is generally left fallow and merely turned once a year to keep weeds at bay.

The summer before the vineyard is to be replanted three major operations take place, each aimed at the improvement of the soil. First, a layer of fresh earth—largely composed of the Tertiary debris whose magic properties I described in the opening pages of this book —is laid on the vineyard. The earth is brought down from the forests in lorries as soon as the mud on the vineyard tracks has hardened, and is dumped in great piles all over the vineyard; the spreading of the piles consumes much time and labour.

Secondly, the vineyard is given a heavy ploughing. This is usually done nowadays with a specially-designed plough, drawn by a powerful tractor; one man drives the tractor, another guides the plough. On very steep slopes a lighter plough and a winch are used.* Both

* The hillsides of the vineyards are seldom steep enough to render terracing necessary. In the years to come such terracing as does exist is likely to disappear

the driver of the tractor and the man guiding the plough need to be acrobats if the job is to be done with dispatch; so great is the resistance which the plough meets in the soil that it is continually being jerked up into the air, and even the tractor, given half a chance, behaves like a bucking bronco. Behind the plough follow a team of men who collect together the old roots and place them in piles to be burnt. Sometimes a root which has not been killed by the chemical injections turns up, and it is astonishing to see how throbbing with life it still is, despite years spent with no direct contact with the air: its fibres are the colour and consistency of underdone roast beef.

Apart from ridding the vineyard of old roots, the main object of *défoncement* (as the heavy ploughing is called) is to aerate the soil and make it easier for the root systems of the young vines to take rapid possession laterally and vertically. The roots resemble the hidden portion of an iceberg: that part of the vine which is above ground and visible is never allowed to ramify to nearly the same extent as the part which is below ground. They establish themselves at many different levels. At an advanced age some roots attain a length of forty feet, and have forced themselves deep into the subsoil; in them the circulation of the sap is slow. The more active roots are near the surface: they are more active because they are younger and because they are in closer contact with the air, with the rain that falls on the soil and with the manure and fertilizers that the vine grower puts into the soil.

The third major operation that takes place during the summer preceding the replanting is the manuring of the vineyard. The deep furrows caused by the ploughing help the manure to penetrate the soil. Natural manure is always used, and is applied lavishly. Phosphatic fertilizer is also administered.

In the late autumn, before the advent of hard frost, preparations for the actual planting begin. First, the stakes to which the young vines will be tied are inserted. These are made of wood or of iron; wooden ones are cheaper, but are more difficult to maintain. The wood must be hard—acacia, chestnut, fir or pine. The height of a stake is generally between two-and-a-half and three feet.

altogether, for a curious reason. When the ground is heavy, a horse pulling a plough is physically incapable of working up an exceptionally steep slope; in the course of the descents, much of the soil at the top of the slope is carried down by the plough. Consequently, in the olden days there was no alternative but to terrace an exceptionally steep slope so that ploughing could take place on the level. With a modern tractor or winch, however, ploughing can be done uphill; soil that has slid down is carried up again; and terracing is no longer necessary.

The insertion of the stakes is extremely exacting work: *"on doit être bon vigneron"*. The slightest error in alignment will not only destroy the disciplined look of the vineyard but, far more important, will increase the risk of machines damaging the young vines as they pass between the rows. The aligning is done with string and long pieces of wood with nails knocked into them at whatever distance apart the stakes are to be inserted.

Experience has proved that vines in the Champagne district produce the best results when planted fairly close together; within reason, competition for whatever riches the soil may contain suits them. The most usual spacing allowed between each row of stakes is 1 metre (just over three feet) in a Pinot vineyard and 1 metre 20 in a Chardonnay one. The distance apart allowed in line is usually between 1 metre and 1 metre 20 for the Pinot and between 1 metre 20 and 1 metre 50 for the Chardonnay. The more lavish foliage of the Chardonnay needs room to spread itself. When the stakes are inserted at a distance of one metre apart, they number 10,000 per hectare (4,000 per acre).

As soon as the stakes are in, a hole is dug beside each one to receive the vine. The holes have to be fairly big to allow the vine to be surrounded by an ample quantity of manure when it is planted. The application of the manure takes place in March, when the hard frosts are over.

By April, having rested for three or four years, the soil should be in perfect condition to accept the young vines.

The vine grower's main concern at the time he plants a vine is to ensure that it will receive a plentiful supply of water; while its tissues are forming, a vine has an almost unquenchable thirst. For this reason, he sprinkles some very light earth on top of the manure with which he lines the hole; and before he plants he checks to see that there are no stones or pebbles in the hole, which might obstruct the penetration of water towards the roots. For preference, he does his planting in April —even, sometimes, in late March—rather than later in the spring, because the last rains of winter can then be counted on to keep the light earth round the roots damp. As he places the plant in the hole he makes sure that the join is exactly at ground level.

Once the vine is in the soil three and a half summers elapse, on an average, before it yields its first full crop of grapes. Some vines take four years to bear their first crop, particularly those grown on very chalky soil.

Throughout these years of non-production the grower's efforts are aimed at developing vigorous vines, capable of bearing rewarding crops for many years to come. Grafting, followed by transplanting, has inevitably enfeebled the vines; infinite care and attention are required to turn them into strong, healthy adults.*

There are four ways in which the grower helps the vine through these difficult years. First, he keeps the earth round the stump banked up; by so doing he protects the join in the vine from the sun, and at the same time he artificially lowers the level of the vine's root system. Secondly, he gives the vineyard continual hoeings, both to kill weeds and to help the flow of water to the roots. Thirdly, he takes endless care to protect the plants from pests and diseases, spraying them with fungicides and insecticides at least two or three times a week during danger periods. Finally, each October he practises a careful *sevrage* on each vine. *Sevrage*, it will be recalled, consists of snipping off the radicles which develop on the upper (French) portion of the plant. Once the vine is in the vineyard these radicles, if allowed to develop, would not only consume sap but would also establish themselves in the soil. This the grower must avoid at all costs, because the top half of the vine is vulnerable to attack from phylloxera, and if phylloxera obtained a grip on an extremity of this top half the whole vine would die and have to be pulled up.

In the course of the vine's third spring in the ground, the grower attaches its shoots to the wires between the stakes; by then the vine should be on the verge of producing its first crop of grapes. But, despite all his efforts, the grower will be lucky indeed if all the vines which he planted three years previously have developed perfectly. Nearly always a certain number have failed to "take", have become stunted and must be replaced.

A modern grafted vine reaches its zenith, from the point of view of the quality of its grapes, in its tenth year; by its fifteenth year it is becoming middle-aged. Such brevity in the productive life of the vine today adds considerably to the cost of champagne.

* Were it not for the fact that the Petit Meslier fares particularly badly after grafting in a northern climate, the Champenois might well grow this vine more extensively. Its grapes produce an excellent white wine which has a bouquet all its own: that the bouquet should be so singular is not surprising, in view of the fact that the Petit Meslier is responsible for the highly perfumed Sautérne wines. The only vineyard where it is grown today in any appreciable quantity is at Venteuil in the Marne valley.

CHAPTER 20

THE ANNUAL CYCLE OF GROWTH
OF THE VINES

THE NATURE AND timing of the vine grower's labours are inextricably linked with the seasonal development of the vines, so, before describing the annual cycle of work in a mature vineyard, I give a brief description of the vines' annual cycle of growth.

All winter long the vines rest. Their branches are bare and sapless: the sap has retreated to the centre of the plants and into the roots. In January, when snow carpets the ground, the stark geometry of the rows of naked vines reminds one of the clinical harshness of a Buffet painting.

The vines do not become active again until the soil reaches a temperature of about 9°C. This generally occurs, in Champagne, late in February or early in March. Thenceforward, they require between 162 and 200 days to reach their full development. This period is divided into eleven distinct phases.

The Weeping (Les Pleurs). The signal that the vines have finished their winter rest is a discharge of liquid from the wounds caused by the pruning of the vine shoots the previous spring. This liquid is pure sap, and sometimes it flows abundantly until the wounds heal. It is the greyish-white colour of melted sugar, and very sticky. In olden days the tears of the vine were believed to have valuable medical properties.

The Opening of the Buds (Le Débourrement). The rise of the sap, heralded by the weeping, gradually forces the buds on the old shoots to open and the new shoots to sprout. The process takes about three weeks. By the end of March, in a normal year, all the buds are open; the period when frosts are to be feared has begun.

The Foliation (La Feuillaison). In early April the first leaves and tendrils emerge from the shoots. As the shoots grow so do more appear, until, around mid-June, each shoot has produced its full complement of sixteen leaves and sixteen tendrils. In a warm spring the rate of growth is very fast indeed: it is not uncommon for a shoot to grow six to eight inches in twenty-four hours. Such rapid growth involves a high consumption of the reserves of sap.

The tendrils might be described as the hands of the vine. They enable it to cling to nearby objects. They wind themselves round the wires joining the stakes, and thus help to support the branches. There is a tendril opposite each leaf.

The Emergence of the Embryo Bunches of Grapes (La Montre ou Sortie du Raisin). By mid-April, generally coinciding with the appearance of the fourth leaf, the embryo bunches of grapes have emerged from the buds on the shoots. The more bunches that appear the more likely is the vintage to be plentiful, so the news everyone wants to hear at this season is *"la montre est belle"*.

The Flowering (La Floraison). At the end of May or very early in June, when the fifteenth or sixteenth leaf has appeared on each shoot and daytime temperatures have risen to at least 15°C., the vines flower. The flowering starts at the bottom of the vine, where the flow of sap is stronger, and spreads upwards. The flowers are yellowish green in colour; they each have five petals. They exhale a most agreeable odour which resembles that of the passion-fruit flower and is particularly powerful at sundown; it is said to be an aphrodisiac—and I find it is. Depending on the weather, the vines remain in flower from one week to three.

During the flowering the anxiety of the Champenois, which has been on a fine edge for weeks on account of the danger from spring frosts, reaches fever pitch. For the amount of fruit which the vine will bear, and the abundance of the harvest, depends on successful pollination. Three Saints' Days—those of St. Mamert, St. Servais and St. Pancrace—fall during the period of greatest danger, and it is often referred to as *la période des Trois Saints*; the Saints themselves are known as *les Saints de Glace*. If, as happened in 1913 and 1921, there is heavy frost while the vines are actually flowering, disaster is complete: the cold nips the flowers in the bud, and the vine may produce no grapes at all. If, as happened in 1957, frost occurs just before the flowering, the damage can be almost as grave: leaves and buds wither and die and many vines may only bear a quarter, or less, of their normal crop of grapes.

For centuries the vineyard owners have been trying to find a satisfactory method of protecting the vines from spring frosts. An eighteenth-century traveller mentions having seen flannel petticoats and pine branches draped over the vines during *la période des Trois Saints*. Before the First World War, when labour was cheaper, straw matting, suspended from iron stakes, was installed in some of the most important vineyards; it was kept horizontal at night and vertical during the day. But certain vines reacted unfavourably to the matting, and the expense soon proved prohibitive. Smoke screens were then tried, produced by burning the residue of gas plants and therefore relatively inexpensive; but the smoke only afforded protection from slight lowerings of temperature, and if a breath of wind appeared it blew away.

Recently, at a vineyard near Romont, where the ground is flat and frosts are always more severe than on the slope, I was shown a new method of frost protection. At intervals of about twenty feet along each row of vines, cone-shaped metal heaters had been installed, connected by plastic pipes to a drum of fuel oil at the side of the vineyard. A worker who lived nearby had received standing instructions to telephone the *maître-vigneron* the moment the thermometer dropped below freezing-point. This he had done at four a.m. on the morning of my visit. The *maître-vigneron* had immediately collected together a team of men and they had rushed out to the vineyard to ignite the heaters. The heaters had been left on for four hours, during which time there had been a further drop in temperature. The results, as we could easily see, had been sensational. Whereas in the rest of the vineyard frost had nipped at least 40 per cent of the vines, in the area affected by the heaters only an odd vine here and there had been caught. The system is being extended to other vineyards on the flat, but there is little likelihood of its being adopted throughout the planted area. The cost would be prohibitive, and there are not enough vineyard workers available to ignite the heaters throughout the length and breadth of the winefield at the vital moment. Expense is always the bugbear in the fight against spring frosts.

The Pollination (La Fécondation). For pollination to be successful, the temperature in the vineyard must be 20°C. or over. Ideal conditions are an overcast sky, warmth, and a moderate wind to cause the pollen to disperse. A little humidity is desirable; too much dryness and too much sun may cause the surface of the ovary which receives the pollen to dry up, while a heavy rainfall carries off the pollen before it has had time to operate. In Champagne weather conditions are seldom ideal, so a number of ovaries nearly always remain non-pollinated, a condition known as *Coulure*.

It is particularly important that pollination should be complete in three or four days, and not be spread over two or three weeks, as happens in changeable weather. In this event the first grapes to form are already big by the time the last flowers have pollinated, and they attract to themselves an excessive quantity of sap, to the detriment of the last berries to be formed. This condition is known as *Millerandage*.

If the flowers absolutely refuse to pollinate, the Champenois have been known, in desperation, to take the bull by the horns and spray sulphur on the vines. The resulting rush of air will often stir the pollen into action.

Once pollination is complete the grower hopes for a little rain, to drive away the dried up remains of the flowers.

The Setting of the Grapes (La Nouaison). Throughout the months of June and July, and sometimes into August, the main preoccupation of the vines is the setting and filling out of their grapes. Immediately after pollination takes place the grapes are no larger than pellets of shot, spherical in shape, green and hard; by the end of July they are still green and only a little less hard, but they may be very nearly the size they will be at the time they are picked in the autumn. The outsides of the skins are beginning to acquire a coating of waxy substance, impervious to rain, to which the yeasts will attach themselves later on. This is the period when the vines are burning up energy at a very high rate: not only are the grápes growing in size, but the length of the shoots and the size of the leaves are increasing too. The demands that will be made on them have not yet, however, reached their peak because the grapes, for the moment, contribute to their own growth. They are rich in chlorophyll (which is why they are green), and the chlorophyll enables them to assimilate carbon dioxide from the air.

During the setting the grapes contain tannins and acids in addition to the chlorophyll, but practically no sugar.

The Ripening of the Grapes (La Veraison). Some time in August, if all is well, the grapes start to ripen. They become softer and more transparent; the skins of the Pinot grapes start to change colour. Unless there is a lot of rain the size of the grapes will not alter much now, but their content will greatly change. The chlorophyll disappears altogether and so, to a large degree, do the acids; in their place appear sugars, and substances which will later have an effect on the wine's bouquet. The more warmth and sunshine *le bon Dieu* provides now, the more sugar there will be and the smaller the proportion of acid. Finally the time comes—usually between mid-September and early October, but sometimes as early as the beginning of September or as late as mid-October—when the transformation is complete and the proportion of sugar ceases to increase: the point of maturity has been reached and, other things being equal, that is when the grapes are picked.

As soon as the ripening begins, the growth of the shoots slows down rapidly. This is because the grapes, no longer possessed of chlorophyll, have ceased to assimilate part of their nourishment from the air, and are competing with the rest of the vine's vegetation for the sap. To supply all its needs during this period, the vine is forced to draw on its reserves of sap.

The Hardening of the Branches and Shoots (Aoûtement). Up to the end of July the branches and shoots breathe, transpire and, to a certain extent, assimilate nourishment from the air, as do the leaves. Early in August (which is why, in French, the process is called *Aoûtement*) the tissues of the branches and shoots start hardening—or lignifying—and become darker in colour. A thin outer skin of cork forms on the new shoots. In this way the vines prepare themselves to face the rigours of winter. Once the grapes have been picked, the hardening speeds up and becomes the principal activity of the plants; it continues until the leaves fall off.

As they harden, the tissues of the wood enrich themselves with reserve matters. It is essential, when cuttings are taken in the spring for grafting purposes, that the cuttings should be well *aoûté*: otherwise they will not contain enough reserves to grow new radicles, nor will the wounds heal.

The Turning of the Leaves (Le Dessèchement des Feuilles). Meanwhile, the chlorophyll disappears from the leaves and they turn yellow or red.

The Fall of the Leaves (La Chute des Feuilles). Late in October or early in November they begin to dry up, and the gentlest wind causes them to fall. The sap now starts retreating to the stumps of the vines and to the roots, there to remain until the spring.

CHAPTER 21

THE ANNUAL CYCLE OF WORK IN A MATURE VINEYARD

OFFICIALLY, THE VINEYARD year begins in Champagne on 1 November and ends when the grapes are picked the following autumn. Between the vintage and 1 November, the vineyard worker is in theory taking a well-earned rest or, if he is a wine-maker as well as a viticulturist, is busy in his cellar; in practice he often begins his annual cycle of work considerably before 1 November, especially when the previous year's vintage occurred early.

Altogether there are twenty-seven tasks that have to be attended to in the course of the year in a vineyard containing adult vines. I begin my description of each task with an English rendering of its French name, with the French name in brackets, often abbreviated (as it would be, for instance, on a *chef des vignes'* notice-board), and with an indication of the month or months in which it is generally performed.

The Scattering of Fertilizers (Epandage des Engrais), November–December. The object here is not so much to enrich the soil as to ensure that it is healthy and that a correct balance is maintained between its major chemical constituents, such as potash, nitrogen and phosphorus. The job is normally done by men. They wear dark blue overalls and a white apron—which does not remain white for long. Each man has attached to his waist a semicircular bowl, often bright red, which contains the blue-grey pellets of fertilizer, each one the size of an orange-pip. Usually three men work as a team, advancing up the rows in unison. They work extremely quickly, with a highly professional panache. From a distance their progress is a beautiful sight to watch: a blue fountain appears to be playing on the vines.

The Banking Up (Buttage), November–December. This consists of driving an angled blade into the soil between each row of vines to a depth of between five and six inches, with the result that a thin slice of earth is thrown over the base of each vine and a shallow channel is ploughed between the rows. It is the deepest working given to the soil in the course of the year. It is done to achieve six objects: to bury the pellets of fertilizer; to open up a trench for the manures that will be applied later; to protect the sensitive grafting wounds in the stumps of the vines from winter frosts; to rid the earth of weeds; to expose the earth to the beneficial effects of winter frosts; and to facilitate the infiltration of rain into the soil.

The bladed instrument with which the ground is cut is known as a *buttoir*. Since 1948 a specially designed tractor, which straddles the row of vines, has been widely used to pull it on flat ground and on easy slopes. Great skill and concentration are required of the driver. At the end of each run—by which time he is already sweating heavily in spite of the winter cold—the mud which has attached itself to the tractor's wheels has to be scraped off. On very steep slopes a winch is used instead of a tractor. Even with the aid of such powerful traction it is far from easy to force a plough through heavy ground up an eighty degree slope. The man behind the *buttoir* has to flex every muscle to keep the blade in the ground and hang on to the handles like grim death. The reaction of the team to the frequent snappings of the winch-cable is unprintable.

When horses are used to pull the plough, as they still are by small proprietors, the blasphemy tends to be more picturesque. Once I was in a graveyard beside a vineyard when, on the other side of a high wall, I head a succession of grunts interrupted by endless repetitions of "Bad horse, Poulette, ready for the sausage machine". On peering through a hole in the wall I saw that Poulette was a strapping Ardennaise, performing her duties admirably, but that her poor master was having to press so hard to keep the plough in the soil that the entire weight of his body was being taken by his arms and he was advancing across the vineyard behind Poulette with his feet off the ground.

The Untying of the Shoots (Enlèvement des Pailles), November–December. Once the vines have been banked up tractors do not enter the vineyard again during the winter, so the shoots can safely be freed from the wire to which they were attached the previous spring. If the attachment was done with short pieces of straw or reed it is essential that these should be removed and burnt, because they tend to harbour pests, especially cochylis caterpillars; but even if strips of wire or little S-shaped hooks were used instead, the shoots must still be untied to enable pruning to take place in the spring. The untying is often done by women.

The Digging of Water-Stops (Arrêts d'Eaux), November–December. On particularly steep slopes winter rain flows down the trenches formed when the vines were banked-up, and carries away the soil. Holes the size of footballs are therefore dug in the trenches about fifteen yards apart, to force the water to concentrate in pools. The digging is considered a man's job, but one often sees a fine young Champenoise engaged upon it.

The Laying of New Earth (Reterrage), mid-December to mid-February. Every four or five years, as I have already mentioned, the vineyard needs to be refreshed with new earth. The laying of it is a far more laborious process than it was during the vineyard's rest period, when there were no vines in the way; the labour involved gives rise to a local saying that a vineyard worker marries in order to have a wife to carry the soil on her back while he spades it out.

The Application of Manure (Epandage des Fumiers), mid-December to mid-February. In the years when new earth is not laid, the vineyard is supplied with manure, Here again a wife comes in useful, as the manure has to be carried into the vineyard from the dumps and deposited in the channels carved out between the rows of vines during the banking up operation. For centuries the vine growers accumulated the necessary reserves of compost for the purpose in what were called *magazins*: these were rectangular mounds, formed of alternate layers of organic manure, vegetal earth, sand and cinders, which the vine growers erected in a corner of their vineyards during the summer and drew upon in the winter according to their needs. The *magazin* was an ideal means of supplying the topsoil with the extra nourishment which it needs, but today it is entirely impractical for the simple reason that the necessary supplies of organic manure are no longer available. It used to be composed of the droppings of cavalry horses stationed in the military camps that abound on *Champagne pouilleuse* and of horses employed on farms in the neighbourhood or used in the vineyards themselves: the roar of the tank and the tractor sounded the death knell of the *magazin*.

Today, if supplies of local organic manures are available, the vine grower uses them—the droppings of cows and sheep, *marc* (what remains of the grape-skins after the pressing), the dead leaves of certain trees, peat from the valley of the Vesle or the Marais de Saint-Gond, roasted horn, the rubbish of slaughter-houses. But when they are not available he uses fish manure or *les boues de ville de Paris* instead. The latter is neither more nor less than the contents of Parisian dust-bins. Each autumn consignments arrive in the winefield by rail in sealed tanks, transport during the summer being forbidden on account of the stink. In theory, each consignment has been finely ground to remove danger from broken glass, and metal objects have been extracted by electro-magnets; but in fact a walk through the vineyards after an application has been made is as intriguing for the eyes as it is unpleasant for the nose: one catches sight of old bits of the *Figaro*, crumpled packets of *Gauloises*, ice-cream cartons, oyster shells, potato peel and orange skins; one feels like Tom peeping into the intimate recesses of Parisian life. The temptation is strong to inspect more closely, for the hawk-eyed vineyard workers commonly retrieve such objects as gold rings, and sometimes booty of even greater value: not long ago, in a Veuve Clicquot vineyard near Le Mesnil on the Côte des Blancs, three of them noticed something bulky wrapped in newspaper; that something turned out to be a bundle of bank-notes worth £300.

Artificial manures, made from straw or white sawdust, are also used. The big vineyard owners make them themselves. Poles are stretched across a concrete tank the size of a small swimming-pool, and on the poles are put bales of straw to form a rectangle about twenty feet high. In each bale are inserted pellets of an ammonia compound. The bales are then sprayed with water. The water (or rain) drips down through the straw into the tank, whence it is pumped out and sprayed over the straw again. After fifteen days of such treatment, the temperature inside the rick has risen to 60°C. and the straw is decomposing. At the end of three months the conversion process is complete: what is so extraordinary is that the straw looks exactly as manure should, dark brown in colour, steaming and gooey. White sawdust is treated in much the same way, but the process takes six months.

The Pruning of the Vine (Taille), March. Of all the vineyard worker's tasks, the pruning of the vine is the most important, and, with the possible exception of grafting, the one that requires the greatest skill and experience. A vine is pruned in order to restrict the quantity of grapes which it produces each year and to force it to grow in a particular form.

There are two main reasons why it is necessary to ration the number of bunches the vine bears. First, only by so doing can grapes of high quality be achieved; and, secondly, a vine which is allowed to produce large quantities of grapes year in year out quickly becomes exhausted.

There are also two main reasons why it is necessary to force the vine to grow in a particular form. In the first place, men and machines must be able to approach it easily, without risk of causing damage, while they are tending the soil it grows in, tending the vine itself and applying fungicides and insecticides. In the second place, it is essential for the bunches of grapes to grow at a specific height above the ground.

Filling a press

Mannequins drying out after the vintage

Casks for the first fermentation

Vats for the first fermentation

Grapes grown far from the soil tend to be watery and acid; the closer they are to the soil, provided they do not actually touch it, the better they will mature. This is because in the daytime the reflection of the sun's rays off the warm earth complements the benefits of direct sunshine, and at night the soil radiates back into the vines the warmth it has absorbed during the day. Vines with luxuriant vegetation rising to roof-top level are all very fine in the sunny south; in Champagne, if the grapes are to have half a chance of reaching maturity, the vine must be kept stunted and never allowed to rise more than three or four feet off the ground.

Three methods of pruning are allowed in the Champagne district: the Chablis, the Cordon de Royat and the Guyot. Each is a classic system, designed to produce grapes of high quality by restricting production in a normal year to a maximum of 7,500 kilos of grapes per hectare (7,000 lb. per acre). As each system requires the vines to be grown in straight lines, with their shoots trained along wires attached to stakes, access to the vines is easy at all times of the year and the grapes grow close enough to the ground to favour maturity. Three systems are allowed to enable the vine grower to choose which-ever one is best suited to the soil of the vineyard, the type of vine he grows and the type of root on to which it has been grafted. Beyond this choice the law gives the vine grower no latitude whatsoever. Since January 1938 the appellation "champagne" has only been granted to wine produced from vines pruned according to the three systems; a vine grower who engages upon a practice such as annular incision,* which increases the size of the crop at the expense of quality, not only forfeits the right to the appellation but is also heavily fined.

In order to understand how the pruning is conducted, two points must be grasped first: the manner in which a vine develops if it is never pruned, and the anatomy of a vine shoot.

If a vine is left to its own devices, this is what happens. During the late spring there emerge from the stump of the plant a very large num-ber of pencil-thin shoots which grow to a great length and scatter themselves in haphazard fashion across the ground. The effect is some-thing like this (and is precisely what took me so much by surprise during my visit to the *vignes-mères* vineyards in the Midi):

---

* If annular incision is practised, which it is not in the Champagne district, it is done two or three weeks before the vintage. A shallow incision is made round the shoot a couple of inches below the first bunch of grapes. As the sap rises through the centre of the shoot and falls through its periphery, the effect of the incision is greatly to increase the quantity of sap at the disposal of the bunches.

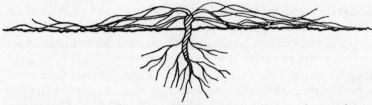

Each shoot is round and smooth, but its roundness and smoothness
are interrupted at intervals (the intervals vary greatly according to the
type of vine) by swellings on which three buds have formed. This is
what each shoot looks like when closely inspected immediately the
buds have formed:

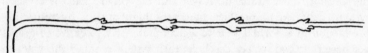

It will be noticed that the arrangement of the buds is the same on
alternate swellings: the first swelling has two buds facing the sky and
one facing the earth, the second has two buds facing the earth and one
facing the sky. This arrangement is as inevitable in the vine's anatomy
as a right and a left hand are in a human being. The bud that is the
nearer of the two to the stump of the vine in each pair of buds is
always the one that produces the leaf. This, therefore, is the appearance
of the vine in the early summer:

The single bud opposite the leaf is always the one that produces the
bunch of grapes. At the time of the vintage, therefore, the shoots
look like this:

As for the third bud, the constant companion of the leaf, that one lies
dormant all summer long, all winter long; the following spring it
wakes up and grows into a new shoot, identical in every way with
the shoot that gave it life. The previous autumn, at the time the leaves
fell off, the wood of the original shoot will have thickened (become
aoûté), so this is what the original shoot and its progeny look like late
in the second spring of the original shoot's existence:

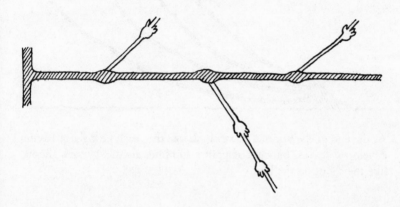

Left to itself the vine will continue year in, year out, to reproduce itself
in the same lavish fashion—each trinity of buds on each shoot producing
a leaf, a bunch of grapes and a new shoot. And unless the process is
checked by pruning, not only will the grapes be far too numerous to
be of good quality but the vine-shoots, climbing to the tops of the
highest trees and then distributing themselves horizontally in all
directions, will render the disciplining of the vine quite impossible.

The Chablis system of pruning gives the vine the following form:

(i) three, four or five main branches, the precise number depending
on the distance apart in line of the vines. If the distance is one metre,
four main branches are allowed. These main branches are in reality
the previous year's shoots which became *aoûté* in wintertime and will
never be fruitful again.

(ii) one shoot at the extremity of each main branch, pruned back so
that there remain on it no more than four swellings containing the
trinity of buds in the case of the Pinot and a maximum of five swellings
in the case of the Chardonnay. The extra length is permitted on the

Chardonnay because the buds in the swelling nearest the main branch are infertile.

Immediately after it has been pruned for the first time, therefore, a Pinot Noir vine, planted four feet away in line from its neighbour, has this appearance:

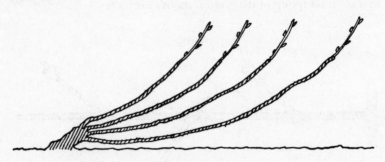

At the end of the summer it will look like this, each new shoot having developed leaves, bunches of grapes and buds for next year's shoots, like the shoot on the left:

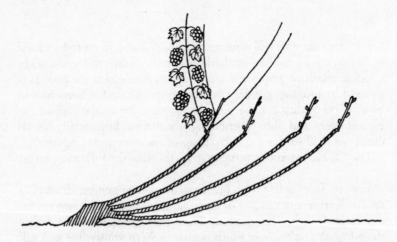

In the autumn the grapes will be picked and the leaves will fall off, and during the winter the shoot which gave birth to the four new shoots will become slightly thickened or *aoûté*. So this will be the appearance of the vine the following spring, just before it is pruned for the second time:

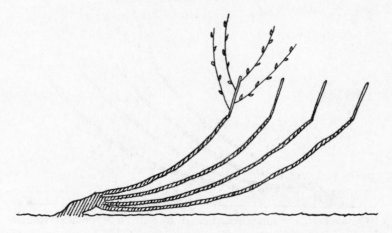

If the vine was *not* pruned for the second time, each shoot which gave birth to leaves and fruit the year before would blossom forth like this:

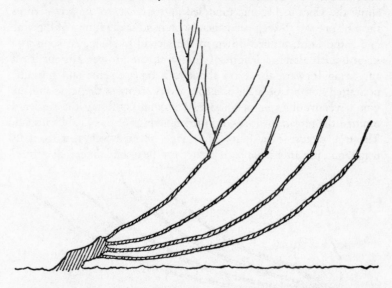

But the Chablis system stipulates that all the shoots which bore fruit the year before must be cut off, except one; and that one must be pruned back to the extent that no more than four swellings containing the trinity of buds remain. Immediately after its second pruning according to the Chablis system, therefore, this is what a Pinot vine looks like:

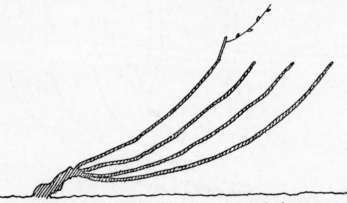

On average, the main branches advance towards the next vine at the rate of one foot a year. This means that, if the vines are planted four feet apart, after five years the main branches of one vine will have reached the stump of the next vine. It would be unthinkable to allow the vines to become muddled up together, so the law permits the vine grower to keep permanently on hand at the stump of the vine one extra shoot, pruned down to the second swelling. As soon as a main branch attains a length of four feet, the grower can cut it off and bring forward the extra shoot as a replacement; and thus the permitted number of main branches always remains the same and the vine never troubles its neighbour. To avoid confusing the reader, I omitted the replacement shoot in the drawings of the Chablis system. The true picture of a Pinot Noir vine, planted four feet from its neighbour, just after it has been pruned for the second time, is therefore:

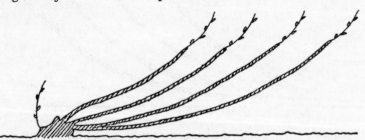

The fact that the Chablis system of pruning allows the vine to have three, four or five main branches makes it a somewhat difficult one to manage, and some growers lack the patience or the time to use it; but it is generally recognized to be the best of the Champagne systems of pruning, and it is used for almost all the Chardonnay vines.

The Cordon de Royat system is worked on a single branch which must be trained horizontally at a maximum height of twenty-eight inches from the soil. Shoots may only be formed on the horizontal part of the branch, and they must be about six inches apart. After pruning, only two swellings may remain on each shoot of the Pinot Noir and the Pinor Meunier; three may remain in the case of the Chardonnay. The Chardonnay is also allowed to have two extra long shoots, pruned to the sixth swelling, per metre of main branch. The farthest shoot away from the stump may be pruned to the fourth swelling on the Pinot and the fifth on the Chardonnay. All replacement shoots must be pruned back to the second swelling.

The Guyot system allows for no permanent main branch. Instead, either one or two shoots issue directly out of the stump of the vine, one if the Guyot Simple is used, two if use is made of the Guyot Double. For the Guyot Simple, the main shoot must be pruned at the eighth swelling, the replacement shoot at the third. For the Guyot Double, the two main shoots must be pruned at the sixth swelling and the two replacement shoots at the second. The Guyot system may not be practised in *catégorie hors classe* growths because it is less inclined to produce quality grapes than the other two systems. For growths rated below 80 per cent a slightly different Guyot system is allowed.

March is the best month for Champagne vines to be pruned, as an old saying confirms:

> *Taille tôt . . . taille tard,*
> *Rien ne vaut la taille de mars.*

February is too early: the great winter frosts are still about and they prevent the wounds caused by the pruning secateurs from healing. April, on the other hand, is rather late: by then the warmth of the soil has caused the sap to rise into the vine, and to cut off a shoot is to waste precious sap. The visitor to the Champagne district does not need to enter a vineyard to know that pruning secateurs are at work: tiny puffs of smoke floating up into the soft spring sunshine indicate from far off that women and children have been following in the pruner's footsteps to collect the discarded shoots, and have set the little bonfires alight.

Maintenance of the Vineyard Installations (Entretien des Installations), late March–April. As soon as he has finished pruning, the vine grower inspects the stakes and the wires supporting each row of vines, and if necessary repairs them. A tractor may have damaged a vine prop; the wire may be rusty. This is the moment in the year when the vine grower makes most use of his *pince universelle*, a type of adjustable spanner which he always carries in his pocket.

The Securing of the Branches (Attachage des Charpentes), late March–April. Tractors will soon be back in the vineyards, so the vine branches must now be attached to the wires again. S-shaped metal hooks are the simplest and quickest means of securing the branches, but they are expensive and many vine growers prefer to use strips of wire, wicker, straw or rush.

It is vital for the securing to be done with extreme care, because the angle at which the branch is made to grow has considerable effect on the productivity of the vine. This is due to a botanical phenomenon which causes the highest buds to exercise a special attraction on the sap. On a vertical vine-branch the buds at the top consume so much sap that the buds near the base sometimes fail completely to blossom; whereas if the branch is fixed horizontally the sap is evenly distributed, and the shoots near the base of the vine have the same diameter as those farther away. For this reason the branches of Champagne vines are always arched steeply at their bases at the time they are secured, so that for the greater part of their length they lie horizontally; on a slope they are always trained uphill, rather than downhill, for the same reason.

The Levelling of the Soil (Débuttage), April. This, in a sense, is the reverse of the banking-up process which is applied to the vineyard in the late autumn. No machine has yet been invented which can remove the banked-up earth from the stumps of the vines without damaging them, so this part of the job has to be done by hand; but a special light plough is used to fold in the furrows of earth between each row of vines which were formed during the banking-up operation. The manure is thus buried and the soil is turned and flattened, all in one go, in readiness for the kinder weather ahead.

The First Spraying (Première Pulvérisation), May. The emergence of the fourth or fifth leaves from the shoots is the signal for the annual campaign against pests and diseases. The vine grower knows that at an absolute minimum he will have to spray each row of vines seven times between now and the end of August, and he is faced with the possibility of having to administer no less than fifteen or sixteen sprayings should the summer turn out to be particularly humid. Only by so doing can he hope to keep mildew, oïdium and the other enemies of the vines at bay during the summer.

Nowadays the product most commonly used for spraying is a mixture of copper compounds (often copper sulphate) and soluble sulphur: the copper compounds combat mildew and rougeot; the sulphur combats oïdium, the Red Cochinelle larvae and the *Phytoptus vitis* tick. Both arrive in the winefield in powdered form and are mixed together in water; when insecticide is required it is added in liquid form to the solution. At a time when the vines are in full vegetation 1,000 litres of water, 20 kilos of copper compounds and 15 kilos of sulphur are needed to spray one hectare of vineyard. Transporting such huge quantities of water out to the vineyards presents many difficulties. Moët & Chandon have solved the problem with an installation that is virtually unique in Europe: the powder is mixed with water in tanks erected at central points in the winefield and the solution is then pumped out to their vineyards through pipes; all their employees have to do is to turn on a tap in the vineyard, fill up and start spraying. Other big vineyard proprietors have water storage tanks scattered around the winefield and a fleet of small motorized tankers that ply to and fro between the tanks and the vineyards, keeping the workers supplied with the solution.

The small proprietor has no such aids. His vineyard may be a quarter of a mile away from the nearest water supply, so he has to lug a wheelbarrow laden with a barrel containing ten gallons of solution (probably with another gallon in the sprayer on his back) along uneven paths, perhaps up a steep slope, to his vines—and then retrace his steps time and time again in the course of the day for refills. In the full heat of summer no more back-breaking task can be imagined.

The owners of large stretches of vineyard do the spraying with huge tractor-mounted sprayers designed to straddle six or eight rows of vines; the machines progress through the vineyard at a terrific speed, belching forth the bluish-green solution like snorting dragons. (The skill of the drivers is given public display at tractor gymkhanas held each May in Rheims and Epernay: the Calgary stampede has nothing on the spectacle of the participants whizzing through a crazy obstacle course rigged up on a parking lot.) In smaller vineyards the sprayers may be pulled by horses. But owing mainly to the subdivision of the winefield into so many small properties, partly to the steepness of some of the inclines, partly also to the inaccessibility of certain plots, the spray is most commonly applied from a sprayer carried on the vineyard worker's back. The more modern types are equipped with a small motor which vaporizes the liquid: with one of these on his back a tough young vineyard worker will half-run, half-walk through the vines, with only short breaks, for hours on end. Other types are equipped with compressed air cylinders to force out the liquid; their weight greatly hampers the carrier. The most ancient models are worked by a hand-pump; with them it is the strong arm of the vineyard worker that draws the liquid up into the nozzle and projects it into the vines, and the pumping reduces progress to a snail's pace.

A man may spend all day in fierce heat spraying his vines and then as he returns home, his eyes watering and burning, he and his horse covered from head to foot in the bluey-green liquid, a thunderstorm breaks. In five minutes his day's labour is washed away, and he has to start all over again on the morrow.

In 1963, for the first time, helicopters were used by some of the big firms to spray their vineyards. The job was entrusted to a Parisian firm with extensive experience of spraying agricultural land in France and North Africa. The helicopters manœuvre like great fish, taking long swoops down towards the vineyard, swishing over it, then twirling round for the next run in. The flights prove an irresistible attraction to passers-by, despite the fact that they and their cars are apt to get splattered with the bluey-green spray.

Spraying by helicopter has two great advantages: (i) the helicopters can spray steep hillsides on which it is impossible to operate tractor-mounted sprayers, and which have therefore to be treated by a vine-yard worker with a portable sprayer; (ii) after a rainstorm or during a period of great humidity, when attacks of mildew are to be feared, the whole of the winefield can—in theory, anyway—be sprayed in a matter of hours, whereas at present the job takes about ten days.

The use of helicopters, however, is still very much in the experi-mental stage. Basically the problem is one of equipping the helicopter with a sufficiently powerful engine to enable a really powerful vaporizer to be run off it. At present the drops of spray are too large, and they fall at too widely dispersed intervals on the leaves for perfect results to be obtained. For this reason some of the leaves in the vineyards being sprayed by helicopters have round pieces of paper stuck on them which look like huge white beauty spots. These are later sent to the Paris laboratories of the helicopter firm for inspection as regards the progress being made in fining down the spray. Twice so far a heli-copter has caught its undercarriage in the wires joining the stakes and crashed—ruining an expanse of vines.

The First Hoeing (*Premier Binage*), *May*. The vineyard must be lightly hoed to a depth of just over an inch three or four times a summer, partly to prevent a crust forming on the soil, partly to kill the weeds. The latter are particularly harmful when the vine is in full vegetation, as they consume much water; also, the humidity they throw off in the proximity of the plants tends to favour the development of mildew. A violent rainstorm followed by sunshine and dry winds invariably cakes the soil, and in years when such conditions occur frequently the number of hoeings may have to be increased to five or six. The vine grower must always take care not to injure the roots of his vines by hoeing too deep.

The Removal of the Leaves from the Old Wood (Ebourgeonnage), May. Only the shoots that emerge from the previous year's growth of wood are fertile; any shoots that appear on older branches are sterile. It is consequently well worth the grower's while to remove all the leaves growing on the vine except those on new shoots and on the replacement shoot: if left on, they consume sap and increase the surface area of the vine vulnerable to disease. The leaves are picked off by hand. The slight wound heals quickly.

The Second Spraying (Deuxième Pulvérisation), late May. This is administered when the eighth or ninth leaf emerges from the shoots.

The Third Spraying (Troisième Pulvérisation), early June. This is administered between the emergence of the twelfth and thirteenth leaves, which coincides with the appearance of the first flowers at the base of the vine.

June is a month of "*travail fou, à quatre bras*", as the vine grower so aptly puts it. The vegetation on the vine is in tumultuous growth and requires endless attention.

The Second Hoeing (Deuxième Binage), June. This may be done at any time in the course of the month except when the vines are actually flowering. Experience has taught the vine grower to keep out of the vineyards at that critical moment of the vines' lives.

The Fourth Spraying (Quatrième Pulvérisation), June, is followed by *The Tying-Up of the Shoots (Palissage), June.* The shoots lack the strength to support the weight of the vegetation and the fruit. Left free, they might break; in any case they would swing about on windy days, exposing their precious cargo of grapes to injury. So either they must be tied up to the four or five fixed wires that run the length of the rows between the stakes or some other method must be used to secure them. A Chardonnay vine, pruned according to the Chablis system, has about twenty-five shoots; the job therefore involves a great expenditure of time and manpower.

The First Trimming of the Leaves (Premier Rognage), June. It has always been the practice in the Champagne district, which it is not in many other French vineyards, to remove the leaves that grow at the extremities of the new shoots, so that only between ten and twelve leaves remain per shoot. The trimming diverts sap to the leaves that remain; it facilitates the penetration of fungicide and insecticide into the body of the vine; it increases the amount of sunshine enjoyed by the bunches; and it helps the passage of tractors. The trimming is practised in Champagne because both the Pinot and the Chardonnay vines produce comparatively little fruit; their grapes are never sufficiently abundant to temper their vegetation. When the grapes are in the process of ripening the development of the vegetation must therefore be stopped, or else there will be an excess of vegetation and not enough fruit. Too drastic a reduction would be detrimental to the grapes, however, as the leaves play a vital part in their nourishment; the trimming must always be done with circumspection. It is carried out with shears, and the sooner it is done after the pollination the better.

July is also a frantically busy month for the vine grower. He administers *The Fifth and Sixth Sprayings* and tackles *The Third Hoeing* and *The Second Trimming of the Leaves*.

August begins with *The Seventh Spraying*. This is the last of the sprayings administered in a normal year, and it must be completed one month at least before the estimated date of the vintage, to ensure that poisons in the spray will be washed off the grapes by rain before they are picked. Then follows *The Third Trimming of the Leaves* and *Hand Hoeing (Sarclage à la Main)*. During the last weeks of their growth the grapes need plenty of water to fill out their tissues, so it is essential to rid the vineyards once again of water-consuming weeds. The only way the job can be done effectively round the stump of the young vine is by hand; contact with the blades of the mechanized hoes, even though the blades are equipped with springs which retract when pressure is exerted on them, would injure the stumps. In a normal year one sees practically no weeds in a Champagne vineyard, but in very humid summers they sprout so profusely that the vine grower, to his chagrin, is unable to keep them in check.

The Thinning of the Leaves (Effeuillage), early September. This consists of picking off leaves, usually two or three in number, that surround the bunches of grapes growing on the north and north-eastern side of the vine, in order that these bunches shall receive the maximum benefit from the few hours of sunshine which their position on the vine affords them. At the same time any leaves that are diseased or are seen to be harbouring parasites are removed. The thinning is only done in cold and humid summers, for in exceptionally sunny summers there would be danger of the bunches being roasted; and it is never practised in vineyards frequently hit by hail, as the leaves afford the bunches some protection.

From 1909 to 1914 there was a vogue in the Champagne district for a special type of gun that fired a rocket into a hail-cloud and caused it to disperse. It so happened that no great damage was inflicted by hail during these years, but the majority of the installations were destroyed in the First World War and few of them were renewed afterwards. Some people contended that the rockets caused hail to descend that would not otherwise have done so; others complained that their main effect was to move the storm so that it broke over another vineyard. Relatively successful attempts have since been made to disperse hail clouds by dropping explosives into them from aeroplanes, but the expense of the procedure precludes any likelihood of its being adopted as standard practice in the winefield.

Once he has completed these jobs there is practically nothing more the vine grower can do to influence the size and quality of the vintage. His day from now on is occupied with preparations for the picking and the pressing; but his thoughts seldom stray far away from the vines on which for nine months he has lavished so much care, and which are now at long last laden with ripening bunches.

There is nothing remotely happy-go-lucky about viticulture in Champagne, and the endless time and care which are expended cost a great deal of money. There can be few cultures more expensive than that of Champagne grapes, which is one of the principal reasons why champagne is an expensive drink. But the most indispensable element in the culture of the grape in the Champagne district is not money or time or hard work or dedication, although all these are needed in great measure; it is courage. With the sole exception of the vine growers of the Rhine and the Moselle, the Champenois are the only professional vine growers in northern climes who have persevered in the struggle against the climate. Most of the others—the wine growers of Ireland, Wales, Picardy, Flanders, Artois, Hainault and the Paris region—gave up centuries ago, or downed tools as soon as the advent of the railways enabled wine from the south to be transported cheaply to the north. To go on tending vines and working the soil as if nothing has happened after an aggressive April frost has nipped the buds and destroyed all hope of a crop, to keep going when hail has wiped out all prospects of making a sou from a vineyard for at least another twelve months, that is the nature of the challenge. Meeting it requires an obstinacy, a refusal to succumb to more than a momentary fit of depression, and a determination to take the long-term view which adds up to courage.

CHAPTER 22

PESTS, DISEASES AND DISORDERS

FUNGI ARE RESPONSIBLE for four diseases to which the vines are prone: mildew, oïdium, rougeot and *pourriture grise*. Mildew and *pourriture grise* tend to be the most troublesome today.

The cause of mildew is a tiny mushroom called *Plamosphora viticola*. It thrives on rain and humidity, so the Champagne vineyards are more vulnerable to its attacks than vineyards situated farther south, where the climate is drier and warmer. The mushroom attaches itself to different parts of the vine—shoots, leaves and grapes—and so alters their tissues that life within them ceases to function. Once its spores have penetrated the tissues no cure is possible. All treatment for mildew is thus preventive, designed to hinder the germination of the spores; it consists of spraying the vines with copper compounds. During the Second World War there was a grave shortage of these products and many vines died of mildew in consequence.

The disease struck for the first time in America in the early nineteenth century. It crossed the Atlantic on the American vines which France acquired to fight phylloxera and reached Champagne in 1885, before phylloxera itself. In 1910 it so ravaged the vineyards that there was virtually no vintage at all. From then on the vine growers started applying earlier and more frequent doses of copper compounds; during wet or humid summers they have been known to apply no less than sixteen doses.

Oïdium is caused by a mushroom called *Uncinula spiralis* which also thrives on humidity. It plants itself on the surface of the vine, digging in at certain spots to obtain nourishment, and thereby causing the tissues to disintegrate in much the same manner as they do when suffering from mildew; in the course of its attacks, it emits a grey dust which has a most offensive smell. The disease was first diagnosed on English hothouse grapes belonging to a Mr. Tucker of Margate in 1845; two years later it appeared in a hothouse near Paris; soon after it began attacking vineyards in France; and by 1852 its ravages in vineyards throughout Europe had reached the proportions of an epidemic. For the first time in modern history France was compelled to import wine. Just in time to prevent the complete destruction of the vineyards of Europe it was discovered that, if sulphur solutions were sprayed on the vines in warm weather, gases would be emitted that would be lethal to the mushroom and the spores. Today the sulphur treatments, applied throughout the summer, generally succeed in keeping oïdium at bay.

Attacks of the rougeot mushroom are to be feared when the third leaf sprouts on the shoot, round about the first fortnight of June. Little sores appear on the leaves, greeny-red on a Pinot Noir leaf, yellow on that of the Chardonnay; if the sores spread the leaves die and fall off. The copper compounds applied in late May to combat mildew usually prevent the spores from developing. The vine grower never knows whether rougeot will attack or not: unlike mildew, which is a constant threat, it disappears from a vineyard for years and then suddenly appears again.

Pourriture grise is a grey woolly growth which forms on the grapes themselves in wet autumns, giving them a diseased, rotted appearance and causing them to shrivel. The growth is formed by a mould called *Botrytis cinerea*. The mould is responsible for the exceptional sweetness of certain white wines, notably Sauternes, Montbazillacs, and Spätaus-leses of the Rhine valley: in the winefields where these wines are made the grapes are left on the vines long after they have ripened, and the filaments of the mould suck out the water in the grape-juice, thereby greatly increasing its richness in sugar; in that form, the rot is known as *pourriture noble*. *Botrytis cinerea*, however, is only benevolent on white grapes, like the Sauvignon, the Riesling and the Sylvaner, which have skins thick enough not to disintegrate when the filaments penetrate them; its advent on red grapes is always a calamity, even if they have thick skins, as the moulds destroy the colour cells in the skins.* In the Champagne district, where none of the grapes grown have particularly thick skins and where wet autumns are a frequent occurrence, *pourriture grise* often ruins a considerable portion of the crop and compromises the quality of the rest. It is impractical to destroy the moulds before they attack, as they float about in the air of the vineyards; nor is any treatment practical once they are on the grapes, because the filaments penetrate to the centre of the grape, where no fungicide can reach them. All the *vigneron* can do is to remove the leaves in the neighbourhood of the affected bunch and pray for sunshine and a breeze, which will dry out the dampness on the skins and check the spread of the disease.

* This might be thought to be an advantage in the Champagne district, where it is desired to produce a white wine from red grapes, but it is not, because, as they are destroyed, the colour cells taint the juice.

There are five species of moth against which the vine grower has to be on constant guard. The Cochylis or Night Moth was first found in Champagne in 1771. It has a pale yellow body about a quarter of an inch long. It starts flying in the month of May, usually at night. It lays its eggs on the buds. As soon as the eggs hatch the caterpillars attack the flowers of the vine, nibbling away the pistils and stamens. Then, to protect themselves against wind and rain, they string threads of silk between the flowers and the buds; it is these little curtains that announce the presence of the parasite. Later in the summer a second generation settles on the grapes, pricks them and causes them to turn mouldy. The Cochylis likes moderate warmth and humidity, but dislikes extreme heat; it is particularly to be feared, therefore, in rainy summers.

The Eudemis is a cousin of the Cochylis. It arrived in Champagne in 1914, but did not become a serious menace until 1924. It has a light green body and grey wings, and is slightly smaller than the Cochylis. It is mainly active at dawn and dusk. Its cycle of reproduction occurs rather later than that of the Cochylis, so normally it attacks the grapes, not the flowers. It likes great heat and dryness, and is consequently rather less to be feared in Champagne than the Cochylis.

The ravages of both Cochylis and Eudemis have been considerably reduced by the introduction of metal vine-props and the training of the shoots along wires, as the chrysalis of neither moth can survive on a metallic surface. It still, however, seeks refuge in the bark of the vine. The only effective treatment against both moths is spraying with insecticide in late May or early June and in late August or early September.

The Ver Blanc du Hanneton, or White Moth of the Cockchafer, is the particular enemy of the young vine and of the grafted cuttings. It is a very small, fragile moth which for some unaccountable reason only takes wing and reproduces every third year. It is difficult to kill with insecticides, as it lives mostly in trees situated beside roads. In recent flight years the Conseil Général de la Marne has voted credits to reward individuals who collect them; the majority of the collectors have been schoolchildren. The job is done in summer, early in the morning, while the moths are still benumbed by the cool of the night.

The Red Cochenille moth lays its eggs in June; about a month later the young larvae start planting their suckers on the vine-shoots and the lower surfaces of the leaves. The mahogany coloured, black-flecked female is a much greater menace than the yellow male, as the latter dies as soon as it has mated. The species thrives in hot weather. The sulphur sprayings administered to combat oïdium generally destroy the Red Cochenille larvae.

The Pyrale moth has been in Champagne since 1773. It devastated the vineyards of Ay in the 1850s and continued to be a serious nuisance in the neighbourhood until it was confronted by a bout of exceptionally cold weather in 1860. It is a large moth whose body is yellow and whose yellow wings, about an inch broad, have three transversal bands. The caterpillars hibernate in the bark of the branches all winter and emerge in the spring; after spinning silken webs over the vine they proceed to devour the buds, the young shoots and the leaves. Before the First World War acetylene lamps with sheets of sticky paper attached to them were used extensively to catch the moths: over 8 million were destroyed in this way one summer. The high cost of labour today renders the use of these lamps impractical, but spraying with insecticide in the spring keeps the pest well under control.

There are two insects which are unwelcome visitors in the vineyards. One is the red spider; it is very small, but a person with good eyes can just see it without the aid of a microscope. It made its first appearance in the vineyards in the early 1950s. It sucks out the sap and enfeebles the vine. Insecticide applied in July and August gets rid of it.

The other unwelcome intruder is a type of tick (*Phytoptus vitis*). It causes a swelling to occur on the leaves which is known as Erinose. The culprit is normally killed by the sulphur sprays administered against oïdium.

The Chardonnay vines are particularly susceptible to a mysterious disorder known as *Court-Noué*. The shoots start to flatten out, U-shaped indention appear on the leaves and eventually the vine become sterile. Experts have spent years studying the ailment, but opinion is still divided as to what causes it or how best it can be treated. Viruses, a mushroom living off the bark of the roots and poisons in the soil have been variously suggested as possible causes. What is certain is that an enfeebled vine is more likely to succumb to *Court-Noué* than a vigorous one: during the Second World War, when shortages of manures, fertilizers and fungicides weakened the vines' resistance to sickness, *Court-Noué* was rife. The disorder occurs more frequently in large holdings than in small ones. It is apparently not infectious, as it remains localized, but it can be transmitted by grafting, which makes it particularly important that the shoots of both the vine of American ancestry and the French vine should not be suffering from the ailment at the time grafting takes place. At present the only satisfactory method of ridding a vineyard of *Court-Noué* is the drastic one of uprooting the vines.

Another disorder which is much feared is Chlorosis or Green Sickness. Outbreaks of it are believed to indicate that there is a serious mineral deficiency (or excess) in the soil of the vineyard. The condition is most likely to occur after a cold or wet spring. The leaves of any affected vine turn yellow as they sprout. Often, when the full heat of summer arrives, the condition disappears; but if the case is a serious one the shoots wither, the grapes, if there are any, do not ripen and the vine dies. The classic treatment is to paint sulphate of iron on the wounds inflicted on the vine at the time of the pruning. The treatment is applied in the late autumn, immediately after the leaves have fallen, when the sap is about to descend towards the roots and will carry the sulphate of iron with it.

These are the principal pests, diseases and disorders to be feared in a Champagne vineyard, but there are many more which strike less regularly, and the vine grower must be constantly on the alert for signs of them. Fortunately, there is much less likelihood today of calamities occurring such as the oïdium epidemic of 1852, the pyrale epidemic of the same decade or the mildew epidemic of 1910. For one thing, chemical progress has placed at the disposal of the modern viticulturist a range of fungicides and insecticides which should enable him to cope with any crisis before it reaches the proportions of an epidemic. Moreover, the vine grower is no longer alone in his fight against pestilence. At the laboratories of the Comité Interprofessionnel du Vin de Champagne in Epernay pests, diseases and disorders are under constant study and new treatments are for ever being tested. Also, the Station d'Avertissements Agricoles de Champagne, run by the Ministry of Agriculture, has outposts in the vineyards and gives the growers daily advice. A law passed in 1941 compels the vine grower to administer the majority of the treatments which are recommended; if he fails to do so he can be fined, and for failing to take certain other precautions against disease he can be sent to prison.

But progress has created new problems. One is the time it takes to apply preventive treatment; another is the cost of applying it. In a year when there is much humidity, staggering sums of money are spent on fighting mildew alone.

CHAPTER 23

THE VINEYARDS IN PRE-PHYLLOXERA DAYS

Aɴʏoɴᴇ ᴡʜᴏsᴇ ᴇʏᴇ has grown accustomed to the present-day appearance of the vineyards, with the vines trained along dead-straight wires, would receive quite a shock if he was transported back to a Champagne vineyard of the pre-phylloxera days. For then there were no straight lines and no wires: the vines grew *en foule*, that is to say, anywhere and everywhere within the plot, with all the apparent casualness of an English garden, although in fact the arrangement was carefully planned.

The vines were grown *en foule* because the system of *provignage* (layering) which was then used demanded that they should be. When a new vineyard was started, the vines were planted in much the same way as they are today: each plant was deposited in a hole, and as soon as it began to grow it was attached with straw to a stake. Two (sometimes three) years later it was pruned: in the course of the pruning all the vine's branches were cut off except one, and that one was shortened. A small trench, six to eight inches deep, was then dug beside the vine, and the remaining branch was laid in the trench, with only its extremity protruding above the soil. Next the trench was dressed with light manure and filled up again, and after that the extremity of the vine-branch was tied with straw to a stake inserted in the ground beside the point where it protruded. In the course of time, the part of the branch which was buried in the soil formed roots; and the part which protruded developed shoots that two years later bore grapes: in other words, an entirely new vine was created. This layering

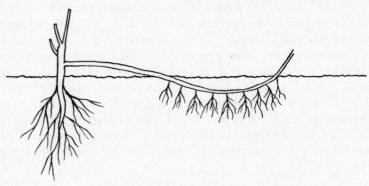

operation was repeated each year until the original vine was five years old; it was then given a couple of years' rest, after which the operation began again, the branches destined to form new vines being dispersed in a slightly different direction each time. And as each new vine was created so was *provignage* practised on it, the result being that the vineyard was perpetually rejuvenating itself, perpetually expanding and for ever growing more untidy.

Any Champenois will tell you that the *en foule-provignage* system is the perfect method of growing grapes in his homeland. For one thing the strain imposed on the roots of the vine is reduced to a minimum, enabling it to remain vigorous and healthy for seventy years or more, whereas a grafted vine grown *en ligne* normally becomes exhausted after twenty-five to thirty-five years. For another, many more plants can be packed into an acre, 16,000 to 20,000 on an average, compared to an average of just over 4,000 when the *en ligne* system is used; and such density, reminiscent of the cabbage-patch, makes it more difficult for the wind to circulate: the vineyard is calmer, less exposed to sudden changes of temperature. Besides, the short pruning rendered possible by *provignage* produces a better distributed foliage, and smaller but more handsome leaves: the grapes thus tend to be of slightly better quality. Finally, being nearer to the ground, and profiting to the maximum from the heat reflected by the soil, the vines tend to flower earlier and the grapes to ripen sooner. The vintage nearly always took place a little earlier in pre-phylloxera days, and that is a great advantage in a northern winefield where a wintery autumn may appear all too soon.

In short, when the vines were grown *en foule* the grower stood a greater chance of providing the champagne-maker, year in, year out, with more grapes and better quality grapes than he does today: he could grow more vines in a given area, his vines lived longer, the foliage was more lustrous, and there was less risk of summer having vanished before the grapes were ripe. One could put it this way: if the weather conditions during the summer of 1974 are as perfect as they were during the summer of 1874, there is no earthly reason why 1974 champagne should not be as stupendous as 1874 champagne was; on the other hand, between now and 1974 there may be years when the grapes have to be left on the vines a little longer than would have been necessary under the *en foule* system, and, if during that delay the weather is unkind, the champagne produced with the wine of those years may not be quite up to the standard it would have been in the preceding century.

If the reader will glance at the little drawing of the *en foule-provignage* system, he will see at once why the system had to be abandoned after the phylloxera invasion: the roots formed by the vine branch buried in the soil derive from the top half of the vine, which means that phylloxera would immediately attack them and cause each newly created vine to wither and die. As long as phylloxera continues to haunt the vineyards, new vines can only be produced by grafting. But even if one day someone finds a way of stamping out phylloxera entirely, it is virtually certain that the vines will never be grown *en foule* again in the Champagne district. The new method of cultivating the vine which phylloxera made it necessary for the grower to adopt would have been forced on him anyway by the economic conditions of the twentieth century. Growing the vines *en foule* was all very well while the grower remained a peasant, willing and economically able to do all the work by hand; in a mechanized society it is entirely impractical. Not even a horse could penetrate any except the very biggest vineyards; there were no paths to speak of, and all the new earth and the manure had to be carted in on the grower's or his wife's back. Cultivating the vines in neat rows has transformed the vine grower's life. For instance, under the *en foule* system every autumn, as soon as the vintage was over, up to 20,000 oak stakes per acre had to be taken up by hand and stored away—otherwise the winter damp would have caused them to rot. And then in the spring they had to be re-inserted, and the vines, which had spent the winter curled up in heaps, had to be re-attached to them. The inserting (known as *ficherie*) was a most laborious operation: men did it by pressing against the stakes with their chests, which were protected by stout leather pads; women used either a mallet or a special appliance that could be worked by foot. Today stakes have to be inserted only once in the lifetime of the vine. The *en ligne* system has two other minor advantages, which help to compensate for its drawbacks: the vines are easier to see and treat, and the greater aeration to some extent discourages parasites.

There still exist in the winefield a few vineyards which are planted with ungrafted French vines. There is one such plot at Bouzy, belonging to Bollinger, and another at a place with the tantalizing name of Boutavent, near Montmirail. The soil of these plots is exceptionally siliceous.

CHAPTER 24

THE VINTAGE

THREE GIANT QUESTION-MARKS loom over the Champagne district as the grapes ripen. What is the vintage going to be like from the point of view of quality and quantity? What date will the picking begin? What price will be paid for the grapes?

The answer to the first question remains in the laps of the gods until the very last moment, and invariably gives rise to the most profound pessimism on the part of the Champenois. They are constitutionally incapable of imagining that some disaster will not intervene to ruin the crop, however promising it may be. In fact, the only time in the entire year when they sometimes indulge in the luxury of fleeting optimism is during the winter. For this to happen the ivy on their homes must be bearing much fruit, for that is said to be, and often turns out to be, the harbinger of a memorable vintage. Alternatively, the previous two or three crops must have been exceptionally small, for a succession of small crops rests the vines and is often followed by an exceptionally large one. But as soon as the grapes appear on the vines the Champenois' faith in such comforting thoughts vanishes completely, and is replaced, at best, by a keep-your-fingers-crossed attitude.

The decision as to when picking may begin is taken by the Comité Interprofessionel du Vin de Champagne and announced in an *Ouverture des Vendanges* proclamation. Two dates are given—one for the red grapes and a slightly later one for the whites.

In order to understand how the dates are chosen and how the individual vineyard owner decides whether to start picking at once or to wait a day or two, one must be quite clear what it is that the champagne-maker looks for in grape-juice in order to produce a high class champagne: namely, a sugar content sufficient to produce 10° to 11° of alcohol, an acid content sufficient to give the wine that freshness which is the hallmark of champagne, and a total absence of colour in the juice of the red grapes.

One must also understand what goes on inside a grape during the last stage of its development. Between the time it sets and the time it has ripened, a grape increases daily in weight (and therefore in the quantity of juice it contains); for a few days after it has ripened its weight remains stationary; thereafter it diminishes. The sugar content increases slowly in the early stages of the ripening, increases rapidly in the later stages, remains stationary for a while after the grape has ripened, and thereafter increases again. The acid content is highest at the moment when the grape starts to ripen, and thereafter constantly diminishes. As soon as a red grape has ripened, the colouring in its skin starts tainting its juice.

Other considerations apart, the earlier the grapes are picked the better, because the longer they remain on the vines the greater is the danger that a sudden rainstorm will cause the dreaded *Botrytis cinerea* mould to alight on them and give them *pourriture grise.*

With so many factors to be taken into account, the decision when to start picking is always a delicate one. As a general rule, the date chosen is that which most nearly coincides with the full ripening of the grapes. Seldom are they picked before they are fully ripe, even though waiting increases the risk of their being ravaged by *pourriture grise.* Grapes that are not quite ripe invariably lack the sugar which the champagne-maker needs, and their acid content has not had time to diminish sufficiently. Seldom, too, are they left for long on the vines once they are ripe, even if their juice is lacking in sugar. For grapes that are over-ripe not only have too low an acid content for their ever-developing sugar content but also, if they are red, contain juice that is tainted with colour. Furthermore, fully ripe grapes always contain more juice than under-ripe or over-ripe grapes.

The question now arises, how does one know when a grape is fully ripe? An old hand at the game can tell with amazing exactitude what stage of its development has been reached by making a series of simple tests. He notes the colour of the skin, the ease with which the grape comes away from the stalk, the appearance of the fragment of pulp which adheres to the stalk, the texture of the stalk, the elasticity of the grape when squeezed, the colour, size and texture of the pips, above all the taste of the juice, and he draws his conclusions accordingly.

There are some Champenois, however, who believe that there is an even simpler method of telling when the grapes are fully ripe. They maintain that the ripening process is similar to a gestation, and that weather conditions have no influence upon it. Nature, they say, decrees that a grape will be ripe one hundred days after the flowers of the vine reach full bloom as immutably as she decrees that a child will be born ten lunar months after conception takes place. All that the weather affects is the chemical composition of the juice: if there is plenty of sun during the summer, the grapes will contain lots of sugar by the time they are ripe; if the summer is chilly and wet, they will contain a miserable amount of sugar and, for that quantity of sugar, too much acid; but the date the grape becomes fully ripe will be practically the same in either case. Convinced of the correctness of their theory, they like to pick their grapes one hundred days after the flowers of their vines reach full bloom.*

The more modern minded vineyard owner prefers to rely on less empirical methods. As his grapes ripen he sends samples of them to a laboratory where a chemist squeezes out the juice in a miniature press and tests it, among other things, for sugar and acid content. And the decision as regards picking is based largely on the information which the chemist provides.

The vintage nearly always begins some time in September, but it has been known to start as early as the third week of August (1893, 1929, 1955) and as late as the second week in October (1860, 1938, 1965). A late vintage is usually a nightmare: the cold weather takes half the fun out of the picking, and the operation is long drawn out because the days are short. Speed, where picking is concerned, is essential in the Champagne district, in order to lessen the risk of the juice of the red grapes becoming tainted with colour, and of *pourriture grise* ruining the entire crop. Normally the vast majority of the grapes have been removed from the vines within ten days of the start of the vintage.

The price the grapes are to fetch is decided by the C.I.V.C., as I have already explained. No longer, therefore, do sordid squabbles over this vital question overshadow the aura of lusty gaiety with which the vintage is traditionally associated; the *négociants* merely give vent to their dissatisfaction over the highness of the price and the *vignerons* complain vociferously that it is ludicrously low.

In a last-minute order, called the *Réglementation de Vendange*, the C.I.V.C. also makes certain rulings that must be adhered to. These include the minimum alcoholic strength the must will have to attain in order to qualify for the appellation, and the maximum weight of grapes with the right to the appellation that may be extracted from each hectare. The weight limit is generally fixed at 7,500 kilos. As the law states that only the first 100 litres of juice extracted from each 150 kilos of grapes may be used to make champagne, it follows that one hectare normally produces only 5,000 litres of juice for the champagne-maker (approximately 2,000 gallons per acre). When one

---

* It is also said in the Champagne district that the grapes will be ready to pick ninety days after the first lilies flower; often they are.

compares this figure with the 3,000 gallons of juice per acre that is commonly extracted for wine-making purposes from vineyards in the South of France and Algeria, one realizes to what extreme lengths the Champenois are willing to go to achieve quality.

Out in the vineyards, a sure sign that the vintage is about to begin is a merry twinkling among the vines. The twinkling is caused by pieces of silver paper which the vineyard workers string along the rows to frighten away birds. At night, some vineyard owners use maroons for the same purpose set to go off with a loud report every two or three minutes (the noise also scares away wild boar, foxes, badgers, dogs, dormice, wasps and other creatures that devour grapes). The shooting of the birds, however, is strictly forbidden, because many of them fly on to fulfil a useful function in Brie—that of picking maggots out of the backs of sheep and cattle. Now and again at this time of the year one sees a starling or some other bird in desperate plight, zooming wildly skywards, plunging dizzily earthwards; it has just eaten a grape with a cracked skin and the juice inside was fermenting: the poor thing is drunk, blind drunk, on Champagne wine.

In Rheims and Epernay and Ay there is a great heightening of tension. From Rio de Janeiro, New York, Venice, Capri, Deauville and other places far and near, jets and fast cars are whisking home the champagne magnates who have been away on business trips and on holiday. Journalists, wine merchants and wine lovers from all over the world are arriving in force to be their guests. And all the while, by road, by rail, on Vespas, on bicycles, by truck, by bus, on foot, the army of grape-pickers is converging on the winefield.

Altogether, nearly 10,000 people come to the Champagne district each autumn to pick the grapes. They come mostly from the Ardennes, the Argonne, Lorraine and Northern France. The Lorraine contingent has been coming almost every year since 1095. The hard core of the army consists of miners and industrial workers and their families from towns like Amiens, Arras, Douai, Lille, Longwy and Roubaix. The big champagne Houses maintain recruiting agents in such centres, and the local inspectors of health encourage their efforts, as no finer cure for silicosis and similar ills exists than ten days in the clean air of the vineyards. The remainder of the army? Well, some are agricultural workers who are for ever on the move, harvesting there, picking fruit or grapes here, threshing somewhere else; some are gypsies (they turn up in long, windowless, horse-drawn caravans which sleep ten); some are students—not many, though, for they tend to find the exacting rhythm of the picking too much like hard work; a few are tramps; a few are undesirables. Some come for their health, as I have already explained; some because this is the only holiday they can afford; some because they have been coming for fifty years or more, and it has become a habit; some because they thoroughly enjoy themselves; some for lust; few for the money. The pickers get paid about £1 a day nowadays, with board and lodging thrown in, which means they should be about £10 in pocket at the end; but they seldom are, as most of their pay goes on bottles of champagne and *eau-de-vie-de-marc* for the winter.

A small vineyard owners generally puts up the pickers he engages in his own home or in outbuildings. The big champagne firms house their pickers in *vendangeoirs*, buildings erected specially for the purpose at various points in the winefield. Some *vendangeoirs* will house 250 people. Many of them are almost luxurious, considering they are only used for ten days to a fortnight a year: the dormitories are whitewashed; each picker is provided with a camp-bed, a straw palliasse, army blankets and a locker for his clothes; there may be central heating and showers (the latter are used by the firm's vineyard workers during the winter); a few even have a reading-room which can be converted into a dance-hall in the evenings. In the summer the *vendangeoirs* are occasionally lent to organizations which run *colonies de vacances* for poor children from Paris and other large cities.

This thought for their comfort is necessary, for grape-picking in the Champagne district was, is and always will be a job for people with strong constitutions. For one thing, there is seldom a broiling sun to brighten up the job, and if there is some sun wasps, to quote a young Englishman who recently took part in the vintage, become "a bloody nuisance". Much more often it is a question of being drenched to the skin one day, frozen stiff the next and covered in mud the day after. Secondly, because the vines are trained low the picker bends double, he kneels, he sits, he lies stretched out to pick, but he never finds a position that prevents his back from feeling it has red hot coals on it at the end of the day. Thirdly, there is the little matter of the overseers. Thanks to these gentlemen, who are responsible vineyard workers, it has never been considered necessary, as is the case with hop-picking in England, to pay for services rendered on a piece-work basis. The newcomer is apt, at first, to imagine that the overseers have soft hearts, for they insist on a slow pace being maintained and frown on excess enthusiasm; it takes him a little while to realize that they do this because they keep the picker relentlessly at it without the slightest let up, except for meals, from dawn to dusk,. and, unlike the Army sergeant, do not know the meaning of such words as "breaks" and "smokes". They have the knack of appearing out of thin air whenever anyone is thinking of slacking off, and they are said to be immune to bribery, even—and this is rare for a Frenchman—to that of a pretty face.

But I must not give the impression that grape-picking is a solemn, sad affair in the Champagne district. Far from it. The pickers may return to the *vendangeoir* each evening with aching limbs, hot, tired and sweaty, or wet through and frozen to the bone, longing for that shower, but out in the vineyards one rarely sees a bad tempered face. The extraordinary variety of dress and headgear around is in itself conducive to gaiety: dungarees below, a coolie hat and pigtails above; a multi-coloured shirt and corduroy trousers; a prim cotton dress and a *bagnolet* (the great white butterfly of a hat that a countrywoman in the Champagne district wears to protect her face from the sun); blue overalls and a beret; anything and everything goes. There is much singing, and the singing is encouraged by the vineyard owners, who believe in the old French saying, "*Bouche qui mord à la chanson ne mord pas à la grappe*". Not that the vineyard owners have much to fear on this latter score from the old-timer, who knows that fearful tummy-aches result from over-indulgence. And even in the most trying conditions the teasing, the flirting and the backchat that go on are nobody's business.

Of course, the food the pickers are given is partly responsible for their good humour. Before leaving the *vendangeoir* in the early morning they have steaming coffee (as black as your hat), bread and Maroilles cheese.* At nine o'clock they have breakfast in the vineyards; it generally consists of soup, *charcuterie*, hot vegetables, more black coffee, more bread and more Maroilles, and it is often washed down with a swig of *marc*. At midday lunch is brought out in canisters and huge thermoses, and is eaten at the edge of the vineyard. The menu is usually soup, bread, meat, vegetables, Maroilles cheese, of course, and strong red wine. Around half-past-three there appears what the English call tea and the French call a *goûter*: this consists of—it sounds a bit monotonous, but it's fortifying—black coffee, bread, Maroilles

---

* Maroilles cheese is renowned for what the French call *agressifs aromes et saveurs violentes*. I know an Englishman who took one back to London and finally decided to bury it in his garden. It has been made in a village called Maroilles in the *département* of Nord for over a thousand years (it used to be known as *merveille du pays de Hainault*), but those given to the pickers are made by a cheese factory in Rheims, which sees to it that they reach smelly maturity at the time picking begins.

cheese, naturally, and red wine. Upon returning to the *vendangeoir* the pickers find waiting for them yet another huge meal, comprised of soup, a gigantic *pot-au-feu* or perhaps a great dish of cabbage and *lard*, Maroilles cheese, a dessert and coffee. And throughout the day—and night—unlimited quantities of red wine are at their disposal, provided by the thoughtful vineyard owner. Water is also available; it is far less popular.

The art of grape-picking in the Champagne district consists of getting as many grapes as possible to the presses before they start fermenting, for the champagne-maker wants to be able to control the fermentation, and in the case of the red grapes premature fermentation causes the colour in the skins to taint the juice. For this reason picking always starts at dawn, when the grapes are cool; later in the day, particularly if the sun is shining, it is often impossible to prevent a number of grapes from fermenting on the journey to the press-house. For this reason, too, great care has to be taken to avoid bruising the grapes, for a bruised grape immediately starts fermenting. There can be no question of wrenching off a bunch of grapes and chucking it into a basket: the picking has to be done gently, and the bunches, particularly those of the Chardonnay, whose grape-skins are exceptionally fragile, have to be treated as if they were made of glass.

To remove the bunches, the picker is provided with a pair of *épinettes*, an instrument which is a cross between scissors and secateurs: *épinettes* are very sharp and very cheap—gardeners, who have never come across anything quite like them, go mad about them. Armed with his pair of *épinettes* and a small wooden basket, the picker takes up position at the bottom of the row of vines allotted to him. Another member of the team or *hordon* is positioned directly opposite him, to pick the grapes on the other side of the row. The pair of pickers start to pick, and as soon as their baskets are full another member of the team, who is known as a *porteur*, takes away their baskets and hands them empty ones. The overseer sees to it that the *porteur* is always beside the picker as his basket is filling up, and in this way the slow but relentless movement of the *hordons* across the vineyard is maintained throughout the day.

In a year when the grapes are in perfect condition, the *porteur* takes the filled baskets to the head of the row and tips the contents straight into huge wicker baskets, known as *mannequins*, in which the grapes make the journey to the press-house; but in years when some of the grapes are imperfect, the *porteur* tips out the contents on to large osier trays, resting on a couple of *mannequins*, for sorting to take place. The sorting is done by elderly women chosen for the job because of their sharp eyes. They remove all the unsound and unripe grapes and place them in a separate pile, to be made later into what is known as *vin de détour*, wine that will never be called champagne and will be consumed locally. Sorting the grapes is a time-consuming and costly operation, but it is indispensable for high quality champagne. Indeed, I have heard champagne-makers say that the future of champagne as a high quality wine depends to a larger extent on the maintenance of the tradition that the grapes must be sorted with extreme care in years when some of them are imperfect than on any other single factor.

The *mannequin* is a very remarkable basket. Oval in shape, its tall sides slant inwards towards the base; it is exceedingly strong, and it will hold 176 lb. of grapes. In the Musée d'Art at Geneva there is a fragment from a Roman sarcophagus which has a vintage scene sculpted on it, and the baskets depicted are identical to the *mannequin* in shape, in size and in the way the wicker is woven. The Champenois use them for a great variety of purposes, including the carting of wood in winter and the erection of enormous triumphal arches, sometimes thirty feet high, when a village is *en fête*. But their days appear to be numbered. Many firms are now using rectangular baskets or wooden boxes instead; they find their clean lines save so much space that the number of journeys which the carts and lorries have to make to the press-house is reduced. Also the rectangular containers, being smaller and lighter than *mannequins*, make life easier for the *colporteurs*, the men who load the carts and lorries; even with the aid of sticks with hooks on their ends, considerable beef is required to hoist aboard a filled *mannequin*.

After being loaded, the carts and lorries set off post-haste for the press-houses (the wheels of the carts have rubber tyres to prevent the grapes from being shaken and bruised). And so the picking, the basket-carrying, the sorting, the loading and the transporting of the grapes continues.

One can always tell when a Pommery or a Veuve Clicquot vineyard is being picked because a flag is flown, white for Pommery, yellow with an anchor design for Veuve Clicquot.

Dull indeed is the *vendangeoir* where of an evening, as a prelude to sleep or further frolics, someone does not organize a singsong or play the concertina for people to dance to; and there are always the fairs for evening entertainment. The Champagne district is a great place for fairs, never more so than during the vintage. All the local girls

attend; they are heavily chaperoned by Mum and other members of
the family, but an enterprising young *vendangeur* is soon flying one of
them through the air with the greatest of ease in a jet fighter, dancing
with her by moonlight, or making love to her in the dark of a covered-
in merry-go-round. There are trout in tanks to be fished for—and to
be taken away alive in water-filled plastic bags. There are ducks, pigs
and geese to be won—provided you can outwit the unashamed rigging
of the sideshows.

All the same, the great complaint of the veteran *vendangeurs* is that
the *vendange* isn't what it used to be. You see their point if you pick
their memories or read about the old times. The arrival of the *vendangeurs* was a tremendous spectacle in itself: they travelled in great carts,
with shaky wheels, drawn by mules, the children and old women aloft,
the parents trudging along behind on foot. (Not, when you come to
think about it, that the spectacle is really any less amazing today, what
with the antiquity of some of the conveyances, the over-crowding,
the leanings-out-of-the-windows, the catcalls and the general hulla-
baloo.) The church bells used to peal as the *vendangeurs* set out each
morning. The donkey—not the lorry—used to be the focal point of
the *vendange*, as the mighty oxen of the Médoc still are (just) in that
winefield today; the donkeys, incidentally, were partial to grapes and
had to be muzzled. As for the songs, they were more robust, like this
one:

> *"Allons en vendange*
> *Pour gagner cinq sous,*
> *Coucher sur la paille,*
> *Ramasser des poux,*
> *Manger du fromage*
> *Qui pue comme la rage*
> *Boire du vin doux*
> *Qui fait . . . partout!"*

(For the benefit of the non-linguist, the gist is that there were fleas in
the straw and the cheese stank to high heaven.) And the agents of the
champagne-makers used to appear out in the vineyards in swift but
rickety cabriolets, instead of in Peugeot 404s or Citroën 2CVs, and
they would bargain for the grapes on the spot, the small proprietor
making his calculations on his fingers.

But it is not so much what went on during the vintage itself that the
veterans miss as what went on afterwards. To the back of the last cart
or basket-laden donkey to leave the vineyard would be attached a

large bouquet of wild flowers and vine-leaves, which was later presented to the owner of the vineyard by a pretty girl; the owner gave the girl a great hug and handed round champagne. In some villages there were spellbinding *cortèges* led by a *Roi des Vignerons* crowned with vine-leaves; in others the vineyard workers themselves paraded through the streets, carrying the tools of their trade—baskets, *épinettes*, buckets, shovels—and a broomstick to which had been attached a lighted candle. The parades were followed by *cochelets*, handsome repasts for which many a cockerel had been killed—hence the name; and then there was a ball.

Not all the old traditions have died out yet, however. *Cochelets* still take place in the homes of many vineyard workers; formidable meals they are too. As the picking draws to an end, one still sometimes sees carts with bunches of flowers tied on behind. And the *grappillage*, the gathering of grapes that were unripe or missed at the time of the vintage, which takes place three weeks later, is still considered by some vineyard owners to be a charitable occasion, the poor and young children being encouraged to take away with them as many bunches as they like. There is one custom, however, that the personnel managers of the big firms must be thankful has died out. This was the *vendangeurs'* habit of bringing with them an old lady, selected for her forthrightness and known as the *mère des vendangeurs*, whose job it was to act as intermediary between them and the vineyard owner, to bargain and to settle grievances.

PART V

THE MAKING OF THE WINE

CHAPTER 25

SOME INTRODUCTORY REMARKS

THE MAKING OF champagne is an art, not a science. Centuries of experience have, it is true, enabled the Champenois to reduce the art of champagne-making to a system which has come to be known as the *méthode champenoise*. But the system is not a rigid one, and only certain of its stages are prescribed by law. In the main, custom and precedent are responsible for its application, and plenty of room is left for the enterprise of the individual producer. I ask the reader, while reading about the *méthode champenoise* in the pages that follow, to remember this. A factual description of its various stages inevitably gives the impression that if the grapes are good, and as long as certain rules are followed, excellent champagne is bound to result; in reality, a champagne-maker of genius can produce a good champagne from mediocre grapes and a dunce will produce dull champagne with perfect grapes. The Champenois always insist on this point.

The most remarkable thing about the *méthode champenoise* is the exceptional extent to which it enables man to manipulate grape-juice. The second fermentation in bottle exploits latent riches in grape-juice which normal wine-making methods leave untouched. In a sense, the manufacture of champagne begins where that of ordinary wines ends. Time-and-motion study experts have estimated that the wine in a bottle of champagne is attended to by nearly 300 pairs of hands before it is ready to drink.

The making of champagne is surrounded with little mystery. There is no secret formula to protect, as there is for instance in the processes by which Chartreuse, Angostura and Campari bitters and Coca-Cola are manufactured. Virtually the only facts about the process that the Houses are unwilling to reveal are the exact composition of their blends and the precise amount of sugar they add. In most firms visitors are allowed to watch all the more important operations, and the workmen are encouraged to answer questions. This does not mean, however, that champagne-making is completely devoid of mystery. Many things that happen in the course of the conversion of the grape-juice into champagne are still not properly understood.

A grape is composed of three parts: pulp, skin and pips. The pulp constitutes 80 to 90 per cent of the weight of the grape. It is made up of innumerable cells which are separated by thin membranes, and each of which contains a drop of juice. As a grape ripens the membranes jellify; that is why the pulp of a ripe grape is gelatinous in appearance and responds like lazy elastic when touched. The Chardonnay grapes always contain slightly more pulp than do those of the Pinot Noir and the Pinot Meunier.

The skin of a grape is made up of three protective envelopes. The outer envelope is known as the cuticle, and is covered with a waxy substance called the pruina; the second envelope is known as the epidermis; the third, innermost envelope is known as the hypodermis and contains the colour cells of the grape. The envelopes enclose odorous matters which, when highly developed, give grape-juice a slight perfume; this perfume disappears in time, and has absolutely nothing to do with the bouquet the wine eventually gives off.

The grapes grown in the Champagne district normally contain two, three or four pips. The pips are not crushed at the time the grapes are pressed, so they have little or no effect on the juice.

The drops of juice that lie squeezed between the membranes of the pulp of the grape are of an exceedingly complex chemical composition; they contain several substances that chemists cannot identify. Until these substances are identified, it will be impossible to distinguish a great wine from an ordinary one by chemical analysis; tasting will remain the only means of doing so. The principal ingredients of grape-juice and the proportions in which they are normally found at the moment of ripening are:

Water: 70–80 per cent
Sugar: 10–25 per cent
Acid: 2–5 per cent

Of these three ingredients the most important is the sugar, because it is this that in the course of fermentation is transformed by the wine-yeasts into alcohol and carbonic acid gas. The sugar is of two types, glucose and levulose: when the grapes reach maturity both are present in equal proportions. Both are fermentable.

The role of the acids is a most important one. They give the wine its freshness, and help it to remain healthy in old age, for they are the enemies of illness-provoking bacteria. Moreover, they favour the development of the bouquet, because when an organic acid comes in contact with alcohol a reaction takes place, and sweet-smelling substances, known as esters, are formed; it is these esters that are largely responsible for the bouquet of a wine. Acids, however, must not be present in the grape-juice in too great quantity, or the champagne will be "*vert*", too green and astringent.

Grape-juice also contains certain mineral salts and other substances of known origin, which contribute to the personality of the wine.

If a grape is carefully examined at the time it is picked, its pruina—the waxy substance on its outer skin or cuticle—is seen to be covered with a misty grey down; this is called the bloom of the grape. If it is examined through a microscope it is seen to consist of a veritable world of living creatures. A proportion of these are bacteria; some of them are capable, under certain conditions, of causing illness in the wine, while others are perfectly benevolent. The remainder of the living creatures are minute fungi, known as yeasts. By far the greater number of these yeasts play no role in wine-making and are referred to by wine-makers as wild yeasts; but the pruina always harbours a percentage of a special type of yeast which, because it has the capacity of converting sugar into alcohol and carbonic acid gas, is known as a wine-yeast. It is estimated that, on average, each grape brings with it to the wine-press upwards of a 100,000 wine-yeasts; the wild yeasts on it may number upwards of 10 million.

The majority of the wine-yeasts spend the winter in the intestines of animals and insects such as dormice, bees and flies. In the spring, when their hosts emerge from hibernation, the wine-yeasts are disseminated: some float about in the air; some settle on dust and on particles of earth; others alight on flowers, feed on the sugar which the flowers contain and, thus fortified, multiply. In August and September the wind, or animals and insects that feed off grapes, carry the wine-yeasts on to the grape-skins. Most of them get stuck on the waxy pruinas and remain there until the grapes are picked; but a few are carried off again by animals and insects, in whose intestines they spend another winter, thus ensuring that there will be no shortage of wine-yeasts in the vineyard the following year.

In actual fact, wine-yeasts themselves have little or no effect on grape-juice; they merely feed upon the sugar it contains. Each wine-yeast, however, contains thousands of minute enzymes (they used to be called "ferments"), which it secretes; and it is these enzymes that turn grape-juice into wine. For when the enzyme comes into contact with certain substances in the grape-juice, it attacks them; a chemical reaction takes place and the substances are transformed. By far the most important transformation, or "fermentation", that takes place is

that of sugar into alcohol and carbonic acid gas; but the other fermentations produce substances (glycerines, acids, esters, among others)
which affect the colour, taste, bouquet and longevity of the wine and
help to form its character. Some of these fermentations take place
when the sugar is transformed, but most of them occur later, while
the wine is ageing.

The wine-yeasts multiply at a fantastic speed when they have sugar
to feed upon. The rate at which they do so depends mainly on the
prevailing temperature, but it is also determined by the amount of
oxygen available. Like all living matter, wine-yeasts respire, and must
have access to oxygen. But when they are feeding on grape-juice
access to too great a supply of oxygen means that the wine-yeasts
multiply at a tremendous rate but secrete practically no enzymes, the
result being that the transformation of the sugar into alcohol proceeds
very slowly. Inversely, if the supply of oxygen is kept short, the rate
of multiplication of the wine-yeasts is slowed down and the secretion
of enzymes is increased, so that the sugar is quickly and completely
transformed into alcohol. That is why, after the grapes have been
pressed, the juice is well aired, to enable the wine-yeasts to multiply,
but is then immediately placed in a cask or vat (which has only a small
opening to allow the carbonic acid gas to escape) so that the multiplication of the wine-yeasts is slowed down, lots of enzymes are
produced and a quick and complete transformation of the sugar into
alcohol takes place.

There are many different types of wine-yeasts. Some cease to work
once a small amount of sugar has been converted into alcohol; some
work very slowly; some only work at high temperatures. In the
Champagne district the predominating type of wine-yeast is the *Saccaromices allypsoideus*, but there are many varieties of it and the variety
inhabiting one vineyard may be quite different from that in the next.
Luckily for the Champenois, most varieties of *Saccaromices allypsoideus*
"fall" easily: that is to say, they do not cloud the wine during *remuage*.
The variety most sought after will transform the sugar completely,
work at low temperatures and work fast.

CHAPTER 26

THE GRAPES AND THE MUST

The Weighing of the Grapes (Pesage)

As soon as the lorries with the newly-picked grapes arrive at the press-house, the *mannequins* are unloaded and laid out in neat piles in a large shed, the produce of each vineyard being kept separate. The baskets are then weighed and the weight is inscribed on a ticket, attached to the basket, upon which has already been recorded the origin of the grapes and the time they were picked. As soon as a press is available the baskets are moved forward into the press-house. When the vintage is in full swing many hundreds of baskets, crammed full with luscious booty, may be lined up outside the press-house awaiting their turn to go in; they are a sight wonderful to behold.

The Pressing of the Grapes (Pressurage)

The press-house may belong to a village, to a co-operative of vineyard owners or to a champagne firm. Most of the big firms prefer to press the grapes themselves, as then they can be sure that the job is done with every possible care, but the cost of a press is such that it is only worth while for a big vineyard proprietor to own one.

Throughout the vintage the press-house becomes a little world of its own, in which the rhythms and interests of normal life are laid aside and forgotten. Once the first basket of grapes arrives pressing goes on twenty-four hours a day until the last basket has been accounted for, and nothing (except, calamity of calamities, the breakdown of a press) is allowed to interfere with the remorseless extraction of juice. The staff, *en bleu* and wearing gumboots, work twelve-hour shifts and eat beside the presses; a Champenoise considers it a great honour to be chosen to do the cooking at the press-house, and she and her helpers lay on beautifully presented, sit-down meals which no man except a Frenchman could hope to enjoy in similar circumstances. If the vintage is a large one, the staff will be bleary-eyed and at the point of collapse by the time the presses come down for the last time, but their cheerfulness and their courtesy to visitors (whom they ply with bunches to taste) remain unfailing. There is something intensely stimulating, awe-inspiring too, about the spectacle of nature's bounty pouring forth from the presses in such abundance.

As I have already had frequent occasion to mention, the technique used to press the grapes in the Champagne district is quite different from that used in other wine regions, because of the need for the juice of the red grapes to be extracted without becoming tainted by the colouring matter in the skins. Treading the grapes by foot is out of the question; it takes so long that the juice extracted from red grapes invariably comes out red. Not only must the pressing be rapid, but the juice must be conducted in such a way that the mass of grapes which it traverses as it descends is as thin as possible.

The key to the technique is the design of the champagne press. It is a comparatively simple instrument, made of oak, consisting of a receptacle, known as a *maie*, which generally holds 4,000 kilos of grapes, and of a heavy lid, known as a *mouton*, which is suspended above the *maie* and comes down into it to press the grapes. The *maie* can be square or round—the modern ones are round—but its depth is seldom greater than two feet; this shallowness in relation to considerable breadth or diameter (a round *maie* is generally about ten feet in diameter) ensures that the juice extracted from the grapes on top never remains for long in contact with the skins of the grapes below as it falls towards the hole in the bottom of the *maie* through which it flows out. The sides of the *maie* are made of closely-knit oak railings which can be taken out, and this facilitates the removal of the grape husks and the cleaning of the *maie* once each lot of grapes has been pressed. The *mouton* is always a little smaller in breadth or diameter than the *maie*, so that it just fits into the *maie* as it descends. It is attached by a shaft to a huge oak beam which is supported by two pillars. In the olden days this shaft was operated by a wheel turned by manpower. In the eighteenth century a wheel was used which men turned by climbing up its spokes like squirrels—there is an example of this *écureuil* type of press in the museum at Epernay; but by the nineteenth century a different type of wheel, known as a *calandre*, which seven men could turn by hand, was in use. Today the *mouton* is operated by electric or hydraulic power, and is capable of exerting a pressure of 40,000 kilos per square metre on the grapes; with such pressure available, they can be pressed really quickly.

The 4,000 kilos of grapes that fill the *maie* are known as a *marc*. One *marc* produces between 2,700 and 3,000 litres of juice, the exact amount depending on the plumpness of the grapes and their type: a Chardonnay grape always gives a little more juice than a Pinot grape. But as the law lays down that only the first 100 litres of juice extracted from each 150 kilos of grapes has the right to the appellation, it follows that only the first 2,666 litres of juice extracted from a *marc* can be made into champagne.

To extract these 2,666 litres of juice, it is necessary to press each *marc* several times. The juice of one pressing is always kept separate from that of another, because the juice of the first pressing is invariably more desirable for the purpose of making champagne than the juice of the second pressing, and each successive pressing produces juice of a lower quality. There are two reasons why this is so. One is that the juice of an early pressing is less tainted with colour, and contains a larger share of wine-yeasts, than the juice of a later pressing. The other is that, owing to the way in which the sugars and acids are positioned in a grape, the juice that flows out of the grapes during an early pressing is better constituted chemically than the juice that flows out later. For the juice in the centre, near the pips, and next to the skin contains a fair amount of sugar, but very little acid; the juice in the intermediary zone, half way between the pips and the skin, is rich in both sugar and acid.

The first 2,000 litres of juice to be extracted from a *marc* are known as the *vin de cuvée*.* The extraction usually involves bringing down the press three times and normally takes between one-and-a-half and two hours. The first 1,000 litres of the *vin de cuvée* are known as the *première cuvée*, the next 600 litres as the *deuxième cuvée*, and the final 400 litres as the *troisième cuvée*. The *vin de cuvée* is used in the production of the best champagnes. 2,000 litres is sufficient to make 2,500 bottles.

The next 666 litres of juice to be extracted are known as the *vin de taille*. It is becoming much harder to extract the juice by now, so, although the volume of the *vin de taille* is very much smaller than that of the *vin de cuvée*, three pressings are generally required to obtain it; the pressings take, on average, an hour-and-a-half. The first 200 litres obtained are known as the *première taille*, the next 200 as the *deuxième taille* and the final 266 as the *troisième taille*. The *première taille* makes a perfectly agreeable champagne, but it will be fruitier, less fresh and generally less elegant than one made with the *vin de cuvée*; also, it will not last as long because, although it contains almost as much sugar as the *vin de cuvée*, it contains much less acid (the juice being derived from the centre or periphery of the grape), and it is the acids in a wine that enable it to live a long time. The *deuxième* and *troisième tailles* have

* *Une cuve*, in French, means a vat. *Une cuvée* means, literally, a vatful; besides using the word in connection with the first 2,000 litres of juice extracted from a *marc*, the Champenois use it to describe the blend of wines of which champagne is composed; they say, for example, "that was a highly successful *cuvée*".

all the disadvantages of the *première taille*, but to a more marked degree. Most of the firms that have great reputations to maintain sell their *deuxième* and *troisième tailles*, if not all three, to firms that specialize in cheaper champagnes or make Buyers Own Brand champagnes, i.e. champagnes that are sold under the name and label of firms other than those of leading Houses.*

After the *vin de cuvée* and the *vin de taille* have been extracted, what remains of the grape pulp—it is known as the *rebêche*—is generally removed, to save time, to a more powerful press in which it is pressed again several times until the last drop of juice has been extracted. The *vin de rebêche* is not allowed to be made into champagne, because it is bitter, and if the grapes were red it is much tainted with colour; also, its lack of acidity gives it a feeble resistance to microbial alteration in old age. It is sometimes known as *Tisane*. It is made into a still wine to be consumed by the maker's staff, or to be sold as *vin ordinaire*.

Each time the *mouton* is pulled up between the various pressings the press-house staff have to perform what is known as a *retroussage*. This consists of breaking up the mass of grapes with a blunt wooden spade (no metal must come into contact with the grapes until the *vin de cuvée* has been extracted) and of manœuvring the grapes at the sides of the *maie* into the centre, where the pressure of the *mouton* is greatest, in readiness for the next pressing. It is notoriously hard work in any year; in years when the skins of the grapes are particularly thick it requires the strength of a Hercules. "Slave labour at its worst" was the comment of a sturdy young Liverpudlian *vendangeur* who had been warned, but insisted on joining a twelve-hour *retroussage* shift.

In most press-houses the loading, the pressing, the *retroussage* and the unloading of a *marc* of grapes takes six hours or longer. Moët & Chandon have an extremely modern press-house installation that reduces the duration of the various operations to between two and three hours, and enables 280 tons of grapes to be handled every twenty-four hours.

* This exceedingly fair comment on B.O.B. champagne appeared in *The French Vineyards* by Dennis Morris:

"I asked one of the great ones of the champagne world what he thought of B.O.B. and the much lower quality champagne. 'You could say,' he smiled, 'that they are good for launching enemy ships, but that would be cynical and unfair. All champagne is good—it has to be by the very strict law which controls its making, and the extremely strict control of every process. Some is a good deal better than others and this is reflected in its price. Besides, what should we do with our *taille* if we had not got these very good customers to sell it to? They are doing a job—everyone can't afford the best.' "

The grape-juice, at the time it emerges from the presses, is sticky and syrupy. To the untrained palate it always seems just plain sweet, although, of course, it is in fact much sweeter some years than others. The sweetness completely masks the taste of the acids. The juice of the white grapes is almost devoid of colour; that of the red grapes is sometimes practically colourless too, but more often it has a distinct reddish tint at this stage. The reddish tint, as long as it is not too pronounced, does not worry the champagne-maker; by the time the juice has finished fermenting it will have disappeared, for the wine-yeasts absorb it.

The Purging of the Must (Débourbage)

The must (as I shall now call the juice) leaves the press-house via a rubber pipe inserted in the hole in the bottom of the *maie*. Ideally, the liquid will be propelled throughout the journey by the force of gravity. In other words, the press-house will be situated on the side of a small hill; directly underneath it there will be a two- or three-storied building, set into the side of the hill, in which the must is turned into wine; and directly underneath this building, below ground-level, there will be two or three levels of cellars in which the wine, having been bottled, is turned into champagne. In such a set-up the original grape-juice—whether it is must or wine—can if necessary be transferred from the press-house all the way down to the deepest cellar without recourse to pumping or the man-handling of casks. But only rarely does the lie of the land render such an installation possible.

The immediate destination of the must upon leaving the press-house is what is known as a *cuve de débourbage*, a round open vat made of wood, or of cement lined with glass tiles, situated directly underneath the presses. Here it is purged of certain extraneous substances, the most undesirable of all being metal particles which may have been left behind by the wires between the stakes or the strips of wire with which the vines are tied up. The nature of the other substances depends largely on what the weather was like during the period when the grapes were on the vines. If it was kind, and in consequence the grapes were radiantly healthy when picked, they will probably consist of nothing more serious than bits of torn grapeskin, pips, stalks, dust, or particles of earth that got splashed on to the grapes during a rainstorm. If, on the other hand, the summer was wet and humid and in consequence the grapes were suffering from rot when picked, the substances may include all sorts of moulds and bacteria capable of perpetrating unpleasant tastes and smells and of causing the wine to fall ill. To allow them to remain in the juice would be to invite disaster;

and they must be got rid of straight away, before fermentation starts in earnest, because most of them are insoluble in cold watery must but highly soluble in angry alcoholic must.

If the temperature at the time when the must reaches the *cuves de débourbage* is low, fermentation will begin so sedately that it suffices to leave the must alone for a period of between twelve and thirty hours —the exact time depending on the temperature and the amount of impurities the must contains—and the impurities will fall to the bottom of the vat on their own accord; the clean must can then be drawn off through a hole in the vat just above the point at which the impurities have settled. But if the temperature is high at the time the must reaches the *cuves de débourbage* the must will start fermenting boisterously at once, and instead of falling the impurities will start dissolving. A hundred years ago the champagne-maker confronted by this situation could do nothing, except curse and resign himself to the prospect of turning dirty must into champagne. Today there are two ways of overcoming the problem. One is to pass the must, on its way from the presses to the *cuves de débourbage*, through refrigerated pipes, and slow down the fermentation in that way. The other is to add a very small quantity of sulphur dioxide to the must as soon as it reaches the *cuves*.

The effect on the must of the sterilizing gas which a tablet of sulphur dioxide emits is positively miraculous. In the first place, it does not kill but merely dazes the tough wine-yeasts, with the result that they temporarily cease to operate and fermentation is thus postponed. In the second place, it does kill most of the germs and moulds that are harmful to wine. Thirdly, it causes particles of metal, earth and dust to coagulate, and their fall to the bottom of the vat is thus hastened. Moreover, it is perfectly harmless in small quantities, as incapable of altering the character of wine as an aspirin is of changing the character of the human body. Virtually all wine-makers use it nowadays, and so, incidentally, do the makers of canned food—to stop their wares from fermenting and as an antiseptic. The quantity that French wine-makers may use is rigidly controlled by the *Code du Vin*. When sulphur dioxide is added, the must may be spotlessly clean and ready to be drawn off from the *cuves de débourbage* after a mere five to six hours, instead of after twelve to thirty hours (and in an impure condition), as might be the case were it not available.

The Transfer of the Must to the Casks or Vats

From the *cuves de débourbage* the must is transferred to the vessel in which it is to undergo its first fermentation. If the champagne-maker's cellars are directly below his press-house, the must can be piped from the *cuves de débourbage* into the fermentation vessel; but if his cellars are many miles from the press-house the must has to be put in cask for the journey and transferred to the fermentation vessel on arrival. In hot weather the danger exists that during the journey the must will embark on a precipitous fermentation, in which event, unless certain precautions are taken, it will start spurting out of the casks or the casks will explode. So a pocket of air is left in each cask, and a corn stalk is placed in a small hole drilled through the wood near the bung, through which the carbonic acid gas generated by the fermentation can escape.

Two types of vessel are used for the first fermentation: casks and vats. Champagne casks are made, ideally, of oak from Hungary, just as, ideally, cognac casks are made of oak from Limousin, bordeaux casks of oak from Aragon (among other places) and sherry casks of oak from America. They are shaped with an axe; sawing disturbs the grain of the wood, and wood particles seep into the wine. Before use, the casks are fumigated with brimstone and tested with water to make sure they are water-tight. The majority of the casks used for fermentation purposes have a capacity of two hundred litres, but a few are bigger.

Fermentation vats are a comparatively recent innovation, and there are still some champagne-makers who contend that a finer, more exquisitely bouqueted champagne is produced when fermentation takes place in a cask. Those who favour vats say this is nonsense and point to two advantages which a vat has over a cask: the conditions of fermentation are easier to control, and less wine is wasted when the racking takes place. Whoever is right, one thing is certain: vats are here to stay. Very small champagne-makers will presumably continue to use casks exclusively until kingdom come, but the economic advantages of vats are such, and their merits are so firmly established, that all the big firms are bound to use them, in conjunction with casks, in the end.

The first vats to be installed in champagne cellars were made of concrete lined with steel, which in turn was faced with glass tiles. They had one drawback: the glass frequently cracked, and maintenance and repair costs were exorbitant. Today one or two firms are using a new type of vat in which the glass tiles, of English manufacture, are replaced by a coating of a phenolic synthetic resin known as Prodor-Glas. Prodor-Glas had already been successfully used to line containers for penicillin and blood-plasma, so there was never any fear that it might impart an odd taste to the wine; it looks like becoming a standard lining for champagne vats in the future. Some of the fermentation vats in use today have a capacity of 33,000 litres.

After they have been filled, a label is attached to each cask or vat denoting, among other things, the number of the *marc* from which the must originated and the abbreviated name of the vineyard the grapes came from: "Vzn" for Verzenay, "By" for Bouzy.

The bungs of the casks are always removed at the outset of fermentation, to allow the carbonic acid gas to escape; but, to prevent dust from entering, either a vine-leaf or a piece of carboard, held down by a brick or a tile, is placed over each bung. The casks are never filled more than two-thirds full, for two reasons: to expose a large surface of the juice to aeration, thus encouraging the yeasts to multiply, and to prevent loss through overflowing. The screw-tops of vats are likewise left off at the outset of fermentation.

The Assistance of the Must

If there was a great deal of rain just before the grapes were picked, and it is thought that a considerable percentage of the yeasts on the skins was washed away, or if the weather just after the pressing is exceptionally cold and the yeasts are likely to be unusually slow in multiplying, so that too few enzymes will be available to attack the sugar, it is often an advantage to add to the must, before fermentation begins in earnest, a quantity of particularly vigorous yeasts.

This can be done in two ways: by adding a small quantity of must from a cask that is already fermenting boisterously, or by preparing a leaven with what are known as "Selected Yeasts", and adding some of this to the must.

Selected yeasts are yeasts which have been developed, in isolation from their inferior brethren, from the choicest yeast cells to be found in the very best growths. The isolating process is a complicated and extremely costly one, and few champagne-makers undertake it themselves; the majority of them buy their selected yeasts from local laboratories which specialize in yeast culture. A great advantage of selected yeasts is that, being of pure strain and known ancestry, their behaviour follows a familiar pattern and produces no nasty surprises, such as the imparting of an unpleasant taste to the wine; besides, provided they have been allowed to acclimatize themselves to the vinous surroundings in which they are to work, they can be counted on to be vigorous and achieve a complete fermentation. Often, if selected yeasts from a great growth are allowed to dominate the yeasts in the must of a secondary growth, the fermentation proceeds in a particularly happy manner. Consequently, it is becoming more and more the practice to assist with selected yeasts must originating from secondary growths. Often a mixture of selected yeasts from the great growths is used, those of Ay, Verzenay and Cramant making a particularly favourable combination. It is important that, whatever the type of yeast used, it is active at the time it enters the cask or vat: there is no difficulty in telling whether it is or not, because yeast in action hisses.

CHAPTER 27

THE STILL WINES

The First Fermentation (Fermentation des Moûts)

THE FERMENTATION OF the must in the casks and vats begins with a stormy phase known as *bouillage*. The must swells and appears to be boiling; it foams, it bubbles, it hisses; it looks very angry. *Bouillage* should be over in eight to ten days. Thereafter the fermentation proceeds more calmly for another ten to twenty days. The whole process thus generally takes a little under three weeks.

The storminess of *bouillage* is caused by the intense activity of the enzymes inside the casks and vats. The yeasts are forever multiplying and secreting enzymes which engage upon the wholesale destruction of the sugar in the must. By the end of *bouillage* only three grams of sugar normally remain in each litre of wine: the rest has been converted into alcohol (which mixes with the must and turns it into wine) and into carbonic acid gas. The latter, being heavier than air, falls into the cellars after being forced out of the vats and casks, with the result that a visit to the cellars while *bouillage* is in progress is a rather unpleasant experience.* The second stage of fermentation is quieter because the yeasts are becoming exhausted and are secreting fewer enzymes; by the time it is finished the sugar content of the wine should have been reduced to two grams per litre.

Now, in order to produce perfect wine, the champagne-maker has to maintain strict control over the fermentation. His main concern is to ensure that it proceeds slowly, because a wine that takes some time to ferment has a much finer bouquet and more finesse than one that has done so in a mad rush. The key to the rate at which the wine ferments is temperature. The ideal temperature for the fermentation of Champagne wines is 15°C.; no great harm is caused if it is between 15°C. and 20°C., but below 15°C. champagne yeasts operate sluggishly, and above 20°C. they are in danger of being killed; if this happens, the fermentation "sticks". That is why the casks and vats in which fermentation is to take place are always positioned at ground level in a *cellier*; the cellars would be far too cold, but the temperature of a *cellier* in September or early October (when fermentation is normally

---

* Carbonic acid gas is harmless in small quantities, but harmful in large ones.

in progress) is usually somewhere between 15°C. and 20°C. It can happen, when the vintage takes place exceptionally early, that temperatures higher than 20°C. are registered, but the more frequent problem is a cold autumn with temperatures below 15°C. In the latter event the *celliers* may have to be heated (smoke must be avoided); in addition, blankets may have to be placed over the casks and electric heating cones inserted in the vats.

The champagne-maker's second concern is to see that fermentation proceeds at a regular rate. He endeavours, by opening and closing the doors and windows of the *celliers*, and above all by avoiding draughts, to keep the temperature constant. Draughts and sudden bouts of cold are particularly dangerous at the end of fermentation, as the yeasts are old and tired, the alcohol in the wine makes it difficult for the enzymes to go on decomposing the sugar, and fermentation may come to an abrupt halt before all the sugar has been decomposed. Getting fermentation going again once it has stopped is a tiresome business. Sometimes raising the temperature of the surroundings suffices; more often the wine has to be transferred to new casks, to aerate it, and a leaven of selected yeasts has to be added.

The champagne-maker's final concern is to achieve a complete fermentation, complete to the extent that not more than two grams of sugar per litre remain in the wine. The yeasts can be counted on to achieve this for him if, before fermentation began in earnest, when the must was still in the *cuves de débourbage*, it was thoroughly aerated.

The *vin de taille* and the *vin de rebêche* invariably ferment more quickly than the *vin de cuvée*, because they contain less acid: acids slow down the rate at which the ferments work.

In a few firms, the difficulties concerning temperature during fermentation have been surmounted by the installation of a temperature control system in the *celliers* which contain the vats. In this way all danger is avoided of high temperatures causing the wine to turn into vinegar—a very real risk when fermentation takes place in large vats.

Some of the bigger firms are also equipped to produce a malolactic reaction in their wine. This recently discovered method of reducing acidity is always applied just as the first fermentation ends.

The Topping-Up of the Casks and the Vats (Ouillage)

In the course of fermentation, the level of the wine in the casks and vats gradually falls. The shrinkage is caused by the release of carbonic acid gas and by evaporation. Evaporation is particularly marked in the casks because a little wine inevitably seeps out through the pores of the wood; as alcohol penetrates the wood more easily than water, there is a tendency for wine fermented in casks to end up slightly weaker than wine fermented in vats.

If the loss of volume were not made good at once, the foam adhering to the top of the vessel would dry and impart a nasty taste to the wine; also, bacteria would make use of the oxygen in the vacant space at the top of the vessel to propagate themselves and alter the character of the wine. As fermentation ends, therefore, the casks and vats must be topped up every three or four days or so until the loss of volume ceases.

The Analysis of the Still Wine

As soon as the wine has cooled off after fermentation, it is analysed and tasted. Being a living matter, composed of many different substances, nearly all of which are attractive to germs and susceptible to chemical change, wine is highly vulnerable to disease and alteration; but as long as certain elementary precautions are taken—such as the removal of diseased grapes from the bunches before pressing, the use of scrupulously clean and suitably constituted wine vessels, frequent *ouillages*—the champagne-maker has not much to fear on this score, particularly with the *vin de cuvée*. The *vin de taille* and the *vin de rebêche* are more susceptible to disease and alteration.

Cold Air let into the Celliers

As soon as analysis of the wine confirms that the enzymes have finished turning the must into wine, the doors and windows of the *celliers* are opened to let in the cold winter air. This is done for four reasons: to bring the fermentation to a complete halt; to prevent the wine from ageing too rapidly; to discourage the development of illness-provoking bacteria; and to cause the yeasts to fall to the bottom of the cask so that what is known as the *vin clair* may be prepared.

Some firms simulate the cold of winter by pouring liquid glycol on to cloths draped over their vats. This causes the temperature of the wine to drop by as much as 4°C.

The First Racking (Premier Soutirage)

Champagne yeasts, as I have already mentioned, have the tendency to fall heavily when inactive. The sudden inrush of cold air into the *celliers* hastens their fall, as it does that of other foreign matters in the wine. Soon the wine above the point in the cask or vat to which the deposit of yeasts and foreign matter has fallen is seen to be bright and clear. The time has come to draw it off. The job is known as racking.

It is important that it should be done as soon as possible after fermentation is complete, because the lees contain micro-organisms capable of causing illness in the wine.

The separation of the wine from the lees can be accomplished in several different ways. The method most commonly used in the Champagne district is to insert the nozzle of a rubber pipe into the bung of the cask—or, in the case of a vat, into the faucet fitted for that purpose into the wall of the vat just above the point to which the lees fall—and to draw off the wine into another cask or vat with the aid of a suction pump. As the last of the wine leaves the old cask or vat, great care must be taken to see that it does not carry away with it particles of the lees.

Normally, the wine is not passed directly from the old cask or vat to the new one: instead, one pipe transfers it to a large wooden bowl, where it is allowed to froth for a minute or two, and another pipe transfers it from the wooden bowl to its new home. In this way the wine is given a thorough airing, and any carbonic acid gas that may still be suspended in it escapes into the atmosphere. Whether or not the airing takes place depends on the result of a test.

Two days before the racking is to be performed, a glassful of wine is removed from the cask or vat, and left uncovered. On the day of the racking another glassful is removed, in order that the colour of the wine in the two glasses may be compared. If the wine removed two days previously is noticeably the yellower of the two it means that there are bacteria in the wine, which, if they were exposed to oxygen, would start multiplying and cause an illness in the wine—for healthy wine, when exposed to air, should not turn yellow. Wine discovered to be in that condition (which the French call a *casse*) has to be passed into the new receptacle direct, *à l'abri de l'air*, and given special treatment therein; wine that has revealed no tendency to turn yellow may be racked via the wooden bowl, *au large contact de l'air*.

(That description of what happens during the racking is faithful and brief—but it makes it sound so easy. Well do I remember how, at the school for trainee cellarmen which I attended, my fellow-learners and I were drenched in sweat after we had heaved the casks up ramps to position them for the racking, and how narrowly our toes escaped extinction as, inexpertly aping the antics of the professional cellarman, we twirled the casks away, empty, to be stored.)

The lees left behind in the cask or vat are not an attractive sight: they are the consistency of mud, the colour of sand. There is a surprising amount of them: they take up between 1 and 4 per cent of the volume of the vessel containing them. Mixed with a little wine to make them more liquid, they are pumped out of the cask or vat and placed in a cask. Later—after being declared to the *Régie*, for they are considered to be part of the wine—they are sold to a distiller who proceeds to make a rough alcohol out of them, known as *eau-de-vie-de-lys*.

If the grape-juice contained an unusually high percentage of tartaric acid, or if a little tartaric acid was added to the juice before fermentation began—which normally only happens in the case of the *vin de taille* and the *vin de rebêche*—the wine leaves behind another deposit, known in French as *vin pierre*, in English as wine-stone. Wine-stone is the consistency and colour of rough sand; in the old type of vat, it sticks to the cement which joins the glass tiles together and has to be scraped off. It used to be bought eagerly by dry-cleaning firms, on account of the tartar it contains, for conversion into dyes, but chemicals have been invented which today's dry-cleaners prefer, and it is no longer in great demand.

The wine emerges from the racking mud-coloured, with practically no bouquet. It is a little rough on the tongue, but not in the least bitter.

The best time to do the racking is on a cold day, when it is not raining and there is no north wind; in such conditions the wine is unlikely to be fretting and cloudy.

The Assemblage of the Still Wines (*Assemblage*)

After the first racking, most champagne-makers proceed to assemble together in vats the various categories of wine originating from the different vineyards. For example, the *deuxième cuvée* from Cramant is mixed together, and so is the *première taille* from Verzenay. If the wines underwent their fermentation in vats, however, the assemblage will already have been done—just before the musts were transferred to the vats.

The Second Racking (*Deuxième Soutirage*)

Towards the end of January the still wines are racked for the second time. This serves the double purpose of separating them from any lees that may have formed recently, and of giving them a good airing.

The Five-Week Rest Period

For approximately five weeks after being assembled together, a period embracing Christmas, January and the early part of February, the wines are allowed to rest. The intense cold causes certain substances, which were not removed by the racking, to fall to the bottom of the casks and vats. Also the enzymes of certain yeasts, which remained in the wine and are impervious to cold, attack some of the acids in the wine and slightly lower its acidity.

The Preparation of the Cuvée

Throughout this five-week period the champagne-maker engages upon the most important, the most difficult and the most distinctive phase of the entire *méthode champenoise*: the selection of the still wines that are to compose his blends. The selection is called the preparation of the *cuvée*.

The selection is conducted with two main objects in view: the production of champagne of a definite flavour and quality and of a consistent type—year in year out, despite the inconsistencies of the harvests—and the enhancement of the qualities of the individual wines. The latter object, it should not be forgotten, is just as important as the former, for, if champagne is made with the wine of only one growth, even if that growth is of a *catégorie hors classe*, the result is rarely as good as a skilful blend.

The preparation of the *cuvée* is a most difficult and lonely task. Unlike the tea, the tobacco or the perfume blender, the person who engages upon it is dealing with living materials that still have the greater part of their lives to lead: he cannot say of his blend, "Ah, this is delicious"; he knows that, the day he makes it, it will appeal only to someone with experience of champagne-making similar to his; its merits and defects will not become apparent till years hence, when the materials he has been working with have changed beyond recognition.

The responsibility of preparing the *cuvée* rests with the *chef de cave*. He is invariably the most important employee in the firm (often, of course, the owner is his own *chef de cave*), and he is frequently a man of great personality. Nowadays, he will almost certainly have attended the wine-school at Montpellier and have earned a degree in biochemistry; but what makes an outstanding *chef de cave* is not a diploma but a pair of good eyes, a nose and a palate capable of detecting and defining the minutest nuances of smell and taste, an amazing memory, and long experience, experience both gained in his own lifetime and transmitted to him in his blood by his Champenois forebears. For in the final analysis the art of blending depends not on chemical or mathematical formulae, but on gift and flair.

The *chef de cave*'s headquarters are not in the cellars themselves, as their temperature and the smell emitted by the wine and the fungi on the walls and bottles render them entirely unsuitable for such delicate matters as blending. He works above ground, in the firm's main buildings, whither he orders samples of the wine in the cellars to be sent to him. His establishment includes a laboratory and a tasting room, the latter equipped with a long table, chairs and spittoons; it is always light, airy and clinically clean. Whatever the size of the firm, these rooms are a holy of holies to which few outsiders gain admittance. They are sacrosanct not because the *chef de cave* works in an atmosphere of cloak-and-dagger secrecy, but because he needs calm in which to carry out his experiments, and surroundings unpolluted by cigarette smoke and whiffs of perfume. Besides, there is seldom any reason for an outsider to penetrate his sanctuary. The situation is quite different from that of Burgundy and Bordeaux, where wine-merchants and wine-lovers are perpetually turning up to taste the new wines and re-taste the old ones: champagne is not submitted to public examination until it is ready to be sold.

The first decision the *chef de cave* has to make is whether or not the new wines are sufficiently noteworthy to be turned into vintage champagne. If he decides they are, he then has two types of *cuvée* to prepare—vintage and non-vintage—and the problems which he has to solve are complex in the extreme: how much of the new wine to use for the vintage *cuvée*, how much to use for the non-vintage *cuvée*, and how much to store for use in future years (generally at least one-eighth of the new wine is put into reserve); which of the new wines for the vintage *cuvée* and which of the old wines for the non-vintage *cuvée* will "marry" most happily, and in what proportions; how much wine derived from red grapes and how much from white grapes there shall be in each *cuvée*; and how much each *cuvée* shall contain of the various pressings.

In order to resolve these problems—and a host of related ones which I have not mentioned—the *chef de cave* makes endless sample *cuvées*, tastes them, has them analysed, tastes them again, discards them, tries again, tastes, tastes and tastes. He continues this routine for weeks until, finally, he believes he has worked out the best formulas possible. He then calls in the heads of his firm; they taste his trial *cuvées*, and if they approve the blending can at last begin.

The Blending (Coupage)

The wines must be blended together, according to the formulas worked out by the *chef de cave*, before the cold weather ceases. Within reason, the earlier the blending takes place the better, because when wines of different ages and different origins first encounter each other certain minor chemical reactions take place, and time is needed for the precipitations thus caused to fall and settle, and for the blend to stabilize itself.

The blending takes place in enormous casks or vats equipped with internal appliances which quickly mix the wines together. Some of them hold the equivalent of 90,000 bottles of champagne.

Having been blended the wine, now resembling in taste and colour an ordinary acrid white wine and giving no hint of the exquisite delicacy and aromas it is destined to develop, is drawn off into smaller casks and vats.

The Fining (Collage)

Before being bottled, the blended wines are submitted to a final racking. In order that this shall be completely successful—in the sense that the foreign matters are removed to the last particle—it is necessary beforehand to fine the wine. Fining consists of adding a gelatinous substance which, in the course of its fall to the bottom of the cask or vat, attaches to itself foreign bodies that would otherwise continue to float about in the wine. The most satisfactory substance for fining the wines of the Champagne district is fish-glue obtained from the floats of certain types of sturgeon found in Russia. Gelatine extracted from the bones and cartilages of animals can also be used.

Both fish-glue and gelatine depend for their efficacy as fining agents on the tannin in the wine: unless this is present in fairly large quantities they, and the impurities in the wine, will not coagulate and sink. Champagne wines contain relatively little tannin because, at the time of the pressing, neither the skins nor the stalks, both of which contain tannin, are for long in contact with the juice. In order for the fining to be successful it is therefore necessary, twenty-four to forty-eight hours before it takes place, for a small quantity of tannin to be added to the wine. It is extracted from nutgalls, which are spherical excrescences produced by insects on the foliage of various types of oak trees. The tannin, which has certain antiseptic properties, also helps the wine to remain healthy as it ages.

When the fish-glue or gelatine has been added, the wine in the cask or vat is vigorously stirred and then left alone to await the final racking after the deposit has had time to settle.

The Storage of the Reserve Wines

After being fined and racked, the wines that are to be kept for use in future years are taken down to a very cold cellar and stored there, in vats, casks or magnums. The storage vats are never anything like as big as the fermentation vats: on average, they have a capacity of about seventy gallons.

The Transfer of the Blended Wines to the Bottling Vat

In early April the first lot of blended wine destined for bottling is pumped into a huge vat, known as a *foudre de tirage*, situated in the bottling plant. Some of these bottling vats will hold 400 hectolitres of wine (8,800 gallons). It is vital that just before it enters the bottling vat the blended wine should be exposed to contact with the air; otherwise, for want of oxygen, the yeasts will not multiply when the wine is bottled, and the second fermentation will be a fiasco.

The Addition of the Liqueur de Tirage

When the bottling vat is nearly full, what is known as the *liqueur de tirage* is added. This consists of still champagne wine—from the same *cuvée* as the wine in the bottling vat—in which a small quantity of sugar has been dissolved. Before the Second World War cane sugar from Martinique (refined, as it still is, at Nantes) was used exclusively; but nowadays beet sugar of such high quality is produced in France that many firms use it instead. Once the wine is bottled, the sugar in the *liqueur de tirage* will be attacked by yeast enzymes and converted into alcohol and carbonic acid gas; unable to escape because of the cork, the carbonic acid gas will become suspended in the wine; and there it will remain until such time as the cork is drawn and it can escape—in a flourish of effervescence. The amount of sugar put into the *liqueur de tirage* therefore depends on two things: the degree of effervescence it is desired to produce in the champagne, and the amount of natural sugar the wine already contains.

The degree of effervescence which it is the custom to give a champagne today is that produced by a pressure of carbonic acid gas inside the bottle amounting to approximately six atmospheres,* measured at 10°C. Now, as four grams of sugar per litre of wine will later give a pressure of one atmosphere, it follows that the total amount of sugar the wine must contain when bottled is approximately twenty-four

---

* Air compressed to half its volume acquires twice its ordinary force, and to a quarter of its volume quadruple its force—hence the use of the word "atmosphere" in connection with the measurement of compression. One atmosphere is the equivalent of fifteen lb. per square inch.

grams per litre.* The quantity of sugar incorporated in the *liqueur de tirage* is therefore always twenty-four grams per litre of wine minus whatever quantity of natural sugar the wine already contains. Owing to the efficiency with which the first fermentation is conducted nowadays, it seldom happens that more than two grams of natural sugar per litre remains in the wine, so one can safely state that the *liqueur de tirage* contains, on average, about twenty-two grams of cane or beet sugar for each litre of wine in the bottling vat.

No champagne yeast enzymes can continue transforming sugar into alcohol and carbonic acid gas once the degree of alcohol of the wine in which it is operating rises above 13·8°. Now, the twenty-four-odd grams of sugar per litre which the wine in the bottling vat contains after the addition of the *liqueur de tirage* produces on average 1·2° of alcohol per litre. It follows that the wine in the bottling vat, before the addition of the *liqueur de tirage*, must on no account contain more than 12·6° (13·8° minus 1·2°) of alcohol; otherwise, to the great detriment of the champagne, there will be unconverted sugar in it once the second fermentation is over. In practice, the wine in the bottling vat has normally been blended in such a way that it contains between 10° and 11·5° of alcohol (and will thus become a champagne containing between 11·2° and 12·7° of alcohol);† but I mention what would happen if its alcoholic content was only a little higher to show the problem that confronts a *chef de cave* when the still wines at his disposal at the time of the blending are particularly rich in alcohol (some of the wine produced in 1893 and 1959 contained 14° of alcohol). He cannot just produce a champagne with a higher alcoholic content than usual because, if he did, there would be unconverted sugar in it. Somehow or other he must procure extra supplies of champagne wine

* During the latter half of the nineteenth century and the first two decades of the twentieth century, most firms sold champagnes of varying degrees of effervescence, just as today most firms sell champagnes of varying degrees of sweetness. *Grand mousseux* champagne was fully sparkling; a *crémant* champagne sparkled more than a *pétillant* one but considerably less than a *grand mousseux*. One or two firms still produce *crémant* champagnes; normally, at the time they were bottled, they contained twelve grams of sugar per litre and thus the pressure of carbonic acid gas inside them is three atmospheres. Sometimes *crémant* Cramants are produced (though they are rarely sold): they are semi-sparkling champagnes made exclusively with the wine of Cramant.

† Most high quality champagnes contain just over 12° of alcohol. The potency of champagne is always slightly reduced, however, by the fact that it releases its alcohol by easy stages—on the drinker's tongue, on the roof of his mouth, in his larynx, wherever, in fact, the bubbles encounter a rough surface and explode— and not in one go in his stomach, as is the case with still wines.

whose alcoholic content is low and, by blending them with the wines
already at his disposal, keep the alcoholic content of the blend, at the
time it is bottled, below 12·6°.

The Addition of the Wine-Yeasts (Levurage)

In the olden days, the task of breaking down the sugar in the wine
after it had been bottled was left to the yeasts that had survived the
first fermentation and the rackings. This method had a number of
disadvantages: the champagne-maker could not be sure the yeasts
were of a type that would fall easily during the *remuage* and not stick
to the side of the bottle, or that their resistance to alcohol would
enable them to go on working in highly alcoholic surroundings; or
they might not be the kind that could work well in the low temperatures of the cellars. It has therefore become the almost invariable
custom to add to the wine in the bottling vat, immediately after the
addition of the sugar, a small quantity of carefully chosen yeasts which
are unlikely to have these disadvantages and which will assist the
yeasts already in the wine to transform the sugar into alcohol and
carbonic acid gas with dispatch and efficiency.

These can either be selected yeasts, purchased from a yeast culture
specialist, or they can be obtained from the champagne-maker's own
wine. In the latter case, the leaven is prepared either with wine from a
cask that has fermented particularly well that winter, or with wine from
a bottle of year-old champagne that passed through its second fermentation the previous spring in a particularly satisfactory manner.
Both have the disadvantage that the champagne-maker can never be
sure the yeasts involved are precisely and exclusively the ones required;
they could have one or all of the drawbacks mentioned above. The
yeasts used for *levurage* tend, therefore, more and more to be selected
ones.

The Final Examination before the Bottling

Before the wine is allowed to leave the bottling vat a sample of the
liquid is submitted to examination by microscope, to ensure that it
contains no germs likely to cause illness during the second fermentation,
and to a sugar content test, to check that it contains precisely the
required amount of sugar.

The Bottling (Tirage)

The modern champagne-maker, having at his disposal selected yeasts
which will operate within a very wide temperature range, is capable

of bottling the blended wines at any season of the year, in the certain knowledge that they will undergo their second fermentation in bottle successfully. Nevertheless, probably 95 per cent of all champagnes are still bottled in the months of April, May and June. This is because the *chef de cave* nearly always wishes to incorporate some, if not the greater part, of the produce of the most recent vintage in his blends, and April is the earliest month when a blend thus composed can be got ready for bottling.

Nowadays, all but the smallest firms have mechanical bottling plants which fill the bottles automatically to the required level. In the big firms the plant is concentrated in a huge hangar or room beside the bottling vat. Throughout the bottling operation the blades in the vat keep turning, to ensure that the *liqueur de tirage* and the yeasts penetrate uniformly into the wine. The wine passes from the bottling vat to the bottling plant through stainless steel or silver-plated brass pipes.

Before being inserted in the bottling plant each bottle is carefully washed and inspected; if the slightest flaw or malformation is detected, it is rejected. Some firms now use what might be called virgin bottles —bottles which were placed in airtight plastic bags the moment they emerged in a pristine state from the ovens, and which consequently never need washing.

The Insertion of the Temporary Cork (Bouchage)

As soon as the bottle has been filled the cork—known as the *bouchon de tirage*—which will protect the wine until *dégorgement* takes place, is inserted. It has previously been soaked in water to make it more supple. The diameter of the cork is double that of the neck of the bottle, so the machine responsible for the insertion has to be capable of applying tremendous compression; but the compression must be applied gently, or the corks will crack. Even in the big firms the corking machines are only semi-automatic, for no machinery has yet been devised which can feed them automatically without damaging the corks. A man has therefore to drop each cork into the corking machine by hand—and a curious sight it is to see this solitary worker, surrounded by other working examples of man's genius with machinery, a genius which one feels should by now have relieved him of his boring occupation, solemnly popping the corks into the slit provided, as each bottle passes by on a conveyor-belt. As soon as the cork is in the neck of the bottle, a little hammer on the machine that inserted it proceeds to thrust it farther downwards.

The Securing of the Cork (Agrafage)

In order to prevent the carbonic acid gas which will shortly be generated in the bottle from expelling the cork, it is now necessary to secure the latter with an *agrafe*, a strong metal clip shaped like an inverted U. A machine clamps the *agrafe* over the cork and then bends both ends of it under the raised rim with which champagne bottles are provided for this very purpose. The *agrafe* and the machine that attaches it to the bottle have only been in use since the middle of the nineteenth century; before that the cork was tied down with string. The directors of the museum at Epernay had it brought home to them a few years ago how ingeniously the string was manipulated, for, having decided to put on display a life-size model of a Champenois in the act of tying down a cork, they could find no one who remembered, or could fathom, how it was done. Eventually an ancient retired employee of one of the Houses succeeded, with much difficulty, in recalling the process, and the result of his handiwork is today on show in the museum.

Bottling, corking and *agrafage* continue throughout the months of April and May and into June—and, if a great deal of wine is being bottled, for even longer. A firm equipped with the most modern machinery can fill between 80,000 and 100,000 bottles a day if the bottles are sealed with crown caps insteads of with corks and *agrafes*, which is one of the reasons (another is the high cost of cork, yet another is the impossibility of the wine becoming "corked") why virtually all firms have for some time used these caps for their non-vintage champagnes up to the stage of *dégorgement*, and are now using them more and more for vintage too.

It is the custom in most firms for a party to be held in the bottling room on the day bottling ends. At the one I attended, tubs of magnificent hydrangeas had been brought in to brighten up the rather gloomy surroundings, and the health of the young wine, about to set off on fresh adventures in the cellars, was drunk in ... one guess? ... champagne.

The Transfer of the Bottles to the Cellars

In the smaller firms the bottles are conveyed to the cellars in baskets, by trolley, by lift or by a brawny Champenois arm; in some of the larger firms they descend on a conveyor-belt equipped with slots for the bottles.

The particular part of the cellars to which the bottles are dispatched depends to a large extent on the type of champagne which the maker aims at producing. High quality champagnes invariably undergo their second fermentation deep in the cellars, where the temperature is between 10°C. and 12°C. At such temperatures fermentation proceeds much more slowly than in the higher temperatures of the top cellars, and for that reason the sparkle which the wine develops is infinitely finer and more persistent, the bouquet has more personality, and the deposit thrown off by the yeasts is more regular and therefore easier to get rid of during the *remuage*; also the risk of bottles bursting is less. Lower quality, cheaper champagnes are generally put through their second fermentation in a *cellier* at, or just below, ground level, where the temperature may approach 18°C.

At whatever level the bottles are placed, they must not be in the proximity of north walls, doors and air ducts, where draughts or sudden changes of temperature are to be feared.

The Stacking of the Bottles (Entreillage)

As soon as they arrive from the bottling plant the bottles must be laid flat, so that the wine will be in constant contact with the cork and will prevent it from drying up; and they must be stacked in piles that are as neat and large as possible. Neatness is essential to save space, and if the piles are large the second fermentation proceeds far more satisfactorily than if they are small. No one knows quite why this is so, but it is assumed that the heat generated by each individual bottle slightly raises the temperature of the whole pile with beneficial effect.

The piles or *treilles*, as they used to be called in French, are built up in magnitude unique to Champagne. The pile is begun by putting a number of bottles on the floor in front of a wall, very close to each other but not actually touching, with their corks facing alternatively inwards and outwards, like sardines in a tin. Two thin strips of wood, known as *lattes* (hence the bottles are described as being *sur lattes*), are then laid on top of the bottles the length of the row, and these provide a flat surface for the next layer of bottles. Altogether twenty such layers can be built upwards in this way. Then up to nine similar rows, each comprising twenty layers, can be erected in front of the original row, so that the pile becomes a rectangle seven feet high, ten feet deep and of whatever length the original row was laid out to. In the big cellars the length of a pile may be anything up to 200 feet, and may contain as many as 250,000 bottles. The beauty of the arrangement is that, despite the great size of the piles, it is easy to remove single bottles from the side and front, even when they are low down, without disturbing the remainder. Not one bottle is actually touching its neighbour, so that if a bottle bursts it does not set up a chain reaction; yet so solid are the piles that you could safely dance the highland fling on top of them.

Before stacking each bottle the *caviste* shakes it, to scatter the yeasts. He then tilts the neck of the bottle towards the floor and, having smartly brought the neck up again just above the horizontal, keeps it there until he stacks it horizontally. He does this to ensure that the air bubble (which corresponds to the empty space between the cork and the wine when the bottle was filled) is forced back to the centre of the bottle; if allowed to remain between the cork and the wine it would cause the cork to dry up, in which event the carbonic acid gas about to be produced could escape.

As he places each bottle in position, another *caviste* puts a dab of white paint on the punt: this is done in order that next time the bottle is moved it can be re-stacked in exactly the same position. In this way the sediment that appears in the wine is always kept on the same side of the bottle, a state of affairs which greatly simplifies the *remuage*.

CHAPTER 28

THE SPARKLING WINE

The Second Fermentation (Prise de Mousse)

THE WINE IN the carefully-stacked piles now undergoes the process which, if no longer exclusively Champenois, is particularly suited to the wines of Champagne: the second fermentation in bottle. In normal conditions this takes place spontaneously, without help or interference from the champagne-maker. This is what happens: the yeasts multiply and the enzymes which they produce set vigorously to work on the sugar; a series of complex chemical changes take place which result in the sugar being converted into alcohol and carbonic acid gas and in certain useless matters being thrown off as sediment; the alcohol mixes with the wine, raising its alcoholic content by between 1° and 1·2°; and the carbonic acid gas, unable to escape from the bottle despite the terrific pressure which it exerts on the cork, has no alternative but to mix with the wine too. Thus when the second fermentation is over (it proceeds more slowly at the end because the yeasts are impeded by lack of oxygen, by the pressure of the gas and by the alcohol which they have produced) the situation inside a bottle of wine that contained 10° of alcohol and twenty-four grams of sugar at the outset is this: the sugar has disappeared; the alcoholic content of the wine has risen to at least 11°; the pressure of the carbonic acid gas inside the bottle is approximately six atmospheres; and sediment is floating about in the wine or, having fallen, has settled on the lower part of the bottle.

The time it takes for all these things to happen varies enormously from *cuvée* to *cuvée*. The phenomenon of effervescence is affected in many, often inexplicable, ways. The temperature prevailing in the cellar or *cellier* has great influence; so does the alcoholic content of the wine at the outset; the type and vigour of the yeasts used is also important. Sometimes the second fermentation is over in eight days; but when the champagne-maker is working with great wines, rich in alcohol at the outset, he sees to it, by positioning the bottles in a cold part of his cellars, that the process takes place slowly, in which case three or more months may go by before it is complete.

The progress of the fermentation is always closely watched. Each day the piles are inspected. From time to time the quantity of sugar remaining in a sample bottle is measured; a check is kept on the build-up of pressure in the bottles by inserting an *aphromètre*, an instrument that resembles a large hypodermic syringe, through a cork. Sometimes a pile will be so slow to embark on fermentation that it has to be moved to warmer surroundings; another pile, seemingly hopeless, may suddenly flush up on its own accord. Whatever happens, breakages are to be expected. Thanks to the exactitude with which the sugar content of a wine can be ascertained nowadays, these no longer assume fantastic proportions, as they did in the eighteenth and nineteenth centuries; but the modern champagne-maker considers himself lucky if the loss through breakage is less than half of one per cent.

The Ageing of the Wine (*Vieillissement sur Lattes*)

When the champagne has undergone its second fermentation and has impregnated itself with carbonic acid gas, the champagne-maker's next concern is to let it age. Champagne requires much time to reach perfection. For that reason the law of France lays down that the wines that compose the blends of a non-vintage champagne must be at least one year old, and that a vintage champagne cannot be sold for at least three years after the vintage date on the bottle. In practice, this is a *minimum ad absurdam*: the wines that compose the non-vintages sold by the great Houses are invariably considerably more than one year old, and their vintages are seldom sold until four or more years have gone by since the grapes were picked.

The bottles spend the greater part of the ageing period (on average two to three years for non-vintage, three to five years for vintage) in the position they were in for the second fermentation, that is to say, lying horizontally *sur lattes* in enormous piles. As with the fermentation itself, the lower the piles are placed in the cellars, the longer the wine takes to mature, and the longer it takes to mature the better it will be; but the piles are not normally placed in the lowest, coldest part of the cellars, as intense cold has a tendency to cause the sediment to dry up, which is inconvenient later on.

During the ageing period the wine undergoes several subsidiary fermentations: the alcohol, for instance, reacts with the acids to form the esters which help to develop the bouquet. Slow but incessant changes occur all the time, the result being that the uncouth wine gradually becomes mature, well-balanced, radiant with bouquet.

The Unstacking and the Restacking of the Bottles (*Déplacements*)

At the beginning of the ageing period, and at least once a year in the course of it, the piles of bottles have to be unstacked and stacked up again. This is necessary to enable broken bottles and bottles whose corks are showing signs of "weeping" to be removed from the piles, and to permit those which are to continue ageing to be given a *poignetage*, a shaking, so that the sediment inside them becomes more homogeneous. Before the shaking is administered the sediment is composed of three strata, superimposed upon one another: one layer comprises organic substances that have detached themselves from the wine; the next, dead yeast cells; the next, chemical precipitates. If the different components were not mixed together, the eventual removal of the sediment from the bottle would be rendered extremely difficult, if not impossible.

The bottles are removed from the piles two at a time. First the corks are inspected. If there is any sign of leakage, the bottle is placed on one side in order that the wine which it contains may later undergo a process, used by all wine-makers, called "*remise en circulation*"; this involves returning the wine to a cask or vat in which grape-juice is fermenting and starting it again on the long business of becoming champagne. Next, the bottles whose corks are intact are shaken in a special way. (A machine exists which will perform the *poignetage*, but most firms prefer it to be done by hand.) With the corks pointing downwards, the *caviste* grips a bottle firmly in each hand at the point where the neck thickens, digs his elbows into his sides and then, keeping his forearm stiff, twirls the bottles to the right and to the left as fast as he can. An experienced *caviste* gives about three twirls each way with the nonchalance of a conductor waving his baton, and when he holds the bottles up to the light to inspect them not a speck of sediment will be stuck to the insides; it will all be floating in the wine. Furthermore he will continue his gyrations for an entire day without showing signs of fatigue. A novice like myself has to twirl twenty times each way before the sediment budges, and most twirls lack elegance; after a quarter of an hour his wrists are becoming acutely conscious that each bottle filled with champagne weighs nearly two-and-a-quarter pounds; by the end of the day his wrists are so exhausted that his writing is as shaky as an old lady's of ninety-two; and at dinner, when he handles a knife and fork, he appears to be suffering from St. Vitus's Dance.

The shaking accomplished, the bottles are generally transported to another bay in the cellars to be re-stacked horizontally. The bottles that were on top before are placed at the bottom, and vice versa. The restacking is done with the same care and precision as it was when the bottles were first placed *sur lattes* just before the second fermentation.

The Working of the Sediment down on to the Cork (Remuage)

When the *chef de cave* considers that the champagne has matured for a sufficient length of time, he gives instructions for the sediment to be removed from the bottles. The removal, as the reader is already aware, is carried out in two stages, *remuage* and *dégorgement*: English-speaking manufacturers of sparkling wine by the *méthode champenoise* call *remuage* "riddling".

As the piles of bottles destined for *remuage* are being unstacked the *caviste* gives each bottle a good shake, with the usual wrist movement, so that the sediment is forced back into suspension, and the various strata of which it is composed become mixed together again. The bottles are then inserted horizontally, neck foremost, with the dab of white paint on their punts facing the six o'clock position, in stands known as *pupîtres*; these are situated deep down in the cellars, where the temperature is even and the risk of the wine being disturbed by vibration is nil. In the language of the cellars the bottles are now said to be *mises sur pointe*. *Remuage* cannot begin until the sediment has resettled on the bottom of the bottles lying horizontally in the *pupîtres* and the wine is perfectly limpid again; this generally takes between one and three weeks.

The *pupîtres* are made of two planks of oak, nearly five feet tall and two-and-a-half feet broad, which are hinged together at the top so that when placed in position on the floor of the cellar they form an inverted V. The face of each plank is pierced with slots which are large enough for the entire neck of a champagne bottle to penetrate. The planks are hinged so that the angle they stand at can be changed at will, and the slots are bevelled, which means that the angle of the bottles can also be changed; the latter, therefore, can support themselves by their necks in the *pupître* at any angle between the horizontal and the almost vertical. Each plank contains sixty slots, arranged in ten rows of six slots each, so that each *pupître* can hold 120 bottles. *Pupîtres* designed to hold magnums have larger slots and fewer of them, while those designed for half-bottles have smaller ones and a greater number.

It takes years to learn how to perform *remuage* properly. The *cavistes* entrusted with it are the highest paid workers in the cellars. They are called *remueurs*. The tools of their trade are their hands: great big hands which a boxer would envy, but which are capable of performing the sort of delicately controlled manipulations a masseur applies. The job has three distinct phases: the bottles are first rotated, then oscillated, and finally slightly tilted. The bottle remains in the *pupître* during the whole process.

To perform the rotative movement, the *remueur* grips the punt of a bottle in each hand and gently but firmly gives it an eighth of a turn to the right so that the dab of white paint on the punt moves up to the $22\frac{1}{2}$-minutes-before-the-hour position. (An eighth is the usual degree of the turn, but *remuage* is a highly individual art and some *remueurs* administer a quarter or a sixteenth of a turn). The rotative movement ensures that the main mass of sediment, as it descends towards the neck, does so at a different point on the circumference of the bottle each time *remuage* is practised, and does not leave behind specks of sediment separated from the main mass.

To perform the oscillating movement, he grips the punt of a bottle in each hand as before, keeping his wrists steady, and sharply oscillates the bottles. The vibrations set up as he does so cause the glass to move *under* the sediment; the sediment is thus wrenched free of the glass. The contact of the glass with the wood of the *pupîtres* during the oscillations produces a sound similar to the "clickety-click-ta-ta-ta-ta" set up by British trains as they cross the sleepers. I know a *remueur* who, when English-speaking visitors are watching him perform, grins broadly and says, "Voilà, mon British Railways mouvement!".

As he wedges the pair of bottles in the slots again, the *remueur* takes care to see that the dabs of white paint point to $22\frac{1}{2}$ minutes before the hour, and he tilts the bottles slightly, so that their necks point down a shade and their punts point up a shade. Gravity will now cause the sediment to slide down a fraction of an inch towards the cork.

At regular intervals, usually every second or third day, the *remueur* repeats this treatment, rotating the bottles an eighth of a turn at a time through many complete circles, oscillating them with ever increasing vigour, tilting them ever higher; now and again he alters the angle of the *pupître* in order to render the tilt even more pronounced. Eventually the punts of the bottles are sticking up in the air almost vertically. By then, if all has gone well, the sediment should have been screwed down, in the form of a muddy ball, into the neck of each bottle and have settled on top of the cork, leaving the wine above perfectly clear.

The whole process generally takes between six weeks and three months to complete, but sometimes it needs longer, for it is never easy to force the sediment to descend to the cork. The sediment, as I have already mentioned, is not homogeneous: it is composed of many different substances—dead yeasts, gum arabic, tartrate, calcium, bicarbonate of potassium, among others—of varying sizes and weight.

The heavy substances are fairly willing to descend, but the lighter ones have a tendency to float up into the wine at the least provocation.

The art of *remuage* resides in using the propensity to fall of the heavier substances to bring down the lighter ones. I was soon made aware of this fact when, at the school for trainee champagne-makers which I attended, I practised *remuage*. The rotative movement and the tilting action were easily learnt (or so I thought); grasping the intricacies of the oscillating movement proved much more difficult, but by the end of the morning I was producing some fine clickety-click-ta-ta-ta-tas, the sediment in my bottles appeared to be descending nicely and I was quite pleased with myself. Then the *remueur* came along, carrying the little lamp, called a *lampe pigeon*, which *remueurs* use to inspect the bottles they handle. He worked the air pocket in one of the bottles I had manip- ulated into the widest part of its belly, spat on the glass above the air pocket and put the *lampe pigeon* on the reverse side of the bottle: the combination of light below and spit above the air pocket enables the sediment to be seen as if through a magnifying glass. "Zut, alors !" ex- claimed the *remueur*, pointing out minute specks of sediment floating about in the wine; the specks, he informed me, were lighter substances which I had failed to attach to the heavier ones as they fell; and he added, somewhat acidly, that the bottles would now have to be rested and the whole process of *remuage* would have to be begun all over again.

But then, to cheer me up, he told me that the same thing sometimes happens to a professional *remueur* when the wine is young (the sediment in young wines being less homogeneous than in older ones), when the yeasts are of a type that do not fall easily or when the wine was racked with insufficient care; in the last case the sediment contains particles of *vin pierre* which stick to the side of the bottle. And he showed me what to do if the sediment assumes the shape of a coil of thread—a phenomenon known as a "claw"—or of a ball—known as a "mask" —and completely refuses to budge: to dislodge it, you tap the bottle with a piece of iron. Before doing so you have to put on a wire mask or a gigantic pair of wire spectacles, as the danger always exists that the bottle will explode. The same *remueur* told me that so recalcitrant was the sediment in a *cuvée* which he handled in 1938 that *remuage* took two-and-a-half years to accomplish.

It took me the better part of half-an-hour to treat the 120 bottles in the first *pupître* I was allotted. *A professional remueur can rotate up to 100,000 bottles in a single working day and oscillate up to 40,000;* his hands whirl at a dazzling pace over the face of the *pupître*. A machine exists —it is called a thabius—that is capable of doing the *remueur's* job. It is composed of a series of little padded hammers that hit the sides of the bottles and induce vibrations similar to those produced by the *remueur's* oscillations; but it has its drawbacks and is rarely used. There is also a machine that passes electric currents through the wine, causing the sediment to collect together; it is used by one or two firms before *remuage* takes place.

In a very bad novel, *Vin de Champagne*, M. Pierre Hamp had this to say about *remueurs*:

"Out of every ten *remueurs*, five have to give up the job on account of swellings in the wrist; nervous contractions have interfered with the flow of blood to the hand."

Thirty years before, Mr. Henry Vizetelly, a much more reliable observer, had written in *Facts about Champagne*:

"Fancy being entombed all alone all day in vaults which are invariably dark, gloomy and icy cold and dank, and being obliged to twist 60 to 70 bottles every minute throughout a 12-hour day. . . . Maddeningly monotonous occupation . . . which combines hard labour, with the wrist anyway, with next to solitary confinement. . . . Gloomy and taciturn . . . [the *remueurs*] sometimes say that they see devils hovering over the bottle-racks and frantically shaking the bottles beside them, or else grinning at them. Still, it may be taken for granted that the men who reach this stage are accustomed to drink freely of raw spirits, and are paying the penalty of over-indulgence."

All I can say is that, although the nature of the work and the surroundings in which it is carried out have changed little since these lines were written, shorter working hours, better medical attention and vastly increased rates of pay have transformed *remuage* into an occupation in which a man can happily engage without fear for his health. Most modern *remueurs*, I believe, while admitting that the work does not suit everybody, would stoutly declare that the lines quoted above had no application to them. The ones I have talked to are cheerful people, immensely proud of their odd occupation. There is one, I am told, who wiggles champagne bottles in *pupîtres* to give a sensational rendering of "Hang out your washing on the Siegfried Line".

The Stacking of the Bottles in an Upturned Position (Mise en Masse)

Remuage accomplished, the bottles are removed from the *pupîtres* and stacked together upside down in enormous piles, away from draughts and variations in temperature. They are then said to be *mises en masse*. The operation is not an indispensable one: the bottles can be submitted to *dégorgement* straight away; but, more often than not, the *chef de cave* wishes the wine to age a little longer, and, if the bottles are stacked rather than left on the *pupîtres* during this period, not only are the latter freed for the next consignment of bottles destined for *remuage* but precious cellar space is saved. It will be appreciated that, whether they are stacked or not, the bottles must be kept upside down between *remuage* and *dégorgement*; otherwise the sediment would slide back into the wine and foul it.

The system used to stack the bottles *en masse* is extremely ingenious. First, a row of bottles is placed against the back wall of a stone bay, with the corks touching the floor and one side of the punts resting against the wall, so that each bottle is almost completely upside down. Similar rows are then built forwards, and upwards, each one supported by the one behind and below. The ground floor story is sometimes composed of fifty rows, and the height of each pile, with the neck of each bottle resting in the punt of the one below, often attains four feet or five stories. The immense amount of space which this manner of stacking saves is the main reason why champagne bottles still have punts, even though bottles of sufficient strength to withstand six atmospheres of pressure could be made without punts today.

Champagne-makers sometimes leave a few hundred bottles of their greatest *cuvées* in the *en masse* position for decades, to provide their children or their grandchildren with the exquisite pleasure of drinking old champagne. Such a pile is left completely alone until the bottles are removed to undergo *dégorgement*, a few days before being drunk. By then the bottles are in need of a good scrub, because grey fungi, which thrive in the cellars, have attached themselves to the glass, giving the bottles an appearance of hoary old age.

The Removal of the Sediment (*Dégorgement*)

Two methods of *dégorgement* are used: *à la "volée"* and *à la glace*. Both require the services of a specialist cellarman, known as the *dégorgeur*, who ranks second among the skilled manual workers in the cellar. The perfect *dégorgeur* works with the maximum of speed and the minimum loss of wine and pressure. His equipment consists of a knife with a special blade, curved and pointed at the end, known as a *crochet de dégorgeur*, for the removal of the *agrafe* round the cork; a pair of pincers, called *pattes de homard* on account of their resemblance to lobster claws, for the extraction of the cork; and a small cask, sawn in half vertically and supported on a tripod, called a *guérite*, into which he directs the sediment as it spills from the bottle. To remove crown caps he uses a bottle opener.

Dégorgement à la "volée" is the older and more difficult to execute of the two methods. Standing in front of the *guérite*, the *dégorgeur* takes hold of the neck of the bottle with the thumb and the three last fingers of his left hand, hooks his index finger around the cork, sticks the punt into his stomach and points the cork towards the floor. On his left forearm and wrist, which are bearing the weight of the bottle, he wears a stout leather sleeve as protection in the event of the bottle exploding. Keeping the neck pointing downwards, he takes the *crochet de dégorgeur* in his right hand and removes the *agrafe*. Then, while his left index finger maintains strong pressure on the cork, he proceeds to ease out the cork with his *patte de homard*. At the precise second when he feels that the pressure of the gas inside the bottle is about to force the cork out, he removes his index finger, thrusts the bottle away from his body, and in the same swift movement raises its neck, so that the cork is pointing upwards at an angle of about 30 degrees into the gaping mouth of the *guérite*. This swinging thrust has the effect of causing the air bubble inside the bottle to dart up into the neck, where, as the cork and sediment fly out into the *guérite*, it acts for one vital second as a sort of cushion between the wine and the sediment, with the result that astonishingly little wine is lost. Or should be lost. A short, sharp report like a revolver shot at the time the cork flies out signifies that little has been; a "whoosh" means the *dégorgeur* is a duffer.

Dégorgement à la glace was first used in the Champagne district in 1889. It is the quicker and easier of the two methods and results in even less wine being lost. It works on the principle of imprisoning the sediment between the cork and a tiny pellet of frozen wine. A refrigeration machine is required, capable of reducing a solution of calcium chloride to a temperature of between $-16°C$. to $-18°C$. The calcium chloride ensures that the liquid, though very cold, does not freeze solid. The bottle is brought to the zinc freezing tank upside down. Its cork and a couple of inches of its neck are then inserted in the liquid, where they remain for approximately eighteen minutes. During that time a pellet of frozen champagne forms directly above the sediment. This pellet sticks to the inside of the neck of the bottle and thus, for the first time since *remuage* took place, the bottle can be stood upright without fear of the sediment sliding back into the wine. This fact greatly facilitates the task of the *dégorgeur*. He inserts the bottle in a special leather envelope attached to a stand in front of the *guérite*, which not only protects him in case of explosion but ensures that the bottle is held firmly pointing at an angle of 45 degrees into the mouth of the *guérite*. He then eases out the cork with his *pattes de homard*. A second later the sediment flies out of the bottle, propelled by the ice pellet behind it, which shoots out too with terrific force.

From this point on the *dégorgeur's* actions are the same whichever of the two methods he is using. He puts his thumb over the spout of the bottle, to prevent the foam from bursting out; he twists the bottle round in his hands, letting just a little foam escape while he does so, in order that it shall carry out with it the specks of sediment that may still be sticking to the inside of the neck; he puts the bottle beside an electric light bulb and looks through it, to check that the wine really is completely free of sediment; he sniffs the champagne, to make sure it has not developed any unpleasant odours since it was bottled; finally he puts the bottle on a nearby stand underneath a rubber cork attached to a spring, where it can wait, without losing pressure, until the next operation begins.

When the *dégorgement à la glace* method is used, a single *dégorgeur* can handle up to 1,500 bottles in an eight-hour day, as opposed to approximately 1,000 by the older method; only about 2 per cent of the wine is lost, instead of 3 per cent to 5 per cent; and the loss of pressure in the bottles is less, the freezing of the necks having the effect of temporarily reducing the desire of the carbonic acid to escape. In view of these advantages, most firms use *dégorgement à la glace* almost exclusively and only employ the older method when the batch of bottles requiring *dégorgement* is too small to warrant the operation of the refrigeration plant or when the wine is very old and its sediment needs removing with special care.

Monsieur Hamp painted a dismal picture of the *dégorgeur's* lot:

"The escaping liquid bruises the benumbed thumbs of the men, whose hands are drenched in icy wine. Their aching fingertips lack the agility which might otherwise prevent painful wounds being inflicted on their frozen flesh."

As usual, he was making a mountain out of a molehill. *Dégorgement* does roughen the hands, as do a lot of other jobs, and occasional accidents do occur—they are bound to when a man spends all day working with glass. But the profession is a highly responsible one. If, at the time when he sniffs the bottles, the *dégorgeur* fails to detect a "corky" smell, the champagne arrives at our table in that condition, to the detriment of the good name of the wine. And, despite the repetitiveness of the occupation, *dégorgeurs* are seldom gloomy men, as a pretty visitor to the cellars learns quickly: a short, sharp jet of foam strikes her in the face as she passes the *guérites* (two jets if she is very pretty), projected with such cunning that only his guilty face enables her to spot the culprit.

The Topping-up and the Sweetening of the Wine (Remplissage and Dosage)

Before a new cork is inserted in the bottle, the small quantity of champagne that was lost during *dégorgement* must be replaced: otherwise the consumer might think he was being cheated. The wine used for the purpose must be the produce of the best possible year and growth, completely fermented, mature and perfectly limpid; the *remplissage* (as the topping-up process is called) of very great champagnes is always done with a supply of the same wine as that already in the bottle, to ensure that the champagne's bouquet is not changed in any way.

Before the topping-up process takes place, a small amount of pure cane sugar of the finest quality is nearly always dissolved in the wine to be added. The wine-plus-sugar is known as the *liqueur d'expédition*, and the act of adding it is known as *dosage*. In small firms the operation is carried out by hand. The bigger firms have machines which automatically measure the exact quantity of *liqueur d'expédition* that each bottle requires and inject it under pressure, thus preventing any escape of carbonic acid gas. These machines are extremely expensive, because a considerable length of the piping through which the *liqueur d'expédition* passes must be made of pure silver, for other metals might impart an unpleasant taste to the champagne. When, as occasionally happens, there is not enough room in the bottle for the volume of *liqueur d'expédition* that the *chef de cave* wishes to add, a small quantity of champagne must be removed from the bottle; this is done with a syphon which has the delightful name of a "*trop de vin*".

Sugar is added to almost all champagnes because, in the course of the second fermentation, all the sugar in the bottle is normally converted, with the result that champagne ends up dryer than almost all other wines. If the edge was not taken off by slight sweetening, the wine would be just a little too dry for most people's taste. Virtually the only champagnes which can be drunk with pleasure without the addition of any sugar whatsoever are exceptionally old ones.

The amount of sugar that is added depends mainly on the taste of the clientele. Just as the aerated water companies in Great Britain have found that their products need to be sweeter when sold in Aberdeen than in Brighton, so the champagne-makers know that certain nations prefer their champagne to be sweeter than others; and they go to a great deal of trouble to cater for these preferences. Most of the champagne sold in Great Britain and the United States, where it is mainly consumed at receptions, and the champagne destined for French connoisseurs is so slightly sweetened that it can justifiably be called dry; the champagne sold to the average Frenchman, who drinks it at the end of a meal with dessert, is sweet, although now that the acidity of the still wines can be reduced by malolactic reaction, thus obviating the necessity of masking taste at a later stage by the addition of sugar, the vogue for dry champagne is gaining ground yearly in France. In Scandinavia and South America most of the champagne sold is very sweet. In addition there exist, or existed, certain customers—the Russians before the Revolution, the odd Oriental prince today—who have such a sweet tooth that they ask for their champagne to be sweetened to an even greater extent. When such exceptionally strong *dosages* are administered the alcoholic strength of the champagne is reduced, and in order to maintain it a small quantity of cognac or Fine Marne* has to be added to the *liqueur d'expédition*. In general it may be said that sweetening conceals the qualities and masks the defects of a champagne; the really great ones are therefore seldom sweetened to any appreciable extent, but the less perfect ones are.

The precise amount of cane sugar which a champagne-maker incorporates in his *liqueurs d'expédition* is one of the very few matters connected with the making of champagne that are treated as secret. There is no reason whatsoever why the Houses should reveal to outsiders the compositions which they use, but the fact that they do not has led to much misunderstanding. For instance, in a report issued in 1885 the director of the Paris Laboratoire Municipal described *dosage* in these terms:

"The liquid lost is replaced by a sauce [*sic*] composed of white wine, Madeira or Port, candy sugar and alcoholic liquors such as Cognac, Rum, Kirsch, etc."

The indignation of the champagne-makers knew no bounds, and a sizzling protest was whisked off to Paris by the Rheims Chamber of Commerce. Further misunderstanding has been caused by champagne-makers in expansive mood referring to a *dosage* as being of such-or-such a percentage, the inference being that a bottle "dosed", for

* See page 381.

instance, to 2½ per cent contains 2½ per cent sugar and 97½ per cent champagne. In actual fact the percentage ratio is worked out according to an extremely complicated technical formula, and is of service to an outsider only as a basis for comparison.

But what has caused even greater confusion is the plethora of terms which the individual champagne-makers have coined to indicate on the bottle the various degrees of sweetness of their champagne. There is no method in the madness—the word "Sec", for instance, on one firm's label may turn out to denote a far sweeter champagne than it does on another firm's label—but this is roughly the meaning of the various terms:

BRUT, NATURE, DRY	Very Dry
EXTRA-SEC	Dry
SEC or GOUT AMERICAIN	Slightly Sweet
DEMI-SEC or GOUT FRANCAIS	Sweet
MI-DOUX or DEMI-DOUX	Very Sweet
DOUX	Exceptionally Sweet

There is no danger of the sugar in the *liqueur d'expédition* causing the champagne to undergo a third fermentation, for all the yeasts were expelled from the bottle at the time of *dégorgement*.

The Insertion of the Permanent Cork (Bouchage)

The bottle is now ready to receive its *bouchon d'expédition*, the cork that will stand sentinel over the wine and the carbonic acid gas until such time as the champagne is consumed by the purchaser. The new cork must be of irreproachable quality, finer than the *bouchon de tirage* which acted as a stopper during the second fermentation and the *remuage*; the type of cork selected depends mainly on the period of time that is expected to elapse before the champagne is drunk. Previous to insertion, the corks are sterilized in a solution of tartar and then softened in warm water.

The insertion is done by a workman called a *boucheur*. The special machine which he uses works on the same principle as the one that inserts the *bouchons de tirage*, but it is more complicated as it performs two jobs, the insertion of the cork and the securing of the wire muzzle. The *boucheur* drops the cork into a hole at the top of the machine; four metal fingers immediately grip it and squeeze it with immense force to half its diameter; finally a kind of hammer, weighing sixteen lb. and capable of exerting a pressure of over 2,000 lb., drives the cork about halfway into the neck of the bottle.

The Securing of the Cork with a Wire Muzzle (Ficelage)

The moment the cork is in position the *boucheur* places a metal capsule on top of it; he then covers the capsule and the cork with a wire muzzle. A little gadget on the machine immediately takes hold of the wire loop on the muzzle and twirls it round and round; within a second the muzzle is in tight embrace with the cork. Simultaneously the hammer descends once more on top of the cork, ramming it into its final position in the neck of the bottle.

The purpose of the capsule is to prevent the muzzle from cutting into the cork, but very large firms have found a subsidiary use for it: they use capsules of specific colours for champagnes destined for specific markets or to denote the different types of champagne (vintage, non-vintage, pink champagne, dry and sweet, etc.).

The purpose of the muzzle, of course, is to prevent the cork from being blown out by the pressure of the carbonic acid gas. There is evidence to show that muzzles were first used to secure champagne corks in 1795. However, string appears to have remained in wide use for the purpose for at least another hundred years.

The Shaking of the Bottles (Poignetage)

Each bottle is now minutely inspected. A workman examines the cork and the muzzle to ensure that both are secure and undamaged, and he holds the bottle against an electric light bulb to make absolutely sure that no sediment was left behind and that the level of the champagne is correct. Then he takes a bottle in each hand and gives them a vigorous *poignetage*; this spreads the *liqueur d'expédition* evenly. A remarkable machine of German invention is used in some firms for this job: it puts the bottles through six vigorous somersaults, yet miraculously never causes breakages.

In a few very large firms the operations of *dégorgement, dosage, bouchage, ficelage* and *poignetage* are done in one huge *cellier*, the bottles being moved from one batch of workers to the next on narrow conveyor belts. With eight *dégorgeurs* working at the head of the chain, about 1,500 bottles can be handled in one hour.

The Final Rest Period (Empilage)

The champagne is now made, but it is still not ready to be sold and drunk. It needs to remain in the peace of a *cellier* for a period, to recover from the shock of *dégorgement* and to assimilate fully the *liqueur d'expédition*. Four to six months is considered the minimum time it should thus rest, but many firms allow a year or more, particularly if the champagne is a *brut*, for when not masked by a lot of sugar champagne's natural acidity, which is responsible for the wine's intense cleanness on the palate, is often a little too pronounced at this stage. Given time, the alcohol in the champagne will work on the acidity and diminish it, greatly enhancing the wine's bouquet in the process.

The bottles are stacked horizontally during the rest period. The same system of stacking is used as for the second fermentation, but this time it is generally referred to as *empilage* instead of *entreillage*. An incidental but important advantage of the rest period is that the bottles can be kept under observation and the corks inspected from time to time.

CHAPTER 29

THE FINISHED PRODUCT

The Dressing of the Bottles (Habillage)

WHEN THE *chef de cave* decides that a *cuvée* has aged and rested for long enough the bottles are washed, polished and brought up in lifts to rooms above the cellers to be dressed.

Champagne bottles are the most gaily and smartly dressed of all wine bottles. Some of the big Houses enlist the aid of designers in their keenness to ensure that their bottles are decked out with all the elegance—and the touch of fantasy—that the world has come to expect of them. The dressing up is sometimes a little excessive, but usually it bespeaks the innate good taste of the French and their flair for colour; one has only to see how bottles of sparkling wine are got up in other lands to realize how easy it is to let a false note creep in and ruin the effect.

A champagne bottle generally has two labels, a narrow one round its neck or shoulder, which is called a *cravate*, and a larger, rectangular one on its body. Between them, the labels display the firm's name, its licence number (preceded by the letters N.M. or M.A., the former to indicate that the champagne is to be sold under the name of the firm that made it, the latter to indicate that it was bought from the maker to be sold under another name), its badge, crest or trademark, the name of the town or village where its cellars are situated, the date of vintage if the champagne is vintage, an indication as to the dryness or sweetness of the wine, and, if the firm holds a very important royal warrant, the grantor's coat-of-arms; the lower label is often ornamented with rich borders and an eye-catching diagonal line. Exceptionally legible type is generally used for the lettering, what the French call *de l'Anglaise* type, which is quite different, for instance, from the *gothique* type generally used in Burgundy; subtle contrast is often established between the lettering and the background. A code-number is always stamped on the back of the lower label, to enable the maker to determine from which *cuvée* the champagne derived, in the event of a complaint being made about it. Flour-and-water paste is used to stick on the labels; it has to be particularly adhesive, to prevent the labels from coming off if the bottle is placed in an ice-bucket.

As about a third of the cork in a champagne bottle is left protruding, champagne-makers have always had to pay more attention to the manner in which the tops of their bottles are dressed than have other wine-makers, whose corks are normally driven in level with the rims. In the eighteenth century champagne corks were nearly always protected from dust and dirt by being dipped in sealing-wax; Moët & Chandon still use this system with their super-de-luxe brand, *Dom Pérignon*. In the early part of the nineteenth century, however, it became the custom to cover the cork and the upper part of the neck of the bottle with a thin sheet of tin or pewter foil, and this remains standard practice today. The foil may be of any colour, but gold and silver are the usual choices. In all probability the switch from sealing-wax to foil was made because the foil gives the bottle a more festive appearance and is slightly cheaper than sealing-wax. Some people say, however, that the motive was to deceive, to prevent the eagle eyes of our ancestors from spotting that the bottles were not quite full. Others claim that the original purpose of the foil, which contains lead, was to poison the rats that roamed in householders' cellars and dined off the string with which the corks were secured before wire muzzles were used.

The dressing of the bottles is nearly always done by women workers. In large firms the women sit in front of a conveyor-belt which brings the bottles to them and carries them away again. The way in which they hold the bottles while putting on the labels and the foil proved too much for the vivid imagination of Monsieur Hamp; this is what he wrote in *Vin de Champagne*:

"They place the punts on their abdomens, which are protected by jute pads. Handling fifteen hundred bottles a day, they press as many times on their sexual organs and find in this posture of the onanist the means of delaying pregnancies until such time as they leave to sit more comfortably making wire muzzles or branding corks."

It used to be common practice for a champagne firm to have different dressings for different countries: gold foil, perhaps, for Great Britain, silver for the United States, purple for France. Now that people are travelling more a need has arisen—and is gradually being met—for the dressings to be standardized, so that an American on a trip to Paris, for example, can easily recognize the champagne he is accustomed to having at home.

The Packing of the Bottles (Emballage)

After being dressed the bottles are wrapped in tissue paper, to keep the labels and the foil bright and clean. Next, either a straw or a papier mâché envelope is slipped over each bottle to protect it during transit; until recently papier-mâché envelopes were used only if the champagne was destined for countries like the United States and Eire, which forbid the importation of straw, owing to the risk that it may harbour foot-and-mouth disease germs; but now papier-mâché envelopes are in much wider use—to the despair of persons who used the straw to cover strawberry patches, thatch dovecots, make cribs at Christmas time or build guinea-pig hutches. Finally, the bottles are placed in the cases, neck to punt, punt to neck.

Standard champagne cases hold a dozen bottles, six magnums, twenty-four half-bottles or forty-eight quarter-bottles. Occasionally bigger cases are used; in the nineteenth century, champagne used to be sent to China in 120-bottle cases. The cases are made of poplar. Their outer surfaces are always branded with the champagne-maker's name and the name of the person to whom they are to be delivered. Generally, the latter is one of the champagne-maker's many agents in France or abroad, but deliveries are made direct to French Ambassadors, certain Heads of State and some organizations, such as airline and shipping companies, which are able to sell champagne duty free.

A few countries, among them Venezuela, levy duty on the gross weight of an import; champagne is sent to such countries in cardboard cartons. In recent years more and more champagne firms have been using cardboard cartons to supply other markets as well: they are easier to open than wooden ones, the risk of the bottles breaking is very little greater and they are considerably cheaper. The only persons likely to deplore this trend are men who are handy about the house and use wooden champagne cases to make shelves and odd bits of furniture.

Shipment

The filled champagne cases begin their journey to the consumer by train, lorry or barge. The makers endeavour to avoid making shipments during exceptionally hot or cold weather. Icy draughts in stations and warehouses and on quaysides are apt to cause tiny crystals, known as *paillettes*, to form, which give the champagne a cloudy look. The *paillettes* are perfectly harmless and disappear as soon as the wine has rested, but they are best avoided.

If the journey is a long one, particularly if it includes a sea voyage, a conscientious agent of a champagne firm always let the wine rest for a month or two before sending it out to wine merchants. "Landing", as the rest-period is called, gives the wine a chance to recover from the journey and acclimatize itself to its new surroundings.

CHAPTER 30

THE BOTTLES

CHAMPAGNE BOTTLES OF eleven different capacities have been made:

Quarter-Bottle	6½ fluid ozs.
Half-Bottle	13 fluid ozs.
Imperial Pint	19½ fluid ozs.
Bottle	26 fluid ozs.
Magnum	2 bottles
Double Magnum or Jeroboam	4 bottles
Triple Magnum or Rehoboam	6 bottles
Quadruple Magnum or Methuselah	8 bottles
Salmanezah	12 bottles
Balthazar	16 bottles
Nebuchadnezzar	20 bottles

However, only the quarter-bottle, the half-bottle, the 26-oz. bottle, the magnum and the double, triple and quadruple magnum are obtainable today. Far and away the greatest quantity of champagne is sold in the 26-oz. bottle. Quarter-bottles are consumed mostly in bars, in air-liners, by people who are ill and by those who live alone. The demand these days for imperial pints (known in France as *médiums* or *impérials*) is restricted almost entirely to doughty champagne-lovers, like the late Sir Winston Churchill, who find a half-bottle too meagre an allotment for their individual requirements and a whole bottle just too much. What prompted the Champenois to choose such splendid biblical names for their larger bottles remains a mystery: a few of the names suggest magnitude—Jeroboam means "increase of the people", Nebuchadnezzar was the most powerful king of Babylon—but others do not.

All the champagne sold in quarter-bottles, and much of what is sold in bottles larger than a magnum, is aged and submitted to *remuage* and *dégorgement* in standard-sized bottles, and then transferred under pressure into the smaller or larger receptacle. *Transvasage*, as the system of transfer under pressure is called, is practised in the case of the quarter-bottle because the expense of *remuage* and *dégorgement* for such a tiny quantity of wine is prohibitive, and in the case of bottles larger than a magnum partly because the *remueur*'s task is rendered exceedingly difficult by the size of the punts, partly because the risk of breakage is so considerable that the bottle-makers refuse to guarantee that the bottles will survive the process. Although the machines which perform *transvasage* are highly efficient and allow very little loss of pressure, the champagne-makers are the first to admit that the process slightly impairs the perfection of the wine. It follows, therefore, that champagne is likely to emerge from half-bottles, bottles and magnums in a more perfect state than from the other sizes.

But there is another consideration to be taken into account in determining the relative perfection of the champagne sold in bottles of various sizes. Air is the enemy of champagne. Now, of the three sizes of bottle upon which *transvasage* is never practised—the half-bottle, the bottle and the magnum—the magnum is the one that contains the smallest air-bubble in relation to the liquid it contains, and the one, consequently, that produces the most perfect champagne. Some people believe so implicitly in the theory "the bigger the bottle, the better the champagne" that they maintain that champagne laid down in bottles larger than a magnum becomes in time even more perfect than the contents of a magnum, even if *transvasage* took place. They may be right; but a wise man will be content to consider the magnum as the ideal container for champagne.

In Dom Pérignon's time the champagne bottle was squat and round, not unlike the modern armagnac bottle. As time passed its body continually grew in height and its shoulders became increasingly sloping, until by the reign of Napoleon III it had more or less attained its present slim cylindrical form. The evolution was dictated by two main considerations: the need for the bottle to have all possible strength to prevent breakages during the second fermentation and during *remuage*, when it acts as a tool of the trade—a very roughly handled tool at that; and the fact that it must have a shape that facilitates the fall of the sediment and the extraction of the cork. Strength was achieved by giving the bottle a large body, sloping shoulders, sides of uniform thickness (able to expand and contract uniformly during sudden changes of temperature), and a punt, above all by increasing its weight: tipping the scales at just over two pounds, the champagne bottle is by far the heaviest wine bottle in existence. The fall of the sediment and the extraction of the cork was facilitated by giving it a perfectly conical neck, widening smoothly towards the shoulders. That an evolution dictated by such practical considerations should have resulted in *le vin des cocottes* being encased in a phallic symbol is a measure of the Champenois' ingenuity.

The composition of the glass of the champagne bottle is a matter of capital importance. It has to be particularly insoluble. Mr. Vizetelly records that, towards the end of the last century, a new type of glass, charged with alkaline sulphurates, was tried out; it disengaged hydro-sulphuric acids which ruined an entire *cuvée*. The glass has to be perfectly smooth, as roughness in the interior causes the carbonic acid gas to fret and increases the risk of explosion. It has to be dark in colour, as light is injurious to such a delicate wine as champagne: brown gave way to deep pond green as the standard colour of the champagne bottle late in the nineteenth century.

Until 1882 a champagne bottle was created by blowing a small quantity of glass through a metal rod. The bottles made in this way were uneven in shape and form. In 1882 special moulds were invented which to a large extent cured the unevenness. After the First World War blowing by compressed air replaced blowing by mouth, which was considered by some to be unhygienic. A few champagne firms, however, remained faithful to mouth-blown bottles until as late as 1932, believing them to be stronger and more supple than those blown by compressed air. The first fully automatic machine for the manufacture of champagne bottles was invented shortly before the outbreak of the Second World War, and it is these machines which are in use today.

In the eighteenth century, when wood was used to heat the glass-ovens, the manufacturers of champagne bottles were all established in or near forests, principally, as I mentioned in the chapter on Dom Pérignon, in the Argonne region. When coal became more economic than wood the numerous small firms resettled themselves, either in the coal-producing area itself in the *département* du Nord, or beside the champagne-makers (the sand near Rheims being of high quality), or between the two, near Soissons. As a result, during the First World War the majority of them were in the thick of the fighting, and their plants suffered severe damage. After the Armistice few of them could afford either the changeover from coal to fuel oil, which was necessary if competitive prices were to be maintained, or the new plant which mechanical blowing called for. Many of them disappeared; a few amalgamated. Today there are only five left to produce the 70-odd million bottles which the champagne-makers require each year: the Verreries de Fourmies at Fourmies (Nord), the Verreries Charbonneaux at Rheims, two factories in the famous St. Gobain group, one at Saumur, another at Chalon-sur-Saône, and the Verreries de Vauxrot at Soissons.

CHAPTER 31

THE CORKS

CORK IS THE name given to bark stripped from an evergreen member of the oak family known in Latin as the *Quercus suber* and in English as the cork-oak tree. Some of these trees attain a height of sixty-five feet; their leaves, like those of the holm (which is also an evergreen oak), are roughly the shape and colour of holly leaves, but flatter, softer and devoid of prickles.

No other material, natural or man-made, combines as marvellously as does cork the qualities of compressibility (unlike rubber, it compresses without horizontal spread), elasticity (it rarely takes a permanent set), adherence (when compressed, it takes up the inequalities of the surrounding surface), impermeability (this is accounted for by its unique cellular structure—it contains 200 million cells per cubic inch), imputrescibility (it is little affected by temperature or moisture) and durability. The fact that cork, in addition to possessing these qualities, is sufficiently supple to be removed easily when inserted in the neck of a bottle, and does not impart an unpleasant taste to wine, makes it the ideal substance with which to stop a wine-bottle.

Because of the tremendous pressure to which the corks that they use are submitted, champagne-makers, from Dom Pérignon's time to the present day, have always gone to immense pains to obtain the best quality cork available. Up to the end of the nineteenth century their supplies came from a single source: the forests of cork-oak trees situated on the southern foot-hills of the Pyrenees in northern Catalonia. For that area, as I intimated in the chapter on Dom Pérignon, is as special regarding cork as is the Champagne district regarding sparkling wine. Owing to the poverty of the soil and to certain peculiarities of the climate, cork-oak trees grown there produce bark that is not only of exceptional quality but is also capable of growing up to three inches thick, so that a cork long enough to stop a champagne bottle can be cut from its width. Majorcan missionaries who took cork-oak trees from Catalonia to the Sacramento area in California, and others who attempted transplantation elsewhere, discovered that only in Catalonia will the cork-oak tree produce such magnificent bark.

In 1880 winds and frost of unprecedented intensity struck the Catalan cork forests. The resulting damage might not have affected their long-term future had not the disaster occurred at a time when the sales of champagne were rising giddily, and the champagne-makers needed more cork than ever before. To keep up supplies, the forest owners started stripping the bark off their surviving trees prematurely. As a result of this shortsighted policy not only did champagne-makers have to look round for other sources of supply, but the whole process of cork-making underwent a revolution. To understand the reason for the latter, it is necessary to know more about the characteristics of Catalan cork-oak trees and about cork in general.

Cork-trees grown in Catalonia should not be stripped for the first time until they are twenty years old. The cork obtained from this stripping is of poor quality, and can only be used for insulating purposes. Thenceforward the strippings may safely take place every eighteen to twenty-five years, and the cork will be of excellent quality; but only from the fourth stripping onwards—over a century, in other words, since the tree was planted—will the bark have that three-inch thickness which is the unique feature of Catalan cork. The length of the waiting period is amply compensated for, however, by the tree's whale-like longevity: it is by no means rare to find cork-oak trees in Catalonia producing thick and healthy bark at the age of four hundred years, whereas in other parts of the world the normal life of the tree is a century.

Even when a strip of Catalan cork is three inches thick, only about 70 per cent of it can be used to make champagne corks. Why this is so becomes evident if the structure of a strip of bark is examined upon its removal from the tree. The strip is seen to have veins running down it, and the closer these veins are to the inner surface of the strip the less space there is between them. Each vein represents one year of growth; and the irregularity of the spacing is explained by the fact that the cork that grew the first year did so without encountering any resistance whatsoever, whereas the growth of each subsequent layer was impeded to an ever-increasing extent by the effort of having to push the old cork outwards. It follows that the thin layers are possessed of greater resistance, more "body", than the thick layers; and thus in each strip of bark there are two completely different types of cork: "hard" cork, whose veins are close together, and "supple" cork, whose veins are farther apart.

Because of the strain imposed upon it by the carbonic acid gas, a champagne cork must be composed largely of "hard" cork. The percentage of "hard" cork in a narrower strip, however, is lower still: the inevitable result, therefore, of the policy of stripping the Catalan trees every twelve to fifteen years instead of every eighteen to twenty-five years was that strips of cork thick enough to permit the making of one-piece corks became rarer and rarer. What are known as "laminated" corks had to be made instead, corks composed of two or more fragments of cork stuck together lengthwise with glue.

A laminated cork proved to be a reliable substitute for a one-piece cork; but by 1935 "hard" cork had become so scarce, owing to the forest-owners' persistence in stripping the trees prematurely, that the cork-makers were even finding difficulty in producing enough laminated corks to satisfy the Champagne district's needs. It was then that Senor José Sagrera Perxés of Palafrugell invented what is known as a "four-piece" cork. This type of cork is composed of two fragments of cork glued together lengthwise and two circular cork discs glued on underneath. Its great advantage lies in the saving of "hard" cork, which needs to be used only for the discs, as they alone are in contact with the champagne; the top fragments can be of the "supple" variety. Later yet another type of cork was invented, which is known as an "agglomerated" cork. It is composed entirely of discs, the bottom one being made of "hard" cork and the top ones of cork dust pressed into a homogeneous whole. In the Champagne district it is only used for bottles undergoing their second fermentation in the cellars, never for bottles that have been disgorged and are being corked for shipment.

Only Catalonia could supply the Champagne district with the cork to make one-piece corks, but the invention of laminated, four-piece and agglomerated corks enabled the cork-makers to look around for other sources of supply. Until the Spanish Civil War broke out, they never went farther afield for their supplies than Andalusia and Estremadura. Hills, a dry climate and comparatively poor soil make the region around Carcares and Plasencia in Estremadura almost as suitable for the growing of the cork-bark tree as Catalonia itself. Although the bark produced is thinner than Catalan bark it is wonderfully compact, and as long as the trees are well-aired it can be taken off the branches as well as the trunks.* During the Spanish Civil War, however, cork from both Andalusia and Estremadura became extremely scarce, and for the first time the cork-makers went outside the borders of Spain, to

---

* The cork-oak tree, like all members of the oak family, litters the ground with acorns, and the Estremadurans, who are very thrifty people, dispatch their pigs into the forests to eat the acorns. In the forests there are wild boar, and when they set eyes on the pigs they mate with them. The issue of this cross-breeding is the animal from whose hind-quarters that delectable commodity, Estremaduran smoked ham, is made.

Portugal, to buy cork. The Lusitanian connection has been maintained, and today about a quarter of the cork for champagne comes from Portugal.* A little Algerian cork is also used.

The vast number of corks that the champagne-makers require each year are supplied by about forty firms, almost all of them Spanish-owned and staffed by Spaniards. Some of them import the bark in strips and cut it up in Champagne; others find it more economic to have the corks roughly made in Spain and then trimmed in Champagne; others still deliver the finished article direct to the champagne-maker from Spain. Altogether there are about 500 Spaniards engaged in cork-making in the Champagne district itself, many of them refugees from the Franco régime. As a colony, they are now almost completely assimilated. The headquarters of virtually all the cork firms are situated in the Gerona–Figueras area of Catalonia, the funnel through which the cork is channelled from the cork forests to the Champagne district.

The stripping of the cork bark is always done at the period of the year when the sap is high up in the tree; in the Iberian peninsula this means the months of June, July and August. The stripping is accomplished as follows. First, two vertical incisions are made with a hatchet down opposite sides of the tree. Then two horizontal incisions are made round the circumference, the first at the foot of the tree, the second at a height determined by the tree's age, and only increased gradually if the tree is not to suffer exhaustion. On a young tree it can be at about three feet, on an old one anything up to twenty feet. Finally the hatchet is inserted into the incisions, and the two strips are levered off. The inside of each strip varies in colour between orange, ochre, beige and fawn, and is as smooth as planed wood, but the outside is black, rough and so crinkled that, when the strips are wired together in bundles with their outsides uppermost for dispatch to Catalonia, they could easily be mistaken for rhinoceros hides.

As soon as the bundles reach Catalonia, they are soaked for three-quarters of an hour in very hot water. Large stone tubs are used that have brick tunnels underneath into which the heating material (usually olive wood) is fed. The object of the hot water treatment is to cause the strips to expand and become more pliable, and to encourage the pores of the cork to open. The bundles are then put out in the open and left there, completely exposed to the elements, for twelve months;

---

* In Portugal, as in Andalusia and Estremadura, trees that furnish cork for the Champagne district are nowadays stripped on average every nine years.

during this period the cork matures and becomes fit for processing. Several times, in the course of the year, the bundles are untied and each strip is smelt, for cork often harbours an evil-smelling parasitic fungus—and if cork with the fungus in it is used as a stopper for champagne or any other wine the contents of the bottle will inevitably be "corked". The slightest whiff of the fungus is therefore enough for the strip to be discarded out of hand for the making of champagne corks: at the factory which I visited in Catalonia, 40 per cent of the strips are normally rejected in the forest and a further 50 per cent in the factory compound. The strips that are fungus-free are then sorted according to the number of pores they contain, their thickness and their sheen,* and tied into fresh bundles. At the end of the twelve-month period a second boiling is administered; this, in conjunction with the first one, has the effect of increasing the thickness of the strips by 30 per cent. Then the strips are taken into the factory.

There begins the process, so specialized that it can truly be called a craft, of turning the strips of bark into champagne corks. Let us assume that the type of cork being made is a four-piece one, composed of two fragments of "soft" cork and two discs of "hard" cork. Strips of "soft" cork are first cut by a big electric saw into fragments just under two inches long, the fragments from each strip being placed in separate baskets to ensure that only pieces of precisely the same origin will be joined together later. Then each fragment is cut by a hand electric saw (the slightest jolt or misjudgement, and off goes the worker's finger) into further fragments half the width of a champagne cork. Next, the rough, black outside bark is removed by a saw. After that, each little rectangle is placed against a revolving wheel, covered with sandpaper, to smooth it off.

The next job is generally done by women: it involves minutely inspecting each rectangle and pairing off those which most resemble each other in colour, sheen, texture and vein structure. Each pair of

* The powers of resistance and the durability of cork are judged by (a) the number of its veins (in other words, by its age) and (b) the regularity in the spacing between the veins (regularity producing a more consistent homogeneity); but its quality is judged by its sheen. If cork is healthy-looking, shiny, bright, a treat to the eye, it is special and will last for years; if it is dull, opaque, lifeless, it is mediocre. There is no denying that a pore is a hole, and it seems odd that a hole should be stopped with a substance that has holes in it; however, as the volume of gas (nitrogen in particular) is as high as 89 per cent in cork cells, pores do not necessarily detract from a cork's quality. Certainly a cork that has many pores and a healthy-looking sheen is a better cork than one that has few pores and no sheen.

rectangles is now glued together lengthwise, and the two thin discs of "hard" cork are glued on above. The cork (for that is what it is now) is then clamped into a frame, and the frame is put in a slow oven for twenty-four hours. Upon its removal from the oven, whirring sandpaper changes its shape from a rectangle to a cylinder; another machine smooths off its top and bottom; and then, after being washed in rainwater, it is put outside for several days, in a special frame of wood and bamboo, to bask in the generous rays of the Catalan sun.

After the sun treatment the corks—by now smooth and shiny—are placed on hammocks made of sacking to be smelt and closely examined by women. Depending on the colour, smoothness and vein structure, the women chuck them into one of two baskets, the first for perfect specimens, the second for less perfect ones—or reject them altogether if they detect the slightest "corky" smell. The contents of each basket are then emptied on to two more hammocks, there to be inspected and smelt yet again, so that in the end each batch of corks has been divided into four qualities. After being branded with the maker's name and that of the champagne firm for which they are destined, the corks are finally placed in huge sacks, resembling hop-pockets, and sent off to Barcelona for dispatch to the Champagne district.

Who is to blame for that distressing but happily fairly rare contingency—the cork that, no matter how it is twisted and pulled and wrenched, simply will not leave the bottle? The cork-maker, for having supplied poor cork, or the champagne-maker, for having selected the wrong type of cork for the bottle? An independent expert would probably place the greater share of the blame on the shoulders of the champagne-maker, but at the same time point out that the mitigating circumstances are considerable. For if the champagne-maker knew in advance exactly when each of his bottles was to be uncorked and the storage conditions to which it was likely to be submitted, there would never be mistakes. If he had a sufficient quantity (for they are always in short supply) he would use one-piece Catalan corks for champagnes that were to be laid down in the purchaser's cellar for a considerable period and for champagnes destined for long voyages: no cork will last as long or endure sterner treatment, but, being so "hard", a certain length of time elapses before it becomes easy to pull. For a non-vintage champagne likely to be drunk immediately, he would use a fairly "supple" laminated cork. For a non-vintage champagne that was to be drunk fairly soon but that had to go on a short voyage first, he would probably use a four-piece cork: its "supple" top would ensure an easy extraction and its great strength—derived from its discs of "hard" cork and from the fact that the veins are at right-angles to each other so that there is no weak point lengthwise—would make it a more suitable choice than a laminated one, which might start "weeping" on the voyage. In practice, however, the champagne-maker rarely does know precisely what is going to happen to his bottles once they are sold. And his choice is further complicated by the question of expense; corks, particularly "hard" corks, are expensive; if he is to keep the price of champagne at a reasonable level, he cannot always use the type of cork that would bear up stoutly under all the conditions to which the bottle could conceivably be submitted.

It remains to be seen, in fact, how long champagne-makers will be able to go on using cork in their bottles in an age when new, cheaper materials are continually appearing on the market. One thing is certain: plastic stoppers will never be used on a large scale, if at all, by the Champenois; experiments stretching over more than a decade have proved beyond doubt that plastic does impact a faint but unwelcome taste to the wine. So do rubber and gutta-percha. However, experiments with crown caps lined with a cork disc are proving very interesting. As I have already mentioned, many firms use them nowadays to stop non-vintage champagne while it is undergoing its second fermentation in the cellars, and only use corks once *dégorgement* has taken place. One champagne-maker I know, a man whose aristocratic appearance and conservative outlook do not prevent him from being extremely open-minded and daring where champagne is concerned, is convinced that crown caps will eventually replace corks altogether, at any rate for non-vintage champagne. He maintains that, just as glass-lined vats have remove the taste of wood from the wine and rendered it purer, so do crown caps remove the taste of cork from it and render it purer—and better. To prove his point, he recently stopped a dozen quarter-bottles with crown caps and asked some fellow members of the Jockey Club in Paris, all connoisseurs of wine, to drink them and tell him honestly what they thought. He claims they all agreed that his quarter-bottles were the best they had ever tasted.

On the other hand, the cork-maker asserts that the wax in cork cells plays a definite chemical role in the maturing of champagne and helps to bring out the wine's qualities; and this opinion is shared, I would say, by the majority of champagne-makers. What will probably happen is that before very long quarter-bottles, which are normally drunk within a few months of their sale, will be sold with crown caps on them; and once the public has grown accustomed to the innovation crown-capped half-bottles will be sold. Later, if half-bottles with crown caps prove to be lasting well, the practice may be extended to standard-sized bottles of non-vintage; but I doubt very much whether vintage champagne will ever be sold without a good, solid, old-fashioned cork from the Iberian peninsula.

PART VI

THE CONSUMPTION AND ENJOYMENT OF
THE WINE AND ITS BY-PRODUCTS

CHAPTER 32

BUYING, CHOOSING, APPRAISING AND LAYING DOWN CHAMPAGNE

THERE ARE TWO golden rules by which the purchaser of champagne should be guided. He should restrict his patronage to those firms that have great reputations to lose, and whose experience and resources enable them to blend and market champagnes of a consistently high quality; and he should always pay a price commensurate with the cost of production of a luxury wine: a very cheap champagne, however highfalutin its name and presentation, invariably stems from the last pressings of second-rate grapes. Those who like to seek out novelties and bargains when buying wine will find this advice dampening to their enthusiasm, but it is sound. Experiment, where champagne is concerned, nearly always ends in disappointment. It is often possible to "discover" a little-known cheap burgundy or bordeaux of quality, but the quality of little-known cheap champagnes is rarely high.

It does not follow that the selection of the champagne best suited to the purchaser's needs is an altogether simple matter. Even if he decides to restrict his choice to the product of the well-known firms, he has to decide which of them to patronize, whether to have non-vintage or vintage, and, if the latter, which year to have. All this requires skill and experience.

The Scots delight to tell of the appeal of heather to each of our five senses; our eyes approve its colour, our noses appreciate its perfume, our ears enjoy the tinkle of its bells when a wind sweeps across the moor, our palates respond to its taste in honey, and our sense of touch is attracted by its springy softness. Champagne, unlike still wines, also appeals to all five of our senses; and the best way to judge its quality is to test methodically the extent of its appeal on each sense in turn.

As the cork is removed, a fragile puff of smoke should emerge from the bottle, spiral momentarily and disappear. As soon as it has disappeared a little of the champagne should be poured into a glass, to a level roughly two inches above the stem; the stem should be gripped tightly with the thumb, index and middle fingers; and the glass should be twirled briskly, so that the champagne is thoroughly woken up. The appraisal of the wine can now start.

Begin with the eyes. Quickly, because it will soon disappear, take a look at the white froth which is playing around on top of the wine. Is is snow-white? Does its agitation, its anxiety to vanish into thin air, convey an impression of force? If so, excellent.

Now hold the glass by the stem against the light and study the wine's colour. Good champagnes vary in colour through a range of yellows which extend from straw through primrose and buttercup to bright gold and bronze. A hint of green is exciting; a tinge of brown is a danger signal, because it may mean the champagne is past its best. Whatever the shade of yellow, it should be limpid, distinctive and pleasing; a champagne that is wishy-washy in colour, whatever its other qualities, is imperfect.

Now inspect the bubbles. An Australian widow I know tells me that her husband used to say, "Champagne should laugh at you", which is an excellent description of how the bubbles should behave. They should be plentiful, uniform in shape, extremely animated and persistent: when the glass is held to the light, it should be possible to spot them forming right down near the stem and watch them rocketing upwards like balls in a juggler's hands. There is some difference of opinion concerning the size the bubbles should be. Most Champenois insist, "The smaller the bubbles, the better the champagne". A few pooh-pooh this theory, and maintain that the regularity and persistence of the bubbles are a surer guide to the quality of the champagne than their circumference.

Next, project the nose over, and well into, the glass, screw up the nose, sniff hard, and pass judgement on the champagne's bouquet. It should be subtle, interesting and pleasing. Detecting the finest nuance of the bouquet is an art:

> ". . . it is a ghost's right,
> His element is so fine
> Being sharpened by his death,
> To drink from the wine-breath
> While our gross palates drink from the whole wine . . ."*

but, with practice, mere mortals can acquire it.

Next, put the glass close to the ear and listen to the minute crackling sounds made by the bubbles. It would be absurd to suggest that by so doing anything much can be learnt about the quality of the champagne, but it is fun to do so now and again. Maurice Hollande, in *La Connaissance du Champagne*, tells of a film about an Indian girl suddenly

---

* From *All Souls' Night* by W. B. Yeats.

transported to the drawing-rooms of New York who put her first glass of champagne to her ear and exclaimed, "It sings !"

Finally, proceed to the most important test of all: the impression the champagne makes on the palate, and its "feel" in the mouth. For this it is essential to take a large sip—having first twirled the glass again—and swill the liquid round with the tongue so that it reaches the gums and the remotest corners of the mouth. The swilling process is a horrible sight to watch, but it is no good skimping it: the lips must be forced backwards and forwards two or three times, and the facial muscles must be extended and contracted: only thus will the champagne fully pervade the palate; and only when it has done so should it be swallowed. The first reaction of the palate should be one of delight at the cleanness and purity of the wine; this impression of cleanliness is a vital characteristic of champagne. Next, a faint prickly sensation should register on the tongue and in the throat, for, although champagne should slide down the throat with the greatest of ease, it is never meant to be soft and velvety like many a good still wine; the bursting bubbles should agitate the oral membranes and in so doing refresh and stimulate the drinker. Finally, the palate should become aware of the champagne's exquisite taste, not too "grapey", gloriously even in character, but possessed of a slight tang that recalls the chalk from which it springs. A perfect champagne has one taste in the mouth and leaves another at the back of the throat after it has been swallowed; the latter, known as the Farewell, is often more of a glow than a definite taste.

It is best to take a wine merchant's advice about the different vintages available. In practice, however, most wine merchants only have the current vintage in stock, so the real problem is to decide whether to buy non-vintage or to pay a little extra and have vintage. The purchaser cannot go far wrong if he makes this his policy: vintage for small, intimate occasions; non-vintage for such functions as balls, wedding receptions and cocktail parties, at which the attention of his guests is likely to be concentrated more on what is going on around them than on the finer points of the champagne.

Champagne has the sweetest temper of all great table wines. Taken to Timbuktu, Antarctica or Tibet, the chances are that it will arrive in better condition than the person with whom it travelled. This is because the carbonic acid gas helps, in a most remarkable way, to keep stable the various matters of which it is composed. But like Rolls-Royce cars, which are also shaped by craftsmen to withstand trials and shocks, the better champagne is looked after the better the service it will render. Remember that one bottle of wine constitutes a cellar, and that even one bottle is worth coddling.

The ideal place to store champagne is in a cellar hewn out of chalk. The next best place is in any well designed cellar. A person who has no cellar need not despair. He should reflect for a moment on what constitutes good cellarage: a constant temperature of 50–55°F. (10°C.– 12·7°C.); ventilation; protection from draughts and vibration; cleanliness. He should then set about finding the corner in his home which comes closest to combining these conditions. Dampness, within reason, will cause no great harm; bright lights will: if it can possibly be arranged, champagne should be stored in complete darkness. If other wines are being laid down as well, the champagne should be placed at the bottom of the pile, where the temperature is lowest. Clarets, ports and burgundies should come next, sherries and sauternes at the top.

The most important moment of all, when champagne is being laid down, comes just before the bottles are placed in position. If the correct drill is performed then, half the battle is won, and, however makeshift the cellarage, the chances are that the champagne will be bursting with life when it is removed to be drunk. The drill is: hold the bottle in the hand in a horizontal position; allow the neck to dip forward to an angle of 45°; raise it to the horizontal position again; and then, immediately, place the bottle in a horizontal position in the rack or on the shelf. The drill is the same as that performed by the workers in champagne cellars when they are stacking the bottles for the second fermentation; the object is to force the air bubble that exists in every bottle of champagne back towards the centre of the bottle. For if this air bubble happens to be situated between the wine and the cork at the moment the bottle is laid flat, it will remain in that position indefinitely; the cork, having no contact with the wine, will dry out—with much rapidity in hot climates; and there is every possibility that the champagne will be "flat" by the time it is removed from the cellar to be drunk.

It follows that at all times it is best to keep champagne in the horizontal position, with the wine in contact with the cork. Now and again, one notices a shop which has champagne bottles standing upright in the window. Clearly the owner knows nothing about champagne; the corks are gradually drying out, shrinking and losing their elasticity. Even when a person buys a single bottle of champagne at a wine merchant's, he should carry the bottle home with him in the horizontal position. And if for any reason the contents of a case of champagne cannot be stacked away immediately, care should be taken to see that the case is lying flat, and not on its side: otherwise half the bottles inside will be standing upright and running the risk of deteriorating.

There is one other precaution that should be taken if the champagne is stored away for several years. That is for the bottles to be inspected from time to time for signs of "weeping". If the look of a cork arouses suspicion, the bottle should be consumed straight away.

CHAPTER 33

SERVING CHAMPAGNE

CHAMPAGNE IS A difficult wine to serve correctly. It does not require decanting, as the sediment has already been removed by the manufacturers, and this saves time and effort; but to remove the cork efficiently, to serve the wine at the right temperature, and to pour it out without spilling involves taking trouble and, above all, concentration.

Champagne, whether served in Lapland or Liberia, must be chilled. The firms do not advertise this fact on their labels because most people who drink champagne know it and would be insulted if the point was pressed home so crudely. It is rather tough, though, on beginners. Now and again a big champagne firm receives a pathetic letter from someone who has recently visited the cellars, usually with a coach party, and gone away with a bottle of champagne. Generally the letter arrives from Interlaken or Nice or the Black Forest, the final destination of the coach tour, and it describes a calamity. It was rather a hot evening, the correspondent announces, and, having dined in the hotel, she thought it would be nice to invite one or two fellow passengers upstairs to refresh themselves from the precious bottle. Glasses were laid out and when everyone arrived the bottle was opened. The cork flew to the ceiling, the wine gushed out all over the carpet and her best frock, and by the time order was re-established there was only enough champagne left for everyone to have one sip. What, the writer asks, was wrong with the champagne? The answer, of course, is that there was nothing wrong with the champagne; the calamity occurred because the eagerness of the carbonic acid gas to escape from the bottle had not been restrained by icing. Also because the lady was inexperienced: with experience and agility a bottle of champagne can perfectly well be opened without loss, even if it has not been cooled.

The temperature of champagne at the time it is served should be between 44°F. (6·6°C.) and 48°F. (8·8°C.). At such temperatures, not only are the taste and bouquet of the wine at their best, but the pressure of the carbonic acid gas inside the bottle is reduced to approximately one atmosphere, and there is thus no danger of the wine or even of the foam spurting out when the cork is removed. An indication that the correct temperature has been achieved is that a slight mist forms on the outside of the glass when the champagne is poured.

The ice-bucket and the refrigerator are equally effective in achieving the correct temperature. When two people are dining alone it is preferable to serve champagne in an ice-bucket, as, presumably, they will take a considerable time to consume the bottle, and unless it is kept on ice the wine at the bottom of the bottle will be warm by the time they are ready to drink it; but when several people are being served from the same bottle it will, one hopes, be finished so quickly that an ice-bucket is redundant. If an ice-bucket is used, water as well as ice should be put in it, as the water helps to speed up the cooling process, which should then take between twenty minutes and half-an-hour. By adding marine salt to the ice the cooling process can be speeded up still further, but the treatment is somewhat brutal, and care should be taken lest the temperature of the champagne is too greatly reduced, to the momentary detriment of its taste and bouquet. If champagne is being drunk out-of-doors in sunshine (spoil-sports say champagne is too delicate a wine to drink in the sun, but they miss one of life's pleasantest experiences), it is essential to serve it in an ice-bucket and to twirl the bottle from time to time, so that its entire surface is brought into occasional contact with the ice. Ideally, a refrigerator in which champagne is to be cooled should be set at 41°F. (5°C.), and the bottle should be left in it for about an hour-and-a-half before being served. Those who wish to be able to serve champagne straight away to guests who arrive unexpectedly are justified in leaving a bottle or two (lying flat) in a refrigerator for several days at a time, but after a longer period the intensity of the bouquet will have diminished and the extraction of the cork may present difficulty. Whatever happens, a bottle that has been in a refrigerator should not be returned to the cellar with a view to being iced again and consumed later, as the contraction and expansion which such action imposes is a strain on the cork.

It is a surprise and a disappointment for people for whom part of the fun, the glamour, the mystique of champagne is the "popping" of the cork to discover that the makers of champagne disapprove of "pops" and insist that the cork should be removed so slowly that the accompanying sound more closely resembles a "sigh". There can be no doubt that the champagne-makers' attitude is the correct one, because what causes the "pop" is the sudden, brutal discharge of a considerable quantity of the carbonic acid gas in the bottle; it is far better for the champagne if the release of carbonic gas is allowed to take place slowly and gently *through* the wine once it has been poured. But the fact remains that there is nothing like the "pop" for making a party "go", and even the champagne-makers have been known to recognize it:

when Mr. Khrushchev visited a champagne cellar in 1960, he was greeted by the thunder of 300 corks being jerked out simultaneously.

In the Champagne district, champagne corks are usually extracted with the aid of a pair of blunt-toothed tweezers specially designed for the purpose. When tweezers are used, the procedure should be as follows:

1. Make sure there is a glass handy, in case the extraction is mishandled and wine spurts out of the bottle.

2. Remove the gold foil surrounding the cork, and cut or twist off the wire muzzle.

3. Having stood the bottle on a flat surface, grip its neck with the left hand, leaving the forefinger free to curl itself over the cork and hold it firmly down.

4. Holding the tweezers in the right hand, grip the cork with them and ease it upwards.

5. As soon as the pressure of the gas on the bottom of the cork is felt by the left forefinger, put down the tweezers and gradually change the position of the left hand, so that the pressure of the cork is taken by the palm, and all five fingers, pointing downwards, are gripping the neck of the bottle.

6. Finally, tilt the bottle up to an angle of 45°, and, while the palm of the left hand takes the pressure, gently ease the cork out with the thumb and forefinger of the right hand.

If tweezers are unavailable, it is possible to extract the cork by twisting it with the strength of the wrists, by working it backwards, forwards and upwards with the thumbs, or by holding on to it with one hand while the other twists the bottom of the bottle; but the risk of the cork breaking is greater than when tweezers are used, and it is less easy to avoid a "pop". Whichever method is used, the main thing to remember is that, as soon as the cork starts to "give", the bottle should be inclined at an angle and the palm and fingers of the left hand should act as a shield to prevent the cork from flying out.

If the cork refuses to budge, there is a simple way of removing it: dip the neck of the bottle in hot water for a minute or two and then pull it; the heat has the effect of softening the wax in the cork and eases the extraction.

A host who intends to open and serve the champagne himself should, before serving it, pour a small quantity into a glass, twirl the glass to liven up the wine, and then sniff and taste it. If he suspects that the champagne is "corked" he should immediately smell the cork, which in such cases has a mouldy smell. Normally it expands, after being removed from the bottle, and assumes the shape of a mushroom; the fact, however, that it does not spread out, but remains peg-shaped, is not necessarily an indication that the champagne is out of condition: all it may mean is that the wine is not in its first youth or has been stored incorrectly, and that, with age or maltreatment, the cork has lost its elasticity.

The inspection over, the host can now fill the glasses. He should remember never to fill them more than three-quarters full; otherwise his guests will be unable to twirl their glasses and savour the bouquet without spilling the champagne.

When a butler or a wine-waiter is serving champagne at a dinner-party, the bottle should be swathed in a white napkin, as iced champagne bottles tend to drip, and women in *décolleté* evening dresses are apt to object if tiny drops of icy water land on their bare shoulders. A napkin, however, has one grave disadvantage: it makes it difficult for the guests to see what type of champagne is being served (hosts wishing to palm off inferior brands on their guests would, I suppose, account this an advantage). A Member of Parliament tells me that, while attending a large luncheon at Chartwell as the guest of Sir Winston Churchill, he nearly died of curiosity because the champagne was superb and obviously very old, but so expertly were the bottles swaddled in white napkins that he was unable to ascertain the year or the make. Queen Victoria, had she been present at that luncheon, would have thoroughly approved of the champagne's anonymity being preserved, as Colonel Frank Hedges Butler's rolling prose informs us in *Wine and the Wine Lands of the World*:

"I once had the honour of playing at a Command Concert before Her Majesty Queen Victoria, at Windsor Castle, with the Imperial Institute Orchestral Society. Next day the Court Circular recorded that 'Refreshments were served in the Audience and Presence Chambers for the Ladies and Gentlemen of the Orchestra'. The refreshments consisted of a gorgeous champagne supper, with the Royal servants in powdered hair and knee-breeches standing round the table.

"But what struck me particularly was the appearance of the champagne bottles. They were naked as the day they were blown! Of the proud panoply of label and gold foil, with which custom has decked 'the wine of duchesses' to stimulate anticipation and guarantee its fulfilment, not a vestige remained; everything had been scrupulously removed. And the wine, as I happened to know, was of the famous vintage of 1884, brought across from the Golden Valley of St. James's

—that wondrous vault beneath the Palace where the gilded necks of the foiled champagne bottles stretched away in two, tight dazzling ramparts. So repugnant was the age of advertisement to the Victorian Court."

To return to the butler and wine-waiter. He should always, without fail, give the host or hostess—or, to put it more crudely, the person who is paying for the champagne—the opportunity of tasting the champagne before it is served round the table. Wine-waiters nearly always do; butlers frequently do not, particularly if their employer is a woman. I know a number of hostesses who serve wonderful champagne, but who fail to insist on this courtesy to their guests. They should pull their stockings up.

In the Champagne district a butler, instead of putting his hand round the bottle to serve it, places his thumb in the punt and takes the weight on his fingers outstretched along the bottle's belly. This method of serving requires a strong wrist and is not recommended for the butter-fingered, but, when executed with panache, it looks professional and impressive. Sometimes, in the Champagne district, the bottle is placed in a special light metal frame, equipped with a handle, and served from that; the advantage of the contrivance is that the warmth of the pourer's hand does not come into contact with the bottle.

Champagne should never be served from a decanter. Having recorded that statement I am free to suggest that, if one is very sure of what one is doing, it is often a good idea to break a rule. Mr. George Howard, the owner of one of England's most stately homes, Castle Howard in Yorkshire, nearly always decants champagne, with conspicuous success. He has two types of receptacle for the purpose. One is a modern Spanish wine-jug, slender at the neck, bowl-shaped at the bottom: the champagne is poured in through a hole at the top, which is closed with a raffia bung, and poured out through the spout. Fitted into the upper swell of the jug there is a glass tube for ice (or snow), which is secured with another raffia bung. The great advantage of this receptacle is that the last drop of champagne is as cool as the first. The other containers which he uses are Georgian glass jugs, twelve inches tall and of most graceful design; they were presumably intended for cups and hocks. They hold over a magnum of champagne and are thus particularly useful when there are large parties to be served. As the jug is inclined over their glasses, the guests catch a glimpse of the lovely colour and the happy foam of a large quantity of champagne, a sight that is normally concealed by the pond green of the bottle.

Once, at the Norwegian Embassy in London, I saw champagne

shown off to as great advantage as in the Georgian jugs. It was at a Christmas party arranged by the Ambassador's daughter. About twenty tables for four had been placed in the dining-room, each decorated with traditional Norwegian Christmas ornaments. These included apples from which there sprang, at rakish angles, long, thin, porcelain-white candles. They were of a special kind that do not drip, and their flames hovered a couple of inches over the champagne glasses. The lights had been turned out, and in the darkened room the flickering candlelight glowed through the crystal, transforming the champagne into a pool of dancing golden bubbles. One could study the wine—and marvel at its vitality and its infectious gaiety—with greater ease than in any *salon de dégustation* that I know in Rheims or Epernay.

Many people imagine that if a bottle of champagne is only partially consumed it is impossible to keep the residue alive and sparkling. In reality, if the cork of an ordinary wine bottle is inserted in a partially consumed bottle of champagne, and the bottle is replaced in the refrigerator, the champagne remains in remarkably good form for at least twenty-four hours; and if one of the stoppers specially designed for the purpose is used—they cost only a few shillings—the champagne keeps its form for even longer. The stoppers are useful when a person is ill and can only take a few sips of champagne at a time; in bars where champagne is sold by the glass; and particularly when a champagne cocktail party is being given and the host has no one to open the bottles for him. A host who has continually to disappear to the kitchen in order to pull champagne corks cannot be a good host; if he invests in a few stoppers he can open the bottles in the afternoon (he must, of course, cool them first, and keep them cool), or even the evening before the party, and then, when his guests arrive, remove the stoppers with a flick of his fingers as and when the bottles are needed. I believe caterers sometimes solve the difficulty of serving a large number of guests in the shortest possible space of time in a different manner. The bottles are opened before the guests arrive, and, to prevent the foam trickling out as the temperature of the champagne rises, minute quantities of cream are dabbed on the rims, which are wiped clean just before the champagne is served. The idea is ingenious and no doubt it could be applied successfully for smaller parties in the home; but great care would have to be taken to ensure that guests did not find cream floating about in their glasses.

Earlier on I had to explain that when a champagne cork is pulled there should be no "pop"; now I must state that the conventional champagne glass, the wide-mouthed *coupe*, sometimes known as the inverted ballet-skirt glass, is looked upon by the Champenois as being entirely unsuitable for champagne. They complain that the gaping mouth not only exposes too large a surface of the wine to contact with the air, thus causing the bubbles to form and explode with undue haste, but also prevents a concentration of the bouquet; and they deplore the tendency which the *coupe* has of causing the champagne to spill when it is being "nosed" and when a toast is being offered. They insist that only one type of glass is perfectly suited to champagne: a tall-stemmed, tulip-shaped one, soberly elegant and unornamented, a type of glass, incidentally, which suits almost all wines, still and sparkling. They like the glass to be colourless, so that the colour of the wine can be seen, and to be very thin, despite the danger of breakages; indeed, the Champenois would applaud Cyrus Redding's remark that "if we could divide a soap bubble in half while floating on a zephyr", we should have the perfect wine-glass. They also prefer it to be full-sized, big enough to hold about an eighth of a bottle of champagne when filled to within two inches of the brim. In their advertisements in the glossy magazines of the world, most of the big champagne Houses engage in a not particularly successful campaign to oust the *coupe*: in the hand of the beautiful girl in the beautiful dress, who is poised in front of a background of luscious green Chardonnay grapes, there is nearly always, nowadays, a beautiful tulip-shaped glass.

There can be no doubt that the Champenois are right: the tulip-shaped glass not only holds the foam and the bouquet much more successfully than the *coupe*; it also makes it much easier for the drinker to "play" with the wine, which is particularly important in the case of champagne because, for the full beauty of the sparkle to be brought out, the bubbles need agitating now and again. Since the tulip-shaped glass is so infinitely more desirable than the *coupe* for the proper appreciation of champagne, it seems extraordinary that the latter has so firmly established itself on the dining-tables of Great Britain, the United States, Belgium and, indeed, France itself (apart from the Champagne district).

The *coupe* came into fashion in the early Victorian era. The most charitable explanation of its invention I have heard is that people felt that a wine of such unique character as champagne deserved to have a completely distinctive glass. The more likely explanation is that Victorian glass manufacturers saw in champagne's rising popularity a golden opportunity of shaming people into buying a separate set of glasses for champagne, just as Victorian cutlers invented the fish-knife and fork to shame people into buying more cutlery. The world hastened to adopt the *coupe*, we may be sure, because it was unmistakable: sitting on crimson plush at Delmonico's or the Café Royal, a person could be certain that even people sitting on the other side of the room could see that he or she was drinking champagne. Even today, I find, when one walks into a dining-room and notices *coupes* beside the ordinary wine-glasses, one experiences a momentary thrill of expectation. For the *coupe* has become a symbol of champagne itself.

There is something else to be said in its favour: *coupes* have a most romantic ancestry. This is the story, as told by Maurice des Ombiaux in *Le Sein d'Hélène*:

"One fête day, Dionysus, Phoebus Apollo and Venus Aphrodite decided to associate Helen with the enchanted juice of the grape by in future raising to their lips a chalice moulded from her breast, in place of an Egyptian ryhton. . . . But to whom was to fall the honour of taking the cast of the fair Grecian's divine globe?

"The Gods had already made their choice: it fell on Paris, the shepherd, Apollo's protégé, who had learnt the art of working metal from Cibelus on Mount Ida. He was led into the hall where the princes of Greece were engaged in libations in the beauty's honour.

"Helen appeared with her attendants, looking as radiant as Phoebe among the stars. The princes of Greece stood up to gaze upon her. The veil which covered her bosom was lifted and one of the two globes was revealed, pink as the dawn, white as the snows of Mount Rhodopus, smooth as the goat's milk of Arcadia. It is said that the Gods chose this moment to look down from the heights of Olympus, in order to contemplate this marvel through which life glowed like light through an alabaster vase.

"With wax provided by the golden daughters of Hymettus, the shepherd Paris, whose capable hands were raised in an attitude of adoration, took the cast of the breast, which looked like a luscious fruit on the point of falling into a gardener's hand.

"When Paris had removed the wax cast, the attendants hastened to replace the veil over Helen's gorgeous breast, but not before her admirers had glimpsed a teat whose freshness was as tempting as a strawberry.

"As soon as the *coupe* had been fashioned under the aegis of Apollo, it was handed to the suitors, each of whom raised it to his lips in turn, thereby experiencing the divine illusion that he was drinking from the breast of the daughter of Jupiter and Leda."

That is the origin of the *coupe*; and lest anyone should doubt the story let me point out that four *coupes* of rose-white Sèvres porcelain, moulded from the breast of Marie-Antoinette, adorned the Queen's Dairy Temple at the château de Rambouillet, and that one of them survives today in the care of the Antique Company of New York Inc.

There are three other types of glass in which champagne used to be drunk and sometimes still is: the *flûte*, the *pompinette* and the tumbler. The *flûte*—the tall, tapering glass which Dom Pérignon is credited by some historians with inventing, and which was much in vogue during the French Regency—holds no wine to speak of; the bouquet is given no chance to express itself and too much froth is promoted (the *flûte's* effect of whipping up the foam was, of course, the reason why it was so popular in the days when champagne's sparkle was weak and irregular); hollow-stemmed *flûtes* have the further disadvantage of being extremely insanitary, since it is practically impossible to clean them properly. The *pompinette*—a scimitar-shaped *flûte* with a round knob at the bottom instead of a stem and a base—can never be put down when there is wine in it: it is said to have been invented to stop chatterboxes, the absent-minded and people in love from letting their champagne grow warm. As for tumblers, Mr. George Saintsbury has written all that need ever be written about them: after explaining that wine never tastes quite right in them, he continued, "In the second place there is no stem for the finger tips to play with; now a wine-glass without a stem is as bad as some other creatures without a waist".

Whatever type of glass is used for champagne, it is particularly important that the glass retains no trace whatever of a detergent and is absolutely dry and well polished: the bubbles hardly rise at all in a glass contaminated with detergent, and sluggishly in a damp one. Many a healthy bottle of champagne has been sent away from table in disgrace, accused by some nincompoop of being "corked", when in reality detergent or damp in the glass was to blame. To obtain a perfect sparkle, the glass should be dried with a newly ironed cloth and polished with shammy-leather.

CHAPTER 34

WHEN TO DRINK CHAMPAGNE AND WHAT TO DRINK IT WITH

WITH HIS CUSTOMARY felicity of phrase, M. André Simon has written: "Champagne is the best of all wines—at times." With equal felicity, he continued:

"There is no wine that is the best all the time: so much depends upon not only our taste but our mood, upon conditions, circumstances and the company. Let us imagine, for instance, that we are having lunch at Ascot or Goodwood. The choice is lobster salad or cold Scotch salmon; you have the one and I have the other, but we both will call for champagne, because champagne is the best wine we can possibly think of. Claret and burgundy would be entirely out of place and vintage port quite unthinkable."

And he ended by inviting the reader to imagine that he had backed three losers and then, finally, had a big win:

"You must celebrate. Are you going to call for a bottle of Château Latour 1929 or Les Grands Echezeaux 1923, or Cockburn '08? They are all great wines, and you or I could write whole books about them . . . but what you want is champagne and no other wine is acceptable."

Many people consider, myself included, that the best time of all to drink champagne is around eleven-thirty in the morning; some people would add, with a chicken sandwich. There is a magic about champagne before lunch to which it never quite aspires later in the day. But one of the glories of champagne, which distinguishes it from every other wine, is that there is never a moment in the twenty-four hours of the day and the night when it cannot be drunk with pleasure: Mr. Winston Churchill, settling into his seat for a wartime Clipper flight to America, calls for champagne—to the horror of Lord Alanbrooke; Mr. Macmillan, so the newspapers report, calls with Edwardian gusto for "Bubbly" immediately after the audience with Queen Elizabeth II during which he became Prime Minister; a similar cry goes out from the chairman in his plush office after the morning's conference, from the tired travellers who started at six in the morning and arrive at three-thirty, from the couple just off to the theatre, from the couple just back from the theatre, and thenceforward till dawn from the couples dancing away their cares in the night-clubs of the world. King Albert of the Belgians, I am told, drank champagne for breakfast with two poached eggs.

If one analyses the situation, one finds that there are three main ways of drinking champagne: by itself between meals or before meals; by itself with a meal; in conjunction with other wines at a meal.

That champagne is the most perfect apéritif in existence hardly anyone denies, even sherry-makers, which is nice of them. At the Elysée Palace and at the Royal Palace in Brussels, where the wine and food for official entertaining are probably planned with an eye to greater classical perfection than anywhere else in the world, champagne is nearly always served as an apéritif. No other wine so effectively sharpens the appetite and stimulates the flow of gastric juices,* thereby enhancing the pleasure to be gained from the meal that follows. When champagne is being served as an apéritif or by itself between meals, dry salty biscuits should be served with it: the salt brings out the flavour of the wine. In theory, ice-cubes should never be added to a glass of champagne, even if it is being drunk between meals on a terrace during a heat-wave; but I have seen champagne-makers add them on scorching hot days and I suffer no qualms in following their example.

There is only one type of meal for which champagne by itself is the absolutely ideal accompaniment: a meal that is light and probably cold, consisting, perhaps, of smoked salmon, cold chicken, salad and strawberries and cream, or of gulls' eggs, slices of cold ham, new potatoes and a sherbet. But it does not follow that to serve champagne alone throughout a different type of meal is a gastronomic sin. If people feel like drinking champagne throughout a much heavier meal, they should go ahead and do so with a light heart.

When champagne is being served in conjunction with other wines at a meal, it is often difficult to decide which is the best moment to introduce it. The average Frenchman today delays drinking it until the

---

* There is a perfectly good reason why this is so. Champagne releases its alcohol far more quickly than a still wine. The moment it comes in contact with the rough surfaces that line our mouths the resulting friction causes the carbonic acid gas suspended in it to force its way out in the form of bubbles—and each of these bubbles carries away with it a drop of alcohol. In the case of a still wine, the release of alcohol does not take place until the liquid reaches our stomachs.

dessert is served for two reasons: because he likes, rightly, to drink a red wine with his cheese (which he has before his dessert), and therefore tends to stick to red wine during the courses served before the cheese; and because he is still a devotee of "sweet" champagne and, quite logically, considers the best moment to drink it is with a sweet dessert. The practice, however, of delaying the service of champagne until the dessert is passed round has survived in many French families who now drink dry champagne, and many gourmets deplore it, because they dislike drinking dry champagne with anything sweet. Personally, although I detest drinking dry champagne between meals with something sweet—which is often done in France—I like drinking it with rich desserts very much indeed; and, quite apart from that, I find that when champagne is produced at the end of an elaborate and memorable meal the meal becomes doubly memorable, mainly because the gaiety the champagne engenders lingers with the guests long after they have left the table. There is, however, a way of serving "dry" champagne in conjunction with other wines which caters for both those who dislike drinking it with dessert and those who do not: this is, to start filling the champagne glasses as soon as the first of the other wines has been served, and to keep on filling them throughout the meal, thus enabling the individual guest to drink the champagne when he chooses. I find that more and more French families are adopting this custom.

I purposely refrain from listing dishes and foods with which champagne is particularly agreeable or particularly horrible, because the matter is largely one of personal taste, and I believe that this type of list often leads to misunderstandings. For instance, if I wrote that champagne and steak-and-kidney pudding make bad bed-partners, which most people agree is a fact, then someone who wanted to drink champagne by itself throughout a meal which included steak-and-kidney pudding might be put off doing so, which, in my opinion, would be a pity if he was in the mood for champagne. But I intend to mention the subject of oysters and champagne. In *Notes on a Cellar-Book* George Saintsbury wrote: "Champagne, with oysters, though it has Thackeray's sanction, seems to me a sin without a solace." Gourmets generally agree with Saintsbury; but one has only to walk along the sidewalks of Paris on a sunny day and observe the relish with which Parisians are consuming a dozen oysters and a half-bottle of champagne at a café table to know that the combination can be a pleasing one; very pleasing, my stomach instructs me to add.

Finally, a word about whisky and champagne. In France, at the time I write, whisky is the rage, and even in the Champagne district one runs the risk of being offered whisky either before one is to drink a lot of champagne or just after one has done so. I always find the combination one of the quickest ways of acquiring a sore head, and I know many people who are of the same opinion. So beware.

The very thought of mixing champagne with other drinks is anathema to the Champenois. They would prefer to drink *vin ordinaire*, perhaps water even, rather than pollute the result of their labours with alien liquid. But in other parts of the world, where different ways of life and different climates prevail, a drink to which champagne contributes can, it must be admitted, be very pleasant indeed.

The most popular way of serving champagne in a mixed form is the champagne cocktail. Personally I have never seen the point of these concoctions, as almost as much champagne is required to make them as when champagne is served neat, so that they are no cheaper than champagne by itself, which is a much "cleaner" drink. But there is no doubt that they do give many people great pleasure, and, this being so, one has no right to disparage them. The simplest way to make a champagne cocktail is to place a lump of sugar, soaked in Angostura bitters, and what the French call a *zeste* of orange in the bottom of the glass, add a little brandy and fill up with iced champagne. Some people prefer to use curaçao or vermouth instead of brandy, and lemon peel instead of orange peel; whatever modifications are made, the secret of success is to serve the cocktail ice-cold without adding ice.

In 1921 the barman of Buck's Club in London, Mr. McGarry, invented a delicious pre-luncheon drink, composed of one-third orange juice, two-thirds champagne and a teaspoonful of grenadine, which came to be known as Buck's Fizz; at the Ritz Bar in Paris a mixture of one-third orange juice and two-thirds champagne is served without the grenadine, and is called a Mimosa; at the Carlton Hotel in Cannes a somewhat similar cocktail, made with one-third orange juice, one-third champagne and one-third cognac plus two dashes each of grenadine and cointreau, is known as a Pick-me-up. Another cocktail to which champagne contributes and which has achieved world-wide popularity is the French 75. This is the recipe:

Serve in a tall glass: the juice of half a lemon, one teaspoonful of sugar, two ozs. of gin; mix well and fill up with champagne, adding one cube of ice.

A Black Velvet or, as it sometimes is called, a Bismarck—champagne and stout in equal quantities—is claimed by its devotees to be an effective cure for a hangover if drunk with breakfast; but I prefer to drink it without a hangover before lunch on a foggy winter's day in an English country pub. With the French 75 and the Black Velvet the cardinal sin is, of course, committed of mixing grape and grain, but then, few cardinal sins are without their satisfactions.

Finally, on a summer's evening a champagne cup served in a beautiful bowl, with succulent fruit floating in it, can be delicious, and as much in harmony with the season as cucumber sandwiches for tea at Henley regatta or cherry brandy at a hunt meet. There are many different ways of making it. The basic ingredients should be a little sugar, some brandy and some curaçao, some syrup of strawberries, an orange, half a lemon, half a banana, a few strawberries, cherries, grapes, perhaps half a slice of pineapple and, whatever happens, borage. These should be placed in the bowl, the bowl should be left on ice for an hour and then, at the very last minute, ice-cold (non-vintage) champagne should be poured in; ice in the cup takes the kick out of it and tends to make it wishy-washy.*

* The recipe for Regent's Punch was given on page 142.

CHAPTER 35

OLD CHAMPAGNE, STILL CHAMPAGNE AND PINK CHAMPAGNE

CHAMPAGNE IS NOT immortal like certain Madeiras; nor will it remain in perfect condition for over a century like certain clarets. One of the principal reasons why it has a shorter life span than many great still and fortified wines is that the carbonic acid gas which it contains makes it impractical for the cork to be changed every decade or so.

Non-vintage champagne should be drunk within a matter of months of its purchase; then it will be young and gay and frivolous, as its makers intended. As a general rule, vintage champagne should be drunk within eight to ten years of the date on the bottle—much sooner if storage conditions were imperfect. If they are perfect there is always a chance that the wine will still be alive and kicking in its teens; but by the time it reaches its twenties the average bottle is undrinkable. Certain very great vintages, however, do possess a life force that carries them on into their thirties and forties, even into their fifties and sixties, and, in that event, whoever is lucky enough to drink them is in for a treat.

Champagnes that have survived for decades are so different from young champagnes that someone tasting one for the first time might well imagine that he was drinking the product of another world (which in fact he is). Generally, but not always—the 1911s and the 1914s being drunk in the Champagne district today are magnificent exceptions—there is very little effervescence left;* as the cork is removed the pressure on it is light, and the wine, when poured, is *pétillant*—just faintly sparkling. More often than not, its alcoholic strength is also reduced: through the years the acids in the wine have been reacting with the alcohol, thereby producing an abundance of sweet-smelling esters. But what the champagne has lost in sparkle and alcoholic strength, it may have gained immeasurably in other ways. Once the eyes have feasted on the rich gold or copper or bronze of a fine old champagne, a young one seems a trifle anaemic. The flavour, too, is nearly always a revelation: stoutly proclaiming the year of its birth, strong, full-bodied, delicious, so delicious, in fact, that old

---

* To encourage the remaining effervescence, some people prefer to serve old champagnes a little less *frappé* than young ones. Others prefer to serve them more *frappé*, to deaden the beery, or *madérisé*, flavour that they sometimes have.

champagnes are one of the very few wines to which the word "nectar" can justly be applied.

As for the bouquet, it is often so pronounced and fruity (owing to the abundance of esters in the wine) that one feels one is smelling the scent of the sun-drenched vineyards in which the grapes ripened decades before. There is often, too, a creamy head to an old champagne which, by its spread and tenacity, reflects a solidity and a homogeneity seldom attained by young champagne. As Mr. Warner Allen has put it, old champagne is "a wine in which time has obliterated all traces of human handiwork, so that one could almost swear that nature alone could have produced such a masterpiece".

"Well, well," I can imagine someone saying, "old champagne sounds so delectable, I shall ring up my wine merchant at once, order a case of champagne, lay it down, and drink it in my old age." I hate to pour cold water on such enthusiasm, but it would be criminal not to counsel caution. If someone lays down a recent vintage of exceptional quality, and sticks to his resolution not to drink it until he is in his dotage, his patience may well be rewarded; but the makers themselves would be the last people to raise his hopes. It must be remembered that a champagne is far more likely to attain healthy old age in the Champagne district than outside it. There are two reasons why this is so. In the first place, in very few other areas of the world do cellars exist which are so perfectly suited to the maturing of the wine. Secondly, champagnes laid down in the Champagne district do not have to be disgorged until a day or two before they are drunk: they live their entire life without ever coming into contact with oxygen (provided the cork is good); whereas champagne laid down in London, New York or Paris has already been disgorged, and the disgorging process has to some extent lessened the chances of longevity (even in the Champagne district, an average of two or three out of every six bottles of very old champagne is discarded as undrinkable; and the casualty ratio elsewhere is usually higher still).

The answer is that if, like Oliver Goldsmith, you "love everything that's old: old friends, old times, old manners, old books and old wines", as far as champagne is concerned it is a justifiable risk to lay it down provided you have first-class cellarage at your disposal; but, if you have not, it is wiser to buy a case or two of old champagne at a time in a saleroom and consume it fairly soon afterwards.

There are many Champenois who dislike their still wines being referred to as "*Champagnes natures*" (with "*rouge*" or "*blanc*" added, to differentiate between the red and white variety), because the term implies—which of course is not the case—that there is something unnatural about sparkling champagne. There are also some Champenois who dislike it when people refer to the still white wine of the Champagne district simply as *"blanc de blancs"*. They point out that *"blanc de blancs"* is a way of describing any white wine made from white grapes (just as *"blanc de rouges"* is a way of describing any white wine made from red grapes), and that the correct term to describe the still white wine of the Champagne district is *"Champagne blanc* (or *rouge*) *non-mousseux"*. However, as this is somewhat of a mouthful, it seems doubtful whether it will ever be widely adopted by those who drink rather than make the wine.

The trouble, today, with the still wines of Champagne is that it is exceedingly difficult to lay one's hands on a really outstanding bottle. Paris, the Ile-de-France and the Champagne district are the only places in France where *Champagnes natures* are commonly found on restaurant wine lists; and, even in the Champagne district itself, rare is the wine merchant or restaurateur who has supremely good bottles to offer a customer. When one recalls that until Dom Pérignon's lifetime all the wine that was made in the Champagne district was non-sparkling, and that as recently as a hundred years ago the fame of the winefield rested to a far greater extent on its still wines than on its sparkling ones, the present-day situation does seem very odd indeed.

Many Champenois explain away the shortage by stating that still champagnes are ruined by travel. That they are very bad travellers indeed compared to sparkling champagne there can be no doubt. In the 1870s Mr. Vizetelly was informed by a champagne-maker that even the journey from the Champagne district to Paris was enough to sicken a bottle of still red champagne. The fact remains, nevertheless, as anyone who has read the historical section of this book knows, that during the seventeenth, eighteenth and nineteenth centuries considerable quantities of still champagne—most of it white, but some of it red or at any rate the produce of red grapes—did survive the journey to England, and won praise from experienced connoisseurs of wine.

The true explanation of why good still champagnes are difficult to obtain nowadays is that, so greatly does the demand for first-class grapes to make sparkling champagne exceed the supply, few of the great firms have enough available to market still wine. Most of the still champagnes that find their way into the cellars of French wine merchants and restaurants today are made by very small firms, who in some cases have no great tradition of wine-making behind them, and who may not, in the normal course of events, have access to the grapes of the finest growths. And this means that virtually the only way a wine-lover can taste a really unforgettable bottle of still champagne is as the guest of one of the great champagne Houses; for most of them do make just a little still wine with grapes from the great growths to drink themselves and to give to their guests.*

A perfect still white champagne is a fairly light, dry wine, with a fruitiness of flavour, a subtlety and intensity of bouquet and a rich yellow sheen that give it a distinction possessed by few other white wines. If drunk young, it sometimes contains the trace of a sparkle, but in that case it is no longer perfect, as a still champagne should be completely still. The growths which produce perfection are all situated on the Côte des Blancs. Still white champagne is traditionally served at the annual Académie Goncourt luncheon at which new candidates are proposed.

The growths which produce the best still red champagnes are Ambonnay, Ay, Bouzy, Cumières, Dizy, Rilly, Verzenay and Villedommange.† Of all the still red champagnes, a Bouzy is the most outstanding. A Bouzy of a great year is lighter and less complex than outstanding bordeauxs and burgundies, but as regards colour (often deep purple), body, cleanliness and smoothness on the palate, bouquet and the manner in which it penetrates to the remotest corners of the mouth, it is a wine that neither of those winefields would be ashamed to call their own.

If ever in the future, as the result of war or economic depression, the bottom should fall out of the market for sparkling champagne, the Champenois could always, as a last resort, do what they did during the depression in the early 1930s—make less sparkling champagne and more still champagne. But there would be a limit to the amount of still champagne that they could produce, for, although very large quantities of superb *blanc de blancs* could be made virtually every year, the quantity of saleable red still wine would be very small indeed, in relation to the size of the red-grape vineyards. This is because, in a winefield as far north as the Champagne district, it is much

* As these rare and wonderful bottles are the private property of the wine-maker and are consumed within the four walls of his home or office, they are seldom properly labelled. Usually a small rectangle of white paper is glued to the neck of the bottle, on which is inscribed in ink the name of the growth and the year of the vintage.

† These vineyards are all mainly planted with Pinot Noir vines. The Pinot Meunier produces a red wine which has less character and less bouquet; it is ready to drink earlier, but does not last as long.

more difficult to make a good red wine than a good white one.

The maker of red wine in the Champagne district is really faced with two quite separate problems. The first concerns colour: how to produce any of those full-blooded tints of red which are the *sine qua non* of a red wine? Visitors to the Champagne district, when they see the rich purple of the Pinot Noir grapes, find it hard to believe that such grapes could fail to produce a magnificently coloured wine; but the fact is that in normal circumstances they produce a wine which is only, one might say, half-heartedly red. This is because there are not normally enough sunny days in Champagne for the colour cells in the skins of the Pinot grapes to develop fully. Even in exceptional years, when there has been an abnormal amount of sunshine during the summer, the majority of the Pinot Noirs cannot be turned into a truly red wine. Happily, however, in such years—and only in such years— the wine-maker can resort to certain subterfuges to obtain the colour he requires. This is what he does:

1. He only uses grapes that have been grown on old vines. As we have seen, the skins of such grapes are more fragile than the skins of grapes produced by young vines, and impart more colouring matter to the juice.

2. After the bunches have been picked, he leaves them out in the sun for between twenty-four and forty-eight hours, to encourage the colouring matter to start dissolving in the juice.

3. Before pressing the bunches, he submits them to a process known as *foulage*, which consists of whirling them round in a special container. This has the effect of bruising the colour cells and of forcing the colouring matter which they contain to mix with the juice.

4. He conducts the pressing in a manner diametrically opposed to that which he employs when he is making sparkling champagne. Instead of forcing the juice out of the grapes as quickly as possible and evacuating it from the press immediately, so that colourless juice is obtained, he extracts it slowly and allows the skins to remain in contact with the juice the whole time.* He has to take great care to

---

* The grapes are normally removed from the stalks after the *foulage*, because the stalks contain a lot of water and practically no sugar, and, if they are pressed, they slightly lower the alcoholic content of the wine. If, however, it is desired to produce a wine that can be drunk at a great age, the stalks are left attached to the grapes during the pressing, as the tannin which they contain must be squeezed out to help conserve the wine.

Altogether three pressings are administered, and the juice of each one is kept separately; the juice of the first pressing invariably produces the best wine.

avoid crushing the pips, as they contain substances that impart a disagreeably bitter taste to the wine.

5. He leaves the skins in the juice when it is transferred to open wooden receptacles to undergo fermentation. Not until the first hectic stage of fermentation is complete, five or six days later, and the young wine is ready to be transferred to casks to finish fermenting and to age, does he remove the skins.

Such contrivances enable the wine-maker to produce a truly red wine in the Champagne district. But the difference between a good red wine and a bad one is very far from being solely a question of colour. A good red wine, in addition to possessing an agreeable, well-developed bouquet, must be comparatively strong (the must should have an alcoholic strength of at least 12°); it should be full-bodied and velvety; and whatever happens it must contain no trace of acidity or astringency. Now, in a winefield as far north as Champagne the requisite bouquet, alcoholic strength, body and smoothness can only be obtained—and acidity and astringency avoided—if the red grapes are slightly over-ripe. To ensure that they are is the second problem with which the maker of red wine has to deal.

The fact that the grapes with which he is to work must in any case be the produce of old vines helps the wine-maker to some extent to solve this second problem, because old vines produce fewer, smaller grapes than young vines, and in consequence their grapes always mature better than those of younger vines. Nevertheless, even old vines will not provide him with grapes of a maturity sufficient for his purposes unless the following conditions have been fulfilled:

1. The vines are exposed to the south or south-west and planted in mid-slope; vines facing other directions or situated on the plain or near the forests crowning the slopes seldom produce exceptionally ripe fruit.

2. The grapes are picked at the very end of the vintage.

3. All perished, dry or immature grapes are removed from the bunches, so that only healthy, over-ripe grapes remain.

4. The summer is a particularly favourable one. In the past four decades exceptional maturity has been attained, even by grapes which fulfilled the first three conditions, only about fifteen times; and in those years alone could superb red wine be made.

Once made, the red wines of the Champagne district are normally left in cask for between one to three years. They are then bottled, and the bottles are transferred to a cold deep cellar, where they remain until they are shipped. If, at the time of the pressing, the stalks were left attached to the grapes, with the result that the tannin in the stalks entered the juice, and if the juice originated from the first pressing, the wine will last for decades. It is these old red wines of the Champagne district—the old Bouzys, Rillys, Dizys, etc.—that compare so favourably with burgundies and bordeauxs.

No wine is more difficult to make than pink champagne. As this one fact explains nearly everything that needs to be explained about pink champagne, I shall begin with a short description of the two methods that are used to make it.

The first method is the older of the two, and may well have been invented by Dom Pérignon. It can only be used in very good years, as it relies for success, in its initial stages, on precisely the same circumstances and procedures as those required in the making of the still red wines of the Champagne district. The same small, exceptionally mature red grapes (the produce of old vines) are called for; the same devices are used to ensure that the skins colour the juice (late picking, exposure to sunshine after picking, etc.); the grapes are pressed in the same manner. Only the length of time the skins remain in the fermenting must is different, for, as the tint of red required for pink champagne is considerably lighter than that required for red still wine, the skins are withdrawn sooner. From that stage on, the wine is treated in more or less the same way as it would be if it was white and the object was to produce a golden sparkling champagne. It is blended after Christmas with similarly made pink wines, perhaps even with a small proportion of wine made with white grapes. In the spring sugar and selected yeasts are added to the blend before it is bottled. The bottles are then taken down to the cellars, whence they emerge three or four years later in the form of pink champagne, having passed in the normal manner through a second fermentation and the processes of *remuage* and *dégorgement*. At least, that is the form in which the maker hopes they will emerge: all too often, however, instead of pink champagne there emerges a champagne that is blue or green or yellow or brown or orange; and all too often, if such a catastrophe has been avoided, the pink champagne turns out to be undrinkable because unwanted deposits have formed in the bottles or because it has developed a peculiar taste.

The advantage of the second, more modern method of making pink champagne is that the grapes do not have to be the produce of old vines or of an exceptionally favourable year; it is also, in theory, much simpler. Exactly the same principles and ingredients are used as when golden sparkling champagne is being made, except that at a particular stage (the stage may vary from House to House, and is each House's secret) a proportion of still red champagne, ideally some Bouzy, is added to the blend to produce the rosé colour.* But, here again, the best endeavours of the *chef de cave* sometimes, though less frequently, result in the catastrophes which occur when the first method is employed. In other words, neither method is fool-proof. Furthermore, there exists little likelihood of either of them being rendered so until a lot more is understood about the reaction of red and white wines upon one another after marriage, and the effect of oxygen and of wine itself on the colouring matters in the skins of grapes.

Once it is understood that the champagne-maker who embarks on the manufacture of pink champagne runs the risk of losing his entire *cuvée*, composed perhaps of thousands of bottles, several mysterious points concerning pink champagne become clear. One understands, for instance, why pink champagne is more expensive than golden champagne. It is clear also why so few Houses make it: its manufacture requires considerable commercial courage, particularly if Method I is used.

The firms that do make pink champagne seldom serve it to their guests; they prefer to develop a taste for, and interest in, golden champagne. Indeed, pink champagne, in the Champagne district, is considered somewhat of a *question délicate*, and is best avoided. If, however, a visitor succeeds in penetrating the taboo, he is usually astounded by the remarks that the Champenois is likely to make. "*Plutôt une originalité*", he is apt to say. I was once told by a champagne-maker—who would never be so flippant about golden champagne—that the most suitable occasion to serve pink champagne is on a summer's evening when you are having supper at a table decorated with a pink tablecloth, pink flowers and pink candles—and the menu includes lobster and strawberries.

* In the olden days, cochineal was added to golden champagne to give it a rosé colour. In his textbook on champagne-making, published in 1877, Professor Robinet recommends the use of Teinture de Fismes (a preparation of elderberries boiled in cream of tartar) for the same purpose. The law now forbids such admixtures. As regards the addition of still red champagne to obtain the rosé colour (Method II), the law remains mute: but the propriety of the practice cannot be questioned, as the wine added is pure wine of the Champagne district, and the fact that it has been added is always mentioned in the official declarations to the *Régie*.

The patronizing, and at times confused, point of view of the Champenois can perhaps be explained by the fact that pink champagne is in some ways a less remarkable wine than golden champagne: it lacks what one might call the fragility of the latter. But I believe their attitude also stems from subtler considerations: from a deep-seated, passionately-held assessment of the fundamental nature of champagne as a wine, of its uniqueness. The twentieth-century Champenois is intensely aware, and proud, of his inheritance. He knows that immense efforts were expended by his forebears to build up the smooth-running businesses with which he is connected today. And, being a realist, he knows perfectly well that the Rock of Gibraltar on which his inheritance rests is a golden sparkling wine. To him there is something unreal about pink champagne, because he can only make it by the traditional method in exceptional years, and even then he cannot be sure that it will turn out perfect. He considers it alien to the mainstream of his destiny; he makes it because many of his own countrymen and many foreigners like it; but he would not consider that the end of the world had come if not another drop was ever made again.

A few Houses market a *Blanc de Blancs* sparkling champagne, implying that it is made exclusively from white grapes. As no control is exercised over the producer as regards the ratios of his blends, the purchaser must have confidence in the House to believe in the authenticity of the designation. Having no juice of the red grape to give it "body", many Champenois consider true champange *blanc de blancs* too light a wine, lacking "follow through"; its taste, they say, vanishes with undue haste, without leaving champagne's characteristic imprint on the palate and the throat. Even the purists will admit, however, that there are one or two growths on the Côte des Blancs whose grapes in an exceptionally fine year will produce a *blanc de blancs mousseux* that gives the impression of being a complete wine.

CHAPTER 36

OTHER PRODUCTS OF THE CHAMPAGNE VINES

OF ALL THE members of the vegetable kingdom, none is more bountiful to man than the vine. There is virtually no part of the plant for which he cannot find several uses if he so desires. Vine-leaves, for instance, perform other services than that of covering the private parts of nudes: they will cleanse wounds; they can be used as poultices; they can be brewed to make a hot drink; pressed, they produce a liquid which, after fermentation, becomes a sort of wine; they are excellent food for cattle and goats. The fibres of vine-bark can be spun into a material suitable for basketry work and for attaching vines to stakes. The grapes can be eaten, consumed as grape-juice or turned into wine. Mme. de Sévigné treated an ulcer on her leg by dipping it in fermenting must. Evaporated must, in Mediterranean countries, is turned into sweets and, in concentrated form, into a parody of honey. The oil of squashed grape-pips can be converted into oil-paint, margarine, cooking fat, soap, even lamp-fuel; the last is said to be extremely practical, as it has no smell and does not smoke. Grape husks can be dried and used as fuel.

The modern Champenois makes little or no use of any part of the vine other than the grapes, but the manufacture of champagne and still wine is far from being the sole use to which they are put. The oil derived from the pips after the grapes have been pressed is sold to a firm in Marseilles to make soap (in the war years it saved many a Frenchman from soapless ablutions). The wine-stone left at the bottom of the fermentation vats after the rackings can be sold, as I mentioned earlier, to dry-cleaning establishments for conversion into dyes. The grape-husks are either returned to the soil as manure or sold as fodder for cattle. There is a considerable world-wide sale for Champagne vinegar, which is made with the still wines of the countryside. But the most important uses to which the grapes of the Champagne vines are put, apart from the manufacture of champagne and still wines, are in the making of Ratafia de Champagne, Fine Marne and *eau-de-vie-de marc-de-Champagne*.

Ratafia is the thick, sweet, peach-coloured apéritif of the Champagne district. In many ways it resembles Pineau des Charentes, the apéritif of the Cognac winefield. It is extremely and deceptively strong (between 18° and 24° alcohol); people who drink it for the first time are often disconcerted halfway through their second glass by the joyful effect it is having on them. Its manufacture is comparatively simple: a few moments after the juice has been pressed out of Champagne grapes brandy (ideally cognac) is added to it; the brandy kills the wine-yeasts and stops the juice from fermenting. The mixture is then put in cask and later bottled. It is usually ready for sale a year after being made. Only a few firms sell ratafia, and those that do employ Jean Goyard & Cie, the distillers in Ay, to make it for them. Goyard make a good ratafia of their own and export a little of it. That ratafia is not better known outside the Champagne district is a pity, because, although not everyone likes a sweet apéritif, it is a highly suitable drink to have before a meal at which champagne is to be drunk exclusively. It should be served in small balloon-shaped glasses. Half a cantaloup melon with a little ratafia in the centre is delectable, infinitely preferable to half a cantaloup with port in the centre.

It is believed that ratafia de Champagne was being drunk in the eighteenth century, but the first known reference to it in a champagne firm's records is in those of Veuve Clicquot for the year 1823; it was not sold commercially to any great extent until the late nineteen-twenties.

The origin of the name "ratafia" is curious. It is derived from two Latin words, *rata fiat*, which formed part of the following formula used to validate legal transactions in the Middle Ages: *De quibus est res, ut rata fiat, publicum fecimus instrumentum* ("We have executed a public document concerning the matters with which the transaction deals, so that it may be confirmed"). Once these words had been spoken by both parties in front of a notary, the deal was "ratified"; custom then required the signatories to drink to the occasion from a bottle provided by the notary, a little ceremony which came to be known as the "ratafia".

Through the ages the name "ratafia" has been given to a number of different types of drinks. Technically, I believe, it can be correctly applied to any liqueur prepared by infusion as opposed to distillation; but in the eighteenth and nineteenth centuries, when people asked for a ratafia, they expected to receive a non-alcoholic fruit cordial. Presumably it was a soft drink that Alfred de Musset had in mind when, in *Mimi Pinson*, he made the young student list the attractions of the Parisian shop-girls: after explaining that they are virtuous, honest and clean, the student adds, "Fourthly, they are sincere because they drink ratafia". On the other hand, in the late seventeenth century ratafias may well have been alcoholic, for, when Mirabell mentions ratafia in the following speech addressed to Mrs. Millamant (with whom he is in love) in Congreve's *Way of the World*, the reference is apparently to something stronger than a fruit cordial:

"Lastly, to the dominion of the tea-table I submit: but with proviso, that you exceed not in your province, but restrain yourself to native and simple tea-table drinks, as tea, chocolate, and coffee. As likewise to genuine and authorized tea-table talk, such as mending of fashions, spoiling reputations, railing at absent friends, and so forth. But that on no account you encroach on the men's prerogative, and presume to drink healths, or toast fellows: for prevention of which, I banish all foreign forces, all auxiliaries to the tea-table, as orange-brandy, all aniseed, cinnamon, citron and Barbados waters, together with ratafia and the most noble spirit of clary."

Fine Marne is a brandy distilled from the still wines of the Champagne district. It is sold exclusively by the firms of Goyat & Cie of Ay and Jolly & Fils of Epernay. It cannot, of course, bear comparison with cognac, but it is an extremely pleasant drink, superior, in my opinion, to the majority of brandies made outside Cognac.

It must not be confused with Fine Champagne, which has nothing whatsoever to do with the Champagne district. It happens that two of the finest vineyard areas in the Cognac winefield are called Grande Champagne and Petite Champagne, and a cognac produced with grapes grown within their boundaries is thus entitled to be called Champagne Cognac or, loosely, Fine Champagne.

Before the war, when grapes were more plentiful, a few champagne firms used to send a small quantity of still wine of the Champagne district to Cognac to be distilled by the firm that supplied them with cognac for their ratafias. No commercial use was ever intended for this cross between a Fine Marne and a cognac; it is simply a curiosity designed to entertain—and baffle—connoisseurs of wine.

Most modern wine-makers follow in the footsteps of the Romans and make a poor man's brandy called *eau-de-vie-de-marc*. It is distilled not from a good wine, as brandies like cognac and Fine Marne are, but from the liquid that is squeezed out of the mess of skins and pips left over after the grapes have been pressed for wine-making. To confuse matters, Frenchmen sometimes refer to the resulting spirit as *eau-de-vie-d'aignes*, or even as *eau-de-vie-de-dédaine*: *aignes* and *dédaine* and *marc* are all words which can be correctly used to describe the grape husks, but *marc* is the one most commonly used today in connection with the spirit.

The majority of *eaux-de-vie-de-marc* are fiery enough to make a goat dance, as the French say. The *marcs* made in Burgundy, Beaujolais (where they are known as Rikiki) and Champagne, however, are rather more genteel. Personally, I really enjoy a good *marc-de-Champagne*, particularly after a meal at which I have been drinking champagne; by sticking to the same grape throughout the evening I find I can be 100 per cent sure of avoiding a headache the next morning. But *marc-de-Champagne* is one of those subjects on which people's opinions are entirely unpredictable. Women generally dislike it, but then one comes along who says she has at last found the perfect after-dinner drink; one connoisseur of wine refuses to touch the stuff, the next one relishes every sip.

Only two firms—Goyat and Jolly—sell *marc-de-Champagne*, but most champagne Houses send a percentage of their left-over skins to these two firms to be turned into *marc* for use within the House.* Most of this *marc* goes down the thirsty throats of the grape-pickers attached to the House at the time of the vintage; but a little is aged in casks. The ageing improves it vastly; some of these old *marcs* which the Houses keep for their private use are finer than any *marc* to be found on the market. A *marc-de-Champagne* made from the skins of Chardonnay grapes is generally superior to one made from the skins of the Pinot.

A French vineyard owner who distils his own spirits, either in his own pot-still or in a perambulating one, is known by his countrymen as a *bouilleur de cru*. In the Champagne district, as in other French vineyard areas, *bouilleurs de cru* used to be a menace. They would convert good wine or *vin de rebêche* or the lees left over in their casks after the rackings into a spirit strong enough to make a lion dance—and consume it. In recent years the law has clamped down considerably on their activities. Nowadays a wine-maker has to send his lees to a properly run distillery, and the distillery turns it into a rough alcohol (*eau-de-vie-de-lys*) which may not be sold for human consumption. And the small travelling distilleries which a firm like Goyat sends out to isolated villages these days produce only Fine Marnes and *marcs-de-Champagne*.

* A champagne House is obliged by law to hand over to the Government a certain percentage of the alcohol derived from each batch of grape husks in lieu of tax. The Government uses the alcohol for industrial purposes.

PART VII

THE PEOPLE

CHAPTER 37

THE CHAMPENOIS

"QUATRE-VINGT-DIX-NEUF *moutons et un Champenois, cela fait cent bêtes*",* runs an old saying known to every Frenchman. Napoleon adapted it to coin another: "*Quatre-vingt-dix-neuf Champenois et un mouton, cela fait cent Braves*". The visitor to Champagne generally gets wind of both sayings fairly soon after his arrival, and he may accept them at face value after an encounter with a moronic shopkeeper or inspection of the multiplicity of names on the war memorial of the tiniest Champagne village.

But stupid shopkeepers are to be met with everywhere, and on close acquaintance the average Champenois does not really seem to be particularly *bête*; indeed, he seems just the opposite. Upon reflection, how could a people be *bête* who have produced Rheims Cathedral, Gobelins tapestries, La Fontaine and "Bubbly"—to mention just a few of their major accomplishments? The original saying is, in fact, not libellous at all, but a tribute to the cunning of the Champenois. It evokes the time when Champenois shepherds used to madden Roman tax-collectors by arriving at the toll-gates with exactly ninety-nine sheep in tow, thereby avoiding payment of a tax due on flocks numbering a hundred head or more. And Napoleon's remark is just a pretty compliment, thoroughly deserved but of no great import, for, though the Champenois are as ready to lay down their lives for their fatherland as any self-respecting people, there is no evidence, in history or anywhere else, of their being an outstandingly martial race.

In addition to misleading sayings, there are other obstacles in the path of a visitor who is endeavouring to understand the Champenois and to grasp in what ways they differ from other Frenchmen. One is the amount of foreign blood that flows in their veins. I am not referring to the fusion of races—Celts, Gauls, Romans, men of the north—that produced the original inhabitants of Champagne (the men from the north were tall, fair-haired, blue-eyed, and the type still exists in Champagne; they stand out a mile to a visitor from Italy, for instance, but Anglo-Saxon eyes, so accustomed to the type, hardly notice them). Nor am I referring to the blood transfusion that left such a startling

* "Ninety-nine sheep and one Champenois make one hundred animals (or fools)"—depending on the sense given to the word *bête*.

mark on a number of Champenois, the Mongolian one, administered by Attila's hordes and by the Hungarian pony invaders of the ninth century. I refer to the number of foreigners and Frenchmen from other provinces—Alsatians, Austrians, Belgians, Poles, Spaniards mainly—who have moved into the Champagne district and its environs during the past fifty years. Most of the Alsatians arrived in 1914, flourishing false papers in the faces of the authorities, who knew perfectly well they were false but turned a blind eye; the majority of the Belgians slipped over the border during the invasions of 1914 and 1940, took root and stayed (they tended to settle on farms, whereas the Poles gravitated towards the vines); the Spaniards are mostly refugees from the Franco régime, or friends or relations of their countrymen in the cork industry ("*visitant l'Espagnol*", in Epernay, is a synonym for "going to the grocer's"). There are said, with only fairly slight exaggeration, to be more foreigners and Frenchmen from other provinces in the Champagne district than there are Champenois. The hazard of taking for a typical Champenois someone who possesses not one drop of Champenois blood is particularly great in the big champagne firms. So often the *gros Monsieur*, who makes you feel so welcome and has you in fits of laughter in a trice, was born in Burgundy or Brittany or Paris and married a champagne heiress; so often the elegant young man with the exquisite manners is a nephew or cousin of the family, from some other province, who was brought into the business because there were no direct heirs.

Then, when finally one does start meeting genuine Champenois, there remains the little problem of their reserve. A Champenois is the least expansive of Frenchmen, particularly where strangers are concerned, and no one could be less of a busybody. Ask him a question and he will answer you politely; but until he gets to know you he leaves most of the talking to you. He would not dream of asking a newcomer who he is or what he is doing in Champagne; and even when he gets to know a stranger fairly well he hesitates to broach such subjects—pounced upon with alacrity by other Frenchmen—as the state of the stranger's liver or what he was up to in Paris the previous weekend. As acquaintance grows he becomes a most obliging friend and a generous host, pulling corks at the slightest provocation, but a certain reserve always remains. Shyness is not responsible, for rare is the adult Frenchman who suffers from that disease. It cannot be attributed to boorishness, for unlike many of his countrymen in the extreme north a Champenois, however dead-pan his expression, is at heart as springy, as alive, as the wine he makes. Nor can it be explained by want of curiosity, for the Champenois is passionately interested in his fellow human-beings. I think it stems partly from the solidity of his make-up, which makes him abhor superficiality, and partly from a conviction, drummed into him and his forebears by the overdose of invasions of which Champagne has been the victim, that minding his own business—in appearance, at least—is, all in all, the best policy.

If one succeeds in piercing the Champenois' reserve, what does one find? First, that he is not a *bon vivant*. Of course, like every other Frenchman, he does not stint himself of wine: *"Bien met l'argent qui en bon vin l'emploie"* wrote the thirteenth-century Champenois poet, Colin Muset. If you are strolling in a garden in the Champagne district where gardeners are at work, you are sure to spot a bottle or two hidden in the pink begonias—a nip every twenty minutes or so is the rule, I find. Once, from a distance, I saw a workman on a building project gazing up at the sky through a pair of field-glasses. A helicopter? A plane looping the loop? Nothing of the kind. The field-glasses turned out, on closer inspection, to be a jolly bottle of wine being downed, judging by the time it took, to the last drop. But perhaps because sparkling champagne is expensive, and no less expensive in the Champagne district than anywhere else in France, more probably because the goddess of plenty is stumped by the chalky soil of Champagne, the Champenois bears little resemblance to his hefty, red-faced Burgundian neighbour, tongue a-hanging out in anticipation of the next bewitching *plat*.

Another thing that strikes one straight away is that the Champenois is a terrific worker. How often in Champagne have I heard the remark *"le travail, ça c'est sérieux"*! Half-an-hour in a Champagne cellar or in the vineyards is long enough to show that the Champenois is industrious. However boring the job—and God knows that many of the processes in the manufacture of a bottle of champagne are rather dull—the Champenois tackles it with unflagging, painstaking concentration. Not for him sudden spurts of industry interspersed with let's-forget-about-it indolence; his is the patient, persevering temperament of the craftsman. Whatever his job, I believe every true son of Champagne considers it an art.

The extent to which this attitude can be applied was revealed to me during a visit which I made with friends to the little factory at Magenta, across the river from Epernay, which turns out mustard with still Champagne wine in it. The founder of the firm received us, sat us down on stiff-backed chairs in a semi-circle round his desk, and proceeded to tell us how he became a mustard-maker. Throughout his childhood and adolescence, he explained, he had dreamed of becoming a composer, but the First World War interrupted his studies, and when it was over a musical career was no longer open to him. It then became an obsession with him, he told us, to find a profession in which the creative force he felt he possessed might find expression. The challenge he was seeking presented itself, to his considerable surprise, in the realms of mustard. To produce a mustard different from that of Dijon, possessing the subtlety of champagne, that became his aim; and for two years he conducted experiments, striving for perfection. Eventually he arrived at what we can buy today as *Moutarde Florida* (sold in small green champagne bottles, it is stocked by the great grocers of the world, from Fortnum & Mason in London to S. S. Pierce in Boston); but, he insisted, as much to banish the thought that his childhood dream had been frustrated as from commercial necessity, he still approached the brewing of each new batch of mustard with artistic fervour. Had not the burning sincerity of the man shone through every word his discourse, coming from a businessman, would have been embarrassing; as it was we were deeply moved.

A great capacity for hard work, common sense, integrity, thriftiness, these are Champenois virtues, and ones which the Champenois have been credited with possessing throughout history. For this reason Colbert, whose father was a draper in Rheims and who possessed these traits to a superlative degree, is often presented as the prototype *par excellence* of a Champenois. His titanic achievement of balancing Louis XIV's budget (the word itself derives from the little black bag, the *bougette*, containing France's accounts, which he always carried around with him); the tremendous impetus which he gave to the French economy; tenacity, business acumen, a flair for organization, these are reflected in a humbler degree in the way the Champenois manages his vines and his wine, and were reflected, in former days, in the way he managed his trade in textiles. Nor can there be any doubt that because the fate of France has been decided in Champagne four times during the past 150 years; because the invasions entailed great suffering and unhappiness; because he has had to rebuild his home and start again from scratch so often, the modern Champenois has become an even more disciplined person than his forebears, perhaps the most disciplined Frenchman of all, with a stuffing of courage inside him that would impress even his worthy ancestors.

Being thus constituted, he is naturally a rather serious person, fond of routine. Early to bed, very early to rise is his motto; few chinks of light pierce the heavily shuttered windows of a village in the Champagne district after nine p.m., and by ten p.m. Epernay is as dead as mutton. The Champenois are stay-at-homes, content with family life, occasional visits to the cinema, and—for a lark—a visit to the fair. But behind the seriousness, the respectability, the reserve, lurks something else which is ready at every moment of the day to explode. This is their sense of humour. It is a rather special sense of humour.

I have referred already to the dead-pan expression which so often immobilizes a Champenois' face. Well, the moment his sense of humour is tickled, which happens very frequently indeed, a metamorphosis takes place which, if I had not observed it in action on innumerable countenances, I should hesitate to describe as being specifically Champenois. In a flash a smile chases away the dead-pan expression, revealing the face to be extremely mobile, and the eyes light up and begin to dance. Nowhere in the world, I swear, are there more dancing eyes than in Champagne; they dance as brightly and as tirelessly as the bubbles in the wine itself.

The impulses that set a Champenois' eyes a-waltzing are varied. A frequent one is some devastating rejoinder he is making, for the Champenois delights in repartee and is a maestro at it. Indeed, it is often said that every Champenois has a bit of Voltaire in him. But his mind is neither as quick nor as sophisticated as Voltaire's: his sallies take time to hatch, and sometimes they are a trifle ingenuous. I believe that both Michelet, the French historian-geographer, and Mlle. Geneviève Dévignes, the expert on the defeat of Attila and a Champenoise herself, came closer to the truth by suggesting that the historical figure in whom the Champenois' gift for guileless but devastatingly effective repartee found supreme expression is Joan of Arc. The Maid's replies at her trial, they say, and indeed nearly every one of her recorded remarks, reflect that *sentiment moqueur*, that artless astuteness, which are so typically Champenois and not at all typical of the more irascible Lorrainer.*

Another impulse that can be counted to set Champenois eyes alight is anything remotely risqué. The Champenois is extremely earthy, but seldom lewd. It is absolutely inconceivable that Champagne could ever

* In support of this theory, Mlle Dévignes points out that Joan of Arc should more properly be considered a Champenoise than a Lorrainer; her father was born in Champagne, at Ceffonds near Montier-en-Der (where Dom Grossard hid the relics of St. Helena); her mother, although born in Lorraine, had a Champenois father. The Maid had no frontier to cross to reach Chinon; indeed, if she was Lorrainer she was not French, because Lorraine did not become part of France until 1766.

have produced a Rabelais: his rough, long-winded lavatory humour is utterly alien to the Champenois' immensely civilized, delicate approach to bedroom jokes. In the old songs and ballads of Champagne, the delicacy of the approach stands out a mile. Some of them are, to say the least, frank:

> *"Je dois coucher une nuit*
> *Entre ses bras toute nue"*

runs an eve-of-marriage song for brides. In certain villages of the Mountain of Rheims a newly-married girl is expected to this day to kneel on thorn-bush faggots and sing a song called *La Requête* which runs:

> *"Mon mari,*
> *Mon petit mari,*
> *Mon amour me porte,*
> *Mon ami doux,*
> *A coucher avec vous . . ."*

Ça m'fait rire ends up:

> *"Quand femm' dit à son mari*
> *Que vingt fois elle a trahi:*
> *'C'est pour toi seul' que j'respire'*
> *Ça m'fait rire, ça m'fait rire,*
> *Vraiment ça m'fait rire!"*

Lusty, naïve, yes; smutty, no.

The intriguing, paradoxical nature of the sons of Champagne, their wit and love of a risqué joke—if not their more solid, sober virtues—are reflected in the life of one of the most illustrious of them, Jean de La Fontaine, who was born in 1621 in Château-Thierry. All his life he displayed a marked distaste for work and a huge capacity for enjoying himself—"I like gambling, poetry, books, music, town life, country life, in fact everything," he wrote. He squandered his own patrimony and his wife's dowry, and his love of a pretty face eventually caused his wife to apply for a legal separation. Until he settled in Paris, where he became the constant companion of Racine, Molière and Boileau, he gave no sign of his literary genius, and not till 1665 did the first of his *Contes* appear. Three years later he published a small collection of *Fables*, which was an immediate and thundering success. But his greatest *Fables*, the ones which have made his name famous the world over, did not appear until the 1670s, when he was over fifty. Seemingly so innocuous to us, they were political dynamite at the time. "His little verses," Taine reminds us, "skipped and jumped like a schoolboy on holiday over everything respected and respectable, jeering at women, the Church, the great of the land and the monks." For years La Fontaine cheerfully endured the terrifying frown of Louis XIV and the cold shoulder of the Church: not until 1684 did the King finally allow him into the Academy, and not until 1682 was he allowed to attend Mass again—and then only after disavowing his *Contes*.*

What tickles a Champenois' sense of humour most readily of all are the frailties and foibles of his fellow human beings. Nothing escapes him, and he is utterly shameless in making fun of what he sees. Read what Taine, the nineteenth-century critic, has to say on the subject; he was a Champenois, born at Vervins, and he ought to know:

"Here, fifty leagues from Paris . . . the people are very much 'all there': they lack the verve and the garrulous gaiety of the man from the Midi, but they have sharp, nimble minds, they are quick to see the irony in a situation and they take malicious pleasure in the follies of others. The householder, watching you from his doorstep, is quietly chuckling to himself; the apprentice behind his work-bench is nudging his neighbour, ludicrous creature that you are. A visit to a work-shop here is always a somewhat alarming experience: were you a prince and covered in gold braid, you know perfectly well that these youngsters in soiled overalls will not have been taken in by your lordly manner and will have sized you up in a moment; the odds are you will serve as the butt of their jokes as they leave for home in the evening."

Anyone at all intuitive, who has been on a conducted tour of a cham-pagne cellar and observed the workers, will recognize the truth of Taine's remarks. The dead-pan expression of the *dégorgeur* or of the little man stacking the bottles (the average Champenois is short of stature but robustly built) in no way conceals the intense activity going on behind his small moustache (little moustaches are very much the

---

* Many of the *Contes* are extremely risqué. *Les Effets de la Nature* is about an ass of a handsome young Champenois who mistook a certain swelling connected with his first *mouvements d'amour* for a malady and, having paid out good money to a doctor to have the swelling reduced by the administration of towels soaked in cold water, eventually discovered a pleasanter, more effective cure in the arms of the doctor's wife.

vogue in Champagne these days). Bet that old bag's still game for a fling, he's thinking to himself. Or, what a fright of a dress. Or, that chap's playing footy-footy with the nun. Or something much worse.

It may be some comfort to the prospective visitor to know that the Champenois is at his most outrageous when taking the mickey out of other Champenois. There exists in the Champagne district something known as the *Parler champenois*, which one would expect to be a local dialect. In reality it embraces a vocabulary of about 300 words peculiar to the area and a collection of no-holds-barred sayings and rhymes in relatively correct French about people and places in the winefield, most of them libellous, most of them (I am assured) containing at least a grain of truth. According to the *Parler champenois*, the men of Haut-villers are cuckolds; of Tauxières, beggars (*gueux*); of Cumières, *glorieux*; of Chouilly, toads (*crapauds*, which also means brats); of Rilly, asses; of Mareuil-sur-Ay, *Messieurs*, which means they're stuck-up; of Ay, *gens*, which might mean almost anything. The citizens of Damery are said to be saint-drowners, because they threw a statue of St. George —in France the patron saint of cherry tree growers—into the Marne when their cherry trees got caught by frost on his Saint's Day (legend adds, incidentally, that the wooden statue floated down-river to Reuil, another vineyard village, where it was fished out and erected in the church). The Holy Virgin of Grauves is said to have performed more turns than miracles, in reference to the fact that during the Revolution the statue was turned into the screw of a wine press. Bergères-les-Vertus is honoured with a couplet stating that its daughters are neither shepherdesses nor virtuous. Cramant, in another couplet, is described as containing a large steeple, ill-natured people and girls worth marrying for their looks but not for their dowries. Avize is dismissed in five words: *belles cottes, pas de chemises*—pretty skirts, no underclothes.

Of course, the *Parler champenois* is not meant to be taken too seriously. We must remember that all Frenchmen have to laugh. "Our need to laugh is our outstanding national trait," wrote Taine, "and foreigners are often shocked by it." He assures us that Champenois banter is never really unkind, never meant to wound. "If it stings, it does so like a bee, without hurting; a moment later the Champenois is thinking of something else . . . his only desire is to foster in you and in himself a fizz of pleasing thoughts." This I believe to be true, because wrapped round everything that is singular about a Champenois—his reserve, his industry, the strain of seriousness in him which so easily disintegrates into hilarity—there exists something equally singular, an icing that sweetens and tempers the whole: the French call it *la douceur champenoise.*

I must admit that it took me some time to understand this trait. I soon became aware that there is a gentleness about the Champenois which is truly remarkable. Nowhere else have I come across a people who speak so softly and so seldom raise their voices, or whose gait, movements, gestures are so quiet, so totally devoid of arrogance. And nowhere else have I come across a people more passionately devoted to that gentlest of all pastimes, fishing. Walk along the Marne or any other fishable river in Champagne and you will find, every thirty yards or so, a mooring, a landing-stage (on the Marne it often consists of half a *remueur*'s stand), a plaque indicating the licence-holder's number and a flat-bottomed boat. You can count on it that whenever he has a moment to spare the owner of that boat will be sitting in it, anchored against the current, rod in hand. "What are you going to do when you retire?" I asked the hale-and-hearty chap in charge of incoming mail at a big champagne firm. "Fish," he replied.

But the longer I spent in Champagne the more convinced I became that there was much more to *la douceur champenoise* than these indications of it which I had observed. To my surprise, what I believe to be the truer significance of it was revealed to me not, as I had expected, in day-to-day dealings with the Champenois, but as the result of a visit which I made to the exhibition of Champenois art of the Middle Ages held at the Musée de l'Orangerie in Paris during the summer of 1959.

Never was the idea for an exhibition more happily conceived. For, although it is perfectly easy to appreciate the originality and fecundity that the Champenois displayed as architects between the twelfth and sixteenth centuries by visiting the six cathedrals and countless churches which they built during that period, it is more difficult to assess their accomplishments as sculptors and artists during the same period: so many outstanding examples of their work are either tucked away in museums or set so high in the fabrics of cathedrals and churches that they are almost invisible to the naked eye. Thus the display, in one suite of rooms, of masterpieces in wood, stone and ivory from the Rheims school of sculpture of the thirteenth century (including many figures and ornaments from the Cathedral itself), masterpieces from the Troyes school of sculpture of the fifteenth century (including the astounding statue of Ste. Marthe from the Church of the Madeleine in Troyes), statues from the Maison des Musiciens at Rheims, the Ebbon Manuscript from Epernay and many beautiful rood-screens and retables—to mention just a few of the delights of this exhibition—

provided art-lovers and those interested in Champagne with a unique opportunity of viewing Champenois art at close quarters and of assessing its diversity and range. Not only were the exhibits beautiful in themselves, but they showed very clearly that the art of Champagne is a happy art, full of fun and *douceur*.

On my way back to Epernay in the train, I started reading the exhibition catalogue. In the preface I came across this sentence:

"Perhaps no art so effectively puts us in touch with the soul of a people, *with the harmony that sometimes exists between men and the countryside they live in*, as does that of the Champenois in the Middle Ages."

Pondering over the words which I have italicized, I looked out of the train window. We were puffing along beside the Marne. Delicate sunshine was filtering through the clouds that seldom leave the Champenois sky, softening what was soft already—rustling reeds, small swishy willows that looked as if they had been dusted with silver powder, poplars planted as a windbreak in a meadow, vine-clad hills, seasoned woods, golden cornfields, the subdued outline of a village. Down on the river, a fisherman and his rod were just discernible. Suddenly I realized why it is that the Champenois is such a dyed-in-the-wool fisherman. It is not just the thought of all those free dinners; nor is it because he knows his wife will transform his catches into *quenelles* and other mouth-watering dishes. Nor is it just because he is basically a calm, reflective person, for whom long hours passed on a river's bank or on some secluded mere provide peace and the opportunity to think. It is also because, in those hidden corners of Champagne where he goes to fish, he finds empathy, complete and perfect, between his vision of life and his surroundings.

Like him, the rivers of Champagne are patient: the green Marne, the silver-streaked Vesle, the lonely Petit Morin—none of them is in a hurry to wed the Seine. Like him, the landscape is "slow", moderate, possessed of grace, measure and equilibrium. There is a *douceur* about both which found supreme expression in the great period of Champenois art, and finds everyday expression now in *la douceur champenoise*. Not that, now and again, like one of those fierce-winded storms that occasionally break over Champagne, the Champenois is incapable of sudden outbursts of violence, if provoked, as he was, for instance, at the time of the Ay Riots.

At Ay there lives today a family, the Louys, who have been vine-growers, father to son, since the thirteenth century. Then there are the

Gimmonet and Philipponat families: both are mentioned in connection
with grape purchases in the mid-eighteenth-century account books of
one of the big firms; at the time I write M. Guy Gimmonet and
M. René Philipponat are respectively *chef des vignes* and *chef des caves* of
that same firm.

This tradition of continuity of service in the winefield shows no
signs of dying out. From the middle of the nineteenth century up to the
outbreak of the First World War, the attractions of town life caused the
population of nearly every agricultural village in Marne to dwindle, but
in most of the vineyard villages, particularly in those situated beside
the great growths, the populations remained constant or even increased.
Immediately after the First World War they did dwindle slightly, but
this was owing to the housing shortage and the damage which the
vineyards had suffered from enemy bombardments, and the decline
was not nearly so marked as in the agricultural villages. Today, while
the great problem in French agriculture remains the drift of the farm-
workers towards the factory, the problem in the vineyards of Champagne is over-employment: the young people would like to stay, but
mechanization has so effectively reduced the manpower requirements
of the vineyards that there are not enough jobs to go round.

The necessity to adapt to modern, scientific methods of viticulture
has naturally had the effect of making the modern Champagne vine-
grower a far more sophisticated person than his forebears. Writing in
the 1870s, Mr. Vizetelly described him as "a remarkably intelligent
peasant, considering what dunderheads the French peasants are as a
rule". Today the vine-grower is no longer a peasant, seldom a dunder-
head. He still has to be strong, as well able as his ancestors to keep a
plough in sticky ground and manhandle a heavy barrel. He still lives
his life close to nature, in rhythm with the seasons. But today, in
addition to understanding the mysteries of the internal combustion
engine, he has to have a nodding acquaintance with biology and
chemistry. At the school of viticulture and œnology which I attended
at Avize, I heard a master say to a sixteen-year-old trainee whose father
owned vines and made a little champagne: "You mustn't make spelling mistakes—you're going to sell a de luxe product"! Nowadays,
if the vine-grower does not arrive at the vineyards on a Vespa or a
motor-bicycle, he comes in a car; renowned since time immemorial
as a spender, unlike the French agricultural worker who has miserly
inclinations, he is busily equipping his home with modern
conveniences.

More prosperous, much more mobile than ever before, the vineyard workers and cellar workers have quietly discarded most of the curious beliefs and customs of their ancestors, and the picturesque ceremonies and pageants which once punctuated the year and gave so much pleasure to their simpler-souled forebears. However, the cult of St. Helena and of St. Vincent, the patron saint of French vine-growers, is still fairly widespread.

The reasons for the Champenois' devotion to St. Helena I have already explained. Why St. Vincent, the young deacon from Saragossa who was martyred at Valence in 304, was adopted by vine-growers as their patron is much less clear. It is known that he was venerated as a national saint by the Burgundians in the Middle Ages, so perhaps the vine-growers of Burgundy adopted him first and in time his influence spread to the vineyards of Champagne and elsewhere. However this may be, St. Vincent has been revered in the Champagne district for centuries, and many churches in the vineyard villages are dedicated to him.

St. Vincent's Day, which falls on 22 January, is a gala day in the Champagne district. In former times the vine-growers, to a man, would start pruning their vines the day before (some still do), and in the evening young people would scour the countryside soliciting the ingredients of a hearty meal from the prosperous, and then light little bonfires (made of the vine-branches that had been cut off during the pruning) around which young and old would dance late into the night. Nowadays the celebrations begin in the morning of the day itself and are organized by fraternities, known as *confréries de Saint-Vincent*, to which only vineyard workers may belong. Around ten a.m. a procession, headed by the *bâtonnier* elected for that year, forms in each village and proceeds to the house of the vine-grower who held the office the year before. There the *bâton*, a long gilded pole surmounted by a tiny crowned statue of St. Vincent, often of exquisite workmanship and always decorated for the occasion with vine sprigs and sometimes with the tools of the trade, is handed over to the new *bâtonnier*, and then the procession, banners flying, band playing, moves off to the church. During Mass the *bâton* is placed in a position of honour in the choir; local wine in midget casks is provided by the *confrérie* for Communion. Afterwards a *vin d'honneur* is held in the home of the new *bâtonnier*, in the village hall or a *vendangeoir*, during which the mayor presents prizes to the best pupils of the *Centre d'Apprentissage Viticole de Champagne* and diplomas to veteran members of the *confrérie*. Family lunches follow, whopping great meals, as I have cause to know; and in the evening as many balls take place as there are vineyard villages.

The name-day of the patron saint of cellar-workers, St. Jean, falls at the end of June. It is celebrated in most of the towns and villages of the Champagne district with processions and open-air parties for children, but nowhere with more *éclat* than in Rheims. There, at nine a.m., the Confederation of Cellar-Workers and Coopers gives a champagne reception, in a cellar lent by one of the big Houses, which is attended by thousands of cellar-workers and their families in their Sunday best, and by guests of honour such as the Archbishop, the préfet and the sous-préfets of the Marne, local military commanders and the heads of the great champagne firms. The reception is followed by High Mass in the Cathedral. Afterwards the congregation repairs to the public gardens for more champagne, provided this time by the corporation of Rheims.

That evening, at sunset, the vineyard village of Cumières (St. Jean is its patron saint) is invaded by huge crowds who come to watch a ceremony which is probably a survival from the pre-Christian era. In a field beside the Marne a stout sixty-foot pole, festooned with vine-branches, has banked up beside it an amazing collection of combustible material, ranging from old chairs and casks to antiquated *mannequins* and vine-stakes. The pile is lit by Monsieur le Maire, who arrives in state, accompanied by members of the village council, a band and—sensible man—a strong detachment of the local fire-brigade. Legend has it that if the flames reach a huge bouquet of flowers (previously blessed by the curé) at the top of the pole, the vintage will be a good one. As the flames leap up, spectators form circles round them and dance. Fireworks zoom into the sky, causing the poplar trees to cast great shadows on the Marne and revealing what appeared to be giant fireflies on the river's surface as the winking flashlights of intrepid canoeists. Later everyone moves on to the fair: to shoot (for live ducks) at decoys on the farther side of the river; to shake up their livers in bumper-cars; to fish in tanks for trout, which can be taken away alive in water-filled plastic bags; to dance in the balmy air till dawn.

CHAPTER 38

CHAMPAGNE GASTRONOMIQUE

CHAMPAGNE IS A region of slight interest to the gastronome.* Unlike the inhabitants of most of the other great vineyard districts of France, the Champenois have never succeeded in founding a school of cookery appropriate to or worthy of their wine. The most probable explanation of their failure to do so is that, in the days before *Champagne pouilleuse* was rendered fertile, the only livestock that could be raised on it were the sheep and the pig, and these have remained the principal standbys of the farmers of Champagne; by French standards, no region can attain Olympian heights gastronomically unless it is backed up by the cow and her attendant glories of beef, veal, milk, cream and cheese.

This does not mean to say that, if you eat in a home or at a restaurant in Champagne today, you are more likely to be served mutton than roast beef; the Champenois are much too fond of eating well themselves to inflict such a fate on their guests. All it means is that the meal will resemble one which you might have in a home or restaurant in Paris, and that the great majority of the ingredients will have come not from Champagne but from *les Halles* in Paris. I found it hard to take in this latter fact at first: after attending a luncheon at which a magnificent pike cooked in champagne was served, I enquired whether the pike had come out of the Marne (having at five o'clock one summer's morning counted no less than fifty Frenchmen fishing for pike and roach and bream at Epernay, I felt sure it had). "Good gracious, no," replied my hostess, "far too many drains—my fishmonger always orders direct from *les Halles*."

Apart from first-rate pork and lamb, just about the only local food produce of which the Champenois are specially proud are the trout caught in the rivers and lakes (nearly every restaurant in the Champagne district has a trout tank) and the wild boar, venison and thrushes (for *pâte de grives*) shot in the forests. And there are only four or five specifically Champenois *spécialités du pays* which enjoy any degree of popularity today. (Among them I do not include a dish such as *coq au*

* For years after the Second World War, no restaurant in the Champagne district proper was honoured by a star in the *Guide Michelin*. Recently the Buffet de la Gare at Epernay and Royal Champagne at Champillon on the Mountain of Rheims have been awarded one.

vin de Bouzy, which, it is true, is only likely to be found on a menu in the Champagne district, but which is nevertheless only that classic dish, *coq au vin*, made with an outstandingly good local red wine.) They are *andouillettes de Troyes*—thick, rather bitter sausages made with mutton tripe; *pieds de cochons* (pig's trotters) *à la Sainte-Ménehould* (the place to eat them is in Sainte-Ménehould itself, where the hotels purchase them from the establishment of Gaston Bazinet, who prepares them according to a special recipe handed down by his forebears, who regaled Victor Hugo, Alexander Dumas and King Louis-Phillippe with them; so singular are they, on account of the tenderness of the bone, which can be eaten, that it has even been suggested that the reason Louis XVI made the fatal stop in Sainte-Ménehould on the way to Varennes was to have a plate of them in the hotel which the Bazinets ran in those days); and *salade au lard*. The last dish (it originates from Aisne) is made with the stalks and leaves of dandelions brought home by the sackful by the vineyard workers in February and March, just before the dandelions flower. The wives of the vineyard workers melt pork fat in a saucepan, throw in the dandelions and add vinegar, salt and pepper. Ten minutes later, when the dandelions are cooked, they add chopped boiled potatoes and serve the mixture piping hot. The secret of success is to be liberal with the vinegar.

There are three local food products to be bought at any grocer, which many people find useful as souvenirs of a visit to the Champagne district. One is *jambon* (or *jambonneau*) *de Reims*, ham cooked in herbs and veined with grated bread; it goes well with salad. Another is Boursault cheese, creamy but possessed of a "kick", a post-war miracle produced in Brie (near La Ferté-sous-Jouarre) by the gentleman whose name it bears. The other is the *biscuit de Reims*. An English lady of my acquaintance, having tea in Rheims after visiting the cathedral, asked for a biscuit, was given a *biscuit de Reims* and promptly complained: she thought she had been given a stale sponge finger. Her mistake was understandable because, although the vanilla-flavoured *biscuit de Reims* can be eaten dry, it is much better dipped in coffee or champagne. It is said to have been invented by an eighteenth-century Rheims baker who was anxious to make use of the warmth of his oven after baking bread. Originally the *biscuit* was white; nowadays it is usually tinted with cochineal.

Of the truly local dishes, by far the best known is *potée champenoise*. It is a heavy dish, not something most people would want to indulge in more than two or three times a year, so it seldom appears on the menus of hotels and restaurants; but, when cooked by a genius and served in the right circumstances, it can be a memorable gastronomic experience. The genius I have in mind is Mme Allard, the wife of the keeper of Moët & Chandon's *vendangeoir* at Verzenay; the circumstances, one of the lunches which she serves in her private dining-room for Moët's guests at the time of the vintage.

Mme Allard's fame as a cook is widespread, but her appearance belies her skill: there is nothing about her of the big-bosomed, well-rounded *maîtresse de maison* presiding over her cooking pots in slippers and blue apron. She is petite, gaily dressed and pretty.

I did not at first grasp how seriously she and her husband treat all matters concerning food and drink. One boiling hot summer's day another Englishman and I, having been shown round the *vendangeoir* by M. Allard, asked in all innocence for a glass of water. Of course, said M. Allard, but wouldn't we rather have champagne? We declined gratefully, explaining that we thought it was too hot and that anyway we were in rather a hurry. We had hoped a glass would be forthcoming from the *vendangeoir* cookhouse, but M. Allard ushered us into his private dining-room and Madame was called for. Having shaken hands with us, she swung into action: but we *must* have champagne; if we wouldn't, she had some very nice cognac which would go well with Perrier water and ice; well then, what *kind* of water would we like—Vittel, Evian, Contrexeville or Vichy; and were we quite sure we wouldn't like some raspberry juice or some orange juice with it? Madame pretended to be deaf when we repeated our assurance that all we wanted was a glass of water from the tap as we were in rather a hurry. Would we please be seated? From a cupboard she carefully selected two glasses, took them to the kitchen, came back with them shining brightly, disappeared again for what seemed an age and eventually reappeared again with a plate of biscuits and a bottle of Evian which, she assured us, would be perfectly cool as she had brought it up herself from the cellar. It can be imagined, therefore, with what formality Mme Allard approaches the challenge of initiating her guests into the mysteries of *potée champenoise*.

Her preparations begin the day before. She visits the butcher and orders salted breast of pork, salted ham, stewing beef, shoulder of beef, an old fowl and some heavily seasoned continental pork sausages, and she lays in a supply of carrots, turnips, leeks, savoy cabbages and potatoes. At eight o'clock the next morning she places the beef in a large casserole containing stock, and starts simmering it slowly; about nine she adds the salted pork, the salted ham and the cut-up fowl; about ten she puts in the sausages, the carrots, the turnips and the leeks;

about midday, in go the savoy cabbages. At about half-past-twelve she removes the sausages, which she places in the oven to keep warm; she takes out the shoulder of beef, which was only included to add flavour and will be eaten up the day after; and she adds the potatoes. By a quarter-to-one, when her guests arrive, she has changed and is on the doorstep to meet them, looking as fresh as a daisy. She ushers them into the dining-room, where each place has been set according to time-honoured French custom: knife and fork and soup spoon (no dessert cutlery yet); a piece of bread, crisp and newly-baked, on top of each napkin; three wine glasses in a row in front, not, as in Anglo-Saxon countries, in a cluster to the right. She offers her guests ratafia or champagne, and, as it is probably freezing and wet outside and they have been taking more exercise, walking through the vines to watch the pickers at work, than they normally do in a month of Sundays, they gratefully accept.

A few minutes later Mme Allard brings in the first course, the traditional prelude to *potée champenoise*: a great bowl filled to the brim with the stock in which the *potée* has been simmering. It is thin, a little fatty, but bursting with goodness. The *potée* itself she brings in on a huge china platter, with the ham, pork, beef, chicken and sausages in the centre, and the vegetables banked up along the sides. As you tuck in, she explains that the addition of the beef, even of the chicken, is not quite *de rigueur*, but that she feels they make the *potée* more palatable; by the time you have accepted a second helping and have been offered a third you are agreeing with her wholeheartedly, and are quite ready for coffee. But this is France. Next comes a tender beef-steak with fried potatoes, a separate vegetable and a platter of cheeses, accompanied by Moët's best Cramants and Bouzys; and then, when you are about to burst, in walks Mme Allard with her *pièce de résistance*, a *tarte au raisin de Champagne*, with which more champagne is served. The tart is another local dish, very simple and perfectly delicious. The Pinot Noir grapes, picked that morning a hundred yards away, are placed on a bed of pastry, sprinkled with sugar and put in a medium oven for twenty minutes; they emerge without having lost a drop of juice, and their piping-hot winy sweetness lands you in a second helping. You accept more champagne; you have coffee; you have *marc-de-Champagne*; you have more *marc*; by the time you leave it is four, maybe half-past. *That* is the way to enjoy *potée champenoise*.

Many good cooks claim that champagne is the ideal wine to cook with, as it lends a subtle flavour to the food, has a less acid taste, when heated, than any other wine, and, because of its lightness, renders even the heaviest dishes digestible. Admittedly, a very large bank account or the determination of the gourmet is necessary if champagne is to be used regularly in the kitchen, but there is no reason why people with limited purses should not occasionally cook with champagne. If the idea of allocating a full half-bottle to the kitchen strikes a person as rank extravagance, he or she should have a look at the supposedly finished bottles after a champagne cocktail-party; it is often surprising how much in fact is left. And it is madness not to use a bottle of champagne that is "corked" or "flat" for cooking; the "corkiness" miraculously disappears as soon as the wine is heated.

Champagne is exactly the same price in the Champagne district as in other parts of France, but, because it is a local product, it is used there more extensively for cooking than in other French provinces. The Champenois enjoy ham and rabbit and snails cooked in champagne; and they frequently liven up strawberries and other summer fruits by soaking them in champagne overnight. However, the most common uses to which champagne is put in champenois kitchens are for a *fumet* and for *poularde étuvée au champagne*.

The *fumet* is the basis of the sauce which a French cook prepares to accompany fish. The ingredients vary according to the cook's whim, but they generally consist of mushrooms, onions, a *bouquet garni* and chives, plus the bones and leftovers of the fish itself, which is cooked separately. The preparation of a champagne *fumet* involves simmering the ingredients in the wine; when the champagne has been reduced to roughly a quarter of its volume,* the liquid is drained off and thickened, ideally with cream, more mundanely with a white sauce. For turbot, sole or pike a *fumet au champagne* is the cat's whiskers.

The most delicious *poularde étuvée au champagne* I have eaten was cooked by M. François Benoist, a former *patron* of the Buffet de la Gare at Epernay, who has allowed me to print his recipe. "Melt some butter in a casserole," he writes, "cover the bottom of it with mushrooms, chives and mirepoix,† and add a chicken cut up into four portions. Do not allow the ingredients to brown. When the chicken is half cooked, add some cognac and set it alight. Then drench the chicken in champagne. As soon as the chicken is cooked, pass the sauce through a sieve, add cream and melted butter, and serve it with

---

* A long reduction should always be allowed when champagne is used for cooking: a half-bottle should end up the volume of a small glass.

† A flavouring of diced carrot, onion, thyme, garlic, bay, ham and fat bacon, which has been fried slowly in butter for about eight minutes.

the chicken. The sauce," he adds, "should be a moiré colour, very reduced and just slightly tangy on account of the mushrooms and the champagne."

Dishes cooked with champagne have always figured prominently on the menus of the great restaurants of France. At the end of the nineteenth century M. Cubat, a former chef of the Tsar of Russia, used to serve at his restaurant on the Champs Elysées *rognons sautés au champagne, les coulis d'écrevisses au champagne, les côtelettes de Paravay au champagne* and *les bécasses à la Strogonoff au champagne*. M. Paillard, another famous restaurateur of that period, regaled his international clientele with *truffes du Périgord au champagne, filet d'ours au champagne à la François-Joseph, les foies gras au champagne, la sole à la russe au champagne* and *choucroute impériale russe au champagne*; the last dish, in particular, was said to be a masterpiece of the culinary art.

The *sorbet au champagne*, a water-ice made with champagne, was customarily served at banquets during the Edwardian era in France, Great Britain and the United States; it was also a favourite of the Russians. It appeared at the halfway point in the meal, just before the roast, and gave the diners a breather, so to speak, before they tackled the remainder of the feast. It could be called a first cousin of the *trou normand*, the glass of calvados which the Normans drink in the middle of their meals. Today, about the only nation who sit down regularly to meals lavish enough to require a *sorbet au champagne* are the Belgians. The virtual disappearance of the *sorbet au champagne* from menus in other parts of the world need not be a cause of regret, however, as it never has been a very satisfactory confection: nearly all the champagne's flavour is lost in the process of icing.

PART VIII

SOME GREAT MAKERS OF THE WINE

Note

In my choice of the firms to include in this Part, I have been guided by the judgement of generations of champagne drinkers. All the firms to which a chapter is devoted have enjoyed the patronage of a discriminating clientele in France and the traditional export markets for champagne since the Victorian era—one or two of them since the reign of George II—and still continue to do so. The fact that the chapters are of uneven length has no bearing whatsoever on the quality of the individual firms' products. They all make the very best champagnes (as do several other firms), but some are able to provide richer pickings for the historian than others.

CHAPTER 39

THE BRULARTS OF SILLERY

Apart from the monks of Hautvillers, by far the most important of the early makers of wine in the Champagne district were a *grande famille* of France, the Brularts of Sillery.

The Brularts established themselves in Champagne in the twelfth century, but their career as wine-makers did not begin until 1543. In that year Pierre Brulart married the heiress of twin properties, Sillery and Puisieulx, which surrounded two villages, similarly named, situated a few miles south-east of Rheims, the former in the valley of the Vesle, the latter a mile or so nearer the Mountain of Rheims. In the woods on the northern bank of the Vesle at Sillery, Pierre Brulart built one of the most imposing châteaux in all Champagne; and thenceforward successive generations of the family divided their time and their resources between two main objects: achieving and maintaining a high position at Court and in society, and making first-class wine.

The most famous of the Brularts was Pierre's son, Nicholas: he negotiated the peace of Vervins between France and Spain (1598), and later became successively Keeper of the Seals, Chancellor of Navarre and Chancellor of France under Henri IV. In his honour Champlain, the founder of Quebec, gave the name of Sillery to a village on the St. Lawrence which is now a thriving suburb of Quebec City. In 1621 he was created Marquis de Sillery; exactly ten years later the marquisate of Puisieulx was conferred on his younger son. During the ensuing hundred years there was seldom a time when some high office of state at home or a governorship or embassy abroad was not held by a Marquis de Sillery or a Marquis de Puisieulx.

We do not know what state the vineyards on the Sillery-Puisieulx property were in when the Brularts first acquired them, but we do know that the family proceeded to pour money into them, always came down from Paris to take part in the vintage, and generally did their utmost to merit their coat-of-arms—wine-casks entwined in vine-branches. By the early seventeenth century they owned 110 *arpents* (acres) of vineyard, situated on the sunny slopes of the Mountain of Rheims, in the growths of Sillery and Verzenay, just below where the Moulin de Verzenay stands today—vineyards which were acclaimed by the family's seventeenth-century contemporaries as being, as they are today, in the class of those of Ay.

In the middle of the seventeenth century Roger Brulart, 4th Marquis de Sillery, who was a leading light of the *Ordre des Coteaux*, the band of young noblemen dedicated to the promotion of the wines of the Champagne district, embarked on exports to England: the account books of the 5th Earl of Bedford in the Muniment Rooms at Woburn Abbey reveal that, on 25 March 1667, £12 10s. 0d. was paid out for Sillery wine. The archives of Verzenay disclose that in 1680 the Brulart family, who were always in the advance guard of œnological practice, were making white wine from red grapes, in application of Dom Pérignon's invention.

The Brulart wines—always sold as Sillery whether the grapes came from Sillery or Verzenay—attained the summit of quality and fame, however, when they were produced by Maréchale d'Estrées, the only child of Louis-Philogène, 6th Marquis de Sillery. The Maréchale seems to have been an exceedingly unattractive character: she was perpetually involved in litigation with the city of Rheims, and she was hated by the peasants; but of her ability as a wine-maker there can be no doubt. She vastly improved the family vineyards with tri-annual dosings of *cendres noires*, carted down from the Mountain of Rheims at great expense; and she thoroughly mastered the art of blending. "It is the mixture of Fromenteau and Pinot grapes that gives the wines of Sillery their superiority and earmarks them for the King's mouth," wrote Béquillet in 1770. Under her tutelage the wines of Sillery became known as les Vins de la Maréchale. In 1775, ten years before she died, her cellars in the château de Sillery contained 61,650 bottles of wine; her *vendangeoir* had no less than four presses; her annual profit amounted to 96,000 livres.

The Maréchale's father, in default of male heirs, had left not only the reversion of his property but also the marquisate of Sillery to his distant cousin Charles-Alexis Brulart, Comte de Genlis, the husband of Félicité Durcrest de Saint-Aubin, who is better known to students of French history as Mme de Genlis.* Never had the prospects of the Brulart property seemed brighter when the Genlis took over. The new Marquis, as far as we can gather, had brains, and the property was in tip-top shape. "Stopped at Sillery to view the wine-press of the Marquis de Sillery," wrote Arthur Young in *Travels in France*. "He is

---

* The new Marquise was the most erudite woman of her age: her literary production finally amounted to eighty volumes, which included novels, historical and theological works and books on education.

the greatest wine-farmer in all Champagne, having in his own hands 180 *arpents*. Till I got to Sillery, I knew not that it belonged to the husband of Mme de Genlis, but I determined, on hearing that it did, to pluck up impudence enough to introduce myself to the Marquis, should he be at home; I did not like to pass the door of Mme de Genlis without seeing her; her writings are too celebrated." But four years after the Genlis inherited Sillery the Revolution broke out. The mob, overjoyed at the opportunity of settling accounts with the legatees of the detested old Maréchale, ransacked the château; even the flooring and panelling of the main rooms were torn up—because they sported her arms. The vineyards became national property, and in 1793 the Marquis was guillotined. He was the last of the Marquesses of Sillery, there being no male heir.

During the Consulate Mme de Genlis's son-in-law, the Comte de Valence, bought back much of the Brulart property, including the château. Mme de Genlis became a frequent visitor; she was now more or less educating Napoleon,* writing him weekly letters on morality, literature and the secrets of the *ancien régime* in exchange for a pension of 6,000 livres. In 1811 splendour returned to Sillery for one fleeting moment: Archduchess Marie-Louise of Austria lunched with the Comte de Valence. She was traversing Champagne on her way to marry Napoleon, as her aunt Marie-Antoinette had traversed it before her marriage to the future Louis XVI. But the management of the mutilated estate proved too much for Valence. According to Major-General Lord Blayney, author of *Narrative of a Forced Journey, 1810–1814*, in 1814 the Brulart vineyards were rented to M. Jean-Remy Moët and their "whole produce conveyed to his cellars", which may or may not have been true; his Lordship's insistence on referring to M. Moët as Mr. Mowhil renders his statements on matters concerning champagne somewhat suspect. What is certain is that in 1821 Valence sold the château to M. Hédin, a notary of Verzy, and the vineyards mainly to M. Moët and the Ruinart family.

For many decades it looked as if the fame of Sillery wine would survive the Brulart family's demise. Such was the magic attached to the name that up to Edwardian times far more Sillery—still and sparkling—was sold than the Brulart vineyards could possibly have produced, a situation which still plagues certain other famous French growths. Thackeray's characters consumed gallons of it. At a dinner

* Before the Revolution she had been governess to the Duc d'Orléans' daughter and tutor to his sons, one of whom, the Duc de Valois, was to become Louis-Philippe, King of the French.

given in the last century by a Scottish landowner for his tenants, Sillery made by Moët & Chandon was paid one of the prettiest compliments any wine can ever have received. Going round the table serving it himself, the laird stopped beside an old lady. "I'm sorry, Mrs. Macdoodle, ye canna take a glass on account of your temperance principles." "Hoot, laird," exclaimed the old lady, "ye just pour it on ma bread an' I'll eat it." Genuine still Sillery made at this period was rich in body, of a fine amber colour and pleasantly bouqueted; wine connoisseurs said it was hard to find a wine that was drier or cleaner on the palate.

Sillery wine is still made, of course, by the firms who own the Brulart vineyards, but it all goes into the *cuvées* that produce champagne, and its lovely name, which once seemed immortal, is now hardly known even to wine-lovers. Everything connected with the Brularts seemed fated to oblivion. In the 1870s Henry Vizetelly wrote: "After crossing the railway, we pass the trim, restored turrets of the famous château de Sillery, with its gateways, moats and drawbridges, flanked by trees and floral parterres"; but if you cross the railway now there is a great void: four years in the no-man's-land of the Great War reduced the massive building to dust. Until recently two little islands on the Vesle—l'île de Genlis and l'île Louis-Philippe—recalled happier times, as did a beech tree planted by Mme de Genlis; but today even they are gone. The islands made way for a canal, and as for the tree, well, no one seems to know quite what happened to it. It is a fair guess that, had fate been kinder, the Marquesses of Sillery would nowadays be not only the best-known champagne-makers of all, but the most celebrated wine-makers in the world, for none of the champagne firms, and not even such aristocratic veterans of the wine world as the Princes of Isenburg at Hochheim (hence the word "Hock"), have a past in wine so ancient or so glittering as theirs would have been. But it did not work out that way.

CHAPTER 40

RUINART PÈRE ET FILS, RHEIMS

THE HOUSE OF Ruinart is the oldest of the existing champagne firms. Preserved for all to see, on parchment so rich that it has never faded, is the record of the firm's first transaction, made on 1 September 1729, *"au nom de Dieu et de la Sainte Vierge"*.

Nicholas Ruinart, the founder, was an Epernay textile merchant. In his portrait he is shown wearing a dark blue velvet coat and waistcoat, a lace ruff and a flowing snow-white wig; the wig frames a pair of wise brown eyes, a finely-shaped nose and a firm mouth. His account books suggest that at first he gave away his champagne to important customers of his woollen business, and that it was the appreciative comments of the recipients, and their requests for regular supplies, that prompted him to sell his wines. The explanation of his skill as a champagne-maker may well rest in the fact that his uncle, Dom Thierry Ruinart, a priest of Rheims, a monk of Saint-Germain-des-Prés and a well-known scholar, was a friend and contemporary of Dom Pérignon. A slab in the central aisle of the church at Hautvillers records that Dom Thierry was "attacked by a grave fever" while visiting the monastery to do research, and that he died there on 29 January 1709.

The founder's tenth son, whose Christian name was also Nicholas, and the second Nicholas's second son, Claude, who joined his father in 1764, expanded the business. It was Claude who moved the firm to its present premises in Rheims, above the fabulous Roman chalk-pits which I described in chapter 6. Louis XVI made him Seigneur of Brimont, a village four miles north of Rheims, where his descendants still have a château. His brother-in-law, Tronson du Coudray, defended Marie-Antoinette at her trial. But business is business, and his Royalist connections did not deter him from supplying many prominent personalities of the Revolution with champagne.

The account books of Claude Ruinart's eldest son, Irénée (1770–1850), who in his youth had been to England to sell Ruinart champagne, are liberally sprinkled with the great names of the Empire: Bonaparte himself, Joseph Bonaparte (deliveries to the rue Saint-Honoré), Talleyrand and Bonaparte's brother-in-law, Murat, King of Naples; Josephine Bonaparte too, but after the divorce she declined to pay for the champagne she had ordered while she was the Emperor's wife, and her bills had to be relegated to the "bad debt" pigeon-hole. During the retreat through Champagne in 1814, Napoleon dined and spent a night in the château de Grands Sillerys, a mansion close to the main Sillery château, which Irénée Ruinart had recently bought. (He had also acquired some of the former Brulart vineyards at Sillery and Verzenay, including one called *le clos de la Maréchale*, which are still in the possession of the firm.) But it seems that, at heart, the Ruinarts were Royalists. As soon as the Bourbons returned, Irénée Ruinart became Mayor of Rheims and a député of Marne. In the former capacity, he received Charles X on the city's behalf when the King arrived in Rheims on 28 May 1825 to be crowned; later the King conferred on him the viscountcy of Brimont. After the Revolution of 1830 the new Vicomte retired, and devoted the rest of his days to the study of viticulture. He published a treatise on a subject of perennial interest to the Champenois, *The Culture of Chalky Soil*.

Irenée Ruinart's successor as head of the firm was his son, Edmond. In 1832 Edmond Ruinart visited America, and he has left a vivid description of his preparations for the journey and of the perilous, uncomfortable voyage across the Atlantic. His diary shows very clearly the extent to which a champagne-maker needed to have a spirit of adventure in the days before the task of selling champagne abroad was entrusted to agents or representatives on the spot.

He spent three weeks in New York, and then visited Philadelphia, Baltimore and Washington. He was received by President Jackson at the White House, and presented him with a case of Ruinart champagne. As champagne magnates away on business trips invariably do today, he returned home in time for the vintage, in early October.

Edmond Ruinart's son, Edgar, was as intrepid a traveller as his father. In 1860 he went to Russia, travelling by diligence, hired carriage and sled. In his diary he recorded every detail of the 4,000-mile journey: his audience with the Tsar in St. Petersburg, nights at the opera, the business calls he made, his expenses—9,600 francs for the three-month trip. It was thanks to men like him and his father that exports of champagne rose from a mere 5 million bottles in 1850 to 10 million in 1865 and 21 million in the 1890s. We may judge of the popularity in England of Ruinart champagne during the late Victorian period by these words from a song:

> "I asked him out to dine one night
> At my place near Kempton Park,

I said the wine was Ruinart
—I'd shifted every mark—
'You lie, it's three-and-sixpenny,
I know it by the cork,
For I've found it on the floor,'
Said Sherlock Holmes."

Throughout the First World War the front line lay within a stone's throw of the firm, and its premises were completely destroyed. The head of the firm, André Ruinart, set up an office in one of the chalk-pit cellars. When shells burst a water-main and his lair became flooded, he put his desk on a raft and calmly went on conducting the firm's business, afloat, eighty feet below the ground. The story would have its place in the annals of high comedy if it had not ended in tragedy: the cold and the damp seriously affected the doughty champagne-maker's health, and he died a few months after the Armistice. His son Gérard supervised the reconstruction of the firm's buildings.

In 1950 Baron Philippe de Rothschild acquired an interest in the business, and advertisements like this one, immensely impressive to wine-lovers, began appearing in high-class French magazines

Château Mouton Rothschild
Baron Philippe de Rothschild
propriétaire
PAUILLAC
&
Champagne Ruinart
père et fils
Vicomte G. Ruinart de Brimont
Baron Philippe de Rothschild
associé
RHEIMS
deux noms prestigieux maintenant unis

The controlling interest was recently bought by Moët & Chandon, but Vicomte de Brimont's nephew, M. Bertrand Mure, continues to run the firm.

Ruinart Père et Fils is one of the smallest of the champagne firms that have a world-wide reputation. Today it is rapidly expanding its production.

CHAPTER 41

MOËT & CHANDON, EPERNAY

F ROM LILLIPUT WE turn to Gargantua. Moët & Chandon is by far the biggest of the champagne Houses; until 1962, when it became a *Société Anonyme*, it was one of the largest businesses in France entirely owned and run by one family. Few, if any, wine firms in the world have a more remarkable record of achievement.

Precisely when the Moëts first appeared in Champagne is not known for certain. Some say there was a Moët in Rheims in 1369. Others credit the family with a slightly later and more spectacular début. They claim that the first Moët was a Dutchman called LeClerc who, while helping the Rémois to repulse an attempt by the English to prevent Charles VII from entering Rheims, shouted "Het moet zoo zijn"—"It must be so"—so lustily that the English vanished, and he was known for ever after as M. Moët. The following is certain: the annals of Rheims record that Jean and Nicolas Moët were magistrates of the city in the early fifteenth century; a Moët (perhaps the one with a lusty voice) was present in the capacity of municipal magistrate when, with Joan of Arc beside him, Charles VII was crowned in Rheims Cathedral in 1429; and a Moët was ennobled in 1446 by the same King. The diæresis on the *e* of Moët is as French as the name is Dutch, one might say Double Dutch: cheerful supporters of Moët & Chandon in Holland ask waiters for bottles of *Moed en Schande*—bottles of "Courage and Shame".

Not until 1716, however (the year following Dom Pérignon's death), is there mention of the name Moët in connection with wine. In that year, or thereabouts, Claude Moët, who lived at Cumières and owned vineyards in the valley of the Marne near Epernay, purchased one of the offices of *courtier de vin*; he and other vineyard owners on the southern slopes of the Mountain of Rheims were fed up, it is believed, with having to send their wine to the Rheims *courtiers de vin* for sale, and were determined to turn Epernay into a wine centre in its own right. It is clear that Claude Moët became a champagne-maker in the true sense of the word, as opposed to a *courtier de vin*, in the 1730s. Possibly he was one even in the 1720s, for in the earliest account book of his that his descendants still possess—it opens in 1743—he frequently refers to sales of his wine that he entered in an earlier account book. But as this earlier account book has been lost, and as French law requires a firm to show documentary proof of its foundation date before allowing it to publicize the fact, Moët & Chandon is stated to have been founded in 1743, which makes it the third oldest of the existing firms.

Claude Moët's account books are documents of fascinating interest; they record not just the dry details of his business transactions, but also the day-to-day activities of his whole family: what they ate and what they wore, the treatments they received while ill, the cost of the funeral when one of them died. But no entry is more significant than the first one to record full details of a sale of wine: 1 May 1743, 391 bottles for Charles Gauthier, "*un des Douze*", the invoice to be made out for 380 bottles in order to save Gauthier tax at the Paris toll-gates. Shipment was to be by boat; and therein we have confirmation of the importance of the Marne to the early champagne-makers. Subsequent entries in the account book show Mareuil-sur-Ay to have been the point where the barges were usually loaded, although Mareuil-le-Port, as its name suggests, was also used. Enquiry reveals *les Douze chez le Roi* to have been the twelve wine merchants accredited to the Court. Claude Moët visited these very important customers each July, choosing that month, no doubt, in order to be able to give his main suppliers of wine—among them the monks of Hautvillers and the Bertin de Rocheret family—advance warning of his requirements for the coming vintage.

Around 1743 Claude Moët was joined in the business by his son, Claude-Louis Nicholas. Soon the family account books became studded with the great names of eighteenth-century France, and the seal was set on their success in 1750, when Mme de Pompadour became a regular customer; her orders were always for about 200 bottles at a time, to be sent to Compiègne in the month of May, just before the Court moved there.

That same year father and son made their first foreign sale: 2 *poinçons* of still champagne for a Mr. Gruppty of London. Before long the son was pioneering other foreign countries, and between 1755 and 1791 markets were opened up in Germany, Spain, Russia, America, Poland and Bohemia. In 1780 the firm had sent its first traveller to England in the person of a M. Jeanson, vineyard owner at Ay, who often sold his wines to the Moëts for inclusion in their *cuvées*. In 1790 M. Jeanson was sent to London again, whence he wrote on 17 May:

"As yet I have only gone on preparatory and often useless errands. I have distributed samples of which I have no news. Patience is necessary, and I endeavour to provide myself with it. How the taste of this country has changed in the last ten years! Almost everywhere they ask for dry wine, but at the same time require it so vinous and strong that there is scarcely any other than the wine of Sillery that can satisfy them."

Two years later Claude-Louis Nicholas died, leaving the business to someone whose name I have probably already mentioned in this book almost as often as that of Dom Pérignon: his son, Jean-Remy Moët.

Jean-Remy Moët was born in Epernay in 1758. He was educated by the Jesuits at Metz and then spent about a year travelling in the Low Countries and Germany. He married in 1792, the year of his father's death. With the Revolution approaching its most catastrophic stage, it was a difficult moment for a young man of thirty-four to inherit sole control of what was already an important business. But Jean-Remy had qualities of mind and heart far above the average, and such blows as the sudden rupture of much needed supplies of wine from Hautvillers did not fluster him (the last consignment arrived under the signature of a monk with the delightful name of Dom Gourmet). One of his first acts on taking over was to dispatch the firm's second shipment of champagne to America. He even got some champagne through to England in 1792, but a line in one of his letters informs us that during the rest of the Revolutionary period he was unable to do so. In May 1793 M. Jeanson invested the not inconsiderable sum of 185,000 livres in the firm, a sure sign of his confidence in the new *patron*. That December, when the Reign of Terror was well under way, the word *citoyen* began to be inserted before the surnames of all Jean-Remy's customers, but it is evident that Jean-Remy himself had little sympathy with the Jacobins: the moment the Directoire was established he switched back to the normal formulas.

It was during the Consulate that Jean-Remy Moët met with the greatest challenge of his business career. In 1798 the Monneron Bank, which held the majority of his capital, failed. He rushed off to Paris, sat on the doorstep of the bank and asked all callers if they had bills signed by him; if they did, he extracted money from a leather satchel and paid the debt. The next day he returned to Epernay without a sou, but with his credit intact. Many years later, when Louis Monneron was completely down and out, Jean-Remy had him to stay, and gave him money to get on his feet again.

Jean-Remy himself appears to have recovered remarkably quickly from this upset to his financial fortunes. In 1802 he became Mayor of

Blending

Blended wine maturing *sur lattes* after the second fermentation

Epernay. Two years later, when Napoleon was proclaimed Emperor of the French, there opened for him a ten-year period of giddy business and social success such as no other wine-maker in history can have experienced. At the root of this success lay his friendship with Napoleon.

The closeness of their relationship is not surprising. Quite apart from his genuine admiration for the Emperor, which clearly amounted to hero-worship, Jean-Remy could only benefit from the imperial favour; and Napoleon, who certainly had a genuine affection for Jean-Remy, also stood to gain. For Jean-Remy's vast cellars, stocked with the best champagne, lay on the direct road from Paris to Germany, along which Napoleon must have known he would spend much of the rest of his life travelling. Besides, history records no other Emperor blessed with a subject so responsive to the imperial will that, at a mere hint, he erects at his own expense not just one house to put up the Court, but two.

That is what Jean-Remy did. He commissioned Jean-Baptiste Isabey, the miniaturist, the favourite painter of the Incroyables and of Napoleonic society, to design for him, opposite his own house at 20 Avenue de Champagne (now part of the offices of Moët & Chandon), the two identical sugar-white buildings and the sunken formal French garden which I described in the chapter on Epernay.

One of the first of the distinguished visitors to accept Jean-Remy's lavish hospitality was the Empress Josephine; she spent the night of 16 October 1804 in one of the two new houses. In 1807 she returned, this time on her way back to Malmaison from Plombières in the Vosges, where she had been taking the waters. Plombières, though madly fashionable, was notorious for being as dull and uncomfortable as its waters were nasty: as her *berline* came spanking down the Avenue de Champagne, how eagerly the Empress must have been looking forward to her pretty bedroom overlooking the French garden, champagne galore and Jean-Remy's jokes; it was said of him that he "never entered a salon without chasing away boredom".

That summer the Emperor himself, fresh from his Austrian victories, arrived in state. Jean-Remy conducted him round the cellars, through lines of cellar-men holding lighted candelabra, and explained the intricacies of the *méthode champenoise*, in much the same terms, no doubt, as champagne magnates and the guides whom they employ use today. Then, ever attentive to his guest's slightest whim, Jean-Remy escorted the Emperor to a splendid bedroom, not in the twin buildings but in his own house; for this room had a large glass-enclosed balcony and there the Emperor, famed for needing very little sleep, would be able to pace up and down at dawn, his mental labours sweetened by the enchanting prospect of Isabey's French garden on the other side of the road, ablaze at this time of the year with rare roses imported from Holland and hundreds of pink begonias. A plaque in the entrance hall of Moët & Chandon's offices commemorates the visit:

"On 26 July, 1807, Napoleon the Great, Emperor of the French, King of Italy and Protector of the Confederation of the Rhine, honoured commerce by visiting the cellars of Jean-Remy Moët, Mayor of Epernay, President of the Canton and member of the General Council of the Département, within 3 weeks of the signature of the treaty of Tilsit."

Plaques do not record the Emperor's other visits, partly because they were not state ones, partly because they were so frequent: entries like "The Emperor arrived on 22 September 1808 on his way to Châlons-sur-Marne" and "The Emperor arrived at eight p.m. on 26 October 1809 on his return from Austria" are one a penny in Jean-Remy's journal.

In 1811, in addition to the Kings of Bavaria and Saxony, Jean-Remy entertained Jérome Bonaparte, King of Westphalia, who arrived on 24 June en route to Paris for the christening of the King of Rome. After placing an order for 6,000 bottles Jérome added:

"In happier circumstances, I would have taken twice the amount; but I'm afraid the Russians would drink it for me."

"The Russians! . . . I don't understand you, Sire," exclaimed Jean-Remy.

"All right, I ll let you into a state secret. War with Russia has just been decided upon in my brother's cabinet. It's terrible, terrible. I see no hope of success."

"But, Sire . . ."

"Yes, I know what you're going to tell me: 'The Emperor's genius overcomes all obstacles!' That's what everybody says. . . . I hope I'm wrong. . . . Only time can tell."*

The battles of Berezina and Borodino the following year confirmed Jérome's sombre predictions.

* *Histoire de l'Abbaye et du Village d'Hautvillers* by l'Abbé Manceaux, Vol. II, p. 552.

Two years later, just before his abdication at Fontainebleau, Napoleon visited his friend for the last time. It was during this visit that Jean-Remy, ever the perfect host, carried up his guest's breakfast consommé himself and was rewarded—not for that, but for ten years of faithful service—with Napoleon's own Chevalier's cross of the Legion of Honour.

That summer, while Napoleon was hatching his plans on Elba for the Hundred Days,* Jean-Remy must have thanked his lucky stars that he had built two houses for distinguished guests instead of one, for everybody who was anybody in Europe was passing through the Champagne district en route from Paris to the Congress of Vienna, and they all wanted to visit the celebrated champagne-maker. Indeed, Jean-Remy's guest list for the summer of 1814 reads like the index to a book on the Congress:

> Alexander, Tsar of all the Russias
> Francis II, Emperor of Austria (Napoleon's father-in-law)
> The King of Prussia
> The Prince Royal of Prussia (later Emperor of Germany)
> Grand Duke Nicholas of Russia (the future Tsar Nicholas)
> Grand Duke Michael of Russia
> The Prince Royal of Würtemberg
> The Prince of Baden
> The Duke of Wellington
> Marshal Blücher
> Prince von Schwarzenberg
> Prince von Metternich
> Prince Souvaroff
> Prince Linar

In 1815 Jean-Remy resigned as mayor of Epernay. The following year his daughter Adelaide married Pierre-Gabriel Chandon de Briailles. The surmise is permissible that Jean-Remy viewed with relief the prospect of being less in the limelight and of having a son-in-law to help him run his business. He had suffered severe losses during the invasion; besides, although the honour of being a courtier had been tremendous, the expense must have been terrific—and it is known that he was exhausted.

* The Sparnaciens claim that Napoleon lost the battle of Waterloo because he was in such a hurry that he could not visit Jean-Remy Moët and stock up with champagne, and thus had to fight on Belgian beer.

As it turned out, however, this was to be the busiest period of his entire life. His ten years in the Napoleonic limelight had made him the most famous wine-maker in the world, and orders for his champagne began pouring in with such profusion that he hardly knew how to fulfil them. The list of his customers between 1814 and 1839 is fantastic: it includes a dazzling array of monarchs and sovereign princes, headed by Queen Victoria; of dukes, royal and otherwise—no less than fifteen British dukes were among his customers; a vast and glittering company of members of the lesser order of the peerage, both in Great Britain and in most of the other countries of Europe, including France herself; and many famous men of the day.

To state that Jean-Remy enjoyed a virtual monopoly in the supply of champagne to fashionable circles in Great Britain and the Continent during the quarter century that followed the battle of Waterloo is no more than the truth. Talleyrand was exaggerating only slightly when he said one night, while dining with Jean-Remy in Paris,

"*Mon cher Monsieur*, you are assured of immortality . . . I predict that, thanks to this *coupe* and its contents, your name will *mousse* far more and far longer than mine. . . ."

In 1832 he decided to retire from active participation in the business, as his health was failing, and handed over control to his son, Victor, and his son-in-law, Pierre-Gabriel Chandon de Briailles. Ever since the firm, which between 1807 and 1833 had been trading as "Moët & Cie", has been known as Moët & Chandon. A month or two later Jean-Remy once more handed in his resignation as Mayor of Epernay (he had been reinstated in office in 1826 on the express order of Charles X). During his two terms as mayor he had handled Epernay's affairs with all the energy, imagination and business acumen he was wont to bestow on his firm. He was responsible for the construction of a new bridge across the Marne and for the erection of Epernay's present-day theatre. Something he did while the theatre was being built was typical of the man: hearing that the Théâtre Montansier, today the Théâtre du Palais Royal, was in liquidation, he bought all the decorations and accessories, and presented them to Epernay.

A never-failing source of pleasure to Jean-Remy in the autumn of his life was his 120-acre estate of Romont, situated at the point below Mailly where the valley of the Vesle merges into the northern slopes of the Mountain of Rheims. He had bought the land, which included forty-four acres of former Brulart vineyard, from the Comte de

Valence, and in 1827 he built a château on it; this he surrounded with a seventeen-acre park, planted with many trees which soon became a landmark for miles around in that treeless plain. The château was severely knocked about in the First World War and today hens lay eggs in some of its principal rooms; but little imagination is required to picture what a charming and comfortable retreat it must have been.

It was while he was at the château de Romont that the postal authorities grappled with a problem that caused them considerable embarrassment. A large envelope had been consigned to the post with the following inscription:

Au plus grand poète de France, à Paris.

At a conference specially convened by the *directeur des Postes*, the decision was taken to send the letter to Lamartine at the rue de l'Université. When the postman handed him the envelope, however, the poet looked at it, hesitated, and said, "My friend, you have made a mistake. This letter is not for me. Take it to M. Victor Hugo." The postman scribbled *refusé* across the face of the envelope, and the following day one of his colleagues rang the bell of Victor Hugo's house in the Place Royale. "But," exclaimed the great writer, who was unaware of what had happened the day before, "you are mistaken, this letter is for M. de Lamartine." As the missive seemed destined to ply to and fro between the two men, the *directeur des Postes* decided to open it. Inside was written:

> *Au plus grand poète de France,*
> *A Monsieur Moët,*
> *fabricant de Champagne,*
> *tous mes hommages.*
> *Zirow, prince russe.*

And it was at the château de Romont that Jean-Remy died, on 31 August 1841, aged eighty-three. The Archbishop of Rheims administered extreme unction. The entire population of Mailly and Ludes, the two vineyard villages nearest to Romont, followed the coffin across the Mountain of Rheims to Epernay, where it was laid to rest in the family mausoleum.

Jean-Remy's heirs enormously expanded the flourishing concern which he had bequeathed to them. They bought up vineyards at almost any price; by 1879 they had become the greatest vineyard proprietors in all Champagne, with a total of 900 acres of such famous *crus* as Cramant, Le Mesnil, Bouzy, Ay and Verzenay in their possession. They extended the firm's premises on the Avenue de Champagne in Epernay until the buildings covered an area of over twenty acres. Some idea of the complexity of the organization which they had built up by the 1880s can be gained by the facts that the inventory of objects in daily use was divided into 1,500 headings, and that, in addition to thirty clerks, 350 cellarmen and 800 vineyard workers, the list of persons in their employ included cork-cutters, *agrafe*-makers, packers, carters, wheelwrights, adlers, carpenters, masons, slaters, tilers, tinsmiths, firemen, needle-women, basket-makers, sweepers, cleaners, coachmen and stable-boys.

Long before the State began to concern itself with such matters, the firm was running an elaborate system of social security for its employees. A doctor and a nurse were always on duty to deal with sickness and injuries; medicines were dispensed without charge; free baths were provided; in the winter each worker was given warm clothing and boots and issued with coal at cost price; the firm either built houses for its employees or advanced the money in lieu; every time a married woman had a baby, she was presented with a layette and a cradle; free legal advice was available, and those momentarily in financial difficulties were assisted; when ill, a worker received half-pay, when incapacitated as the result of an accident, full pay; liberal pensions were paid out on retirement, and not a sou was deducted from the recipient's wages for this during his working life. As a result of this wise stewardship, the firm prospered and sales soared. In the 1820s Moët's average annual sales are believed to have been in the region of 20,000 bottles; by 1872 the figure had risen to 2 million, and by 1880 to nearly 2½ million.

Although, true to its tradition, the firm continued to supply innumerable crowned heads and famous statesmen, its most interesting customer during this period was Wagner. The connection arose through Wagner's friendship with M. and Mme Paul Chandon de Briailles (Pierre-Gabriel's son and daughter-in-law), who were keen music-lovers. Many well-known musicians visited them at 9 Avenue de Champagne (one of the twin buildings which Jean-Remy Moët had erected to house his guests), gave concerts there and played the superb Cavaillé-Coll organ which the Chandons had installed in the music-room (the organ is still in the house). In 1861, shortly before *Tannhäuser* was performed for the first time in Paris, Wagner wrote to M. Paul Chandon from 3 rue d'Aumale, Paris:

"Most precious friend, thank you for your sumptuous present. Please forgive the two-week delay in my reply, for I have not one minute to myself at the moment. In any case, here are two tickets for you, if you do not mind sitting in the pit. I am ashamed to say I have been allocated very few seats to give to friends, for the management has reserved most of the seats for people with season tickets and for members of the Imperial House."

As every opera-lover knows, *Tannhäuser* was a complete flop in Paris. Wagner's next letter, written some weeks later, contains the handsomest tribute ever paid to champagne by a great artist:

"Most esteemed friend . . . I would never have risen above the bitterness I have been feeling these last few weeks if I had not constantly recalled your friendship. . . . Believe me, that magnificent wine you sent to my house proved my sole means of mending my broken spirits, and I cannot speak too highly of the effect it had on me at that moment when there was so much I wanted to forget. It had the same effect on the small group of friends who stood by me. I assure you that for several evenings in succession I remembered with nostalgia the pleasant impressions it left me with . . ."

The third letter M. Chandon received from Wagner was written from the Villa Tribschen, near Lucerne, in 1868:

"A line, most honoured and considerate friend, to ask you to send a consignment from your world-famous cellars to my modest refuge in Switzerland, where it looks as though I shall be stranded for a long time. I should like, for my personal consumption, a good champagne, not the type for ladies but something hearty for men. I am sure that with your usual kindness you, who are so eminently qualified to do so, will select the quality for me. Please send me 30 bottles and 100 half-bottles. Draw a bill on me, payable at the end of the half-year.

"If it would give you pleasure to be present at a performance of one of my new works, I invite you to Munich in mid-June.

"I shall never forget the part you took in that ill-fated performance of *Tannhäuser* in Paris, or the worries it caused us."

The last letter in the correspondence was headed "Bayreuth-in-Bavaria" and was dated 25 May 1875; it was written in French, not, like the others, in German:

"Since the war I have had no champagne, as I was afraid of offending you by asking for your assistance, to which I have been accustomed for so long.

"I now venture to renew our former relations by asking you to instruct your House to send me 50 big and 100 half-bottles of the excellent produce of your vineyards."*

Wagner's reticence is understandable, because M. Paul Chandon had had a lively time during the Franco-Prussian War. It had fallen to him, as a municipal councillor, to collect the 200,000 franc indemnity imposed on Epernay in August 1870, and when this proved impossible because so many of the inhabitants had fled, taking their savings with them, he had been obliged—to save his life—to make out a cheque for that sum on his personal account with a Berlin banker. On several occasions he had been forced by the Prussian railway authorities to act as a hostage against sabotage on their trains, riding beside the driver, getting covered with soot in the process. And then there had been the incident at the hospital for 600 beds in Epernay which M. Chandon ran at his own expense. One day the Germans refused him entry to it. Returning home, he donned the full robes and insignia of the Order of Malta, of which he was a member, and reappeared at the hospital thus garbed, there to be greeted by salutes from the sentries and bows and curtsies from the German medical staff.

Moët's premises were severely damaged by long-distance shelling during the First World War; virtually all that survived of the eighteenth-century building in which Jean-Remy Moët had lived and worked were the little Salon Vert where Napoleon had lunched in 1807 (ever since that luncheon the walls have been painted green, the Emperor's favourite colour) and the Salon Gris, a beautifully proportioned room next door, overlooking the English garden; both are now used for the reception of visitors. The present yellow-brick building adjacent to the Salons, which replaces the premises destroyed by shelling, was erected in 1929; at the time it was thought to be shell-proof and bomb-proof.

An indication of the world-wide popularity which the firm's wines

* These letters from Wagner are published for the first time by kind permission of Comte Chandon-Moët.

continued to enjoy throughout the 'twenties is given by two lines of a popular American song of the period:

> "The platform I stand on
> Is Moët and Chandon."

At this period the firm launched a new brand of vintage champagne, a super-de-luxe one, called "Dom Pérignon". The extremely elegant bottle and label were copied from eighteenth-century specimens in the firm's possession. In the opinion of many connoisseurs, "Dom Pérignon" is the most perfect champagne on the market; it was served to President Kennedy the evening before he was assassinated. But it always has been and always will be in very short supply: a wine merchant who manages to procure some usually reserves it for his biggest and best customers; only the most exclusive restaurants stock it. The basis of Moët & Chandon's fame and fortune continues to be its "Brut Impérial" or "Dry Imperial", as it is known in Great Britain; the name, and the imperial crowns on the label, commemorate the firm's Napoleonic connections.

Since the Second World War the firm has broken all its previous records, and it now sells in the region of 10 million bottles of champagne a year. The imaginative way in which its public relations are handled is partly responsible for this thumping success: Moët is the only champagne firm, indeed one of the few wine firms in the world, that runs an establishment where important visitors—agents, wine merchants, writers, journalists, wine connoisseurs, etc.—are housed and entertained. Anyone who has been a guest at the château de Saran, which was formerly the summer home of the Moët branch of the family and is situated in the heart of the vineyards at the northernmost point of the Côte des Blancs, will testify to the uniqueness of the hospitality dispensed there.

Another factor which has contributed to the firm's post-war success is its willingness to modernize: its wine-presses are the most up-to-date and efficient in the winefield; so are its arrangements for *dégorgement*; so are its new offices, which are equipped with IBM computers, partitions of Saint-Gobain glass and a sound-proofing system. As for its five miles of pipelines in the vineyards, which carry insecticide to the vineyard worker and save him having to make endless journeys to refill his canister, the installation is virtually unique in Europe and has resulted in a vast saving of labour. Although their vineyards are as extensive now as they were in 1879 (900 acres), the firm needs to employ only 200 full-time vineyard-workers, as opposed to 800 then.

Yet another factor that has helped the firm to go from strength to strength is the excellence of the relations that exist between labour and management: a system of incentives, known as *Travaux à la Roye*, is applied to most of the work done by hand in the cellars and the vineyards. Agreement is reached, for instance, between management and workers as to the number of bottles a *remueur* can be reasonably expected to treat in the course of a working day, and if the *remueur* treats more than that number the profit on the extra bottles goes into his pocket, not the firm's. Similarly, when there is a job to be done like the untying of vine-shoots in November and December, each worker is allocated a certain area of vines and it is mutually agreed how many days it should take him to cover it; if the worker happens to have work to do on his own vines during the period, the firm raises no objection if he arranges with his wife or someone else to do the job for him—as long as it is done well. In fact, the worker is at perfect liberty to go off on the spree to Paris if he so desires, and if he can find a competent stand-in.

The firm is at present controlled by the President, Comte Robert-Jean de Vogüé (whose wife is a descendant of the Moëts and whose son, Ghislain, is the Secrétaire-Général), Comte Chandon de Briailles and Comte Chandon-Moët.

No monograph on Moët & Chandon, indeed no book on champagne itself, would be complete without a word about Comte Robert-Jean de Vogüé (he is a Commandeur of the Legion of Honour and was made a Member of the Victorian Order by King George VI). For nearly forty years he has been an outstanding personality in the winefield (I have already mentioned the part he played in the foundation of the C.I.V.C., and the reaction his arrest by the Germans in the Second World War caused). It is not in the least surprising that M. de Vogüé should have made such a mark, because wine flows as freely as blue blood in de Vogüé veins: so widespread are the ramifications of the family in the great vineyards of France (his brother runs Veuve Clicquot-Ponsardin) that, it is sometimes said, a cellar stocked exclusively with the wines which they make would be of unbeatable quality and range. But the energy, intelligence, imagination and charm with which the gods endowed M. de Vogüé (the word is pronounced "vŏg-u-é") are manifest in many other members of the family, and have helped them to make their mark in a number of other fields besides that of wine: Eugène-Melchior de Vogüé, M. de Vogüé's great-uncle, was an expert on the Russian novel and a close friend of

Maréchal Lyautey; Melchior de Vogüé, his grandfather, was a noted archaeologist to whom Doughty turned for advice when writing *Arabia Deserta*; Louis, Marquis de Vogüé, his father, was for many years president of the Suez Canal Company; Comte Arnaud de Vogüé, a cousin, is the guiding spirit of the mammoth Saint-Gobain glass company.

Similar catholicity of interest is displayed by M. de Vogüé in the friends he has made and in the activities he pursues in addition to champagne-making: the former include the Comte de Paris, Maurice Chevalier, Pierre Mendès-France, Assis Chateaubriand, the Brazilian newspaper magnate, and the late Aneurin Bevan; the latter include a directorship of the Société des Bains de Mer de Monte Carlo, sheep-farming and agriculture; he keeps bees, he will tell you with characteristic gaiety, because when the crop of grapes is poor and his sheep are not doing well, the cartons of honey are always a consolation.

The pace at which he lives would be the undoing of most men. However, like all true Champenois (in his case by adoption—the de Vogüés stem from Ardèche), he does occasionally take time off to fish; and another never-failing source of refreshment to him is his lovely home at Mareuil-le-Port, where the lawns are kept almost as smooth and green as English ones and on which, in summer, his numerous grandchildren romp, surrounded by white doves, white dogs, white pheasants and whatever other white pets may recently have taken his fancy.

CHAPTER 42

LANSON PÈRE ET FILS, RHEIMS

THE HOUSE OF LANSON was founded in 1760 by a Rémois, François Delamotte, whose name the firm at first bore. Around 1810 Jean-Baptiste Lanson, a member of a family originating from Rethel in Ardennes which had long been associated with the Delamottes, assumed complete control of the firm, and in 1838, when the last of the Delamottes died, Jean-Baptiste began trading under his own name. In about 1848 he was joined by two of his eight sons, Victor and Henri. In 1889 Victor's son, Henri-Marie, entered the business.

At that time the company was still very small. Virtually its entire output went to Great Britain where, at the very end of her reign, Queen Victoria gave it the Royal Warrant. Henri-Marie Lanson set vigorously to work to expand his inheritance, and by the time the First World War broke out Lanson champagne was as well known in France itself, Belgium, Holland and the Scandinavian countries as it was in Great Britain.

The firm's premises were almost completely destroyed during the First World War, but long before the damage had been repaired Henri-Marie's two sons, Victor Lanson (the present Chairman) and Henri Lanson, had determined to make the name of Lanson known all over the world, an ambition in which they have manifestly succeeded, thanks largely to indefatigable globe-trotting. During the economic crises of the late 'twenties and early 'thirties, the Lansons paid no attention to prophets who foretold a grim future for champagne and quietly went on buying vineyards—red-grape ones at Sillery, Verzenay, Verzy, Ambonnay, Bouzy, Mareuil-sur-Ay and Dizy, white-grape ones at Oger, Avize, Cramant and Chouilly. The result is that today the firm has enough of its own grapes each year for about half its requirements.

Henri-Marie Lanson died in 1938. Apart from his two sons, five of his grandsons now work for the firm: Etienne, Pierre and François in Rheims, Jean-Baptiste as a traveller and Dominique as agent for Belgium and Congo.

The firm sells 85 per cent of its champagne as an Extra-Dry non-Vintage under the name "Lanson Black Label". The quality, the degree of sweetness and the label are the same for all countries.

The reserve wines of which it is composed are matured in magnums. The firm's history is not a spectacular one, but its success is. Any champagne-maker will tell you that to get a champagne known in all four corners of the world is an unbelievably lengthy and difficult undertaking. Yet the Lansons have succeeded in doing this in a half-century that included two World Wars and a long period of economic uncertainty.

CHAPTER 43

LOUIS ROEDERER, RHEIMS

LITTLE IS KNOWN about the early days of the House of Louis Roederer apart from the facts that the firm was founded in 1765 by a M. Dubois, that it started trading under the name of Dubois et Fils, and that by the beginning of the nineteenth century it was owned and managed by M. N-H. Schreider.

M. Schreider had no sons, and in 1827 he called in his eighteen-year-old nephew, Louis Roederer, to help him run the firm. He was so impressed by the young man's intelligence and ability that when he died in 1833 he left him the business.

Louis Roederer's first act on assuming control was to give the House his own name. Then, with the boundless energy of youth, he set about converting it from a very small, almost unknown firm, with annual sales of scarcely 100,000 bottles, into a power to be reckoned with in the champagne trade. The markets he concentrated on were Russia, the United States and Great Britain, in that order. At that time Russia was the almost exclusive preserve of the Veuve Clicquot, M. Moët and the Ruinarts; but thanks largely to the persuasiveness of a M. Krafft, who had joined the firm as a traveller in 1836, it was not long before the Tsar himself was drinking young M. Roederer's champagne, and the monarch's wine steward was paying annual visits to Rheims to taste the Louis Roederer *cuvées*. On one of these visits the steward complained that, although the *cuvées* were excellent, there was nothing to distinguish the Louis Roederer champagne served at his master's table from the Louis Roederer champagne consumed by his master's subjects, apart from the labels on the bottles. Louis Roederer immediately arranged for special "Cristal" bottles to be made—they were the same shape as ordinary champagne bottles, but so strong that the punt could be dispensed with—and ever after these were used for the Louis Roederer champagne supplied to the Russian Court.

With his house growing yearly in importance and renown, Louis Roederer erected the firm's present-day premises on the Boulevard Lundy in Rheims: an attractive two-storied building which completely surrounds an immense courtyard. He became a member of the Rheims municipal council, and gave the town a hospital which bore his name. When he died, in 1870, the ambition of his youth had been richly fulfilled: he was selling approximately 2½ million bottles of champagne a year; he was famous in Russia; and he was the third or fourth largest supplier of champagne to the United States.

Louis Roederer's son, whose Christian name was also Louis, inherited the House. He was a well-known bibliophile: his library of eighteenth-century works with original drawings was considered to be the richest in France outside the château de Chantilly. He died young, in 1880, leaving the champagne firm to his sister, Mme Jacques Olry. When she died in 1888, she left the firm to her two sons, Louis Victor and Léon; the latter was only seventeen at the time. In accordance with their mother's wishes, the two young men promptly applied to the Garde des Sceaux for permission to add the name of Roederer to their own. Under their stewardship the firm continued to prosper, and the prosperity was reflected in their possessions: in 1895 the Olry-Roederer equipage at hunts in the Forest of Compiègne was described as the handsomest in France, while their collection of pictures included works by Teniers, Fragonard and Isabey. Louis Victor Olry-Roederer died in 1903, and for the next thirty years the firm was managed by his brother.

At the time when the First World War broke out, three-quarters of the firm's output was being sold to Russia: in the 'twenties, Léon Olry-Roederer therefore had to find bigger outlets for his champagne in the four remaining important markets, France, Belgium, Great Britain and the United States. The task was made easier for him by the fact that Louis Roederer champagne had long been drunk by a discerning coterie of people in these countries.

When Léon Olry-Roederer died in 1932 he left the champagne firm, his vast estate in Normandy and his stable of trotting-horses, one of the most famous in Europe, to his widow, Mme Camille Olry-Roederer. The stories that circulate about Mme Roederer in Champagne point to her being a most colourful and determined lady. They range from the way she bamboozled the Germans during the Second World War into giving her a larger ration of sugar than she actually needed for the *dosage*, in order to pass on the balance to her workers, to her habit of wearing a man-sized wrist-watch ("to give masculine authority") even when she has on a Dior dress, ear-rings composed of clusters of gold grapes and a bracelet of miniature gold champagne bottles; from her concern for the welfare of cart-horses' feet, which she has a special method of washing, to her practice of starting off on business trips with a briefcase bulging with documents . . . and needlework.

Male champagne magnates have a healthy respect for her business acumen. I have heard more than one complain that no sooner have they started to make headway in a foreign market, say Sweden, than Mme Roederer enters one of her champion trotters in the local races, turns up to watch it win, staggers everybody at the subsequent celebration party with her fabulous diamonds, and generally stirs up such interest in the name of Louis Roederer that her champagne is all the rage for months to come. It is no coincidence that Mme Roederer's racing colours and the predominant colours on her firm's brochures, etc., are the same—red and dark blue.

During the 'thirties, Mme Roederer increased the size of the firm's vineyard holdings to 430 acres, so that today hers is one of the few champagne Houses that in normal years does not need to buy any grapes. She was also responsible for making it possible for champagne-lovers to indulge in a luxury previously monopolized by the Tsars, Louis Roederer champagne in "Cristal" bottles. Louis Roederer "Cristal" is expensive, hard to obtain and very good. The Lord Mayor of London—with his tongue in his cheek?—served it to Mr. Khrushchev and Marshal Bulganin when they attended a banquet at the Mansion House in 1956.

CHAPTER 44

VEUVE CLICQUOT-PONSARDIN, RHEIMS

In 1772 Philippe Clicquot, a young banker and woollen merchant of Rheims, married a Mlle Muiron. Later that year, as a side-line to his other activities, he founded a champagne firm, in order, no doubt, to make good use of his wife's dowry, which included some excellent vineyards at Bouzy and Verzenay.

At the outset, Philippe Clicquot sold most of his champagne to friends and business acquaintances in France, but by the time the Revolution broke out he had customers in America, and he was even sending small shipments to Russia, via Archangel. The Reign of Terror put a stop to the firm's export sales, but this setback in no way shook Philippe Clicquot's confidence in the future: round about that time he bought a property in Rheims that had belonged to the Knights Templars—la Commanderie du Temple—to house his champagne-making establishment. The firm still occupies the site, and today, as in Philippe Clicquot's time, workmen engaged in extending a cellar often come across a skeleton, as the cellars lie directly underneath the Templars' graveyard.

The Clicquots had only one child, a son called François, whom they sent to Switzerland to be educated. In 1797, shortly after being invalided out of the Revolutionary Army on account of a wound, François Clicquot did something that was to have momentous consequences for the entire champagne trade. He fell in love with Nicole-Barbe Ponsardin, a young Rémoise, daughter of a rich textile manufacturer. The marriage took place in 1798, and because the churches of Rheims had not been restored to public worship the ceremony was performed—nothing, as it turned out, could have been more appropriate—in a champagne cellar. The bridegroom was just twenty-three, the bride twenty.

Shortly before the marriage François had joined his father in business. Realizing that France at that time was an insufficient market for champagne, François determined to concentrate on exports, and he made several journeys to Swabia, Bavaria, Austria and Switzerland on the firm's behalf. One day, in Basle, he met a young German from Mannheim, called Bohne, who wanted a job. François was impressed by the tubby little man's forceful personality and, as the prospects for peace seemed good (the Treaty of Amiens had just been signed), he engaged him as travelling salesman. M. Bohne was to serve the firm loyally and brilliantly for twenty years, but the first mission he undertook for the firm, to England, was a flop: champagne, he complained, was too expensive for the English. Nor was his second mission—to Italy, Venice, Trieste, Austria, Saxony, Poland and Russia—particularly successful: in a letter he wrote from Frankfurt in 1803 he mentioned the difficulty of competing with Jacquesson champagnes, "as they have found a way of manipulating their wines so that there are practically no breakages". Later in the same year he wrote from Danzig, "M. Ruinart is the Matador here". Nevertheless, by that time the firm's customers already included such names as the Duke of Saxe-Coburg, the Duke of Würtemberg, the Margrave of Anspach and the Prince of Hohenlohe; and by 1804 things were going so well that François felt justified in liquidating the banking and textile interests which his father had handed over to him when he retired in 1802.

Early in October 1806, when he was thirty, François Clicquot suddenly contracted a fever; fifteen days later he was dead.

Philippe Clicquot immediately decided that the business must close, and letters announcing its liquidation were actually sent out (copies of them are still in the firm's possession). M. Clicquot, however, had failed to take into account the determination of his twenty-seven-year-old daughter-in-law. Within four months of her husband's death she had revived the company, taken in M. Bohne as a partner, arranged with a M. Jerome Fourneaux, the head of another champagne firm, to do the blending for her, borrowed capital from the Clicquots and the Ponsardins, and launched out as "Vve. Clicquot-Ponsardin, Fourneaux et Cie".

In any age and in any country, the young widow's decision would have been considered a brave one: the business was still young and needed consolidating; most of the employees were men. Furthermore, the firm's archives reveal that, except to accompany her husband to Bouzy at the time of the vintage (the house they stayed in still stands, as does the wine-press, built in 1790), Mme Clicquot had previously played no part whatsoever in the firm's affairs. Moreover, she had a three-year-old daughter to look after. We may be sure that, to her contemporaries, her decision seemed not only foolhardy but rather shocking. However, her small frame and delicate features concealed an excellent brain and a will of iron, and she set about her self-appointed task with rare courage and energy.

Her plan, from the start, was to ignore the French, English and American markets, and to concentrate on sales to Italy, Central

Europe, Scandinavia, and above all Russia. M. Bohne was to base himself on St. Petersburg, covering the East German, Austrian and Russian markets from there.

During her first few years in business she had to contend with many difficulties. The English Blockade was one of them. Her first shipment of champagne to M. Bohne—50,000 bottles—got hemmed in at Amsterdam by the British Navy, and she had to sell it off at a *vil prix*. Later she incurred further losses when a ship in which she had a half-interest, the *Pactole*, was forced into the Spanish port of Gijon while on its way to Martinique, and the crew were taken prisoner.

"May the genius of our great monarch rid humanity of these maritime harpies!" railed M. Bohne in a letter.

Then there was the Russian censorship. Even communicating with M. Bohne was a hazardous business. In a letter dated 1807, which slipped past the censor, M. Bohne wrote:

"Honoured Friend, in the name of God, never mention politics in your letters, unless you wish to compromise my liberty and my life, for the slightest indiscretion results in deportation to the mines of Siberia."

Then he went on to explain why, in a previous letter, he had announced his intention of retiring to Switzerland, his native land:

"You may have heard that a law has just been passed here, directed against foreigners, particularly the French, which forces one to choose between becoming a Russian subject and leaving the country. Luckily, my passport gives no indication of where I come from, so I am exempt. The letter in which I spoke of my wife and children must have seemed quite extraordinary to you, but all letters are opened here and I wanted the authorities to suppose that I am a Swiss family man resident at Hamburg."

Thereafter, Mme Clicquot's letters to M. Bohne were all headed "from Lübeck".

A third problem was the disruption caused by the Napoleonic Wars. In 1806 M. Hartmann, one of Mme Clicquot's travellers, arrived in Copenhagen on business and found the city being bombarded by the British fleet. Two years later he wrote from Vienna deploring the fact that the Viennese aristocracy had deserted the capital. In 1810, M. Bohne commented from Stettin: "It is no longer *en vin*, it's *en vain* that I am a traveller nowadays; all I get for my trouble is a succession of noses,

slammed doors and insults, and you get no business." In 1811 M.
Boldemann, another of the firm's travellers, wrote from Bohemia to
say that he had had to buy a carriage, not to make his journeys more
comfortable, but to sleep in, as all the hotels were shut and the rooms
of the peasants and Jews were *abominables*.

Moreover, Mme Clicquot was short of capital. She was forced to
sell her jewels to raise money. Once she gave a traveller a large diamond
and a pearl necklace to sell to the *"riches seigneurs"* of Central Europe.

Time and again, M. Bohne complained that the wines she was sending him did not compare in quality with those which her husband had
produced. In 1806 he wrote from Berlin to say that the bubbles in the
latest shipment were far too large. "I like big eyes everywhere," he
added, "except in champagne." "Never forget," he wrote from St.
Petersburg in 1808, "that only the best will do for Russia. No country
pays a better price for quality, none quibbles more if the quality is
poor." Her 1809 wines, he said, lacked that "after-taste of pineapples
which should perfume the mouth and cause one to meditate deliciously
over the wine's aroma long after one has put down one's glass."

However, although Mme Clicquot's first years in business were one
long uphill climb, she had much to be thankful for. No beginner could
have had a more inspired adviser than M. Bohne. This is what he wrote
when, in 1806, a happy event was impending at the Russian Court:

"I am told the Empress is pregnant. What a blessing for us if she were
to have a Prince! In this immense country, torrents of champagne
would flow. Don't breathe a word about this in Rheims. All our
competitors would want to rush North!"

This was his advice when, in 1808, an important customer was on
his way to Rheims:

"He is a man of no education, formerly an ironmonger. I recommend
him to you in the most pressing manner. Monopolize him, put him up,
feed him, entertain him, flatter him, show him your cellars (but not
the work), and yet make him feel that he is the guest of a House of some
standing. He will make many wise remarks, tell lies, yawn, get bored,
but *he will buy* if you succeed in surrounding him with those civilities
you excel at, and *if you cling on to him like a spider to a fly*."

And, despite all the difficulties, her wines were getting sold, in
Warsaw, Vienna, Riga, Danzig, Constantinople, Malta, above all in

Moscow and St. Petersburg. Mme Clicquot must have purred with delight when, in 1808, M. Bohne wrote:

'You are becoming as famous here for your wines as M. Maille is in Paris for his mustards and vinegars. . . . The demand is fantastic, sure proof that champagne is no longer considered a luxury in Russia, any more than coffee is in Prussia."

In the summer of 1810 Mme Clicquot dissociated herself from M. Fourneaux, engaged a M. Antoine Muller as *chef des caves* and changed the style of her House to "Veuve Clicquot-Ponsardin'.* Never again did M. Bohne have cause to criticize the quality of the firm's wines.

However, in 1812 fresh troubles arose. Napoleon invaded Russia, and the Russians immediately forbade the import of French wines. No longer, in M. Bohne's eyes, was Napoleon "our great monarch", but "that infernal genius who has tormented and ruined the world for the past five or six years". Somehow or other, during the next eighteen months, he managed to visit or keep in touch with Memel, Riga, Hamburg and Vienna, but, in those cities and in Russia, he was reduced to collecting orders "for the end of the war".

By 1814 the tide had turned, and the Russians and the Prussians were in occupation of Rheims. But though Mme Clicquot had foreseen catastrophe, in fact she suffered no loss whatever. To celebrate her deliverance, and the news of Napoleon's abdication, she allowed herself a rare indulgence: she wrote off to St. Petersburg for some Russian tea. The Frenchman who was looking after her interests in Russia in M. Bohne's absence hastened to send her a large consignment, imploring her to accept it as a gift. "It is black and green," he wrote, "the very best available, straight from the China Caravan."

In late April M. Bohne, who had recently married and bought a

* M. Muller remained in the employ of Mme Clicquot until 1822. On 16 March of that year, having recently married a Mlle Ruinart, he founded his own champagne-making establishment. The advertisements that he inserted in Russian newspapers to announce his début contained the following somewhat impertinent statement: "Having been for a number of years in charge of the production and clarification of the House of Veuve Clicquot wines, to which he succeeded in giving perfect limpidity . . . he is confident that his own wines merit absolutely the same respect." Needless to say, Mme Clicquot's reaction was one of lofty in-difference: "The methods the said gentleman is using to make himself known in Russia do not bother me, as his resignation has in no way affected the limpidity of my wine."

house in Heilbronn, turned up in Rheims, intent on executing a plan
that he had had up his sleeve since 1812. This was, at breakneck speed
and in deepest secrecy, to load an entire vessel with Veuve Clicquot
champagne and send it to Russia, so that the firm's wine would be on
the market there long before that of competitors. The enterprise was
full of risks: France and Russia were still technically at war; the
Russians had not yet lifted the ban on French wines imposed in 1812;
but M. Bohne, who was to accompany the precious cargo, intended to
call in at Koenigsberg on the way to St. Petersburg, and he was
convinced that there he would find some way of getting the wine
across the frontier. If all else failed, he was prepared to smuggle it over.

Throughout April and May 1814 Mme Clicquot's cellars were a
hive of activity. At last, late in May, the cases containing 10,000 bottles
were ready for dispatch to Rouen. M. Bohne arrived at the port on
1 June. The *Gebroeders*, a Dutch vessel, was lying alongside the quay.
"My cabin surpasses description, there isn't even a bed!" wailed
M. Bohne. But his spirits rose when, among the cases being loaded,
he found one addressed to him from Mme Clicquot: it contained
eighteen bottles of the red still wine of Cumières, five bottles of
cognac and—a six-volume edition of *Don Quixote*.

The *Gebroeders* sailed on 6 June. A month later a letter arrived
from M. Bohne, posted at Elsinore in Denmark, to say that all was well
so far, apart from the fact that bed-bugs two inches long had drunk
half the blood in his body. Meanwhile, news had reached Rheims that
Russia had lifted the embargo on French imports. Without a moment's
hesitation, Mme Clicquot arranged for a second shipment to be sent
to St. Petersburg; this time her contract with the shipowners included
a clause forbidding any wines except her own to be included in the
cargo.

M. Bohne did not learn of the lifting of the embargo until the
Gebroeders reached Koenigsberg on 3 July:

"This is what I have decided to do. As everybody is delighted to see
me and my wine, I am going to accept offers for part of the cargo to
pay expenses here and bring you in a little money; then, as the freight
charges to St. Petersburg are dirt cheap, send the rest up there. In the
meantime, I am letting it be known that the whole shipment is already
sold and destined elsewhere, but that, if I obtain a very high price, I may
be able to oblige a few people."

This first message enchanted Mme Clicquot:

"Praise be to God! You have arrived safe and sound at your destination. Really, one was so used to seeing things go wrong that it all seems like a dream."

She must have been even more pleased by M. Bohne's next letter:

"I am adored here because my wines are adorable!... Oh! Honoured Friend, what a spectacle, and how I wish you were here to enjoy it. You have two-thirds of the best society of Koenigsberg at your feet over your nectar.... Of all the good wines that have so far titillated northern heads, none has had the effect of Mme Clicquot's *cuvée* 1811 ... I seek orders from no one, I just reveal the number of my hotel room and a queue forms outside it."

When the champagne eventually reached St. Petersburg each bottle fetched twelve roubles. The second consignment sold equally well. The success of their Russian gamble marked a definite turning-point in both their careers. Madame Clicquot, growing richer every day, was soon able to give up the Central European market altogether and concentrate exclusively on sales to Russia. As for M. Bohne, he eventually built up such an efficient sales organization in St. Petersburg that he was able to go into semi-retirement at Heilbronn, and spend his remaining days with his family.

In October 1816 Mme Clicquot's only child, Clementine, completed her studies at the Couvent des Anglais in Paris. According to M. Bohne she was a charming girl; but she was desperately shy. Sometimes the strain of trying to shine at a party would reduce her to tears. "Don't cry, Mentine, don't cry," Mme Clicquot would say, "I'll buy you *esprit* when I marry you off." Mme Clicquot soon found, however, that this was easier said than done. Word had got around that she was now rich, and the eligible young men, produced by her socially well-connected cousin in Paris, asked for impossibly large dowries.

Eventually she had to set a sum for the dowry beyond which she was not prepared to go. After a lot of bargaining her terms were accepted by Comte Louis de Chevigné, a penniless but intelligent and handsome young member of the *ancien régime* aristocracy. The marriage took place in Rheims on 13 September 1817.

Mme Clicquot's business continued to prosper exceedingly: in 1821 the demand for her champagne exceeded the supply by 100,000 bottles, a situation which prompted one of her competitors to send *his* champagne into Russia with corks branded with the magic letters V C P.

His explanation, when brought to court, that the letters formed part of the formula "*Véritable ChamPagne*" was not accepted; he was convicted of fraud and sentenced to have the letter "F" for "Fugitif" branded on his shoulder.

Mme Clicquot was now forty-four and a grandmother: Comtesse de Chevigné had given birth to a daughter, Marie-Clementine, nine months to the day after her marriage. But neither the management of a flourishing champagne firm nor the demands of family life were proving a sufficient outlet for her boundless energy. On 1 June 1822 she astounded her friends by opening a bank in Rheims, under the name of Veuve Clicquot Ponsardin & Cie. The enterprising manner in which she sought to combine her new profession with her old is revealed in a letter which she wrote to friends in England in 1824, shortly before Charles X came to Rheims to be crowned:

"As you know, the brother of your King, the Duke of Northumberlan (*sic*), is to attend the coronation as Ambassador Extraordinary. There can be no doubt that during his visit to our town the prince and his suite will consume a great deal of red and white champagne wine, and will need a banker to supply them with money. If you can find a way of offering my services to the noble Lord, either directly or through the intermediary of some influential personage of your acquaintance, I believe he might accept them; in that case I would pay you a good commission on the wine I am able to sell him."

Nothing came of this particular proposal as, much to Mme Clicquot's annoyance, the Duke of Northumberland stayed with the Ruinarts (she herself put up the Duc de Berry and the Duc d'Orléans, the future King Louis-Philippe); but her other attempts to build up an international clientele for her bank were much more successful. She is known to have had clients in Amsterdam, St. Petersburg and Vienna.

In 1822 she embarked on yet another business activity, the placing of wool. Letters which she wrote to sheep-farmers in Berri, Burgundy, Bresse and Picardy inviting them to send her their wool for sale in Rheims are still in existence, as are others which she wrote to Rheims textile merchants offering to obtain wool for them from Aachen, Frankfurt, Hanover, Holland, Austria, Moravia and Switzerland.

A year or two later she bought a large spinning-mill at Esslingen, near Stuttgart. She visited it twice—in a luxurious *berline* built to order by a firm of Strasbourg coachmakers.

Wise M. Bohne had died during the winter of 1821. He had tripped while crossing the bridge over the Rhine at Strasbourg, fallen into the icy river, and contracted a fatal chill. To help her run her e˙er-expanding business empire, Mme Clicquot was relying more and more on her principal partner, a German called M. Kessler. Another German in her employ, young Edouard Werle, held M. Kessler in low esteem. He considered that Mme Clicquot's attempts to become a second Rothschild overstepped the bounds of prudence and were directly attributable to the *folie de grandeur* of M. Kessler. Edouard Werle, however, was only a very junior member of the firm—he had entered it in 1821, mainly to learn French—and he kept his thoughts to himself.

In 1828 his worst fears were realized. Rumours spread that Mme Clicquot was pledged for a very large sum of money indeed to a Paris bank that had recently failed, and her creditors began besieging her offices. She was away at the time. On hearing what was happening, Edouard Werle did not hesitate. He rushed up to Paris, arranged for a loan of two million francs by pledging securities left him by his father, and returned to Rheims in the middle of the night. The next morning he installed himself in Mme Clicquot's bank and honoured every bill. Word immediately spread that Mme Cliquot was not ruined after all, and by the time she returned to Rheims her business was running normally again.

After this crisis great changes took place in the House of Clicquot. M. Kessler was given the Esslingen spinning-mill and Mme Clicquot's other German assets in exchange for his stake in her French businesses, and he returned to Germany; there he founded a Sekt firm, with headquarters in Esslingen, which is still a flourishing concern and claims to be the oldest Sekt-making establishment in Germany. The bank and the woollen business were closed down. In July 1831 Edouard Werlé became Mme Clicquot's principal partner. A day or two previously he had become a naturalized Frenchman and had added an acute accent to his surname.

Edouard Werlé, whose birthplace was in Hesse, was a man of exceptional gifts and rare ability. As the years went by, Mme Clicquot entrusted him with more and more responsibility. His devotion to her was complete, and the skill and care which he lavished on the firm for over half a century were undoubtedly largely responsible for the world-wide celebrity that Clicquot champagne has enjoyed ever since. It was he who gradually reduced the firm's dependence on the Russian market, by increasing the sale of its wine in America, England, Germany—and France. Amazing as it seems, hardly a bottle had been sold in France previously. There is a letter in the firm's archives from an important Paris hotelier in which he literally implored Mme Clicquot to let him have six bottles; and it is known that certain Frenchmen, determined to have some, used to go to the trouble and expense of having bottles sent to them from abroad. In 1850 Edouard Werlé was appointed mayor of Rheims. During his term of office he supervised the erection of the city's railway station, and he organized the most glittering social event Rheims has known for over a hundred years: the state visit of Napoleon III and Empress Eugénie on 11 October 1858.

The de Chevigné marriage was an extremely happy one and, if this observation by Richard Castel, Louis de Chevigné's former tutor, is any guide, Clementine developed in the course of it precisely that *esprit* which Mme Clicquot had promised to purchase for her:

"What a charming, mischievous letter of Clementine's: it reminded me of champagne—all sparkle, wit and fire."

Mme Clicquot soon found, however, that Clementine's dowry was a mere fraction of the price she was expected to pay Louis de Chevigné for curing her daughter's shyness: he was incurably extravagant and a reckless gambler. When he was not spending Mme Clicquot's hard-earned money he wrote verses, and attended parades of the Rheims Garde Nationale, of which he had been appointed Colonel. Nevertheless, she retained a warm regard for her son-in-law, and soon after her granddaughter's marriage, in 1839, to Comte Rochechouart de Mortemart she gave her consent to a project on which Louis de Chevigné had been itching to embark for nearly twenty years. This was to restore to its former glory, for use as the family's summer home, the ruined château de Boursault, situated in vineyards high above the left bank of the Marne, five miles west of Epernay.

Hitherto, Mme Clicquot had spent her rare moments of leisure in her pretty but unpretentious house at Oger-le-Mesnil on the Côte des Blancs. What she must have felt at being forced to foot the bill for the vast new building, with its many towers and turrets, its monumental fireplaces of Burgundy stone, its specially-woven Aubusson tapestries, its richly carved panelling, its innumerable crystal chandeliers, all rivalling in magnificence anything produced by sixteenth-century artists on the banks of the Loire, is better left to the imagination. But no doubt her heart swelled with pride at the sight of the words *Mater Filiae* that her tactful son-in-law had had inscribed above the main doorway, and of the Chevigné and Mortemart arms emblazoned in the panelling of the dining-room. And no doubt her thrifty nature became reconciled to Boursault every time she looked out of its northern windows, for the view across the Marne valley, and along it in both directions, is superb.

It was against the background of Boursault, where she lived in grand style until her death, that the legend of the Widow Clicquot as a formidable but kindly Grande Dame, the uncrowned Queen of Champagne, took shape. Sitting in a throne-like armchair beside the fire, dressed in a many-tiered crinoline, a silk blouse and a frilly lace cap (which framed her exceptionally broad and determined mouth, her prominent nose and her large intelligent eyes), she received the homage of all Europe. A tribute to her fame which must have pleased her greatly was the nickname of "King Clicquot" conferred on Frederick William IV of Prussia by his subjects—on account of his passion for her wine. But, in her remaining years, what gave her greatest pleasure were the attentions showered upon her by her family. When she was over eighty they arranged for her to be painted, with her great-granddaughter, Anne de Mortemart, playing among flowers at her feet; inscribed underneath were the words, *Natis Mater*. On one of her last birthdays, Louis de Chevigné composed a poem in her honour, which was sung by Anne de Mortemart during dessert:

> *"Jadis on se battait Anglais contre Français,*
> *Aujourd'hui chacun boit et chacun vit en paix.*
> *Ce secret inconnu qui fait tant de merveilles,*
> *La dame de Boursault l'a mis dans ses bouteilles."*

Behind the façade of the cosy matriarch, however, there remained the shrewdest business woman of the day. Edouard Werlé never bottled a *cuvée* or engaged in a major transaction without consulting Mme Clicquot first. To the very end she remained resourceful. In 1836 Louis de Chevigné had published a book, called *Les Contes Rémois*, which contained certain passages that Mme Clicquot found shocking. Without saying a word to her family, she calmly bought in each edition as it appeared—there were twelve of them altogether—and had it burnt.

She died at Boursault on 29 July 1866, at the ripe old age of eighty-nine.

Madame Clicquot left the champagne firm and certain of her vineyards to M. Werlé; the remainder of her vineyards she bequeathed to her descendants.

On M. Werlé's death, the ownership of the firm passed to his son, Comte Alfred Werlé, a cultured and amiable gentleman who married the granddaughter of the Duc de Montebello. When he died in 1907, the firm was managed for about fifty years by his son-in-law, Comte Bertrand de Mun, aided by Prince Jean de Caraman-Chimay. Today the firm is controlled by Comte Bertrand de Vogüé (who is married to Comte de Mun's daughter), his son Comte Alain de Vogüé, and the Marquis de Nazelle.

Anne de Mortemart, Mme Clicquot's great-granddaughter, married the Duc d'Uzès, by whom she had three children: the Duc d'Uzès, the Duchesse de Luynes and the Duchesse de Brissac. In addition to her other accomplishments, Mme Clicquot thus obtained a niche for herself in the family trees of three of France's oldest dukedoms.

Anne, Duchesse d'Uzès, lived at the château de Boursault; during the Great War, she invited many Allied officers to hunts and champagne lunches there. However, the large sums of money which she had given to General Boulanger, in support of his movement to restore the French monarchy, eventually compelled her to sell the château; today it is the mere shadow of its former self. The vineyards that she had inherited from Mme Clicquot she sold to M. Werlé's descendants. The firm now possesses 600 acres of vines, distributed between fourteen *grands crus*, enough for about a third of its requirements.

Literature and music have both paid posthumous tribute to Mme Clicquot. The chapter "Old Veuve", in George Meredith's novel *One of our Conquerors*, is largely devoted to an appreciation of her wines. *La Valse de Clicquot*, with its catchy little refrain,

> "*J'aime bien boire avec Margot*
> *Un petit verre de Clicquot*"

was played for the first time at the Scala in 1900; it is a favourite of French disc-jockeys.

CHAPTER 45

HEIDSIECK & CO. MONOPOLE, RHEIMS
PIPER-HEIDSIECK, RHEIMS
CHARLES HEIDSIECK, RHEIMS

ON 23 NOVEMBER 1749, at Borgholzhausen near Bielefeld in Westphalia, the wife of a Lutheran pastor gave birth to a son, Florenz-Louis Heidsieck, whose life was to have a profound and lasting influence on the champagne trade. The Heidsiecks originated in Schleswig-Holstein, which probably explains why, when he was fifteen years old, Florenz-Louis Heidsieck was sent to Lübeck to obtain a grounding in commerce. At the age of twenty-four he moved to Berlin. Four years later, in 1777, he visited Rheims (in connection with a lawsuit, it is believed). There he made friends with a woollen merchant, M. Nicolas Perthois, whose confidence in the future of Rheims's two staple trades—wine and wool—appears to have impressed him as greatly as did the gentleman's daughter, Agathe. In 1785 Florenz-Louis married Agathe Perthois, and in the same year he founded a firm in Rheims—for *"vins et tissus"*—called Heidsieck & Co.

Florenz-Louis enjoyed almost instantaneous success as a champagne-maker, and before long he gave up the woollen side of his business in order to concentrate exclusively on wine. Soon he was in need of help to run the firm. The only child of his marriage had died, but he had a plentiful supply of German nephews to call upon, and over the years four of them came to join him.

In 1811 one of them, Charles-Henri Heidsieck, who was only twenty-one at the time, was sent to Russia on the firm's behalf. He went first to Moscow, then 200 miles east to Nijnii-Novgorod on the Volga, where people from all over Russia congregated once a year for the great fair at which furs, leathers and tea were the principal articles exchanged. Throughout the journey he rode a white horse; his servant accompanied him on another horse, and a packhorse trailed along behind, loaded with luggage and samples. When Napoleon's soldiers arrived in Russia the next year, they found that the young champagne-maker on his white horse had made quite a name for himself; and even his grandson, Charles-Eugène Heidsieck, who visited Russia late in the nineteenth century, met people who had heard tell of him.

Subsequently he travelled for the firm in the Balkans, but in 1818, the year he married the daughter of a Rheims textile manufacturer, he left Heidsieck & Co. to work in wool and cotton. In 1824 he died, aged thirty-four, leaving a two-year-old son, Charles-Camille Heidsieck, later to become a prominent champagne-maker himself.

Florenz-Louis Heidsieck died in 1828, and thereafter Heidsieck & Co. was run jointly by his three remaining nephews. But in 1834 they decided to separate: one of them, Auguste Delius, became a banker, while the other two, Henri-Louis Walbaum and Christian Heidsieck, continued to make champagne, but in cousinly rivalry.

The present-day House of *Heidsieck & Co. Monopole* is the direct descendant of the firm which Henri-Louis Walbaum ran. At first the firm was known as Walbaum Heidsieck & Co., but in 1846 its name was changed to Heidsieck & Co. Since then the name under which the firm has traded has been changed on three occasions: first to Walbaum, Luling, Goulden & Co, then to Walbaum, Goulden & Co, and finally, in 1923 (when the firm was acquired by M. Edouard Mignot, founder of the great chain of grocery stores, Comptoirs Français), to Heidsieck & Co. Monopole. The words *"Successeur de Heidsieck & Co., Maison fondée en 1785"* have, however, always figured prominently in the firm's style and title.

The reason why the word "Monopole" was incorporated in the firm's name in 1923 was that, in 1860, the House had registered the word as a name for their brand of champagne, and the brand had meanwhile achieved such fame that champagne-drinkers were in the habit of referring to it as "Heidsieck Monopole". Today the brand is, if anything, even better known, and it is not surprising that the word "Monopole" is printed in larger letters on the firm's labels than the word "Heidsieck".

Since 1947 the firm has been controlled by M. Edouard Mignot's son, M. Jean Mignot. It owns just over 400 acres of vineyard, situated mainly at Verzenay, Cramant and Avize. It is a leading brand in Germany and Switzerland, and is also one of the main suppliers of champagne to Great Britain.

The present-day House of *Piper-Heidsieck* is the direct descendant of the firm that Christian Heidsieck ran. As we have seen, it was in 1834 that he started in business on his own, selling his champagne as "Heidsieck". In the course of the first year he took in three assistants: Henri Guillaume Piper, a great-nephew of Florenz-Louis Heidsieck, who had been working in the cellars of Heidsieck & Co. for several years; Christian Walbaum, his cousin; and J. C. Kunkelmann, the son of the Chief of Police of Mannheim, who spoke fluent German, French and English. In the following year he died, leaving a daughter but no son; and his widow decided to continue the business under the name "Veuve Heidsieck", with the help of her husband's three assistants.

In 1837 she married Henri Piper, and the newly married couple changed the name of the firm to "H. Piper & Co.", but continued to market their champagne as "Heidsieck". Meanwhile J. C. Kunkelmann had visited America and Christian Walbaum Russia; and the former, who was convinced of the great possibilities of the American market, decided to base himself permanently in New York as the firm's representative.

Its internal affairs thus neatly sorted out, the firm prospered, and nowhere more so than in the United States, where J. C. Kunkelmann created a tremendous vogue for H. Piper & Co.'s "Heidsieck". Only one problem remained: the Americans would refer to the firm's champagne as "Piper's 'Heidsieck' ". Eventually the firm decided to call all the champagne it sold "Piper-Heidsieck"; and it has continued to do so ever since, although it has never abandoned the right to either the commercial name or the brand name "Heidsieck", and it still sells some of its champagne labelled just "Heidsieck". Like Heidsieck Monopole & Co., the firm considers Florenz-Louis Heidsieck to have been its true founder.

In 1850 J. C. Kunkelmann returned to Rheims from the United States with a handsome fortune and was taken in as a partner in the firm, as was Christian Walbaum. Walbaum died in 1866, Henri Piper in 1870. J. C. Kunkelmann now acquired control of the firm, and changed its name to Kunkelmann et Cie. Upon his death in 1881 his son inherited the firm. The second Kunkelmann, an extremely hand-some man, sported a magnificent short curly beard, curled moustaches and side-burns; he dressed in London and was renowned for his British phlegm. One day he received a telegram announcing that the firm's American agents, Osborne & Sons, had failed. "What do they owe us?" he enquired. "1,500,000 francs," came the reply. That was a princely sum in those days, and America, as it is today, was the firm's prize market. But all M. Kunkelmann said was, "Well, I can't attend to this now—I've already committed myself to be absent for three days." Not for three weeks was someone sent to the States to make the best of a bad job. Making the best of a bad job proved to involve selling 26,000 cases of Piper-Heidsieck in London, where the brand was—and still is—little known, at what the firm today graphically describes as a *"vil prix"*. But Piper-Heidsieck, as M. Kunkelmann was evidently aware, was perfectly well able to withstand such a shock. When he died, in 1930, he passed on a flourishing firm to his daughter, the Marquise de Suarez d'Aulan.

During the 'thirties the Marquis, who helped his wife to run the firm, was famous for his dash: a member of the French bobsleigh team in the 1936 Olympic Games at Garmisch-Partenkirchen, he later flew his own Percival Vega Gull. The war offered even fuller scope for his mettle. Unknown to the great majority of his workmen, he turned part of the Piper-Heidsieck cellars into a depot for arms parachuted into the district by the Allies. The Germans eventually got wind of what was going on, and one morning they converged on the firm, bent on arresting the Marquis; but, tipped off ten minutes before, he had already left—for Spain. Franco put him in prison (meanwhile a German overseer had been installed in his firm). He bribed his way out and headed for Algeria. There he joined the Lafayette Thunderbolt Squadron, pretending to be thirty-four when in fact he was forty-four. He was sent on missions over Sicily and Italy. In 1944 his plane was shot down over Mulhouse and he was fatally wounded. The Marquis was awarded posthumously the Croix de Guerre and the Légion d'Honneur.

After the war his widow married Général d'Alès, a former French Military Attaché at The Hague. The firm is now run by Baronne d'Alès, her husband, her son by her first marriage, François, Marquis de Suarez d'Aulan, and M. Jean Dapremont.

Piper-Heidsieck owns one small vineyard at Avize. Its cellars are among the largest in Rheims and visitors are welcome there.

The House of *Charles Heidsieck* was founded in 1851 by Charles-Camille Heidsieck, whose father, Charles-Henri, had caused a sensation in Russia with his white horse. Before starting his own business, Charles-Camille had worked for four years in the Piper-Heidsieck establishment.

He appears to have inherited that magic touch with champagne which Florenz-Louis Heidsieck and so many of his descendants had already proved themselves to possess. Starting off as a champagne-maker at the age of twenty-nine, he had built up a fine business before he was forty. But Charles-Camille also had a highly developed love of adventure which very nearly proved his undoing when he decided to invade that favourite haunt of the mid-nineteenth-century champagne-maker, the United States.

A *remueur* at work

79,528 bottles awaiting *dégorgement*

A *dégorgeur* at work

His first visit took place in 1857. One of the finest shots in France, he resolved to combine business with sport—shooting bear and buffalo. The spectacle of a pistol-packing champagne magnate tickled the fancy of the Americans: he made troops of friends, his receptions were crowded, and his sporting feats were reported in the newspapers from one end of the country to the other. He became known as "Champagne Charlie", and in New York and New Orleans people fell over each other to buy his champagne. It became his practice to make annual visits to America, and on these visits he always took with him the latest models of sporting guns. On 28 January 1860 the *Illustrated Newspaper* reported: "We have had the pleasure of examining some of the weapons Monsieur Heidsieck has brought with him. More perfect specimens of the fire-arm we have never seen; they are marvels of beauty, strength and, withal, so light that the sportsman can never tire of their weight." It was further recorded that M. Heidsieck would make an extended tour through the Southern States, Cuba, Florida and Texas, then ascend the Missouri river and visit Minnesota. "M. Heidsieck is young and agile," the paper added, "and we do not doubt will bear the fatigue as well as the backwoodsmen and trappers who will accompany him."

There is no evidence that he ever went to Cuba or ascended the Missouri, but he certainly had his fill of adventure the following year, the year the American Civil War broke out. Anxious about his stocks of champagne, he left by the first available boat for New York. After settling his business there he set off, against advice, for New Orleans, where he was selling over 3,000 baskets, of 25 bottles each, a year. Having tried for months to cross the fighting lines, and after several close escapes from death, he eventually enlisted as a barman on a Southern ship for the day's voyage from Mobile to New Orleans. As a favour to the French Consul in Mobile, he agreed to take the diplomatic bag with him and deliver it to the French Consul in New Orleans, Comte de Méjan. Unknown to him, the bag contained offers from French textile manufacturers to provision the Southern Armies; unknown to the captain of the ship, the Yankees were already in New Orleans. The bag fell into the hands of General Butler, the Yankee commander, and, notwithstanding the energetic protests of Comte de Méjan, Charles-Camille was arrested and imprisoned in a fort in the middle of a particularly unhealthy stretch of the Mississippi delta. American friends sent him food and medicines, but four months went by before the French Government was able to obtain his release.

Shaken but unbowed by this experience, Charles-Camille collected

important sums of money owed him by his American agents, bought
two ships and lots of cotton that was going cheap, stuffed the ships
with the cotton and packed them off to England, expecting to make
a fortune. One ship sank in a gale, the other was captured by the
Yankees. Unable to draw more of the money owed to him by his
American agent, who had gone bankrupt, he headed home, only to
find that in his absence his business had more or less collapsed. Trusting
friends made him loans and he fought his way back, but the going was
hard. When his son, Charles-Eugène Heidsieck, succeeded him as head
of the business in 1871, not all the loans had been repaid.

Late one winter's evening several years afterwards, an astounding
thing happened. Father Raverdy, a missionary priest, who is mentioned in Willa Cather's *Death Comes to the Archbishop* and whose home
was near Rheims, walked into the firm's offices and announced to
Charles-Eugène Heidsieck that a brother of the firm's former American
agent who had been ruined in the Civil War had since moved to
Denver, Colorado, and had there staked claims on the Heidsieck
family's behalf, hoping in this way to pay back what was owed.
Enquiry revealed the property to have risen greatly in value already;
most of it was sold at once to repay the money that Charles-Camille
had borrowed to get his business going again. In 1923 the family gave
away the last of their Denver holdings—a bit of land sandwiched
between two railways: they did so because American law prevented
either railway from buying it, nobody else was prepared to do so, and
they were having to pay taxes on it.

The Heidsiecks who have been active in the firm during the
twentieth century have shown the same willingness as Charles-Camille
to travel to remote corners of the world in the firm's interest. In 1907
Charles-Marcel Heidsieck, the founder's grandson, started on a series
of journeys which took him to Australia, New Zealand, Burma, India,
South America and many other lands; from Peru and Chile he brought
back a collection of Inca pottery that is said to be one of the best in
France. His brother, Charles-Robert, spent much time in Poland and
the Balkans just before the First World War. The two brothers, now
both over eighty, retired in 1965.

The firm is today headed by four directors: two brothers, Charles-
Christian and Jean-Charles Heidsieck, and their nephews, Charles-Remy
and Charles-Henri Heidsieck; a third brother, Pol-Charles Heidsieck,
looks after the interests of the firm in Paris. M. Charles-Christian
Heidsieck is the chief delegate of the *négociants en vin de champagne*
to the C.I.V.C. M. Jean-Charles Heidsieck has made over thirty trips

to Canada, the United States and the West Indies since 1923 and is a frequent visitor to London, where he has many friends. His son, Jean-Marc, in addition to being concerned with United Kingdom and other markets, is technical supervisor of the cellars in Rheims.

M. Jean-Charles Heidsieck's thirty-year-old younger son, Eric, is an international pianist of world renown. He gave his first piano recital in Rheims at the age of nine. Aged ten, he played his first concerto. After that he became a pupil of Cortot, and studied at the Conservatoire in Paris, where he won first prize. One of the first concerts that he gave abroad was in front of an audience brought together in London by Queen Victoria's granddaughter, Princess Marie-Louise, who considered him her protégé; he was sixteen at the time.

The Charles Heidsieck offices in the rue de la Justice in Rheims are among the most modern in the Champagne district. The two-storied white building encloses a flower-filled patio; in the marble entrance hall the nook for the reception clerk is faced with a huge sheet of concave glass. The firm owns no vineyards. Its main markets are France, Great Britain, the United States and Belgium; 60 per cent of its output is exported.

All Heidsiecks connected with the firm are christened Charles, and they use the name, in conjunction with another Christian name, if they work in the firm.

CHAPTER 46

PERRIER-JOUËT, EPERNAY

THE HOUSE OF Perrier-Jouët was founded in 1811, in the middle of the Napoleonic Wars, by Pierre-Nicolas-Marie Perrier-Jouët. The Perrier-Jouëts were cork-makers; Mme Clicquot is known to have been a customer of theirs.

By the mid-1850s the firm had built up a highly distinguished clientele, which included Napoleon III, Leopold I of the Belgians and Queen Victoria. Orders from the British Royal Household were always hand-written, and models of exactitude:

BUCKINGHAM PALACE

12 April 1861

Dear Sirs,

You may send me as soon as you think fit the following, marked as under; the Bill of Lading to Messrs Maclean & Wooley, Lower Thames St., London, Her Majesty's Custom House Agents.

100 Dozen 1857 Champagne (part of reserve) to be packed in three dozen cases, and marked G.W.C. as before.

48 Dozen 1857 Champagne (part of reserve) to be packed in six dozen cases, and marked H.R.H.

P.W.

9 Dozen 1857 Champagne (part of reserve) to be packed in three dozen cases, and marked R.W.C.

W.P.

The price we agreed was to be 50/- *per dozen, for the period of reserve.*

The Invoices are to be made for,

G.W.C.	to Her Majesty
H.R.H.	to H.R.H. The Prince of Wales
P.W.	
& R.W.C.	to myself, and all sent to me.
W.P.	

Believe me to be,
Dear Sirs,
Yours very sincerely,
WILLIAM PAYNE

Messrs Perrier Jouët & Co.
Epernay

Towards the end of his life, M. Perrier-Jouët built and lived in the huge building halfway up the Avenue de Champagne, which today houses Epernay's municipal library. Upon his death, control of the firm passed to his nephew, M. Henri Gallice, and then to his great-nephew, M. René Gallice. The latter was succeeded by his brother-in-law, M. Louis Budin, who was Mayor of Epernay during the Second World War. M. Budin retired in 1959, and was succeeded by his son, M. Michel Budin.

Perrier-Jouët has always remained a very small firm, specializing in first-class champagnes. Many a testimonial to the high quality of its products is to be found in the literature of wine. The firm owns 250 acres of vineyards, situated mainly at Cramant, Avize, Ay, Verzenay and Mailly. Its offices are housed in an elegant eighteenth-century building, which surrounds three sides of a well-tended courtyard overlooking the Avenue de Champagne; they are flood-lit at night.

CHAPTER 47

G. H. MUMM & CO., RHEIMS

THE HOUSE OF MUMM was founded in 1827 by M. P. A. Mumm
and a M. Giesler; it was known at first as P. A. Mumm, Giesler & Co.
M. Mumm, who was a Protestant, came from Rudesheim on the Rhine,
where the family owned important vineyards bordering on the Schloss
Johannisberg property. In 1837 M. Giesler severed his connection with
the firm and started his own champagne-making establishment at
Avize on the Côte des Blancs. The following year M. P. A. Mumm's
grandson, M. G. H. Mumm, joined the firm; in 1853 it was given his
name. During the ensuing half-century, the firm continued to be
owned and run by members of the Mumm family, but they never
took out French citizenship; when the First World War broke out,
the firm was therefore considered to be the property of enemy aliens,
and was confiscated by the French Government. In 1920 it was put
up for public auction and bought by its present owners, who trade
under the name "G. H. Mumm & Co., Société Vinicole de Champagne, Successeur". The Société, whose headquarters are in Paris, has
10,000 shareholders. M. René Lalou, who has been with the company
since 1920, is the Chairman, M. M. G. Snozzi is the Managing Director
and M. Jean Couvreur is in charge of the firm's establishments at Rheims.

Mumm is one of the largest of the champagne firms, selling on
average 4 million bottles a year. In 1952 the firm made its first sale to
America; ever since the U.S. has been its principal market, and there
have been few periods when the firm has not been the leading exporter
of champagne to the States. The name *Cordon Rouge*, which is given to
both vintage and non-vintage Mumm, and the diagonal red line on the
labels, are almost better known today than the name of the firm itself.
The rose on the labels of the firm's pink champagne is a detail of a
painting by Leonard Foujita, *La Petite Fille à la Rose*, which hangs in
the firm's Paris offices.

Mumm's cellars, which extend underground for ten miles and are
open to the public, contain some of the most up-to-date champagne-
making equipment in the winefield. A temperature conditioning
system has been installed in the four galleries which house the firm's
484 vats for the first fermentation (they have an aggregate capacity of
32,828 hectolitres).

The firm owns 500 acres of vineyard, situated at Mailly, Ambonnay, Bouzy, Avenay, Ay, Cramant and Avize. A hundred full-time vineyard workers are employed. The firm's slogan is "Mumm's the Word for Champagne".

Recently, on some ground adjacent to Mumm's cellars, M. René Lalou commissioned at his personal expense the construction of a chapel dedicated to Notre-Dame de la Paix. His friend Foujita, in fulfilment of a promise made at the time of his baptism in Rheims cathedral in 1959, has embellished the interior with more than a thousand square feet of frescoes. This joint undertaking has been given the name of the Foujita-Lalou Foundation and has been presented to the city of Rheims for the benefit of various causes. It is already attracting numerous visitors.

CHAPTER 48

J. BOLLINGER, AY

THE HISTORY OF Bollinger is closely linked with that of the de Villermont family, who established themselves in Champagne in the fifteenth century, if not earlier. Their home was at Cuis, three miles north of Epernay. Here they owned vineyards and made wine, but not on a truly commercial basis—the aristocratic family who engaged in commerce prior to the Revolution was the exception rather than the rule; all they did was to sell in cask to friends and relatives what they did not need themselves, in much the same way that people who own small properties with vines on them in France and Spain and Italy do—in cask or in bottle—today. In the course of the centuries, however, by purchase, marriage or inheritance, the de Villermont holdings gradually grew, until by the early 1800s they owned important slices of the growths of Ay, Verzenay and Bouzy in addition to their acreage at Cuis. At this time they moved from Cuis to Ay, which proved a happy chance, for only a few years later, when the invading Russians were about to ransack the town, it transpired that Admiral Comte de Villermont had known the Russian commander while in Russia as an *émigré* from the Revolution, and Ay was spared.

A happier day still, however, was in store for Ay. In 1829 the Admiral's son-in-law, Jacques Bollinger, who came from Würtemberg, decided that it was folly not to exploit commercially the family's ever-growing vineyard holdings. With this aim, a partnership was formed, comprising the Admiral, Jacques Bollinger and a M. Renaudin. The Admiral, as an aristocrat of the old school, refused to allow his name to appear on the labels, so the first bottles were sold as Champagne Renaudin, Bollinger. In fact, M. Renaudin resigned his partnership a couple of years later, but his name has remained part of the firm's trade mark ever since, although that of Bollinger has gradually been given greater prominence.

The firm specialized—and still specializes—in the production of quality non-vintage champagnes; Bollinger "Special Cuvée" has been a favourite of the British for over a hundred years.

Jacques Bollinger died in 1884, leaving what was already a solidly established business to his sons, Joseph and Georges. They introduced Bollinger champagne to the American market.

In 1937 Monsieur Jacques Bollinger (the son of Georges Bollinger) considerably expanded the firm's premises by purchasing the offices and cellars (but not the name) of the champagne House of Duminy. The two cellars were immediately joined together, and as a result it was possible to establish a direct subterranean connection between the Bollinger offices in the Boulevard Maréchal and the family's home in the rue Jules Lobet. Today that home—a long, low house forming one side of an attractive courtyard, with an old coach-house beside it and an ancient *cellier* opposite, where casks stacked six feet high are lined up like guardsmen on parade—is presided over, as is the firm itself, by Madame Lily Bollinger, the widow of Jacques Bollinger.

Madame Bollinger, a member of an old Touraine family, the de Lauristons, assumed complete control of the firm's affairs when her husband died in 1941. It is impossible to imagine a more awkward moment for a woman to have had such a responsibility thrust upon her: the firm's premises had recently suffered considerable damage from bombing—as had much of Ay—and there were still three long years of Occupation to face. But Madame Bollinger is just as formidable a person in her own way as was the Veuve Clicquot. She steered her inheritance through the war years and the difficult post-war ones with consummate skill—as she does today; the 1961 Bollinger was the tenth vintage *cuvée* the production of which she had personally supervised. And she has not been afraid to take an independent line: while most of her male competitors have been busy modernizing their plants with vats for the first fermentation and the storage of their reserve wines, she has stoutly maintained that there is nothing to beat the cask for these purposes. What counts, she says, are traditional methods, even if they appear old-fashioned; and her champagnes, she asserts, prove it.

Sheer hard work must also be part of Madame Bollinger's recipe for success, however. Every morning she is at her desk at nine o'clock, and few days go by when she is not acting as hostess at lunchtime in her elegant dining-room to agents from France, friends from abroad or journalists anxious to find out how a modern champagne widow conducts her business. On these occasions she is generally supported by her two nephews, M. Claude d'Hautefeuille and M. Christian Bizot; the former concentrates on the internal affairs of the firm, the latter keeps in contact with its world-wide interests. And then there are her trips abroad. She visits New York annually and London several times each year. On such occasions the clothes she wears are made for her by one of the great French *couturiers*; but to the citizens of Ay she is a more familiar figure in tweeds or a simple dress, riding . . . a bicycle.

Consciously or unconsciously, Madame Bollinger has an innate understanding of the importance of the personal touch. Well do I remember how, at a large dinner-party which she gave in her home for a group of young British wine merchants, she handed round the coffee, the *marc* and the cognac herself, letting drop as she did so that she had been out since six in the morning inspecting the vines. The hour was very late; it would have been easy for the servants who had served the delicious dinner to serve the coffee and the *digestifs* too; but when you are young, and when you yourself were still in bed at eight or nine, it is quite something to have been offered your coffee and your *marc* or your cognac by a great lady of Champagne who was out in the vineyards at six.

less unmistakable, the plain castellated façade of the central block of Mellerstain as conceived by Robert Adam. And Mme Pommery did not forget that other hallmark of the English country estate: the park. The Butte was soon surrounded by a stout stone wall and planted with trees, lawns and flower-beds, through which there wound a broad drive, announced by massive cast-iron gates impaled with the words "Pommery & Greno" in large gold letters. The Rémois invited to the opening of the new establishment in 1878 can hardly have believed their eyes, but its capacity to surprise is perhaps even greater today, especially on a summer's night, when it is flood-lit and the words "Pommery & Greno" in neon lights line the top of the Mellerstain block.

1879 was also a memorable year for Mme Pommery: she married off her daughter to Comte Guy de Polignac, a member of one of France's oldest families; and her 1874 champagne, launched by M. Hubinet in England, caused such a sensation there on account of its exceptional quality and its startling "dryness" that appreciative Englishmen were still writing odes about it more than a decade later.

Mme Pommery was now at the pinnacle of her fame; she had not reached this position without making an enemy or two on the way. One day she heard that her detractors were taking their revenge by circulating rumours that she was in financial difficulties. She handled the situation with characteristic aplomb, spiced with the originality that marked so many of her actions. It so happened that the newspapers were stirring up a row about the impending sale to America of a masterpiece of Millet's, *Les Glaneuses*. She bought the painting for 300,000 gold francs and presented it to the Louvre (where it hangs today), a gesture which promptly killed the rumours and at the same time gave her pleasure as an art-lover and a patriot.

A three-quarter-length portrait of Mme Pommery was painted about this time. She is standing beside a tall blue chair, her left fore-arm resting on its back. The clothes she is wearing are extremely elegant: a black silk dress, tight-fitting from the waist upwards, bouffant below, its cuffs and shoulders edged with black velvet to match the buttons down the front; at her wrists, frilly white lace; at her neck, a narrow Eton collar with a gold brooch in the centre; on her head, a tiny blue toque attached to a black mantilla which hangs down behind her shoulders. Her blonde hair is parted in the centre and swept down across her broad forehead, hiding her ears. Everything about her suggests the *femme du monde*, in complete control of herself and her world: the hands, with their long pointed fingers, are completely

CHAPTER 49

POMMERY & GRENO, RHEIMS

POMMERY & GRENO was founded in 1836 by M. Pommery, a young member of a Rheims woollen family, and by M. Narcisse Greno, who was older and already had experience in the wine trade. The capital for the venture was provided by M. Pommery, and he dealt with the day-to-day business of the firm in Rheims. M. Greno, a born salesman—hearty, happy-go-lucky, quick to make friends—spent most of the year travelling. The business was soon on a sound footing, but neither of the founders appears to have been particularly ambitious: the red still wines of Champagne were their speciality, not sparkling champagne. The north of France was their principal market, although they did sell a little wine in Belgium, Holland and western Germany. In 1858, however, Pommery died; his place was taken by his widow, *née* Louise Mélin; and in the course of the next thirty years she transformed the modest little business into one of the largest and most prosperous, and certainly the most spectacular, of all the champagne firms.

Mme Pommery was thirty-nine at the time she was left a widow; her son, Louis, was seventeen, her baby daughter, Louise, was still in the cradle. As far as is known, she had previously taken no part in the running of the firm, and had never intended to do so; but evidently M. Greno was already convinced that she was an extremely able woman, because it was he who persuaded her to assume an active role. One of the first things she did after taking over was to invent a motto—*Qualité d'abord*—which, for the rest of her life, she did her utmost to live up to. Then she introduced two major changes in policy: in future, the firm would produce sparkling champagne, not the still variety; and at the earliest possible opportunity it would invade the English market.

The team which Mme Pommery formed to carry out her plans was still with her in 1890 when she died, which shows she must have been a good employer. (It did not include M. Greno, who, because of failing health, had given up the partnership in 1860; but he remained a firm friend of Mme Pommery, and she would often discuss a difficult question with him or ask him to give a pep-talk to some agent or traveller who was flagging.) In charge of the cellars were M. Victor

Lambert and M. Olivier Damas; the latter was a cousin of M. Greno's. As her right-hand-man in the office she chose M. Henry Vasnier, a young man aged twenty-five, who had already been in the firm two years and had proved himself to be remarkably efficient, particularly at creating new agencies, a form of occupation after Mme Pommery's own heart. M. Adolphe Hubinet became her agent in England. It is said that she gave him the job because, having bought some ribbons from him in a draper's shop in Rheims, she found, upon returning home, that he had sold her far more than she had intended to buy—a sure sign that he was a good salesman. The story may well be true, as it is known that, at the time Mme Pommery first met him, Hubinet was staying with a draper in Rheims, having recently returned from the English Midlands, where he had been representing a group of French wine and liqueur firms; in any case, Mme Pommery could not have made a wiser choice. On 22 January 1861 Hubinet set off for London, armed with a thousand franc note given him by Mme Pommery and a contract which entitled either party to back out of the arrangement after the lapse of one year. His first office was at 5 Norfolk Street, off the Strand, but later he moved to 24 Mark Lane. There he had a long and brilliant career, in the course of which he built up a formidable following for Mme Pommery's champagne in England, Scotland and Ireland.

At the outset of her career Mme Pommery's home, offices and cellars were grouped together in the rue Vauthier-le-Noir in Rheims, within a stone's throw of the cathedral. The firm expanded so rapidly that she was soon contemplating a move, particularly of her cellars. But, before she had made up her mind where to go, the 1870 war broke out.

M. Vasnier, together with over half of her workmen, was called up at once. For the greater part of a year, therefore, she had to manage the firm by herself. The force of character and the courage which she displayed during the Occupation are perfectly illustrated by an incident that occurred at her luncheon table while the Prince of Hohenlohe, the Governor of Rheims, was quartered in her house (he was there for six months):

"At last," said the Prince, "there are no more armed civilians left. My proclamation has been obeyed."

"I can assure you," replied Mme Pommery, "some citizens still have arms," and so saying she produced a tiny revolver from her bag.

"Madame, in the Governor's house!"

"Prince, I must remind you that this is *my* house. And that is not all.

I still have firearms belonging to my family hidden away. Perhaps you would like to search for them." (They were under the floor-boards.)

A deathly silence followed, which was finally broken by Graf von Waldersee, a member of the Prince's staff: "Madame, it is not we who disarm the ladies, it is they who disarm us!"

Soon after the Germans left she acquired the site for her new cellars—the Butte Saint-Nicaise, a barren hillside about a mile beyond the ramparts of Rheims, which had been used for centuries as a municipal dumping-ground. I have described elsewhere how she converted the 120 abandoned chalk-pits underneath the Butte into one of the largest and most original cellars in all Champagne, its galleries supported by Norman and Gothic arches, its walls decorated with pictures, carved out of the chalk, by Navlet. But what I have not yet described are the equally original buildings which she erected above the cellars for use as offices.

From 1864 onwards Mme Pommery had been making regular trips to England with her son, partly on business and to visit friends, of whom she had many in England, but also to sight-see. While the plans were being drawn up for the new buildings, she had an inspiration: why not use the British style of architecture, which she had always much admired, and erect something on the lines of a British stately home? The more she thought about it, the more the idea appealed to her: such a radical departure from conventional design would startle people and attract attention to her House; besides, her British clientele, the corner-stone upon which her ever-increasing prosperity rested, would presumably be flattered. Bursting with enthusiasm, she dashed off letters to five of her British customers who owned famous country houses and asked them to send her plans to work on.

Whether all five obliged and who they all were her descendants, alas, do not know; but that two of them were the Duke of Argyll and the Earl of Haddington is evident to anyone who has ever visited or seen a picture of the Argyll and Haddington family seats, Inveraray Castle in Argyll and Mellerstain in Berwickshire. For among the perfectly hideous but delightfully bizarre conglomeration of buildings which arose—and still stands—on the Butte Saint-Nicaise, half of them built of brick, the other half of stone, some of them toned up with red and blue tiles in the Byzantine fashion, some of them boasting a tower, a spire or a dome, there peep out, unmistakably, the round corner towers with hats of Inveraray and, considerably reduced in size but no relaxed; the broad mouth, with its rather narrow lips slightly curled up at the corners, is on the point of breaking into a smile; the long, finely-shaped nose denotes breeding; the blue oval eyes are frank, confident and compelling. She must have been a very attractive woman.

She also had an excellent sense of values. She could have well afforded it, but she never felt the need of a château de Boursault (not that the Veuve Clicquot did either—at the outset!). She was far too fond of the little chalet which she owned, surrounded by woods and vines, at Chigny-les-Roses on the northern slopes of the Mountain of Rheims. There she kept ducks and turkeys, grew roses and worked at her crochet. Like Colette, she had a passion for butterflies and, as Colette did too, she spared no expense in framing them, showing them off as if they were precious stones. There were visitors, but not too many, except at the time of the vintage and during the shooting season: then both the chalet and the house in the rue Vauthier-le-Noir would be crammed with friends, important customers, agents and travellers from France, England, Belgium and Holland. M. Vasnier and M. Hubinet, both excellent shots, would organize the shoots.

But Mme Pommery was far too much of a realist to imagine that her children and grandchildren would necessarily share her simple tastes as regards living accommodation. So, as soon as the offices had been built, she turned her attention to the desolate ground on the opposite side of the Rheims-Châlons road. Having arranged for it to be covered with new soil she engaged Redon, the artist, to lay out a park to be planted with rare trees and shrubs, and a garden to be watered by artificial streams: her idea being that, if ever her descendants wished to build a château there, the grounds would already be mature and welcoming. They did: in 1907 the château des Crayères arose in Redon's park; a little later the chalet at Chigny-les-Roses was supplanted by another big family home, the château des Rozais, which is now a holiday home for children.

In 1889, the year before she died, aged seventy-one, Mme Pommery calmly bought up one-sixth of the entire crop of grapes produced in the Champagne district.

For a decade after her death the firm continued peaceably on its way, administered jointly by her son, Louis (who had been helping his mother since 1866), her daughter (by then the Marquise de Polignac, the father-in-law having died) and M. Henry Vasnier. The new century, however, dawned bleakly: her son-in-law died in 1901, M. Henry Vasnier in February 1907, her son Louis in May of the same year. In April 1907 her grandson, Melchior, Marquis de Polignac, took over the direction of the firm. He was a great sportsman, a member of the International Committee of the Olympic Games, and the organizer of the world's first important air show, *La Grande Semaine d'Aviation de la Champagne*, which took place in Rheims in 1909;* but it was as the founder of the Parc Pommery that he made his greatest contribution to sporting life in France.

His original idea was to provide the firm's workmen with a sports ground and their families with a pleasure ground in which to walk and take the air—a project quite unique in the France of that day. He handed over eighty acres of land on the southern side of the Butte Saint-Nicaise for the purpose, and in 1911 the Parc Pommery was inaugurated, complete with football and hockey fields, tennis courts, an athletics track and a swimming-pool. In 1912 France put up such a poor showing at the Olympic Games that he extended the Parc's facilities and put them at the disposal of everyone in Rheims, not just his workers and their families. Throughout the First World War the Parc lay within 1,500 yards of the front line, and was totally destroyed; once the firm's buildings, which had suffered a similar fate, had been repaired, it was restored—just in time to undergo a second battering during the Second World War. Today, however, the Parc Pommery is once again the centre of Rheims's busy sporting life. The city's football team, one of the best in France, trains there, and the annual four-day Concours Hippique International organized by the Rheims Société Hippique is held in it; if no longer unique, it is still one of the best-equipped and most attractive sports and pleasure grounds in France.

From 1902 to 1932 M. Hubinet's good work in England on the firm's behalf was continued by M. André Simon, the author, gourmet, and founder of the Wine and Food Society.

The Marquis de Polignac retired in 1947. For the next three years the firm was run by Louis Pommery's widow, a Mme Pommery once again. In 1952 Prince Guy de Polignac was appointed Président Directeur-Général. He is the Bailiff of the French branch of the Knights of Malta, and Pommery champagne, in bottles with labels

* Twenty-eight pilots, among them Louis Blériot, Glenn Curtiss, Louis Paulhan, Hubert Latham, Henry Farman and Bunau-Varilla, competed, and many new records were set up: Speed (45 miles an hour) by Blériot, Long Distance (111 miles) and Endurance (3 hours 4 minutes) by Farman. In 1959 a committee, presided over by the head of Pommery & Greno, Prince Guy de Polignac, himself a pilot, organized an air show at Rheims to celebrate the fiftieth anniversary of *La Grande Semaine d'Aviation*, but this time what made the crowds gasp was the screaming antics of jet-fighters.

incorporating the words *Ordre Souverain de Malte* and the white cross on a red background of the Order, is always available for the Knights' receptions. Both he and his wife are Chevaliers of the Légion d'Honneur and they were both awarded the Croix de Guerre for their services in the last war. He runs the firm with his brothers, Prince Louis and Prince Edmond.

The three Princes are Polignacs on both sides of the escutcheon. Their mother, Princesse Henri, born Comtesse Diane de Polignac, is a sister of the late Melchior, Marquis de Polignac, and thus a grand-daughter of Mme Pommery (today she is Honorary Chairman of the firm). Prince Henri was a member of the senior branch of the family. As the firm is thus doubly linked with the Polignacs, as as the Polignacs rank second to none among the nobility of Europe, I feel that a word is called for about the family.

The present head of the family, which dates from A.D. 860, is Armand XXVII, sixth Duc de Polignac (the dukedom dates from the reign of Louis XVI). The family seat is the château de Polignac at Puy-en-Velay in Haute-Loire, but there are no less than fifteen Polignac ancestral homes scattered about France. Louis XVI and many of his forebears addressed all Polignacs as Cousin; but the most poignant mark of royal confidence which the family has received in its colourful history was when Marie-Antoinette, riding in the tumbril to the guillotine, penned a note to her friend, Yolande, Duchesse de Polignac, entrusting the royal children to her care.

There scarcely exists a great French family into which the Polignacs have not married at some time or another. In 1825 the fourth Duc married Amélie de Crillon, thereby acquiring as his Paris home that masterpiece of the architect Gabriel, the Hôtel de Crillon. Their next important acquisition through marriage was Mme Pommery's champagne firm. After that they allied themselves with *haute couture* and perfume: Comte Jean de Polignac, Princesse Henri's brother, married Marie di Petro, the only child of Mme Jeanne Lanvin, the fashionable *couturière*, who subsequently created Lanvin perfumes. In her beautiful Paris *hôtel*, surrounded by Christian Berard murals and one of the finest collection of Impressionist paintings in France, Comtesse Jean was hostess to the musical and literary *élite* of Paris of the twenties and thirties. When she died she bequeathed the house (and stakes in Lanvin perfumes and Lanvin *couture*) to Prince Louis; it is there that Princesse Henri, mother of the three brothers who run Pommery & Greno today, still lives, gaily queening it over her enormous family.

Yet another marriage closely relates the Polignacs to the Prince of Monaco. On several occasions recently Pommery & Greno have prepared special bottles, appropriately labelled, in honour of this connection: in April 1956, for the marriage of Prince Rainier to Miss Grace Kelly; in March 1957, for the baptism of Princess Caroline; and in March 1958 for the baptism of Prince Albert, Marquis des Baux. In 1959 Prince and Princesse Guy de Polignac gave a very special luncheon, a luncheon *au robinet*, for Prince Rainier and Princess Grace at the château des Crayères: in front of each guest's plate stood a crystal pipe, about six inches high, surmounted by two small taps which, when opened by the guest, produced—the one an unending supply of the white still wine of Avize, the other an unending supply of a vintage sparkling Pommery. This most sumptuous method of serving Champagne wine was first devised by Melchior, Marquis de Polignac, in 1914; it was used at a luncheon for no less than 500 people to celebrate the House's centenary in 1936; and it has been used at luncheons, given either at the château des Crayères or in the cellar buildings, in honour of Queen Marie of Rumania, the future Queen Juliana of the Netherlands, Mr. Walt Disney, M. Mikoyan, Mr. John F. Kennedy, the future President of the United States, Miss Sonya Henje, Monseigneur Roncalli, later Pope John XXIII, and the Comte de Paris.

No account of the House of Pommery & Greno would be complete without reference to the exquisite fourteenth-century statue of the Virgin and Child, almost certainly of Champenois origin, which stands in one of the firm's chalk-pits. It was given as a wedding present by an American friend to Melchior, Marquis de Polignac, in 1919; his wife later gave it to the firm, and in 1940 Princesse Henri de Polignac had the happy thought of placing it on a pedestal in a chalk-pit a hundred feet below the ground. It was blessed by the Archbishop of Rheims during the Christmas of 1948, and since then has been known as Nôtre-Dame-des-Crayères. Flood-lighting of the most delicate tint of blue fills the sanctuary, causing the semi-precious stones with which the statue is encrusted to shimmer, and revealing in all their incomparable beauty the Virgin's face, the folds of her dress and the gesture of the infant Jesus, who is stretching out his hand to take his mother's shawl.

KRUG & CO., RHEIMS

JOSEPH KRUG, the founder of the House, was born in Mainz, which was then a free town, in 1800. Exactly when he emigrated to France is not known for certain as virtually all the Krug family papers were burnt in the basement of his grandson's home in Rheims during a German artillery bombardment in 1915. He may have done so in his middle teens, at the time when Mainz was incorporated into the Grand Duchy of Hesse-Darmstadt; he may have waited until his twenties or even until his late thirties, when his father died. All the family know for sure is that in 1841, at the British Embassy in Paris, he married Emma Ann Jaunay, an English girl, whose sister Louisa was married to Adolph Jacquesson, the head of the prominent champagne firm of that name, which was then situated at Châlons-sur-Marne; that he worked for a time with the Jacquessons; and that in 1843 he moved to Rheims where, with a M. de Vives as an associate, he launched out as a champagne-maker on his own.

At first he rented cellar space, three floors of underground galleries in the rue Saint-Hilaire, considered at the time to be very up-to-date (the firm's present premises were not built until the 1870s). This purely temporary arrangement subsequently brought him quite a bit of business, as the owners of the cellars which he had rented noted that he had a tremendous flair for blending—a flair that he passed on to his descendants—and for many years they commissioned him to compose *cuvées* for them. He appears to have formed an early connection with America: the firm has in its possession today an empty bottle whose label has printed on it an effigy of George Washington and an American eagle. The firm also still possesses one or two bottles with M. de Vives' names on the labels, which must date back to its début, as M. de Vives is known to have died two or three years after the association was formed.

Joseph Krug was succeeded by his only son, Paul, who was born in 1842. Paul Krug had ten children, but none of them displayed the slightest inclination to become champagne-makers. Eventually the eldest son, Joseph Krug II, who had always wanted to be a sailor, was persuaded to join the firm. By 1893 he was running it jointly with his father, and in 1910, when his father died, he assumed complete control.

In 1915 he was wounded and taken prisoner in the Ardennes, while serving as a captain in the Artillery; when he returned to Rheims, aged forty-nine, his health was in such a lamentable state that it was thought that he might never be able to attend to his business again; and as his only son, Paul Krug II, was six years old at the time, it was eventually decided that his nephew, M. Jean Seydoux, should be asked to join the firm as joint manager, which he did in 1924. However, the medical reports proved unduly pessimistic: M. Joseph Krug II's health gradually improved, step by step he got back in the saddle again, and he did not hand over the reins to M. Seydoux and Paul Krug II (who had joined the firm in 1941) until 1959—the year he celebrated his ninetieth birthday! Even then he did not retire completely: he remained Technical Adviser to the firm until the end of 1965. At the time I write he is ninety-seven, and still, I should add, one of the most popular and respected figures in the Champagne district. M. Seydoux died in 1962, since when M. Paul Krug II has run the firm alone, with the help of his two young sons, Henri and Remi.

Krug is—and always has been—a very small firm with a world-wide reputation for producing the very best champagne. I asked M. Paul Krug why the firm had never expanded and how it has succeeded in maintaining its enviable reputation for quality. He said there were three reasons why it had remained small. One was that both the founder and his grandson had each fathered only one son apiece, thus to some extent obviating the necessity, indeed the possibility, of expansion. Another was that the Krugs were a bourgeois family who for many decades had shared the French bourgeoisie's distrust of bank loans, preferring to finance themselves out of profits; and that what with wars, high taxation and devaluations, very little had been left to finance expansion. The third was, quite simply, that the firm's policy had always been voluntarily to limit supplies in order to uphold quality. For, he insisted, quality is invariably a matter of choice, and of severity in the choice. Even the most skilled champagne-maker will sometimes blend a *cuvée* that is not up to par: he then has the choice of letting it go out under his own name or of selling it to another firm whose standards are less exacting. Similarly, in years when the grapes are poor he has the choice of buying them and producing a mediocre champagne or of sticking his toes in and producing no champagne at all.

At this point I asked M. Krug whether he considered that the fact that the firm owned no vines had any bearing on the quality of its champagnes. He replied that his great-grandfather had always felt strongly that a champagne-maker was more likely to succeed if he

POMMERY & GRENO, RHEIMS

POMMERY & GRENO was founded in 1836 by M. Pommery, a young member of a Rheims woollen family, and by M. Narcisse Greno, who was older and already had experience in the wine trade. The capital for the venture was provided by M. Pommery, and he dealt with the day-to-day business of the firm in Rheims. M. Greno, a born salesman—hearty, happy-go-lucky, quick to make friends— spent most of the year travelling. The business was soon on a sound footing, but neither of the founders appears to have been particularly ambitious: the red still wines of Champagne were their speciality, not sparkling champagne. The north of France was their principal market, although they did sell a little wine in Belgium, Holland and western Germany. In 1858, however, Pommery died; his place was taken by his widow, *née* Louise Mélin; and in the course of the next thirty years she transformed the modest little business into one of the largest and most prosperous, and certainly the most spectacular, of all the champagne firms.

Mme Pommery was thirty-nine at the time she was left a widow; her son, Louis, was seventeen, her baby daughter, Louise, was still in the cradle. As far as is known, she had previously taken no part in the running of the firm, and had never intended to do so; but evidently M. Greno was already convinced that she was an extremely able woman, because it was he who persuaded her to assume an active role. One of the first things she did after taking over was to invent a motto— *Qualité d'abord*—which, for the rest of her life, she did her utmost to live up to. Then she introduced two major changes in policy: in future, the firm would produce sparkling champagne, not the still variety; and at the earliest possible opportunity it would invade the English market.

The team which Mme Pommery formed to carry out her plans was still with her in 1890 when she died, which shows she must have been a good employer. (It did not include M. Greno, who, because of failing health, had given up the partnership in 1860; but he remained a firm friend of Mme Pommery, and she would often discuss a difficult question with him or ask him to give a pep-talk to some agent or traveller who was flagging.) In charge of the cellars were M. Victor

Lambert and M. Olivier Damas; the latter was a cousin of M. Greno's.
As her right-hand-man in the office she chose M. Henry Vasnier, a
young man aged twenty-five, who had already been in the firm two
years and had proved himself to be remarkably efficient, particularly at
creating new agencies, a form of occupation after Mme Pommery's
own heart. M. Adolphe Hubinet became her agent in England. It is
said that she gave him the job because, having bought some ribbons
from him in a draper's shop in Rheims, she found, upon returning
home, that he had sold her far more than she had intended to buy—a
sure sign that he was a good salesman. The story may well be true, as it
is known that, at the time Mme Pommery first met him, Hubinet was
staying with a draper in Rheims, having recently returned from the
English Midlands, where he had been representing a group of French
wine and liqueur firms; in any case, Mme Pommery could not have
made a wiser choice. On 22 January 1861 Hubinet set off for London,
armed with a thousand franc note given him by Mme Pommery and a
contract which entitled either party to back out of the arrangement
after the lapse of one year. His first office was at 5 Norfolk Street, off
the Strand, but later he moved to 24 Mark Lane. There he had a long
and brilliant career, in the course of which he built up a formidable
following for Mme Pommery's champagne in England, Scotland and
Ireland.

At the outset of her career Mme Pommery's home, offices and cellars
were grouped together in the rue Vauthier-le-Noir in Rheims, within
a stone's throw of the cathedral. The firm expanded so rapidly that she
was soon contemplating a move, particularly of her cellars. But, before
she had made up her mind where to go, the 1870 war broke out.

M. Vasnier, together with over half of her workmen, was called up
at once. For the greater part of a year, therefore, she had to manage the
firm by herself. The force of character and the courage which she
displayed during the Occupation are perfectly illustrated by an incident
that occurred at her luncheon table while the Prince of Hohenlohe, the
Governor of Rheims, was quartered in her house (he was there for six
months):

"At last," said the Prince, "there are no more armed civilians left.
My proclamation has been obeyed."

"I can assure you," replied Mme Pommery, "some citizens still have
arms," and so saying she produced a tiny revolver from her bag.

"Madame, in the Governor's house!"

"Prince, I must remind you that this is *my* house. And that is not all.

I still have firearms belonging to my family hidden away. Perhaps you would like to search for them." (They were under the floor-boards.)

A deathly silence followed, which was finally broken by Graf von Waldersee, a member of the Prince's staff: "Madame, it is not we who disarm the ladies, it is they who disarm us!"

Soon after the Germans left she acquired the site for her new cellars—the Butte Saint-Nicaise, a barren hillside about a mile beyond the ramparts of Rheims, which had been used for centuries as a municipal dumping-ground. I have described elsewhere how she converted the 120 abandoned chalk-pits underneath the Butte into one of the largest and most original cellars in all Champagne, its galleries supported by Norman and Gothic arches, its walls decorated with pictures, carved out of the chalk, by Navlet. But what I have not yet described are the equally original buildings which she erected above the cellars for use as offices.

From 1864 onwards Mme Pommery had been making regular trips to England with her son, partly on business and to visit friends, of whom she had many in England, but also to sight-see. While the plans were being drawn up for the new buildings, she had an inspiration: why not use the British style of architecture, which she had always much admired, and erect something on the lines of a British stately home? The more she thought about it, the more the idea appealed to her: such a radical departure from conventional design would startle people and attract attention to her House; besides, her British clientele, the corner-stone upon which her ever-increasing prosperity rested, would presumably be flattered. Bursting with enthusiasm, she dashed off letters to five of her British customers who owned famous country houses and asked them to send her plans to work on.

Whether all five obliged and who they all were her descendants, alas, do not know; but that two of them were the Duke of Argyll and the Earl of Haddington is evident to anyone who has ever visited or seen a picture of the Argyll and Haddington family seats, Inveraray Castle in Argyll and Mellerstain in Berwickshire. For among the perfectly hideous but delightfully bizarre conglomeration of buildings which arose—and still stands—on the Butte Saint-Nicaise, half of them built of brick, the other half of stone, some of them toned up with red and blue tiles in the Byzantine fashion, some of them boasting a tower, a spire or a dome, there peep out, unmistakably, the round corner towers with hats of Inveraray and, considerably reduced in size but no less unmistakable, the plain castellated façade of the central block of Mellerstain as conceived by Robert Adam. And Mme Pommery did not forget that other hallmark of the English country estate: the park. The Butte was soon surrounded by a stout stone wall and planted with trees, lawns and flower-beds, through which there wound a broad drive, announced by massive cast-iron gates impaled with the words "Pommery & Greno" in large gold letters. The Rémois invited to the opening of the new establishment in 1878 can hardly have believed their eyes, but its capacity to surprise is perhaps even greater today, especially on a summer's night, when it is flood-lit and the words "Pommery & Greno" in neon lights line the top of the Mellerstain block.

1879 was also a memorable year for Mme Pommery: she married off her daughter to Comte Guy de Polignac, a member of one of France's oldest families; and her 1874 champagne, launched by M. Hubinet in England, caused such a sensation there on account of its exceptional quality and its startling "dryness" that appreciative Englishmen were still writing odes about it more than a decade later.

Mme Pommery was now at the pinnacle of her fame; she had not reached this position without making an enemy or two on the way. One day she heard that her detractors were taking their revenge by circulating rumours that she was in financial difficulties. She handled the situation with characteristic aplomb, spiced with the originality that marked so many of her actions. It so happened that the newspapers were stirring up a row about the impending sale to America of a masterpiece of Millet's, *Les Glaneuses*. She bought the painting for 300,000 gold francs and presented it to the Louvre (where it hangs today), a gesture which promptly killed the rumours and at the same time gave her pleasure as an art-lover and a patriot.

A three-quarter-length portrait of Mme Pommery was painted about this time. She is standing beside a tall blue chair, her left fore-arm resting on its back. The clothes she is wearing are extremely elegant: a black silk dress, tight-fitting from the waist upwards, bouffant below, its cuffs and shoulders edged with black velvet to match the buttons down the front; at her wrists, frilly white lace; at her neck, a narrow Eton collar with a gold brooch in the centre; on her head, a tiny blue toque attached to a black mantilla which hangs down behind her shoulders. Her blonde hair is parted in the centre and swept down across her broad forehead, hiding her ears. Everything about her suggests the *femme du monde*, in complete control of herself and her world: the hands, with their long pointed fingers, are completely relaxed; the broad mouth, with its rather narrow lips slightly curled up at the corners, is on the point of breaking into a smile; the long, finely-shaped nose denotes breeding; the blue oval eyes are frank, confident and compelling. She must have been a very attractive woman.

She also had an excellent sense of values. She could have well afforded it, but she never felt the need of a château de Boursault (not that the Veuve Clicquot did either—at the outset!). She was far too fond of the little chalet which she owned, surrounded by woods and vines, at Chigny-les-Roses on the northern slopes of the Mountain of Rheims. There she kept ducks and turkeys, grew roses and worked at her crochet. Like Colette, she had a passion for butterflies and, as Colette did too, she spared no expense in framing them, showing them off as if they were precious stones. There were visitors, but not too many, except at the time of the vintage and during the shooting season: then both the chalet and the house in the rue Vauthier-le-Noir would be crammed with friends, important customers, agents and travellers from France, England, Belgium and Holland. M. Vasnier and M. Hubinet, both excellent shots, would organize the shoots.

But Mme Pommery was far too much of a realist to imagine that her children and grandchildren would necessarily share her simple tastes as regards living accommodation. So, as soon as the offices had been built, she turned her attention to the desolate ground on the opposite side of the Rheims-Châlons road. Having arranged for it to be covered with new soil she engaged Redon, the artist, to lay out a park to be planted with rare trees and shrubs, and a garden to be watered by artificial streams: her idea being that, if ever her descendants wished to build a château there, the grounds would already be mature and welcoming. They did: in 1907 the château des Crayères arose in Redon's park; a little later the chalet at Chigny-les-Roses was supplanted by another big family home, the château des Rozais, which is now a holiday home for children.

In 1889, the year before she died, aged seventy-one, Mme Pommery calmly bought up one-sixth of the entire crop of grapes produced in the Champagne district.

For a decade after her death the firm continued peaceably on its way, administered jointly by her son, Louis (who had been helping his mother since 1866), her daughter (by then the Marquise de Polignac, the father-in-law having died) and M. Henry Vasnier. The new century, however, dawned bleakly: her son-in-law died in 1901, M. Henry Vasnier in February 1907, her son Louis in May of the same year. In April 1907 her grandson, Melchior, Marquis de Polignac, took over the direction of the firm. He was a great sportsman, a member of the International Committee of the Olympic Games, and the organizer of the world's first important air show, *La Grande Semaine d'Aviation de la Champagne*, which took place in Rheims in 1909;* but it was as the founder of the Parc Pommery that he made his greatest contribution to sporting life in France.

His original idea was to provide the firm's workmen with a sports ground and their families with a pleasure ground in which to walk and take the air—a project quite unique in the France of that day. He handed over eighty acres of land on the southern side of the Butte Saint-Nicaise for the purpose, and in 1911 the Parc Pommery was inaugurated, complete with football and hockey fields, tennis courts, an athletics track and a swimming-pool. In 1912 France put up such a poor showing at the Olympic Games that he extended the Parc's facilities and put them at the disposal of everyone in Rheims, not just his workers and their families. Throughout the First World War the Parc lay within 1,500 yards of the front line, and was totally destroyed; once the firm's buildings, which had suffered a similar fate, had been repaired, it was restored—just in time to undergo a second battering during the Second World War. Today, however, the Parc Pommery is once again the centre of Rheims's busy sporting life. The city's football team, one of the best in France, trains there, and the annual four-day Concours Hippique International organized by the Rheims Société Hippique is held in it; if no longer unique, it is still one of the best-equipped and most attractive sports and pleasure grounds in France.

From 1902 to 1932 M. Hubinet's good work in England on the firm's behalf was continued by M. André Simon, the author, gourmet, and founder of the Wine and Food Society.

The Marquis de Polignac retired in 1947. For the next three years the firm was run by Louis Pommery's widow, a Mme Pommery once again. In 1952 Prince Guy de Polignac was appointed Président Directeur-Général. He is the Bailiff of the French branch of the Knights of Malta, and Pommery champagne, in bottles with labels

* Twenty-eight pilots, among them Louis Blériot, Glenn Curtiss, Louis Paulhan, Hubert Latham, Henry Farman and Bunau-Varilla, competed, and many new records were set up: Speed (45 miles an hour) by Blériot, Long Distance (111 miles) and Endurance (3 hours 4 minutes) by Farman. In 1959 a committee, presided over by the head of Pommery & Greno, Prince Guy de Polignac, himself a pilot, organized an air show at Rheims to celebrate the fiftieth anniversary of *La Grande Semaine d'Aviation*, but this time what made the crowds gasp was the screaming antics of jet-fighters.

incorporating the words *Ordre Souverain de Malte* and the white cross on a red background of the Order, is always available for the Knights' receptions. Both he and his wife are Chevaliers of the Légion d'Honneur and they were both awarded the Croix de Guerre for their services in the last war. He runs the firm with his brothers, Prince Louis and Prince Edmond.

The three Princes are Polignacs on both sides of the escutcheon. Their mother, Princesse Henri, born Comtesse Diane de Polignac, is a sister of the late Melchior, Marquis de Polignac, and thus a grand-daughter of Mme Pommery (today she is Honorary Chairman of the firm). Prince Henri was a member of the senior branch of the family. As the firm is thus doubly linked with the Polignacs, as as the Polignacs rank second to none among the nobility of Europe, I feel that a word is called for about the family.

The present head of the family, which dates from A.D. 860, is Armand XXVII, sixth Duc de Polignac (the dukedom dates from the reign of Louis XVI). The family seat is the château de Polignac at Puy-en-Velay in Haute-Loire, but there are no less than fifteen Polignac ancestral homes scattered about France. Louis XVI and many of his forebears addressed all Polignacs as Cousin; but the most poignant mark of royal confidence which the family has received in its colourful history was when Marie-Antoinette, riding in the tumbril to the guillotine, penned a note to her friend, Yolande, Duchesse de Polignac, entrusting the royal children to her care.

There scarcely exists a great French family into which the Polignacs have not married at some time or another. In 1825 the fourth Duc married Amélie de Crillon, thereby acquiring as his Paris home that masterpiece of the architect Gabriel, the Hôtel de Crillon. Their next important acquisition through marriage was Mme Pommery's champagne firm. After that they allied themselves with *haute couture* and perfume: Comte Jean de Polignac, Princesse Henri's brother, married Marie di Petro, the only child of Mme Jeanne Lanvin, the fashionable *couturière*, who subsequently created Lanvin perfumes. In her beautiful Paris *hôtel*, surrounded by Christian Berard murals and one of the finest collection of Impressionist paintings in France, Comtesse Jean was hostess to the musical and literary *élite* of Paris of the twenties and thirties. When she died she bequeathed the house (and stakes in Lanvin perfumes and Lanvin *couture*) to Prince Louis; it is there that Princesse Henri, mother of the three brothers who run Pommery & Greno today, still lives, gaily queening it over her enormous family.

Yet another marriage closely relates the Polignacs to the Prince of Monaco. On several occasions recently Pommery & Greno have prepared special bottles, appropriately labelled, in honour of this connection: in April 1956, for the marriage of Prince Rainier to Miss Grace Kelly; in March 1957, for the baptism of Princess Caroline; and in March 1958 for the baptism of Prince Albert, Marquis des Baux. In 1959 Prince and Princesse Guy de Polignac gave a very special luncheon, a luncheon *au robinet*, for Prince Rainier and Princess Grace at the château des Crayères: in front of each guest's plate stood a crystal pipe, about six inches high, surmounted by two small taps which, when opened by the guest, produced—the one an unending supply of the white still wine of Avize, the other an unending supply of a vintage sparkling Pommery. This most sumptuous method of serving Champagne wine was first devised by Melchior, Marquis de Polignac, in 1914; it was used at a luncheon for no less than 500 people to celebrate the House's centenary in 1936; and it has been used at luncheons, given either at the château des Crayères or in the cellar buildings, in honour of Queen Marie of Rumania, the future Queen Juliana of the Netherlands, Mr. Walt Disney, M. Mikoyan, Mr. John F. Kennedy, the future President of the United States, Miss Sonya Henje, Monseigneur Roncalli, later Pope John XXIII, and the Comte de Paris.

No account of the House of Pommery & Greno would be complete without reference to the exquisite fourteenth-century statue of the Virgin and Child, almost certainly of Champenois origin, which stands in one of the firm's chalk-pits. It was given as a wedding present by an American friend to Melchior, Marquis de Polignac, in 1919; his wife later gave it to the firm, and in 1940 Princesse Henri de Polignac had the happy thought of placing it on a pedestal in a chalk-pit a hundred feet below the ground. It was blessed by the Archbishop of Rheims during the Christmas of 1948, and since then has been known as Nôtre-Dame-des-Crayères. Flood-lighting of the most delicate tint of blue fills the sanctuary, causing the semi-precious stones with which the statue is encrusted to shimmer, and revealing in all their incomparable beauty the Virgin's face, the folds of her dress and the gesture of the infant Jesus, who is stretching out his hand to take his mother's shawl.

KRUG & CO., RHEIMS

JOSEPH KRUG, the founder of the House, was born in Mainz, which was then a free town, in 1800. Exactly when he emigrated to France is not known for certain as virtually all the Krug family papers were burnt in the basement of his grandson's home in Rheims during a German artillery bombardment in 1915. He may have done so in his middle teens, at the time when Mainz was incorporated into the Grand Duchy of Hesse-Darmstadt; he may have waited until his twenties or even until his late thirties, when his father died. All the family know for sure is that in 1841, at the British Embassy in Paris, he married Emma Ann Jaunay, an English girl, whose sister Louisa was married to Adolph Jacquesson, the head of the prominent champagne firm of that name, which was then situated at Châlons-sur-Marne; that he worked for a time with the Jacquessons; and that in 1843 he moved to Rheims where, with a M. de Vives as an associate, he launched out as a champagne-maker on his own.

At first he rented cellar space, three floors of underground galleries in the rue Saint-Hilaire, considered at the time to be very up-to-date (the firm's present premises were not built until the 1870s). This purely temporary arrangement subsequently brought him quite a bit of business, as the owners of the cellars which he had rented noted that he had a tremendous flair for blending—a flair that he passed on to his descendants—and for many years they commissioned him to compose *cuvées* for them. He appears to have formed an early connection with America: the firm has in its possession today an empty bottle whose label has printed on it an effigy of George Washington and an American eagle. The firm also still possesses one or two bottles with M. de Vives' names on the labels, which must date back to its début, as M. de Vives is known to have died two or three years after the association was formed.

Joseph Krug was succeeded by his only son, Paul, who was born in 1842. Paul Krug had ten children, but none of them displayed the slightest inclination to become champagne-makers. Eventually the eldest son, Joseph Krug II, who had always wanted to be a sailor, was persuaded to join the firm. By 1893 he was running it jointly with his father, and in 1910, when his father died, he assumed complete control.

In 1915 he was wounded and taken prisoner in the Ardennes, while serving as a captain in the Artillery; when he returned to Rheims, aged forty-nine, his health was in such a lamentable state that it was thought that he might never be able to attend to his business again; and as his only son, Paul Krug II, was six years old at the time, it was eventually decided that his nephew, M. Jean Seydoux, should be asked to join the firm as joint manager, which he did in 1924. However, the medical reports proved unduly pessimistic: M. Joseph Krug II's health gradually improved, step by step he got back in the saddle again, and he did not hand over the reins to M. Seydoux and Paul Krug II (who had joined the firm in 1941) until 1959—the year he celebrated his ninetieth birthday! Even then he did not retire completely: he remained Technical Adviser to the firm until the end of 1965. At the time I write he is ninety-seven, and still, I should add, one of the most popular and respected figures in the Champagne district. M. Seydoux died in 1962, since when M. Paul Krug II has run the firm alone, with the help of his two young sons, Henri and Remi.

Krug is—and always has been—a very small firm with a world-wide reputation for producing the very best champagne. I asked M. Paul Krug why the firm had never expanded and how it has succeeded in maintaining its enviable reputation for quality. He said there were three reasons why it had remained small. One was that both the founder and his grandson had each fathered only one son apiece, thus to some extent obviating the necessity, indeed the possibility, of expansion. Another was that the Krugs were a bourgeois family who for many decades had shared the French bourgeoisie's distrust of bank loans, preferring to finance themselves out of profits; and that what with wars, high taxation and devaluations, very little had been left to finance expansion. The third was, quite simply, that the firm's policy had always been voluntarily to limit supplies in order to uphold quality. For, he insisted, quality is invariably a matter of choice, and of severity in the choice. Even the most skilled champagne-maker will sometimes blend a *cuvée* that is not up to par: he then has the choice of letting it go out under his own name or of selling it to another firm whose standards are less exacting. Similarly, in years when the grapes are poor he has the choice of buying them and producing a mediocre champagne or of sticking his toes in and producing no champagne at all.

At this point I asked M. Krug whether he considered that the fact that the firm owned no vines had any bearing on the quality of its champagnes. He replied that his great-grandfather had always felt strongly that a champagne-maker was more likely to succeed if he concentrated exclusively on his own profession and left the growing of grapes to the professional grape-grower, just as there is generally division of labour between the textile manufacturer and the sheep farmer; that was why his great-grandfather had never bought any vineyards. On the other hand, times change, and he felt that if his great-grandfather were alive today, when the competition to obtain first class grapes is so much greater than it ever was before, he would adopt a different policy; at any rate he himself would not decline fifty hectares of good vines in good places, as then he could cultivate them with quality in view—not like some people, just to produce more and more grapes each year!

I gained the impression, however, that in his heart of hearts M. Paul Krug still clings to the view that the champagne-maker who elects to concentrate on quality is better off sticking to one profession. His office, unlike those of other champagne-makers I have seen, is crammed with pictures and mementos connected with the firm's English agents, Reid, Pye & Campbell. When I remarked on this he said, "We've had a perfect relationship with them for exactly eighty years . . . no fuss, no bother . . . *they leave us alone* while we're making the champagne and we can count on them to sell it for us." The "us" really is the Krug family, for Krug & Cie employ no *chef des caves*. Each spring, when the time comes for the *cuvées* to be made, M. Krug locks himself up in the tasting room with Henri and Remi and they get on with the job. *"Je suis le cuisinier et mes fils sont les marmitons en attendant de devenir chefs cuisiniers eux-mêmes"*, was the way he put it. A trusted workman will often be asked to give his opinion of the result, but, in the final analysis, it is the *patron* who takes the blame or, as is more generally the case, the credit. "We find it works better that way," M. Krug added with a smile.

Once, the *cuvées* of Krug were made by a woman—Mme Joseph Krug II. It was in 1915, the year her husband was taken prisoner. Ian Maxwell Campbell describes in *Wayward Tendrils of the Vine* how Mme Krug apparently favoured the red grape, as she produced a much fuller-bodied and deeper-coloured champagne than is normally connected with the name; the real reason for the preponderance of red grapes, her son told me, was the difficulty of transporting white grapes from the Côte des Blancs to Rheims in the middle of the war; anyway, it sold in record time and was a huge success. Mme Krug was a very brave lady indeed. During the First World War she not only did hospital work but also ran a dispensary in the firm's cellars; she was gassed twice. During the Second World War she found hiding-places near

Rheims for British and Canadian airmen and then helped them on their way back to England via Spain. The Gestapo eventually found out what was going on, and she and her husband were arrested and put in Châlons gaol; on that occasion the Gestapo were unable to prove anything and M. and Mme Krug were released, but later Mme Krug was arrested again and imprisoned at Fort de Romainville near Le Bourget airport. She should have been on the famous train, crammed with deportees, that was stopped at Bar-le-Duc as a result of the entreaties of M. Nordling, the Swedish Consul-General in Paris, but she was among the twelve women left behind because they were too ill to travel. During the last forty-eight hours of their captivity they were looked after by Mongol guards. Mme Krug never recovered her health after this terrible experience, although, when the war was over, she continued her work with *Le Retour à Reims,* an organization which she and some of her friends had founded in 1919 to help those returning to Rheims to re-settle themselves, and which was at that time giving assistance to returning prisoners and deportees. She died in 1954.

CHAPTER 51

POL ROGER & CO., EPERNAY

THE HOUSE OF POL ROGER was founded in 1849 by a gentleman of that name whose family came from Ay. It must have required considerable courage to start a business at the time because Europe was in a state of ferment: France had not yet recovered from the agitations of the 1848 Revolution, which had toppled King Louis-Philippe's throne. Similar troubles beset Italy, Germany and Austria, while England was grappling with Chartist demonstrations and with rioting in Ireland.

To begin with, M. Pol Roger made champagne for other firms, but he was soon selling under his own name in France; and in 1876 he began shipping to England. Between the First World War and 1934 the firm shipped more champagne to England than any other, which was a triumph of the first order, as the House has always remained comparatively small, stressing quality rather than quantity. Today, 70 per cent of its produce is exported, most of it to Great Britain, the United States, Belgium and Italy.

M. Pol Roger died in 1899, whereupon control of the firm passed to his two sons, Maurice and Georges, who at the time were respectively thirty and twenty-six years old. One of the first things the Roger brothers did was to apply for permission to append their father's Christian name to their surname. It is much more difficult to change your name in France than in England: normally, permission is only given if your name is *Idiot* or something like that. On 15 December 1899, however, the President of the Republic signed a decree giving the family the right to bear the surname Pol-Roger, hyphenated. The House and the champagne continued to be known as Pol Roger without the hyphen. It has been said: "*De deux petits prénoms on a su faire un Grand Nom!*"

Within a year of assuming control of the firm, the Pol-Roger brothers were the victims of probably the worst disaster that has ever befallen a champagne firm. At two o'clock one morning in March 1900, M. Maurice Pol-Roger was awakened by the sound of a crash; he imagined two goods trains had collided in Epernay station, and went to sleep again. At about four a.m. he was awakened by the sound of another crash, much louder this time, followed by a long thundering boom. He jumped out of bed and looked out of the window;

immediately, his worst fears were realized. For some weeks workmen
had been engaged in extending the firm's cellars and adding supports to
the existing cellarage. There had been a collapse; where the warehouse
had stood there was now a gaping hole in the ground, 250 feet long,
180 feet wide. Inspection revealed that two entire galleries had fallen in,
one to a depth of sixty feet, the other to a depth of eighty-three feet,
destroying in the process 500 casks of wine and over 1,300,000 bottles
of champagne. The monetary loss was estimated at four million francs.

The brothers faced up to this calamity with great fortitude and
unshakable calm, qualities M. Maurice Pol-Roger was to stand in need
of again: when the Germans arrived on 4 September 1914, he was
Mayor of Epernay. The occupation of the town lasted only seven days,
but those seven days were probably the most chaotic of any in
Epernay's long and chequered history. The town was crammed to
bursting point with wounded, refugees, German troops and French
prisoners; and the Prince of Mecklenburg, Prince William of Prussia
(the Kaiser's fourth son) and General von Moltke had each set up his
headquarters there. To add to the confusion, the police and the other
civil authorities had moved out just before the arrival of the Germans,
taking the municipal funds with them: M. Pol-Roger coped with this
situation by issuing small paper notes, signed and guaranteed by himself, letting it be known that anyone who refused to accept them would
be arrested. A day or two later, however, he himself was arrested by
the Germans, who accused him quite falsely of having cut off Epernay's
gas and electricity supplies in order to hinder them. So incensed were
the Germans that at one point they threatened to burn down the town
and shoot the Mayor; but eventually tempers cooled and Epernay was
fined 176,550 francs instead.

In recognition of the services that he had rendered Epernay during
the occupation, M. Pol-Roger was later presented with a beautifully
bound volume containing the signature of every single citizen who
had remained behind; he was also made a Chevalier of the Legion of
Honour. Except for one short period, he remained Mayor until 1935;
that year, faced by his refusal to accept re-election, the people of
Epernay conferred a unique distinction upon him: they made him their
honorary Mayor for life.

It always remained a mystery to his friends and admirers how M.
Pol-Roger managed to run his champagne firm so successfully and
administer the affairs of Epernay with such brilliance when so much of
his time was devoted to sport. He would go off on trout or salmon
fishing expeditions each spring, shoot grouse in England or Scotland

in August, and join wild-boar shoots in Champagne almost daily in the late autumn (he bagged a record total of 525 wild-boar in his lifetime); he also regularly entered pigeon-shooting competitions at Deauville and Monte Carlo (in 1912 he was classed fourth among 180 crack competitors at Monte Carlo). Once, when asked when he actually did work at his business, he replied, "Principally, between saying my morning prayers and the time I go to shoot", which, at times, was just about the literal truth: he would leave his office at 9.30 a.m., having spent an hour or two dictating letters, change in the car, shoot or fish, change again in the car, and be back at 5 p.m. to sign his letters.

M. Maurice Pol-Roger died in 1959, having recently been made an Officer of the Legion of Honour. His son, M. Jacques Pol-Roger, and his nephew, M. Guy Pol-Roger, both partners in the firm and like him shrewd businessmen and keen sportsmen, died in 1956 and 1964. Now the firm is run by another nephew, M. Jean Pol-Roger, and by his grandson, M. Christian de Billy, helped by Guy's son, M. Christian Pol-Roger; a somewhat wistful look enters their eyes whenever their predecessor's time-table is mentioned: they *know* that the nine-to-six routine, which present-day convention imposes on a champagne-maker, is not the only recipe for success.

Pol Roger was the favourite champagne of Sir Winston Churchill, as British cartoonists often reminded the public on the great man's birthdays; he preferred the firm's older vintages, bottled in Imperial Pints. Sir Winston's loyalty to Pol Roger was no doubt partly explained by his friendship with Mme Jacques Pol-Roger (M. Maurice Pol-Roger's daughter-in-law), whom he met for the first time at a luncheon party given by Lady Diana Cooper at the British Embassy in Paris in November 1944. After the war, Sir Winston named one of his racing fillies "Odette Pol-Roger" after her (although it ran under the name "Pol Roger"); it won four races, including the Black Prince Stakes Handicap at Kempton on the day of the Queen's Coronation in 1953. The bound volumes of his War Memoirs that Sir Winston sent Mme Pol-Roger were inscribed as follows:

Cuvée de Réserve
Mise en Bouteille
au château Chartwell

When Sir Winston died, a black border was added to the labels of Pol Roger champagne in memory of him.

Mme Pol-Roger is a great-granddaughter of Sir Richard Wallace and one of the three ravishingly beautiful daughters of the late Général Wallace; the sisters are known to *Tout-Paris* as the Wallace Collection. Her garden on the Avenue de Champagne in Epernay proclaims her love for England: when summer comes, it is always a riot of roses, peonies, phlox, lilies, tobacco plants and huge delphiniums.

BIBLIOGRAPHY

A Brief Discourse on Wine, anonymous, London, 1861.

Allen, H. Warner, *Wines of France*, London, 1924.

— *Natural Red Wines*, London, 1951.

— *White Wines and Cognac*, London, 1952.

Anglade, Lucien, *Résumé du Cours de Viticulture*, C.I.V.C., Epernay.

Aubry, Octave, *Eugénie, Empress of the French*, London, 1939.

Barrelet, James, *La Verrerie en France*, Paris, 1953.

Barroux, Robert, *Saint Remi et la Mission de Reims*, Paris, 1947.

Barry, Sir Edward, *Observations on the Wines of the Ancients*, London, 1775.

Beaujean, F., *Jean de La Fontaine à Château-Thierry*, Société Historique et Archéologique de Château-Thierry.

Belloc, H., *Sonnets and Verse*, London, 1954.

Benstead, C. R., *Hic, Haec, Hock!*, London, 1934.

Berget, Adrien, *La Pratique des Vins*, Paris, 1899.

— *Les Vins de France*, Paris, 1900.

Berry, C. W., *A Miscellany of Wine*, London, 1932.

— *Viniana*, London, 1934.

Bertall, *La Vigne*, Paris, 1878.

Bird, William, *A Practical Guide to French Wines*, Paris.

Blanchet, Bernard, *Code du Vin*, Montpellier.

Bloch, Marc, *Les Rois Thaumaturges*, Strasbourg, 1924.

Bourgeois, Armand, *Le Vin de Champagne sous Louis XIV et sous Louis XV*, Paris, 1897.

Brillat-Savarin, Jean-Anthelme, *Physiologie du Goût*, Belley, 1948.

Brunet, Raymond, *Sa Majesté Le Vin de France*, Paris, 1929.

Bulletin de l'Institut National des Appellations d'Origine des Vins et Eaux-de-Vie, No. 72, Janvier 1960, Paris.

Butler, Frank Hedges, *Fifty Years of Travel by Land, Water and Air*, London, 1920.

— *Wine and the Wine Lands of the World*, London, 1926.

Campbell, Ian Maxwell, *Wayward Tendrils of the Vine*, London, 1948.

Caraman Chimay, Princesse Jean de, *Madame Veuve Clicquot-Ponsardin, Sa Vie, Son Temps*, Reims, 1956.

Carling, J. E., *The Complete Book of Drink*, London, 1951.

Catel, Maurice, *Visages de la Champagne*, Paris, 1945.

Chamberlain, Samuel, *Bouquet de France*, New York, 1952.

Champagne, "La France à Table", No. 33, Paris, 1951.

Chancrin, E., et Siloret, G., *Le Vin*, Paris.

Chandon et Cie., *Successeurs de Moët & Chandon, contre Edg. François et Léon Chandon*, Epernay, 1909.

Chappaz, Georges, *Le Vignoble et le Vin de Champagne*, Paris, 1951.

Chatelle, Albert, *Reims, Ville des Sacres*, Paris, 1951.

"*Commerce*", 24 November 1897, London.

Congrès Archéologique de France, Session XXVIII, Paris, 1862.

Congreve, William, *The Comedies of William Congreve*, London, 1895.

Couanon, Georges, *Les Vins et Eaux-de-Vie de Vin de France*, Paris, 1921.

Crabellier, Maurice, et Juilliard, Charles, *Histoire de la Champagne*, Paris, 1952.

Crouvezier, G., *La Cathédrale de Reims*, Paris.

Crozet, René, *Histoire de Champagne*, Paris, 1933.

Delamain, Robert, *Histoire du Cognac*, Paris, 1935.

Des Travertins Anciens de Sézanne, Mémoires de la Société Géologique de France, Deuxième Série, 8.

Dévignes, Geneviève, *Chansons Champenoises*, Paris, 1929.

— *Ici le Monde Changea de Maître (Attila)*, Paris, 1953.

— *Rheims Magnifique*, Paris.

Devlétian, Artin, *The Protection of Appellations and Indications of Origin*, International Bureau for the Protection of Industrial Property, Berne.

Dill, Sir Samuel, *Roman Society in Gaul in the Merovingian Age*, London, 1926.

Dion, Roger, *Histoire de la Vigne et du Vin de France*, Paris, 1959.

Diot, Robert, *Résurrection d'un Port Antique*, "La Banque", Revue de la Banque de France, Octobre 1958.

Dutton, Ralph, and Holden, Lord, *The Land of France*, London, 1952.

Epton, Nina, *Love and the French*, London, 1959.

Etablissement Moët & Chandon à Epernay, "Les Grandes Usines de Turgan", Janvier 1892.

Eyland, Dr. J.-M., *Vin et Santé: Le Champagne*, "Cuisine et Vins de France", Décembre 1957.

— *Promenade Littéraire en Champagne*, "Cuisine et Vins de France", Décembre 1959.

Feuerheerd, H. L., *The Gentleman's Cellar and Butler's Guide*, London, 1899.

Fiévet, Victor, *J.-R. Moët*, Paris, 1864.

— *Mme Veuve Clicquot*, Paris, 1865.

— *Histoire de la Ville d'Epernay*, Epernay, 1868.

Françot, Paul, *Résumé du Cours d'Oenologie Champenoise*, C.I.V.C., Epernay.

Gandon, Yves, *Champagne*, Neuchâtel, 1958.

Genlis, Mme de, *Souvenirs de Félicie*, Paris.

Geoffroy, Pierre, *Cours d'Oenologie: Les Constituants Chimiques du Moût et du Vin*, C.I.V.C., Epernay.

Hamp, Pierre, *Marée Fraiche, Vin de Champagne*, Paris, 1913.

Healy, Maurice, *Stay me with Flagons*, London, 1949.

Henry, E., and Loriquet, Ch., *Journalier ou Mémoires de Jean Pussot*, Reims, 1858.

Hodez, Roger, *La Protection des Vins de Champagne par l'Appellation d'Origine*, Paris, 1923.

Hollande, Maurice, *Connaissance du Champagne*, Paris, 1952.

— *Trésors de Reims*, Reims, 1961.

Hugo, Victor, *Le Rhin*, Paris, 1838.

Hyams, Edward, *Vin*, London, 1959.

Jofra, Ramiro Medir, *Historia del Gremio Corchero*, Madrid, 1953.

Krudener, Mme de, *Le Camp de Vertus*, Paris, 1815.

La Champagne, La Marne, Paris, 1952.

La Chronique de Champagne, Vol. 4, Reims, 1838.

La Fontaine, *Contes et Nouvelles*, precédées d'une étude sur La Fontaine par H. Taine, Paris.

La Réglementation de la Taille pour l'Appellation "Champagne", Institut National des Appellations d'Origine des Vins et Eaux-de-Vie, Paris.

"La Revue Vinicole", Novembre 1954, Novembre 1956, Paris.

Larousse Gastronomique.

L'Art en Champagne au Moyen Age, Musée de l'Orangerie, Paris, 1959.

Le Champagne, "Opinion, Economique et Financière", Paris, 1956.

Le Comité Interprofessionel du Vin de Champagne, Epernay, 1960.

Leedom, William S., *The Vintage Wine Book*, New York, 1963.

"Le Figaro", Supplément, 12 Février 1895.

Legislation Viti-Vinicole en Matière de Champagne, C.I.V.C., Epernay.

Lenôtre, G., *Le Drame de Varennes*, Paris, 1906.

— *Histoires Révolutionnaires: Vieux Papiers, Vieilles Maisons*, Série 5, Paris, 1928.

Le Page, Louis, *Epernay pendant la Guerre*, Paris, 1921.

Lermontov, Michael, *Le Héros de Notre Epoque*, traduction Marc Chapiro, Genève, 1946.

Le Siècle d'Offenbach, Cahier de la Compagnie Madeleine Renaud-Jean-Louis Barrault, Paris, 1958.

Le Vin de Champagne, C.I.V.C., Epernay.

Le Vitrail du Champagne en la Cathédrale de Reims, Reims, 1954.

Lichine, Alexis, *Wines of France*, London, 1953.

Lomax, Alan, *Mister Jelly Roll*, New York, 1950.

Macqueen-Pope, W., *The Melodies Linger On*, London, 1950.

Manceaux, l'Abbé, *Histoire de l'Abbaye et du Village d'Hautvillers*, Epernay, 1880.

Marrison, L. W., *Wines and Spirits*, London, 1957.

Menin, *Traité du Sacre des Rois*, Paris, 1823.

Menu, Henri, *Le Camp de Vertus: Revue de l'Armée Russe sur le Mont-Aimé*, Epernay, 1896.

Meredith, George, *One of Our Conquerors*, London, 1912.

Michelet, Jules, *Tableau de la France*.

Milsand, Ph., *Procès Poétique Touchant les Vins de Bourgogne et de Champagne*, Paris, 1866.

Mommessin, Jean, *Les Origines du Vignoble Français*, Mâcon, 1954.

Montorgueil, Georges, *Monseigneur Le Vin*, Etablissements Nicolas, 1927.

Moreau-Bérillon, C., *Au Pays du Champagne*, Reims, 1923.

Moreau, Emile, *Le Culte de Saint Vincent en Champagne*, Epernay, 1936.

Moret, L., *Précis de Géologie*, Paris, 1958.

Morinière, Jacques de la, *Champagne*, Wine Trade Club Lecture, London, 1948.

Morison, Samuel Eliot, *Christopher Columbus, Mariner*, New York, 1942.

Morris, Dennis, *The French Vineyards*, London, 1958.

Mouillefert P., *Les Vignobles et les Vins de France et de l'Etranger*, Paris, 1891.

Muir, Augustus, editor, *How to Choose and Enjoy Wine*, London, 1953.

Néret, Chanoine L., *Dom Pérignon*, Epernay, 1924.

Nollevalle, J., *L'Agitation dans le Vignoble Champenois*, Numéro Spécial de "La Champagne Viticole", Epernay, Janvier 1961.

Northcliffe, Lord, *At the War*, London, 1916.

Nouvelle Revue de Champagne et de Brie, Vol. 7, Châlons-sur-Marne, 1929.

Ogrizek, Doré, *France Observed*, London, 1959.

Ombiaux, Maurice des, *Le Gotha des Vins de France*, Paris, 1925.

Oppenheimer, Sir Francis, *Frankish Themes and Problems*, London, 1952.

Pacottet, P., et Guittonneau, L., *Vins de Champagne et Vins Mousseux*, Paris, 1918.

Partridge, Burgo, *A History of Orgies*, London, 1958.

Pasteur, M. L., *Etudes sur le Vin*, Paris, 1866.

Péchenart, Abbé L., *Sillery et Ses Seigneurs*, Reims, 1893.

Pestel, H., *Les Vins et Eaux-de-Vie à Appellations d'Origine Contrôlées en France*, Mâcon, 1959.

Pierre, Frère, *Traité de la Culture des Vignes de Champagne*, Epernay, 1931.

Poinsignon, Maurice, *Histoire Générale de la Champagne et de la Brie*, Paris, 1885.

Pushkin, A. S., *Poésies et Nouvelles*, traduction F.-E. Gauthier, Paris, 1888.

— *Doubrovsky et Autres Contes*, traduction Whyms, Bruxelles.

Pouillaude, Ch., *Le Liège et les Industries du Liège*, Paris, 1957.

Quintilien et Pline le Jeune, *Oeuvres Complètes*, traduction M. Nisard, Paris, 1942.

Rabelais, *Le Sixième Livre des Haultz Faitz et Dictz de Pantagruel*, Paris, 1933.

Redding, Cyrus, *A History and Description of Modern Wines*, London, 1836.

— *French Wines and Vineyards*, London, 1860.

Robinet, E., *Fabrication des Vins Mousseux*, Paris, 1877.

Root, Waverly, *The Food of France*, New York, 1958.

Saintsbury, George, *Notes on a Cellar Book*, London, 1920.

Schoonmaker, Frank, and Marvel, Tom, *The Complete Wine Book*, London, 1935.

Scott, J. M. *Vineyards of France*, London, 1950.

Seeger, Alan, *Poems*, London, 1917.

Seltman, Charles, *Wine in the Ancient World*, London, 1957.

Sergent, Abbé R., *Hautvillers*, Epernay, 1928.

Shand, P. Morton, *A Book of Wine*, London, 1926.

— *A Book of French Wines*, London, 1928.

Shaw, Thomas George, *Wine, the Vine and the Cellar*, London, 1863.

Sheen, J. R., *Wines and other Fermented Liquors*, London, 1864.

Simon, André L., *In Vino Veritas*, London, 1913.

— *Wines and Spirits*, London, 1919.

— *The Blood of the Grape*, London, 1920.

— *Bottlescrew Days*, London, 1926.

— *Champagne*, London, 1934.

— *Vintagewise*, London, 1945.

— *A Wine Primer*, London, 1946.

— *Drink*, London, 1948.

— *By Request*, London, 1957.

— *The Noble Grapes and the Great Wines of France*, London, 1957.

Simon, André L., *A History of Champagne*, London, 1962.

Simplicissimus, Ein Rückblick auf die Satirische Zeitschrift, Hanover, 1954.

Stern, G. B., *Bouquet*, London, 1927.

Sutaine, Max, *Essai sur l'Histoire des Vins de la Champagne*, Reims, 1845.

"*The Times*", Wines of France and Germany Supplement, 26 May 1953.

Thudichum, J. L. W., and Dupré, August, *A Treatise on the Origin, Nature and Varieties of Wine*, London, 1892.

Trofimoff, André, *Ciels et Décors de France*, Paris.

Vallery-Radot, René, *La Vie de Pasteur*, Paris, 1900.

Visages d'Epernay, Epernay, 1954.

Vizetelly, Ernest, and Vizetelly, Arthur, *The Wines of France*, London, 1908.

Vizetelly, Henry, *Facts about Champagne and other Sparkling Wines*, London, 1879.

— *A History of Champagne*, London, 1882.

Vogüé, Bertrand de, *Madame Veuve Clicquot à la Conquête Pacifique de la Russie*, Reims, 1960.

Waugh, Evelyn, *Helena*, London.

Wechsberg, Joseph, "A Dreamer of Wine", *New Yorker*, 17 and 24 May 1958.

"*Wine and Spirit Trade Review*", 13 June 1925, and 13 and 20 March 1936.

Young, Arthur, *Travels during the Years 1787, 1788 and 1789*, London, 1792.

INDEX

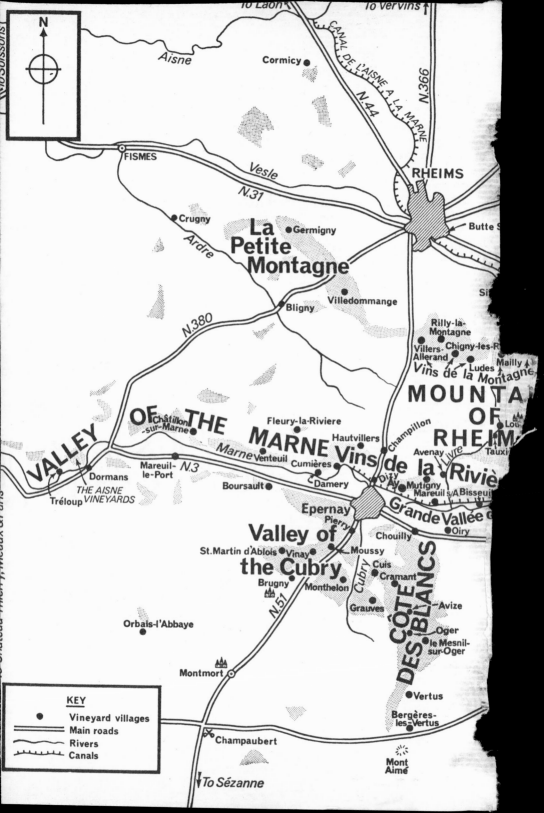